Reconstructing Human Origins:
A Modern Synthesis

Reconstructing Human Origins: A Modern Synthesis

GLENN C. CONROY

Washington University
St. Louis

W · W · NORTON & COMPANY

NEW YORK · LONDON

The text of this book is composed in Baskerville with the display set in Optima.
Composition by University Graphics, Inc.
Manufacturing by Maple-Vail
Cover art: *Le Tremoin* by Pierre-Yves Tremois, © 1997 Artists Rights Society (ARS), NY/
ADAGP, Paris.

Library of Congress Cataloging-in-Publication Data

Conroy, Glenn C.
      Reconstructing human origins : a modern synthesis / Glenn C. Conroy.
         p.   cm.
      Includes bibliographical references and index.
      ISBN 0-393-97042-6 (pbk.)
      1. Man—Origin.   2. Fossil man.   3. Human evolution.   I. Title.
   GN281.C587   1997
   573.3—dc20   96-25161

W. W. Norton & Company, Inc., 500 Fifth Avenue, New York, N.Y. 10110
http://www.wwnorton.com

W. W. Norton & Company Ltd., 10 Coptic Street, London WC1A 1PU

1 2 3 4 5 6 7 8 9 0

Contents

Preface

This book is nonfiction. The story is true, and the people are real.

Richard Preston
The Hot Zone (1994)

We are all ONE, say the gurus. Aye, I might agree—but one WHAT?

Edward Abbey
A Voice Crying in the Wilderness (1989)

To know what will come is the same as to make it so.

Cormac McCarthy
Suttree (1979)

A waggish commentator once observed that the sciences could be conveniently lumped into three categories: the soft sciences, like political science and sociology, the hard sciences, like physics and chemistry, and then the really difficult sciences, like paleoanthropology. What makes paleoanthropology so "difficult" is the realization that human evolution is a unique evolutionary experiment—one that cannot be repeated. For this reason it is not unusual (or unreasonable) to encounter honest disagreements among knowledgeable paleoanthropologists about the nature, but not the fact, of human evolution. As in my previous book, *Primate Evolution* (1), I have tried to convey this state of dynamic tension fairly and honestly without promoting my views to the exclusion of others. While I am certain that my own biases percolate through on occasion, I have made every effort to present the reader with what I take to be a balanced view of the major events and issues in human evolution. My hope is that by the time readers have reached the end of the book, they will have come away with a reasonable grasp of the fossil evidence for human evolution and how that evidence is interpreted in modern paleoanthropological research. I am less concerned, and I hope students agree, if my interpretation or emphasis differs somewhat from that of their own professors. After all, that is what teachers and books are for.

While this book is written mainly with anthropology undergraduate and graduate students in mind, anyone interested in the natural sciences can easily follow the major episodes of human evolution as outlined here by simply starting at the beginning and reading through to the end. Bearing in mind that the fossils themselves are the main "stars" of the book, I have tried to integrate the impact that recent advances in such areas as radiometric dating, functional morphology, molecular biology, and archeological inference have had on modern interpretations of how hominids lived and dispersed across the globe over the last 5 million years or so.

Writing a textbook can be a forbidding and sometimes lonely task. "Like fly-fishing, writing is an elaborate conspiracy to make lyrical an activity that is inherently a business of barbs and worms" (2). However, the process was made so much more pleasant by the congenial atmosphere provided by friends and colleagues here in what I would consider to be the golden age of physical anthropology at Washington University. I am grateful to them for sharing with me over the years their considerable and diverse insights into many of the topics discussed in this book. To all those who graciously gave of their time to review and improve the manuscript— Robert Blumenschine, Russell Ciochon, Robert Eckhardt, David Frayer, Michael Little, Jim Moore, Jane Phillips-Conroy, D. Tab Rasmussen, Betsy Schumann, Jeffrey Schwartz, Richard Smith, Frank Spencer, Mark Teaford, Alan Templeton, Erik Trinkaus, and Tim White—I thank you for your strong words of encouragement and your gentle words of criticism.

Finally, I must add to this list my gratitude to my editors at W. W. Norton, particularly Jim Jordan for sharing his wise counsel for many years, Rachel Warren for all her administrative efforts, David Sutter for his copyediting skills, Mike Reingold for his beautiful illustrations, and John Byram, who saw it through to the end.

Reconstructing Human Origins:
A Modern Synthesis

CHAPTER 1

Time, Climate, and Human Evolution

Time is but the stream I go a-fishing in. I drink at it; but while I drink I see the sandy bottom and detect how shallow it is. Its thin current slides away, but eternity remains.

Henry David Thoreau
Walden (1854)

Sometimes we need to be close to the earth and feel its true age and contemplate its real history. We need to contemplate, as well, the history of man's imaginings about the earth and to remind ourselves that truth has many tellings, only one of which we call science.

Howell Raines
Fly Fishing through the Midlife Crisis (1994)

INTRODUCTION

The question of human origins has provoked the collective imagination for as long as recorded history. Indeed, humankind's interest in the subject is as pervasive today as it was in ancient times.

The modern study of human evolution encompasses many fields and is based on a large body of empirical research. Paleoanthropology is a subject that appeals to a remarkably wide range of people. There are a number of reasons why this is so. To some, much of its colorful history conjures up images of romance and adventure in far away and exotic places, a tale of dramatic discoveries and heated controversies amidst the sound and fury of clashing egos. In others it evokes sublime reflections about our place in nature, about our collective past and future. And then there are simply those who believe in the aphorism that those who neglect the past are condemned to repeat it.

The major emphasis in this book is on the discovery and interpretation of the fossil evidence for human evolution. To many dedicated students of human evolution, fossil discovery is the very heart and soul of paleoanthropology because fossils are the most direct and unequivocal evidence documenting the course of our evolutionary history. Fossil discoveries connect us to eternity, giving us the privilege of glimpsing, if ever so briefly and imperfectly, the blurred image of those who walked the earth hundreds of thousands or millions of years before us. We may not always be certain about their proper taxonomic label, or their exact place on the human evolutionary tree, but that does not diminish the wonder. We still recognize them as somehow a part of us, and ourselves as a part of them.

Even though it is fossil discovery that usually stokes the fire of public imagination, intellectual adrenaline flows into paleoanthropology from a number of other interrelated disciplines. Such diverse fields as geochronology, archeology, phylogenetic reconstruction, functional morphology, paleoecology, behavioral ecology, and molecular biology all play a critical role in modern paleoanthropological research. For this reason, one of my aims in this book is to try to integrate information from these and other fields into our ever expanding knowledge of, and appreciation for, the human fossil record.

Human evolution should not be considered to have a definite beginning or (barring a nuclear holocaust, "hot" virus disaster, or asteroid impact) a definite end. Humankind is part of an evolutionary continuum of primates stretching back to the origins of the order some 70 million years ago. What we think of as "human" evolution has occupied only about the last 7 percent of that time, approximately the last 5 million years or so, and that story is the subject matter of this book.

What Distinguishes Humans from Other Primates?

Before launching into the story of human evolution, perhaps it is best to start with the more basic considerations of what distinguishes primates from other mammals and what distinguishes humans from other primates. Carolus Linnaeus, the originator of the modern scientific system of classifying and naming organisms, put forward the first definition of the mammalian order **Primates** in the tenth edition of his great work *Systema Naturae* (1). He characterized Primates as possessing several distinctive anatomical features including four cutting teeth, the **incisors**, at the front of the jaw; two collarbones, or **clavicles**; two mammary glands, or **mammae**, on the chest; and at least two grasping, or **prehensile**, extremities that function as hands in the sense of being able to grasp objects by means of an opposable first digit. He divided the order into four genera, to which he gave the Latin names *Homo, Simia, Lemur,* and *Vespertilio.*[1]

Linnaeus' taxonomic lumping together of humans and apes did not meet with universal approval and a succession of comparative anatomists in the eighteenth and nineteenth centuries devoted much effort and ingenuity to devising anatomical and behavioral criteria that could convincingly distinguish the two groups. They pointed not only to measurable anatomical characters, such as bone structure and dentition, but also to such qualitative traits as the human capacity for speech, reason, and what were called other "higher" brain functions (2,3). None of their alternative classification schemes made much headway, however, and the Linnaean formulation stood more or less unchanged for more than a century.

The true evolutionary link between apes and humans was finally recognized in the midnineteenth century by Charles Darwin. Having established the general principles of his theory of natural selection in *The Origin of Species* (4), he went on to apply them specifically to the question of human evolution in *The Descent of Man* (5). He wrote:

> It is notorious that man is constructed on the same generalized type or model with the other mammals. All the bones in his skeleton can be compared with the corresponding bones in a monkey, bat or seal. So it is with his muscles, nerves, blood vessels and internal viscera. The brain, the most important of all the organs, follows the same law. . . . It is, in short, scarcely possible to exaggerate the close correspondence in general structure, in the minute structure of tissues, in chemical composition and in constitution, between man and the higher animals, especially the anthropomorphous apes.

Darwin even speculated on the likely geographic site where primate evolution led to the emergence of the human species. He noted that

> in each great region of the world the living mammals are closely related to the extinct species of the same region. It is therefore probable that Africa was formerly inhabited by extinct apes closely allied to the gorilla and chimpanzee; and as these two species are now man's closest allies, it is somewhat more probable that our early progenitors lived on the African continent than elsewhere.

The first significant post-Darwinian modification of the Linnaean system of primate classification was proposed in 1873 by the English anatomist St. George Mivart (6). Removing bats and colugos ("flying lemurs") from the order, he reorganized the remaining members into two suborders; the primitive **Prosimii**, or "premonkeys" (lemurs, lorises, and the like), and

---

[1]He included within the genus *Homo* not only humans but also the orangutan (naming it *Homo sylvestris*). Under *Simia* he included the monkeys and the rest of the apes. Under *Lemur* he grouped the lemurs and other "lower," less humanlike forms, and under *Vespertilio* he put various species of bats.

the more advanced **Anthropoidea** (monkeys, apes, and humans). He also proposed an expanded list of traits to further distinguish primates from other mammals. Primates, he wrote, were

> unguiculate [having nails or claws], claviculate [having clavicles], placental mammals, with orbits [eye sockets] encircled by bone, three kinds of teeth [incisors, canines, and molars], at least at one time of life; brain always with a posterior lobe and a calcarine fissure [a transverse groove along the medial surface of that lobe]; the innermost digit of at least one pair of extremities opposable; hallux [big toe] with a flat nail or none; a well-developed caecum [a pouchlike part of the large intestine]; penis pendulous; testes scrotal; always two pectoral mammae.

Although none of these characters, it turns out, are peculiar to primates, their combination has long been accepted as diagnostic of the order.

An alternative approach to the problem of defining the primates, advocated chiefly by the English anatomist Sir Wilfred LeGros Clark several decades ago, sought to characterize the order in terms of a complex of evolutionary trends rather than a simple listing of morphological traits (7). According to this view, the distinctive evolutionary trends that set the early primates apart from other placental mammals include progressive enlargement of the brain, convergence of the axes of vision, shortening of the snout, atrophy of the olfactory sense, prolongation of the postnatal growth period, and specializations of the extremities for grasping. Most of these hypothesized trends, it was thought, were related to a tree-living, or **arboreal** way of life.

More recently, a much more elaborate definition of the living primates has been proposed that takes into account such diverse factors as geographic distribution, habitat, means of locomotion, influence of major sense organs on the shape of the skull, relative brain size, reproductive biology, and dental patterns (8). For example, living primates are typically arboreal animals living mainly in tropical and subtropical ecosystems (there are some obvious exceptions, such as the more savanna-dwelling baboons of Africa and the temperate forest–dwelling macaques of Asia). Anatomical features of the hands and feet, the **manus** and **pes** respectively, are adapted for prehension (grasping). This is clearly evidenced in the foot by the widely divergent big toe, or **hallux**, in all primates except humans. In addition, the digits have nails instead of claws, which serve as supportive structures for the tactile cutaneous ridges on the fingertips that reduce slippage on arboreal supports.

In all modern primates the visual sense is emphasized over the olfactory sense. For this reason the eyes are usually relatively large and are protected either by a **postorbital bar** (typical of lemurs and lorises) or by a complete bony cup referred to as **postorbital closure** (typical of monkeys, apes, and humans). The emphasis on vision has other anatomical consequences. For example, the orbits have become enlarged and have moved from a more lateral-facing to a more forward-facing position in the skull. This feature is associated with **binocular vision**, where both eyes focus on the target object and thereby allow it to be perceived with greater depth perception (Fig. 1.1).

Compared with most other mammals the primate brain is enlarged relative to body size. Indeed, primates are unique among living mammals in that the brain constitutes a significantly larger proportion of body weight at all stages of gestation. Modern primates have long gestation periods relative to maternal body size, and both fetal and postnatal growth are characteristically slow in relation to maternal size. Consequently, sexual maturation is attained late, and life spans are correspondingly long relative to body size. In sum, it takes longer for modern primate populations to reproduce themselves than is the case for populations of most other mammals (8).

In many respects, what distinguishes humans from other primates is simply an extension of what distinguishes primates from other mammals. For example, the trends noted above toward increased brain size, delayed maturational periods, and specializations of the hand for object manipulation reach their most extreme development in modern humans.

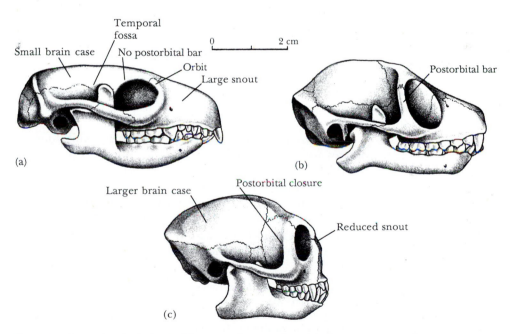

Fig. 1.1. Several morphological features distinguishing modern primate and non-primate skulls.   (a) Insectivoran (hedgehog); (b) prosimian (*Lepilemur*); (c) New World monkey (*Callithrix*). Note relative size changes of brain and snout, development of the postorbital bar and postorbital closure, and position of the eye sockets (106).

Harvard anthropologist David Pilbeam has nicely summarized some of these features that distinguish humans from other primates, in other words, some of the things that "make us human" (9). For example, he notes that in terms of population size, distribution, and genetic structure, modern human populations are found in virtually every environment on the planet, far exceeding the tropical and subtropical ranges characteristic of most nonhuman primate populations. Humans can only accomplish this enormous range extension because we, in a sense, provide our own microenvironments wherever we go (e.g., clothes, shelters, climate control like furnaces and air conditioners, etc.). He also notes that, compared to other primates, humans are a genetically uniform species—so much so that even if all human populations were to disappear except one, about three-quarters of the total human genetic diversity would still be preserved.

We are also distinguished from most other primates by our feeding habits. Whereas most nonhuman primates have fairly restricted or specialized dietary preferences (e.g., fruit-eating [frugivory], leaf-eating [folivory], insect-eating [insectivory], human populations are eclectic in their feeding preferences, selecting from almost every type of plant and animal food available. As we shall see in later chapters, the type of food our ancestors ate, and the way they procured that food, had a tremendous influence on human evolution. Much of our ancestor's cranial and dental anatomy directly reflects the types of stresses generated by powerful chewing muscles (Fig. 1.2a); in addition, the development of increasingly sophisticated tool technologies beginning over 2.5 million years ago has clearly been influenced by food procurement strategies throughout all of human evolution. Indeed, probably the most distinctive feature of modern humans compared to other primates is our now complete reliance on material culture (i.e., tools) for survival.

Probably the most unique skeletal adaptations distinguishing humans from other primates are those of the pelvis and lower limb that permit our unusual type of locomotion—bipedalism (Fig. 1.2b). The origins of bipedalism remain one of the intriguing mysteries of human evolution, and we will discuss it fully in later chapters. For now, let us just note that bipedalism frees the hands from the locomotor function that characterizes all other primate groups and allows them to be used in other critical roles, such as making tools, holding infants, and gathering food.

Fig. 1.2. There are many anatomical and behavioral distinctions between humans and other primates. (a) The size and shape of the human skull have changed dramatically over the past 4 million years. Most of these changes relate to 1) the gradual reduction in the size of the teeth, jaws, and chewing muscles and 2) the threefold increase in brain size. (b) Adaptations of the pelvis and lower limb for bipedal walking are another one of the major anatomical distinctions between humans and other primates. In this model of *Australopithecus afarensis* dated to over 3 mya, many of these unique adaptations were already well underway (107). Photographs courtesy of David Brill.

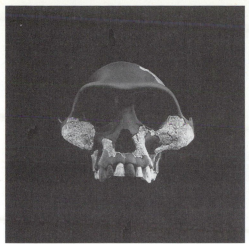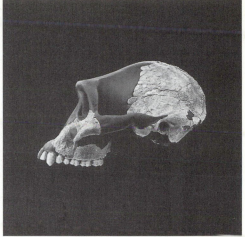

Australopithecus afarensis (composite specimen)

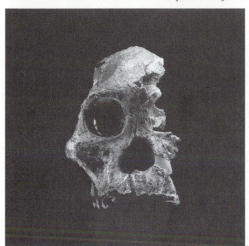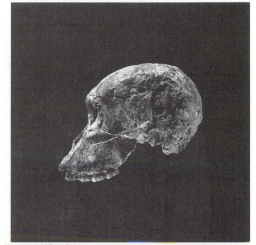

Australopithecus africanus (Sts 71)

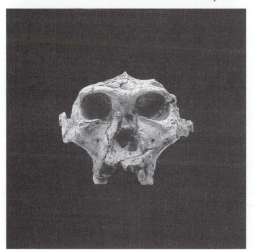

(a)

Australopithecus robustus (SK 48)

(Continued)

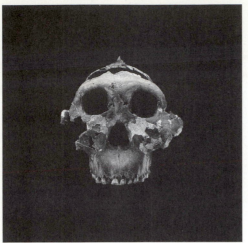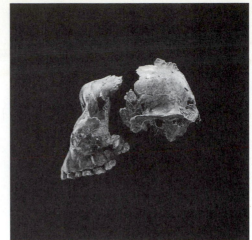

Australopithecus boisei (OH 5)

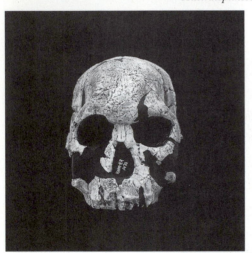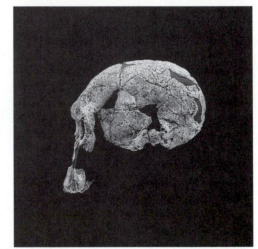

Homo habilis (KNM-ER 1470)

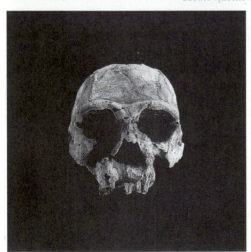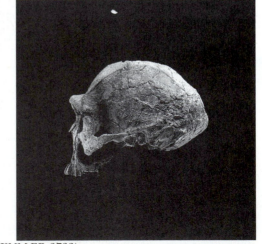

(a)   *Homo erectus* (KNM-ER 3733)

(Continued)

"Archaic" *Homo sapiens* (Petralona 1)

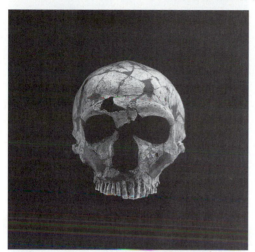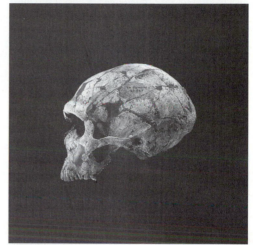

Homo sapiens (Ferrassie 1 Neandertal)

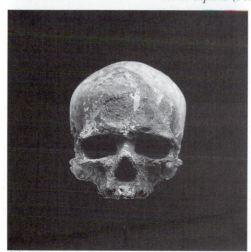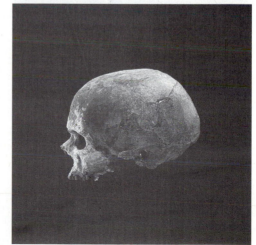

(a)

Homo sapiens (Cro-Magnon 1)

(Continued)

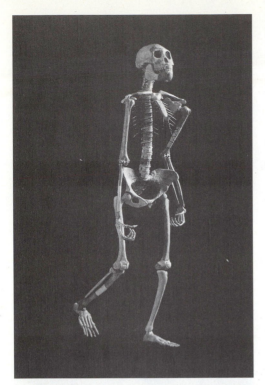
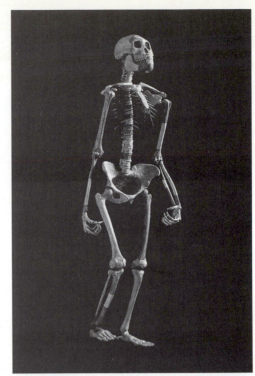
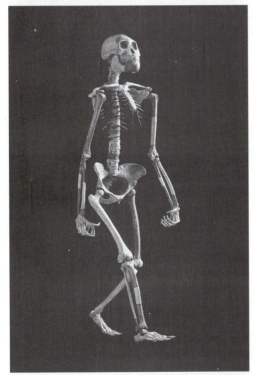
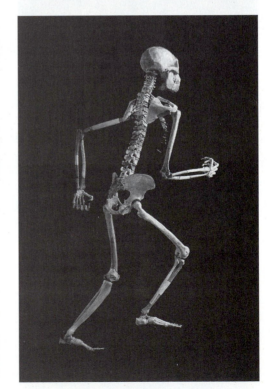

(b)

As alluded to above, a number of life-history variables distinguish humans from other primates. Modern humans have long gestation periods relative to maternal body size as well as prolonged periods of infant dependency. Sexual maturation occurs relatively late, and life spans are correspondingly long. Therefore, compared to other primates, human females have a much longer postreproductive phase to their life cycle. Unlike other primates that usually have peak periods of sexual receptivity, or **estrus**, human females remain receptive throughout the duration of their monthly reproductive cycle.

Finally, one of humanity's most distinguishing characteristics is the evolution of language and the type of symbolic thinking associated with it. Without language, much of our social behavior and interactions would be impossible. The evolution of articulate human speech involved major structural reorganization in both the brain and in the laryngeal apparatus (i.e., the voice-box). As Pilbeam notes, language "makes possible sharing, exploitation and the delay of reward or punishment; the structuring of relationships; propaganda; art; the division of labour; warfare; and the aggregation and socialisation of masses of people. Its most essential feature is that it allows human behavior to be governed by the complex and subtle rules that together make up human culture."

Box 1.1. Some Features Characterizing Living Primates that (in General) Distinguish Them from Other Mammals (8)

1. Lifestyle is typically arboreal; range is mainly restricted to tropical and subtropical ecosystems.
2. Extremities are adapted for prehension; sensitive tactile pads are present on the digits.
3. Locomotion is hindlimb dominated, with the center of gravity of the body located closer to the hindlimbs.
4. The visual sense is greatly emphasized, and the olfactory sense is reduced.
5. The bony housing for the middle ear is formed by a separate bone called the petrosal bone.
6. The brain is moderately enlarged relative to body size (at all stages of gestation) and has a true lateral, or Sylvian, sulcus separating the frontal and parietal lobes from the temporal lobe and a triradiate calcarine sulcus.
7. Males are characterized by early descent of the testes into a scrotal sac.
8. Gestation periods are long relative to maternal body size, and small litters of precocial neonates (i.e., infants born with at least a moderate covering of hair and both ears and eyes open) are produced.
9. Both fetal growth and postnatal growth are characteristically slow in relation to maternal size; sexual maturity is attained late, and life spans are correspondingly long relative to body size (i.e., reproductive turnover is slow).
10. The dental formula exhibits a maximum of two incisors, one canine, three premolars, and three molars in each quadrant of the upper and lower jaws.

ORGANIZATION OF THIS TEXT

Were the changes in human behavior that distinguish us from other primates causally related to the changes in morphology seen in the human fossil record? Can the emergence of humans be considered an evolutionary "revolution" or was it simply a gradual continuation of previously existing evolutionary change both in terms of morphology and culture? What were the selective advantages of the biocultural changes seen in the human fossil record that ultimately allowed us to become dominant in such a relatively short geological time span? These are the kinds of questions we will explore as we follow the course of human evolution over the past 5 million years. We begin in Chapter I by putting human evolution into its proper temporal and paleoenvironmental context by reconstructing the geologic and climatic history of the past 5 million years, the Plio-Pleistocene.

Chapter II begins with a general discussion of what an appropriate fossil site looks like and how paleoanthropologists go about their work. It is followed by an extensive review of the various dating methods used in modern paleoanthropological research, many of which prove critical to the modern interpretations of the human fossil (and archeological) record discussed in later chapters. We also introduce in this chapter three important topics in modern paleoanthropological research: 1) phylogeny reconstruction; 2) classification; and 3) the tempo and mode of evolution. We consider how failure to appreciate the distinction between phylogeny and classification can lead to confusion and misunderstanding in studies of human evolution. The underlying methods, principles, and assumptions of the two major schools of biological classification predominant in paleoanthropology today, evolutionary systematics and phylogenetic systematics (popularly known as cladistics), are compared and contrasted. Two different views of the tempo and mode of evolution are also presented. Chapter II ends with a summary of the taxonomy used in this text.

If, as all modern biology suggests, humankind is part of a long evolutionary continuum, we need to know who or what preceded us in the evolutionary line. That is the question we address in Chapter III. If we seek humankind's antecedents we must search among the fossil hominoids, or primitive "apes," of the Miocene, the epoch preceding the Pliocene; we review that fossil evidence in this chapter.

As the Miocene drew to a close, a major new episode in primate evolution unfolded as one of these Miocene "apes" began its adaptive radiation throughout Africa—and later the entire world. This unusual "ape" would begin to shape its world in ways no other organism had before it. The story of this last major adaptive radiation in hominoid evolution, the human lineage, begins in Chapter IV with the appearance of the earliest undoubted hominids in the fossil record, the australopithecines. Here we encounter for the first time evidence of hominization, the advent of an animal that walked on two legs rather than four, used tools rather than teeth for tearing and cutting, had a relatively large brain, and had evolved behavioral and social mechanisms enabling it to survive the harsh environs of the African savanna. We discuss these trends in detail in Chapter V.

In Chapter VI we review the fossil evidence pertaining to the origins of our own genus, *Homo*. The genus *Homo* first appears in Africa about 2.4–2.0 million years ago (mya). This new genus reveals several important evolutionary distinctions from earlier (and contemporary) australopithecines, including changes in the skull and postcranial skeleton, more sophisticated stone-tool technology, and most importantly, new levels of cerebral organization in terms of both absolute size and complexity. These trends continue throughout the Plio-Pleistocene in the various *Homo* lineages, culminating in early members of our own species, *Homo sapiens*, several hundred thousand years ago.

Over the past two decades an increasing number of fossils ascribed to early *Homo* have been discovered in both eastern and southern Africa, but as the pace of discovery has quickened, so have the inevitable questions such discoveries raise: How can early *Homo* be distinguished from australopithecines, particularly *Australopithecus africanus*? Is the range of morphological variation being subsumed under the name *Homo habilis* too great for a single species? If all these specimens represent more than one species, what other taxa are represented in this heterogeneous sample? Does the definition of *Homo* need modification, and if so, how? Is *Homo habilis* really ancestral to *Homo erectus*? We explore these, and other, questions in this chapter.

In Chapter VII we encounter a larger and more formidable hominid species, and certainly the first to spread out of Africa to populate much of the Old World, *Homo erectus*. Prompted mainly by new, rigorous applications of cladistic techniques, some paleoanthropologists have recently begun to challenge some time-honored opinions about *H. erectus*. Is *H. erectus* simply an arbitrarily defined stage, or grade, of human evolution, temporally and morphologically sandwiched between Plio-Pleistocene *H. habilis* on the one hand and upper Middle Pleistocene archaic *H. sapiens* on the other? Or is it a "real" species with definable boundaries in time and space? Did *H. erectus* exist only in the Far East, where it was first discovered, or can it also be identified in Africa or Europe? Was Asian *H. erectus* simply an evolutionary dead end, contributing little to modern human evolution? In Chapter VII we consider these questions as we examine the fossil evidence for *H. erectus*. By some 500,000–300,000 years ago, *H. erectus* populations were being supplanted by, or evolving into, a highly varied group of hominids living throughout much of the Old World. These rather ill-defined or "transitional" fossil groups are often considered together under the informal and unflattering designation of "archaic" *H. sapiens* because they had not yet evolved morphological features that can be considered typical of later, anatomically modern *H. sapiens*. Throughout the Old World these archaic *H. sapiens* are usually associated with some form of the Developed

Oldowan/Acheulian (chopper/handaxe) tool complex. The fossil record of this group of hominids is discussed in Chapter VIII.

The issue of the biological and behavioral origins of "modern" humans remains one of the most contentious, and exciting, subjects for debate in contemporary paleoanthropology, and the last two decades have seen a virtual revolution in our thinking about modern human origins. This is the topic we fully explore in the last two chapters, Chapters IX and X. Virtually all anthropologists agree that sometime during the Middle/Late Pleistocene transition, important biological and cultural changes were taking place in human evolution between populations of (what are best called) "late archaic humans" and "early modern humans." What is not uniformly agreed upon is exactly where, when, and how these "modern" humans first arose. In these last two chapters we will discuss the molecular, fossil, and archeological evidence that bears on a number of vexing questions about this important transitional period in human evolution. For instance, was the biocultural transition from "late archaic humans" to "early modern humans" restricted in time and space, occurring first in Africa, then radiating outward, or did it develop independently in several different places across the continents?

RECONSTRUCTING PLIO-PLEISTOCENE CLIMATES

Darwin realized over 150 years ago that organisms evolve adaptations that suit them to their habitats, including both the plants and animals they eat and the climate they inhabit. Therefore, the study of human evolution begins properly with the study of climate and geology. Primates, the mammalian order to which humans belong, have been evolving over the past 60–50 million years of earth history. The interval of geologic time over which this process has taken place, the **Cenozoic era**, is subdivided into the Paleocene, Eocene, Oligocene, Miocene, Pliocene, and Pleistocene **epochs**[2] (Fig. 1.3). The story of the evolution of the human primate mainly unfolds over the last two of these epochs, the 5 million years collectively referred to as the Plio-Pleistocene.

The major divisions of earth history that we recognize today—eras, epochs, and others—derive from the work of early geologists who had no way to determine the actual ages of the different rocks they studied. Instead, divisions were defined by the kinds of fossilized animals found in the rocks or sediments or by evidence of major climatic changes. The term for the last epoch of the Cenozoic, the "Pleistocene" (meaning "most recent"), was introduced by Sir Charles Lyell in 1839 to describe those sediments in which 70 percent or more of the molluscan fauna consisted of extant, or

---

[2]The last 10,000 years are sometimes considered a separate epoch, the Holocene.

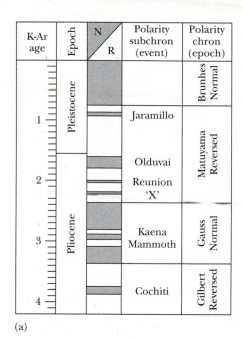

Glaciation sequence		Time kya	Temp.
Alpine	Description		cold ⟶ warm
Holocene	Present Interglaciation	10	
Würm IV		20	
Würm III/IV			
Würm III		30	
Würm II/III	Last Glaciation	40	
		50	
Würm II		60	
		70	
Würm I/II	Last Interglaciation	80	
Würm I		90	
Riss-Würm		100	
Riss	Penultimate Glaciation	200	
Mindel-Riss		300	
Mindel		400	
Günz-Mindel			
Günz		500	

(a) (b)

Fig. 1.3. The paleomagnetic chronology of human evolution over the past 4.2 million years. The Earth's geomagnetic field is known to have gone through a series of complete reversals in its polarity. At various times in the geologic past, its magnetic field has been directed, as it is today, toward the north (normal polarity) and at other times toward the south (reversed polarity). Short-term magnetic reversals of opposite polarity within each chron are called "events." In (a), the normal magnetic polarity chrons, or epochs, are shaded; reversed magnetic chrons are white. Shown expanded in (b) are the Alpine glacial sequences and corresponding temperatures over the past 500,000 years (see text). From (108).

living, species. Soon thereafter, however, other midnineteenth century geologists began the misleading practice of equating the Pleistocene with the "Glacial period," a concept that developed out of an emerging **Glacial theory** that extensive glaciers had formerly covered much of the Northern Hemisphere. Thus began the era of defining the Pleistocene and its subdivisions on the basis of glacial stratigraphy rather than on Lyell's original faunal concept.

Evidence of Climatic Change from Glacial Stratigraphy

The Pleistocene was in fact a time of highly variable global climate and is characterized today by abundant geological evidence of alternating periods of glacial ice advances, or **glacial periods**, and retreats, or **interglacial periods**. Irregular but well-defined episodes of somewhat milder climatic conditions occurring during glacial periods, so-called **interstadials**, are known

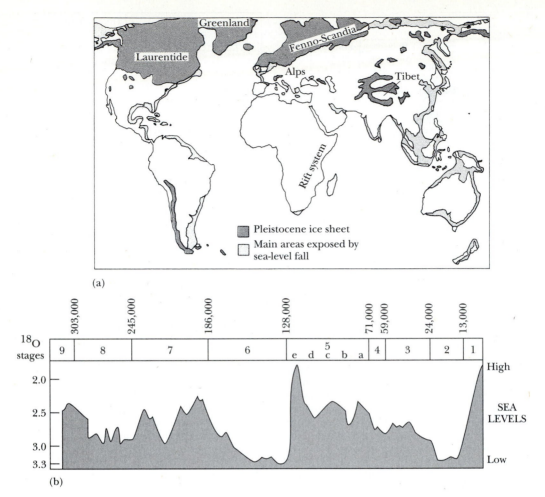

Fig. 1.4. (a) During the last Ice Age glacial ice covered extensive areas of the Northern Hemisphere, causing sea levels to fall by more than 100 m. This lowering of sea level dramatically changed coastlines worldwide by exposing shallow continental shelves. Adapted from (109). (b) Variations in ice and sea levels over the past 300,000 years are recorded in this ^{18}O record. Values on left side represent the proportion of ^{18}O in the sample. The last interglacial (isotopic stage 5e) is notable for its high sea level. Conversely, low sea levels (indicating maximum glacial conditions) are seen in stages 2 and 6 especially (110). (c) Schematic representation of the vegetation during an interglacial and during a glacial, in a north-south section through Europe (111).

from this epoch, and recent analyses of ice cores drilled in central Greenland show that extreme climatic instability characterizes both interglacial and glacial periods, with abrupt climatic changes beginning rapidly and lasting in some cases from only decades to centuries (10–16).

Glacial periods were about 7°C colder than interstadial periods, and about 12–13°C colder than present interglacial temperatures (17). Interestingly, deep-sea sediments in the Middle Pleistocene dating from

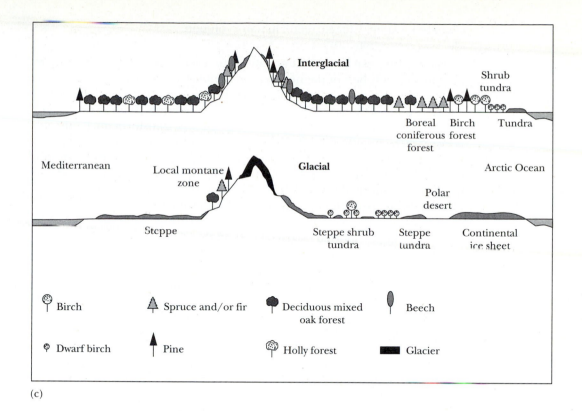

Interglacial

Shrub tundra

Boreal coniferous forest   Birch forest   Tundra

Mediterranean

Glacial

Arctic Ocean

Local montane zone

Polar desert

Steppe

Steppe shrub tundra   Steppe tundra   Continental ice sheet

Birch   Spruce and/or fir   Deciduous mixed oak forest   Beech

Dwarf birch   Pine   Holly forest   Glacier

(c)

400,000–300,000 years ago (the time of the so-called mid-Brunhes climatic event) reveal, in equatorial Africa, a transition to more humid or "interglacial" conditions while more "glacial" ocean conditions were prevailing in the Northern Hemisphere, suggesting that global climatic changes sometimes had opposite effects in the two hemispheres (18).

Alternating episodes of glacial advance and retreat profoundly affected worldwide sea levels, with glacial advances leading to lowered sea levels as seawater was increasingly locked up in the ice sheets and glacial retreats leading to elevated sea levels as seawater was increasingly released from melting ice sheets (19). During Pleistocene glacial ages, the total area covered by glaciers was up to three times as great as today, and many glaciers were 2–3 km thick.[3] Of course, as sea level dropped, more of the continental shelf became exposed and more land corridors were opened up for migrating animals, including early humans. It is estimated that sea levels may have fallen by as much as 100–140 m during glacial periods and risen by as much as 20 m above present day levels during interglacial periods (21–23) (Fig. 1.4).

[3]The total volume of water contained in glaciers outside Greenland and Antarctica is not known precisely, but it is probably equivalent to a sea level rise between about 0.3 and 0.7 m. Global sea level has risen some 10–20 cm over the last century as mountain glaciers have retreated in most parts of the world. Modelling of modern glaciers suggests that for every 1°K warming the area-weighted glacier mass balance will decrease by 0.40 m per year, which corresponds to a sea level rise of 0.58 mm per year (20).

Simply put, glacial ice accumulates whenever snow has not had time to completely melt before the next season's snow begins to accumulate. This is why, given sufficient time, glacial-ice buildup can occur in places like Antarctica even though the total annual precipitation there is no greater than in the Mojave Desert. The power of glaciers to transform the landscape is everywhere manifest, from the gouging out of vast inland lakes, such as the Great Lakes, to the hollowing out of steep cliffs and gorges on mountainsides, or the scooping out of mountain valleys like Yosemite and the fjords of northern Europe. Driven by the force of gravity, glaciers leave other signs of past climatic change including characteristic striations in bedrock inscribed by rocks in the base of overriding glaciers; deposits of rock material transported by glacial ice and then "dumped" by the melting ice on the land surface, known as **glacial drift**; ridges of glacial drift built up from the material riding on the ice that delineates the melting zones along the margins and bottom of the glacier, known as **moraines**; and extensive deposits of windblown glacial dust produced by the grinding down of boulders within glacial ice against bedrock, known as **loess**.

Sometimes layers of glacial drift, referred to as **till**, settle out in thin layers on lake bottoms when currents are calm. Layers of glacial till, known as **varves**, reflect annual cycles of summer melt-off. Varves have proven useful in reconstructing prehistoric time scales (at least back to the end of the last glacial) in the same way that tree rings, in the science of **dendrochronology**, have been used in the southwestern United States.

Evidence of Climatic Change from Deep-Sea Cores

It is becoming increasingly common in modern geological work to investigate Plio-Pleistocene climates using information gleaned from deep-sea cores rather than glacial stratigraphy because deep-sea sedimentation occurs continuously whereas continental sedimentation does not. For example, **oxygen-isotope analysis** from ocean sediments indicates that there have been nearly two dozen glacial advances just within the Pleistocene, many of which would not have been picked up in the terrestrial stratigraphic record (Fig. 1.5a). Today, the powerful technique of analyzing oxygen-isotope ratios in the calcareous shells of deep-sea marine organisms is in-

Fig. 1.5.   (a) The Pleistocene oxygen isotope column as recorded in a deep-sea core from the Pacific Ocean. Note how the amount of ^{18}O isotope varies with the depth of the core. At the 1,200-cm level, the sediments show a change in magnetic polarity that is dated by radiometric means to about 780,000 years ago. The variation in ^{18}O (e.g., $-0.5‰$, $-1.0‰$, etc.) represents changes in the average $^{18}O/^{16}O$ ratio found in bottom-dwelling foraminifera (the ratio increases, i.e., approaches $-0.5‰$, during glacial periods and decreases, i.e., approaches $-2.0‰$, during interglacial periods). From (110). (b) Schematic diagram showing the respective enrichments and depletions of oxygen isotopes 18 and 16 during glacial and interglacial cycles (112).

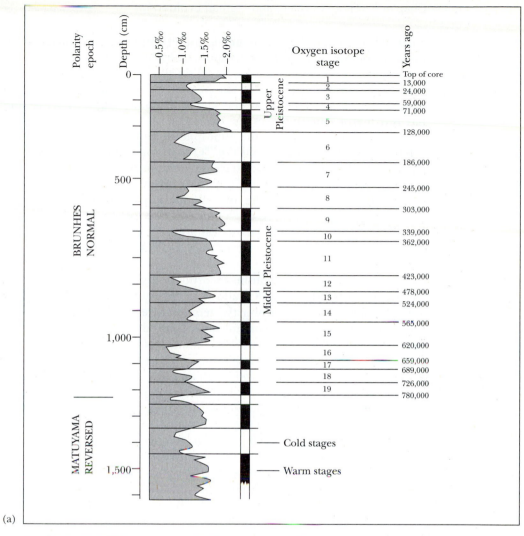

(a)

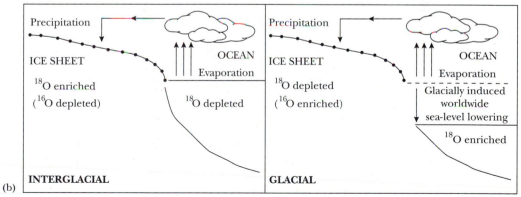

(b)

creasingly used because the oxygen-isotope composition of calcite reflects both ice volume and ocean temperature. In theory at least, oxygen-isotope analysis is relatively simple and is based on the fact that there are two isotopes of oxygen in ocean water, the heavier ^{18}O and the lighter ^{16}O (^{18}O being about 12.5 percent heavier). The differential weight of the isotopes has two useful consequences for the study of ancient environments: as ocean water evaporates into the atmosphere, more of the heavier isotope is left behind in the ocean, and the ^{18}O that does evaporate tends to precipitate out before the ^{16}O, so that precipitation over the interior of continents is relatively deficient in ^{18}O and relatively enriched in ^{16}O, as compared to seawater. Since the overall quantity of the two isotopes is unchanging on Earth, more of ^{16}O tends to be locked up in continental ice during glacial periods, making less available in the oceans. Over time this process leads to an increase in the ^{18}O/^{16}O ratio of seawater during glacial periods.

Since some marine organisms incorporate oxygen when forming their calcareous shells, the ^{18}O/^{16}O ratios preserved in their shells reflect past ocean temperatures—the lower the temperature, the higher the ^{18}O content. Thus, shells of marine organisms recovered from deep-sea sediments provide information about past ice volume *and* ocean temperatures. For this reason, oxygen-isotope stratigraphy can be used to subdivide deep-sea sediments into stages of relatively high and low oxygen-isotope ratios that reflect alternating cold and warm climatic cycles (Fig. 1.5).

Analyses of carbon isotopes in marine fossils provide another independent measure of climatic change with which to cross-check results from oxygen-isotope data. Increases in ocean temperature are associated with increases in atmospheric carbon dioxide: present data indicate a 40 percent increase in atmospheric CO_2 since the last glacial (24). During periods of ocean warming, the lighter isotope of carbon, ^{12}C (compared to heavier ^{13}C), is preferentially evaporated out of the ocean and into the atmosphere as a component of carbon dioxide for the same reason as noted above for the lighter isotope of oxygen. This increase in ^{12}C concentration passes through the atmosphere to land plants as they take up the carbon dioxide and may be detectable in the teeth and bones of animals that fed on the plants (25).

It is now abundantly clear from both oceanic and terrestrial evidence that marked, progressive global cooling began in the early Eocene and culminated in the "Ice Ages" of the Pleistocene. For example, atmospheric CO_2 concentrations can be inferred from the size of fossil leaf **stomata**, the minute respiratory orifices in the epidermis of leaves, and such studies show unmistakable cooling trends through the **Neogene** (Miocene–Pleistocene) (26). This is also clearly reflected in the Cenozoic oxygen-isotope record that shows unequivocal evidence for gradual increases in ^{18}O values (i.e., cooling) through time that were punctuated by several relatively rapid ^{18}O value changes, most notably in the early Oligocene (about 36 mya), the middle Miocene (about 14 mya), and the late Pliocene (about 2.5 mya).

These more rapid cooling events likely correlate with the first major growth of ice sheets on Antarctica, and further subsequent increases in ice volume in Antarctica and in the Northern Hemisphere respectively (27–29).

Causes of Climatic Change during the Plio-Pleistocene

For over a century scientists have hypothesized about the forces that drove these late Cenozoic cooling trends, and we will summarize some of the most popular ideas here. Ample evidence suggests that changes in the Earth's orbit around the Sun were one major factor affecting Pleistocene climates. The Pleistocene record shows that there were about fifteen major cold periods and fifty minor cold advances over the past 1.5 million years, or about one major cold advance every 100,000 years. Virtually all models of the orbital hypothesis of climatic change hold that the **eccentricity** of the Earth's orbit, the **obliquity,** or tilt, of the Earth's axis, and the **precession of the equinoxes** are the controlling variables that influence climate. Each does so through their impact on planetary **insolation,** the geological effect of solar rays on the surface materials of the Earth (30,31).

The influence of these factors may be visualized in the following way. Perturbations of the Earth's orbit are produced by gravitational forces of other planets and periodically alter the geographic distribution of incoming solar radiation. These gravitational forces produce three main perturbations having five primary periods (Fig. 1.6):

1) The Earth's orbit around the Sun varies between near-circularity and more pronounced ellipticity at periods of about 100,000 years and 400,000 years. This is known as the eccentricity of the orbit (Fig. 1.6a). When the orbit is most elliptical the Northern Hemisphere reaches extremely cold temperatures, which may trigger maximum glacial advances.

2) The obliquity, or tilt, of the Earth's axis varies between about 22 and 25 degrees with a period of about 41,000 years (Fig. 1.6a).

3) The third effect is **precession**, which changes the distance between the Earth and the Sun at any given season. There are two components of precession: a) **axial precession**, in which the Earth's axis of rotation "wobbles" like that of a spinning top (the North Pole describes a circle in space with a period of 26,000 years) (Fig. 1.6b); and b) **elliptical precession**, in which the elliptical orbit itself rotates slightly (Fig. 1.6c). The net effect of these two precessions is referred to as the precession of the equinoxes, in which the equinoxes (March 20 and September 22) and the solstices (June 21 and December 21) shift around the Earth's orbit with a period of 22,000 years (Fig. 1.6d).[4] The precession can cause warm winters and cool sum-

---

[4]Equinox is the time when the Sun crosses the plane of the Earth's equator, making night and day all over the Earth of equal length; solstice is the time of year when the Sun is at its greatest distance from the equator.

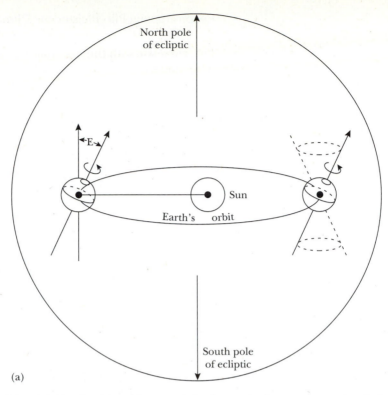

Fig. 1.6. (a) The Earth's orbit around the Sun varies between near-circularity and more pronounced ellipticity at periods of about 100,000 years and 400,000 years (eccentricity of the orbit). When the orbit is most elliptical the Northern Hemisphere reaches extremely cold temperatures, which may trigger maximum glacial advances. The obliquity, or tilt, of the Earth's axis (E) varies between about 22 and 25 degrees with a period approximating 41,000 years. There are two components of precession: (b) axial precession, in which the Earth's axis of rotation "wobbles" like that of a spinning top (the North Pole describes a circle in space with a period of 26,000 years), and (c) elliptical precession, in which the elliptical orbit itself rotates slightly. (d) The net effect of these two precessions is referred to as the precession of the equinoxes (see text). (e) Planetary effects of low orbital insolation correlate quite well with some of the main glacial advances (32).

mers in one hemisphere while having just the opposite effect on the other hemisphere. Presently, the point of closest approach of the Earth to the Sun, or **perihelion**, occurs in northern winter (January). Thus portions of the winter hemisphere receive as much as 10 percent more insolation than they did 11,000 years ago, when perihelion occurred in the summer (32). There now seems little doubt that these planetary effects of low orbital insolation correlate quite well with some of the main glacial advances (Fig. 1.6e).

Other theories also implicate localized tectonic forces as important factors causing major climatic changes. One such force, **continental drift**, is a consequence of powerful convective currents in the Earth's upper mantle, which cause the top 70 km layer of the Earth, including oceanic and con-

Axial precession or "wobble"

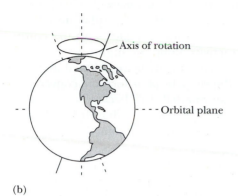

(b)

Precession of the equinoxes

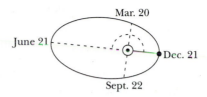

Today

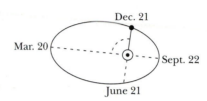

5,500 years ago

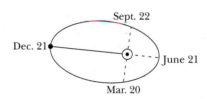

11,000 years ago

● Earth on December 21

 Sun

(d)

Precession of the ellipse

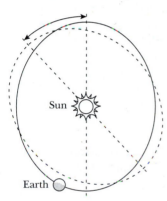

(c)

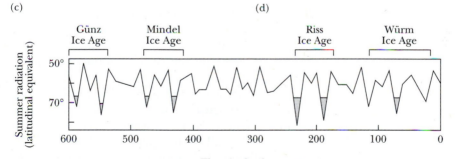

(e)

tinental crust, the **lithosphere,** to move slowly over the underlying layer from 70 to 200 km below the surface, the **asthenosphere**. The top layer consists of independently moving plates, hence the name **plate tectonics**. Probably the single most important factor causing plates, and the continents they bear, to move is volcanic activity along the midoceanic ridges. Along these ridges, new crustal rock is continually being formed and the new rocks are carried to each side of the ridge by plate-tectonic convection (33). Soon after plate tectonics and continental drift became established facts in geological thinking by the late 1960s, the idea that drift of continental plates over the poles may have been a factor in climatic change was proposed.[5]

Another idea was that tectonic movements in critical locations resulted in the formation of ocean gateways that accelerated rapid cooling and glaciation in the Cenozoic by spilling the colder, less salty, and hence lighter waters of the Arctic Ocean over the North Atlantic, eventually covering the entire ocean surface with a layer of low-temperature, low-salinity water (35,36). Another such example is the development of a cold circum-Antarctic current produced when Antarctica separated from South America and Australia (37). The relationship between the emergence of the Isthmus of Panama and the initiation of Northern Hemisphere glaciation is unclear, however. The formation of the isthmus seems to predate widespread Northern Hemisphere glaciation by 2.0 to 0.5 million years (28).

More recently, new "ice-age" theories have focused on the possible climatic effects caused by uplift and erosion of mountain ranges and plateaus during the Cenozoic (38). One such model considers uplift of the Himalayas and the Plateau of Tibet to be *the* main driving force of Cenozoic climate change (28). Although Cenozoic uplift has occurred in other regions of the world (e.g., the Alps, East Africa, and parts of the cordillera of North and South America), nowhere has it reached the immense scale seen in the Himalayas and Tibetan plateau. Formed as a result of the collision between the Indo-Australian and Asian plates beginning in the middle Eocene (about 52–44 mya), and continuing to form today, the Tibetan plateau is the most imposing topographic feature on the planet, having a mean elevation of 5 km and an area half that of the continental United States.

Even though elevation of the Himalayas was initiated in the early Tertiary, the full ecological and climatological impact of the Tibetan plateau uplift has only been fully manifest since the mid- to late Miocene (39–42). We now know that a dramatic ecological shift of plant species occurred at that time, reflected in the transition from a predominance of plants exhibiting the C_3 photosynthetic pathway to those exhibiting C_4 metabolism.

---

[5]It has recently been discovered that the basic elements of the theory of continental drift were first suggested by Abraham Ortellus in 1596, antedating by more than 150 years other writers credited with early formulations of the theory (34).

Indications of the predominance of photosynthetic pathways are gained through **carbon isotope analysis**, specifically by comparing the relative abundance of two carbon-isotopes, ^{12}C and ^{13}C. Distinct carbon isotope "signatures" are passed along the food chain from the plants to the tissues, including tooth enamel, of herbivores. Browsers, for example, display a C_4 isotope signature because of the dominance of foliage from trees, shrubs, forbs, etc., in their diets. Grazers, on the other hand, are mostly C_3, reflecting their more **graminivorous**, or grass-eating diet. Most trees, shrubs, forbs, corms, tubers, and grasses that require cool, wet growing seasons exhibit the C_3 pathway and were dominant before the uplifting of the Tibetan plateau, whereas most grasses that require hot, dry growing seasons exhibit the C_4 pathway and rose in abundance late in the Miocene. C_4 grasses are first detected in Pakistan about 9.4 mya and in Kenya about 15.3 mya, with C_4 grasslands dominating by the Plio-Pleistocene (43). The advent of C_4 plants in the fossil record signals the initial development of the Asian monsoon system of long, dry seasons punctuated by periods of massive rains (44–46). As an example, the basic carbon-isotope signature of modern East African ecosystems is compared with that of Olduvai Gorge (Bed II) in Figure 1.7.

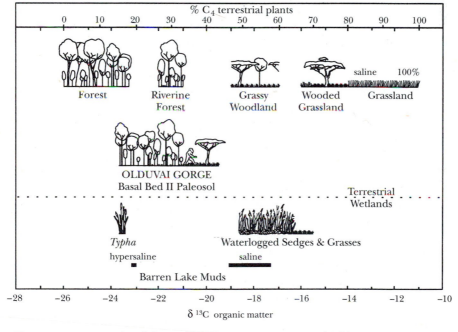

Fig. 1.7. An example of the carbon isotope "signature" of Olduvai Gorge. The upper horizontal scale indicates the approximate equivalent percentage of C_4 flora. The lower horizontal scale indicates that basal Bed II at Olduvai supported a relatively closed riverine forest to grassy woodland habitat (113).

The modern Tibetan plateau is so vast that its weather drives not only the regionally intense monsoon circulation, but also perturbs atmospheric circulation on a hemispheric scale. Computer-simulated climate models that factor in the effects of changing Tibetan plateau topography[6] successfully predict climatic trends from the equable, moist temperate climates characteristic of the early and mid-Cenozoic to the periodic cold/warm and dry/wet regional patterns seen today in the Northern Hemisphere (28, 47). These models propose that over the past 40 million years or so, uplift of the Tibetan plateau resulted in stronger deflections of the atmospheric jet stream, more intense monsoonal circulation, increased rainfall on the front slopes of the Himalayas, greater rates of chemical weathering, and ultimately, lower atmospheric CO_2 concentrations.

Before the rise of the plateau, the Earth's climate was more equable, warmer, and more temperate. Since the uplift of the plateau, however, hot air gathers at its top each year, rises, and is displaced by moist, cooler air from the Indian Ocean, which causes the annual monsoon rains. This continual cycle produces a "chemical weathering" phenomemon: the heavy monsoonal rain contributes to the removal of vast amounts of carbon dioxide from the atmosphere; the carbon dioxide in the rain reacts with silicate rocks that are exposed as the plateau rises; the heavy rain weathers the rock, and the minerals are ultimately washed downriver into the ocean, where they are incorporated into the shells of marine animals, eventually to be desposited as limestone on the ocean floor. The Tibetan plateau and the Himalayas produce up to a quarter of the rock sediment released into the world's oceans, though they make up only 5 percent of the landmass. The removal of so much carbon dioxide from the atmosphere over millions of years has helped cool the Earth's temperatures by reducing the "**greenhouse effect**," the trapping of heat in the Earth's atmosphere by carbon dioxide. Indeed, climate modelling studies have shown that greater mean South Asian summer monsoonal rainfall and warmer surface temperatures are associated with increases in atmospheric carbon dioxide concentration (48).

Fully understanding the forces driving climatic change is difficult by any standard. But we can conclude from the previous discussion that taken as a whole, such factors as change in the tilt of the Earth's axis, continental drift, mountain building, and glacial sedimentation may have initiated strong positive feedback loops to global cooling (28,39). The previous review of glacial and oxygen-isotope evidence of climatic change leads the way for a more detailed look at the geological events and chronology of the Plio-Pleistocene.

---

[6]Such models in fact show that high topography alone is not sufficient to initiate the growth of large terrestrial ice sheets in both hemispheres and so is among the factors contributing to these climatic changes.

THE PLIO-PLEISTOCENE TIME SCALE

As we said earlier, geologists usually divide geological history into divisions that reflect major climatic changes and changes in fossilized flora and fauna. Today, the base of the Pleistocene is defined at its type locality at Vrica, Italy, by the first occurrence there of cold water–adapted mollusks that are today restricted to the North Sea and the Baltic. This abrupt appearance of cold water–adapted mollusks, and hence by definition the base of the Lower Pleistocene, is presently dated to about 1.64 mya and reflects the onset of climates far colder than those of the preceding Pliocene. This Plio-Pleistocene boundary datum coincides quite closely with other more modern indicators that we will discuss below (49,50).

The Pleistocene is traditionally subdivided into **Lower**, **Middle**, and **Upper** (or **Late**) **Pleistocene** time intervals, though there is little evidence now that these original divisions have global significance since they were originally applied to undefined stratigraphic sediments in the Bavarian Alps (22). Much work in the past few decades has gone into refining the Pleistocene time scale using recent advances in glacial stratigraphy, geomagnetic polarity reversal stratigraphy, deep-sea oxygen-isotope stratigraphy, and radiometric dating techniques. Using global glacial criteria, modern stratigraphers correlate the onset of the Middle Pleistocene to the first evidence of continental glaciation in Europe (about 900,000 years ago)[7] and its termination to the end of the next-to-last glacial (Riss or Saale) in Europe and (Wisconsinian I) in North America about 127,000 years ago (51). Thus, on the basis of glacial stratigraphy the Lower Pleistocene was about 1.6–0.9 mya, the Middle Pleistocene was about 900,000–127,000 years ago, and the Late Pleistocene extends from about 127,000 years ago, continuing to the present or to 10,000 years B.P. (before present) if one recognizes the Holocene.

The Contribution of Geomagnetic Reversal Studies

The first indication that the Earth's magnetic field may have reversed its polarity was presented in 1906 by the French physicist Bernard Brunhes, after whom the Brunhes normal polarity epoch was named (see Fig. 1.3). Twenty years later, M. Matuyama concluded that the Earth's magnetic field had a reversed polarity during the early Pleistocene and that it has been normal since then, hence the Matuyama reversed polarity epoch.

---

[7]Some advocate that the beginning of the Brunhes normal polarity chron at 0.72 mya be used to define the beginning of the middle Pleistocene, but this is inconsistent with the requirement that all epochs be defined in fossiliferous marine sediments.

The geomagnetic field is known to have gone through a series of complete reversals in its polarity lasting from 10^4 to 10^7 years (52). At various times in the geologic past, the Earth's magnetic field has been directed, as it is today, toward the north, or normal polarity, and at other times toward the south, or reversed polarity. The cause(s) of these reversals in the magnetic field are not yet clearly understood but are thought to originate from electric currents in the Earth's outer core, which consists mainly of liquid iron. In addition, the intriguing possibility exists that the Earth's magnetic field shifts by following preferred (that is, predictable) paths along longitudinal meridians, and these patterns of change may eventually provide insights into the causes of the changes themselves. For example, over the past 5 million years or so there has been a tendency for the polarity reversals to be characteristically biased along two longitudinal bands, one centered over the Americas and the other over East Asia and Australia, rather than being uniformly distributed around the geographical North Pole (53,54).

Magnetic minerals in rocks preserve a magnetic vector indicating the orientation and intensity of the global magnetic field within which they formed, and this vector can be detected and used to indicate the relative time and position of the rock's formation. The processes by which sediments are magnetized are thought to depend on several factors, including magnetic mineralogy, duration of the transitional field state, and sedimentation rate (55). Hundreds of magnetic field reversals are now well documented in the geological record. In general, it takes about 5,000 years for a total reversal to occur. However, on occasion during a reversal the magnetic field can undergo extremely rapid changes, up to about 6 degrees per day (56)! The magnetic histories of rocks and sediments are used to construct a **geomagnetic polarity reversal time scale** of a field or region that consists of extended intervals called **polarity epochs** during which the field has predominantly one polarity, interrupted by shorter **polarity events** of opposite polarity. By convention, polarity epochs are named after scientists who made significant contributions to studies of the Earth's magnetic field and polarity events are named after the location at which a reversal was first recognized. The reversal scale for the past 5 million years contains four epochs, starting with the present: **Brunhes** (normal), **Matuyama** (reversed), **Gauss** (normal), and **Gilbert** (reversed) (see Fig. 1.3).

Paleontologists can use magnetic profiles if they can fit a sequence of fossiliferous sediments containing fossils of interest into a **paleomagnetic column,** or magnetostratigraphic profile of a region. A viable column requires that the ages of the actual magnetic reversals represented in the profile be dated by independent means, usually by radiometric techniques, which will be discussed later. A radiometrically dated column allows the age of the fossils to be determined within the limits of resolution of that column. Measurements of past reversals in the Earth's magnetic field are important to paleoanthropologists for another reason: they document the progress of continental drift, a phenomenon that has had a profound impact on the distribution of plant and animal species, including primates, and hence on their evolution. Volcanic activity at the midoceanic ridges is continually creating new crustal rocks, which, as they cool, become magnetized in the direction of the prevailing geomagnetic field while they move to both sides of the ridge, creating sea-floor spreading. In effect, sea-floor spreading can be likened to a tape recording of changes in polarity of the Earth's magnetic field on both sides of the ridge. Geologists can play back this recording to reconstruct the past positions of the continents. This paleomagnetic record of sea-floor spreading can be extended back to rocks dating to the middle Jurassic, about 180 mya (57,58).

Recently it has been proposed that Pleistocene subdivisions are better correlated to the geomagnetic polarity record and to the marine oxygen-isotope record than to glacial stratigraphy, since continental glacial stratigraphy is so incomplete and not applicable worldwide. Accordingly, it has been recommended that the Lower/Middle Pleistocene boundary be set at the Matuyama/Bruhnes magnetic polarity reversal about 780,000 years ago (59) and that the Middle/Late Pleistocene boundary be set at the beginning of the previous interglacial incursion of the sea over land about 127,000 years ago (60), a change known as a **transgression** that converts initially shallow-water conditions to deeper-water conditions. This latter date corresponds quite closely to the beginning of marine oxygen-isotope stage 5e, which is assigned a provisional age of about 125,000 years (50,61) (Fig. 1.4b).

A Summary of Plio-Pleistocene Glaciations

Geologists are continually refining the dates for the epoch immediately preceding the Pleistocene, the Pliocene. The base of the Pliocene is currently defined at its type site at Capo Rosello, Sicily, to just above the Chron 5/Gilbert boundary of the paleomagnetic time scale at about 5.3 mya. This essentially coincides to the time interval from the end of the so-called **Messinian salinity crisis** about 5.3 mya, when sea level dropped worldwide, producing the temporary desiccation of the Mediterranean Sea, to the base of the Lower Pleistocene about 1.6 mya. A number of factors, including the sudden increase in global ice volume caused by the expanse of Antarctic glaciers, brought about the drastic lowering of sea level that precipitated the Messinian crisis (62–66). The complete drying up of such a large body of water had profound biological and geological consequences. Of particular interest is the fact that the expanded dry-land connections between Africa and Europe permitted the free exchange of faunas and floras, including increased selection for annuals in the herbaceous flora of the Mediterranean region.

It now seems apparent that substantial glaciation events were already well under way by the late Miocene, perhaps as early as 8 mya in Greenland (67). There is also evidence suggesting that globally significant climatic

Table 1.1   Glaciation during the Plio-Pleistocene

6.0–4.3 mya: Global ice volume fluctuated about a constant mean with an average amplitude of about 0.5 percent

4.3–2.8 mya: Global ice volume fluctuated around a smaller mean

2.8–2.4 mya: Global ice volume began a cyclic but steady increase, culminating in an abrupt increase about 2.4 mya to a volume significantly larger than had been attained in the preceding 4 million years

2.4–2.1 mya: Global ice volume decreased steadily

2.1–0.9 mya: Global ice volume stabilized

0.9–0.7 mya: Global ice volume increased abruptly to a new maximum about 700,000 years ago

0.7 mya–present: Large-amplitude, approximately 100,000-year fluctuations in ice-sheet volume

perturbations were generating glaciers in other parts of the world at about this same time, including the Southern Hemisphere, where glaciers were probably present in Antarctica and in Patagonia (Argentina) about 7–6 mya (68).

By the middle Pliocene, about 3.5 mya, these Antarctic ice sheets had retreated in the face of somewhat warmer temperatures, sea level rose, and there is evidence to suggest that the East Antarctic ice sheet suffered extensive deglaciation, although some geological evidence suggests that this ice sheet has endured for at least 4.3 million years (69–71). However, by about 2.5 mya the cold cycle was back and brought with it the return of lowered temperatures and advancing ice sheets (72). It was this cold phase for which geologists first found evidence of mountain glaciation in the western United States and Canada. These periodic swings between warmer and colder conditions continued into the later Pliocene and reached their peak in the Pleistocene. The main events leading up to and including the Plio-Pleistocene global ice volume retreats and advances are summarized in Table 1.1 (73).

THE ARCHEOLOGICAL TIME SCALE

Over the years, archeologists have developed their own definitions for subdividing the (late) Plio-Pleistocene into **Early** (or **Lower**), **Middle**, and **Late** (or **Upper**) **Paleolithic** based mainly on stone-tool complexes. It should be emphasized that these terms refer to cultural complexes of early humans and are *not* synonymous with the chronostratigraphic terms Early, Middle, and Late Pleistocene as defined above. To add to the confusion, the terms Early, Middle, and Late Stone Age have often been used for subdivisions of the sub-Saharan Stone Age. The approximate chronological arrangement of these major cultural divisions and their characteristic tool types as well as inferred behavioral traits are shown in Figure 1.8.

The Lower Paleolithic spans the interval between the first evidence of stone-tool manufacture about 2.6 mya in East Africa and the first appearance, or predominance, of prepared-core flake technologies and flake tools about 200,000–40,000 years ago.

Depending upon the particular time and place, these Lower Paleolithic industries are characterized by choppers and flakes (e.g., Oldowan industry), handaxes and/or cleavers (e.g., Acheulian industry), and unspecial-

Age and Main Division	Stone Technology		Some Other Tools[a]	Behavioral Traits
	General	Specific		
Present Late Stone Age 0.035 MYA	Specialized composite tools Abstractions Cave art	Many regional traditions Many functionally specific tool sets	Digging sticks — Carrying trays, etc. — Spears — Throwing sticks — Shaped: opportunistic — Bone tools: opportunistic — Fire ?	Population expansion Small bands Intensive seasonal resource use in smaller areas Cohesion for ceremonies and exchange
0.04 MYA Middle Stone Age 0.15 MYA	Simple compound tools Hafting begins	Several regional traditions and chronological sets		Seasonal herding of livestock Resource and task-specific camps Regular reoccupation by large bands in large territories
0.2 MYA Early Stone Age II Acheulian and Developed Oldowan 1.8 MYA	First standard tool forms	Large cutting bifacial tools Chopper/light-duty complex		Organized hunting of large animals Scavenging and planned collecting Widely adapted sites reoccupied
2.0 MYA Early Stone Age I Oldowan 2.5 MYA	Selected opportunistic tools	Choppers Spheroids Light duty Heavy duty Small cutting tools		Scavenging and hunting of small animals Collecting insects, eggs, and plant foods from brief stopovers
No known flaked stone tools 5.0 MYA	Simple opportunistic tools (sticks, etc.)?	Manuports?		Collecting plant foods, insects, and small mammals

[a] – – – Inferred ——— Confirmed

Fig. 1.8. The approximate chronological arrangement of the major cultural divisions of the Plio-Pleistocene. Adapted from (114).

ized flakes (e.g., Clactonian industry) (74) (Fig. 1.9a–d). The main difference between a **handaxe** and a **cleaver** is that the former has a more or less
pointed end while the latter has a straighter cutting edge. More will be said
about these early tool industries in later chapters.

The Middle Paleolithic (about 200,000–35,000 years ago) is often referred to (in Europe at least) as the **Mousterian** after the site of Le Moustier
in France, where it was first recognized (Fig. 1.9e–h). It is characterized by
increasing sophistication of stone-tool technology, particularly in the use
of flake tools made from prepared cores (e.g., **Levallois cores**). A Levallois
core is one that is extensively preshaped in order to produce one or more
flakes having a predetermined shape (Fig. 1.9e). The first appearance of
Middle Paleolithic tools is not a synchronous event throughout the Old
World. Mousterian sites are dominated by sidescrapers and denticulates
that have little regional specificity and are difficult to sort into discrete,
nonoverlapping categories. In Europe, the only fossil hominids found at
Mousterian sites are Neandertals[8]; however, skeletal material associated
with Middle Stone Age (= Middle Paleolithic) industries of southern Africa
and the Near East (e.g., Skhul and Qafzeh) appear much less Neandertallike, approaching anatomically modern humans more closely (76,77). We
shall have much more to say about this in a later chapter.

The Upper Paleolithic (about 45,000–10,000 years ago) is characterized
by the predominance of well-made **blades** (by definition, any flake that is
at least twice as long as wide is a blade), microliths, distinctive bone points,
and the use of **burins** (tools with a chisellike point) and other tools to work
bone, antler, ivory, teeth, and shells, although as one might expect, many
Middle Paleolithic tool types continue with diminished frequency into the
Upper Paleolithic as well (78,79) (Fig. 1.9i–l). As is true of Middle Paleolithic tools, the first appearance of Upper Paleolithic tools did not occur
synchronously throughout the Old World. The oldest Upper Paleolithic
technology in Europe comes from the Balkans (Bacho Kiro and Temnata,
Bulgaria) dated to approximately 45,000 years ago and appears in both
Spain (Castillo) and Belgium (Magrite) at least 40,000 years ago (80). In
fact, recent discoveries from the Semliki Valley, Zaire, suggest that finely
made bone tools were being made in the western rift valley of Africa some
90,000–75,000 years ago (81,82). Decorative beads, pendants, and other

---

[8]British (and older American) authors usually spell Neandertal with an ''h'' (Neanderthal).
Virtually everyone else, including contemporary American authors, now spell it without the
''h'' (Neandertal). For trivia buffs: in 1863 an account of the skull from Neandertal was
read by Prof. W. King to the Geological Association for the Advancement of Science at
Newcastle-upon-Tyne. His address was published using the new specific name *Homo
neanderthalensis* in 1864. According to the International Rules of Zoological Nomenclature,
Article 19, ''The original orthography of a name is to be preserved unless an error of
transcription, a *lapsus calami*, or a typographical error is evident. Since none of these
conditions apply, the scientific name of this species (for those who consider it a distinct
species) must be *neanderthalensis*, although in colloquial and adjectival forms the name can
be modified to Neandertal'' (75).

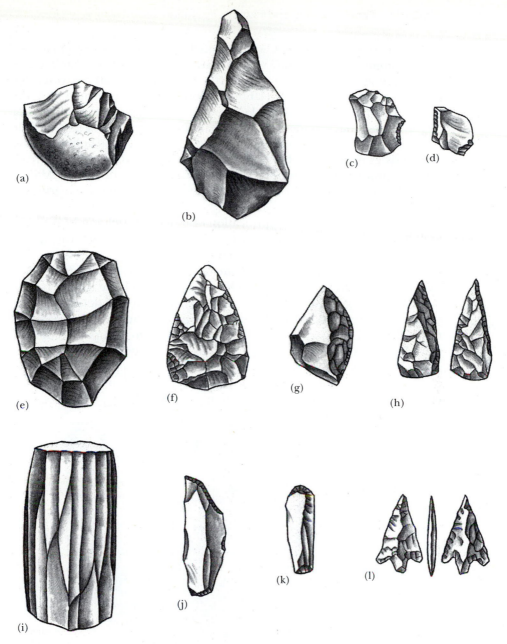

Fig. 1.9. Representative stone tools of the Paleolithic (74). Lower Paleolithic: (a) Oldowan chopper, Africa; (b) early Acheulian handaxe, Africa; (c) Clactonian flake tool, Europe; (d) flake tool, China. Middle Paleolithic: (e) Levallois core with flakes removed from it, Europe; (f) Mousterian handaxe, France; (g) Quina convex scraper, Europe; (h) Pietersburg bifacial point, South Africa. Upper Paleolithic: (i) prismatic blade core; (j) burin on blade; (k) Perigordian end scraper; (l) Solutrean tanged point.

items of personal adornment become much more common, raw materials such as stone, ivory, and shell were traded over long distances, and graves were more elaborate (83,84) (Fig. 1.10). Of particular interest is the appearance in Eurasia of more elaborate dwellings such as mammoth bone huts (85). Upper Paleolithic tool complexes also tend to exhibit a greater degree of regional specificity than those of the preceding Lower or Middle Paleolithic. In the Late Stone Age (= Upper Paleolithic) of southern Africa, one finds clear evidence for better utilization of marine resources (e.g., fishing, capture of fur seals) (86–88). At least one South African Middle Stone Age site, Klasies River, also shows evidence of extensive marine resource exploitation.

In terms of variety and sophistication of tool types, richness of symbolic and artistic expression, and successful exploitation of ever-increasing and diverse food resources, this transition from the Middle to Upper Paleolithic about 50,000–40,000 years ago documents a radical transformation in human behavior, one that Stanford archeologist Richard Klein considers "the most dramatic behavioral shift that archaeologists will ever detect, . . . [one that] almost certainly marks the advent of the fully modern way of doing things or, more precisely, of the fully modern ability to manipulate culture" (79). Upper Paleolithic industries are usually associated with anatomically modern humans although two sites in France are exceptions: at Arcy-sur-Cure and Saint-Césaire Neandertal remains are found in association with early Upper Paleolithic Châtelperronian tools.

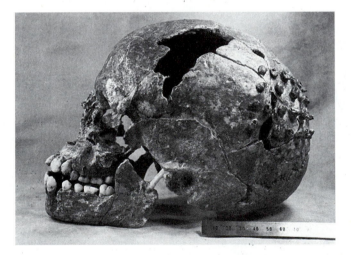

Fig. 1.10.   Side view of an adolescent skull from the Upper Pleistocene burial site of Grotte des Enfants, Grimaldi, Italy.   Many Upper Pleistocene skeletons, like those at Grimaldi, were deliberately buried and their bones colored with red ocher. Shell ornaments and other decorations often surrounded the skeletons. Note the coiffe, or headpiece, made from pierced shells on the back of this adolescent's skull. (Photo courtesy of B. Schumann.)

EFFECTS OF MIOCENE AND PLIO-PLEISTOCENE CLIMATES ON HOMINID EVOLUTION

Events at the end of the Miocene may have had far-reaching implications for hominid paleobiology during the Plio-Pleistocene. During the Antarctic ice-cap buildup, for instance, cold, upwelling water flowed along the west coast of Africa and, by drawing moisture-laden air off the land, increased the aridity of the coastal areas of southern Africa (89). Any flora strongly dependent on high rainfall patterns would have suffered during this period as more open, drought-resistant forms of vegetation spread. This trend, which we will review in detail in later chapters, must have put pressure on arboreal hominoids of the late Miocene in Africa, since the equatorial forests were undoubtedly shrinking. The continuation of this process greatly enlarged the area of the transitional ecological zone between forest and adjacent savanna. It is tempting to view this transitional ecological zone, which is neither forest nor savanna, as the area in which behavioral and anatomical changes were taking place in hominid evolution. These changes, which will be examined in detail in Chapters IV and V, ultimately led from arboreal quadrupedalism to terrestrial bipedalism (90).

Several ecological models of hominid origins and bipedalism stress the importance of such fringe environments as they arose in Africa about 12–5 mya. For example, one such model speculates that at the time the African apes and australopithecines split from their common ancestor, the initial ecological niche available to both would most likely have been rather broad, including dense to fairly open savanna and some even more densely forested areas (91). The result of the growth of the fringe environment might have been to lessen competition between the new sibling species by partitioning the niche occupied by the parent species into two narrower and less overlapping adaptive zones: the australopithecines would have gravitated to the more open areas and the African apes would have moved into the more densely forested regions. This fringe environment model goes on to predict that competition would have been further reduced if the apes and australopithecines had developed their own special dietary, dental, and locomotor adaptations. Such specializations of early hominids would have included the evolution of a powerful masticatory, or chewing, apparatus, bipedalism, the use of rudimentary tools and weapons, and a set of social changes including the use of home bases, the division of labor, and food-sharing.

Recent research casts some doubt on this rather neat scenario that "explains" the origins of bipedality as an adaptive response to the transition from forested to more open habitats. Analyses of stable carbon isotopes from soils in Kenya's East African rift valley indicate that a heterogeneous environment persisted for the last 15 million years in the region and that open grasslands never did dominate this portion of East Africa. If true, there is then no evidence for a sudden or dramatic shift from more forested to more grassland habitats during this early phase of hominid evolution and suggests that if hominids evolved in East Africa during the late Miocene, they did so in an ecologically diverse setting (92). Recent discoveries in Ethiopia also suggest more wooded habitats for the earliest hominids from that region of East Africa (93,94). And finally we should note that recent long-term observations indicate that rain forest–dwelling chimpanzees from West Africa use more tools, make them in more different ways, hunt more frequently and more often in groups, and show more frequent cooperation and food-sharing than their savanna-dwelling relatives do—all behaviors that we tend to associate with models of early hominid behavior (95). We shall come back to a more detailed discussion of these early hominids and the origins of bipedality in Chapters IV and V.

A number of hypotheses have been developed that attempt to relate widespread climatic and associated environmental change, particularly the widespread cooling that occurred around 2.5 mya and affected faunas and floras worldwide, to important events in Plio-Pleistocene hominid evolution (see Box 1.2). These hypotheses are collectively referred to as the **climatic forcing model** and much of the data relating to this model are summarized

Box 1.2.   The Climatic Forcing Model and Plio-Pleistocene Hominid Evolution

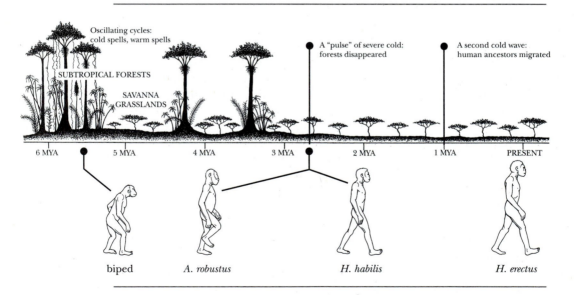

in Figure 1.11. In general, this model concludes that major speciation events in early African hominids (as well as other African mammals) are coincident with shifts to more arid, open conditions in Africa around 2.5 mya, 1.7 mya, and 1.0 mya—time periods that correlate to the growth and subsequent expansion of ice sheets in the higher latitudes. The model's hypothesis is supported by data from many locales, including records of African climate variability from deep-sea drilling of marine sedimentary sequences off the African coasts (96). In southern Africa changes in fossil bovids reflect a shift from moderately moist, or mesic, and bush-covered

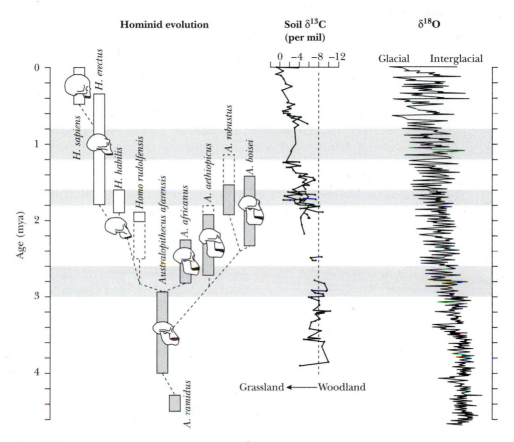

Fig. 1.11. Temporal relations between changes in one scenario of hominid evolution, East African vegetation, and glacial ice volume. Steplike increases in African aridity at about 2.8, 1.7, and 1.0 mya may be related to significant speciation events in early hominid evolution. Increased regional aridity near 1.7 mya is supported by soil carbonate stable isotopic evidence (^{13}C values) and general cooling trends through the Plio-Pleistocene are evident in the oxygen isotope ^{18}O values (96).

environments to more arid and open ones (97). In East Africa this conclusion is supported by changes in micromammals (98), pollen assemblages (99), and bovids that all reflect expansion of arid and open grasslands. Many of the larger African mammals, including elephants, pigs, horses, rhinos, and "robust" australopithecines, all show trends toward increasingly high-crowned teeth, or **hypsodonty,** and/or hypermasticatory development about this time, adaptations associated with grassland diets of tougher and perhaps more abrasive foodstuffs (100). Tundralike open vegetation also first appears in northern-central Europe about this same time, and the major glaciations in the Northern Hemisphere begin. In China one finds widespread and thick loess deposits (101), and in the mountains of Colombia there is evidence for a significant lowering of the tree line (102).

The climatic cooling noted at about 2.5 mya also marks the appearance in Europe of a distinctive mammalian fauna that includes animals particularly well adapted to highly seasonal, drought-resistant grasslands. This fauna characterizes the **Villafranchian** mammal age and is recognized by the presence of mammoths (*Mammuthus*), true bovines (cattle, bison, buffalo), and one-toed horses (*Equus*). None of the widespread Miocene hominoids of Eurasia (e.g., *Dryopithecus, Pliopithecus, Sivapithecus*) survived into the Pliocene of Europe and only *Gigantopithecus* and fossil gibbons and orangutans persisted in Asia. (We will review the Miocene hominoid fossil record in Chapter III.) Likewise, none of the vast array of African Miocene hominoids are known from the Pliocene of that continent, although hominoids must, of course, have existed somewhere in Africa at that time, since their modern descendants, chimpanzees and gorillas, still survive there. Instead, what we do find in the Pliocene of Africa are the first undoubted hominids in the fossil record, the subject of Chapters IV and V.

But how well does the climatic forcing model hold up, compared and contrasted to another general model of speciation, the **Red Queen Model**, which holds that evolutionary change leading to new species is driven by competition among populations that share the same habitat and that sexual recombination evolved to augment a population's capacity to evolve quickly (103)? In contrast to the climatic forcing model, the Red Queen Model would not predict a tight relationship between major climatic change and speciation events but would instead predict evolutionary change to continue even during periods of relative climatic stability. Two recent studies compared speciation events in hominid evolution to climatic patterns over the past 5 million years to see if any correlation between the two emerged (104,105). The results were unequivocal: not a single statistically significant correlation was obtained between the first appearance of hominid taxa (speciation) and any climatic variable. This is not to say that climate does not affect hominid evolution, it most certainly does, particularly on levels of taxonomic diversity and extinction patterns. What it does say is that climatic forcing *alone* cannot explain the pattern of hominid evolution and that such patterns are probably best viewed as resulting from both climatic and intra- and interspecific competition.

Now that we have placed the study of human evolution within a general temporal and paleoclimatological framework, we are now prepared to launch into a more detailed discussion of how paleoanthropologists actually find, date, and name fossil hominids.

CHAPTER II

Finding, Dating, and Naming Fossil Hominids

One reason evolutionary scenarios are so contentious is that palaeoanthropologists continually name fossil species and then create scenarios based on the artificial constructs they have just created.

Glenn C. Conroy
"Closing the hominid gap" (*Nature* 360, 1992)

INTRODUCTION

Establishing plausible scenarios to explain how fossil hominids relate one to another is a central problem in the study of human evolution, and the aspect of evolutionary study most prone to controversy. Before delving into the technicalities of hominid phylogeny and classification, we will first look at some examples of what paleoanthropologists do in the field and laboratory. Nearly all aspects of human paleontology—which include interpreting hominid fossils, establishing phylogenies, and speculating about the tempo and mode of human evolution—depend on some understanding of how and where fossils are found, and on how they are dated.

FINDING FOSSIL HOMINIDS

How do the remains of once-living animals end up as fossils—or to put it another way, how do bones that were once part of the biosphere end up as stones, or part of the lithosphere? The science that concerns itself with the process of fossilization is called **taphonomy**, which literally means "laws of burial" (1,2). Since fossilization usually takes place over thousands or millions of years, and much of the original geological and biological information is lost during the process (such as the ancient environmental context of the site or the form and function of soft tissues, like muscles) one of the main objectives of modern paleoanthropological research is to reconstruct as much of this lost information as possible. In order to do so, the geological and biological conditions responsible for the creation of the particular fossil assemblage under study must be investigated (Fig. 2.1).

Both geological and biological factors determine what type(s) of environment(s) best preserve fossil bones after death (3). Geological factors would include the geometry and lithology of the sediments, i.e. their thickness, composition, and grain size, and their structure or dynamics, which could depend, for example, on the existence of former streams or lake beds. Biological factors affecting fossil preservation might include the presence of predators like leopards or bone scavengers like hyenas and porcupines, or a depositional composition that alters bone chemistry. Geologists refer to the sum of the physical, chemical, and biological changes affecting a fossil-bearing sediment as **diagenesis.** Sedimentary diagenesis involves a temporal element as well: were the fossils deposited over a relatively long or a short period of time, or even over a geologically "instantaneous" period of time, as through a single catastrophic event like a volcanic eruption or flash flood?

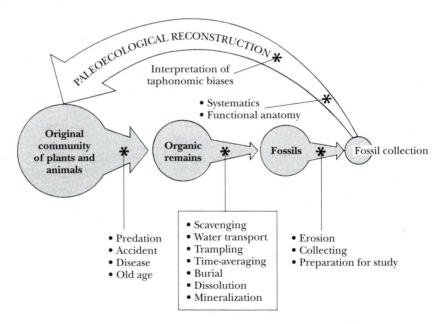

Fig. 2.1. Taphonomy is the study of how fossil samples are related to the original plant and animal communities of the past.   In order to reconstruct these past communities, the biological and geological conditions responsible for the creation of the particular fossil assemblage under study must be investigated (65).

Because the factors that prevent bones from fossilizing far outnumber those that are conducive to fossilization, the chances are exceedingly small that any one previously living hominid individual would ever become fossilized, much less that it would be discovered thousands or millions of years later by paleoanthropologists. And yet there have been many hominid fossil discoveries, some fortuitous and others the result of dogged persistence in the field. The study of taphonomy has led to an improved ability to describe the unique terrains and conditions in which hominid fossils are most likely to be recovered, and these predictions tend to correlate with the history of hominid finds. Virtually all hominid fossils have been discovered in one of four main depositional environments: 1) volcanic deposits associated with large scale tectonic forces such as rift-valley formation; 2) lake, or lacustrine deposits; 3) river, or fluviatile deposits; and 4) cave deposits.

Box 2.1. Two Examples of Depositional Environments in Which Early Hominids Have Been Found

---

Let's consider the set of circumstances associated with fluviatile environments in East Africa, as illustrated in Figure 2.2a. In this case, an early hominid dies alongside a river fringed by riverine forest. The carcass is dismembered and scattered by predators such as jackals, hyenas, and vultures. Some of the bones are washed downstream in a flash flood and then covered by successive layers of sediment, including ash from a nearby erupting volcano. Gradually, as all the organic material in the bone disappears, it is replaced by water-soluble minerals in the soil that ultimately turn the bone to stone. Suppose, in this example, that hundreds of thousands (or perhaps millions) of years change the environment into a stream-dissected region of eroding sediments with little vegetative cover, a topography referred to as **badlands**. *A keen-eyed paleoanthropologist walking over these sediments might be fortunate enough to notice a small piece of fossilized bone or tooth eroding out of one of the many gullies in the region. And if he or she is fortunate enough to be able to match bits of sediment, or matrix, still attached to the fossil to some nearby stratigraphic layer, then a clue may be provided as to the location of the exact stratigraphic level from which the fossils are eroding. This would be a good place to start a test excavation in the hope of finding more of the fossil still embedded in the sediments. Geologists may also be able to radiometrically date the overlying volcanic ash and thereby provide a minimum age for the underlying fossil. These dating techniques will be discussed more fully below.*

A very different environment for the discovery of fossil hominids is the cave sites of southern Africa, first explored by paleoanthropologists early in the twentieth century. Most of the australopithecine-bearing South African cave sites are formed out of two kinds of Precambrian rock: magnesium-containing, or **dolomitic** *limestone, and calcareous deposits known as* **tufas**, *which are chemical sedimentary deposits rich in calcium carbonate typically occurring as incrustations around the mouths of springs (4,5).*

Swartkrans cave in South Africa (Fig. 2.2b) was initially formed by the solution of dolomite in groundwater, the contours of the cave being determined by planes of weakness in the rock (panel 1). As water level dropped in the region, the cavern filled with air and rainwater caused joints or other natural planes of weakness in the rock to form in the dolomite overlying the cave (panel 2). Eventually one or more of the joints broke through to the surface, thereby providing a direct passageway be-

(a)

Fig. 2.2.   (a) One example of how a hominid might become fossilized and then later discovered by paleoanthropologists from a fluviatile deposit in East Africa (66). (b) Four stages in the formation of the Swartkrans Cave Site. Leopards are often attracted to the trees near entrances to dolomitic caves as safe retreats to bring their kills. Cave entrances characteristically support several large tree types that flourish there as a result of protection afforded to them from frost and fire. Thus, many of the fossilized bones found in the cave breccias, including some of the early hominids, were probably part of leopard meals that were stored in these trees near the caves entrance. From (67,68).

*tween the cave and the surface. In caves of this sort, sediment containing the bones of animals that have washed in from the surface usually begins to form beneath the joint into what is called a **talus cone** (panel 3). When the sediment is calcified by lime-bearing solutions dripping from the roof, the resulting deposit is known as a **cave breccia**. Ultimately the cavern fills almost completely with breccia but over thousands or millions of years surface erosion removes much of the dolomitic roof of the ancient cave, thereby exposing the fossil-bearing breccia at the surface (panel*

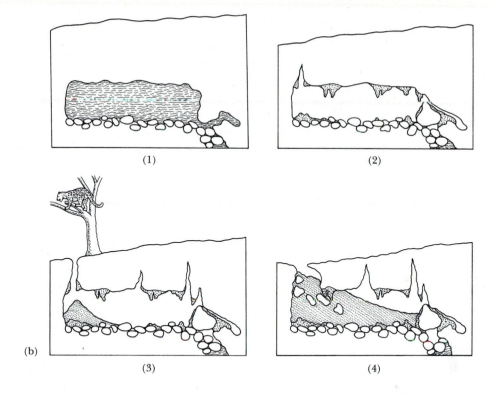

(1)   (2)

(b)

(3)   (4)

4). The South African early hominid sites of Sterkfontein, Kromdraai, Swartkrans, and Makapansgat are currently at this stage of development. Because these cave sites were rich in limestone, they were early targets for mining activity–and in fact it was miners who first noted fossil bones in most of these cave deposits.

DATING FOSSIL HOMINIDS

The technology of dating fossil sites has improved dramatically in recent years, making it possible to construct complex scenarios of geological, floral, and faunal transitions at a given site. Understanding the biological and cultural implications of a hominid fossil or artifact today often requires two types of dating: **relative dating**, which seeks to put fossils and artifacts into a temporal context with other locally associated archeological, faunal, and floral materials, and **absolute dating**, which ties a fossil or artifact to an absolute time scale in years and therefore to other fossils or artifacts discovered at other sites. As our examination of classification disputes later in this chapter will make clear, time is an indispensable factor in any construct of relatedness and evolutionary change. Even though some disregard time when determining phylogenetic relationships (see below), the validity of any phylogenetic analysis depends on its being consistent with temporal considerations. For example, any phylogenetic analysis that concluded that Australian aboriginals were more closely related to *Homo erectus* than to modern Europeans would be obviously absurd based on what we know about the history of these groups in both time and space. Likewise, if we wish to explore how various phases of human evolution relate to major climatic cycles or changes we need to know when in human history these climatic events occurred. Finally, cultural traditions (as seen in the archeological record) evolve just as biological systems do, and to understand the connections between biological evolution and cultural evolution through the Plio-Pleistocene, accurate dating is imperative. In later chapters, we will see many examples of the relevance of dating techniques to all these issues; dating is really the only independent measure of the validity of any evolutionary scenario.

Relative Dating

Before the advent of absolute dating techniques, which we discuss below, paleoanthropologists were limited mostly to relative dating methods, and in many cases, they still are today. Relative dating simply orders objects of interest (fossils, archeological assemblages, etc.) into temporal sequences relative to one another (i.e., older or younger than) and are often only applicable at the local or regional level. For example, if fossils can be securely placed into a local stratigraphic sequence, the so-called **law of superposition** dictates that, assuming the strata are relatively undisturbed, the fossils contained in the lower strata will be older than those higher up in the stratigraphic sequence. It is assumed that fossils found in the same stratigraphic level are roughly contemporaneous, the degree of contemporaneity depending upon how quickly that particular strata was laid down. Of course, if younger fossils are redeposited in older sediments (e.g., in certain burials) then this assumption is violated. One example of relative dating, at several important early hominid sites in southern Africa, is shown in Figure 2.3. None of these sites contain rocks suitable for precise radiometric dating, and yet, by identifying the fossil mammals associated with these early hominids and then comparing them to similar species from radiometrically dated sites in East Africa, paleoanthropologists are able to place these sites into a reasonably secure temporal framework. For example, the bovids from Makapansgat are similar to those found in several East African sites radiometrically dated to 3.7–2.5 mya, suggesting that the Makapansgat sediments are roughly equivalent in age.

Relative dating often relies on chemical as well as geological information. Several chemical tests widely used in paleoanthropology measure the concentrations of fluorine, uranium, and/or nitrogen within fossil bones found together in the same deposit to determine their relative ages. The basis for the **nitrogen test** is that as bone fossilizes, the nitrogen-containing

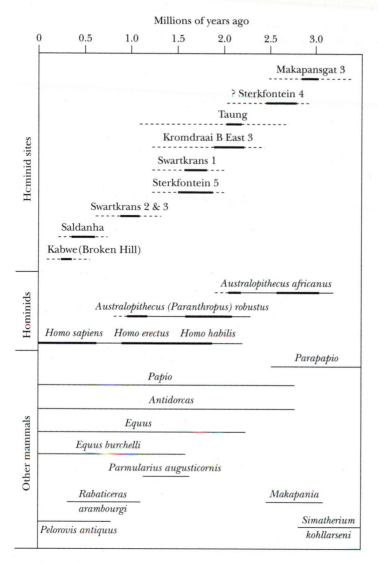

Fig. 2.3.   Relative dating of fossil hominid sites, and associated hominid and mammal fossils, from southern Africa.   Estimated time ranges of fossil hominid species and of some of the mammals used to date them are also shown. Numbers after the site names denote stratigraphic units (Members). *Parapapio* and *Papio* are baboons, *Equus* are zebras; and the others are bovids (buffaloes and antelopes). From (16).

amino acids in collagen break down at a predictable rate, and thus the amount of nitrogen remaining in the bone indicates how long the bone has been fossilizing. Conversely, the basis for the **fluorine test** is that bones absorb flourine from surrounding groundwater, which then combines with bone calcium to form the compound fluoroapatite; the longer the bone has been in the ground, the more fluoroapatite is present. Fluorine and nitrogen relative dating tests are complementary in that bones deposited recently would have higher nitrogen contents and lower fluorine contents than more ancient bones. These chemical tests are site-specific, meaning that the amount of nitrogen lost or fluorine absorbed depends on geological and environmental factors at each particular site. For this reason, these tests usually cannot determine the relative ages of fossil bones found at different sites whose conditions of deposition are different.

A notable early success in using these tests was the unmasking of the infamous Piltdown skull forgery. Flourine dating tests determined that the **calvaria**, or skullcap, had much more fluorine than the "associated" mandible; of course, had they both been in the deposits at Piltdown for the same amount of time they would have absorbed approximately equal concentrations of fluorine. Because of this discrepancy, the fossils were more carefully examined and it was found that the mandible was actually that of a female orangutan whose molars had been filed down to obscure its true identity (6,7).

Absolute Dating with Radiometric and Other Techniques

Contrary to popular belief, most radiometric dating techniques do not date the fossil bones themselves, but rather the geological strata associated with the fossil bones. (As we discuss in detail below, the major exception to this is carbon-14 [^{14}C] dating, which can only date fossil bones younger than about 50,000 years old, the normal outside limit of the technique.) Ideally one would like to date the actual fossiliferous layer of sediment, but when there is any question about the relation between the fossil and the sediment from which it came, one brackets the fossil by dating strata above and below it to provide minimum and maximum ages. This is accomplished by one of several different dating techniques.

Radiometric dating techniques are indispensable to the study of human evolution. All such techniques are based on the principle that when atoms of a radioactive element emit radiation, these "parent" atoms decay at a known constant rate into "daughter" atoms of another element. In such cases, the age of the sample is determined by measuring the ratio of parent to daughter atoms remaining in the sample. This procedure is employed when the radioactive atoms included in newly formed rock contain none of the daughter atoms, the initial daughter/parent ratio thereby being set at zero.

The principles behind radiometric dating are determined by the chemical behavior of atoms. Many atoms are unstable and change spontaneously to a lower energy state by radioactive emission or decay within the nucleus itself. Two atoms that have the same number of protons, and hence the same **atomic number**, but a different number of neutrons, are called **isotopes**. For instance, two commonly used isotopes of uranium (atomic number 92) are ^{235}U and ^{238}U. The superscripts represent the **atomic mass number**, or total number of protons and neutrons. Radioactive decay may occur through one of the following processes, depending on the characteristics of the atom:

- **alpha decay:** the nucleus of the parent atom loses 2 protons and 2 neutrons; thus its mass number decreases by 4 and its atomic number decreases by 2. An example of alpha decay is the decay of uranium to thorium, ^{238}U to ^{234}Th.
- **beta decay:** one of the neutrons in the nucleus turns into a proton; in this case the atomic number increases by 1 but the mass number remains unchanged. An example of beta decay is the decay of rubidium to strontium, ^{87}Rb to ^{87}Sr.
- **electron capture:** a proton in the nucleus turns into a neutron, thus decreasing the atomic number by 1. As in beta decay, the mass number remains unchanged. An example of electron capture is the decay of potassium to argon, ^{40}K to ^{40}Ar.

All radioactive elements are inherently unstable and each has a characteristic decay behavior and a unique constant rate of decay. Thus, if a radioactive element is incorporated into a mineral or rock when it forms, the amount of the radioactive element that decays into its daughter atoms is controlled only by the elapsed time since formation. The principle of radiometric dating can be likened to sand in an hourglass; sand in the top chamber compared to sand accumulated in the bottom chamber always provides a measure of the time that has elapsed since the glass was turned. Just as the hourglass is sealed so that extraneous sand cannot enter or leave the system, so too must the atomic structure of the mineral be "sealed" so that neither the parent nor the daughter atoms can enter or leave from any external source (8).

Each individual atom of a given radioactive isotope has the same probability of decaying within any given year, and this probability remains the same no matter how long the material being dated has been in existence. This probability of decay is termed the **decay constant** (let us call it K), and is simply that proportion of atoms of a particular element that always decays within any given year. The number of atoms that will actually decay is K*N, where N is simply the number of radioactive parent atoms still present in the system at the beginning of the year. At the beginning of the following year, the number of radioactive parent atoms is obviously smaller, having decreased by the amount K*N. Thus, the number of radioactive parent atoms decreases with each succeeding year. The time required for half of the atoms of any particular radioactive element to decay is termed its **half-life**, and each radioactive element has its own specific half-life, which may last seconds or millions of years.

The end of one half-life marks the beginning of the next one. Thus, if

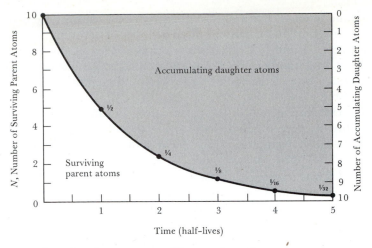

Fig. 2.4. Radioactive decay curve.   The number of parent atoms present when the rock was formed (N_0) is arbitrarily taken here to be 10 units. The points along the curve (N/N_0) represent the ratio of surviving parent atoms to the initial number of parent atoms. Using the right-hand vertical axis, one can also read off the number of daughter atoms present at any given time. From (69).

N_0 represents the initial number of atoms, then half that number ($N_0/2$) remains after the first half-life, half of those ($N_0/4$) remain after the second half-life, half of those ($N_0/8$) are left after the third half-life, and so on. If one plots the number of surviving parent atoms as a function of time, the result is a curve like that shown in Figure 2.4. This relationship forms the basis for most radioactive clocks. As a simple illustration, suppose one wants to determine the age of a sample in which the parent/daughter ratio is found to be 1:32 and the half-life of the element is known to be 1 million years. Since 1:32 equals $(1/2)^5$, this means that the sample has undergone five half-life cycles and is thus 5 million years old.

Carbon-14 (^{14}C)   One of only two techniques that can be applied to fossil bone directly, carbon-14 dating is important and widely used. This technique can date many once living carbon-containing materials, like wood, charcoal, bone, shell, and peat, to within a range of about 200 to 50,000 years B.P.[1] Carbon-14 (^{14}C) is continuously produced in the upper atmosphere by the interaction of cosmic-ray neutrons with stable isotopes of nitrogen (^{14}N).[2] The radioactive atoms of ^{14}C, along with those of the much

[1]It is customary to express radiocarbon dates in terms of years before the present (B.P.), where the present is taken to be 1950. A useful rule of thumb is that it takes about 83 years for 1 percent of radiocarbon to disappear and about 3 days for a millionth part to disappear (9).

[2]$n + {}^{14}N \rightarrow {}^{14}C + H$, where n is the neutron and H is the proton that is emitted by the product nucleus.

Box 2.2. Conditions Required to Use Radiometric Techniques in Paleoanthropological Studies (Fig. 2.5)

- *The radioactive decay process of the samples must not have reached completion; if it has, the sand will all be in the bottom of the hourglass—the isotope will have completely decayed into its daughter isotopes.*
- *All materials to be dated (e.g., bones, artifacts, pottery, minerals, etc.) must lie in a well-defined stratigraphic context.*
- *Any analytical methods used to detect the products of radioactive decay must be sufficiently refined to give dates within statistically acceptable margins of error.*

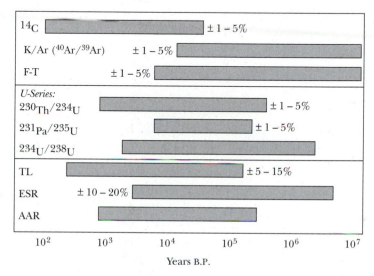

Fig. 2.5. The main dating methods used in paleoanthropology.   From (17).

more numerous nonradioactive isotopes of carbon, ^{12}C and ^{13}C, are rapidly incorporated into atmospheric carbon dioxide (10). Generally, the ratio of $^{14}C/^{12}C$ in the atmosphere remains relatively constant, i.e., the continuous production of ^{14}C is offset by its continuous radioactive decay, a condition referred to as steady state. All living organisms in equilibrium with the atmosphere maintain a small natural concentration of radiocarbon; carbon dioxide enters plants through photosynthesis and/or root absorption and is passed on to animals when they eat the plants. But when an organism dies, or when any carbon-containing compound can no longer exchange carbon freely with the atmosphere, ^{14}C is no longer absorbed and its concentration declines as a result of radioactive decay (the half-life of ^{14}C is 5,730 $\pm$ 40 years). By comparing the atmospheric $^{14}C/^{12}C$ ratio to that of the dead organism and by knowing the half-life of ^{14}C, the time since death can be calculated (Fig. 2.6).

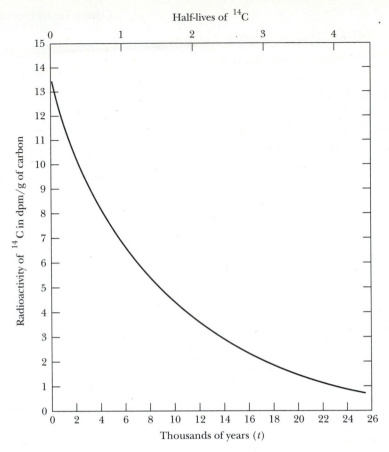

Fig. 2.6. Decay of ^{14}C in plant or animal tissue that was initially in equilibrium with $^{14}CO_2$ in the atmosphere (or hydrosphere). When the plant or animal dies, the exchange stops and the activity due to ^{14}C decreases as a function of time (t) (the half-life of ^{14}C is about 5,730 years). From (15).

Working with carbon-14 samples A number of potential uncertainties are involved in ^{14}C dating. For example, has the activity of ^{14}C in plant and animal tissues been constant and independent of time during the past 70,000 years or so or have there been fluctuations in levels of absorption? Are ^{14}C values independent of geographic location? Do ^{14}C values vary with the species of plant or animal whose tissues are being dated? Have the samples themselves been contaminated with modern ^{14}C or are they in other ways impure?

Recent studies point to systematic variations in atmospheric radiocarbon content in the past that could make radiocarbon dates inaccurate unless the fluctuations are taken into account. For example, the higher radiocarbon content of plants and animals in the polar regions might result from a rate of ^{14}C production that is significantly greater in the polar atmosphere than at the equator. Also, the radiocarbon content of the Earth's atmosphere is influenced by the intensity of both solar activity and the Earth's magnetic field. Finally, the introduction of fossil fuels into the Earth's atmosphere since the Industrial Revolution has also influenced ^{14}C activity in the atmosphere, as has radiation from atomic bombs.

How do anthropologists deal with these potential sources of error in ^{14}C dating? One way is to calibrate the variation of the atmosphere's radiocarbon content by analyzing the carbon content of wood from ancient trees, like the sequoia (*Sequoia gigantea*) or the bristlecone pine (*Pinus aristata*). Trees grow by adding a layer of woody tissue to the circumference of their trunks and branches each year, thereby isolating the underlying woody layers from atmospheric ^{14}C. Therefore, the concentration of ^{14}C in the underlying woody tissues decreases over time because of radioactive decay. Variations in the radiocarbon content of the atmosphere over the past several thousand years can thus be measured by analyzing wood samples whose age is established by counting annual growth rings, that is, by **dendrochronology**. The age-corrected deviations of the radiocarbon content of such trees can then be used to calculate corrections to conventional radiocarbon dates. Unfortunately, such adjustments to the ^{14}C time scale cannot be accurately calibrated by dendrochronology before about 9,000 years B.P. because of the lack of suitable fossil trees for dendrochronological dating. Even so, it does appear that ^{14}C ages are consistently younger than true ages for objects dated to beyond 9,000 years B.P. (11).

A novel application of radiocarbon dating recently has been to rock art in both North America and Europe. For example, charcoal used in prehistoric paintings at Altamira and El Castillo caves in Spain and at the Niaux caves in France have been dated to 14,000 ± 400 years B.P., 12,990 ± 200 years B.P., and 12,890 ± 160 years B.P. respectively (12). Organic carbon found in paint pigment in southwestern Texas rock art has been dated to 3,865 ± 100 years B.P. (13).

Potassium-Argon (K-Ar) and Argon-Argon (^{40}Ar-^{39}Ar)   Two of the most important radiometric techniques in paleoanthropology are potassium-argon (K-Ar) and the closely related argon-argon (^{40}Ar-^{39}Ar) methods. Conventional K-Ar dating relies on the decay of ^{40}K through a complex sequence of intermediate steps into ^{40}Ar. Consolidated volcanic ash, known as **tuff**, and certain **igneous rocks** like basalt that flow in a molten state to the Earth's surface from deeper in the crust are the samples most widely used for K-Ar dating. With a half-life of just under 1.3 billion years, K-Ar decay can date the oldest rocks on Earth as well as rocks less than 100,000 years in age.

Conventional K-Ar dating requires the processing of at least two samples. The first sample has to be chemically processed to measure the amount of stable potassium-39 (^{39}K) it contains and a second sample has to be melted to measure the amount of ^{40}Ar present. Since the ratio of ^{40}K to ^{39}K is constant from rock to rock, the amount of ^{39}K in the sample reflects the amount of radioactive ^{40}K originally contained within the rock. These separate procedures may lead to various degrees of imprecision. Conventional K-Ar dating also requires that all of the argon be extracted from the sample to be dated.

Two types of errors are associated with K-Ar dating that may lead to distorted dates if not accounted for: discrepantly high ages may occur if any ^{40}Ar is incorporated into the rock or mineral to be dated at the time of its formation; and discrepantly low ages may occur if ^{40}Ar is lost from the rock or mineral due to diffusion or various other chemical reactions (14).

More recently, a spinoff of conventional K-Ar dating, the Ar-Ar method, or more specifically, ^{40}Ar-^{39}Ar, has been developed that overcomes some of the limitations of conventional K-Ar dating by allowing both potassium and argon to be measured from a single sample, and by requiring the measurement of isotope ratios of argon only.

Working with K-Ar samples   When potassium-bearing rocks are experimentally subjected to neutron irradiation, a series of reactions are set up that result in the formation of several isotopes of argon. The most important of these reactions produces ^{39}Ar from ^{39}K. Of course, the number of atoms of ^{39}Ar produced is directly proportional to the number of atoms of ^{39}K present in the original sample. As noted above, the atoms of ^{40}Ar in the sample are produced by the radioactive decay of ^{40}K atoms. In one variation of the ^{40}Ar-^{39}Ar method, all the argon gas is extracted at once, yielding dates that are comparable to conventional K-Ar dates; still, they are based only on measurements of isotopic ratios of ^{40}Ar-^{39}Ar and do not require a separate determination of the potassium concentration. However, argon can also be released by irradiating samples at ever increasing temperatures, thereby allowing ages to be calculated for each fraction of the argon gas released from the sample. In this way, a spectrum of dates can be calculated from the ^{40}Ar-^{39}Ar ratio for each step until finally an age plateau is reached that provides the best overall age estimate for the sample (15).

One final variation of the ^{40}Ar-^{39}Ar technique that is becoming more widely utilized in paleoanthropology today is the **single-crystal fusion** method. In this method a laser is used to melt crystals to release the argon gas. This technique has two important advantages over the methods mentioned above: 1) because the laser beam allows such a localized heating of the crystals there is much less chance of background atmospheric argon confounding the final age calculations; and 2) it greatly reduces the amount of sample needed for the age determination (16).

Uranium Series (U-S)   Uranium is present as a trace element in virtually all natural materials, providing a very large potential sample for radiometric dating and a large context for building fossil chronologies. Uranium series (U-S) dating includes several techniques based on the radioactive decay of either ^{238}U or ^{235}U through a series of intermediate steps to various daughter isotopes. The entire uranium series of radioactive elements and isotopes, only some of which are useful in radiometric dating, is shown in Figure 2.7a. The different sets of daughter isotopes used for dating purposes are thorium-uranium (^{230}Th-^{234}U, or simply Th-U), protactinium-uranium (Pa-U), and ^{234}U-^{238}U. The first of these is the most widely used (17,18).

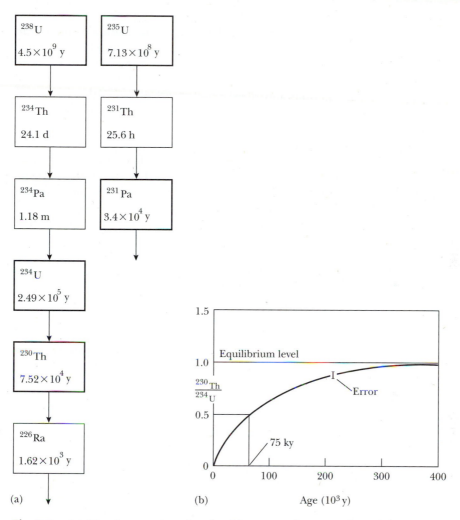

(a)

(b)

Fig. 2.7. (a) The decay series of each of the parent isotopes of uranium. Heavily outlined boxes represent isotopes having half-lives long enough to be useful in dating fossil hominids. The numbers under the elements refer to their half-lives (m, minutes; h, hours; d, days; y, years). (b) Graph of the ^{230}Th-^{234}U activity ratio as a function of the age of a sample. The origin of the graph assumes the sample was initially precipitated with a zero content of thorium. The error bar is an example of the magnitude of typical errors in this dating technique. In this example, a ^{230}Th-^{234}U ratio of 0.50 corresponds to an age of 75,000 years (75 ky in the figure). From (17).

Working with U-S samples   All U-S dating methods are based on the observation that unaltered uranium-containing material contains a certain proportion of each daughter isotope. Most importantly, in any uranium-bearing material that has lain undisturbed for millions of years, the radioactive decay rate of each daughter isotope equals the decay rate of all other daughter isotopes in the same sample. Such a sample is said to be in **secular radioactive equilibrium**.

For example, if atoms of ^{238}U are decaying at the standard decay rate of 1 disintegration unit per minute (dpm) per gram of sample, then all its daughter isotopes (e.g., ^{230}Th, ^{226}Ra) will decay at 1 dpm per gram as well. The decay rate (in dpm/g) is proportional only to the concentration of uranium in the sample and does not depend on any other chemical or physical property of the sample. However, when a sample is altered or disturbed by some physical or chemical process, it departs from secular radioactive equilibrium and millions of years may elapse before equilibrium is reestablished. For radiometric dating purposes, this state of disequilibrium is all important, because it preserves a record of the time when the sample was disturbed; it is the age of the disturbance that is measured in U-S dating. The following example may help clarify the method.

While most geological material at hominid sites are ancient rocks that are in, or close to, equilibrium, other materials such as stalagmites, bones, teeth, or shells may have arrived, or been formed, at the site de novo. Imagine that one wishes to date a calcium carbonate deposit that is associated with a fossil or stone-tool industry. Further suppose the deposit is a travertine, a crystalline calcium carbonate deposit precipitated in solution in ground- or surface water by inorganic chemical processes. As we would expect, the travertine contains a concentration of uranium that can be used to date the sample. However, when freshly deposited, travertine contains no ^{230}Th because this isotope, unlike the uranium that produces it, is relatively insoluble in water and therefore cannot be precipitated within the structure of the travertine. Therefore, the ^{230}Th-^{234}U ratio in the travertine will be zero on the date of its formation: with the passage of time, some ^{234}U decays to ^{230}Th and the ^{230}Th-^{234}U ratio increases (Fig. 2.7b). Remember that equilibrium is defined as the equal radioactive decay rate of each daughter isotope with its parent atom, so in equilibrium ^{230}Th will be decaying at the same rate it is being formed by the decaying ^{234}U. As the travertine approaches equilibrium, the ^{230}Th-^{234}U activity ratio approaches a limiting value of 1.0; on the curve shown in Figure 2.7b the degree of approach to equilibrium is used as a measure of the time elapsed since the sample was formed. The date at which this ratio approaches 1.0 is the effective upper age limit for this dating technique, in this case approximately 350,000 years. The minimum age is typically a few hundred years. Depending upon the procedures used, the accuracy of such dates range from approximately 1 to 5 percent.

The main types of material datable by U-S techniques include various

types of chemically or biologically precipitated calcium carbonate ($CaCO_3$: calcite or aragonite) such as:
- **travertines:** crystalline calcium carbonate deposits formed by chemical precipitation from solution by inorganic processes (e.g., flowstone or dripstone in caves, tufa near springs)
- **speleothems:** any variously shaped mineral deposits formed in caves by the action of water (e.g., stalagmites, stalactites, and flowstones)
- **calcretes:** calcitic deposits formed in soils of semiarid regions
- **biogenic carbonates:** skeletons or shells of some marine organisms made of aragonite or calcite (unfortunately, molluscan shells are unsuitable for U-S dating but stromatolitic [algal] calcite and coral are well suited for U-S dating)

Studies are still being done to see if other materials are suitable for U-S dating, including **apatite** (the phosphate found in teeth and bones), wood, and peat. Recently, tests using the thorium-uranium dating method on corals from Barbados confirmed the high precision of the technique for dating at least the past 30,000 years. In fact, precision of Th-U dating is often better than that achieved for most ^{14}C dating for materials older than 10,000 years. These results suggest that Th-U dating may be used as a first-order tool to calibrate the ^{14}C time scale beyond the range of dendro-chronological tests (11).

Fission Track   Although fission-track (F-T) dating relies on the principle of radioactivity, it differs from the methods previously discussed in that it measures the side effects of **spontaneous fission** within the atomic nucleus of ^{238}U. During spontaneous fission the nucleus splits into two or more high-energy fragments, and these fragments leave damage tracks within the rock crystals that can be enlarged and studied. Instead of measuring parent/daughter ratios, F-T dating counts the number of tracks left behind by the naturally recoiling atoms in the sample; the more tracks per unit volume, the older the sample. Given the right kind of sample, F-T dating can be applied to common minerals such as micas, apatite, and zircon (9,15) that range in age from a few decades to 3.5 billion years, the age of the oldest rocks on Earth. The technique has been particularly useful in archeology for dating pottery. For example, when clays used for making pottery contain crystals of zircon, the fission-track "clock" of the zircon would have been set to zero when the pottery was "fired" (19). Successful F-T dating is based on the assumption that ^{238}U decays at a constant rate, that fission tracks are produced and retained with 100 percent accuracy, and that the concentration of uranium in any specimen remains constant through time.

Thermoluminescence and Electron Spin Resonance   Almost all sediments have a weak level of radioactivity since most contain some traces of the radioactive elements uranium, potassium, and thorium. In addition, various types of ionizing radiation, such as gamma rays, cosmic rays, and even sunlight, sometimes interact with atoms in soils in such a way that electrons are removed and trapped within the crystal lattice of the material. Since these electrons retain the excess energy they received from the radiation source, heating these solids induces the trapped electrons to return to their stable energy states and liberates the excess energy as light in the process. The light emitted by such thermal activation is called **thermoluminescence** (TL), and the intensity of the emitted signal is a measure of the trapped electrons in the mineral.[3] Since minerals within fossiliferous sediments may contain some of these trapped electrons, their radioactive signal may be detected with appropriate instrumentation (15,20,21). A prerequisite for successful TL dating is that at some time in the past the trapped electron population of the material was zero. Some materials may be "zeroed" or "reset" when they are heated to upward of 450°C, or occasionally when exposed sufficiently to daylight. Thus, for burnt stones (e.g., burnt flint or quartz tools) and pottery, the "resetting date" is the time of firing; for unfired calcite, it is the time of crystallization; and for sediments, it is the time of deposition subsequent to exposure to sunlight. As in other radiometric tests, electrons accumulate in the lattice at a standard rate, and the amount of accumulated energy is a measure of the duration of time since the solid was originally formed or subsequently zeroed.

In order to transform the dating signal into years it is first necessary to measure the amount of total radiation that has accumulated in the sample, the accumulated dose, and the amount of radiation the sample receives in 1 year in that particular sedimentary environment, the dose rate. Determining the accumulated dose, or total radioactive signal of the sample, is a two-step process. The radioactivity of the sample is first measured in a spectrometer. To calibrate the result, the sample is given a dose of radioactivity of known intensity after which the radioactivity of the sample is measured a second time. From these two tests one is able to calculate the original level of radioactivity in the sample (or the measure of radiation to which the sample has been exposed since it was last "zeroed," i.e., last heated to about 450°C). The annual radiation dose, or the dose rate per year that the sample has been receiving while buried, is determined from the concentrations of radioactive uranium, thorium, and potassium in the parent rock. The time elapsed since the last heating is thus given by the simple relationship:

$$\text{age} = \frac{\text{accumulated radiation dose}}{\text{annual radiation dose}}$$

TL has been used to date archeological materials such as pottery, glass, bones, shells, and flint heated by fires (20,22).

The presence of unstable electrons in solids can also be detected by

---

[3]In TL the dating signal is stimulated by heat whereas in optically stimulated luminescence (OSL) the signal is stimulated by light (20).

electron spin resonance (ESR) (23,24). Unlike TL dating, where the number of trapped electrons is determined by heating and the emission of light, in ESR dating the number of trapped electrons is determined by measuring their absorption of microwave radiation. The radiation exposure age of a sample dated by ESR is calculated using the same formula as noted above for TL dating. The theoretical age range of ESR dating is from a few thousand years to more than 1 mya, but in practical terms most age estimates beyond about 300,000 years are very uncertain.

For paleoanthropologists, the most useful material for ESR dating is tooth enamel. After an animal dies, its enamel starts to record the radioactivity of the environment in which it is buried. This radioactive signal emanates from minute concentrations of radioactive elements that are in the environment (e.g., uranium, thorium, and potassium) as well as from cosmic rays. Unfortunately, bone as well as other components of teeth like dentine and cementum are not suitable for dating but the technique has been successfully applied to calcite in cave deposits, fossil shells, and corals (22,23,25–29).

One advantage of ESR over TL dating is that TL measurements remove the age information from the sample, whereas an ESR measurement can be taken a number of times on the same sample.

Amino-Acid Racemization   Amino-acid racemization is a nonradiometric test that has been used to date such diverse materials as fossil bone, mollusk shells, and ostrich eggshell ranging from a few centuries to several hundred thousand years old (30–34).

The bones of living animals consist of about 25–30 percent organic material, most of which is protein. At death, these proteins begin to break down into free amino acids through predictable biochemical pathways. The one property of amino acids that makes them potentially useful for dating is that most of them exist in at least two configurations that have the same molecular formula. Two amino acids that have different structures but identical formulas are called **optical isomers**, and are designated D and L forms. Only the L–amino acids are commonly found in living organisms.[4] However, over long periods of time these L–amino acids slowly undergo a conversion from the active L–amino acid form into the inactive D–amino acid form, a process known as **racemization**. Thus, the ratio of D– to L–amino acids remaining in a fossil increases through time and the rate of this reaction is slow enough to be useful in geochronology. Aspartic acid has one of the fastest amino-acid racemization rates and for this reason has generally been used for dating Holocene and Late Pleistocene fossils. Isoleucine, on the other hand, has a racemization rate about ten times slower than aspartic acid and is used to date older fossil bones (31).

Amino-acid racemization rates are very sensitive to both temperature and the physical-chemical environment in which the material to be dated

---

[4]Some D-proteins are found in certain bacteria (31).

has been deposited. For example, the half-life of amino acids undergoing racemization ranges from a few days at 100°C to thousands of years at 20–25°C. For this reason, formulas that convert the degree of racemization to geological age must first be empirically "calibrated" to account for variations in paleotemperatures and other relevant environmental factors of the locality over the time period of interest. In order for amino-acid racemization dating to be practical, the fossil to be dated must have been kept at a relatively constant temperature over time, and the amino acids in the sample must have been separated from any environmental contamination (31,35). Environments that come closest to meeting these criteria are deep-sea sediments, where there has been relatively constant cold-water temperatures over long periods of time, and deep, sealed caves in which the temperature remained relatively constant during the various ice-age cycles.

It is fair to say that the validity of the technique is the subject of intense debate particularly because of this dependence on temperature and on the physiochemical environment (36).

A Summary of Absolute Dating Techniques

The most widely used dating methods in paleoanthropology today are those just discussed: carbon-14 (^{14}C), uranium series (U-S), potassium-argon (K-Ar), fission-track (F-T), thermoluminescence (TL), electron spin resonance (ESR), and amino-acid racemization (AAR), whose resolutions are compared in Figure 2.5. Of these, carbon-14, uranium series, potassium-argon, and fission-track are all based on the radioactive decay of specific isotopes. Thermoluminescence and electron spin resonance utilize aspects of ionizing radiation and require additional information about paleoenvironmental factors that may affect their results. Since fission-track and potassium-argon dating are only applicable where volcanic rocks are present, and carbon-14 is only applicable for ages less than about 50,000 years, electron spin resonance, thermoluminescence, and uranium-series have the most potential for dating stages of human evolution in areas where volcanic rocks are scarce or absent (17). Amino-acid racemization and carbon-14 are the only techniques that date fossil bone directly.

Now that we have explored potential hominid sites and the dating methods used to age hominid fossils, how and what do we name them?

NAMING FOSSIL HOMINIDS

Two important goals of modern paleoanthropological research are the phylogenetic reconstruction of the human lineage and the classification of human fossils. Often the failure to appreciate the distinction between phylogeny and classification leads to much confusion, controversy, and misunderstanding in human evolution studies. **Classification** is simply the process of establishing, defining, and ranking taxa within some hierarchical series of groups (37). **Phylogeny**, on the other hand, concerns the evolutionary history of organisms and includes both cladogenetic and anagenetic information (38). **Cladogenesis**, or dendritic evolution, refers to a branching type of evolutionary process involving the splitting and subsequent divergence of populations. **Anagenesis**, or phyletic evolution, refers to the evolutionary process of gradual accumulation of changes in ancestor-to-descendant lineages through time.

The controversy arises when the relationship between classification and phylogeny is considered. All biological systematists agree that the criteria chosen upon which a classification is based should reflect some aspects of phylogeny, but there is great disagreement about which details to emphasize. As one evolutionary biologist has commented: "That there should be any controversy at all might . . . seem strange. The principle of classification, considered superficially, might seem too straightforward to be controversial: you simply have to define groups by taxonomic characters. . . . And if taxonomists are observed superficially that is what they appear to do" (39). However, as we shall see, the processes by which taxonomic characteristics are selected and employed in classification are more complex, bringing in theoretical and philosophical considerations of a more subjective sort.

Three Analytical Levels of Classification and Phylogeny

Implicit in any Darwinian system of classifying organisms is a set of underlying evolutionary principles, and the classification of any group of organisms, including hominids, depends upon which organizing principles are adopted. Most hypotheses about human evolution can ultimately be boiled down to three analytical levels, each having its own degree of complexity. The first, or simplest, level is represented by the **cladogram**, which is a branching diagram of the distribution of unique character states, a **character** being any feature chosen for study. Membership in a **clade** means that the members have specific characters in common with each other and with their most recent common ancestor, but not with earlier ancestors. These characters, because they can be identified only with immediate ancestors and with members of the clade, are called shared derived, or **synapomorphic**, characters (characters B and C in Figure 2.8a). A character may evolve through several character states, and each state is derived from the one preceding it. Although the common possession of such derived character states (see below) among different taxa implies that they share some type of evolutionary relationship, *the exact nature of the evolutionary relationship is not specified in the cladogram* (40–42).

The second, more complex analytical level is represented by the **phylogram**, or phylogenetic tree, which adds information not present in a cladogram by depicting the nature of the evolutionary relationship among

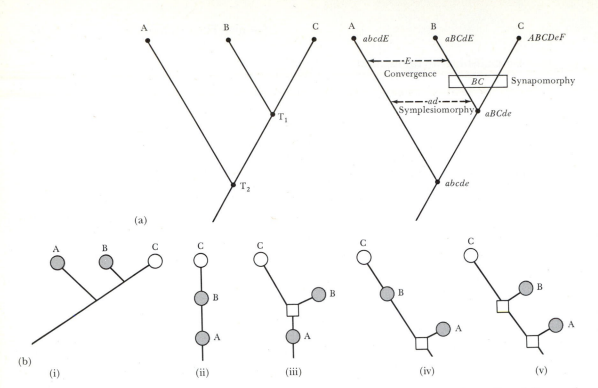

Fig. 2.8. (a) In the simple cladogram on the left, hypothetical taxa B and C are more closely related to one another than either is to taxon A since they share a more recent common ancestor (T_1). Thus taxa B and C together make up a clade that is the sister group of taxon A. In the simple cladogram on the right, characters observed in three taxa and inferred in their common ancestors are given beside each group. Lower-case letters signify primitive (plesiomorphic) characters, and capital letters signify derived (apomorphic) states of those same characters. Taxa B and C are linked by shared derived (synapomorphic) character states *B* and *C*. Characters *a* and *d* linking taxa A and B are shared primitive (symplesiomorphic) characters and thus are not indicative of any special relationship between those two taxa. Character *F* is an autapomorphic character (one that arose for the first time in that group) in taxon C. Adapted from (70). (b) Cladograms and phylograms compared for information content. Open circles represent recent taxa, dark circles represent fossil taxa, and squares represent postulated common ancestors. The four phylograms (ii–v) are all consistent with the given cladogram (i) and provide more information about hypothesized ancestor-descendant relationships than does the cladogram. From (71).

the various taxa. For example, the evolutionary relationship may be an ancestor-descendant lineage or a forked lineage of two daughter species derived from one parental species after a speciation event (Fig. 2.8b). Furthermore, phylogenetic trees convey more information because they depict not only extinct and extant taxa but also ancestor-descendant relationships and degrees of divergence among taxa. By convention, the branches in a phylogenetic tree represent lineages, forks in the branches represent speciation events, the slant and length of the branches reflect the rapidity with which divergence took place, and the branch endpoints indicate terminal taxa, either extant or extinct (Fig. 2.9a). In pictorial terms the main difference between a cladogram and a phylogram is that the former has no time dimension.

To summarize, a phylogram may add to the information contained in a cladogram by specifying the nature of the evolutionary relationships postulated as well as the temporal sequence of the taxa, provided reliable data

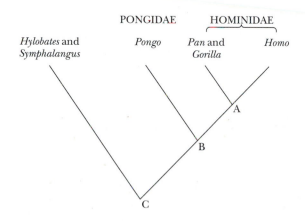

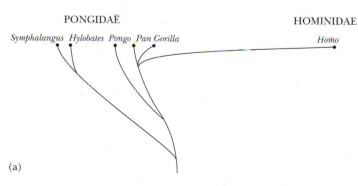

(a)

Fig. 2.9. (a) Contrasting classifications of living hominoid primates. Cladists (top diagram) classify groups solely according to the branching sequence of phylogeny, and sister groups are given the same taxonomic rank. For example, if *Pongo* is placed in the family Pongidae, its sister group (comprising *Pan, Gorilla,* and *Homo*) must also be included in a family, Hominidae. Evolutionary systematists (bottom diagram) take the same phylogenetic information but classify the taxa differently, by taking into account the unique morphological and behavioral features of *Homo* compared with those of the other great apes. Thus *Homo* is placed in its own family, the Hominidae, and the great apes are placed in a separate family, the Pongidae. From (72). (*Continued*)

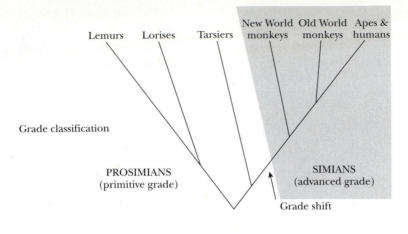

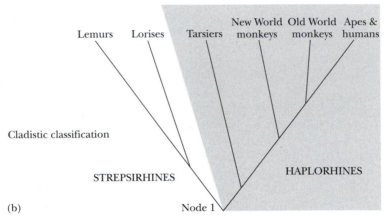

Fig. 2.9. (b) Two approaches to the classification of living primates. In the classical (or grade) classification (top diagram), the classification is based on the general grade of organization of the animal. In this phylogram primates that have retained a relatively high proportion of primitive features are allocated to a lower grade (Prosimii) whereas those primates characterized by a higher proportion of advanced features are allocated to a higher grade (e.g., simians or Anthropoidea). By contrast, in a cladistic classification (bottom diagram) divisions are based solely on the sequence of branching within the tree rather than preservation of the general features of the group. Node 1 represents the point at which organisms ancestral to lemurs and lorises—the strepsirhines—became genetically isolated from the ancestors of the other primates—the haplorines. Individual groups in the cladogram are therefore considered clades rather than grades. From (73).

can be obtained from fossil-bearing rock layers (41). The comparative information content of cladograms and phylograms is shown in Figure 2.8b.

The third and most complex level is the scenario. A **scenario** is not a diagram at all, but an historical narrative that attempts to describe not only phylogenetic relationships among taxa but also the ecological and/or evolutionary forces that most directly influenced the character state(s) under discussion. More abstract, hypothetical, and interpretive than the cladogram or phylogenetic tree, the scenario also inspires the greatest number of verbal fisticuffs in paleoanthropology (41,43–45).

Two Schools of Classification

The two main schools of biological classification popular in paleoanthropology today, **evolutionary systematics** and **phylogenetic systematics**, or **cladistics**, make different uses of the analytical tools outlined above and sometimes arrive at differing classifications. The more traditional approach, evolutionary systematics, evaluates the observed similarities and differences among organisms in terms of their presumed line of evolutionary descent, or phylogeny. In cladistics, the phylogenetic relationship is defined solely by "recency of common ancestry." There are two points of agreement between the schools. First, both agree that branching sequences are important, though the evolutionary systematist believes that classification should reflect more than just branching sequences. Second, both agree that analyses of morphological characters must be taken into account before a classification may be accepted and that some morphological characters are better suited than others for biological classification. Morphological characters that are considered better clues than others to evolutionary relationships are given greater weight in both systems, a practice known as **character weighting**. But this is where the similarities end. The pictorial representation of evolutionary systematics is the phylogenetic tree, which, as we have already noted, shows *both* the branching patterns of ancestor-descendant lineages *and* the degree of divergence of the descendant branches. In this approach the systematist takes into account not only the branching pattern of phylogeny but the subsequent evolutionary fate of each branch as well (46). Phylogenetic systematics (cladistics), on the other hand, employs the cladogram, and tries to represent phylogenetic relationships in a very formalistic way, which we will examine in detail.

The underlying philosophy of cladism is best expressed by its founder, the German entomologist Willi Hennig (47):

> New species originate exclusively because parts of existing reproductive communities have first become externally isolated from one another for such extended periods that genetic isolation mechanisms have developed which make reproductive relationships between these parts impossible when the external barriers which have led to their isolation are removed. Thus, all species [=reproductive communities] which exist together at a given time . . . have originated by the *splitting* [emphasis added] of older homogeneous reproductive communities. On this fact is based the definition of the concept, "phylogenetic relationship": under such concept, species, B, is more nearly related to species, C, than to another species, A, when B has at least one ancestral species source in common with species C which is not the ancestral source of species A.

Thus, in cladistics the degree of phylogenetic relationship is defined solely by "recency of common ancestry" (the more recent ancestry of B and C above) and pictorially represented in the cladogram. The sole aspect of phylogeny that cladists represent is the *order* of branching sequences among taxa, which in turn reflects the distribution of certain characters within a clade or group of related organisms. As noted earlier, members of a clade possess shared derived characters, or synapomorphies, i.e, characters they share in common with each other and with their most recent common ancestor but not with earlier ancestors. Importantly, a distinction needs to be drawn between groups of organisms having a common genetic origin (clade) and those characterized by a certain level of organization and/or adaptation, or **grade** (48,49) (Fig. 2.9b, p. 65).

To the cladist, phylogeny is simply a sequence of dichotomies, or splitting evolutionary branches, with each fork of the branch representing the splitting of a parental taxon into two daughter taxa known as **sister groups**. In its strictest form, cladism demands that sister groups occupy the same taxonomic rank, that is, the same genus, family, superfamily, etc., and that the parent taxon ceases to exist after it splits into its two daughter taxa. Because of this, a cladistic classification can be read directly off a cladogram simply by ranking sister groups in a hierarchical fashion. However, what is sometimes overlooked is the fact that cladistic classifications do not necessarily represent the branching order of sister groups per se, but rather the order of emergence of unique derived characters, whether or not the development of these characters happens to coincide with speciation events (43).

The Problems of Classification

The first step in cladistic analysis, or any classification scheme, is to cluster together those species that seem morphologically similar. However, morphological resemblance cannot be the sole criterion by which phylogenetic relationships are determined because morphological similarity may have several causes. More specifically, two groups of organisms may resemble each other in a given character state for any one of the following reasons:

- The similar character existed in the ancestry of the two groups before the evolution of their nearest common ancestor. This is a shared *primitive* character, or **symplesiomorph**. In Figure 2.8a, *a* and *d* represent symplesiomorphic characters. Clearly, characters can remain unchanged through a number of speciation events. Therefore, the common retention of shared primitive characters cannot be used as evidence of close phylogenetic relationship. If one associates in a group taxa whose similarities are based on shared primitive features, then one may create a group that consists of taxa derived from a single ancestral taxon but does not contain all the descendants of that most recent common ancestor, a so-called **paraphyletic** group (Fig. 2.10).
- The similar character originated in their common ancestor and is shared by all of that ancestor's descendants. In this case the character is a shared *derived* character, a synapomorph. In Figure 2.8a, *B* and *C* represent shared derived characters. Note that B and C are *not* present in the ancestor of all three taxa A, B, and C, but only in the immediate ancestor to B and C. By contrast, two groups may differ from each other because one possesses a character that arose for the first time in that group. This

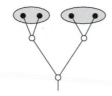 

(a) One paraphyletic group   (b) Two monophyletic groups   (c) One polyphyletic group

Fig. 2.10. Three different ways of forming taxonomic groups. (a) Paraphyletic group: If a taxonomic grouping is based on shared primitive features (symplesiomorphies), the group may consist of taxa derived from a single ancestral taxon but not contain all the descendants of that most recent common ancestor. (b) Monophyletic groups: These groups are based on the common possession of shared derived (synapomorphic) features and include the ancestral species and all descendant species. (c) Polyphyletic group: A taxonomic group whose resemblances are based on convergences. A polyphyletic group consists of taxa derived from two or more distinct ancestral taxa and is a taxonomic category based on convergence rather than common ancestry. From (47).

type of unique derived character is called an **autapomorphy**. Such characters are acquired by a phylogenetic line *after* it has branched off from its sister group. In Figure 2.8a, *F* is such a unique derived character. The supposition that two or more taxa are more closely related to one another than to any other taxon can only be confirmed by demonstrating their common possession of synapomorphic characters. Two or more such taxa constitute a **monophyletic group** (Fig. 2.10).

• The similar character arose independently in several descendant groups. This is a convergent character. A taxonomic group whose resemblances are based on convergences is called a **polyphyletic** group. A polyphyletic group consists of taxa derived from two or more distinct ancestral taxa and is a taxonomic category based on convergence rather than common ancestry (Fig. 2.10).

The similarities in form or structure that are of interest to systematists in building classifications are called **homologous** structures when they are shared between two species and their common ancestor. An example of homology is pentadactyly, as in the five-fingered hand of chimpanzees and humans. Depending upon the school of classification they adhere to, systematists attempt to deal with several other factors in choosing and weighting characters. The opposite of homology, **homoplasy**, is any resemblance not due to inheritance from a common ancestry, e.g., similarities due to parallel evolution, convergent evolution, or analogy. **Parallel evolution** is the independent acquisition in two or more related descendant species of similar character states evolved from a common ancestral condition; **convergent evolution** is the independent evolution of structural or functional similarity in two or more unrelated or distantly related lineages or forms that is not based on genotypic similarity; and **analogy** is functional similarity due to convergent evolution rather than to common ancestry, i.e., a similarity of form or structure shared between two species but not shared with their nearest common ancestor. An example of such a structure would be the wings of birds and bats.

One of the main problems systematists encounter in character analysis arises in the case of **polymorphic** characters, those that change gradually over a continuum of forms, or **morphocline**, from one species to another. The problem is to determine the **polarity** of the morphocline; in other words, which end of the continuum is primitive and which end is derived? For example, the mammalian forefoot can have from one to five digits (e.g., horses versus humans). Which of the two character states is actually the primitive mammalian condition and which is the derived one?

There are several ways of dealing with this problem. If a given morphological character state is typical of a large number of relevant taxa, and particularly if the state is shared with other closely related taxa of similar taxonomic rank, then it is reasonable to regard that state as primitive. Another alternative is to rely on developmental, or **ontogenetic** data. Although the old notion that ontogeny recapitulates phylogeny is no longer accepted in the literal sense, morphological characters typical of an early stage of an organism's development are still generally considered more primitive than features appearing at a later stage (41). Thus in the case of the mammalian forefoot, five digits are regarded as the primitive condition and any reduction in this number is considered a derived state.

Strictly speaking, cladists do not weight characters. Rather, they discard from their analysis any characters that are not synapomorphies. For example, among prosimian primates (lemurs and lorises) the possession of a shared derived trait, like the special alignment of canines and incisors for fur grooming, known as the **dental comb**, has more taxonomic significance than the possession of a shared primitive trait, such as a comparatively small brain. In this view the common possession of such derived characters proves the common ancestry of a particular group, whereas the common possession of primitive characters has little, if any, taxonomic value.

The Harvard zoologist Ernst Mayr has succinctly summed up the distinction between the two taxonomic schools (46):

> The main difference between cladist and evolutionary taxonomists is in the treatment of autapomorph characters. Instead of automatically giving sister groups the same rank, the evolutionary taxonomist ranks them by considering the relative weight of their autapomorphies as compared to their synapomorphies. For instance, one of the striking autapomorphies of man (in comparison to his sister group, the chimpanzee) is the possession of Broca's center in the brain, a character that is closely correlated with man's speaking ability. This single character is for most taxonomists of greater weight than various synapomorphous similarities or even identities in man and the apes in certain macromolecules such a hemoglobin or cytochrome C. The particular importance of autapomorphies is that they reflect the occupation of new niches and new adaptive zones that may have greater biological significance than synapomorphies in some of the standard molecules.

Box 2.3. Two Examples of Cladistic and Evolutionary Systematics Classifications

To illustrate the differences between evolutionary and phylogenetic systematics, let's consider how each school would approach the classification of two very different types of animals—crocodiles and birds. In spite of the fact that crocodiles and birds took very different evolutionary pathways and have obvious morphological differences, a strict cladist would have to classify them as sister groups because they share characters derived from a common reptilian ancestor. In fact, birds have sometimes been referred to as "glorified reptiles" for, with the exception of feathers, almost every character in their skeleton can be matched to that of archosaurian reptiles. They would also have to be classified at the same taxonomic rank, even though one sister group, the crocodiles, still looks very much like the ancestral reptilian group whereas the other, birds, obviously does not.

Looking at the same organisms, an evolutionary taxonomist would take into account the different evolutionary history of each group. Accordingly, the two groups would be assigned to different taxonomic ranks, with crocodiles being classified as an order within the class Reptilia and birds as an altogether separate class, Aves (46). In general, the evolutionary systematist considers the fossil record to be an important arbiter as to whether or not an inferred primitive group is the true one or not. As the eminent paleontologist George Gaylord Simpson once noted, "primitiveness and ancientness are not necessarily related, but they usually are" (50).

Consider how the contrasting schools approach the relationships among humans and apes. A cladist would interpret the cladogram in Figure 2.9a (top) to mean that humans, chimpanzees, and gorillas (Homo, Pan, and Gorilla) share a more recent common ancestor with one another than they do with orangutans (Pongo). Thus Homo forms a clade that is the sister group of the clade formed by Pan and Gorilla and together these three genera form a clade that is the sister group of Pongo. These four genera would in turn make up the sister group of a clade consisting of gibbons (Hylobates) and siamangs (Symphalangus). The classification would necessarily reflect this branching pattern, as follows: if the orangutan clade were classified at the family level, say as Pongidae, then humans, chimpanzees, and gorillas would also have to be classified together at the family level as Hominidae, since sister groups must have the same taxonomic rank. To put a finer point on it, then, a cladistic interpretation suggests that the term "hominid" should be used to refer to humans, as well as chimpanzees and gorillas! To avoid any confusion however, we use the term "hominid" in this text to refer only to humans and their immediate fossil relatives (e.g., the genera Homo and Australopithecus).

An evolutionary systematist might derive a very different classification from the same cladistic relationships depending on how much emphasis is placed on unique derived, or autapomorphic, characters. For example, as we see above the strict cladist classifies chimpanzees and humans as sister groups and accords them the same taxonomic rank even though chimpanzees presumably look much more like the ancestral group than modern humans do. In other words, since diverging from chimpanzeelike ancestors, humans as a lineage have developed an extensive suite of autapomorphies—large brains, bipedal posture, language, delayed maturation and elaborate tool use among others—that the evolutionary systematist takes into account in the phylogram (Fig. 2.9a bottom). Evolutionary systematists therefore usually classify all the apes in the family Pongidae, and humans in the family Hominidae, even though chimpanzees share a more recent common ancestor with humans than with some of the other apes, such as orangutans and gibbons. The justification is that humans have reached a higher grade of evolution (51). In short, evolutionary classifications reflect the adaptive and morphological attributes of a taxon rather than their strict cladistic relationships.

Even though humans may actually be very similar to apes in certain molecular characters, such as in overall protein and DNA structure, the two groups differ so much in mental capacity that no less a figure than famed biologist Julian Huxley once proposed that humans should be placed in a separate kingdom—the Psychozoa!

THE TEMPO AND MODE OF HUMAN EVOLUTION

An important component in debates about hominid phylogeny and classification, and one of great interest to paleoanthropologists, is the issue of at what rate (**tempo**) and by what process (**mode**) hominid evolution actually occurs. Determining the tempo and mode of hominid evolution is a formidable challenge since neither aspect of the evolutionary process is obvious from a human fossil record in which fossilization has occurred by chance and many organic changes in organisms have not necessarily been recorded. As George Gaylord Simpson once put it (52):

> Looking more closely into the pattern of evolution, we see that it involves also the organic changes that have occurred in the (branching) sequence and the rates at which these changes have occurred. Trying to see how these (organic changes) arose, were transmitted, and became what they did, we find ourselves grappling finally with every factor and element that is in life or that affects life.

There are currently two principal models of the tempo and mode of hominid evolution. The first, sometimes referred to as **phyletic gradualism**, holds that a daughter species usually originates through a progressive series of small, gradual transformations of a parental species, the process we have previously described as anagenesis. There are several main attributes of this model:
- new species arise by the gradual modification of an ancestral population
- the transformation is generally slow
- the transformation may involve most of the ancestral population, but more commonly involves **allopatric** populations, i.e., populations occupying different and disjunct geographical areas
- the transformation takes place over all or at least a large part of the ancestral population's geographic range

An alternative model, **punctuated equilibrium**, claims that the creation of a new species is more often than not a comparatively rapid event. Furthermore, its advocates believe it is the mode that best describes the kinds of major evolutionary changes human paleontologists study and that the hominid fossil record contains (53,54). The model is based on the idea that most evolutionary change is concentrated in comparatively rapid speciation events in small isolated subpopulations of the ancestral species, a process known as **allopatric speciation**. A species that originated in such a small, isolated population and then spread to invade the territory of the parental population would appear to the paleoanthropologist to have arisen abruptly in the fossil record; thus speciation in such populations would appear to be essentially instantaneous in terms of geologic time.

What is novel about the punctuated equilibrium model is the idea that most evolutionary change within lineages is concentrated in these rapid speciation events and that the rest of most species' life histories—the time before or after the actual speciation event itself—is characterized by little change, or **stasis**. Thus, the "equilibrium" part is as important to this model as the "punctuated" part. There are several main attributes of this model (55):

- most new species arise from the splitting of existing lineages
- most new species develop rapidly, then stabilize
- a small subpopulation of the ancestral species gives rise to the new species
- the new species originates in a very small, isolated part of the geographic range of the ancestral species
- once they arise, species do not change much throughout their remaining history

Both of these models of the tempo and mode of speciation have important implications for interpreting the fossil hominid record (56–59). For example, a phyletic gradualist might interpret the many obvious morphological discontinuities in the fossil hominid lineage as mere gaps in the fossil record, perhaps using them as convenient temporal boundaries for dividing the fossil lineage into different species, say for example, between *Homo erectus* and *Homo sapiens*. A punctuationist, on the other hand, would regard the same fossil data as a reflection of the normal evolutionary process: long periods of morphological stasis interrupted by rapid speciation events. To the punctuationist, the process of change from *H. erectus* to *H. sapiens* would not be seen as a slow, gradual species-wide evolution but rather as resulting from allopatric speciation in which a *H. erectus* subspecies, as a peripheral isolate of the *H. erectus* parental species, rapidly evolved and ultimately replaced its parental population by migration. In this view, unlike phyletic gradualism, the main body of the *H. erectus* species does not undergo the gradual change to a new *H. sapiens* species. Thus, what are considered missing data by a phyletic gradualist is considered evidence for a critical evolutionary event by a punctuated equilibriumist. In the equilibriumist interpretation, one has to ask what the chances are that a given series or sequence of fossils found at a particular site just happen to coincide with the point of geographic isolation of a subspecies from the parental population.

Strict gradualists, in emphasizing the importance of steady morphological change within fossil lineages, interpret speciation as a special case of phyletic evolution. They see species as arbitrary units, conveniently defined by gaps in the fossil record. Strict punctuationists, in arguing that morphological change is dominated by abrupt speciation events, see species as discrete units having a beginning and an end in time. Thus, although strict

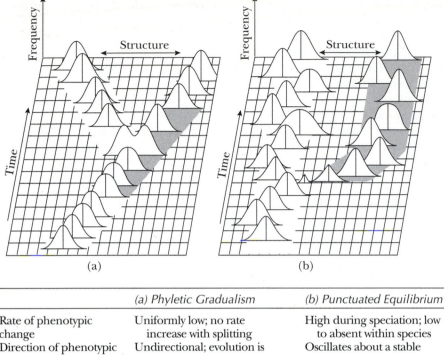

	(a) Phyletic Gradualism	(b) Punctuated Equilibrium
1. Rate of phenotypic change	Uniformly low; no rate increase with splitting	High during speciation; low to absent within species
2. Direction of phenotypic change within a species	Undirectional; evolution is phyletic	Oscillates about a stable mean
3. Population size for speciation	Small or large; can occur in whole species	Only in small isolated populations
4. Whether speciation is purely a function of time	Yes, speeded up by environmental change but does not require it	No, requires environmental change
5. How new species arise	By phyletic speciation or by allopatric speciation in large or small populations	Usually only by allopatric speciation in small, isolated populations
6. Implications for species	Species are arbitrary subdivisions on a continually evolving lineage	Species are real, discrete entities with beginnings and terminations

Fig. 2.11.   Three-dimensional graph illustrating major differences between (a) phyletic gradualism and (b) punctuated equilibrium.   Different species are denoted by stippling. The bell curves simply represent the morphological variability within the populations at any point in time. From (74).

proponents of both models agree that both slow and rapid changes are manifested in the fossil record, they interpret the data differently (Fig. 2.11).

Increasingly, paleoanthropologists and biologists alike seem to view these two models of speciation at opposite ends of a continuum of possibilities, with some lineages being better described by one model and some tending toward the other in their pattern of speciation, but few species being exclusively defined by either.

TAXONOMY USED IN THIS TEXT

There are currently two alternate classification systems for the living primates, the more traditional one based on the grade of organization that divides them into the suborders **Prosimii** (prosimians) and **Anthropoidea** (simians) and the cladistic one that divides them into the suborders **Strepsirhini** and **Haplorhini**, based on branching sequences or clades (Fig. 2.9b). As discussed more fully in a later chapter, this cladistic classification system groups gorillas and chimpanzees together with humans in the family Hominidae (Fig. 2.9a), thus leading to some potential confusion as to what is meant by the term ''hominid.'' Throughout the text various fossils will be referred to not only by their Latin names, but also by the anglicized versions of these names (for example, Hominidae and hominids). The names applied to some of these higher categories follow certain established rules, as illustrated in Table 2.1.

One of the most important attributes of any classification system should be ease of communication. Therefore, for the purposes of this text I plan to adhere to a classification of the hominids as set out by the distinguished paleoanthropologist, Phillip Tobias (60). In Tobias' noncladistic classification scheme, the reader can rest assured that the term ''hominid'' refers solely to humans and their immediate fossil relatives and not to living or fossil ''apes.'' In other words, I will continue to use Hominidae in the sense of the hominoid lineage postdating the ancestor common to them and the African great apes:

Family: Hominidae
    Subfamily: Australopithecinae
        Genus: *Australopithecus*
           Species: *A. ramidus*[5]
                   A. anamensis
                   A. afarensis
                   A. africanus
                   A. robustus
                   A. boisei
                   A. aethiopicus
    Subfamily: Homininae
        Genus: *Homo*
           Species: *H. habilis*
                   H. rudolfensis
                   H. ergaster
                   H. erectus
                   H. sapiens

[5]The fossils first described as *A. ramidus* (61) may ultimately prove to belong to a new genus, *Ardipithecus* (62). In this text we will retain the original name, *A. ramidus*.

Table 2.1a   The Linnaean Hierarchy of Classification Categories

Kingdom
　Phylum
　　Subphylum
　　　Superclass
　　　　Class
　　　　　Subclass
　　　　　　Infraclass
　　　　　　　Cohort
　　　　　　　　Superorder
　　　　　　　　　Order
　　　　　　　　　　Suborder
　　　　　　　　　　　Infraorder
　　　　　　　　　　　　Superfamily
　　　　　　　　　　　　　Family
　　　　　　　　　　　　　　Subfamily
　　　　　　　　　　　　　　　Tribe
　　　　　　　　　　　　　　　　Subtribe
　　　　　　　　　　　　　　　　　Genus
　　　　　　　　　　　　　　　　　　Subgenus
　　　　　　　　　　　　　　　　　　　Species
　　　　　　　　　　　　　　　　　　　　Subspecies

When a taxon occurs in parentheses but is preceded by an equals sign, it refers to alternate usage. Examples are Propliopithecidae (=Pliopithecidae), *Sivapithecus* (=*Ankarapithecus*) *meteai*, and *Gigantopithecus giganteus* (=*bilaspurensis*). Here alternate names for family, genus and species, respectively, are given. Where subgenera occur, the subgenus name is also given in parentheses but without the equals sign, as in, for example, *Dryopithecus (Proconsul) africanus*.

Table 2.1b   Formal and Anglicized Names of Higher Taxa in Primates

Category	Formal Suffix	Genus	Stem	Formal Name of Taxon	Anglicized Name of Taxon
Infraorder	-iformes	*Lemur*	Lemur-	Lemuriformes	lemuriform
		Tarsius	Tarsi-	Tarsiiformes	tarsiiform
Superfamily	-oidea	*Lemur*	Lemur-	Lemuroidea	lemuroid
		Homo	Homin-	Hominoidea	hominoid
Family	-idae	*Lemur*	Lemur-	Lemuridae	lemurid
		Homo	Homin-	Hominidae	hominid
Subfamily	-inae	*Lemur*	Lemur-	Lemurinae	lemurine
		Homo	Homin-	Homininae	hominine

The vernacular form of the two subfamilies, australopithecines and hominines, will be frequently used in the text. Two other colloquial terms, "gracile" and "robust," have often been used in the past as a convenient shorthand to refer to *Australopithecus africanus* and *A. afarensis* (gracile) on the one hand and *A. robustus* and *A. boisei* (robust) on the other. However, as we shall see in a later chapter, these terms are potentially misleading and confusing since it is now thought that there is relatively little difference in body size between the two groups.[6] In addition, new fossil evidence, particularly from South Africa, clearly indicates that dental dimensions in some "gracile" australopithecine specimens greatly exceed those found in the type specimen of *A. robustus*. Therefore, the terms "gracile" and "robust" should probably be abandoned in the future; they are used in this text only for historical continuity with the older literature and are not meant to convey any formal taxonomic implications.

Finally, a word about the practice of taxonomic attribution and nomenclature followed throughout this book, and in the literature, is in order. When a species can be identified, the taxonomic attribution is customarily recorded, as for example *Australopithecus africanus*, and both the genus and species name are either underlined or in italics. When the abbreviation "cf." (from the Latin "confer"—to be compared to) is used, as in *Australopithecus* cf. *A. africanus*, this means that the specimen should be compared to *A. africanus*. Use of "cf." in this context is taken to mean that while the preserved morphology suggests attribution to *A. africanus*, there is insufficient evidence to make an unequivocal judgment. A specimen that can only be identified at the generic level is indicated as, for example, *Australopithecus* sp. indet. (species indeterminate). Likewise, a specimen that can only be referred to family level is referred to, for example, as Hominidae gen. et sp. indet. (genus and species indeterminate) (64). If a fossil belongs to the entire known material of a species available to a taxonomist, or **hypodigm**, that has affinity with, but is not identical to, another taxon, then the designation "aff." (from the Latin, *affinis*) is used, for example, *Australopithecus* aff. *A. africanus*. If a specimen is damaged or incomplete, but is none the less recognizable as part of such a hypodigm, it is referred to as cf. *Australopithecus* aff. *A. africanus*. "Aff." is meant to suggest possible but inconclusive membership in a known species.

Now that we have looked at some of the ways paleoanthropologists find, date, and name fossils, we are ready to delve into the fossil record itself. If, as all modern biology suggests, humankind is part of a long evolutionary continuum, we need to know who or what preceded us in the evolutionary line. That is the question we address in the next chapter.

---

[6]In fact, a recently discovered cranium of *A. afarensis* from Hadar, Ethiopia, dated to about 3 mya is the largest australopithecine cranium (in terms of biasterionic width) yet discovered (63). Asterion is the point where the lambdoidal, parietomastoid, and occipitomastoid sutures meet low down on the lateral side of the skull.

CHAPTER III

Before the Bipeds: Human Antecedents among the Miocene Hominoids

If the immunological dates of divergence . . . are correct, then paleontologists have not yet found a single fossil related to the ancestry of any living primate and the whole host of species which they have found are all parallelistic imitations of modern higher primates. I find this impossible to believe. . . . [I]t is not presently acceptable to assume that all the fossil primates resembling modern forms are only parallelisms, that highly arboreal apes wandered hundreds of miles out of Africa across the Pontian steppes of Eurasia in search of tropical rain forest, or that *Australopithecus* sprang full-blown five million years ago, as Minerva did from Jupiter, from the head of a chimpanzee or gorilla.

Elywn L. Simons
"The origin and radiation of the primates"
(*Ann NY Acad Sci* 167, 1969)

INTRODUCTION

If the earliest hominids didn't spring full-blown, as Minerva did from Jupiter, from the head of a chimpanzee or gorilla 5 million years ago, where did they come from? As we saw in Chapter I, the story of human evolution unfolds mainly over the last two epochs of the Cenozoic Era—the Pliocene and the Pleistocene. But to understand humankind's deeper history, which is the subject of this chapter, we must search among the fossil hominoids (or primitive "apes") of the preceding epoch, the Miocene. **Hominoid primates** encompass the lesser apes (gibbons and siamangs of eastern Asia), the great apes (chimpanzees and gorillas of Africa and the orangutan of Southeast Asia), and humans. The Miocene was the heyday of hominoids, for it was during this epoch that they reached their greatest abundance and diversity, and there is little doubt that human origins lie somewhere within this group.

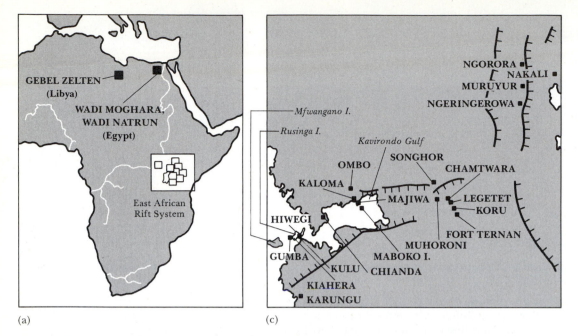

(a)

(c)

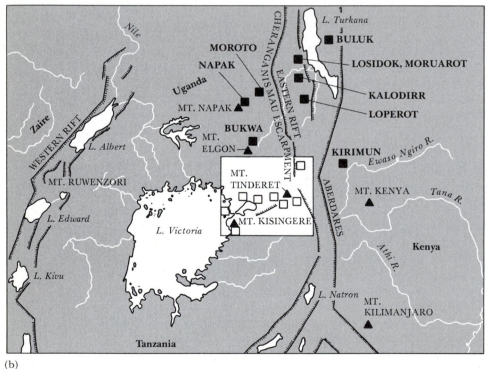

(b)

The Miocene epoch lasted nearly 20 million years, from about 24 to 5 mya (1). Primitive Old World hominoids first appear in the late Oligocene/ early Miocene fossil record of East Africa about 25 mya and become abundant and diverse in a number of East African faunas about 22–17 mya. By

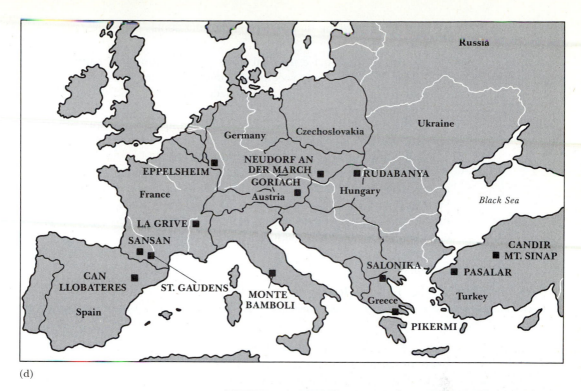

(d)

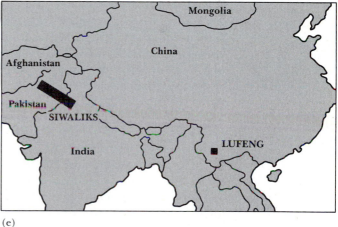

Fig. 3.1. Geographic distribution of Miocene hominoids from Africa and Eurasia. (a) Sites in North and East Africa; area in the square is expanded to give (b), sites in East Africa; the square in (b) is enlarged to give (c), sites in western Kenya. Triangles represent ancient volcanoes. (d) Miocene hominoid sites in Europe and Asia Minor. (e) Miocene hominoid sites in southern and eastern Asia. From (42).

(e)

the middle Miocene, approximately 16–10 mya, this situation changes dramatically, with monkeys becoming more abundant in the fossil record and hominoids less so, a trend that continues to this day. The early/middle Miocene, about 16.5 mya, was also the time African hominoids first emigrated to Eurasia. For reasons that are still unclear, hominoids become extremely rare in the African fossil record by the late Miocene (approximately 11.5–5.0 mya), although pockets of them survived in some abundance in southern Asia and China until about 7 mya (Fig. 3.1). The absence of fossil chimpanzees or gorillas in Africa has led some to suggest that rain forests are not conducive to fossil bone preservation. This cannot be the total story, however, since recent taphonomic studies in the Kibale Forest of western Uganda show that chimpanzee bones can, and do, accumulate on the forest floor (2).

By the end of the Miocene a very different apelike creature—*Australopithecus*, the first hominid—appears in the African fossil record. We will begin the hominid story in the next chapter.

With the exception of a recently discovered hominoid jaw from Namibia in southern Africa, all African Miocene hominoid fossils have been discovered in the equatorial region of East Africa. Therefore, our search for human origins should begin with a brief sketch of the geology and paleoecology of this important region of the African continent.

EAST AFRICA IN THE MIOCENE

Today, East Africa is ecologically isolated from Eurasia even though it has been physically connected to the Arabian Peninsula since the Miocene (3,4). The dominant feature of the landscape is the great **East African rift system**, which stretches all the way from the Red Sea in the north to the southern end of Lake Malawi (bordering Mozambique, Tanzania, and Malawi) in the south. The East African rift is continuous with tectonic spreading centers in both the Red Sea and the Gulf of Aden and all three began to form in pre-Miocene times (5). **Rift valleys** are formed when continental crust is subjected to tension, usually the result of tectonic uplifting. A rift valley can be likened to a fractured arch that has been pulled apart by tension so that the keystone has dropped en bloc or in strips (Fig. 3.2) (6,7).

East African early Miocene landscapes were characterized by large-scale volcanic activity, with some volcanoes rising 1,000 m or more above the surrounding countryside. By the late Miocene floodlike volcanic eruptions had spread over much of the area. The main source of early Miocene hominoid fossils in East Africa is the tuffaceous sedimentary sequences below the Miocene lavas of the Tinderet and Kisingiri volcanoes along the eastern shores of Lake Victoria in Kenya (see Fig. 3.1b). This association with volcanic lavas and tuffs allows many of these Miocene hominoid–bearing sites in Kenya to be radiometrically dated using techniques we discussed in Chapter II (e.g., potassium-argon dating) (8–11). Most of the hominoid fossils associated with the Kisingiri volcano (e.g., at Rusinga Island, Kenya) are about 17 to 18 million years old and those associated with the Tinderet volcano (e.g., at Songhor and Koru, Kenya) are about 19 million years old. Several ancient volcanic regions in Uganda have also yielded important early Miocene hominoid fossils (e.g., Bukwa) and these may be as old as

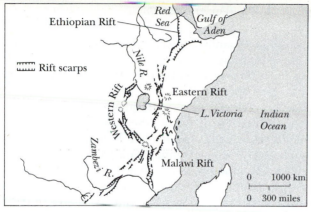

(a)

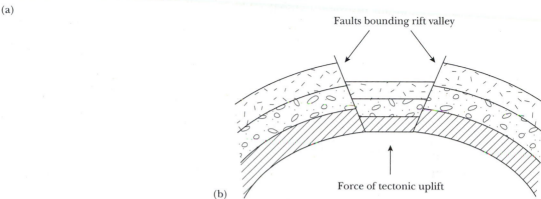

Faults bounding rift valley

Force of tectonic uplift

(b)

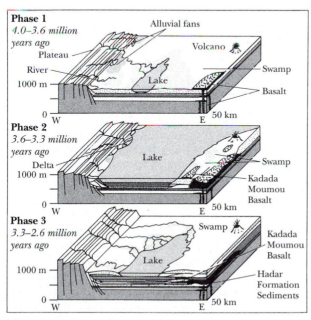

Phase 1
4.0–3.6 million years ago
Plateau
River
Alluvial fans
Volcano
Lake
1000 m
Swamp
Basalt
0
W   E   50 km

Phase 2
3.6–3.3 million years ago
Delta
Lake
1000 m
Swamp
Kadada Moumou Basalt
0
W   E   50 km

Phase 3
3.3–2.6 million years ago
Swamp
Kadada Moumou Basalt
Lake
1000 m
Hadar Formation Sediments
0
W   E   50 km

(c)

Fig. 3.2. (a) The East African rift system stretches some 4,000 km from Mozambique in the south to the Red Sea in the north. Most of the major Miocene hominoid localities are in Kenya and Uganda between the eastern and western rifts. Highlands form the shoulders of both major rifts. (b) Rift systems are caused by underlying tectonic uplift that produces surface cracks in the overlying continental crust. The resulting subsidence of crustal blocks between these fracture lines in the Earth's crust produces a long, narrow trough bounded by faults. (c) Three phases of rift formation using the site of Hadar in Ethiopia as an example. Phase 1 from 4.0 to 3.6 mya; phase 2 from 3.6 to 3.3 mya; phase 3 from 3.3 to 2.6 mya. Adapted from (165).

23 million years (12–15). Unfortunately, Miocene deposits in the western rift valley have not yet been radiometrically dated, but some of the Plio-Pleistocene volcanic tuffs there have recently been correlated to dated tuffs in the Lake Turkana Basin (see Chapter IV) (16).

Many of the early Miocene faunas show similarities to present-day African lowland forest communities. For example, the fauna at Songhor includes several excellent forest-indicator species like flying squirrels, elephant shrews, and prosimians (17). In addition, over a half-dozen primate species are present at the site. In modern African faunal communities, this number of primate species is usually found only in fully forested conditions. As mentioned above, cercopithecoids (Old World monkeys) are rarer than hominoids in these early Miocene faunas, so it seems probable that early Miocene hominoids were occupying many of the ecological niches that came to be more fully exploited by monkeys (18,19).

Several important middle Miocene sites in this area of western Kenya lie stratigraphically below a 12-million-year old lava flow that flooded the region from the northwest. Hominoid fossils from two of the most important of these sites, Maboko Island and Fort Ternan, date to about 15 mya and 14–12 mya respectively (20–26). These, and other, middle Miocene sites are significant because they document the unfolding of a major ecological shift in East Africa from forested environments to more open-country ones (20,27–31). This is evident, for example, in the greater proportions of open-country mammals like bushbucks, buffaloes, gazelles, and giraffids in these middle Miocene faunas (32). Importantly, however, there were still pockets of rain forest and woodland in the East African rift valley as recently as about 12 mya, in contrast to the savannalike conditions found there today (33–35). And as we will discuss in the following chapter, the earliest hominid species yet discovered, the recently named *Australopithecus ramidus* from deposits in Ethiopia dated to about 4.4 mya, is associated with fauna and flora more typical of African woodlands (36,37).

Unfortunately, East African late Miocene faunas are poorly known, making it difficult to infer paleoecological information for that time period. A few isolated primate teeth from deposits near Lake Baringo in Kenya document the presence of hominoids during this period, but these teeth tell very little about the biology of late Miocene apes, or their changing habitats. We do know, however, that the climatic trends toward cooling and drying seen in the middle Miocene continued in the late Miocene and into the Pliocene.

Today's East African climate is greatly affected by the highlands bordering the eastern and western rifts, mainly because these highlands prevent both Atlantic and Indian Ocean rainfall from reaching the interrift region of the interior. Rainfall in the west, brought by warm prevailing winds of the South Atlantic, penetrates inland to equatorial western and central Africa only as far as the shoulder of the western rift valley. In the east, the northeast monsoon and the year-round southeast trade winds bring moisture to East Africa from the Indian Ocean, but this moisture precipitates predominantly at the coast and over the highlands bordering the eastern rift. The result of these rainfall patterns is that much of the interrift area is deprived of rain. Since rainfall is heavy where moisture-bearing winds from the sea are forced up over mountain ranges, the land on the leeward (or rainshadow) side of the two mountain ranges is usually dry, causing the semiarid conditions today of the interior rift valley.

The climate of eastern equatorial Africa was probably wetter in the early Miocene than it is at present because the surrounding highlands had not yet formed (38,39) and rainfall in the interrift region was unlikely to have been as severely restricted as it is today. The prevailing rainfall patterns probably started to change as the highlands began to form in the middle to late Miocene; therefore, early Miocene East African climate and vegetation probably resembled what we see today in the forested volcanic mountains and lowlands along the western rift (see Fig. 3.2).

EURASIA IN THE MIOCENE

The landscapes of Eurasia, like Africa, have changed dramatically since the Miocene, mostly as a result of the mountain-building forces of the Alpine and Himalayan systems and the regression of the **Tethys Sea** to form the Mediterranean, Black, and Caspian sea basins. The Tethys Sea was initially a broad waterway that divided the northern supercontinent **Laurasia** (consisting of what is now North America , Europe, and Asia) from the southern supercontinent **Gondwanaland** (South America, Africa, Antarctica, India, Madagascar, and Australia). From about 25 to 20 mya, southwestern Eurasia was inundated by the extensive Tethys seaway, which acted as an effective faunal barrier preventing African mammals, including hominoids, from reaching Eurasia.

Approximately 20 mya, as the Tethys Sea began to recede, the first significant emigration of African land mammals into Eurasia evidently occurred through a corridor linking the two landmasses. Miocene hominoids first appear in western Europe (France) about 16 mya. In Europe, as in East Africa, more seasonal environments and the evolution of more open-country woodland habitats are in evidence by the middle Miocene. As the Tethys Sea continued to regress the Mediterranean, Black, and Caspian sea basins assumed the form we recognize today.

The period about 10 to 5 mya was characterized by major faunal turnover in Eurasia. As environments became increasingly seasonal, the geographic ranges of Eurasian hominoids began to shrink, so that by about 7 mya most members had disappeared, leaving only residual, or relict populations in the subtropical and tropical environments of Southeast Asia

(3,40). The expansion across Asia of more open-country faunas and plants with thickened cell walls better adapted for resistance to water loss, so-called **sclerophyllous vegetation**, coincides with these hominoid extinctions.

We mentioned in Chapter I the tremendous effect the rising Himalayas had on worldwide climate. The continuing uplift and subsequent erosion of the Himalayas were important for another reason, namely, the resulting thick sequence of fossiliferous sediments that were deposited at their base. These sediments, known as the **Siwalik Group**, and the Miocene hominoid fossils derived from them, have played a very important historical role in discussions of human origins (41) (see Fig. 3.1e). We will come back to them later in the chapter.

OVERVIEW OF MIOCENE HOMINOIDS: MORPHOLOGY AND ADAPTATIONS

Basic Primate Morphology

Virtually all human fossil material studied by paleoanthropologists consists of dental and skeletal remains. For this reason, interpretation of the human fossil record necessarily demands a basic understanding of primate morphology. To better prepare the reader for our discussions of the fossil record that follows, we will begin by reviewing some basic aspects of primate dental and skeletal anatomy. Many of the items mentioned in this brief overview will be more fully discussed when they become relevant to interpretations of the fossil evidence.

Cranial Morphology   The primate skull serves a number of critical functions: it houses and protects the brain and special sense organs such as those of hearing, vision, and smell; it forms the anchoring structure for the dentition; and it provides the bony surface attachment area for both the chewing (masticatory) muscles and the muscles of facial expression. To some extent, the overall shape of the skull in various primates reflects the relative degree of enlargement or specialization of these various functions. For example, primates that rely more on the sense of smell, or olfaction, tend to have longer snouts than those that rely more on vision. Likewise, those primates with well-developed chewing muscles often have accentuated bony crests or muscular markings on the skull, for instance temporal lines marking the origin of the temporalis muscle, that serve as sites of attachment for those powerful muscles.

Posture, or how the head is carried on top of the vertebral column, may also affect cranial morphology. For example, the hole at the base of the skull for passage of the spinal cord, the **foramen magnum**, tends to face more inferiorly than posteriorly in primates that routinely hold their trunk more erect in both resting and locomotor postures. There are, however, other factors possibly affecting the relative position of the foramen magnum. In humans such factors include 1) the relatively large degree of cranial base flexion that brings the face to a position below, rather than in front of, the brain case and 2) the relative enlargement of the **occipital lobes** of the brain that results from an expansion of the visual cortex of the cerebral cortex.

The thin bones forming the roof of the skull, the **calvaria**, are the frontal bone anteriorly, the occipital bone posteriorly, and the parietal, temporal, and sphenoid bones laterally. These bones are joined to one another by fibrous joints called **sutures**. All of the upper teeth are housed in the maxilla except for the incisors, which are housed in the premaxilla. All the lower teeth are contained in the mandible.

The main osteological features of the ape and human skull are compared in Figure 3.3 and the main osteological landmarks of the human mandible are identified in Figure 3.4.

Dental Morphology   The dentition is one of the most informative parts of the human body as far as paleoanthropologists are concerned. Of all the skeletal elements teeth are the most resistant to biological, chemical, and/or physical destruction and, therefore, they are generally the most common skeletal element found in most fossil assemblages. The important clues about past and present human adaptations provided by the dentition pertain to diet, age, sex, health, and phylogenetic relationships.

A major characteristic of the human dentition is that our teeth are regionally differentiated to serve special functions, a condition known as **heterodonty**. Thus, on each side of the upper and lower jaws starting at the front are two teeth adapted for cutting and cropping, the **incisors**, followed by a single-pointed, tusklike tooth, the **canine**, which in turn is followed by the postcanine dentition, two **premolars** and three **molars**, teeth whose complex chewing surfaces are adapted for grinding and crushing. Therefore, all adult fossil and modern humans normally have eight teeth in each quadrant of the upper and lower jaws for a total of thirty-two. A shorthand way to write the **dental formula** for humans is 2.1.2.3. Teeth in the upper and lower jaws are usually identified with superscripts and subscripts, respectively. For example LM^1 is shorthand for a left upper first molar and RM_1 is shorthand for a right lower first molar. One point of potential confusion is that the two premolars in each quadrant of the upper and lower jaws are usually referred to as the third and fourth premolars, e.g., P3 or P4, and not as the first or second premolars as one might expect. Actually, there is a good evolutionary reason for this terminology; lower primates once had four premolars in each quadrant but during the course of primate evolution the ancestors of higher primates, including humans, lost the first and second premolars. Thus, the two remaining premolars are actually premolars three and four of the original set of four.

The adult dentition is preceded by a milk, or **deciduous**, dentition that

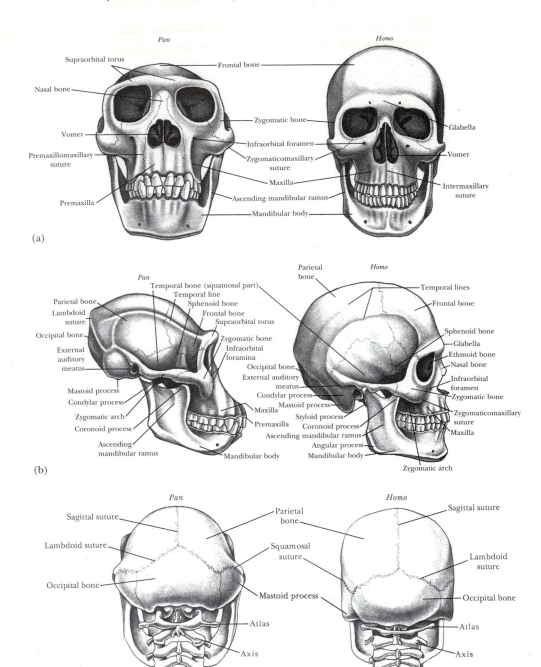

Fig. 3.3. Comparison of the skull in chimpanzees (left) and modern humans (right) with the major bones and bony landmarks identified.   (a) Frontal view. (b) Lateral view. (c) Posterior view. (d) Basal or occlusal view.

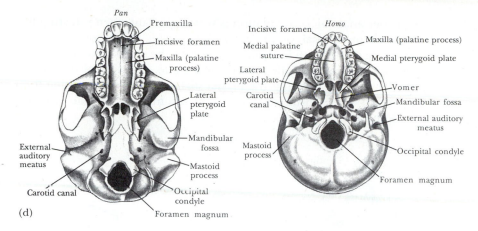

(d)

consists of two incisors, a canine, and two premolars, sometimes referred to as "milk molars," in each quadrant. The three permanent adult molars are not preceded by any deciduous teeth. Shorthand notation for the deciduous dentition would be, for example, Rdi_2 and Ldm^1 for the right deciduous lower second incisor and left deciduous upper first molar, respectively.

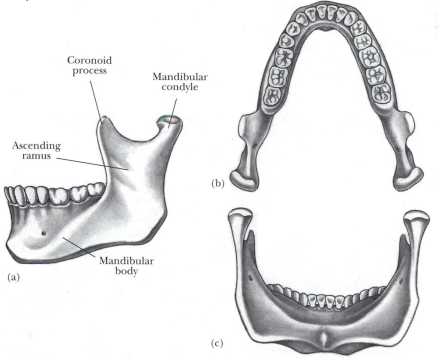

Fig. 3.4. Important bony landmarks of the human mandible. (a) Lateral view. (b) Occlusal view. (c) Posterior view.

The proper anatomical orientation is very important when referring to teeth. A crown, or **occlusal**, view refers to the chewing surface of the tooth. The **buccal** side of the tooth faces laterally toward the cheek and the **lingual** side of the tooth faces medially toward the tongue. The side of the tooth facing the front of the mouth is the **mesial** surface and the side facing the back of the jaw is the **distal** surface. These orientations are labelled in Figures 3.5 and 3.6.

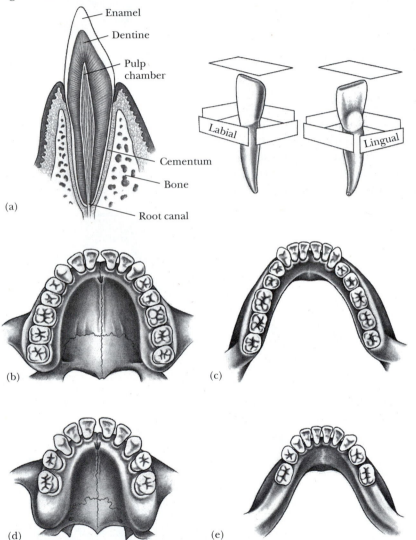

Fig. 3.5. (a) Cross section through a human incisor to show the different tissues (left) and its proper orientation (right). (b) Occlusal view of the upper permanent dentition. (c) Occlusal view of the lower permanent dentition. (d) Occlusal view of the upper deciduous dentition. (e) Occlusal view of the lower deciduous dentition.

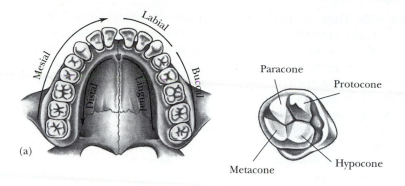

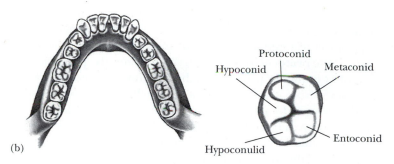

Fig. 3.6. (a) Occlusal view of the upper dentition showing the major cusps of the M^1 (insert). (b) Occlusal view of the lower dentition showing the major cusps of the M_1.

Teeth consist of two main parts, a crown and a root (or roots). The crown projects into the oral cavity and the root is anchored in the bony socket, or **alveolus**, of the mandible or maxilla. The crown is covered by an avascular layer of mineralized tissue known as **enamel** (Fig. 3.5). Enamel is the hardest biological structure in the human body. The root is covered by a thin bonelike layer called **cementum**. Beneath these surface layers and forming much of the tooth's bulk is another very resilient connective tissue known as **dentine**. Dentine differs from enamel in that it is not as highly mineralized a tissue (approximately 70 percent versus 97 percent by weight). The **pulp cavity** is the neurovascular space deep to the dentine that extends for a variable distance into the roots.

In humans the incisors are relatively simple, single-rooted teeth having a somewhat spatulate crown. The single-rooted canine is still a somewhat pointed, tusklike tooth, but it is not the long, sharp weapon that it is in some other primates like baboons. Functionally the human canine has become more incorporated into the incisor tooth row. Humans use these teeth in diverse ways, from cutting and cropping foods to holding objects. The premolars may have one or more roots and are also relatively simple teeth having two main cusps, which is why they are sometimes referred to as **bicuspids**. There is often a thickened ring of enamel around the base of the tooth called the **cingulum**. In some primates with large, stabbing upper canines like baboons, the anterior lower premolar acts as a honing stone to sharpen the posterior edge of the upper canine every time the two teeth come into contact. Such an adaptation is referred to as a **sectorial** premolar.

The upper molars of humans have four main cusps: the protocone, paracone, metacone, and hypocone. Looking at the occlusal surface of an upper molar, the **protocone** is the main cusp on the mesiolingual side, the **paracone** is the main cusp on the mesiobuccal side, the **metacone** is the main cusp on the distobuccal side, and the **hypocone** is the main cusp on the distolingual side (Fig. 3.6). Enamel crests often connect the main cusps; these crests are adaptations for slicing food between the molars during occlusion.

The crowns of the lower molars consist of two parts: an anterior portion, the **trigonid**, and a posterior, heellike projection, the **talonid**. The three main cusps of the trigonid are the mirror image of the cusps of the upper molar trigone: the **protoconid** on the buccal side, and the **paraconid** (which is usually absent in higher primates, including humans) and **metaconid** on the lingual side. Note that the names of the lower molar cusps end in -conid, while those of the upper molars end in -cone. The talonid is usually a basinlike structure surrounded by a raised enamel rim with two main cusps: the **hypoconid** laterally and the **entoconid** medially. Often there is an additional cusp, the **hypoconulid**, toward the middle of the distal margin of the rim. It is often well developed on lower third molars. During chewing, the protocones of the upper molars fit into the talonid basins of the corresponding lower molars, like the action of a pestle in a mortar.

Postcranial Morphology   The postcranial skeleton comprises 1) an **axial skeleton**, consisting of those bones forming the central axis of the body, including the vertebrae, sacrum, ribs, and sternum, and 2) an **appendicular skeleton**, consisting of those bones making up the upper and lower limbs including their respective limb girdles. The postcranial skeleton provides the overall scaffolding that holds up the body as well as the site of attachment for the muscles that move the body. The skeleton acts as a system of levers that facilitate, indeed make possible, movement powered by muscles.

In many respects, the primate skeleton retains many basic mammalian postcranial features. For example, primates, including humans, retain five fingers and toes, a relatively mobile shoulder joint for free movement of the upper limb in all directions, grasping, or prehensile capability in both hands and (in nonhuman primates) feet, a well-developed collarbone, or clavicle, and completely separate bones of the forearm (radius and ulna) and leg (tibia and fibula).

Primates also have developed highly sensitive friction pads on the hands and feet, and in most modern primates the distal finger and toe bones, or phalanges, are covered by flattened nails instead of sharp, curved claws.

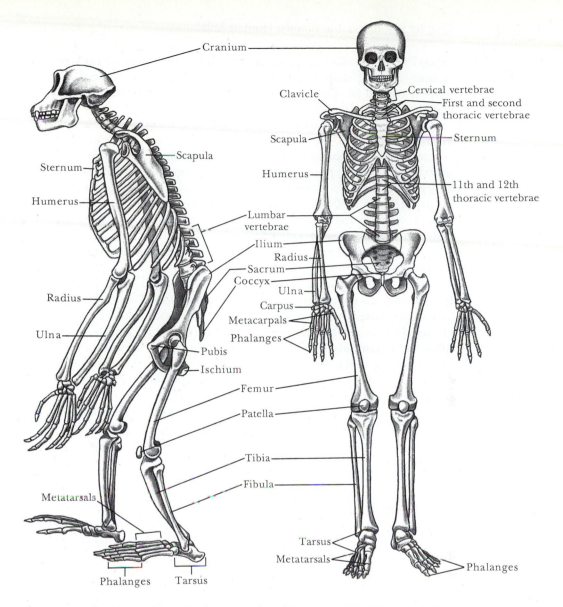

Fig. 3.7. Major bones of the chimpanzee (left) and human (right) skeletons. Note in the human that the right hand is pronated (palm facing backward), whereas the left hand is supinated (palm facing forward).

These nails and friction pads provide an efficient mechanism for both grasping and manipulating objects.

The skeleton of humans and apes consists of the same basic bony elements, although the size and shape of many of these bones of course vary depending on the different functional demands placed on them (Fig. 3.7). These differences are particularly marked in those parts of the skeleton related to locomotion (e.g., the pelvis and lower limb), brain size (e.g., cranial size and shape), and masticatory stresses (e.g., dental size and shape). We will be discussing each of these in much greater detail as they pertain to the fossil evidence for human evolution.

Our purpose in the following section is not to examine in detail all the Miocene hominoids, but rather to identify those that represent trends pertaining to the question of human origins. It is difficult to present a coherent overview of Miocene hominoids within some generally accepted taxonomic and phylogenetic framework. Major taxonomic revisions of these fossils occurred in the 1960s and 1970s, and our concepts of hominoid phylogeny have changed in the years since then. Later in this chapter we will discuss historical taxonomies of Miocene hominoids, conflicting evidence from recent biomolecular and morphological data, and the changing definitions of classical terminology.

In the meantime we must define some nomenclature for these Miocene hominoids in a meaningful and unambiguous way. For this purpose the terminology used in *Primate Evolution* (42) will again apply. Three distinct clusters of Miocene hominoids are recognized: primitive early and middle Miocene hominoids of East Africa and Eurasia, characterized by thin enamel on the molar teeth, called **dryomorphs**; middle Miocene hominoids of East Africa and Eurasia, characterized by thickened enamel on the molar teeth, known as **ramamorphs**; and early and middle Miocene hominoids of Eurasia that share many primitive catarrhine features called **pliomorphs**.

Dryomorphs include such genera as *Proconsul, Rangwapithecus, Limnopithecus, Dendropithecus, Micropithecus,* and *Dryopithecus;* ramamorphs include *Sivapithecus, Ramapithecus* (often considered part of *Sivapithecus*), and *Gigantopithecus;* and pliomorphs include *Pliopithecus* and *Laccopithecus* (Fig. 3.8).

It is important to note from Figure 3.8 that these three ''morph'' categories are not taxonomic terms; for example, dryomorphs include genera classified in the families **Proconsulidae** (*Proconsul*) and **Pongidae** (*Dryopithecus*).

As pointed out earlier, hominoids first appear in the late Oligocene/early Miocene fossil record of East Africa (northern Kenya) approximately 25 mya and become quite abundant and diverse in early Miocene faunas dated to about 22–17 mya. By contrast, hominoids first appear in Eurasia only about 16 mya and, with few exceptions, most disappear from Eurasia about 7 mya.

Fossil hominoids were first discovered in East Africa in 1926 at Koru, Kenya. Shortly thereafter (1931–32) two other richly fossiliferous Kenyan Miocene sites, Songhor and Rusinga Island, were discovered. Subsequent work has resulted in the discovery of several thousand specimens representing a half-dozen or so Miocene hominoid genera from these and other East African sites (Fig. 3.1). Although most of these specimens are teeth

Taxa	Epoch (and Area)
Infraorder Catarrhini	
Superfamily Hominoidea	
Family Proconsulidae	E. Mio. (Africa and Asia)
Dendropithecus	E. Mio. (Africa)
Dionysopithecus	?E. Mio. (Asia)
Limnopithecus	E. Mio. (Africa)
Micropithecus	E. Mio. (Africa)
Proconsul	E. Mio. (Africa)
Rangwapithecus	E. Mio. (Africa)
Family Oreopithecidae	E.– L. Mio. (Africa, Eur.)
Nyanzapithecus	E.– M. Mio. (Africa)
Oreopithecus	L. Mio. (Eur.)
Family Pongidae	M. Mio.– Pleist. (Africa, Eur., Asia)
Dryopithecus	M.– L. Mio. (Eur.)
Gigantopithecus	L. Mio.– Pleist. (Asia)
Lufengpithecus	L. Mio. (Asia)
Sivapithecus	M.– L. Mio. (Africa, Eur., Asia)
Family Pliopithecidae	M.– L. Mio. (Eur., Asia)
Laccopithecus	L. Mio. (Asia)
Pliopithecus	M.– L. Mio. (Eur.)
Family *incertae sedis*	
Afropithecus	E.– ?M. Mio. (Africa, Saudia Arabia)
Turkanapithecus	E. Mio. (Africa)

Fig. 3.8. One classification of Miocene hominoids.

and jaw bones, one genus at least, *Proconsul*, is well represented by both cranial and postcranial material.[1] Since this is the best known of the early Miocene hominoids, we shall use it as our general model of early hominoid morphology and adaptation.

CHARACTERISTICS OF EARLY MIOCENE HOMINOIDS (*PROCONSUL*)

The temporal and geographical distribution of early Miocene hominoids is limited mainly to late Oligocene/early Miocene sites of northern and western Kenya including Rusinga and Mfwangano Islands, Songhor, and Koru (44,45) (Table 3.1). *Proconsul africanus* and *P. heseloni* are the smallest

[1]Much of the more complete postcranial material belongs to the species *Proconsul heseloni* [formerly referred to as *P. africanus* (43)].

Table 3.1a   The Occurrence of Catarrhine Taxa at Early Miocene Localities in Africa

	Meswa Bridge	Koru	Songhor	Napak	Rusinga	Mfwangano	Kalodirr	Others
Micropithecus clarki		X		X				
Limnopithecus legetet		X		X	X			X
Limnopithecus evansi			X					X
Dendropithecus macinnesi		X	X	X	X	X		X
Nyanzapithecus vancouveringorum			X		X	X		X
Kalepithecus songhorensis		X	X					X
Rangwapithecus gordoni		?	X					
Proconsul africanus		X	X		X	X		
Proconsul nyanzae					X	X		
Proconsul major		X	X	X				
Proconsul sp.	X							
Simiolus enjiessi							X	
Afropithecus turkanensis							X	X
Turkanapithecus kalakolensis							X	
?Xenopithecus koruensis		?						
?"Xenopithecus" hamiltoni								X
?Victoriapithecus sp.				X				
?Prohylobates sp.								
Prohylobates tandyi								X
Prohylobates simonsi								
Total	1	6–8	7	5	5	4	3	

Table 3.1b   The Occurrence of Catarrhine Taxa at Middle Miocene Localities in Africa

	Maboko	Fort Ternan	Others
Micropithecus leakeyorum	X		X
Limnopithecus sp.	X		
Small catarrhine A		X	
Small catarrhine B		X	
cf. *Proconsul africanus*		X	
Kenyapithecus africanus	X		X
Kenyapithecus wickeri		X	
Nyanzapithecus pickfordi	X		
Mabokopithecus clarki	X		
Large oreopithecid		X	X
Victoriapithecus macinnesi	X		X
Cercopithecid indet.			X
Total	6	5	

of the *Proconsul* species, being intermediate in dental size between gibbons (*Hylobates*) and pygmy chimpanzees (*Pan paniscus*). Body-weight estimates for these smaller *Proconsul* species range from 9 to 12 kg. *Proconsul nyanzae* is a much larger, sexually dimorphic, species with male body weights estimated at 35–38 kg and females at 26–28 kg (46–49). *Proconsul major* is the largest species, with a dental size approaching that of a female gorilla. Unfortunately, little is known about the postcranial skeleton of this species.

The genus *Proconsul* was first described in 1933 from fossils discovered at Koru, Kenya (50). *Proconsul* was a highly successful genus that diversified into several species in the early Miocene of East Africa. There are currently four generally accepted species of *Proconsul*: *P. africanus*, *P. nyanzae*, *P. major*, and *P. heseloni* (43,51). *Proconsul* was initially considered to be a fossil great ape, or pongid, when it was first described. In fact, it was commonly held well into the 1970s that an ancestor-descendant relationship existed between *P. africanus* and the chimpanzee and between *P. major* and the gorilla (52–55). However, we shall see later in the chapter that recent studies in both paleontology and molecular biology demonstrate the improbability that any modern great ape lineage was already distinct by the early Miocene.

Proconsul is generally associated with forested paleoenvironments and its species are recognized as a group by their common possession of a number of mainly ancestral features of the skull and dentition that characterize Old World monkeys, apes, and humans generally (42). *Proconsul* is, however, linked specifically to hominoid primates, apes and humans, on the basis of several postcranial characters that are discussed below.

Generally speaking, most early Miocene dryomorphs like *Proconsul* had rather lightly built, or gracile, jaws and thinly enamelled teeth, whereas most middle to late Miocene ramamorphs such as *Afropithecus*, *Kenyapithecus*, and *Sivapithecus* had more robust jaws and thicker enamelled teeth. The only major exceptions to this general rule are the genera *Dryopithecus* and *Otavipithecus*, both of which appear to have had teeth more thinly enamelled than other middle Miocene hominoids (see below). By the middle/late Miocene most of the thinner-enamelled dryomorphs were clearly on the wane and the thicker-enamelled ramamorphs become more common in the fossil record of both Africa and Eurasia. This suggests that hominoid craniodental morphology was adapting coincidentally with dietary changes resulting from the ecological factors we noted earlier, namely the replacing of foodstuffs associated with wetter, more forested environments of the early Miocene (e.g., soft fruits, young leaves) by foodstuffs associated with drier, more woodland-bushland conditions of the middle to later Miocene.

One of the finest early Miocene hominoid specimens ever discovered is the beautifully preserved skull of *P. heseloni*, found by Mary Leakey at Rusinga Island in 1948 (Fig. 3.9). The skull is lightly built and lacks both browridges, or **supraorbital tori**, and strong muscular markings. The lower portion of the face projects forward, a condition known as facial **progna-**

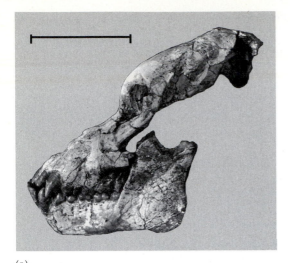

(a)

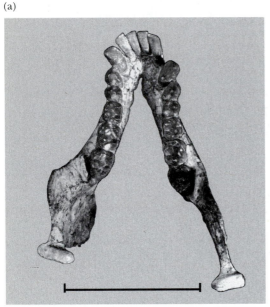

(b)

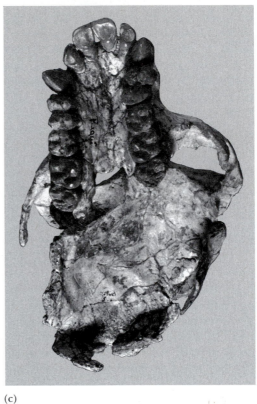

(c)

Fig. 3.9. Skull of *Proconsul heseloni* from the early Miocene of Rusinga Island, Kenya. (a) Lateral view. (b) Occlusal view of lower jaw. (c) Occlusal view of the upper jaw. (Courtesy of P. Andrews.)

thism. When originally found, the back or occipital portion of the skull did not articulate with the rest of the specimen because large parts of the intervening skullcap were missing. Incredibly, 35 years later two of the missing pieces of the skull were found, thereby making it possible to attach the main skull fragment to the occipital portion. As a result of this fortuitous circumstance, a reasonably accurate cranial cavity, or endocranial, volume of 167 cc has been calculated for this specimen.

Box 3.1. Encephalization Quotients (EQ): How Do Paleoanthropologists Interpret Endocranial Volume?

How do researchers determine and interpret a cranial volume of 167 cc for P. heseloni*? Is that a large volume, a small volume, or something in-between? Part of the answer depends on how large the animal in question is. After all, a cow will have a much larger brain than a mouse in absolute terms, but will the cow have a relatively larger brain than the mouse taking body size into account? Biologists have devised a very useful index, called the encephalization quotient (EQ), to explore this question. EQ is designed to measure relative brain size in mammals and is calculated by dividing the endocranial volume of the specimen in question by the endocranial volume expected of a living mammal of the same body size. For example, one (of several) such empirically derived formulae for EQ is:*

$$EQ = observed\ brain\ weight\ (g)/0.0991\ body\ weight\ (g)^{0.76}$$

Given the body weight and brain size estimates for P. heseloni*, its EQ is approximately 1.5 by this formula. An EQ of 1.5 is interpreted to mean that cranial volume in this species is one and a half times larger than the cranial volume we would expect to see in a living mammal of the same approximate body size.*

Relative brain size in Proconsul *can also be expressed as a percentage of human relative brain size by dividing its EQ value by 2.87, the EQ for* Homo sapiens *determined from this same formula (note that other formulae result in different values for EQ—see, for example, Fig. 5.1). The corresponding value for* P. heseloni *is about 52 percent and for chimpanzees, orangutans, and gorillas is about 41 percent, 32 percent, and 17 percent respectively. Similar calculations for various New and Old World monkeys range between 23 percent and 82 percent. Therefore, one might conclude that on this scale the gorilla has the smallest relative brain size of all higher primates and that there is some overlap in relative EQs between monkeys and apes. It is important to note, however, that relative EQs in monkeys of about the same body size as* P. heseloni *range from 23 percent to 41 percent, indicating that* P. heseloni *had a relatively bigger brain than modern monkeys of comparable body size (56).*

The postcranial skeleton in early Miocene hominoids is best known for the species *P. heseloni* and *P. nyanzae*. It exhibits a unique mosaic of rather generalized higher primate features combined with a few shared derived features characteristic of living hominoids, most notably the absence of both a tail and an enlarged bony expansion of the ischium, or **ischial tuberosity** (Fig. 3.10). The absence of enlarged ischial tuberosities indicates that early Miocene hominoids, as in living great apes, lacked the enlarged, fatty sitting pads known as **ischial callosities** found on the ischium of all Old World monkeys and gibbons.

Limb proportions in early Miocene hominoids are unlike those found in any living hominoid. The ratio of upper limb length to lower limb length, the **intermembral index**, is a crude predictor of overall locomotor behavior in many living primates. For example, low intermembral indices, e.g., those less than 70 percent, typify vertical clinging and leaping primates, such as tarsiers and bushbabies; moderate indices, ranging from 70 to 100 percent, typify most arboreal quadrupedal monkeys, like rhesus macaques and ba-

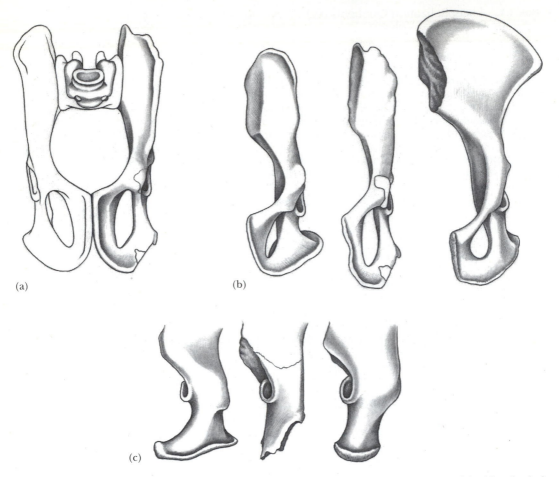

Fig. 3.10. (a) Ventral view of a reconstruction of a *Proconsul* pelvis. Nonshaded lines represent reconstructed regions. Note the very narrow overall shape of the pelvis. (b) Ventromedial views of (from left to right) *Papio* (baboon), *Proconsul*, and *Pan* (chimpanzee) hip bones. Note the widely flaring iliac blade of *Pan*, absent in *Papio* and *Proconsul*. Width of the iliac blade reflects mediolateral breadth of the torso. *Proconsul* probably had a narrow torso like *Papio*. (c) Dorsal view of (from left to right) *Papio*, *Proconsul*, and *Pan* left ischia. Note the flaring ischial tuberosity of *Papio*, with its broad, flat surface, and the flaring of the ischial ramus cranial to the tuberosity. *Proconsul* exhibits virtually no flaring, even less than does *Pan*. This indicates that *Proconsul* did not have ischial callosities. From (62).

boons; and high indices, ranging from 100 to 150 percent, typify hominoids that engage in some degree of suspensory locomotion, like chimpanzees and gibbons. The intermembral index in *Proconsul* was about 85–90 percent, squarely within the set of values for general arboreal quadrupedal monkeys (Fig. 3.11a).

Proconsul hand and foot proportions were also more similar to those of

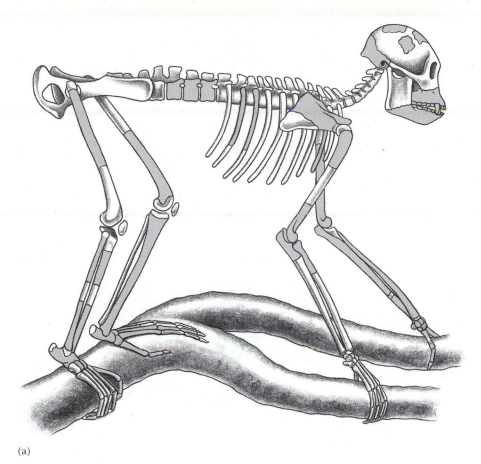

(a)

Fig. 3.11. (a) Reconstruction of the skeleton of *Proconsul heseloni* (about 20 percent natural size). Limb proportions are most similar to those found in some Old World monkeys. The intermembral index is about 87 (length of forelimb/length of hindlimb × 100). From (48).

arboreal monkeys than to apes (Fig. 3.11b,c, pp. 102–103). The size and shape of their finger bones suggest that they were primarily above-branch arboreal quadrupeds. Interestingly, the thumb was relatively long and was clearly adapted for limited rotation and opposition, as in extant great apes. There is no indication of any knuckle-walking adaptations in the wrist or finger bones (57), a point we will come back to at the end of this chapter.

Based on a partial skeleton of *P. nyanzae*, it appears that *Proconsul* had a number of monkeylike features of the trunk as well, including a long, flexible vertebral column, a narrow rib cage or torso, and an habitually **pronograde** posture—in other words, it most likely walked with its palms flat on the ground. These features are very different from the short, inflexible vertebral column (particularly in the lumbar, or lower back, region), broad and shallow torso, and knuckle-walking postures seen in mod-

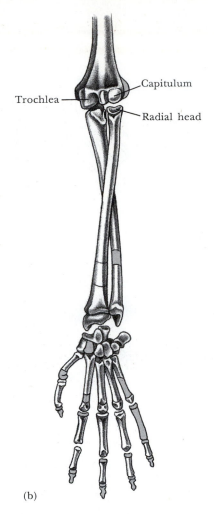

Fig. 3.11.   (b) The hand and forearm bones of *P. heseloni* (about 40 percent natural size). From (48).

ern African great apes (Fig. 3.12, p. 105). Thus, the overall impression we are left with is of an animal having a unique mosaic of monkeylike and apelike postcranial features quite unlike any primate living today. Probably, these morphological features represent the ancestral higher primate or catarrhine postcranial condition (43,58–63).

Discoveries from a number of other early Miocene sites around Lake Turkana (e.g., Kalodirr, Buluk) and Lake Baringo (e.g., Kipsaramon) attest to the great diversity of early Miocene hominoids (see Fig. 3.1). Several recently described genera include *Afropithecus*, *Simiolus*, and *Turkanapithecus* (64–71). Based on faunal comparisons, most of these hominoids date to about 18–16 mya.

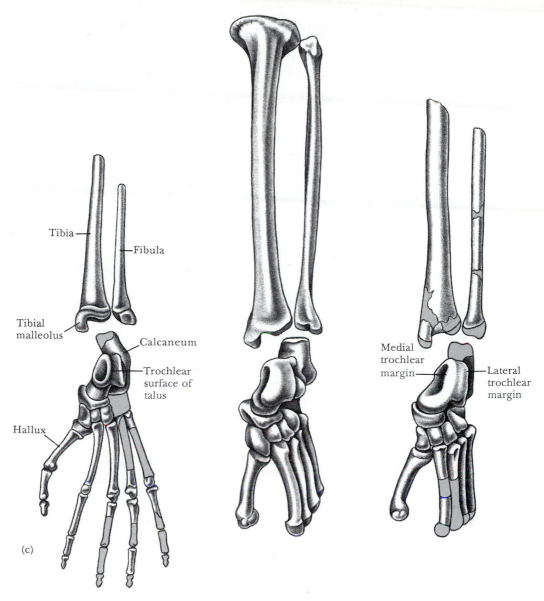

Fig. 3.11.   (c) Comparison of the lower leg in (from left to right) *Proconsul heseloni, Pan,* and *Proconsul nyanzae.* Note the opposable, grasping hallux in all three. About 33 percent natural size. From (48).

One of these taxa, *Afropithecus turkanensis,* is particularly interesting. It is known from a number of specimens including a partial cranium, several mandibles, isolated teeth, and associated postcranial bones. It appears to be a rather distinctive species, quite unlike any other Miocene hominoid. It is particularly distinctive from other Miocene hominoids in the basal flare

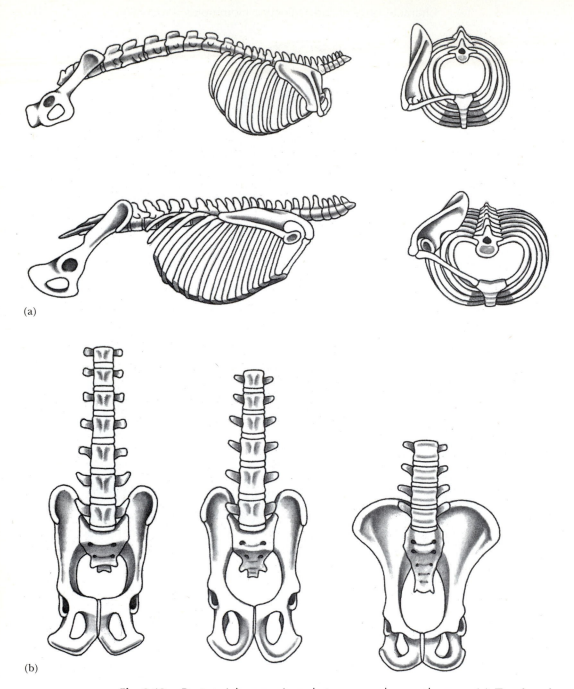

(a)

(b)

Fig. 3.12. Postcranial comparisons between monkeys and apes. (a) Trunk and pelvis of *Macaca* (above) and *Pan* (below), in side (left) and superior (right) views. Note the different orientations of the shoulder joints and the different shapes of the thorax. (b) Anterior views of pelvis and lumbar vertebral column of (left) *Macaca*, (middle) *Proconsul* (reconstructed from fossil evidence), and (right) *Pan*. Note the longer lumbar region in the macaque monkey. From (166).

of the upper cheek teeth, which has the effect of making the cusp tips appear more closely packed together than the cusp bases, and in its very thick enamel (72). Although it resembles some Eurasian middle Miocene hominoids like *Sivapithecus* in some ways (for example in the large, forwardly projecting, or procumbent, central incisors coupled with relatively small, asymmetrical lateral incisors; small supraorbital tori with high hafting of the cranial vault onto the face; and molars with thickened enamel and more flattened occlusal surfaces), its overall facial shape differs markedly from them. It looks more like a blown-up version of the primitive Oligocene anthropoid *Aegyptopithecus* from Egypt (73) (Fig. 3.13). These similarities between Oligocene *Aegyptopithecus* and Miocene *Afropithecus* pose three interesting questions: 1) do they simply represent a retention of primitive facial features for more than 14 million years of hominoid evolution? 2) do they mean that *Afropithecus* represents the last of a long lineage of prim-

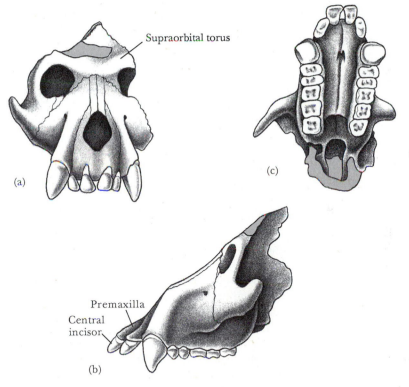

Fig. 3.13.   Skull of *Afropithecus turkanensis* from Kalodirr, Kenya.   (a) Front, (b) side, and (c) basal views of the upper jaw and face. Note the small supraorbital tori, the long premaxilla, and the procumbent incisors, all traits shared with *Sivapithecus*. It differs, however, from *Sivapithecus* in its more linear midface profile. Scale about 33 percent natural size. From (69).

itive Oligocene hominoids from North Africa that survived into the Miocene of East Africa? or 3) do they mean that *Afropithecus* has phylogenetic affinities with other middle Miocene genera such as *Sivapithecus, Kenyapithecus* or *Otavipithecus* (see below)? We cannot confidently answer any of these questions as yet, but in posing them we demonstrate just how complex Miocene phylogenetic relationships really are.

CHARACTERISTICS OF MIDDLE MIOCENE HOMINOIDS

Middle Miocene hominoids are found at a number of sites throughout Eurasia (e.g., Spain, France, Greece, Hungary, Turkey, India, Pakistan, China) and a few sites in Africa (e.g., Fort Ternan and Maboko in Kenya and the Otavi Mountains of Namibia) (Fig. 3.1). The exact number of and phylogenetic relationships among these middle Miocene hominoid taxa are matters of ongoing and spirited debate (74–76). For example, some propose that *Dryopithecus* may be among the earliest members of the great ape–human clade (77,78) whereas others propose that *Ouranopithecus* may be directly ancestral to later humans (79–81). For our purposes, however, it is not necessary to discuss all of these phylogenetic machinations in great detail. Rather, our objective is to highlight some of the more general features of this rather heterogeneous group of middle Miocene hominoids and to discuss how some of them have influenced discussions about human origins.

One of the most controversial of these Eurasian middle Miocene taxa is *Ouranopithecus macedoniensis*, known from a number of sites in Greece dated to about 10–9 mya. What makes this female gorilla–sized taxon particularly relevant to a text on human evolution is the recent claim that it is the sister group of *Australopithecus* and *Homo* (79,80). This claim is based on several general similarities between *Ouranopithecus* and *Australopithecus*, such as low-crowned and thick-enamelled molars; broad, shallow mandibular bodies; the overall appearance of the rounded and swollen molar cusps; and the trend toward both canine and P_3 honing facet reduction.

The according of "hominid" status to *Ouranopithecus*—representing it as the sister group of *Australopithecus* and *Homo*—harks back to views prevalent in the 1960s, namely, that the human lineage had diverged from the African apes by the middle Miocene (see below). This new claim for *Ouranopithecus*, however, has the earliest member of the human lineage appearing in Greece rather than Africa! This view has not gone unchallenged (82). Can another spin be put on the apparent similarity between *Ouran-*

opithecus and *Australopithecus*? First, because sexual dimorphism in body weight and canine size in primates decreases exponentially with decreasing body size (83,84), the reduced canines could be accounted for if the relevant *Ouranopithecus* specimens are shown to be females instead of males. Second, as we noted earlier in our review of basic primate dental morphology, the relative size of P_3 honing facets is functionally related to the size of the upper canine because these honing facets serve to sharpen the back edge of the upper canine; if upper canine size is reduced, the associated P_3 honing facets will be as well. Third, the morphology of the "rounded and swollen molar cusps" is indistinguishable from that of other thick-enamelled middle Miocene hominoids such as *Sivapithecus*. Thus, it is probably safe to conclude that while the roots of Western civilization may rightly be traced back to Greek soil, the same cannot be said, at least yet, about human origins.

Other Eurasian early/middle Miocene hominoid samples that have impacted discussions of human origins come from sites in South Asia (Pakistan, India), Turkey, and China. This century, the most explored area for the recovery of middle Miocene hominoids has been the Siwalik Hills of Pakistan and India. Assorted craniodental and postcranial remains representing over a hundred Miocene hominoids have been found in this extensive area. Unlike the Miocene tuffaceous deposits of East Africa, the Siwalik sediments are generally not amenable to direct radiometric dating. Consequently, most of the Siwalik hominoids have been dated on the basis of paleomagnetic stratigraphy and faunal correlations. Specimens allocated to *Sivapithecus* first appear in South Asia about 13–10 mya in the Chinji Formation, reach their peak of abundance and diversity about 10–8 mya in the Nagri Formation, and disappear about 8–5 mya after the Dhok Pathan Formation (85–88).

Probably the single most important *Sivapithecus* specimen recovered from the Siwaliks is the skull of a single individual preserving much of the face and lower jaw (89,90) (Fig. 3.14). This important specimen provides a number of specific details about *Sivapithecus* facial architecture that demonstrate a more remarkable similarity to orangutans than to *Proconsul* or to any living African great ape. Such orangutanlike features include the deep and widely flared zygomatic process (see Fig. 3.3); the marked prognathism, short upper face, and narrow interorbital distance; the relatively large first incisor compared to the second incisor; and the overall shape of the orbits and facial profile.

Differences in the anatomy of the lower face distinguish early from middle Miocene hominoids and the same differences, in general, also distinguish African apes from orangutans. The differences relate primarily to the disposition of the incisive canal, the passageway in the front of the hard palate for small arteries and nerves running between the nasal and oral cavities, as well as to the morphology of that portion of the premaxilla that

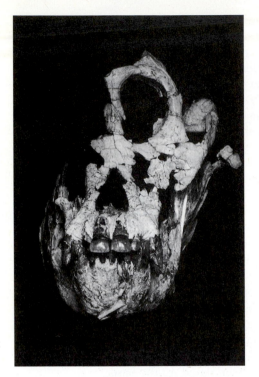

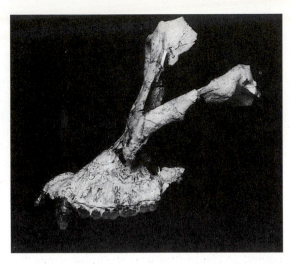

Fig. 3.14.   Skull of *Sivapithecus indicus* from the middle Miocene of Pakistan.   In the shape of the eye socket, the construction of the bony ridge over the orbits, the dimensions of the incisors, and the detailed anatomy of the lower face, *Sivapithecus* can be seen to resemble the orangutan more closely than any other modern hominoid. (Photos by W. Sacco, courtesy of David Pilbeam.)

houses the roots of the upper incisors, the subnasal alveolar process (91,92). As shown in Figure 3.15, the pattern found in middle Miocene hominoids like *Sivapithecus* resembles the pattern found today in orangutans. We shall come back to this morphology in the next chapter when we look at early hominid facial architecture in more detail.

Very few hominoid postcranial remains have been positively identified from these South Asian sites, and none are found in direct association with dental remains. Several foot bones, some finger bones, and parts of the humerus, radius, and femur have been described that range in size from those of a female gorilla to those of a pygmy chimpanzee. The articular surfaces of the finger bones are interesting in that they resemble those found in palmigrade, quadrupedal primates. However, the degree of shaft curvature and robustness implies that the fingers were also subjected to tensile stresses, for instance in hanging from branches. This evidence is compatible with the view that *Sivapithecus* engaged in arboreal quadrupe-

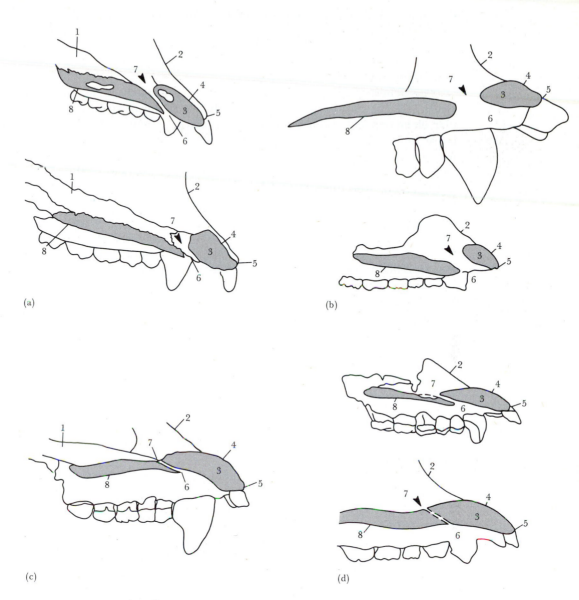

Fig. 3.15. Anatomy of the lower face in Miocene and extant hominoids. Sagittal sections through the premaxilla and palate (shaded areas): (a) *Pan* (top) and *Gorilla* (bottom); (b) *Proconsul major* (top) and *Rangwapithecus vancouveringi* (bottom); (c) *Pongo*; (d) *Sivapithecus indicus* (top) and *S. meteai* (bottom). Anatomical parts: 1, vomer; 2, lateral margin of nasal aperture; 3, subnasal alveolar process; 4, nasoalveolar clivus; 5, prosthion; 6, oral incisive fossa; 7, and arrowhead, nasal incisive fossa; 8, hard palate. Note in both specimens in (b) that the premaxilla is broadly separated from the palate.

dalism and climbing behavior. However, some features of the limb bones, particularly the lateral, rather than straight, curvature of the proximal humeral shaft, are ancestral *Proconsul*-like characters rather than modern orangutan ones (93–96), which complicates the tidy picture of a direct *Sivapithecus*-orangutan relationship.

The richest of the Turkish sites, Pasalar in northwestern Anatolia, has yielded over seven hundred isolated teeth, several maxillary and mandibular elements, and about a dozen postcranial fragments dated by faunal correlation to about 15 mya. These have been provisionally grouped into two species of the genus *Sivapithecus* or, alternatively, into two separate genera. As is typical of middle Miocene hominoids generally, the molar enamel is relatively thick. Dental dimensions in the larger species are about the same size as those in the larger *Sivapithecus* species from the Siwaliks but, unlike most Siwalik hominoids, the lower molars have a prominent buccal cingulum reminiscent of the condition found in *Proconsul*. The smaller Pasalar species is similar in having well-developed molar cingula; low, rounded molar cusps; and thick molar enamel (97–101).

A particularly important Turkish specimen discovered northwest of Ankara is a lower face of *Sivapithecus* that includes the complete palate with all the upper teeth (102). This specimen and the Pakistan specimen mentioned above are the two most significant fossil discoveries linking *Sivapithecus* to the orangutan clade and support the argument that the orangutan clade had already diverged from the other great apes by at least 12 mya (Fig. 3.16). The importance of these discoveries to the history of human evolution studies is in their providing one of the most widely cited divergence dates by which molecular anthropologists set their molecular clocks and in their disproving of the 1960s and 1970s idea that *Sivapithecus* and the closely related specimens referred to at one time as *Ramapithecus* were on the human evolutionary lineage.

In the last few decades important middle Miocene hominoid samples have been recovered from lignite beds at Lufeng in south-central China in deposits representing lake and swamp environments (103–105). Extensive excavations since the 1970s have produced a wealth of hominoid material that includes jaws, skulls, teeth, and a few postcranial bones (106–110). Chinese paleoanthropologists initially divided this hominoid sample into two genera, *Sivapithecus* and *Ramapithecus*, and considered this latter genus to be an early representative of the human lineage. As we shall see, there is some uncertainty about whether these fossil belong to one, both, or neither of these two genera.[2]

The Lufeng crania (three assigned by the Chinese to *Ramapithecus* and two to *Sivapithecus*) have a number of features in common. The two supraorbital tori are poorly developed and the region of the frontal bone be-

---

[2]English translations of many of the original Chinese articles dealing with these fossils can be found in (111).

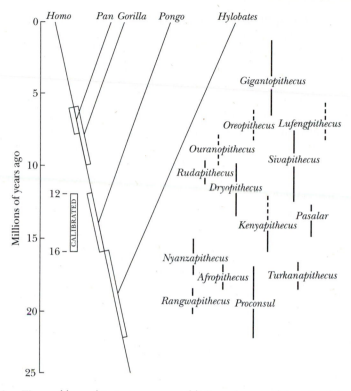

Fig. 3.16. Time of branching sequences of living apes, as determined from comparative genetics and based on calibration dates between 16 and 12 mya for the origin of the orangutan lineage. Temporal ranges of fossil apes are shown to the right. Solid lines reflect relatively well-known time ranges and dashed lines reflect uncertain temporal positions within a probable time interval. From (167).

tween these two browridges, the area of the skull known as **glabella**, is concave. The orbital contours are squarish with rounded corners and the nasal aperture is narrow and pear-shaped. Interestingly, many of the craniodental features found in these specimens are similar to those found in orangutans (112).

A few postcranial remains including a scapula and clavicle have also been described as orangutanlike (113). In contrast, the finger bones are described as being less orangutanlike: for example, the articular surface for flexion and extension is less extensive than in orangutans, suggesting that this movement is more extensive in modern orangutans than in the Lufeng hominoids. However, it seems clear that the fossil finger bones, or phalanges, were adapted to grasping and hanging, as they are very long and strongly curved.

Many of the morphological differences noted between the Chinese *Si-*

vapithecus and *Ramapithecus* specimens are similar to those found between male and female orangutans, so it is possible that these two "genera" simply represent the males and females of a single, sexually dimorphic genus (112,114). Another possibility is that the Chinese *Sivapithecus* and *Ramapithecus* are indeed two separate genera but with very different patterns of dental sexual dimorphism, with *Sivapithecus* more similar to *Pongo* and *Ramapithecus* more similar to *Homo* (115). If the skulls are male and female of a single species, then the original names (*Ramapithecus lufengensis* and *Sivapithecus yunnanesis*) are not valid and the correct name for this sexually dimorphic hominoid species is *Sivapithecus lufengensis*. However, there is one other problem: the crania of *S. lufengensis* bear no significant resemblance to other *Sivapithecus* crania, such as those from Turkey and Pakistan. For that reason most paleoanthropologists now refer the Lufeng material to a separate genus, *Lufengpithecus*.

Only a few fossil specimens document the existence of hominoids in the middle Miocene of Africa (see Table 3.1). Most of these specimens come from the middle Miocene Kenyan sites of Fort Ternan, Maboko Island, Majiwa, and Kaloma (23,27,116–118), but one comes from northern Namibia (74,119,120) The East African specimens are mainly referred to the genus *Kenyapithecus* and the Namibian specimen has been referred to the new genus, *Otavipithecus*. These fossils date to about 16–12 mya.

Probably the richest of these middle Miocene sites is Maboko Island, where at least five hominoid genera have now been recovered, all dating to about 16–14 mya (121).[3] One of these, *Kenyapithecus*, is of particular interest because for many years it was considered, along with *Ramapithecus*, a direct ancestor of the human lineage (122,123). Many of the morphological features of *Kenyapithecus* are similar to those already noted for other middle Miocene hominoids, e.g., the broad, shallow, robust mandibles; low-crowned and thick-enamelled molars lacking cingula; differential molar-wear gradients from M_1 to M_3; and canines that are relatively reduced in size. These features of mandibular robustness, molar morphology, and differential molar-wear gradients are markedly different from the complex of morphological features characterizing most early Miocene hominoids. Once again we note that these morphological differences undoubtedly signify a change in diet from relatively soft and easily chewed foods to more resistant foodstuffs. This is consistent with the paleoenvironment evidence indicating that these middle Miocene sites were more open woodland environments compared to the earlier Miocene sites.

Recently the first Miocene hominoid ever discovered from the African continent south of equatorial East Africa was reported (74,119,120) (Figs. 3.17, 3.18). This represents a major range extension of Miocene Hominoidea in Africa to latitude 20°S, approximately 10 degrees farther south than the limit of extant African apes. As we have seen, most previously known

---

[3] *Micropithecus, Limnopithecus, Kenyapithecus, Nyanzapithecus, Mabokopithecus.*

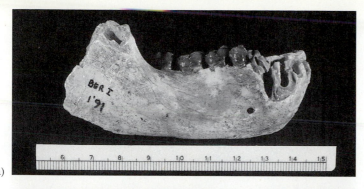

(a)

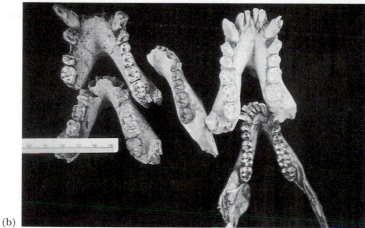

(b)

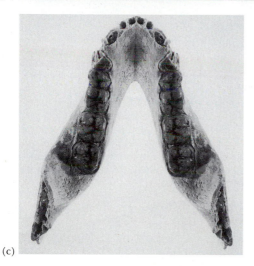

(c)

Fig. 3.17. Holotype mandible of *Otavipithecus namibiensis,* the only known Miocene hominoid from subequatorial Africa. (a) Lateral view. (b) Occlusal view of *Otavipithecus* (middle) compared to *Proconsul nyanzae* (upper left), *Dryopithecus fontani* (upper right), *Sivapithecus sivalensis* (bottom left), *Proconsul heseloni* (bottom right). (c) Reconstruction of *Otavipithecus namibiensis* mandible. (Photos by G. Conroy.)

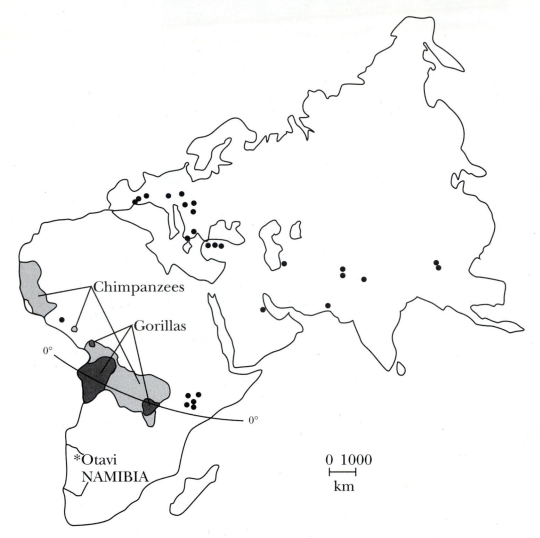

Fig. 3.18.   Distribution of middle and late Miocene Hominoidea (black dots) and extant African apes (shading).   Asterisk indicates site of *Otavipithecus* discovery. From (119).

Miocene hominoids are found in southern Eurasia between latitudes 23°N and 50°N, extending from Spain in the west to China in the east, and in East Africa (Fig. 3.1). The single jaw of *Otavipithecus namibiensis* exhibits a unique constellation of characters that differentiates it from other middle

Miocene hominoids of Africa and Eurasia and represents the only fossil evidence documenting a pre-australopithecine stage of hominoid evolution in southern Africa. *Otavipithecus* has been dated by faunal analyses to the latter part of the middle Miocene, approximately 13 mya. The faunal analyses also suggest that Namibia experienced a relatively humid climate during the middle and upper Miocene that contrasted strongly with the desertic and semiarid conditions that characterize the region today (119,124).

With the exception of the Plio-Pleistocene hominids that we discuss in the next chapter, there are no other hominoids from southern Africa with which to compare *Otavipithecus*. *Otavipithecus* is clearly not an australopithecine; moreover, its dental and mandibular morphology and proportions differ from early Miocene proconsulids. More appropriate comparisons are with middle Miocene hominoids of East Africa and Eurasia such as *Kenyapithecus*, *Sivapithecus*, and *Dryopithecus*.

As noted earlier, *Kenyapithecus* and the closely related *Sivapithecus* are known from a number of sites in Kenya and Eurasia. Both differ from *Otavipithecus* in having molar teeth that are characterized by thick enamel and marked differential wear and by mandibles that are quite robust with broad ascending rami that obscure most of the third molar in lateral view.

Dryopithecus is best known from sites in western and central Europe. In spite of the fact that *Otavipithecus* and *Dryopithecus* share several characteristics including relatively thin enamel, reduced or absent buccal cingula, and a moderately developed shelflike buttress of bone on the inside of the mandibular symphysis, the **inferior transverse torus**, there are enough clear distinctions to identify *Otavipithecus* as a separate genus (125).

Statistical tests relating molar size to body weight in modern anthropoids suggest that *Otavipithecus* probably weighed 14–20 kg, i.e, about the same body size estimated for small *Proconsul* or *Dryopithecus* species but smaller than the 30–35 kg size of living female pygmy chimpanzees. The minimal differential wear on the molars, combined with the thinness of the enamel, suggests that *Otavipithecus* most likely subsisted on nonabrasive foods. The narrowness of the incisor, or symphyseal, region of the lower jaw also argues against a specialized fruit-eating, or frugivorous, diet of tough-skinned fruits but neither molar size nor shape shows any adaptations to a specialized leaf-eating, or folivorous, diet. It is most likely that *Otavipithecus* subsisted on foods such as leaves, berries, seeds, buds, and flowers, i.e., foods that did not require extensive preparation by the incisor teeth prior to mastication.

Because the timing of dental eruption, as inferred from molar wear patterns, is related to the length of the maturational process within major groups of primates, it is reasonable to conclude that the molars of *Otavipithecus* emerged in rapid succession, as they do in living chimpanzees. Estimation of the age at death using chimpanzee maturation rates suggests that this individual died at about 10 years of age (126,127).

Box 3.2.   Summary of Craniodental Adaptations

Although the phylogenetic affinities of many Miocene hominoids are still subject to debate and revision, there seems little doubt that as a group most early Miocene forms can be distinguished from most middle Miocene forms and that human origins trace back to one of these African middle Miocene groups. Distinguishing characteristics of most middle Miocene hominoids include:

- *molars that are thick-enamelled with low, rounded cusps (bunodont)*
- *relatively low-crowned and robust canines*
- *relatively deep, robust mandibular bodies and symphyses*
- *laterally flaring zygomatic arches*
- *anteriorly abbreviated mandibles and premaxillae, suggesting a relatively nonprojecting, or orthognathous face*
- *lower first molars enlarged relative to third molars*

These features are relevant to discussions about human origins because, as we shall see in the next chapter, most of them foreshadow the conditions found in the earliest hominids, the australopithecines. As we shall document, these morphological changes undoubtedly relate to increased masticatory stresses in these animals as they began to exploit the new ecological niches of the African savanna.

PHYLOGENY AND CLASSIFICATION OF MIOCENE HOMINOIDS: HISTORICAL OVERVIEW

Even though Miocene hominoids have been known from Eurasia for over a century and from Africa for over half a century (128–130), it is still a challenge to present them within some generally acceptable taxonomic and phylogenetic framework. This is because the methodology of phylogenetic analysis and our conception of hominoid phylogeny have both fundamentally changed since many of these fossils were first described, and because major taxonomic revisions continue to occur. Therefore, the best introduction for students into the morass of Miocene hominoid phylogeny and classification is through an historical framework, concentrating mainly on those genera that are most pertinent to the question of human origins. We will then briefly follow how these views have evolved over time.[4]

In the mid-1960s two prominent paleontologists, Elwyn Simons and David Pilbeam, both then at Yale, produced a highly influential taxonomic revision of Miocene hominoids (52). They assigned all the then-known Miocene hominoids from Africa and Eurasia to a single subfamily, Dryopithecinae, within the family Pongidae (Fig. 3.19). Most of these fossil pon-

---

[4]For a more thorough discussion of Miocene hominoids, see (42).

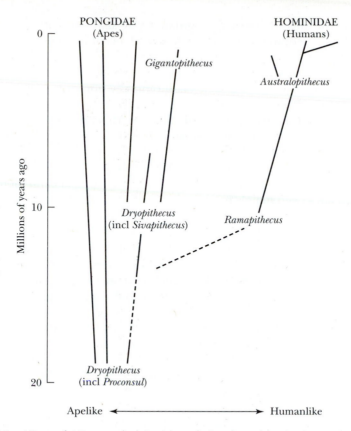

Fig. 3.19. View of Miocene hominoid evolution prevalent in the 1960s, which assigned all the East African and Eurasian Miocene hominoids to the subfamily Dryopithecus within the family Pongidae. From (168).

gids were assigned to the genus *Dryopithecus*, and within this genus they recognized three subgenera: *Dryopithecus*, mainly for the European dryopithecines; *Proconsul*, for the African dryopithecines; and *Sivapithecus*, mainly for the Asian dryopithecines. The European dryopithecines were divided into two species, *Dryopithecus (Dryopithecus) fontani* and *D.(D.) laietanus*, the Asian dryopithecines into two species, *Dryopithecus (Sivapithecus) indicus* and *D.(S.) sivalensis*, and the African dryopithecines into three species, *Dryopithecus (Proconsul) africanus*, *D.(P.) nyanzae*, and *D.(P.) major*. Within this framework, *D. africanus* was considered by Simons and Pilbeam to be ancestral to modern chimpanzees and *D. major* to modern gorillas, thereby implying that the evolutionary lineages leading to each of the African great apes had already diverged from one another by the early Miocene, some 18 and 20 mya (54). It was also suggested that *D. sivalensis* was related to the ancestry of the orangutan. As we shall see, the latter suggestion concerning orangutan phylogeny now seems more likely than the former suggestion concerning African ape phylogeny.

Gigantopithecus was another dryopithecine genus accepted by Simons and Pilbeam. At the time of their taxonomic revision only one species, *G. blacki* from the Pleistocene of China, was known. A second species, *G. bilaspurensis*, was later described from the late Miocene of northern India (131). This latter species was probably directly ancestral to the Chinese species, although in the 1970s some authors had proposed a more direct relationship between both species and *Australopithecus* (132). *Gigantopithecus* was probably the largest primate that ever lived and, because of its great size, must have been mainly terrestrial. Based on dental dimensions it could have weighed anywhere from about 150 to 230 (or more) kg (49), although some workers suggest that *Gigantopithecus* may have stood over 10 ft tall and weighed as much as 1,200 lbs. The dentition of these animals is characterized by small, vertical incisors; short, stubby canines; and enormous cheek teeth with flattened crowns and thickened enamel. As one might expect, the huge jaws housing these teeth are thick and deep. The size and shape of these jaws and teeth indicate a diet consisting of hard, fibrous material, similar perhaps to the bamboo diet of the living giant panda (133).

A second Miocene hominoid family recognized by Simons and Pilbeam was Hominidae, the family of humans and their immediate fossil ancestors. They allocated one Miocene genus and species, *Ramapithecus punjabicus*, to this family and for many years *Ramapithecus* was considered the earliest known hominid in the fossil record, dating to perhaps 14–12 mya. This notion had a profound influence on paleoanthropological thinking for many years (41), but, as we shall see, views about it began to shift dramatically by the early 1980s.

A third hominoid family recognized at the time was Hylobatidae, the family of gibbons and their fossil ancestors. Most paleoanthropologists at the time considered several Miocene hominoids such as *Limnopithecus* from East Africa and *Pliopithecus* from Europe to be ancestral gibbons. Because no one has seriously argued that human origins emerged from this gibbonlike group, it shall not be considered further in this text.

The "party line" in paleoanthropology up through the mid-1970s explained the relationship among the three families mentioned above as follows. The evolutionary lineages leading to chimpanzees, gorillas, orangutans, and gibbons all diverged by the early Miocene about 18 mya, and the lineage leading to humans diverged from the other apes by the middle Miocene about 14 mya. A number of influential anthropologists at the time believed that all the great apes (chimpanzees, gorillas, and orangutans) were more closely related to one another than any one of them was to humans or to the lesser ape, the gibbon. For that reason humans, gibbons, and great apes (and closely related ancestral forms) were classified in the families Hominidae, Hylobatidae, and Pongidae respectively, and consequently all the Miocene hominoids were pigeonholed into one of these three families. Accordingly, all Miocene apelike genera (e.g. *Dryopithecus, Sivapithecus, Proconsul*) were classified as pongids; all small and generalized gibbonlike fossils (e.g., *Pliopithecus*) were classified as hylobatids, and all humanlike fossils (including *Ramapithecus* and *Australopithecus*) were classified as hominids.

With the benefit of hindsight provided by several decades of further discoveries in both paleoanthropology and molecular biology, we now know that this phylogenetic and classification scheme significantly underestimated the diversity of Miocene hominoids. It is now generally accepted that the subgenera *Dryopithecus, Proconsul,* and *Sivapithecus* (for many of the European, African, and Asian Miocene hominoids respectively) should all be elevated to generic rank since this taxonomic allocation more faithfully represents the morphological diversity seen among these groups.

A major rethinking of Miocene hominoid phylogeny began to emerge by the late 1970s, reflecting new fossil discoveries, developments within the field of molecular anthropology, and a wave of enthusiasm for cladistics. The results of these studies led paleoanthropologists to conclude that the traditional taxonomic scheme of hominoid primates outlined above was incorrect. Accumulating data were making two things increasingly clear: the African apes (chimpanzees and gorillas) were more closely related to humans than either one was to the orangutan; and the evolutionary lineages leading to each of the modern African apes (and humans for that matter) could not have diverged as long ago as the early/middle Miocene (95,134–143).

THE ROLE OF MOLECULAR ANTHROPOLOGY (MOLECULAR CLOCKS)

Comparisons of biomolecular data in modern apes and humans have been crucial in confirming both of these points (Figs. 3.20, 3.21). These molecular tests fall into several categories, depending on the resolution of the test: 1) those that measure differences in whole proteins without knowledge of the specific changes in the protein structure, like immunodiffusion and electrophoresis; 2) those that determine the specific amino-acid sequences of proteins, like amino-acid sequencing; 3) those that determine the nucleotide sequences of DNA, like DNA sequencing; and 4) those that detect differences in DNA molecules without indicating exactly which nucleotides have changed, like DNA hybridization (144).

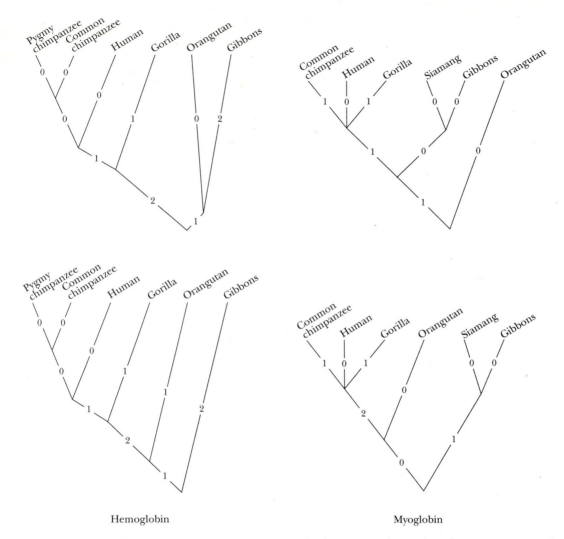

Hemoglobin   Myoglobin

Fig. 3.20. (left) Evolutionary tree for humans and apes based on sequencing of hemoglobins. (above) Relatedness between groups as a function of the lowest number of amino acid replacements needed. For example, gibbons and orangutans differ by two amino acids while gibbons and humans differ by six; therefore, the most parsimonious classification of humans and apes based solely on hemoglobin sequences would group gibbons and orangutans together; however, a number of different molecular lines of evidence place orangutans closest to the chimpanzee-human-gorilla clade, as shown in the figure below. (right) Trees vary depending on the molecular character chosen. Evolutionary tree for humans and apes based on myoglobins. (above) Lowest number of amino acid replacements needed. (below) Amino acid replacements constrained by other molecular evidence. From (169).

Box 3.3. DNA Hybridization

DNA hybridization has had a particularly profound, if controversial, influence on studies of hominoid phylogeny (140,141,145). The technique itself is relatively straightforward. When double-stranded DNA is heated, the bonds between the nitrogenous base pairs adenine-thymine and guanine-cytosine are broken down so that single strands of DNA are produced. When the single strands are allowed to cool, they tend to reassociate into double strands. When single strands of DNA from two different species are combined they tend to produce what are known as hybrid double-stranded DNA molecules. These hybrid DNA molecules will contain a number of mismatched base pairs depending on how genetically different the two species are from one another. The more mismatches, or genetic differences, there are in the hybrid DNA molecule, the lower the temperature needed to disassociate it again into two strands. Thus hybrid DNA from two closely related species will disassociate at higher temperatures than hybrid DNA from two more distantly related species.

Data from such studies show a fairly consistent branching sequence within hominoid evolution: first, the separation of gibbons from the great ape–human clade; second, the separation of the orangutan from the African great ape–human clade; and third, the separation of gorillas, chimpanzees, and humans after a long common evolutionary pathway since separation from the orangutan (Fig. 3.16). The details and timing of this last split among chimpanzees, gorillas, and humans are still the subject of active study and debate. Some molecular anthropologists conclude that humans and chimpanzees are more closely related to one another than either one is to the gorilla; others conclude that chimpanzees and gorillas are more closely related to one another than either is to humans; and still others conclude that this three-way split, or trichotomy, is unresolvable, at least with present molecular techniques (146–155). We will see at the end of this chapter just how important the ultimate resolution of this debate will be for human evolution studies, but for the moment, the best we can do is to keep an open mind on the subject.

Regardless of how this trichotomy is ultimately resolved, molecular anthropologists have still attempted to date each of these major cladogenic events by devising various **molecular clocks**. The use of molecular clocks is based on the premise that many molecular differences among taxa are neutral mutations that accumulate at a relatively constant rate when averaged over geologic time (Fig. 3.21). Therefore, the larger the molecular difference, the earlier the inferred divergence date. The irony, at least as far as paleoanthropologists are concerned, is that molecular clocks must ultimately be calibrated against the fossil record.

Fortunately, the results of molecular anthropology are bolstered by more traditional anatomical and paleontological studies that also support the broad outline of the three major cladogenic events noted above (158). For example, most paleoanthropologists agree that the hominoid primates (gibbons, chimpanzees, gorillas, orangutans, and humans) are a monophyletic group. Within this group there are numerous postcranial features, particularly in the wrist, shoulder musculature, and trunk, that also attest

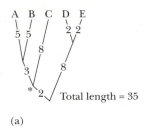

(a)

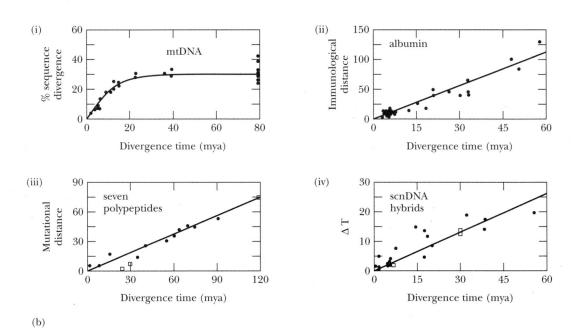

(b)

Fig. 3.21. (a) Calibrating the molecular clock based on a uniform rate of molecular change over time. This hypothetical evolutionary tree shows the number of changes of some particular molecular event along each branch of the tree. Notice that the same number of steps are involved as one follows any pathway from a given branchpoint to the tip of the tree. For example, from the branchpoint marked with an asterisk it is 3 + 5 = 8 steps to taxon A, 8 steps to taxon B, and the same to taxon C. This tree can be drawn against a time scale if a single uniform rate of molecular change is assumed over the whole tree in that the number of changes on each branch reflects the time, in relative units, that has elapsed on that branch. To convert relative time to absolute time, all that is needed is the absolute date for just one branchpoint. For example, if we knew from the fossil record that the common ancestor of taxa A, B, and C (i.e., at branchpoint *) dated to 40 mya, then we could infer that one molecular change occurred every 5 million years (e.g., eight changes occurring over 40 million years). Therefore, taxa A and B must themselves have diverged 25 mya (five changes in each since their divergence); the root of the entire tree would be 50 mya (ten changes) and the divergence of species D and E would be 10 mya (two changes). From (170). (b) Examples of various molecular clock ''calibrations'' for different types of molecular genetic data. All dates along the

Box 3.4. Molecular Clocks

In order to see how molecular clocks work, let us suppose two taxa differ in some molecular parameter by X units and that they diverged Y million years ago judging by the fossil record. Thus, assuming relatively constant rates of change, X number of molecular changes have occurred over Y millions of years and this relationship sets the clock. It is then a relatively simple matter to calculate the divergence times of other taxa by measuring how much the taxa differ in the same molecular parameter. For example, suppose two taxa that diverged 60 mya differed by 20 units of some molecular parameter. Change in this parameter is thus assumed to occur at the rate of 1 unit per 3 million years. Consequently the divergence date of two taxa differing by 10 such units would be estimated at 30 mya, 5 units at 15 mya, and so on. A number of such molecular clocks have been proposed for calculating divergence times within hominoid evolution. Many of the clocks have been calibrated by placing the split between Old World monkeys and apes, the cercopithecoid-hominoid split, at about 25 mya, but this split could be several million years older than this. In general, molecular clock studies suggest the following: 1) separation of the gibbon from the great ape–human clade about 15–12 mya; 2) separation of the orangutan from the African ape–human clade about 12–10 mya; and 3) separation of African apes from humans about 7–4 mya. It is obvious, then, that if any of these dates are even remotely correct, the early/middle Miocene divergence dates for chimpanzees, gorillas, and humans offered by paleoanthropologists in the 1960s and early 1970s are significant overestimations. Be that as it may, while molecular biology has provided paleoanthropology with invaluable insights into evolutionary processes and with more testable means of assessing phylogeny and cladogenesis, it is still by no means the panacea that some claim it is. There are two general points that should not be lost sight of in any discussion about molecular clocks. First, the debate is not whether molecular clocks keep time metronomically, like a watch—they do not. At best their "clocklike" behavior is stochastically constant, analogous to the situation in radioactive decay. Second, there is little doubt that different DNA sequences evolve at markedly different rates (134,156,157). Third, molecular anthropologists sometimes have difficulty in ascertaining which molecular configurations are primitive and which are derived for the taxa under study. In such cases similarity in molecular structure, in and of itself, may be no more informative about phylogenetic relationships than similarity in morphological structures would be if their polarities were unknown (see Chapter II). And finally, there is one other little problem—molecular anthropologists do not even agree among themselves about what their data reveal about the "true" phylogeny of hominoid primates.

---

abscissa are derived from fossil or biogeographic evidence. (i) Solid line: mitochondrial DNA sequence divergence for various mammals. The slope of the linear portion of the curve gives the conventional mtDNA clock calibration of approximately 2 percent sequence divergence per million years between recently separated lineages (note that beyond about 20–15 mya, mtDNA sequence divergence begins to plateau, presumably as the genome becomes saturated with substitutions at the variable sites). (ii) Albumin immunological distances (as estimated by microcomplement fixation) from various carnivorous mammals and ungulates. (iii) Accumulated codon substitutions in seven proteins (cytochrome c, myoglobin, alpha- and beta-hemoglobins, fibrinopeptides A and B, and insulin) for various mammalian species. The three squares below the solid line involve primate comparisons. (iv) Delta T values from DNA-DNA hybridizations of carnivores (dots) and primates (squares). After (156).

to the linkage between the great apes and humans to the exclusion of gibbons. Within the great ape–human group there is also strong morphological evidence linking gorillas and chimpanzees to the exclusion of orangutans, particularly in the many anatomical specializations for knuckle-walking (159–161). Interestingly, many of these relationships were deduced by such early morphologists as Thomas Huxley, G. Elliot Smith, and William Gregory many decades ago.

If we recall some of the principles of cladistics we discussed in Chapter II, it now becomes apparent why most early classifications of hominoid primates were deficient—namely, because they did not correctly reflect these phylogenetic relationships. If, in cladistic terminology, the African apes and humans are considered sister groups (i.e., more closely related to one another than either is to the orangutan), then they should be put in one family to contrast with the family containing orangutans rather than having humans in one family and the three great apes in another.[5] But, as we saw in Chapter II, other systematists believe that novel new adaptive patterns—such as the ones evident in humans—should be reflected in a classification, just as long as polyphyletic groups are not formed. For example, orangutans, chimpanzees, and gorillas are a monophyletic group—they all share a common ancestor. However, not all descendants are included (humans), a crime only to some cladists. Because of this, many new taxonomic schemes have been proposed in the past few years to more accurately reflect these relationships. For example, some paleoanthropologists favor dividing hominoids into two families, Pongidae and Hominidae, with the latter being further subdivided into two subfamilies, Paninae for the African great apes and their fossil relatives, and Homininae for humans and their fossil relatives. In this scheme (or variants of it) the family Pongidae would refer solely to the orangutan and its fossil relatives. Unfortunately, these taxonomic proposals result in the expansion of the term Hominidae to include at least some of the great apes and create havoc with such familiar terms as "pongid," "hominid," and "ape," thereby violating one of the main purposes of any taxonomic classification—ease of communication. However, just to put the reader's mind at ease, this reminder from Chapter I—when we use the vernacular term "hominid" in this text, we refer solely to humans and their immediate fossil ancestors (e.g., the genera *Homo* and *Australopithecus*).

SPECULATIONS

Finally, let's return to the question posed at the beginning of this chapter. If the earliest hominids didn't spring full-blown from the head of a chimpanzee or gorilla 5 mya, then where did they come from? Darwin had it

[5]But see (162) for a different view.

right over a century ago when he wrote (163):

> in each great region of the world the living mammals are closely related to the extinct species of the same region. It is therefore probable that Africa was formerly inhabited by extinct apes closely allied to the gorilla and chimpanzee; and as these two species are now man's closest allies, it is somewhat more probable that our early progenitors lived on the African continent than elsewhere.

If one accepts the paleontological, morphological, and molecular evidence indicating that African apes and humans are closely related sister groups that have only recently diverged from one another (say 10–5 mya), it is perverse to argue that the earliest members of this clade are to be found anywhere else but in the middle/late Miocene of Africa. But as we have seen, there is a long tradition in paleoanthropology of attempting to identify early members of this clade somewhere other than in Africa, for example in the Miocene of Eurasia. However, it seems that if such proposals are carried through to their logical conclusion, the modern descendants of these early members of the African ape–human clade (chimpanzees, gorillas, and humans) would have had to independently walk, hobble, or swing their way back to Africa without leaving any trace of their presence on the Eurasian landmass until one of them, *Homo*, reinvaded the region in the early Pleistocene. It's hard to see this as a parsimonious inference from either the fossil or the molecular evidence.

The ongoing debate about whether chimpanzees are more closely related to humans or gorillas does not pertain to the question of where a common ancestor lived. However, it has profound impact on discussions about early human adaptations. For example, let's do a thought experiment and assume for the moment that the chimpanzee-gorilla-human trichotomy is resolved in favor of a chimpanzee-human clade. Remembering that chimpanzees and gorillas share a unique locomotor pattern—knuckle-walking—and that humans have their own unique locomotor pattern—bipedalism—let's ask what type of locomotor behavior would characterize 1) the common ancestor of the African ape–human clade and 2) the common ancestor of the chimpanzee-human clade? For each question we have three options: some form of knuckle-walking, some form of bipedalism, or some other unidentified form of quadrupedal locomotion.

Given these conditions, if we first assume that some form of knuckle-walking characterized the common ancestor of the African ape–human clade, then we would have to conclude that both gorillas and chimpanzees retained this ancestral form of locomotion and that humans lost it and developed their own unique bipedal locomotion sometime after they had diverged from chimpanzees. This seems plausible. Now let's assume that some form of bipedality characterized the common ancestor of the African ape–human clade. In this case we would have to conclude that humans retained this ancestral locomotor pattern while gorillas and chimpanzees *independently* evolved knuckle-walking adaptations after each had diverged from the human lineage. This seems highly implausible. And finally, if we assume that some other form of quadrupedal locomotion characterized the African ape–human common ancestor, then we would have to conclude that gorillas, chimpanzees, and humans *all* had to independently evolve their specialized modes of locomotion after each diverged from this common ancestor. This seems implausible to the point of absurdity.

Now let's change the conditions of our thought experiment and assume that the trichotomy is resolved in favor of a chimpanzee-gorilla clade. Now we ask the same questions: What type of locomotor behavior would characterize 1) the common ancestor of the African ape–human clade and 2) the common ancestor of the chimpanzee-gorilla clade? Under these conditions, if we first assume that some form of knuckle-walking characterized the common ancestor of the African ape–human clade, then we would have to conclude that gorillas and chimpanzees retained this ancestral form of locomotion and that humans evolved their own unique bipedal locomotion sometime after they diverged from the chimpanzee-gorilla clade. This seems plausible. Now if we assume that some form of bipedality characterized the common ancestor of the African ape–human clade, then we would have to conclude that while humans retained this ancestral locomotor pattern the common ancestor of the gorilla-chimpanzee clade developed knuckle-walking adaptations after it had diverged from the human clade. Again, this seems plausible. Finally, if we assume that some other form of quadrupedal locomotion characterized the common ancestor of the African ape–human clade, then we would have to conclude that knuckle-walking evolved in the gorilla-chimpanzee clade and bipedalism evolved in the human lineage after both clades had diverged from this common ancestor. Again, this seems quite plausible.

However, the Miocene hominoid record puts some constraints on these models. For instance, as we noted earlier, there is no postcranial evidence that any Miocene hominoids were knuckle-walkers. Therefore, models postulating a common knuckle-walking ancestry for the African ape–human clade cannot rely on the fossil record for support. (Of course one caveat is that postcranial evidence for late Miocene hominoids is so poor that future discoveries may alter this view.) For example, the recent discovery of a 9.5-million-year-old partial *Dryopithecus* skeleton from Can Llobateres, Spain, provides evidence that orthograde postures had already evolved in this lineage by this time and that the overall body structure of these dryopithecines resembled extant hominoids in many important features such as 1) a shorter and stiffer vertebral column; 2) a broader thorax with a more dorsally shifted scapula; 3) a relatively high intermembral index; and 4) very large hands adapted for powerful grasping (164). Likewise, we can be fairly confident that bipedality is not a reasonable option for the ancestral locomotor behavior of the African ape–human clade, a point that will become obvious in the next chapter when we discuss the evolution of bipedalism. What we are left with then is postulating some type of unique quadrupedal locomotor behavior (and associated morphology) in the common ancestor of the African ape–human clade that is unlike anything seen today. This scenario, as we saw in our thought experiment above, really only makes sense if the chimpanzee-gorilla-human trichotomy is resolved in favor of a chimpanzee-gorilla clade. Such unique postcranial and inferred locomotor adaptations are exactly what we see in the earliest members of the human lineage that are about to emerge onto the African scene. If the debate is ultimately resolved in favor of the chimpanzee-human clade, then anthropologists will have to answer the question of how two such morphologically and behaviorally dissimilar animals as humans and chimpanzees could possibly share a more recent common ancestor than two such morphologically and behaviorally similar animals as chimpanzees and gorillas. It would imply such rampant parallelisms in African ape–human lineages that paleontologists and morphologists would have very little recourse but to admit that their disciplines are inadequate for resolving such phylogenetic issues. Ironically, the debate will not be resolved without paleontological data.

As the Miocene epoch drew to a close, a major new episode in primate evolution began to unfold: one of these Miocene hominoid species began an adaptive radiation throughout Africa and began to shape its world in ways no other primate had even approached. The story of the last major adaptive radiation of this weird ape, the evolution of the human lineage, is the subject of the rest of this book.

CHAPTER IV

The Earliest Hominids: The Australopithecines

One no longer has the option of considering a fossil specimen older than about eight million years as a hominid *no matter what it looks like.*

Vincent Sarich
"A molecular approach to the question of human origins"
(In *Background for Man*, 1971)

INTRODUCTION

It is remarkable that while there are literally hundreds of prehuman "ape" fossils from Miocene deposits in eastern Africa and Eurasia, there are virtually none from the succeeding Plio-Pleistocene (1). What we find instead in the Plio-Pleistocene record of Africa is the rather sudden appearance of a very unusual higher primate, one that walked on two legs rather than four, used tools rather than teeth for tearing and cutting, had a relatively large brain, and survived, indeed even thrived, in the harsh environs of the African savanna by virtue of newly evolved behavioral and social mechanisms.

These new higher primates, the australopithecines (meaning "southern apes"), first appear in East Africa around 5 mya and in southern Africa around 3 mya. Thus far, australopithecines are only known from sites in Africa (the major australopithecine sites are shown in Figure 4.1). As we shall see in a later chapter, claims for the presence of australopithecines in Southeast Asia (e.g., Java) are generally not given much credence (2,3). Many popular accounts of human evolution give the misleading impression that these early hominids were small-brained and/or small-sized. Although

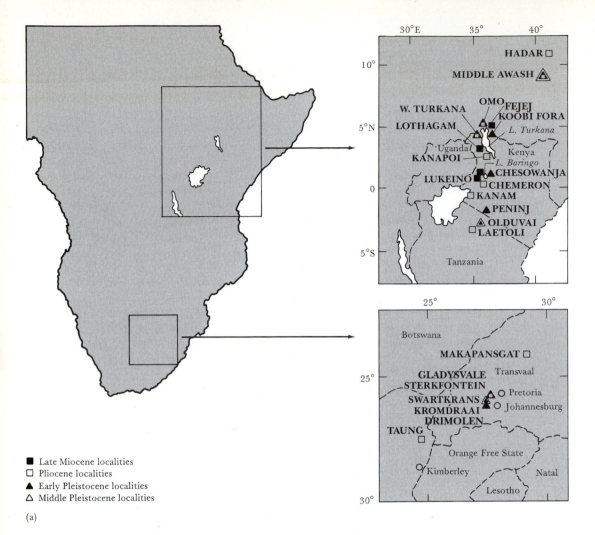

(a)

Fig. 4.1. (a) Australopithecine sites of eastern and southern Africa. Middle Awash sites include Maka, Belohdelie, and Aramis. A new australopithecine species, *A. ramidus,* recently discovered at the Middle Awash site of Aramis, Ethiopia, is dated to >4 mya and may be the stem group from which all later hominids evolved. Another new australopithecine species from Kenya, *A. anamensis,* is dated to about 4 mya. Two new australopithecine sites, Gladysvale and Drimolen, have also recently been found in southern Africa. Both are within a few kilometers of the well-known sites of Sterkfontein, Kromdraai, and Swartkrans. (b) A general chronology of major Plio-Pleistocene australopithecine sites.

they are smaller than modern humans (Fig. 4.2a), australopithecines had brains roughly three times larger than those of Miocene ''apes'' and their body size was within the range of modern chimpanzees, which are very formidable animals indeed and quite capable of hunting and killing a diverse array of other mammals including red colobus monkeys, bushpigs, and bushbucks (4,5).

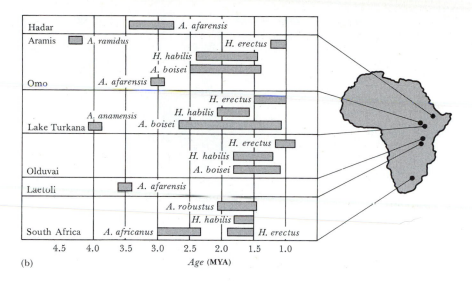

(b)   Age (MYA)

Claims for the earliest appearance of our own genus, *Homo*, date to about 2.4 mya in East Africa (Kenya and Malawi) and to slightly less than 2.0 mya in southern Africa, although some of these earliest specimens are difficult to distinguish from the more "gracile" forms of australopithecine, which we will discuss below (6–9).[1] It appears that *Australopithecus* and *Homo* may have coexisted in eastern and southern Africa for more than a million years, from about 2.4 to 1.2 mya (13). The newer genus, *Homo*, reveals several important evolutionary distinctions from australopithecines, including more gracile jaws and teeth, more frequent use of stone-tool technology, and, most importantly, new levels of cerebral organization reflected in both absolute brain size and increased complexity (14–16). These trends continued throughout the Plio-Pleistocene in the various *Homo* lineages, culminating in early members of our own species, *H. sapiens*, several hundred thousand years ago. We shall discuss the evolutionary journey of *Homo* in more detail in later chapters.

Although most paleoanthropologists recognize at least six to seven australopithecine species, including *Australopithecus ramidus*, *A. anamensis*, *A. afarensis*, *A. africanus*, *A. robustus*, *A. boisei*, and *A. aethiopicus* (see below), it is fair to say that there is no unanimity of opinion (and probably never will be) about the exact number of australopithecine species, or even genera, or about the classification of individual australopithecine specimens. As we noted earlier, the fossils originally assigned to the new species *A. ramidus* may ultimately prove to be distinctive enough to be placed in a new australopithecine genus, *Ardipithecus* (17,18). There has also been a tendency

---

[1]The recent claim for the earliest evidence of *Homo* at 2.4 mya in East Africa, a temporal bone fragment (KNM-BC1) from the Chemeron Formation of Kenya (9), has been disputed by several workers (10–12).

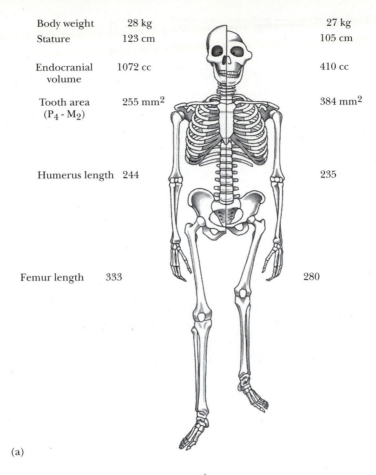

	Body weight	28 kg		27 kg
	Stature	123 cm		105 cm
	Endocranial volume	1072 cc		410 cc
	Tooth area $(P_4 - M_2)$	255 mm^2		384 mm^2
	Humerus length	244		235
	Femur length	333		280

(a)

	Body Weight (kg)		Stature (cm)		
	Male	Female	Male	Female	EQ
A. afarensis	45	27	151	105	2.4
A. africanus	41	30	138	115	2.6
A. robustus	40	32	132	110	3.1
A. boisei	49	34	137	124	2.7
H. habilis	52	32	157	125	3.1
H. erectus (African)	68		180	160	3.3
H. sapiens	65	54	175	161	5.8
P. troglodytes	54	40			2.0

(b)

Fig. 4.2. (a) Estimated body proportions of an early hominid, *A. afarensis* (''Lucy'') (right side) compared to those of a modern pygmy (left side). (b) Estimated male and female body weights and heights and encephalization quotients (EQs) of several early hominid species compared to those of modern chimpanzee (*Pan troglodytes*). After (22).

Table 4.1   Two Schemes for the Nomenclature and Taxonomy of
Australopithecines

	One Genus (Australopithecus)	Three Genera (Ardipithecus, Australopithecus, Paranthropus)
"Gracile" forms	A. ramidus	Ardipithecus ramidus
	A. anamensis	Australopithecus anamensis
	A. africanus	Australopithecus africanus
	A. afarensis	Australopithecus afarensis
"Robust" forms	A. robustus	Paranthropus robustus
	A. boisei	Paranthropus boisei
	A. aethiopicus	Paranthropus aethiopicus

in recent years for some authors to resurrect the genus name *Paranthropus* for both *A. robustus* and *A. boisei*, a practice we do not follow in this text.[2]

Traditionally, australopithecine species have often been distinguished from one another by inferred body and craniodental type as either **gracile** (lighter, smaller toothed) or **robust** (heavier, larger toothed). Two different taxonomic schemes reflecting this somewhat artificial, or at least overlapping, dichotomy are presented in Table 4.1. While the terms "gracile australopithecine" and "robust australopithecine" may be convenient shorthand labels, recent studies strongly suggest that body size and dental dimensions of these species may not differ as much as previously thought (Fig. 4.2b) (19–23). In fact, most of the differences may be restricted to the gracility or robustness of the cheek teeth and chewing apparatus, although as we noted in Chapter II, some specimens allocated to "gracile" forms, like *A. africanus*, actually have larger teeth than some of those allocated to *A. robustus*. In this text we shall therefore use quotation marks for "gracile" and "robust" in reference to australopithecines, to show that we are intending these names only as convenient shorthand labels to provide some continuity with preexisting literature.

One major generalization about australopithecine evolution in Africa seems warranted: only the so-called "gracile" australopithecines *A. ramidus, A. anamensis, A. afarensis,* and *A. africanus* are known prior to about 2.6 mya, whereas the so-called "robust" australopithecines *A. robustus, A. boisei,* and/or *A. aethiopicus* first appear about 2.6 mya and survive until about 1.0 mya (Fig. 4.1b). As we shall see later in Chapter V, this generalization has had a significant impact on theories of australopithecine phylogeny.

[2]Much of this often spirited debate about the number of early hominid genera and/or species might appear to the uninitiated like the paleoanthropological equivalent of how many angels could dance on the head of a pin.

Current evidence suggests that the australopithecines were confined to the African continent, most of their fossil remains having been recovered from the widely separated East African rift valley and South African cave breccias. The East African deposits generally consist of lake and river sediments that bear occasional layers of volcanic tuff. Many of these tuffs have been radiometrically dated by the methods presented in Chapter II. The South African cave breccias, on the other hand, cannot be radiometrically dated as yet, and dates for them are usually based on faunal comparisons to other radiometrically dated African sites.

AFRICA DURING THE PLIO-PLEISTOCENE

The Australopithecine Fossil Record in South Africa

Australopithecine fossils have been recovered from several South African cave sites. Of the major australopithecine-bearing sites, five (Sterkfontein, Kromdraai, Swartkrans, Gladysvale, Drimolen) are located within 10 km of one another just a few miles outside Johannesburg; one, Makapansgat, is located in the northern Transvaal; and one, Taung, is located on the edge of the Kalahari Desert, north of Kimberley in the western Cape. What follows is a brief review of the history and stratigraphy of the major South African cave sites shown in Figure 4.1, beginning with the earliest finds.

Taung

History of excavation   Taung, in the local language, means the place of Tau or Tao, the Lion. Located some 130 km north of Kimberley in the northern Cape Province, it is the most southwesterly site on the African continent from which australopithecines have been recovered.

In May 1924, Josephine Salmons, a young medical student at the University of the Witwatersrand in Johannesburg, was shown by a friend the skull of a fossil baboon that had come from the limeworks at Taung. She, in turn, brought the fossil to her anatomy professor, Dr. Raymond Dart. Australian by birth, Dart had just assumed the chair of anatomy at the new medical school in Johannesburg. Prior to arriving in South Africa, Dart had spent a year as a Rockefeller Fellow in the anatomy department at Washington University in St. Louis under the guidance of Dr. Robert J. Terry and had also worked on fossil human skulls under the tutelage of G. Elliot Smith in London. Both Terry and Smith had strong anthropological interests that were undoubtedly passed on to the young Raymond Dart, who later admitted that "circumstances thrust anthropology upon me after I had chosen to follow even more useless trails as a neurological embryologist'' (24). The fossil baboon skull piqued Dart's latent anthropological interest. Reasoning that a site yielding fossil baboons might also contain fossil hominids, Dart discussed the fossil find with R. B. Young, a professor of geology, who was about to visit the vicinity of Taung to do some economic geology research.

When Young arrived at Taung in November of that year, the limeworks manager, a Mr. Spiers, showed him part of another fossilized skull that had recently been blasted out of the limeworks and was now lying around in his office. Knowing Dart's interest in fossil primates, Young brought the fossil back to Johannesburg and handed it over to Dart on November 28, 1924 (25). Over the next 40 days Dart extracted the fossil from its rocky matrix, analyzed it, and then sent his preliminary conclusions to the British scientific journal *Nature* for publication (26).

The specimen he extracted from the rock consisted of most of the face, lower jaw, and half of a brain endocast of a young ''child'' he named *Australopithecus africanus* (''southern ape of Africa''). In his short article that appeared in *Nature* on February 7, 1925, and despite the name he gave the fossil, Dart described its many humanlike qualities. Dart proposed that his new specimen be regarded as a manlike ape and in keeping with this view proposed that a new family, Homo-simiadae, be created for it. Because of this, and because this was the first truly ancient hominid fossil ever found on the African continent, his article triggered an intellectual revolution about human origins that continues unabated to this day. Indeed, the popular science magazine *Science 84* included the Taung skull among the ''20 discoveries that changed our lives in the 20th century.''

One might think that the humanlike qualities of the Taung skull noted by Dart in his 1925 article would have been accepted with open arms by a worldwide anthropological community obsessed with finding the ''missing link'' between apes and humans. However, the reaction to the Taung discovery (and to the claims of humanlike qualities for australopithecines in general) ranged from total neglect (27), to ridicule (28),[3] to extreme criticism in the most influential textbooks of the day (29). Clearly, Dart's little skull was not consistent with the preconceived notions of Victorian paleoanthropologists, namely, that early hominids must have had large brains (at least 750 cc according to one eminent anatomist of the day[4]) and that early man must have evolved in Europe or Asia, but surely not in the ''Dark

[3]''Cried an angry she-ape from Transvaal,
  Though old Doctor Broom had the gall
      To christen me Plesi-
      anthropus, it's easy
  To see I'm not human at all'' (28).

[4]Sir Arthur Keith, English anatomist extraordinaire, was so far off the mark, so often, in matters paleoanthropological that one might wonder whether there is any necessary relationship between anatomical training and anthropological insight or common sense! One historian has even alleged that Sir Arthur may have been the ''brains'' behind the Piltdown forgery (30).

Continent" of Africa. Since the skull was obviously that of an immature individual, critics were quick to point out that if and when adult specimens were found they would certainly look more like apes than humans, since immature living apes look more "human" than adult apes do. Perhaps European society was just not prepared to accept the view that Africa was the "cradle of mankind," as Dart had referred to it when he exhibited the skull at the 1925 British Empire Exhibition at Wembley. Dart's Taung child remained in taxonomic limbo until adult australopithecines began showing up in other South African sites in the 1930s and 1940s. As we shall see, australopithecines eventually received recognition through the discoveries of Robert Broom and John T. Robinson, and the subsequent efforts of C. K. (Bob) Brain and Phillip V. Tobias.

Since the exact site of discovery of the only *Australopithecus* specimen from Taung was destroyed by limestone quarrying in the 1920s, precise biostratigraphic information for use in dating the fossil remains problematic. Earlier geological and uranium-isotopic investigations suggested an age of about 1 million years for the hominid specimen (31); however, this is clearly at odds with the faunal dating, particularly of the cercopithecids, or Old World monkeys, which suggests an age of 2.0 to 2.5 million years (32,33). In fact, it is now known that the younger radiometric date based on U-S dating can only be considered a minimum age. The older age is more consistent with that of other *A. africanus* specimens from Sterkfontein (Member 4) and Makapansgat (Members 3 and 4), which date to 3.0–2.4 mya (see below) (34–37).

Taung paleoenvironment   An analysis of the Taung sediments suggest that they formed under semiarid conditions similar to those in the area today. The cycle of cave filling that entrapped the hominid seems to have marked the onset of more humid conditions. Within the past several years, paleontological excavations at Taung have resumed, but no further hominid remains have yet been discovered. Taung is therefore unique among South Africa's australopithecine-bearing caves in that it has yielded only the single hominid specimen. The associated fauna is unique as well, consisting mainly of small-sized animals, many of which display unusual damage to the bones and skulls. While early accounts interpreted these characteristics of the Taung assemblage as being due to the carnivorous activities of australopithecines (or of other carnivorous mammals) (38), a more recent suggestion concludes that a large bird of prey with hunting habits analogous to living African black, martial, or crowned eagles may have been the taphonomic agent responsible for the collection of most of the Taung fossils, including that of the Taung child itself (39,40).

Sterkfontein

History of excavation   In a 1935 guidebook to places of interest around Johannesburg, the owner of the Sterkfontein caves wrote, "Come to Sterkfontein and find the missing link." On Monday, August 17, 1936, the South African paleontologist and physician Robert Broom did just that by finding the first adult australopithecine!

Earlier that year two of Dart's former students, G. Schepers and W. Le Riche, alerted Broom that fossil baboons had been found in the cave breccias of Sterkfontein. Broom, who had joined the staff of the Transvaal Museum in Pretoria only 2 years before, was understandably excited by these discoveries and paid his first visit to Sterkfontein on August 9, 1936. Eight days later he was rewarded by the discovery of an adult fossil hominid. In a series of brief communications to *Nature*, Broom initially described this material as *A. transvaalensis* (41–43), but later described it as a new genus, *Plesianthropus*. It turned out to be the first adult australopithecine known to science.[5] The specimen consisted of the anterior two-thirds of a brain cast, the skull base, parts of the parietal bones, a right maxilla containing the P^4–M^2, and portions of the frontal bone.

Following this initial find, Broom made many discoveries at the site until the outbreak of World War II interrupted his fieldwork. After the war, Broom was assisted by John T. Robinson, also of the Transvaal Museum, and discovered many other australopithecines at the site (45). For many years the onsite director of excavations at Sterkfontein was the late Alun Hughes. Work continues there today under the supervision of Phillip Tobias and Ronald Clarke of the University of the Witwatersrand, and over six hundred hominid specimens have now been found at the site. The overwhelming majority of the specimens are attributed to *A. africanus*, but a cranium attributed to *Homo habilis* has also been recovered as have several teeth tentatively identified as *A. robustus* (46–48).

The Sterkfontein deposits have been subdivided (from oldest to youngest) into stratigraphic units, or **Members**, numbered 1 to 6. Fossil hominids have thus far been found only in Members 2, 4, and 5 (49) (Fig. 4.3). The lowest deposits, Members 1–3, are exposed in the Silberberg Grotto. With the exception of four articulating hominid foot bones recently discovered from Member 2 (50), the *A. africanus* sample is all from Member 4 and includes remains of at least fifty individuals represented by skulls of varying degrees of completeness, maxillae, mandibles, isolated teeth, and various postcranial bones. However, the substantial size and morphological variation of the hominid sample suggest that more than one hominid species may be present in Member 4 (51–53). For example, one specimen in particular (Stw 252) has large, pongidlike incisors and canines in combination with cheek teeth that are larger than many specimens from both eastern and southern Africa attributed to *A. robustus* and/or *A. boisei*. In fact, dental variability in these Member-4 hominids is greater than that between *Homo*

[5]Actually, the first adult australopithecine specimen ever found was a lower canine from Laetoli found by Louis Leakey in 1935. However, its hominid affinities were only recognized in 1981 (44).

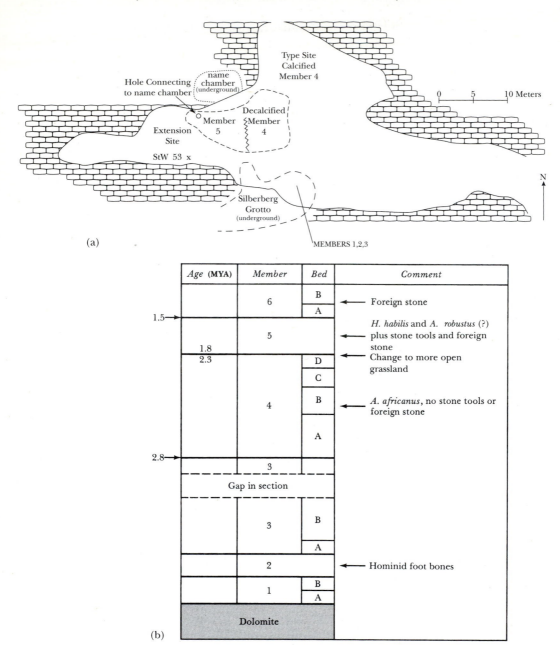

Fig. 4.3.   (a) Sterkfontein excavation plan showing areas referred to in text (55). (b) Stratigraphic sequence of the Sterkfontein Cave Site. Note positions of *A. africanus* and *H. habilis*. Several isolated teeth tentatively assigned to *A. robustus* have also been recovered from Member 5, as have large collections of Oldowan and Acheulian tools. Total depth of section is about 27.5 m (202).

habilis and a large-toothed *A. boisei*. Interestingly, one recent reconstruction of the Stw 252 cranium looks remarkably similar to a recently discovered *A. afarensis* skull from Hadar (54). The hominids from Member 4 are dated to about 2.5 mya. No stone tools have yet been recovered from Member 4.

The distribution of the fossil hominids, as well as that of the fossil wood in the partly calcified breccia, suggests that Member 4 formed as a talus cone beneath a vertical shaft and that large carnivores were dropping in the bones as they fed in the trees above the cave entrance (see Fig. 2.2b) (55).

Remains of both *Homo habilis* and (tentatively) *A. robustus* have been recovered from Member 5, and thus far seem restricted to that Member. This earliest representative of the genus *Homo* in southern Africa, the *H. habilis* cranium Stw 53, was discovered on August 9, 1976, by Alun Hughes, 40 years to the day after Broom's first visit to Sterkfontein (56). The type specimen of *H. habilis* had already been found in the mid-1960s by Jonathan Leakey at Olduvai Gorge in East Africa; the Latin name *habilis* was suggested by Dart to indicate a hominid that was presumably handy or skillful with tools.

Of great importance is the recognition in Member 5 of what may be southern Africa's earliest stone-tool cultures. Both Oldowan and early Acheulian tool types have been recognized and some of the more diagnostic tools are illustrated in Figure 4.4. The three "robust" australopithecine teeth are associated with the Oldowan tools and faunal comparisons suggest the Sterkfontein Oldowan of Member 5 may date to 2.0–1.7 mya. The Member 5 "robust" australopithecine teeth consist of a lower right first molar and an upper incisor and canine, both heavily worn.

The Oldowan tools are characterized by simple toolmaking methods that utilize more easily flaked raw materials such as quartz. The most distinctive tool types are two chopperlike cores, a discoidlike core, and a protobiface. These tools presumably accumulated at the site as a result of repeated visits by hominids to an open site favored for its shelter and for the nearby gravels used for toolmaking.

The early Acheulian compares well with East African Acheulian assemblages dated to approximately 1.5 mya. The *H. habilis* cranium was found about 6 ft from the limit of the early Acheulian tool distribution of Member 5, so it is still not clear whether or not *H. habilis* was the Acheulian toolmaker (46,47).

Sterkfontein paleoenvironment   Unfortunately, the paleomagnetic stratigraphy of Sterkfontein is still poorly resolved. Based on faunal comparisons, the hominids from Member 4 are estimated to date from about 2.8–2.3 mya and those from Member 5 to 2.0–1.7 mya (57). ESR has recently been used to date bovid tooth enamel from Member 4 and gives an average age

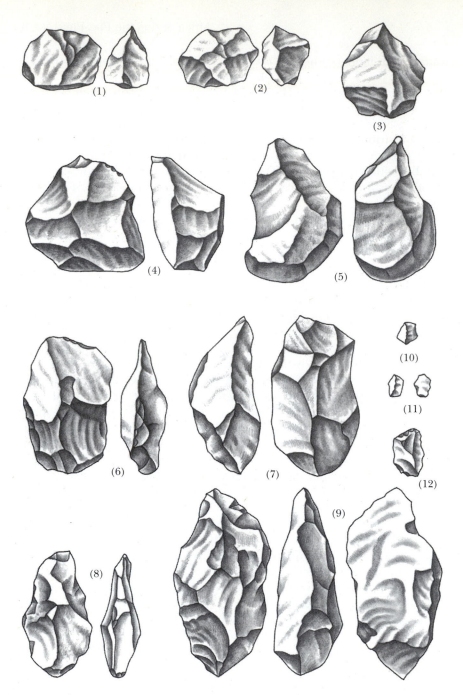

Fig. 4.4. Stone tools from Member 5, Sterkfontein. Oldowan tools: 1, quartz chopper-core; 2, quartz discoid-core; 3, quartz irregular core; 4, quartz chopper-core; 5, quartzite proto-biface; 10, 11, utilized quartz flakes; 12, retouched quartz flake. Acheulian tools: 6, quartzite cleaver on a large flake; 7, quartzite cleaver on a large flake or other detached piece; 8, small chert bifacial handaxe; 9, quartzite unifacial handaxe on a large flake. From (46).

of about 2 million years for this Member (58). Analysis of fossil antelopes from the site suggests a transition to more open grasslands and increasing aridity in southern Africa about 2.5–2.0 mya, i.e., at about the Member 4/5 interval (59,60). The presence of fossilized lianas in Member 4 suggests the presence of large supporting trees and indicates that the local vegetation must have included at least some riparian forest (61).

It has been suggested that the low proportion of juvenile animal bones from Member 5 indicates that some meat was scavenged rather than actively hunted by hominids (62). The presence of indisputable cut marks on the shaft of a small bovid humerus implies that at least some of the bones in Member 5 represent hominid food remains. This conclusion must be tempered, however, by the observation that there are no obvious cut marks on any of the bones associated with the Oldowan tools, suggesting that hominids were not the accumulating agent for the bulk of the fauna (47). At least two bone tools from the site were probably used as instruments for digging up edible bulbs (63).

Kromdraai

History of excavation   The first "robust" australopithecine was discovered at Kromdraai in 1938 under somewhat unusual circumstances (64). The site itself is situated only 1.5 km east of Sterkfontein. The limeworks manager at Sterkfontein, a Mr. G. W. Barlow, sold Robert Broom a well-preserved palate with a molar tooth of a fossil hominid but at first refused to tell him where it had come from. Broom eventually extracted from Barlow the information that the specimen had been found nearby by a schoolboy, Gert Terblanche. Broom took the young boy back to the original finding place, where he soon discovered much of a hominid cranium including part of a palate, much of the left side of the face, almost the whole left zygomatic arch, the left side of the base of the skull, a portion of the parietal bone, and the greater part of the right mandible with most of the teeth. Broom made this skull (TM 1517)[6] the type specimen of a new genus and species that he named *Paranthropus robustus* (43). Subsequent excavations carried out by personnel from the Traansvaal Museum have now recovered a minimum of six "robust" australopithecine individuals from Member 3 of the Kromdraai B East (KBE) Formation, also referred to as the Kromdraai Australopithecine Site (Fig. 4.5). The fossil hominid sample includes the partial skull and dentition of the type specimen, isolated teeth, the proximal end of an ulna, the distal end of a humerus, a second metacarpal, a proximal hand phalanx, talus (or ankle bone), and an ilium. Faunal comparisons suggest an age of about 1–2 million years and this is consistent with the reversed polarity (tentatively correlated to the Matuyama reversal) of the Kromdraai stratigraphic column (see Fig. 1.3a).

---

[6]"TM" stands for Transvaal Museum.

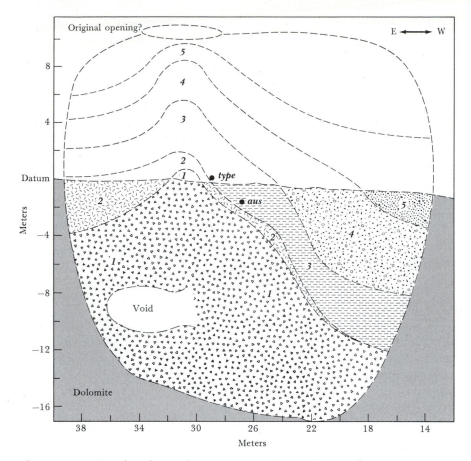

Fig. 4.5. Stratigraphy of Kromdraai Cave Site. Section through the KBE Formation (Kromdraai Australopithecine Site).   Scale at left gives meters above and below present land surface (datum). Dotted lines above datum show hypothetical original cave contours before erosion. Successive breccia Members are labelled 1 to 5. Abbreviations: *type*, possible source of type specimens of *A. (=Paranthropus) robustus*; *aus*, mandible of juvenile *A. robustus* (203).

Only one questionable stone tool flake is known from the site, making it unlikely that early hominid scavenging or butchery was responsible for the Kromdraai animal bone accumulations (63).

Kromdraai paleoenvironment   Sedimentological analyses suggest a more humid environment than that prevailing during deposition of Member 4 at both Makapansgat and Sterkfontein. A wooded local environment is evident from the fauna of KBE Member 3, whereas the pollen recovered from the boundary of KBE Members 2 and 3 suggests that a more open savanna characterized the area at that time (65).

Makapansgat

History of excavation   Located in the northern Transvaal, the Makapansgat hominid site is a cavern of almost pure limestone that was mined for a decade starting in 1925. Approximately thirty specimens (representing about a dozen individuals) of *A. africanus* have been recovered from the site, which are the oldest known remains of this taxon from the fossil record of Africa.[7] During these mining operations a local mathematics teacher, W. I. Eitzman, drew Raymond Dart's attention to the abundance of fossil bones being blasted out of the cave breccia by limeworkers. Inexplicably, Dart did not investigate the site thoroughly until 1947, at which time he discovered that many of the vertebrate fossils contained free carbon, leading him to speculate that the bones had been intentionally burned by early hominids inhabiting the cave. In September 1947, one of Dart's researchers, J. W. Kitching, discovered the back, or occipital, portion of an australopithecine skull on one of the limeworkers' dumps. Reasoning that this early hominid might have been responsible for some of the burned bones in the deposit, Dart named the new hominid *A. prometheus* (66). By the mid-1960s however, most workers concluded that the majority of australopithecine fossils previously described as *Plesianthropus* (named for Broom's adult specimen from Sterkfontein) as well as *A. prometheus* should be included in the single taxon, *A. africanus* (67).

Other important hominid discoveries were made at the site in 1948, including an adolescent mandible, an infant's right parietal bone, several craniofacial fragments and isolated teeth, and two fragments of an adolescent pelvis (68). The discovery of the pelvis was critical, since it proved conclusively that *A. africanus* walked bipedally. Several stone tools were also recovered from the site (69).

Dart also noticed that many of the vertebrate fossils from the site seemed to be artificially fractured and that some animal parts were more commonly preserved than others. This suggested to him that the hominids were in some way responsible for the bone accumulation and he proposed the idea that many of the bones and jaws at Makapansgat had been utilized as tools by the early hominids at the cave: teeth as saws and scrapers, long bones as clubs, and so on (70). He named this the **Osteodontokeratic** (bone-tooth-horn) **Culture**. Dart's theory became the inspiration for the "killer ape" theory made famous by the dramatist Robert Ardrey in his book *African Genesis* (71). However, more recent taphonomic studies have cast doubt on this interpretation, suggesting instead that many of these bone accumulations were the product of carnivore scavengers such as hyenas (63,72,73).

---

[7]A second cave (the Cave of Hearths) is located about 1 km from the Makapansgat limeworks cave, and contains what is probably the most complete archeological record of continuous habitation (up to 220,000 years from the earliest Stone Age to recent historical times) in Africa.

A paleomagnetic record for this site extends from the base of Member 1 to the lower levels of Member 4 (Fig. 4.6), but the calibration of the paleomagnetic record at Makapansgat is open to several different interpretations. The fossil hominids, all assigned to *A. africanus*, are known only from Members 3 and 4 and have been variously dated to about 3.0–2.4 mya (31,32,74). Faunal correlations using fossil bovids (antelope, buck, buffalo, etc.), suids (pigs), and cercopithecoids (monkeys) indicate that Member 3 faunas are most similar to East African faunal assemblages dated to about

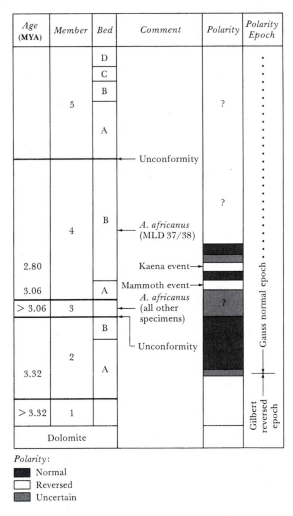

Fig. 4.6.   One interpretation of relative dating of the Makapansgat Cave Site.   Stratigraphic and paleomagnetic sequence of the Makapansgat Formation showing the location of the major australopithecine discoveries from that site. An unconformity represents an interruption of deposition. From (202).

3.0–2.6 mya (60). Such comparisons assume, of course, that eastern and southern Africa had similar enough environments to support the same fauna and that similar faunas are truly contemporaneous (75).

Makapansgat paleoenvironment   Taphonomic, palynological, and sedimentological studies suggest fluctuating climatic and vegetational conditions during the period of sedimentation at Makapansgat (76). Studies of fossil pollen suggest that when australopithecines occupied the area the region may have had higher rainfall patterns that supported patches of subtropical forest and thick bush as well as savanna. Evidence of more episodic rainfall patterns begins to appear after the middle of Member 4 with the presence of a higher proportion of grazing mammals, signalling the onset of more open, drier conditions about this time (31,77,78).

Swartkrans

History of excavation   Toward the end of 1948 Robert Broom decided to investigate Swartkrans, a new cave site less than a mile from Sterkfontein. The excavations had an auspicious beginning: the very first dynamite blast yielded an australopithecine tooth. By the end of the first week a mandible (SK 6) was found that Broom described as a new species of "robust" australopithecine, *Paranthropus crassidens* (now usually lumped together with the Kromdraai specimens as *A. robustus*) (79). Soon afterward, in April 1949, a very different hominid was discovered, first named *Telanthropus capensis* but later reclassified as *Homo erectus* (80,81). This was the first evidence for the coexistence of *Australopithecus* and *Homo* in the fossil record of Africa (13,82). We shall have more to say about African *H. erectus* in a later chapter.

Robert Broom died in Pretoria in April 1951, but the work at Swartkrans was continued by his colleague, John Robinson. Since the 1960s the site has been investigated by C. K. Brain and associates from the Transvaal Museum, who have since recovered a large number of "robust" australopithecines and a lesser number of *Homo* specimens. The hominid sample from the site now includes several hundred specimens representing over a hundred individuals including cranial remains, mandibles, numerous isolated teeth, and limb bone fragments. Remains of *A. robustus* have come from Member 1 (98 individuals); Member 2 (17 individuals), and Member 3 (9 individuals). Temporal coexistence with *Homo* cf. *erectus* is indicated by the fact that four individuals of this hominid were found in Member 1, two in Member 2, but, as yet, none in Member 3 (83). Interestingly, approximately 40 percent of the hominids represent immature individuals (84–93).

There are several major rock units defined at this cave site, designated Members 1–5 (Fig. 4.7) (94,95). Both Members 1 and 2 contain stone and bone tools and, as noted above, remains of both *A. robustus* and *Homo* cf. *erectus*. Similar tools and *A. robustus* remains are also known from Member

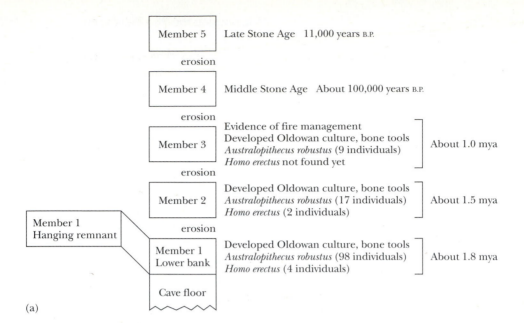

| Member 5 | Late Stone Age   11,000 years B.P. |

erosion

| Member 4 | Middle Stone Age   About 100,000 years B.P. |

erosion

| Member 3 | Evidence of fire management
Developed Oldowan culture, bone tools
Australopithecus robustus (9 individuals)
Homo erectus not found yet | About 1.0 mya |

erosion

| Member 2 | Developed Oldowan culture, bone tools
Australopithecus robustus (17 individuals)
Homo erectus (2 individuals) | About 1.5 mya |

erosion

Member 1
Hanging remnant

| Member 1
Lower bank | Developed Oldowan culture, bone tools
Australopithecus robustus (98 individuals)
Homo erectus (4 individuals) | About 1.8 mya |

| Cave floor |

(a)

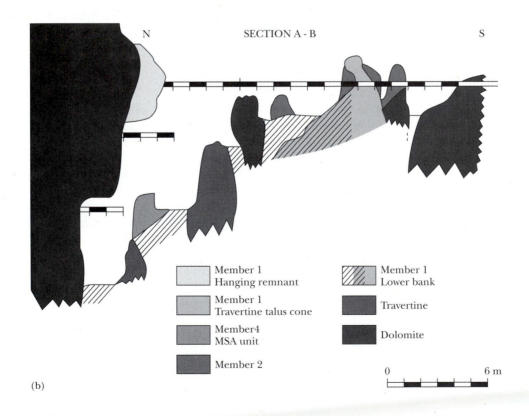

N   SECTION A - B   S

Member 1
Hanging remnant

Member 1
Lower bank

Member 1
Travertine talus cone

Travertine

Member 4
MSA unit

Dolomite

Member 2

0   6 m

(b)

3. Evidence for the earliest use of fire also comes from this Member (96–98).

Faunal analyses suggest that Member 1 is between about 1.5 and 1.8 million years old and that the faunas from Members 2 and 3 do not differ significantly from Member 1. The artifact assemblages from Members 1–3 also show no significant differences and all are classified in the core/chopper/flake tool tradition, sometimes referred to as the Developed Oldowan. In addition to the stone tools, several fossil bones have been discovered from all three Members that appear to have been used as digging tools and some may have even been modified for preparing animal skins (99,100). Interestingly, one delicate bone flake from Member 3 had been fashioned into a pointed awllike tool, similar to those used for the piercing of animal hides. Middle Stone Age artifacts have been recovered from Member 4, although no hominid fossils are known from this level (31). It is now thought that Members 1–3 date from about 1.8 to 1.0 mya. Since the Plio-Pleistocene boundary is about 1.8 mya, the Swartkrans hominids are technically Pleistocene in age. Thermoluminescence dating of quartz sands gives ages of about 1.2 million years for the breccia of Member 2 and about 1.6 million years for the breccia of Member 1 (101). Paleomagnetic results have not proven useful at this site so far.

Swartkrans paleoenvironment   Based on analyses of mammalian skeletal parts preserved at the site, there seems little doubt that large cats, leopards, and sabre-toothed cats were the main agents of bone collection at Swartkrans. However, evidence of controlled use of fire and butchering in Member 3 suggests that hominids could also have been responsible for at least some of the bone accumulation. The paleoenvironment throughout the depositional history of the cave seems to have been very similar to that of today—one of highveld grassland and riverine woodland savanna in the vicinity of the Blaaubank Stream, which currently flows near the site (102).

New Sites: Gladysvale and Drimolen   Although only two early hominid teeth have been described thus far from Gladysvale (an upper premolar

Fig. 4.7.   (a) Stratigraphic sequence of the Swartkrans Cave Site. Hominid remains have been found in Members 1 to 3: *A. robustus* and *H. erectus*, both from Members 1 and 2, but only *A. robustus* from Member 3. Stone tools have been found throughout the sequence, and the earliest evidence of fire comes from Member 3. The oldest deposit, Member 1, is divided into two discrete masses: the hanging remnant clinging to the cave's north wall, and the lower bank resting on the cave floor, both thought to date from 1.8 to 1.5 mya based on faunal considerations. Members 1 to 3 probably fall within a time range of 1.8 to 1.0 mya, and Members 4 and 5 are probably less than 100,000 years old. (b) A section running north-south through the filling of the Outer Cave at Swartkrans showing the vertical relationships among the various Members. MSA in Member 4 stands for Middle Stone Age. It now appears that Members 1 and 2 occupied much of the Outer Cave, south of the hanging remnant. Note that Members 3 and 5 are not shown in this section (95).

and molar), the site is important as the first new australopithecine-bearing locality to be found in southern Africa since Robert Broom discovered the remains of *A. robustus* at Swartkrans in 1948. The fauna, preliminarily dated to about 2.5–1.7 mya, indicates that savanna conditions prevailed during deposition of the cave deposits. The teeth have been designated as *A.* cf. *africanus*. More recently, several other Gladysvale hominid fossils attributed to early *Homo* have been reported from deposits thought to be of early Middle Pleistocene age (103,104).

Of great interest is the recent discovery by Dr. Andre Keyser of new hominid fossils from the nearby site of Drimolen. This site has already yielded a number of isolated australopithecine teeth as well as a mandible and cranium of a female *A. robustus* with almost complete dentition and, next to it, a mandible of a male *A. robustus* (61).

Summary of South African Sites

Throughout most of the time that *A. africanus* was present in southern Africa, the region was characterized by greater humidity and thicker bush cover than it is today. A major ecological change apparently occurred about 3–2 mya that led to increasing dryness and to the spread of more open grassland conditions. Sedimentological and faunal evidence suggests that a more cyclic (and probably seasonal) rainfall pattern emerged after this time and persisted throughout the Pleistocene. However, none of these subsequent fluctuations between wet and dry climates were as dramatic as the event about 2.5 mya that initiated them. For the most part *A. africanus* was replaced in southern Africa by populations of *A. robustus*, which coexisted at first with *H. habilis* and later with *H. erectus.*

Thus, the three major sites near Johannesburg (Sterkfontein, Swartkrans, and Kromdraai) suggest changing patterns of vegetation cover and cave filling over the approximately 2 million years of australopithecine evolution in southern Africa. Among fossil bovids, the Alcelaphini (e.g., hartebeests) and Antilopini (e.g., springboks) are useful faunal markers for inferring past vegetation cover, since both are indicative of open plains and grassland environments (62,105,106). These bovids comprise anywhere from 25 to 90 percent of the bovid remains at these sites. Although the percentage of these bovids generally increases over time, an abrupt increase apparently occurred about 2.5–2.0 mya. This shift seems to fit well with the idea of a general faunal change in southern Africa in the late Pliocene, including the shift from "gracile" to "robust" australopithecines about this time in the Sterkfontein valley (60) (Fig. 4.8).

To sum up, the australopithecine-bearing sites in southern Africa can be lumped together in the following general way: Taung, Makapansgat, and Sterkfontein Member 4 as older than 2.5 million years (the so-called Sterkfontein Faunal Span) and Swartkrans, Kromdraai, and Sterkfontein

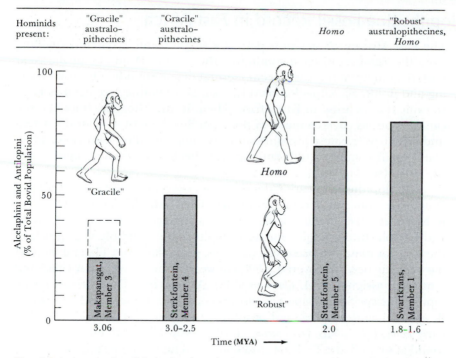

Fig. 4.8. Among fossil bovids, the Alcelaphini (e.g., hartebeests) and Antilopini (e.g., springboks) are useful faunal markers for inferring past vegetation cover, since both are indicative of open plains and grassland environments.   These bovids make up anywhere from about 25 to 90 percent of the bovid remains at South African hominid sites. Although the percentage of these bovids generally increases over time, it appears an abrupt increase occurred about 2.5–2.0 mya. This shift seems to fit well with the idea of a general faunal change in southern Africa in the late Pliocene, including the shift from "gracile" to "robust" australopithecines about this time in the Sterkfontein Valley. The sites are arranged from left to right according to their estimated chronological sequence. The dotted lines represent uncertainty due to possible faunal admixture from several stratigraphic layers. After (60).

Member 5 (and possibly Gladysvale) as younger than 2.5 million years (the so-called Swartkrans Faunal Span). More specifically, these sites can be arranged (from oldest to youngest) in the following sequence: Makapansgat Member 3, Makapansgat Member 4, Sterkfontein Member 4, Taung, Sterkfontein Member 5 and Kromdraai B, Kromdraai A and Swartkrans Member 1, Swartkrans Member 2, and Swartkrans Member 3 (107). In general, *A. africanus* seems restricted to the older sites and *A. robustus* to the younger ones. As we shall see, this has been used as partial support for the view (now in retreat) that *A. africanus* and *A. robustus* were both part of a single evolving "robust" australopithecine lineage.

The Australopithecine Fossil Record in East Africa

The East African rift system is part of a single tectonic system extending from the Zambesi River in southern Africa to the Dead Sea in the Near East. Beginning in the late Eocene, several major episodes of crustal warping and uplift, accompanied by volcanism and faulting, occurred as large volcanic domes arose in East Africa. Then, in the Miocene, floodlike volcanic eruptions covered much of the area. But the East African rift system underwent its greatest transformation during the Plio-Pleistocene, when major uplift combined with faulting and affected the entire length of the rift (108) (see Fig. 3.2).

Australopithecine-bearing deposits associated with the East African Rift System are concentrated in Ethiopia at Hadar, Middle Awash, and Omo; in Kenya at Lake Turkana and Lake Baringo; and in Tanzania at Olduvai and Laetoli. Interestingly, one australopithecine mandible with much of the anterior dentition preserved (canines, premolars, and a lateral incisor) has recently been discovered 2,500 km west of the rift valley in Chad and tentatively assigned to *A. afarensis* (109). At least four East African australopithecine species are now generally recognized: *A. ramidus, A. anamensis, A. afarensis,* and *A. boisei* (and possibly *A. aethiopicus*). Fossils identified as early *Homo* (*H. habilis, H. ergaster, H. rudolfensis, H. erectus,* etc.) have been found at Omo, Lake Turkana, and Olduvai. These will be reviewed in subsequent chapters. What follows is an introduction to the East African australopithecine fossil record.

Early Pliocene Hominids from East Africa   Very few hominids older than 4 million years are known from East Africa and, as we have seen, none at all of this antiquity are known from southern Africa (see Fig. 4.1). Some researchers have pointed to a couple of isolated teeth from two sites in the Lake Baringo area of northern Kenya, Lukeino and Ngorora, as evidence of a hominid presence in East Africa prior to about 5 mya. However, these claims are unreliable because it is sometimes very difficult to assign single hominid teeth at the species or even genus level (110–112). It is of some interest, however, that a piece of mandible and several isolated teeth recently described from deposits in East Lake Turkana dated to about 4 mya include an M_1 said to resemble the Lukeino molar (113).

Arguably the oldest hominid fossil comes from a locality known as Lothagam, Kenya (see Fig. 4.1) (114). In 1967 an expedition to the area discovered a right mandibular fragment preserving the crown and root system of M_1 and the broken roots of M_2 and M_3. The specimen comes from the lower layer designated Lothagam-1, which is bracketed by radiometric dates of 8.3 to 3.7 mya (115–117). Recent biostratigraphic analyses suggest that the mandible may in fact be from the late Miocene since it appears to be older than 5.6 million years (118). The specimen was originally assigned to *A. africanus* (115), while others considered it a possible pongid (119) or a form close to the lineage of a hypothetical ancestral hominid (120). More recent assessments of the fossil demonstrate its similarity to *A. afarensis*, particularly since it shows some adaptations to increased masticatory power and enlarged cheek teeth, or megadontia, characteristic of later australopithecines (110,118,121). If this assessment is correct, it would be the earliest known member of this species.

A second nearby site, Kanapoi, has yielded a distal left humeral fragment, partial right tibia, and jaws and teeth of a newly named australopithecine species, *A. anamensis* dating to about 4.2–3.9 mya (122,123). The tibia appears fully adapted to bipedalism and, if correctly interpreted, would be the oldest anatomical evidence for upright walking in the fossil record. Many features of the jaws and teeth, e.g., enamel thickness, seem intermediate between *A. ramidus* and *A. afarensis*. Other specimens attributed to this new species have been recovered from the Allia Bay region of East Lake Turkana.

A nearly complete left radius was recovered from middle Pliocene sediments east of Lake Turkana. Unlike the tibia from Kanapoi, this specimen includes a number of apelike characteristics and has a distal articular surface (for articulation with the wrist bones) that is arranged like that found in quadrupedal climbers, thus supporting the argument (see Chapter V) that vertical climbing was a significant component of the total locomotor repertoire of early hominids (124).

Two early Pliocene hominid fossils have been recovered from the site of Tabarin in the Chemeron Formation near Lake Baringo, dated to approximately 5 mya: a right mandibular fragment preserving M_1 and M_2, and a proximal humerus. Both have been tentatively assigned to *A. afarensis* (110,125,126).

Several teeth from a single individual have recently been recovered from deposits at Fejej in southern Ethiopia that may also date to about 4 mya. These have also been tentatively assigned to *A. afarensis* (127,128).

A new site at Aramis, Ethiopia (Middle Awash)   Undoubtedly the single most important discovery of a hominid more than 4 million years old comprises dental, cranial, and postcranial elements of a new australopithecine, *A. ramidus*, from Pliocene deposits dating to 4.4 mya at Aramis, Ethiopia (18,129) (see Fig. 4.1). The name "ramidus" is from the local Afar language, in which "ramid" means "root." The antiquity and primitive morphology of the specimens suggest that *A. ramidus* may represent the potential root species of all later hominids. The published specimens include most of the teeth of one individual, several associated postcranial elements, two partial cranial bases, a child's mandible, and other associated and isolated teeth. Further discoveries at the site in the 1994 field season have added a number of new cranial and postcranial specimens to the *A. ramidus* sample, including additional mandibular portions and teeth, humeri, hand and foot bones, and a fragmentary adult skeleton that includes cranial, mandibular, vertebral, and upper and lower limb elements (130). We will have more to say about the morphology of this new species in the next chapter.

A rich fossil fauna and flora has been recovered at Aramis, including thousands of *Canthium* seeds, a genus common in African woodlands and forests. The predominance in the fauna of fossils of medium-sized colobine monkeys and kudus reinforces the idea that *A. ramidus* inhabited closed, wooded habitats, although the caveat should be added that similar floral and faunal elements can be found today along the Awash River in Ethiopia. It is interesting to speculate that *A. ramidus* may have lived before the expansion of hominids into the more open grassland environments that later hominids like *A. afarensis* more typically favored.

Omo Group: Northern Turkana Basin (Kenya and Ethiopia)   First visited by European big-game hunters in the late 1880s, the Omo area produced its first fossils in 1902. In 1933 the French paleontologist Camille Arambourg established a rudimentary geological sequence for the Omo area and published a paleontological survey of the region.

Detailed paleoanthropological studies at Omo, which began in 1966, were organized under the auspices of the International Omo Research Expedition headed by F. Clark Howell from the United States, Yves Coppens from France, and Richard Leakey from Kenya. Conceived as a multidisciplinary effort involving geologists, paleontologists, anatomists, and archeologists, this expedition was one of the most successful cooperative paleoanthropological efforts to date. The Omo Group of sedimentary deposits is now the longest and best-dated hominid fossil–bearing sequence in East Africa.

Richard Leakey's Kenyan team first explored some of the younger deposits in the area and discovered two hominid skulls dating to about 100,000 years ago (131). As we shall see in a later chapter, these fossils have important implications for the origins of modern humans. Meanwhile, the French and American teams explored the older deposits, dated to about 3–1 mya and recovered several hundred early hominid specimens from nearly a hundred separate localities (132). Preliminary assessments of these hominids suggested the presence of both ''gracile'' and ''robust'' australopithecines as well as early *Homo* (7,133).

The Omo Group deposits that yield the bulk of the hominid fossils are part of the depression of the eastern rift valley and are exposed around the northern half of Lake Turkana, Kenya, and in the lower Omo River Valley of Ethiopia (see Fig. 4.1). These Plio-Pleistocene sediments include the Mursi, Usno, and Shungura Formations of the lower Omo River Valley, Ethiopia, and the Koobi Fora and Nachukui Formations on the eastern and western shores respectively of Lake Turkana, Kenya. At last count, 449 hominid fossils have been documented from the Omo Group sediments: 177

from the Koobi Fora Formation, 259 from the Usno and Shungura Formations, and 13 from the Nachukui Formation. The Mursi Formation has yet to yield any hominid fossils (132).

Shungura and Usno Formations (Ethiopia) A number of important hominid fossils have been recovered from the Shungura Formation. These sediments consist of over 700 m of stream (fluvial), lake (lacustrine), and deltaic deposits that are divided into twelve Members (labelled from oldest to youngest as Members A–L) on the basis of widespread volcanic ash layers at the base of each Member.[8] Hominid fossils are known from Shungura Members B–H, K, and L and from levels of the Usno Formation equivalent to Shungura Member B (132) (Fig. 4.9).

It was originally thought that hominids from the Usno Formation, and from Shungura Formation Members B–G, were similar to specimens of *A. africanus* from southern Africa. Even early on, however, it was perceptively noted that some of the oldest specimens (notably those from the Usno Formation) might ultimately prove, with additional material, to represent a distinct but related species, possibly *A. afarensis* (133). Other specimens from Shungura Formation Members E–G were attributed to "robust" australopithecines and compared to *A. boisei* and/or *A. aethiopicus.* A very few localities in Shungura Formation Members G and H (and perhaps L) have yielded teeth and cranial parts that are similar to those attributed to *H. habilis* and some cranial fragments from (the uppermost) Member K suggest *H. erectus* (134).

In a more recent assessment, F. Clark Howell has reiterated that the more "gracile" specimens from the Usno and Shungura Formations previously assigned to *A. africanus* may actually belong to *A. afarensis* and/or *H. habilis.* The fragmentary nature of the material makes it difficult to assign many of these specimens with any great degree of confidence. Howell now considers many of the more "robust" specimens previously assigned to *A. boisei* to belong to *A. aethiopicus* (7).

There is little consensus on the taxonomic placement of all the Usno and Shungura hominids, so a summary statement is difficult. However, the following general chronology can be offered (7,13,132,135–137). Australopithecines (possible *A. afarensis*) first appear at Omo in the Usno Formation just over 3 mya. "Gracile" hominids (*A. afarensis* and/or early *Homo*) are present in Members C–G and L of the Shungura Formation, thus spanning a time range from about 2.7 to 1.4 mya. "Robust" hominids provisionally referred to *A. boisei* and/or *A. aethiopicus* are from Members C–G and K, although the allocation of some of these specimens from below tuff G to *A. boisei* is questionable. Thus, their time range is from about 2.5

---

[8]Each Member is named for the volcanic ash layer at its base, and includes that tuff and all overlying sediments up to the base of the next volcanic ash layer. There is no Member I.

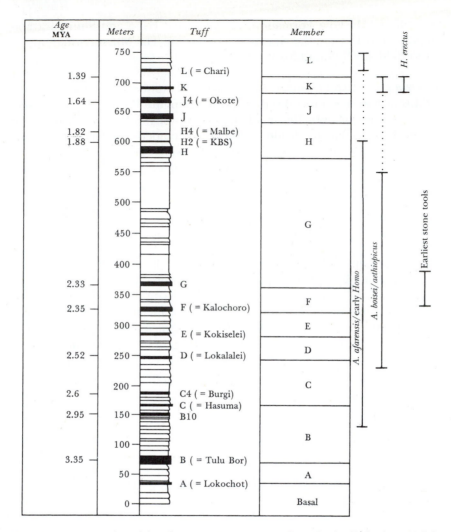

Fig. 4.9.   Stratigraphy of the Shungura Formation at Omo Basin, Ethiopia.   Height of strata above the bottom of the Basal Member is given in meters; names of tuffs in parentheses refer to field names in the Koobi Fora Formation at eastern Lake Turkana. Hominids have been recovered from Members B–H, K, and L (hominids from the Usno Formation correlate with Shungura Member B). Approximate age of fossil hominids and appearance of earliest stone tools are indicated to the right. Modified from (132).

to 1.5 mya. One specimen referred to *H. erectus* from Member K is dated to about 1.5 mya.

The earliest stone tools, mainly quartz flakes, are found in Members F and G and are dated to about 2.4–2.3 mya (132). These, and newly discovered Oldowan tools from Gona, Ethiopia, dated to 2.5 mya, are among the oldest stone tools yet discovered from Africa (138). In only two instances are hominid fossils found at these early Omo archeological sites but, unfortunately, none of them are found in direct association with the tools so it is uncertain which hominids were the toolmakers (7).

Only isolated teeth (twenty-three specimens) have been recovered from the Usno Formation (from the Brown and White Sands localities) (133). This part of the Usno Formation correlates to the lower portion of the Shungura Formation (Member B) and thus the hominid fossils are just over 3 million years old.

The Omo Group paleoenvironment What do the Usno and Shungura Formations reveal about the paleoenvironments in which these early hominids lived? The earlier Pliocene in this region was dominated by an extensive freshwater pre-Turkana lake with a diverse fish fauna and a moderately diverse molluscan fauna. The presence of fossil wood signifies dry wooded or bush savanna habitats in the region as well. By the mid-Pliocene a major north to south flowing river system had emerged with numerous east and west flowing tributaries. Fossil wood and pollen suggest that more humid riparian forest and more open forest/wooded savanna habitats existed at this time. Many of the associated small mammals have equatorial African forest affinities. The reduction in arboreal pollen and the substantial increase of grasses is strong evidence in the pollen record for a change in vegetation and drier conditions about 2.5–2.0 mya. This change to more arid climates and expanding grasslands is also documented in the gradual turnover of the mammalian fauna to more grazing, open-country, and **xeric** (dry)-adapted species, particularly bovids and suids. As we have seen, this parallels paleoclimatic inferences reached for the South African sites (7,139,140).

Koobi Fora and Nachukui Formations (Kenya)

History of Koobi Fora excavation During the first field season (1967) of the International Omo Expedition, Richard Leakey chartered a helicopter to explore the northeastern shores of Lake Turkana (known then as Lake Rudolph). Almost immediately he found stone tools similar to those from Bed I at Olduvai Gorge (see below). Buoyed by the prospects of new discoveries, he pulled out of the Omo expedition and organized his own expeditions to Lake Turkana in 1968. These explorations continue to this day on both the east and west sides of the lake and have been enormously successful (141).

Leakey's first hominid discovery at Lake Turkana was the virtually complete skull of a "robust" australopithecine (KNM-ER 406, for Kenya National Museum-East Rudolf, no. 406) (Fig. 4.10a). Many other australopithecine specimens (Fig. 4.10b,c) have since been found as well as representatives of both *Homo* aff. *H. habilis* and *Homo* aff. *H. erectus*. These latter fossils will be discussed in later chapters.

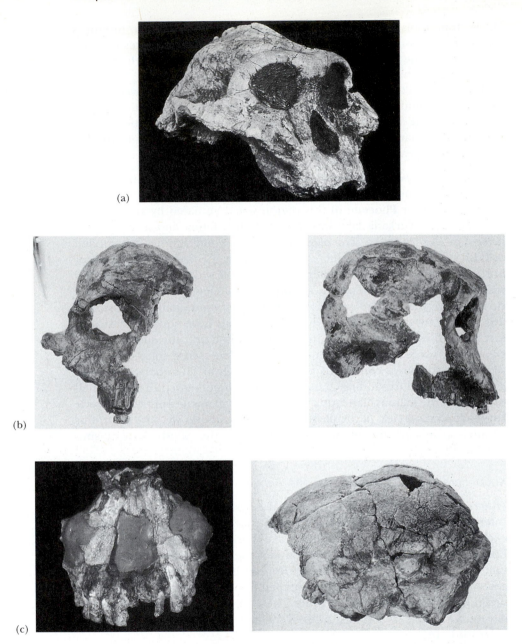

(a)

(b)

(c)

Fig. 4.10. Examples of early hominids recovered from Lake Turkana in northern Kenya. (a) Fronto-lateral view of KNM-ER 406, generally classified as *A. boisei*. The cranium has well-developed sagittal and nuchal crests and a wide, robust face. Endocranial capacity has been estimated at 510 cc. (b) Front and lateral views of KNM-ER 732, possibly female *A. boisei*. Endocranial capacity estimated at 500 cc. (c) Front and lateral views of KNM-ER 1805. Since it has proven difficult to assign this cranium to a particular species, it is often referred to as *Australopithecus* sp. Photos courtesy of Kenya National Museum.

Lake Turkana is one of many African lakes that developed in depressions formed by crustal downwarping and faulting during the Cenozoic. While there is no geological evidence for an extensive and long-lived lake throughout the entire Plio-Pleistocene in this region, there were intervals of lacustrine deposition over restricted areas that were associated with significant lake-level fluctuations (142). This history has resulted in the deposition of more than 500 m of lake, deltaic, and fluvial sediments that record the gradual shift of the lake's eastern shoreline. These sediments, now known as the Koobi Fora Formation, are further subdivided into eight Members, most of which are defined by volcanic tuffs and were given names, rather than numbers (Fig. 4.11). Fossil hominids from the Koobi Fora Formation have been recovered from the Lonyumun, Lokochot, Tulu Bor, upper Burgi, KBS, and Okote Members and span a time range from just over 4.0 to 1.4 mya, although the great majority of Koobi Fora hominid specimens are less than 2.0 million years old (132,143,144).

The Lake Turkana paleoenvironment   The paleoenvironmental setting for hominids at Koobi Fora was certainly one of fluctuating spatial shifts in ecological zones as lake levels rose and fell. One recent paleoecological model found that *A. boisei* from both Koobi Fora and West Turkana appeared to be closely associated with closed/wet habitats, such as those found today at National Parks like Hwange (Zimbabwe), Umfoloze (South Africa), and Kafue (Zambia). This model also suggested that early *Homo* was associated with less restricted habitats, including open and dry bushy areas as well as closed/wet habitats and that *A. robustus* from southern Africa may have preferred more open, arid habitats (145).

Studies of the Lake Turkana region indicate that Plio-Pleistocene environments were generally comparable to the modern environment of the area even though temperature and rainfall fluctuations have certainly occurred over the past 4 million years. However, the recent recovery at Koobi Fora of two plant taxa characteristic of the central African rain forests from a restricted chronostratigraphic layer dating to about 3.4–3.0 mya suggests that the general pattern of environmental stability in East Africa was punctuated at times by brief but significant rain-forest expansions (146).

The Nachukui Fossils   Plio-Pleistocene sediments on the western side of Lake Turkana make up the Nachukui Formation. As in the Koobi Fora Formation, Members within the Nachukui Formation are named for volcanic ash layers at the base of each Member. A total of thirteen hominids have been collected from this Formation thus far, the most important being the 2.5-million-year-old skull of a hyperrobust australopithecine (WT 17000—the "Black Skull") and a beautifully preserved *Homo erectus* skeleton (WT 15000—"Turkana Boy"), both of which will be discussed in greater detail in later chapters. Stone tools have also been found on both sides of the lake, the oldest ones dating to just over 2 mya (147,148).

Extensive geological (149–154) and paleontological (155–158) research

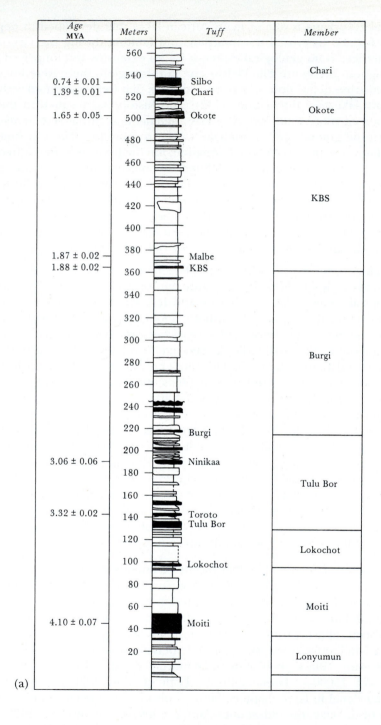

(a)

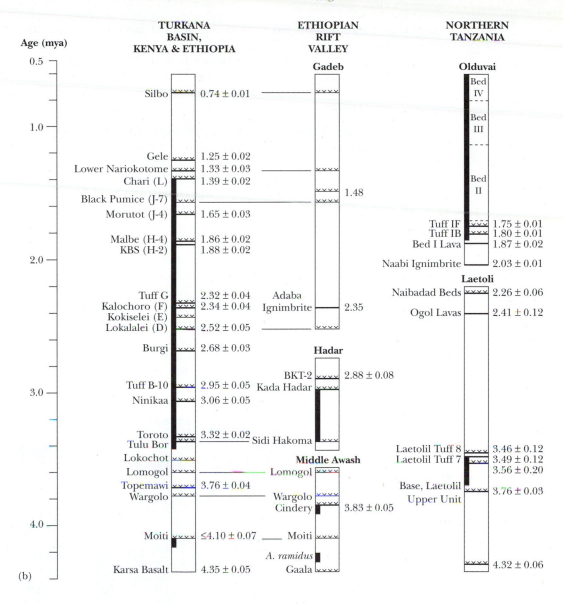

Fig. 4.11. (a) Stratigraphy of the Koobi Fora Formation. (b) Correlations of fossil hominid sites in the Turkana Basin of Kenya and Ethiopia (e.g., Koobi Fora, Omo) (left); sites in the Middle Awash Valley (e.g., Hadar) (center); and sites in northern Tanzania (e.g., Olduvai, Laetoli) (right). The heavy dark line on the left edge of each column indicates a time interval from which fossil hominids have been recovered. Note the stratigraphic position of the new species, *A. ramidus*, just above the Gaala Tuff in the Ethiopian rift valley. Radiometrically dated levels are given to the right of each column (144).

over the past two decades has refined the original radiometric ages first proposed for these sediments. Recently, precise correlations between radiometrically dated tuffs in the Omo Group and the Middle Awash Valley (see below) have been achieved (Fig. 4.11b) (117,143,144,159).

Hadar and the Middle Awash (Ethiopia)

History of excavation   The sites at Hadar and along the Middle Awash River Valley are located within the Afar depression of Ethiopia, a hot, desolate area of badlands situated at the confluence of the East African, Red Sea, and Gulf of Aden rift systems (160–164). The individuals most responsible for paleoanthropological explorations of the Middle Awash were geologists M. Taieb and J. Kalb with anthropologists D. Johanson and T. White, who were investigating the geological evolution of the Awash River. In 1972 the first short geological and paleontological surveys of the area were undertaken and the following year the first hominid remains from Hadar were recovered, an associated knee joint consisting of a distal femur and proximal tibia and fragmentary right and left proximal femora (165).

Nearly 250 australopithecine specimens representing a minimum of thirty-five individuals were recovered from Hadar during the 1970s, the most spectacular being the skeleton nicknamed "Lucy" (A.L. 288-1) and the partial remains of at least thirteen individuals from site A.L. 333 ("the first family"), both dated to about 3.2 mya (166) (Fig. 4.12). One possible

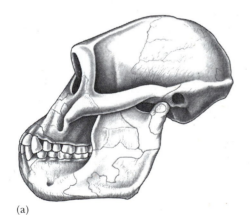
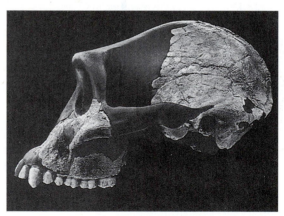

(a)

Fig. 4.12.   (a) Side view of an adult skull of *A. afarensis* reconstructed by W. Kimbel and T. White. Courtesy of Institute for Human Origins. (b) The skeleton of A.L. 288-1 ("Lucy") discovered at Hadar, Ethiopia, in 1974. (c) The skeleton of "Lucy" (left) contrasted with the skeleton of a modern human female of average height (right) in walking position. Although Lucy was only about 105 cm (3′ 5″) tall, other *A. afarensis* individuals have been found up to 150 cm (4′ 11″) tall. Note Lucy's relatively long arms. From (204). (d) Partial skeleton of *A. africanus* from Sterkfontein (Sts 14). (Photo by D. Panagos courtesy of the Transvaal Museum, Pretoria.)

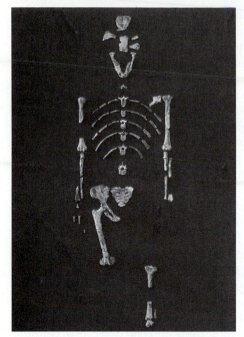

(b)

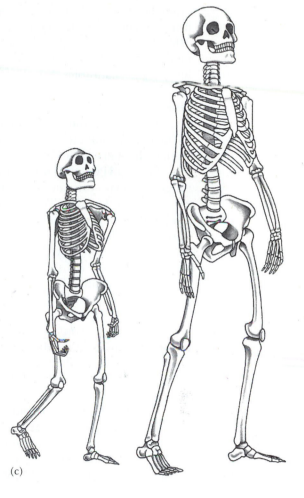

(c)

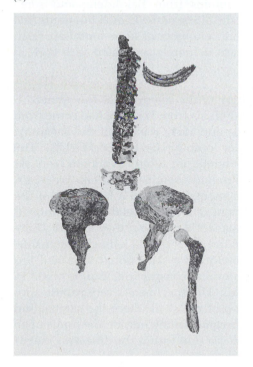

(d)

reason there were so many individuals present at a single locality is that a hominid social group was overcome, buried, and preserved by a sudden flood event (167,168). Three more field seasons beginning in 1990 have yielded an additional fifty-three australopithecine specimens, including the first skull of *A. afarensis* (54).

With the exception of the new *A. ramidus* discoveries from Aramis, (see above), all the other Hadar and Middle Awash australopithecines have generally been attributed to *A. afarensis*, although some researchers question if there is not more than one hominid taxon present in the Hadar sample (169–172). For example, there is great size disparity between presumed male and female specimens assigned to *A. afarensis*. Comparable size differences in mandibles, humeri, and proximal femora are rarely observed in modern humans or chimpanzees and are even rare in the most sexually dimorphic living primates, orangutans and gorillas (173).

Australopithecine fossils from Hadar come from the Hadar Formation, particularly from the Sidi Hakoma, Denen Dora, and lowermost Kada Hadar Members (159,174) (Fig. 4.13). Recent geological work has shown that the Sida Hakoma Tuff near the bottom of the australopithecine time range at Hadar correlates with other tuffs in East Africa dated to about 3.4 mya (e.g., the Tulu Bor Tuff at Koobi Fora). Therefore, the Hadar hominid sample ranges from about 3.4 to 2.9 mya, some 400,000 years or so younger than the oldest Middle Awash hominids from Belohdelie and some 200,000–600,000 years younger than the oldest of the Laetoli hominids (see below and Fig. 4.11b) (175,176). While a number of stone tools have been found in the Hadar region, none are definitely associated with skeletal remains of *A. afarensis*.

Fossils from the Middle Awash   Prior to the discovery of the Aramis *A. ramidus* hominids, the oldest fossil hominids from Ethiopia had come from Fejej (see above) and the Belohdelie and Maka regions of the Sagantole Formation in the Middle Awash Valley south of Hadar (159,177,178). The hominid cranial fragments from Belohdelie are about 3.8 million years old and the estimated age for the Maka hominid assemblage is 3.4 million years. The Belohdelie hominid cranial fragments consist of a large part of the right frontal bone and a small segment of a left parietal bone. Although the incomplete fragments are chimpanzeelike in size, they are not chimpanzeelike in shape. The Belohdelie frontal bone has a much flatter side-to-side, or **coronal**, profile, and therefore the skull would have had less narrowing behind the orbits, or **postorbital constriction**, than is found in extant apes and other early hominids. The specimen is very robust, with the thickness at the point on the top of the skull where the sagittal and coronal sutures intersect, known as **bregma**, falling outside the range of all other australopithecines and early *Homo* (but within the *H. erectus* range) (179,180).

A number of important craniodental and postcranial fossils have re-

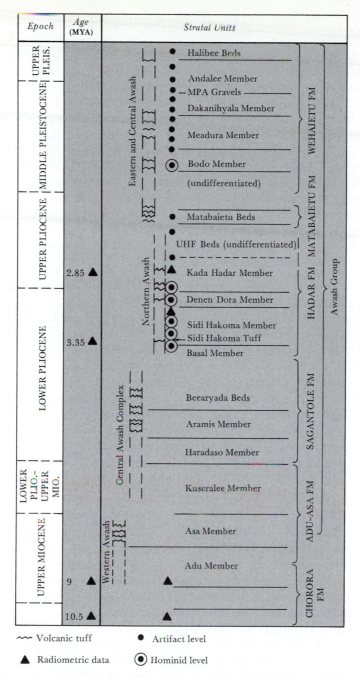

Epoch	Age (MYA)	Stratal Units

Eastern and Central Awash

Halibee Beds
Andalee Member
MPA Gravels
Dakanihyala Member
Meadura Member
Bodo Member
(undifferentiated)

WEHAIETU FM

Matabaietu Beds
UHF Beds (undifferentiated)

MATABAIETU FM

Northern Awash

2.85 — Kada Hadar Member
Denen Dora Member
Sidi Hakoma Member
3.35 — Sidi Hakoma Tuff
Basal Member

HADAR FM

Awash Group

Central Awash Complex

Beearyada Beds
Aramis Member
Haradaso Member

SAGANTOLE FM

Kuseralee Member
Asa Member

ADU-ASA FM

Western Awash

Adu Member

9 —
10.5 —

CHORORA FM

∿∿ Volcanic tuff   ● Artifact level

▲ Radiometric data   ◉ Hominid level

Fig. 4.13. Composite stratigraphic section of the Hadar Formation indicating distribution of *A. afarensis* hominid specimens. Dating of volcanic tuffs indicate that no Hadar hominid is older than about 3.40 million years, and establish ages of about 3.18 million years for the A.L. 288-1 ("Lucy") skeleton and about 3.20 million years for the A.L. 333 hominid assemblage ("the first family"). The temporal range of *A. afarensis* at Hadar thus extends from about 3.4 to 3.0 mya. Adapted from T. White in (205).

cently been described from Maka dating to about 3.4 mya (178). Four mandibular specimens (and several isolated teeth) have been recovered that show certain morphological (and metrical) resemblances to *A. afarensis* from Hadar and Laetoli. In addition, the site has also yielded several post-cranial bones including a proximal femur, humerus, and proximal ulna. The humerus is large and robust, much more so than the humerus of "Lucy" (A.L. 288-1 from Hadar), and is taken to support the view that *A. afarensis* was a highly sexually dimorphic species. The Maka femur shares a number of morphological features with other specimens attributed to *Australopithecus* that differ from later *Homo* and it, along with the Kanapoi tibia of *A. anamensis,* provides the earliest anatomical evidence documenting the evolution of upright walking (122,179).

We shall discuss these, and other, anatomical correlates of bipedal locomotion in more detail in the next chapter.

The Hadar paleoenvironment   Analyses of the Hadar sediments reveal that a lake surrounded by marshy environments once existed in the region and was fed by rivers flowing off the Ethiopian escarpment. In general, the sediments represent marshy, lake-margin, and associated fluvial deposits related to the extensive lake that periodically filled the entire sedimentary basin. The mammalian fauna of the upper Basal Member and lower Sidi Hakoma Member also suggest primarily marshy, lake-edge environments. A little higher up in the Sidi Hakoma Member a transition to more open habitats occurs in apparent association with lake regression. Clearly, a mosaic of habitats existed through time that included closed and open woodland-bushland and grassland. It appears that the relative proportions of these habitat types varied through time in response to the changes in local climatic conditions and/or lake-basin regression (166).

Laetoli (Tanzania)

History of excavation   The oldest well-documented sample of australopithecines from Tanzania comes from Laetoli, a site some 50 km south of Olduvai Gorge in northern Tanzania (Fig. 4.1). Laetoli is most renowned for studies conducted there by Mary Leakey and associates from 1974 to 1979. The Pliocene deposits of this area are known as the Laetolil Beds and all the hominids from these beds (including the type specimen of *A. afarensis*) are attributed to *A. afarensis* (167,181).

Louis Leakey actually discovered East Africa's first australopithecine fossil, an isolated lower left canine, at Laetoli in 1935, though its australopithecine affinities were not recognized until 1981 (44). The first fossils from Laetoli to be recognized as hominids by their discoverers were unearthed in 1939 by Ludwig Kohl-Larsen's German expedition and consisted of a maxillary fragment with P^{3-4} (from Garusi I) and tooth sockets, or **alveoli**, for the canine and incisors, an isolated M^3 (Garusi II), and various other skull fragments among which was a large occipital fragment that has apparently since been lost (182,183). The maxillary fragment and isolated molar probably belong to different individuals, since dental wear suggests the former is from a young individual and the latter from a much older and smaller individual. These hominids were originally named *Meganthropus africanus* because of their alleged similarity to the genus *Meganthropus* described from Java (see Chapter VII) (184). More recent mineralogical analyses indicate that these specimens come from the same level in the Laetolil Beds as the *A. afarensis* specimens discovered in the 1970s by Mary Leakey and her team, and there now seems little reason not to allocate them to *A. afarensis* as well.

The most famous and unusual "fossil" from the site is the trail of hominid footprints discovered in 1978 (Fig. 4.14). These fossil footprints are preserved because of a unique combination of climatic, volcanic, and mineralogical conditions. Approximately 3.6 mya a series of light ashfalls from

Fig. 4.14. Laetoli footprints. These footprints, dated to approximately 3.6 mya, are entirely humanlike in form. This 10-m stretch of trackway shows two hominid trails, made by three individuals. The single hominid trail (G1) is on the left, and the double hominid trail (G2/3)—made by two hominids, the second stepping directly within the tracks of the first—is on the right. Traversing the hominid trail at the lower right are two trails of the extinct equid, *Hipparion*, and its foal. (Photo by T. Moon and reprinted by permission of the J. Paul Getty Trust, copyright 1995.)

a nearby volcano coincided with a series of rainshowers. The carbonate in the ash then hardened as it dried in the sun. Fortunately, several hominids appear to have crossed the ash layer while it was still wet, preserving very humanlike tracks (185). These famous footprints provide the most incontrovertible evidence to date that by about 3.6 mya early hominids were bipedal (186–190). We shall have more to say about the Laetoli footprints in the next chapter.

The Laetolil Beds are subdivided into two units, the lower one approximately 70 m thick and the upper one 45–60 m thick. Almost all the vertebrate fossils, including the hominids, are from the upper unit, which consists principally of **aeolian**, or windblown tuffs. The hominid-bearing strata in the upper unit are well dated to 3.76–3.46 mya (191) (Fig. 4.11b).

The Laetoli paleoenvironment   Several paleoenvironmental reconstructions of Laetoli have been developed from sedimentological analyses. The aeolian deposits suggest an environment in which vegetation was sufficient seasonally to prevent extensive windblown transportation of sand-sized ash particles. The nature of the weathering of these Laetoli tuffs further indicates the presence of a saline, alkaline soil. Perhaps the closest modern analogy to the Pliocene at Laetoli is the eastern semiarid-arid part of the Serengeti Plain, an area of grassland savanna with scattered bush and acacia trees with a dry season and a rainy season averaging about 50 cm per year.

The fossil vertebrate and invertebrate fauna from Laetoli reinforce this model of a semiarid climate: the absence of hippopotamus, crocodile, and other water-dwelling animals characterizes an upland savanna distant from a permanent water source. The fossil fauna is, in fact, quite similar to the fauna living in the area today. Fossil rodents are particularly useful paleoenvironmental indicators because they do not migrate through the year as larger mammals do, and most species live within quite restricted ecological niches. Laetoli fossil rodents also suggest an environment of open grassland with occasional acacia trees, and the presence of the naked mole rat in particular implies that the climate in the Laetoli area was even warmer then than it is today (192).

Olduvai (Tanzania)

History of excavation   Olduvai Gorge is a large gash in the Serengeti Plain of northern Tanzania (Fig. 4.1). Louis Leakey, formerly of the National Museums of Kenya, the husband of the aforementioned Mary Leakey, and father of Richard Leakey, enjoyed telling the story of its "discovery" in 1911 by one Professor Kattwinkel, an absentminded German butterfly collector, who nearly plunged to his death down the gorge in pursuit of some elusive lepidopterous specimen. Recovering from his fall, Kattwinkel descended into the gorge and discovered fossil bones along its slopes.

The elder Leakey first visited the site that was to make him world famous in 1931. Within hours of setting up his camp he discovered stone tools in the gorge. During his explorations at Olduvai in the 1930s, Leakey discovered a number of promising sites for the recovery of stone tools. In 1935 his young research assistant, Mary Nicol, discovered fragments of a hominid skull among the remains of antelopes and pigs and some stone tools. Louis and Mary were married in 1936, beginning one of the most productive husband and wife collaborations in the annals of science.

Constraints of time, money, and other research projects kept the Leakeys away from Olduvai until the early 1950s. During that decade they found and described a number of tool sites and uncovered a few hominid teeth, but nothing particularly newsworthy. That all changed on the morning of July 17, 1959, as Louis remained in camp recovering from a bout of influenza and Mary revisited the area where the first stone tools had been found in 1931. When she arrived at the site she noticed some teeth and parts of a hominid skull just eroding through the surface of the slope. After brushing away the dirt to reveal some of the teeth, she found that she had uncovered the most complete hominid fossil ever found at Olduvai. It was a beautifully preserved skull of a "robust" australopithecine that Louis Leakey named *Zinjanthropus boisei* (*Zinj* for the ancient name of East Africa, *anthropos* meaning "man," and *boisei* to honor Charles Boise, one of the Leakey's financial benefactors). *"Zinjanthropus"* would turn out to be only a temporary taxonomic label (193,194) (Fig. 4.15).

The press was quick to nickname this hominid "Nutcracker Man" because of its enormous teeth and jaws. It was clear that this species represented a taxon distinct from *A. africanus*. The question of whether or not it represented a distinct genus, however, was (and still is) open to debate (195,196). The original describer of the skull, Phillip Tobias (Dart's successor at Witwatersrand University), felt that this "robust" australopithecine should be classified only as a distinct species within the genus *Australopithecus*, appropriately named *A. boisei* (67). However, over the past few years the taxonomic pendulum has begun to swing back to the view that the "robust" australopithecines should be separated at the generic level from the "gracile" australopithecines and that the name *Paranthropus* should be retained for such "robust" forms.[9] However, until the branching sequences of all the "robust" forms are confidently worked out, it seems premature to revert back to the name *Paranthropus*.

A few hundred meters north of the Zinj site, the Leakey's eldest son, Jonathan, found another interesting fossil site. Excavations yielded fragments of a rather thin hominid skull, several foot bones, hand bones, and a mandible of a hominid very different from *"Zinjanthropus."* In fact, what Jonathan had discovered was the type specimen for *Homo habilis*, the subject of the following chapter (197).

The Olduvai sediments are labelled (from oldest to youngest) Beds I to IV, with additional Pleistocene beds above Bed IV (Fig. 4.11b). Olduvai has

---

[9]It seems the more things change, the more they stay the same!

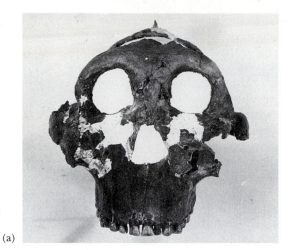
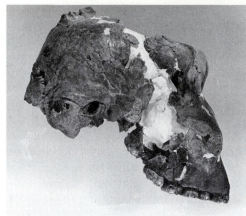

(a)

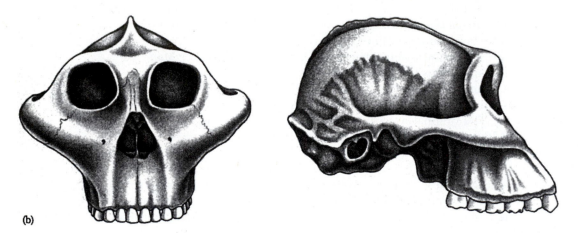

(b)

Fig. 4.15. Crania of *A. boisei.*   (a) *"Zinjanthropus"* cranium from Bed 1 of Olduvai Gorge. (b) Reconstruction based on specimens from Olduvai Gorge and Koobi Fora (Lake Turkana). [a, Photo by R. G. Klomfass, by permission of P. V. Tobias; b, redrawn from (206).] Note the massive face and attachment areas for the powerful chewing muscles, particularly the size of the sagittal crest for the origin of the temporalis muscle and the size of the zygomatic arch for origin of the masseter muscle.

been an unusually rich hominid site. In addition to the numerous *A. boisei* and *H. habilis* fossils recovered from Beds I and II, it has also yielded specimens of *H. erectus* from upper Bed II and lower Bed IV, thus marking the appearance of this species at about 1.2 mya at this site. Louis Leakey found the first of these *H. erectus* specimens at Olduvai himself (OH 9). Considering how strongly the public associated his name with early hominid discoveries, it is ironic that this specimen was the only hominid fossil he personally ever found at Olduvai. We will have a lot more to say about *H. erectus* in following chapters.

The Olduvai paleoenvironment Because australopithecines are restricted to Beds I and II (where most early *Homo* specimens are found as well), the following comments on the Olduvai paleoenvironments will concentrate on these two beds.

The Olduvai Gorge is between 45 and 90 m deep where the lowest unit of the beds (Bed I) is exposed. Varying between 30 and 54 m in thickness, Bed I is probably the most firmly dated of any hominid Lower Pleistocene site: the fossils are on the order of about 1.7 to 1.8 million years old and the fossiliferous part of Bed I may represent a time span of only 50,000 to 100,000 years (198). Bed I can be subdivided into five lithologically different types: lake deposits, lake-margin deposits, alluvial-fan deposits, alluvial-plain deposits, and lava flows. The lake deposits accumulated in a shallow, perennial lake in the lowest part of the basin at the western foot of the volcanic highlands. The lake either did not have an outlet or overflowed infrequently, resulting in fluctuating lake levels. The perennial part of the lake was saline and alkaline. The lake-margin sediments were laid down on a broad expanse of low-lying, relatively flat terrain periodically flooded by the lake. Hominid fossils in Bed I are concentrated in these lake-margin deposits at the eastern end of the lake (199).

Fossilized leaves and pollen are rare in Beds I and II, but swamp vegetation is indicated by abundant vertical root channels and casts possibly made by some kind of reed. Fossil rhizomes of papyrus also suggest the presence of marshland and/or shallow water. Other structures, such as diatoms and traces of algae, point to fluctuating lake levels and saline conditions. The climate was probably semiarid, although wetter than at Olduvai today, as indicated by the presence of ostracods, freshwater snails, fish, and aquatic birds. Climatic fluctuations may have been seasonal or may have lasted a few decades. Studies relating habitat preferences in modern antelopes (Bovidae) and pigs (Suidae) to similar fossil animals from Olduvai indicate that Bed I paleoenvironments may have been more wooded than previously suspected, since no modern grassland-dominated ecosystem contains as many closed- and intermediate-habitat animals as the Bed I assemblages (200).

The paleogeography of the region represented by Bed II was similar to that of Bed I, at least until faulting began, after which time the perennial lake in the basin was reduced to perhaps a third of its former size. This paleogeographical event accounts for the change in mammalian faunas that occurred about this time whereby swamp-dwelling animals decreased in number and plains-dwelling animals such as horses increased in abundance (201).

Summary of East African Sites

As we have seen, the earliest undisputed hominid appears in the fossil record of East Africa as a single mandibular fragment from the site of Lothagam some 5.6 mya. Recently discovered specimens of *A. ramidus* from Aramis, Ethiopia, dated to about 4.4 mya, however, give us the best glimpse of what the earliest hominids in the fossil record looked like. As we noted earlier, these specimens may be distinctive enough to warrant a new generic designation, *Ardipithecus*. The combination of relatively thin enamel and large canine size, together with a primitive P_3 morphology, suggests a canine/premolar complex morphologically and functionally like the presumed ancestral ape condition. Slightly younger than the Lothagam and Aramis specimens are several tantalizing hominid specimens from Kanapoi, Allia Bay (East Lake Turkana), and the Lake Baringo region of Kenya and the Middle Awash Valley of Ethiopia dated to about 4 mya. Of these, the tibial fragment from Kanapoi and the femoral fragment from Maka are particularly important in showing that bipedal adaptations of the hindlimb had commenced very early in hominid evolution, a view dramatically supported by the discovery of fossil hominid footprints at Laetoli dated to about 3.6 mya. With the exception of the Aramis fossils, all of these specimens are currently attributed to *A. anamensis* and/or *A. afarensis*, although this may change when further discoveries come to light.

Beginning with the site at Laetoli at about 3.6 mya and continuing through the sites of Hadar, Omo, Lake Turkana, and Olduvai, the fossil record of East African australopithecines is impressive up to about 1 mya, when it ceases. As we have seen, the most common hominids in the earliest part of this fossil record, from about 5.6 to 2.5 mya, are *A. ramidus, A. anamensis*, and *A. afarensis*. By about 2.5 mya an early species of *Homo*, usually allocated to *H. habilis,* and an early "robust" australopithecine, designated as either *A. boisei* or *A. aethiopicus*, are present in the fossil record. In fact, *Homo* aff. *H. habilis* and *A. boisei* were contemporaneous from about 2.4 to 1.4 mya at Omo, from about 2.0 to 1.5 mya at Lake Turkana, and from about 1.8 to 1.2 mya at Olduvai (13). *Homo* aff. *H. erectus* first appears about 1.5 mya in East Africa and is known from Lake Turkana, Omo, and Olduvai (see Fig. 4.1).

With the possible exception of Laetoli, most East African early hominid sites are associated with water sources of one sort or another, from the ancient lake margins at Olduvai to the dense riverine forests along the Omo Valley. Proximity of hominids to water would be expected, especially if the sites represent campsites or home bases where families or groups gathered repeatedly. The cave sites in South Africa, in contrast, have yielded bones that may have been accumulated by hominids and/or carnivores. The proximity of all of these early hominid cave sites to water cannot be ascertained from the southern African evidence.

The presence of australopithecines in Chad some 2,500 km west of the rift valley strongly suggests that hominids were already widely distributed throughout the woodland and savanna belt from the Atlantic Ocean across the Sahel of Africa by the middle Pliocene (109).

Vegetation types inferred from pollen studies of these various East African hominid sites are summarized in Figures 4.16 and 4.17. Aramis stands out as being the only early hominid site possibly associated with closed woodland environments.

In this chapter we have encountered for the first time in the fossil record

Locality (mya)	Paleoenvironment
Tabarin, Kenya (5.0–4.0)	Lake margin, with locally variable savanna elements
Middle Awash, Ethiopia (4.5–3.9)	Fluvial conditions, with extensive tectonic activity associated with the formation of the East African Rift
Laetoli, Tanzania (3.7–3.2)	Savanna woodland, with well-defined wet and dry seasons
Hadar, Ethiopia (3.6–2.6)	Lake and associated floodplain, with braided streams and rivers
Omo, Ethiopia (Shungura) (3.3–1.4)	After 2.1 million years ago, dry savanna flanking river banks with gallery forest and dry-thorn savanna; before this date, the environment was probably forested
Koobi Fora, Kenya (3.3–1.4)	Before 1.6 million years ago, a freshwater lake with floodplains, gallery forest and dry-thorn savanna; during later times, the lake fluctuated from fresh to brackish
Olduvai, Tanzania (1.9–<1.0)	Salt lake with surrounding floodplains with seasonal streams and rivers and dry woodland savanna; tectonic changes after 1.5 million years ago resulted in the drying up of the lake
Transvaal, South Africa (Makapansgat 3, Sterkfontein 4 and 5, Swartkrans 1, Kromdraai and Taung) (3.0–1.4)	All were mosiac environments, with Makapansgat Member 3 and Sterkfontein Member 4 being less open (more bush/woodland) than Swartkrans Member 1 and Sterkfontein Member 5; this suggests a trend from wetter to drier conditions through time

Fig. 4.16. Summary of early hominid environments in Africa. From (208).

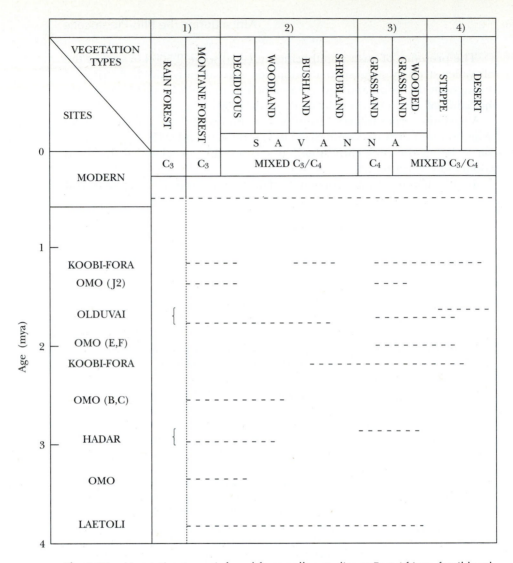

Fig. 4.17. Vegetation types inferred from pollen studies at East African fossil localities. Adapted from (207). 1) Rain forest: a closed stand of trees of several strata, large trees 40 to 60 m high, with an interlaced canopy. Montane forest is an evergreen forest with a smaller height of trees and a homogenous composition above 1,300 m. 2) Woodland: a stand of trees up to 18 m height with an open or continuous canopy cover of more than 20 percent; at least 40 percent grasses and herbs dominate the ground cover. 3) Grassland: land dominated by grasses and occasionally other herbs, sometimes with widely scattered or grouped trees and shrubs; canopy cover not exceeding 2 percent. 4) Steppe: vegetation with short grass, abundant annual plants between widely spaced perennial herbs, and scattered trees (*Acacia* and *Commiphora*) being the most common trees in East Africa. In a broad sense, the term "savanna" includes all categories between woodland and desert.

of Africa evidence of hominization, i.e., the evolution of an animal that walked on two legs rather than four, used tools rather than teeth for tearing and cutting, had a relatively large brain, and had evolved behavioral and social mechanisms enabling it to survive the harsh environs of the African savanna. We have placed these early hominids into their proper geological and paleoenvironmental context. Now we turn to the fossils themselves and to what they tell us about the biological adaptations of our earliest ancestors.

CHAPTER V

Australopithecine Paleobiology and Phylogeny

Even if one were to learn everything about the hominid-pongid common ancestor, many of the most crucial questions about distinctively hominid evolution
would remain unanswered: why are we humans and not chimpanzees, bonobos,
or gorillas?

John Tooby
Irven DeVore
"The reconstruction of hominid behavioral evolution
through strategic modeling"
(In *The Evolution of Human Behavior: Primate Models*, 1987)

INTRODUCTION

Having reviewed the paleoclimatological, biogeographical, and geological
settings of australopithecines in eastern and southern Africa in the last
chapter, we turn now to a discussion of the fossils themselves and what they
can tell us about early hominid life styles. We will be concerned particularly
with two of the most important trends in Plio-Pleistocene hominid evolution, the increase in brain size and the development of bipedalism. The
following two sections focus on distinctions in craniodental morphology in
Australopithecus and early *Homo*; in the section on locomotion we will look
in detail at the postcranial evidence for the onset of bipedalism.

As noted earlier, popular accounts of human evolution often use the
colloquial terms "gracile" and "robust" as a convenient shorthand for
referring to *A. africanus* (and by extension *A. ramidus/anamensis/afarensis* as
well) on the one hand and *A. robustus/boisei* on the other (but remember
the caveat we noted earlier about body size differences among these species). So far, *A. ramidus*, *A. anamensis*, *A. afarensis*, and *A. boisei* seem re-

stricted to East African sites, whereas *A. africanus* and *A. robustus* seem restricted to South African ones. Some "gracile" hominids in East Africa have also been attributed to *A. africanus* (1), but the presence of this species in East Africa is debatable and most workers either consider such specimens to be conspecific with *A. afarensis* or assign most, if not all, of them to *Homo*. Therefore, both East and South Africa contain at least one "gracile" and one "robust" australopithecine species.

Documenting evolutionary trends requires that we determine the chronology of the species. As a first-order approximation, the six australopithecine species can be listed chronologically (from oldest to youngest) as *A. ramidus, A. anamensis, A. afarensis, A. africanus, A. robustus,* and *A. boisei*. In general, the "gracile" species precede the "robust" species in the fossil record, although early forms of *A. boisei* in East Africa evidently coexisted with later forms of *A. africanus* in South Africa (see Fig. 4.1). Not only do the two "robust" species overlap in time, but their accepted chronological relationship may eventually be reversed based on the discovery of the *A. boisei* specimen from west Lake Turkana (WT 17000), which is much older than any specimens of *A. robustus*. This point is still open to debate (2,3).

Compared with modern humans, australopithecines are characterized by relatively small brains, ranging from approximately 413 to 530 cc, housed in skull bones that are generally quite thin. In spite of small actual brain size, australopithecine encephalization quotients (EQs) are relatively high (compared to other mammals), ranging from 2.4 in *A. afarensis* to about 3.1 in *A. robustus* (Fig. 5.1). In addition, trends toward some neural reorganization, like expansion of the temporal lobes of the brain, are evident through time (4–7).

As australopithecine skulls become generally larger and more robust in later species, other cranial trends become evident. The "robust" skull carries forward the adaptive trends already seen, albeit in less-developed form, in the "gracile" australopithecines, namely, that faces become shorter, deeper, and more massive and all the structures associated with powerful chewing, particularly in the dentition, are accentuated (8) (Fig. 5.2). Skull bones of "robust" australopithecines became even more filled with air spaces, or **pneumatized**, in order to reduce the weight of the enlarged skull, a process that had already begun in *A. ramidus*.

The need to generate powerful masticatory forces probably influenced the evolution of australopithecine cranial morphology more than any other single factor. Since the power of a muscle is directly related to its physiological cross-sectional area, one way to increase the bite force of a major masticatory muscle, like the temporalis muscle, is to enlarge its cross-sectional area, an evolutionary change that is documented in the increased size of the **temporal fossa**, through which this muscle passes to its insertion point on the coronoid process of the mandible (Fig. 5.2). Changes in cranial shape, in particular the realignment of the jaw to a position more directly beneath the midface and braincase, also serve to improve the mechanical advantage of some of the masticatory muscles, allowing them to

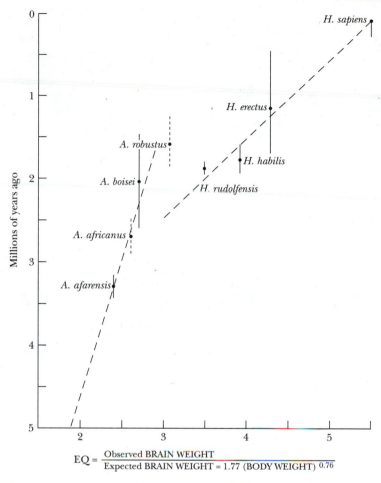

$$EQ = \frac{\text{Observed BRAIN WEIGHT}}{\text{Expected BRAIN WEIGHT} = 1.77 \, (\text{BODY WEIGHT})^{0.76}}$$

Fig. 5.1. Evolutionary trends in hominid encephalization quotients (EQs). Dots represent mean EQ values for each taxon; lines extending from each taxon along the time axis indicate estimated age ranges for each taxon. From (7).

generate greater bite force along the tooth row. Finally, since hominids can rely on their hands for food preparation and uptake rather than on their anterior dentition alone, more of the entire tooth row can become "molarized," thereby increasing overall masticatory chewing surfaces. Many of these features are carried to an extreme in "robust" australopithecines, where the mechanical advantage of the masticatory muscles and the molarization of the premolars (and even canines) reach their greatest development (9).

Trends in australopithecine cranial morphology can be correlated to trends in postcanine tooth size. For example, absolute postcanine dental size is smallest in *A. ramidus* and *A. afarensis* and largest in *A. boisei*. Early *Homo* is indistinguishable from *A. afarensis*. Furthermore, the size of the

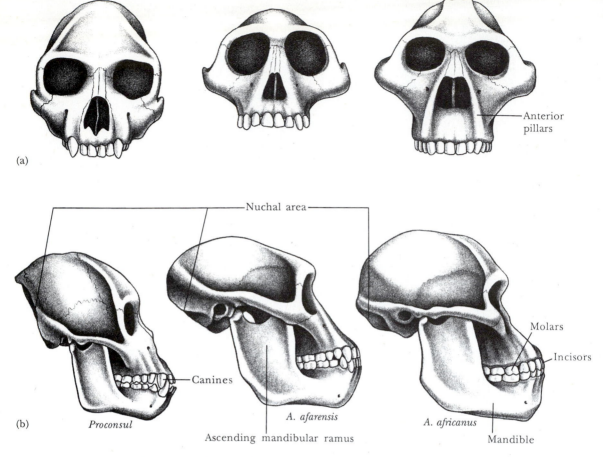

(a)

Anterior pillars

Nuchal area

Molars

Incisors

Canines

(b)   *Proconsul*

A. afarensis

A. africanus

Ascending mandibular ramus

Mandible

Fig. 5.2. General craniodental trends in australopithecines.   (a) Frontal and (b) lateral views of a Miocene ape and four australopithecines. Shaded regions are reconstructions. Note that many morphological features associated with powerful chewing and grinding are more accentuated in ''robust'' than in ''gracile'' australopithecines: faces become shorter, deeper, and more massive, often with strong anterior pillars; skulls may show pronounced sagittal crests; lower jaws become thickened with high ascending mandibular rami; incisors become smaller relative to molars; canines become more incisiform; molars become massive; and the temporal fossa becomes larger for the increased size of the temporalis muscle.

lower cheek teeth in *A. africanus* reveals an unusual pattern in that the M_1 is similar in size to *A. afarensis* (and early *Homo*) whereas the M_2 and M_3 are more similar in size to *A. robustus* (10). Calculation of the megadontia quotient (MQ)[1] shows that in *A. afarensis* the cheek teeth are about 1.7

[1]The megadontia quotient (MQ) is a measure of relative tooth size and compares the size of the tooth area of the specimen in question to that of a mammal of about the same body size. It is calculated by the formula: MQ = P4-M2 tooth area/12.15 (body weight)$^{0.86}$.

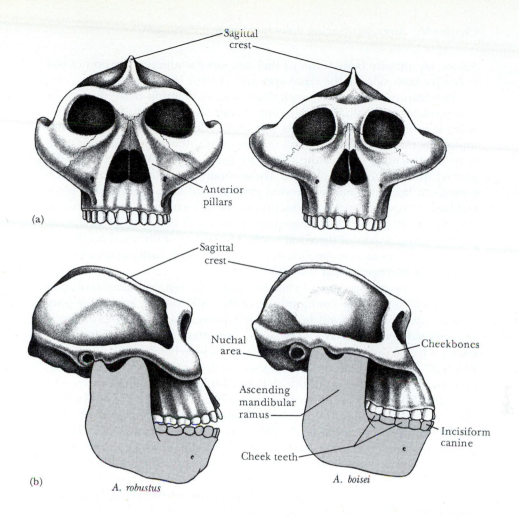

(a)

Sagittal crest

Anterior pillars

(b)

Sagittal crest

Nuchal area

Ascending mandibular ramus

Cheek teeth

Cheekbones

Incisiform canine

A. robustus

A. boisei

times larger than expected from estimated body weight, in *A. africanus* and *A. robustus* they are about 2.0 and 2.2 times larger respectively, and in *A. boisei* they are about 2.7 times larger (11,12). These compare with MQ estimates of 1.6 for *H. habilis* and 0.9 for African *H. erectus, H. sapiens,* and common chimpanzees (13,14). These studies reveal two important things: 1) all species of *Australopithecus* (with the possible exception of *A. ramidus*) are characterized by postcanine megadontia; and 2) relative cheek-tooth size tends to increase through time from *A. afarensis* to *A. boisei* and to decrease through time in the *Homo* lineage.

Larger teeth require larger jaws, which in turn require larger muscles to move them. The larger muscles then need larger bony attachments to the skull and jaw. These include 1) prominent **sagittal** and **nuchal crests** for the attachment of powerful chewing and neck muscles, respectively, and 2) bony struts in the face to withstand powerful chewing stresses set up through the massive jaws and teeth. One pair of struts, the **anterior**

pillars, are massive bony columns that support the anterior portion of the palate on both sides of the nasal aperture (15,16) (Fig. 5.2).

Two features of cranial morphology deserve mention here, the first of which relates to vocalization. The upper respiratory system of modern humans is unique among mammals (Fig. 5.3). Although humans share homologous upper respiratory tract features with other mammals, the positions of structures such as the larynx or pharynx have become markedly altered during human evolution. These anatomical changes have determined our breathing and swallowing patterns and have provided the physical basis necessary for the production of the full variety of human speech sounds, or phonation (17). Phonation is the result of laryngeal activity, in particular the activity of the vocal cords. Movement of the vocal cords produces "puffs" of air into the airspace above the vocal cords, an area known as the **supralaryngeal vocal tract** (SVT).

Several specific anatomical changes have occurred in human evolution that directly impact the configuration of the SVT. In fact, analysis of phonation capabilities in fossil hominids has been based almost entirely on reconstructions of the SVT. The most important of these evolutionary changes is that increased flexion of the cranial base has resulted in a larynx that has "descended" in the neck relative to the position of the soft palate, thereby increasing the size of the SVT. In addition, the human tongue now lies within both the oral and the pharyngeal cavities whereas the nonhuman primate tongue is almost entirely contained within the oral cavity. The primary linguistic function of the SVT is that of an acoustic filter. Therefore, even though nonhuman primate SVTs can produce most of the sounds of human speech, albeit with nasalization, only the human SVT can produce the entire range of vowels and consonants. In nonhuman primates, the size and shape of the SVT is incapable of producing velar stop consonants (like [g] and [k]) and quantal vowels (like [i], [u], and [a]).

An analysis of the base of the australopithecine skull, the **basicranium**, indicates that the unique morphology of modern humans had not yet evolved in these hominids, and by extension the australopithecine SVT was probably more similar in overall structure and function to that of living apes than to modern humans (18–21). While the correlations among basicranial anatomy, laryngeal position, and language capabilities are highly complex and somewhat equivocal (22), it seems reasonable to conclude that australopithecines were probably not capable of speech as we know it, but were limited to the range of vocalizing seen in modern apes (Fig. 5.3).

Second, "gracile" and "robust" australopithecines can generally be distinguished by their differing vascular patterns for draining venous blood from the brain. Although their function is debated, these patterns are believed to have evolved in response to the changing gravitational pressures associated with bipedalism: "gracile" australopithecines (and *Homo*) tend to employ a transverse/sigmoid sinus system in combination with a widely dispersed network of veins that pass within and through the skull bones (the **diploic** and **emissary veins**, respectively) whereas "robust" australo-

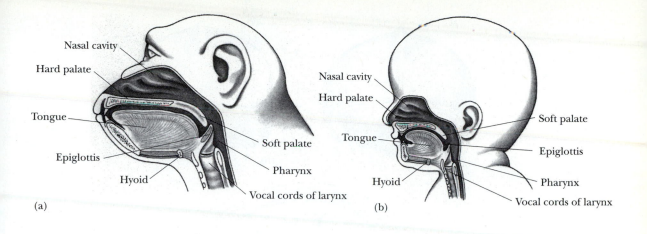

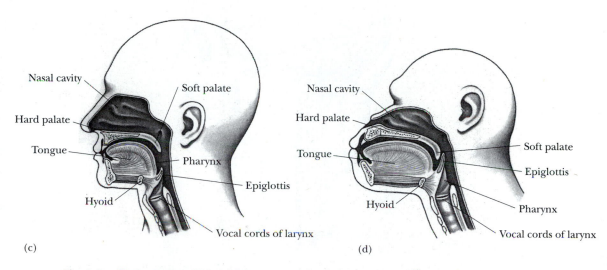

Fig. 5.3. Comparative views of the airway in (a) chimpanzee; (b) human infant; (c) adult human; (d) australopithecine. In the chimpanzee the tongue is situated entirely within the oral cavity, whereas in the adult human its rounded posterior border forms the anterior boundary of the oropharynx. Also note that the larynx (epiglottis) is high in the neck in the chimpanzee, reaching the level of the soft palate. This morphology reduces the amount of space in the airway above the vocal cords, the supralaryngeal vocal tract. In the adult human the larynx is lower in the neck (the epiglottis does not reach the level of the soft palate), thereby increasing the size of the supralaryngeal vocal tract. The human infant and the reconstructed australopithecine appear more like the chimpanzee. From (19,231).

pithecines, as well as the Hadar *A. afarensis* hominids, employ blood channels that are described as the **occipital/marginal venous sinus** system (Fig. 5.4) (23–25).[2]

[2]The true situation is somewhat more complex in that some "robust" australopithecines (e.g., KNM-ER 23000) and some "gracile" australopithecines (e.g., Taung) have both types of vascular patterns (26).

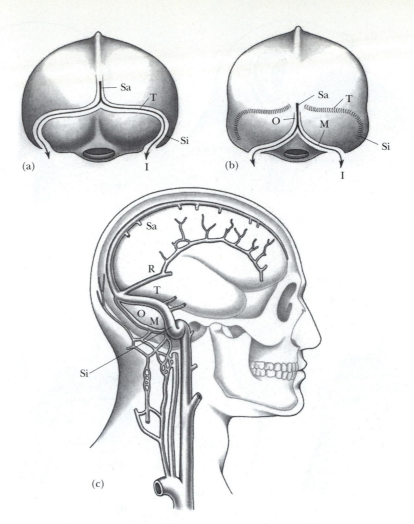

Fig. 5.4. Posterior views of typical cranial venous sinus systems in (a) "gracile" australopithecines and modern humans and (b) "robust" australopithecines and the Hadar hominids. In (a), blood flows from the superior sagittal sinus (Sa) to the transverse (T)-sigmoid (Si) sinuses and then exits the cranium via the internal jugular veins (I). In (b) this transverse-sigmoid system is reduced or missing. Instead, a large portion of blood is drained through the occipital (O)/marginal (M) sinus system to the vertebral plexus of veins that are near the foramen magnum. The O/M sinus can also deliver blood to the internal jugular vein depending on postural and respiratory constraints. (c) Venous sinuses and emissary veins. R, rectus or straight sinus. Emissary veins traverse the skull and communicate with the vertebral plexus of veins around the foramen magnum. From (23,27).

Why such different cranial vascular patterns characterize "gracile" and "robust" australopithecines is not intuitively obvious, but one intriguing theory is that the venous network pattern that ultimately emerged in "gracile" australopithecines, and *Homo*, acted as a radiator to help cool the heat-sensitive brain. This theory is based on the observation that under conditions of heat stress, or hyperthermia, in modern humans, cooler blood in

Taxon	n	Mean (cm³)	95% Population Limits (to nearest cm³)
A. afarensis	3	?413.5	352 – ?500
A. africanus	6	440.3	383 – 499
A. robustus	1	530.0	—
A. boisei	7	463.3	332 – 595
H. habilis	6	640.2	429 – 852
H. erectus erectus	7	895.6	667 – 1125
H. erectus pekinensis	5	1043.0	731 – 1355
H. erectus (Asia and Africa)	15	937.2	647 – 1228
H. sapiens soloensis	5	1151.4	896 – 1407

Fig. 5.5. Endocranial capacity estimates for various early hominid species. $n=$ sample size. There is a 95 percent chance that the "true" endocranial mean value of each species falls within the interval denoted by the 95 percent population limits. From (103).

the scalp flows inward through the skull and toward the brain by way of tiny emissary and diploic veins. A corollary to this theory, then, is that the "gracile" vascular pattern of brain cooling released a thermal constraint in *Homo* that had previously kept brain size in check in earlier hominids (Fig. 5.5) (27,28). Certainly the dense concentration of sweat glands in the face and scalp leaves little doubt that the head continues to function as a specialized evaporative cooling and heat-dissipating structure (29,30). These and other thermoregulatory cooling mechanisms must have been critical to the emerging bipedal hominids, who remain the only mammal capable of sustained running, with the possible exception of the modern horse.[3]

Now that we have considered some of the more general aspects of australopithecine morphology, we will examine each of the species in some detail.

CRANIODENTAL AND POSTCRANIAL CHARACTERISTICS

A. ramidus

As mentioned in the previous chapter, the single most important discovery of an early Pliocene fossil hominid comprises dental, cranial, and postcranial elements of a new australopithecine species, *A. ramidus*, from Aramis,

[3]Modern hunter-gatherers like the Kalahari Bushmen and the Tarahumara of Mexico have been known to pursue animals for hours, even days.

Ethiopia.[4] These fossils derive from a thin stratigraphic interval immediately above the Gaala Vitric Tuff Complex (GVTC) dated by Ar-Ar to approximately 4.4 mya (32,33) (see Fig. 4.11b). The antiquity and primitive morphology of the specimens suggest that *A. ramidus* may represent the potential root species of all later hominids. The specimens include most of the teeth of one individual, several associated postcranial elements, two partial cranial bases, a child's mandible, and other associated and isolated teeth.

Several of the features that distinguish *A. ramidus* from other australopithecines are the larger upper and lower canines relative to the postcanine teeth; the narrow and obliquely elongated lower first deciduous molar (in fact, the Aramis dm_1 is more similar to that of a chimpanzee than it is to any known hominid); and the thin enamel on both molars and canine teeth (Fig. 5.6). The combination of relatively thin enamel and large canine size, together with the primitive P_3 morphology, suggests a canine/premolar complex morphologically and functionally like the presumed ancestral ape condition. In terms of the size of the molar teeth, the *A. ramidus* sample is significantly smaller than *A. afarensis*, and thus shows no evidence of the postcanine megadontia that characterizes all other australopithecine species.

The cranial material also displays a mosaic of apelike and hominidlike features. For example, the marked pneumatization of the temporal bone that invades the root of the zygomatic bone is quite chimpanzeelike, whereas the shortened basioccipital component of the cranial base is more hominidlike.

Published postcranial remains include portions of all three bones (humerus, radius, ulna) from the left arm of a single individual. These bones are larger than the same bones in some *A. afarenesis* specimens (see below) but smaller than other arm bones attributed to *A. afarensis*. The arm also seems to display a mosaic of hominid–great ape features. Discoveries from the 1994 field season have added a number of new cranial and postcranial specimens to the *A. ramidus* sample, including additional mandibular portions and teeth, humeri, hand and foot bones, and a fragmentary adult skeleton that includes cranial, mandibular, vertebral, and upper and lower limb elements (34). It would be premature to attempt to infer locomotor behavior for this new australopithecine species until these recently discovered lower limb bones have been fully analyzed. However, several derived craniodental features that *A. ramidus* shares with all other hominids—such as the anterior placement of the occipital condyles for articulation with the first cervical, or atlas, vertebra; the anterior placement of the foramen magnum for passage of the spinal cord; and the more incisiform canine, indicating reduced sexual dimorphism—may correlate with bipedality, but that remains to be demonstrated.

[4]White et al. (31) have recently given this taxon a new generic name, *Ardipithecus*.

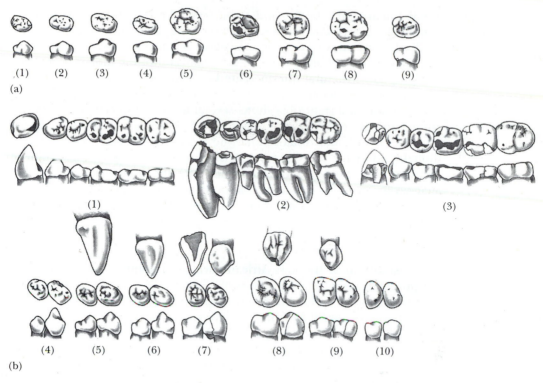

Fig. 5.6. (a) Metric and morphological comparisons of deciduous first molars showing the differences between the dm$_1$ of *A. ramidus* and other early hominid species. 1, *Dryopithecus*; 2, *Pan paniscus* (pygmy chimpanzee); 3, *Pan troglodytes* (chimpanzee); 4, *A. ramidus*; 5, *A. afarensis*; 6, *A. africanus*; 7, *A. robustus*; 8, *A. boisei*; 9, modern *Homo sapiens*. The dm$_1$ of *A. ramidus* is much more like that of chimpanzees, both in terms of size and morphology, and represents a good ancestral morphotype for all later hominid species. (b) Comparisons of upper canine/lower premolar complexes and tooth rows. Top two rows: occlusal and lateral views of (from left to right) the lower canines, premolars, and molars of: 1, *P. troglodytes*; 2, *A. ramidus*; 3, *A. afarensis*. Shaded areas represent dental wear. Bottom three rows, lingual views of upper canines and occlusal and buccal views of lower third and fourth premolars of: 4, *Dryopithecus*; 5, *P. troglodytes* (male); 6, *P. troglodytes* (female); 7, *A. ramidus* (holotype ARA-VP-6/1); 8, *A. afarensis* (LH-3); 9, *A. afarensis* (A.L. 400); 10, *A. afarensis* (A.L. 288-1, "Lucy"). Note absence of upper canines in specimens 4 and 10. From (32).

A. anamensis

The recently named species *A. anamensis* is known from twenty-one cranial, dental, and postcranial specimens recovered from Kanapoi and Allia Bay (East Lake Turkana), Kenya, dated to about 4.2–3.9 mya (35). The species is described as having a mosaic of primitive and derived features suggesting that it may be a possible ancestor to *A. afarensis*. Some of the features by which it differs from other australopithecine species include the nearly parallel mandibular bodies and tooth rows, the long sloping axis of the mandibular symphysis, canines with very long and robust roots, and the small elliptical external earhole or acoustic meatus. In other features, such as enamel thickness and buccolingual expansion of the molars, it appears to be a good structural intermediate between the earlier *A. ramidus* and later *A. afarensis* specimens.

A portion of a right tibia shows several features associated with bipedalism, particularly the size and shape of the proximal articular surfaces for articulation with the distal femur, the relatively straight tibial shaft (although part of the midshaft region is missing), and the configuration of the distal articular facets for articulation with the ankle. Using regression analyses based on human tibia, the body weight of this individual is estimated to be 47–55 kg. A distal humerus from the same site is also human-like.

A. afarensis

The best known of the East African early australopithecine species is *A. afarensis*, well sampled from the period about 4–3 mya. If the Lothagam mandible described in the previous chapter is correctly identified, the species dates back more than 5 mya. *A. afarensis* has been recovered only from sites in East Africa, including Laetoli, Hadar, Maka, and Middle Awash. Fossils that may be of this species have also been found at Omo, Koobi Fora, Fejej, Lothagam, Kanapoi, and Tabarin. At present, however, the 3.6-million-year-old Laetoli sample is the earliest dated large sample of the species.

The craniodental morphology of *A. afarensis* is known from a number of adult and juvenile specimens and, as a whole, seems intermediate between pongids and later hominids (Figs. 4.12a, 5.7) (36–41) (Table 5.1). Much of the postcranial skeleton is also known and reveals an interesting mosaic of humanlike (42–46) and nonhumanlike features (47,48) (Figs. 4.12b,c, 5.8 [pp. 189–90]). The most complete adult skeleton is ''Lucy'' (A.L. 288-1). Dated to about 3.2 mya, the small female was probably no more than 105 cm in height (approximately 3′5″) and about 30 kg in weight. The measure of the length of the humerus divided by the length of the femur multiplied by 100, known as the **humerofemoral index**, is approximately 85 in *A. afarensis*, a value that is higher than in modern humans (about 75). Comparing these two figures gives an intuitive sense of the unique body proportions in *A. afarensis*, which generally had a longer humerus in proportion to its lower limbs than modern humans (49–51). Recently discovered upper limb bones at Hadar also confirm that the *A. afarensis* forearms were relatively long (41). For example, the ulna/humerus index of about 92 percent is much closer to values typical of modern chimpanzees than to those of modern humans. The finger and toe bones also differ from those of modern humans, particularly in their more

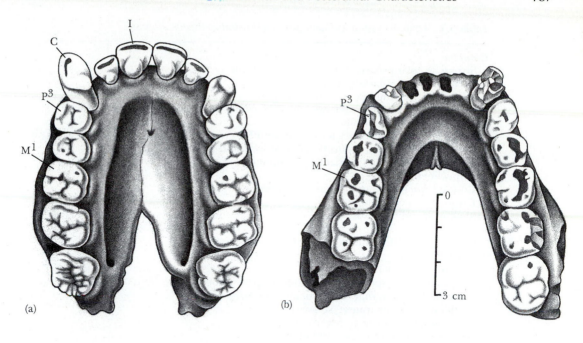

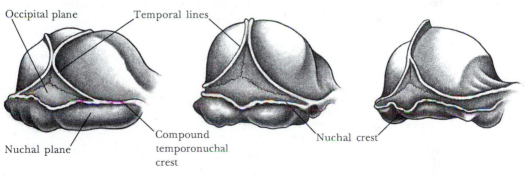

(c)   *A. afarensis*   *A. africanus*   *A. boisei*

Fig. 5.7. Craniodental features of *A. afarensis*. (a) A.L. 200-1a from Hadar; a partial maxilla with a full adult dentition. Note the wide central incisors with worn dentine; the slightly projecting canines with a worn area for honing the lower third premolar; the distinct space, or diastema, between the upper incisor and canine; and the shallow palate with long, narrow, straight-sided dental arcades. (b) The type specimen of *A. afarensis*, the mandible LH 4 from Laetoli. Several features appear to be quite primitive, for example the large dominant cusp on the lower third premolar and the rather parallel-sided tooth rows. (c) Comparison of posterior view of *A. afarensis*, *A. africanus*, and *A. boisei* showing the compound temporonuchal crest, which is absent in all but a few specimens of later australopithecines. From (15,36,232).

Table 5.1   Features Listed as Diagnostic for *Australopithecus afarensis*

Cranium
   Strong alveolar prognathism with convex clivus
   Palate shallow, especially anteriorly
   Dental arcade long, narrow, straight-sided
   Facial skeleton exhibiting large, pillarlike canine juga separated from zygomatic
      processes by deep hollows
   Large zygomatic processes located above P^4/M^1 and oriented at right angles to tooth
      row with inferior margins flared anteriorly and laterally
   Occipital region characterized by compound temporonuchal crest (in larger
      specimens)
   Concave nuchal plane short anteroposteriorly
   Large, flattened mastoids
   Shallow mandibular fossae with weak articular eminences placed only partly under
      braincase
   Occipital condyles with strong ventral angulation
Mandible
   Ascending ramus broad, not high
   Corpus of larger specimens relatively deep anteriorly and hollowed in region of low
      mental foramen that usually opens anterosuperiorly
   Moderate superior transverse torus
   Low rounded inferior transverse torus
   Anterior corpus rounded and bulbous
   Strong posterior angulation of symphyseal axis
   Postcanine teeth aligned in straight rows
   Arcade tends to be subrectangular, smaller mandibles with relatively narrow incisor
      region
Dentition
   Upper central incisors relatively and absolutely large
   Upper central and diminutive lateral incisors with strong lingual basal tubercles
   Upper incisors with flexed roots
   Strong variation in canine size
   Canines asymmetric, lowers with strong lingual ridge, uppers usually with exposed
      dentine strip along distal edge when worn
   P_3 occlusal outline elongate oval in shape with main axis mesiobuccal to distolingual
      at 45–60 degrees to tooth row
   P_3 with dominant mesiodistally elongated buccal cusp and small lingual cusp often
      expressed only as inflated lingual ridge
   Diastemata often present between $I^2/\underline{C}$ and $\overline{C}/P_3$
   $\underline{C}/P^3$ complex not functionally analogous to pongid condition

---

$\underline{C}$ = upper canine; $\overline{C}$ = lower canine.

marked longitudinal curvature (52). The significance of these, and other,
postcranial features will be discussed below in the context of general trends
in the hominids.

   As we noted earlier, there is a great deal of presumed sexual dimorphism in specimens assigned to *A. afarensis*, assuming that all the specimens
are correctly identified as belonging to a single species. The association

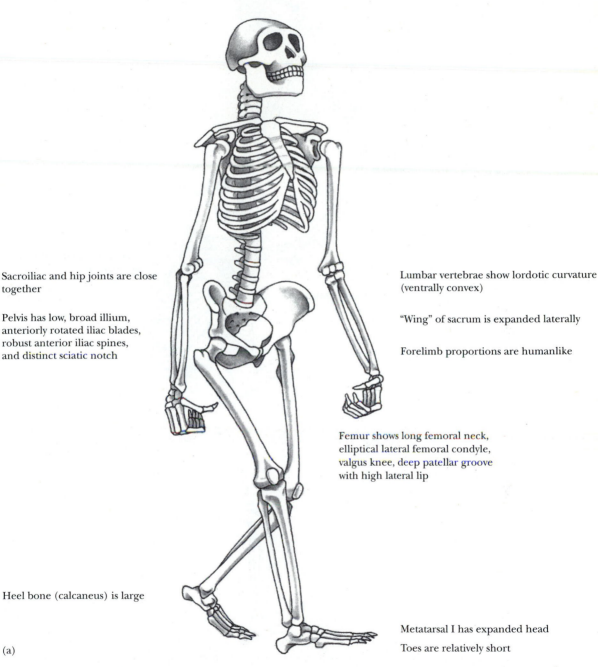

Sacroiliac and hip joints are close together

Pelvis has low, broad illium, anteriorly rotated iliac blades, robust anterior iliac spines, and distinct sciatic notch

Lumbar vertebrae show lordotic curvature (ventrally convex)

"Wing" of sacrum is expanded laterally

Forelimb proportions are humanlike

Femur shows long femoral neck, elliptical lateral femoral condyle, valgus knee, deep patellar groove with high lateral lip

Heel bone (calcaneus) is large

Metatarsal I has expanded head

Toes are relatively short

(a)

Fig. 5.8. (a) Postcranial synapomorphies of *A. afarensis* and *H. sapiens*.

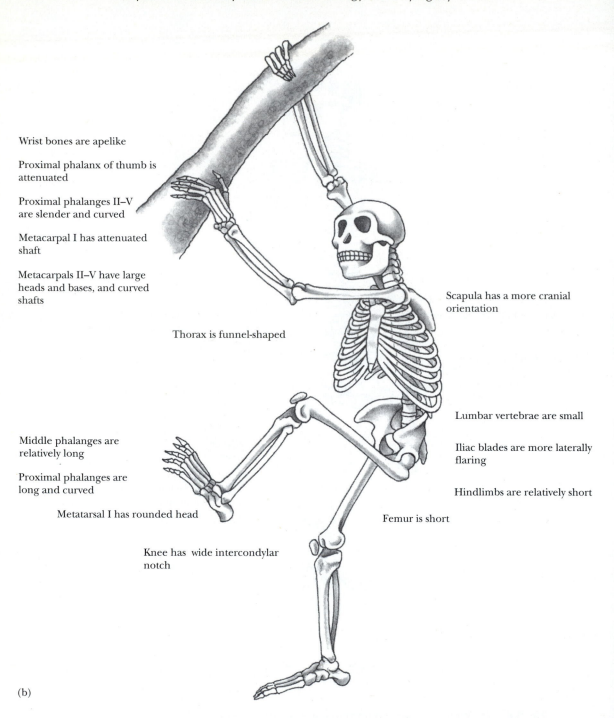

Wrist bones are apelike

Proximal phalanx of thumb is attenuated

Proximal phalanges II–V are slender and curved

Metacarpal I has attenuated shaft

Metacarpals II–V have large heads and bases, and curved shafts

Thorax is funnel-shaped

Scapula has a more cranial orientation

Lumbar vertebrae are small

Iliac blades are more laterally flaring

Hindlimbs are relatively short

Middle phalanges are relatively long

Proximal phalanges are long and curved

Metatarsal I has rounded head

Femur is short

Knee has wide intercondylar notch

(b)

Fig. 5.8.   (b) Primitive postcranial traits of *A. afarensis.* From (48).

between inferred body weight, degree of sexual dimorphism, and primate social systems in living primates has even been used to argue that *A. afarensis* probably did not have a monogamous social structure, but more likely lived in large, kin-related multimale groups with females that were not kin-related, an inference that is tenuous at best (53,54).

A number of important craniodental and postcranial fossils have recently been described from Maka, Ethiopia, that may predate much of the Hadar material (55). Four mandibular specimens and several isolated teeth have been recovered from deposits dated to about 3.4 mya that show certain morphological and metrical resemblances to *A. afarensis* from Hadar and Laetoli, such as large canines and incisors compared to later hominids; asymmetrical third premolars; and a space, or **diastema**, between the canine and P_3.

This site has also yielded several postcranial bones, including a proximal femur, humerus, and proximal ulna. The humerus is large and robust, much more so than the humerus of "Lucy" (A.L. 288-1 from Hadar), and is taken to support the view that *A. afarensis* was a highly sexually dimorphic species. Importantly, the Maka femur (and the tibia attributed to *A. anamensis*; see above) provides the earliest anatomical evidence of upright walking (56).

A. africanus

A. africanus was the first australopithecine ever discovered (57). The species is restricted to the South African sites of Taung, Sterkfontein Members 2 and 4, and Makapansgat Members 3 and 4 (and possibly Gladysvale). The type specimen from Taung consists of the right side of a natural brain endocast, the face, and most of the mandible of an immature "manlike ape." All the deciduous teeth are in place, and the first permanent molars had recently erupted (Fig. 5.9). Based on an analogy with modern children, Raymond Dart originally considered the "Taung child" to be about 6 years old when it died. As we shall see later, this view has been recently challenged (58–61).

Let's consider what made Dart proclaim in 1925 that he had found "an extinct race of apes intermediate between living anthropoids and man." First, there is the long and narrow, or **dolichocephalic**, cranium, which is more humanlike than apelike. Second, there are no browridges, or **supraorbital tori**, as there are in even young apes. Third, the orbital region has a humanlike shape: the orbits are circular in outline, not squarish as in apes, the interorbital distance is very small, and the bones associated with the olfactory apparatus situated between the eyes, the ethmoids, are not inflated laterally as in modern African apes. Fourth, all the other facial bones are delicate structures, and the anterior projection of the face, or facial **prognathism**, is relatively slight.

Even though the specimen was a juvenile, Dart was able to see that the

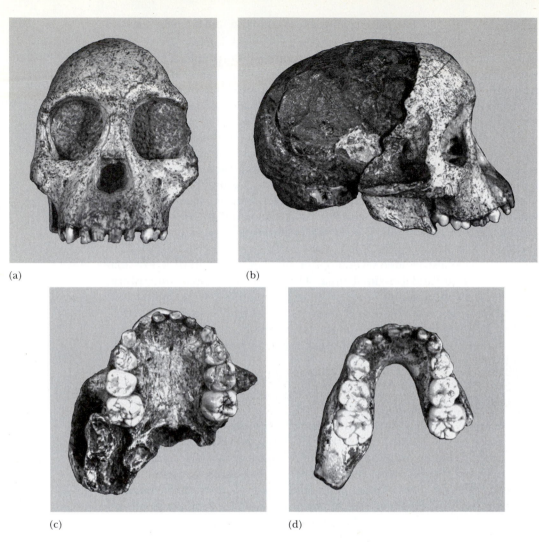

(a)

(b)

(c)

(d)

Fig. 5.9. The Taung child (*A. africanus*). This specimen was the first australopithecine ever discovered. (a) Frontal and (b) lateral views of the skull and brain endocast; (c) upper and (d) lower jaws. Note the long, narrow cranium, the lack of supraorbital tori (browridges), the narrow interorbital distance, the small canines, the parabolic dental arch, and the lack of a simian shelf (scale about 60 percent natural size). (Photos by G. Conroy.)

dentition and mandible were distinctly humanlike. He pointed in particular to the small canines and the absence of diastemata between the lower canines and premolars; the parabolic shape of the **dental arch**; and the lack of the so-called **simian shelf** at the back of the mandible's midline (see Fig. 5.9).

Dart also remarked on the relatively forward position of the foramen magnum, which to him indicated the "poise of the skull upon the vertebral column," and "the assumption by this fossil group of an attitude appreciably more erect than that of modern anthropoids." This more vertical posture suggested to him that the hands were freed from their primitive function as accessory organs of locomotion and were becoming better adapted as organs of manipulation and tool-using.

Finally, Dart pointed to some unusual features of the surface of the brain as revealed by the endocranial cast. An **endocranial cast** is produced in a fossilized skull when the inside of the braincase fills with sediment that hardens, thereby forming a replica, or cast, of the inner surfaces of the cranial bones. The brain size of the diminutive Taung creature equalled or exceeded that of gorillas many times its overall body size. Other features of the endocast suggested neuronal reorganization. For example, the ratio of cerebral to cerebellar matter is greater than in gorillas and the **association areas** of the parietal and temporal lobes, the regions of the cerebral cortex involved with complex functions of comprehension, communication, and consciousness, seemed to be enlarged compared to pongids (Fig. 5.10). The significance of the enlargement of these so-called association areas in the Taung specimen has become the subject of a vigorous debate in the recent literature (62–67). However, one thing is clear: the overall shape of the brain and the configuration of the grooves on the side of the brain, or **sulcal patterns**, on the Taung endocast are apelike, not human-like, particularly in the frontal and temporal lobe regions (68).

Further discoveries over the years of adult australopithecine cranial, dental, and postcranial remains, particularly at Sterkfontein and Makapansgat (Fig. 5.11), completely vindicated Dart's original claims for *Australopithecus*. It became evident from these later discoveries that *A. africanus* had reduced canines, walked bipedally, made stone tools, and had a large brain relative to body size.

A. robustus

Only 13 years after Raymond Dart's publication of the Taung child in 1925, Robert Broom announced the discovery of a much more robust australopithecine from Kromdraai, South Africa (69). This specimen became the type of a new genus and species of australopithecine that Broom named *Paranthropus robustus*. Since 1948 the other site in South Africa that has proven to be an exceptionally rich source of *A. robustus* specimens is Swartkrans. As we noted in the previous chapter, hominids were first discovered there in 1948.

"Robust" australopithecines are also known from a number of sites in East Africa (Omo, Koobi Fora, East and West Lake Turkana, Olduvai, Peninj, and Chesowanja) dating to 2.6–1.0 mya (see Fig. 4.1) (26,70). The "robust" australopithecines from East Africa are usually put in the species *A. boisei* (or *A. aethiopicus*). Only the South African "robust" australopithecines from Kromdraai, Swartkrans, and Drimolen are currently allocated to the species *A. robustus*. As the name implies, the major distinction between *A. africanus* and *A. robustus* is one of greater size and overall robust-

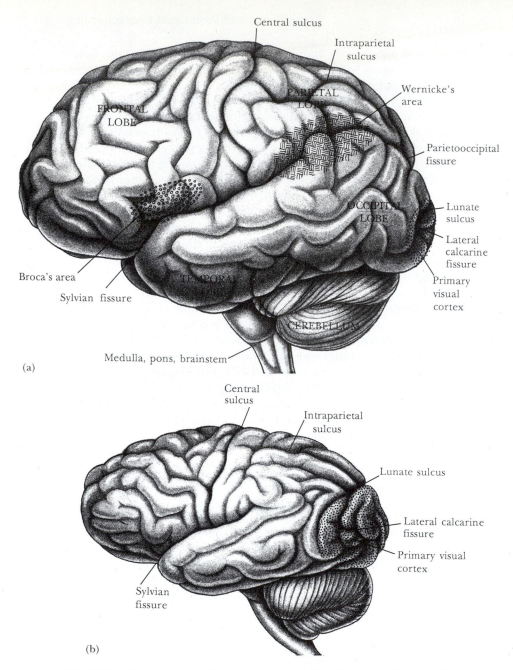

Fig. 5.10. Comparison of the (a) human and (b) chimpanzee brains. The lunate sulcus divides the primary visual cortex posteriorly from the association areas of the parietal and temporal lobes. Note that expansion of the association areas has resulted in a more posterior displacement of the lunate sulcus in the human brain. Two very important association areas in the human brain involved with speech comprehension and production are labelled Wernicke's area and Broca's area respectively. From R. Holloway in (233).

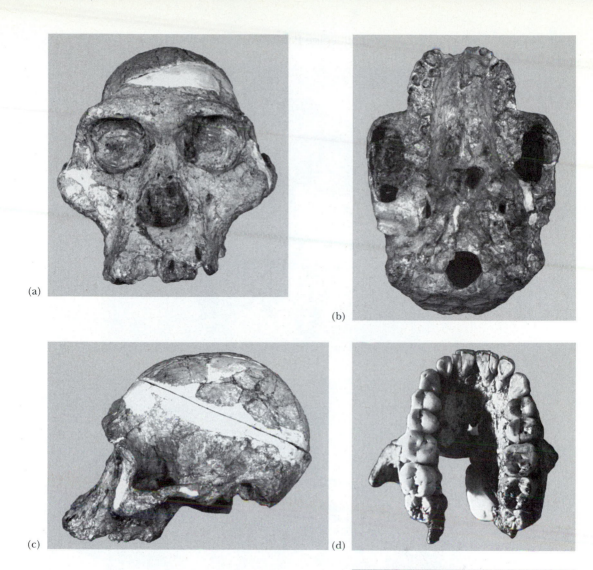

(a)

(b)

(c)

(d)

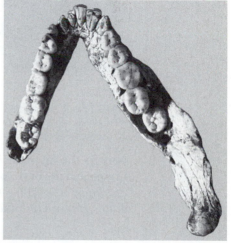

(e)

Fig. 5.11. Craniodental remains of adult *A. africanus* specimens from Sterkfontein. (a) Frontal, (b) basal, (c) lateral view of Sts 5 (''Mrs. Ples''); (d) upper and (e) lower jaws of Sts 52 (scale about 60 percent natural size). (Photos by G. Conroy.)

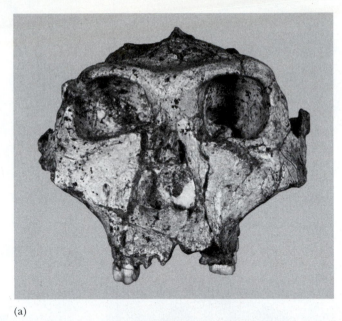

(a)

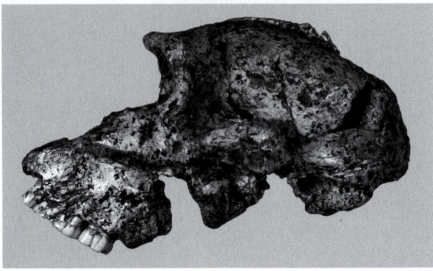

(b)

Fig. 5.12.   Craniodental remains of adult *A. robustus* from Swartkrans.   (a) Frontal view of SK 48; (b) lateral view of SK 46; (c) upper jaw of SK 13; (d) lower jaw of SK 12 (scale approximately 60 percent of natural size). (Photos by G. Conroy.)

ness in the craniofacial and dental features of the latter. While average brain capacity of *A. robustus* (about 530 cc) is slightly larger than that of *A. africanus*, it is still relatively small compared with later hominids of the genus *Homo*. The brain is housed in a skull that is more massive than that

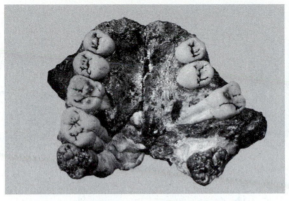

(c)

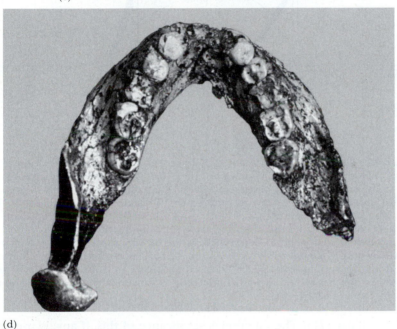

(d)

of *A. africanus* but less so than that of *A. boisei*. The cranial vault is thin-walled and normally has well-developed sagittal and nuchal crests (see Fig. 5.7c). The facial skeleton is hafted onto the roof of the skull, the **calvaria**, at a relatively low level; that is, the forehead rises only slightly above the upper margins of the orbit. The browridges are well developed, and the face is broad with prominent anterior pillars to withstand large chewing stresses passing through the face (Figs. 5.12, 5.13). Both *A. africanus* and *A. robustus* have a long external ear canal, the **external auditory meatus**, which contrasts with the short meatus found in modern humans. However, while *A. robustus* has a more conical meatus, the meatus in *A. africanus* is

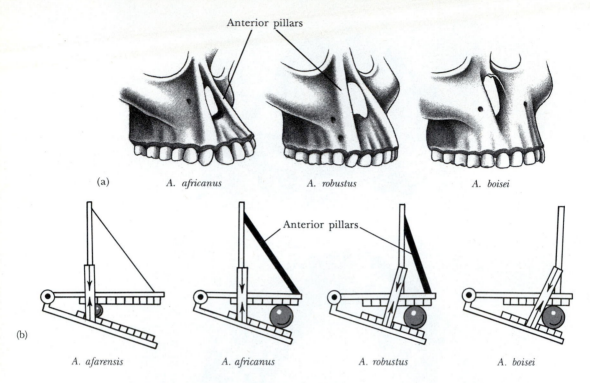

Fig. 5.13.   Facial buttressing in australopithecines.   (a) Three-quarter view of the facial region in *A. africanus*, *A. robustus*, and *A. boisei*. Note the increased extent of the bony buttressing along the lateral side of the nasal cavity; in both *A. africanus* and *A. robustus* this buttressing takes the form of distinct anterior pillars. (b) The mechanical forces requiring facial buttressing. The vertical columns represent the infraorbital region, and the opposing arrows the contracting masseter muscle. As the occlusal load of food to be crushed by the molars, represented by the circle, increases and is extended forward from the infraorbital region, additional buttressing in the form of anterior pillars becomes necessary. In *A. boisei* the whole infraorbital region has moved forward sufficiently to functionally replace the anterior pillars. From (15,226).

more tubular (71). The functional significance of this, if any, is presently unknown.

The dentition is a very distinctive feature of the "robust" australopithecine lineage: the incisors are relatively small, while the premolars and molars are large, crushing and grinding teeth with thick enamel and flat surfaces (8,61,72). The canines tend to be functionally incorporated into the incisor row, and thus are not the kind of projecting, pointed, stabbing teeth found in so many other primates (Fig. 5.14). The high incidence of anterior dental crowding, particularly in the Swartkrans *A. robustus* sample, strongly supports the notion that anterior tooth reduction in "robust" australopithecines was spurred on by posterior tooth expansion and that canine reduction may be related to the need to expand the cheek teeth within

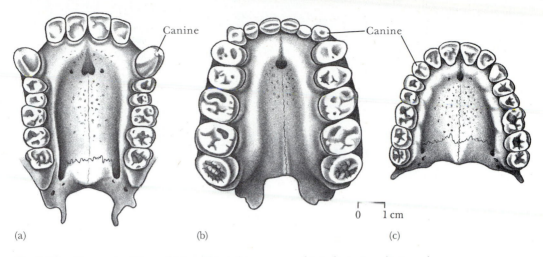

Fig. 5.14. Upper dentition of (a) modern chimpanzee, (b) *A. boisei*, and (c) modern *H. sapiens*. Note the relative size differences between anterior and posterior teeth in *A. boisei* compared with those of the other genera.

given limits of jaw size (73). As one might expect, the mandibles are also large and robust because they house these large teeth; serve as sites of attachment for the powerful chewing muscles; and withstand the large chewing stresses generated during mastication of tough, fibrous vegetation. Both qualitative and quantitative studies show that the "gracile" australopithecine dentition is better adapted to diets consisting primarily of leaves and/or fleshy fruits whereas the "robust" australopithecine dentition is better adapted to a diet consisting of hard food items like seeds and nuts (74,75).

This last dietary conclusion has been tempered somewhat by new evidence from both strontium/calcium (Sr/Ca) ratios and stable carbon isotope studies of *A. robustus* teeth from Swartkrans. In theory, Sr/Ca ratios are lower in carnivores than in folivores (Fig. 5.15). This is because vertebrate digestive systems discriminate against strontium in favor of calcium such that Sr/Ca ratios in vertebrate tissues, including bone, are lower than Sr/Ca ratios in the food eaten by vertebrates. For example, herbivores have lower Sr/Ca ratios than the plants they eat and carnivores have lower ratios than the meat they eat, and these differences are preserved in the Sr/Ca ratio of their bones. When applied to humans, the Sr/Ca ratio is assumed to reflect inversely the contribution of meat to the diet. Recent data suggest that the *A. robustus* diet may have been more omnivorous than previously supposed and probably included both animal matter and fibrous vegetation. By comparison, the elevated Sr/Ca levels found in early *Homo* samples from Swartkrans suggest that its ecological niche may have included intensive exploitation of underground plant resources, since roots and rhizomes have higher Sr/Ca levels than leaves from the same plants (76–80).

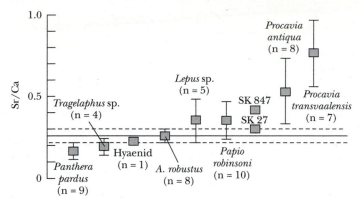

Fig. 5.15. Mean Sr/Ca + 1 S.D. for *A. robustus* (SK 27) and *Homo* sp. (SK 847) from Swartkrans Member 1.   *Panthera* = leopard; *Tragelaphus* = kudu; *Lepus* = hare; *Papio* =baboon; *Procavia* = hyrax. Note general trend of higher Sr/Ca ratios from left to right as one goes from more carnivorous (leopard) to more folivorous (hyrax) mammals, and the higher ratio in the *Homo* sp. specimens compared to the *A. robustus* sample. From (79).

One other intriguing possibility exists, however: the differences in Sr/Ca ratios between *A. robustus* and early *Homo* (SK 847) at Swartkrans may reflect physiological differences between males and females, and not necessarily differences in diet. Sr/Ca ratios are typically higher in females than in males because calcium is reduced in bones of pregnant or lactating females. According to this interpretation, SK 847, a specimen often referred to as early *Homo*, may in fact be a female of the same species represented by specimens with low Sr/Ca ratios usually identified as *A. robustus* (81). In this regard we should note that part of the cranium of SK 847 was initially described as *A. robustus* before it was fitted to cranial fragments that had been earlier attributed to early *Homo* (82).

Remains of the pelvis, ankle bone (talus), and metatarsal of the first toe, or **hallux**, are more humanlike than apelike, indicating that "robust" australopithecines were bipedal, although not identical to modern humans in their bipedalism (83,84). Recent studies on hand bones from Swartkrans suggest that *A. robustus* was capable of using and making stone tools (see below) (85–87).

Features such as stature, body weight, and body proportions are very poorly known. Reasonable estimates of stature and body weight are about 110–132 cm and 32–40 kg, respectively (14).

A. boisei

The hyperrobust hominid *A. boisei* is well-known from several East African Plio-Pleistocene sites, including Olduvai Gorge (from which the type specimen was found), eastern Lake Turkana (Koobi Fora Formation), Omo Basin, and west of Lake Turkana (see Fig. 4.1). These specimens are dated to about 2.5–1.0 mya. The earliest representatives of East African ''robusts'' from Omo and West Turkana are believed by some to represent a distinct species, *A. aethiopicus.*

By most appearances, *A. boisei* represents a more robust extreme than *A. robustus* (Fig. 4.15). The skull is the most robust of any australopithecine and is characterized by accentuated sagittal and nuchal crests. Pneumatization of the skull is more extensive than in *A. africanus* or *A. robustus,* browridges are well developed, the forehead is low or absent, and the face is very long and flat. The jaws and postcanine teeth are extremely large, as are the parts of the skull where the chewing muscles attach, for example, the zygomatic arches for the attachment of the masseter muscles, and the lateral pterygoid plates (see Fig. 3.3) for the attachment of the medial and lateral pterygoid muscles.

Clearly, selection pressures favored increased tooth-chewing areas for both *A. robustus* and *A. boisei,* since in both species molars and premolars are much larger compared with incisors and canines; the differential is greatest in *A. boisei* (Fig. 5.14). Variations in skull and dental size in specimens attributed to *A. boisei* suggest that the species was markedly sexually dimorphic in body size, with males averaging 49 kg and females 34 kg (see Fig. 4.2).

Probably the most spectacular *A. boisei* fossil ever found in terms of overall robustness is the recently discovered specimen (WT 17000) from West Lake Turkana (88) (Fig. 5.16). At 2.5 million years old, it is the oldest

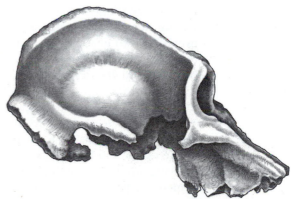

Fig. 5.16. Front and side views of hyperrobust skull of *A. boisei* (WT 17000) from deposits west of Lake Turkana dated to about 2.5 mya.   Some researchers consider it to be a distinct species, *A. aethiopicus.* Note the prognathic face, large sagittal crest, low, flat forehead, and small brain size (about 410 cc). (Photo courtesy of A. Walker and National Museums of Kenya.)

representative of *A. boisei* yet known, although as noted above, it is sometimes classified as a distinct species, *A. aethiopicus*.

This specimen reveals a tremendous amount of information. The skull of this species includes a very flat and shallow palate and a premaxilla showing pronounced subnasal prognathism. The small size of the braincase, combined with the development of enormous chewing muscles (particularly the posterior fibers of the temporalis muscle), has produced a compound temporonuchal crest and a large sagittal crest. Like all "robust" skulls, the forehead is rather low and flat, and pneumatization of the cranial bones is extensive, particularly in the lateral portions of the cranial base. Later in this chapter, we will examine the phylogenetic implications of this important specimen.

A. boisei is currently represented primarily by craniodental specimens. A few isolated limb bones (partial humerus, femur, tibia) have been attributed to *A. boisei*; however, it is difficult to assign postcranial material to this species with any certainty since skeletal parts have not been recovered in direct association with any teeth or crania attributed to *A. boisei*.

COMPARISON OF "GRACILE" AND "ROBUST" AUSTRALOPITHECINES

What if anything distinguishes "gracile" from "robust" australopithecines? Do they represent two distinct lineages, one, *A. africanus*, ancestral to *Homo* and the other, *A. robustus*, doomed to extinction? Are they part of one evolving "robust" australopithecine lineage (*A. africanus–A. robustus–A. boisei*), or are they simply size variants of the same animal? To put these phylogenetic issues into perspective for their examination later in the chapter, we need a clear understanding of the morphological differences between the two groups. The person most responsible for emphasizing distinctions between them, and for relating these distinctions to inferred behavior and ecology, was the Transvaal Museum's John T. Robinson (89–91).

Robinson pointed out that in "robust" australopithecines, the relatively small anterior teeth (incisors and canines) are set in a flattish, or **orthognathous** face, whereas the massive postcanine teeth are set in dense bone of the upper and lower jaws. It is obvious that this animal generated large chewing stresses through the skull via these enormous teeth. This is confirmed by the thickened bone in several areas where these forces would have been dissipated throughout the skull: the robust zygomatic process, the anteriorly thickened palate, and (in *A. robustus*, at least) the robust anterior pillars (15,92,93) (see Fig. 5.13).

The large masticatory muscles also left their mark on skull architecture. The presence of a sagittal crest on most "robust" skulls indicates the large size of the temporalis muscle in relation to the overall size of the braincase. The strong development of the lateral pterygoid plates for attachment of the lateral and medial pterygoid muscles, and the zygomatic arch for attachment of the masseter muscle, also indicates the hypertrophy of these chewing muscles. The combination of large, strongly flaring zygomatic arches with relatively small anterior dentitions gives most of these robust forms a flattish, even dished, facial appearance. The absence of a true forehead, the great postorbital constriction to accommodate a large temporalis muscle, the sagittal crest, and the large browridges combine to give this form a skull shape unique among hominids. Muscle markings indicate that the neck muscles were also powerful. Their size undoubtedly contributes to the fact that in posterior view the broadest part of the skull is low down across the mastoid region.

There are other unique features of the "robust" australopithecine skull that relate to powerful masticatory stresses. In both juvenile and adult *A. boisei* specimens there is an extraordinary degree of overlap along the edges of the temporal and parietal bones at the squamosal suture (see Fig. 3.3b). This overlap is a bony adaptation to offset the forces produced by the combined effect of the massive temporalis muscle acting from a relatively anterior location and the masseter muscle acting from a relatively lateral location. The excessive pressure created along the squamosal suture by this unique masticatory system would otherwise loosen the contact between the temporal and parietal bones (94).

In Robinson's model, the total morphological pattern of "gracile" australopithecines is very different from that of "robust" australopithecines. In the "gracile" form the anterior teeth are relatively larger, the postcanine teeth relatively smaller, the face more prognathous, and the cranial vault higher than in the "robust" form. This implies relatively lower chewing stresses in the "gracile" species, since the great ruggedness of the bones, including sagittal cresting, is for the most part absent (see Fig. 5.2). It is interesting to note that even though the overall appearance of the skull in both forms is of a rather rugged creature, the actual skull bones themselves are quite thin.

To Robinson these craniodental differences reflected considerable differences in diet and behavior between the two groups. The larger anterior teeth in the "gracile" forms were seen as an adaptation to diets that included meat-eating, whereas the emphasis on the postcanine dentition in the "robust" forms was seen as an adaptation to tough vegetarian diets utilizing roots, tubers, and bulbs. Robinson considered *A. africanus* so humanlike in both morphology and implied hunting behaviors that he eventually reclassified it as *Homo africanus*. Robinson's insights have been reinforced by other studies; for example, a recent analysis of incisor microwear indicated that *A. africanus* used its incisors to process a greater variety of foods, including larger, more abrasive items, than *A. robustus* (95).

Many of these craniodental distinctions between "gracile" and "robust" australopithecines are summarized in Table 5.2.

Table 5.2 Differences Between Southern African "Gracile" (Sterkfontein) and "Robust" (Swartkrans) Australopithecines

	"Gracile"	"Robust"
Cranial		
Overall shape	Narrow, with "unmistakable" forehead; higher value for supraorbital height index	Broad across the ears; lacking a forehead; low supraorbital height index
Sagittal crest	Normally absent	Normally present
Face	Weak supraorbital torus; variable degree of prognathism, sometimes as little as "robust" form	Supraorbital torus well developed medially to form a flattened "platform" at glabella; face flat and broad, with little prognathism
Floor of nasal cavity	More marked transition from the facial surface of the maxilla into the floor of the nasal cavity; sloping posterior border to the anterior nasal spine and lower insertion of the vomer	Smooth transition from facial surface of maxilla into the floor of the nasal cavity; small anterior nasal spine that articulates at its tip with the vomer
Shape of dental arcade and palate	Rounded anteriorly and even in depth	Straight line between canines, deeper posteriorly
Pterygoid region	Slender lateral pterygoid plate	Robust lateral pterygoid plate
Dental		
Relative size of teeth	Anterior and posterior teeth in "proportion"	Anterior teeth proportionally small; posterior teeth proportionally large
dm_1	Small, with relatively larger mesial cusps; Lingually situated anterior fovea; large protoconid with long, sloping buccal surface	Larger, molariform, with deeply incised buccal groove and relatively large distal cusps
P^3 roots	Single buccal root	Double buccal root
Upper canine	Large, robust, and symmetrical crown with slender marginal ridges and parallel lingual grooves	Small, *Homo*-like, with thick marginal ridges and lingual grooves converging on the gingival eminence
Lower canine	Asymmetric crown with marked cusplet on the distal marginal ridge and marked central ridge on the lingual surface	More symmetric crown with parallel lingual grooves, weak lingual ridge and featureless distal enamel ridge

BODY SIZE AND BRAIN SIZE

Early hominid body size assumes great importance in paleoanthropological research because of its relationship to a number of important life-history parameters, including brain size, feeding behavior, habitat preferences, and social behavior. How do paleoanthropologists determine australopithecine body size? One statistical method used by researchers is regression analysis, which compares some osteological variable to body weight in modern animals to see how good a body-weight predictor that variable might be when applied to the fossil record. Since in bipedal animals the body weight must be transmitted through the vertebral column, a good test might measure the cross-sectional area of several vertebrae as a predictor of body weight. Using a formula relating vertebral cross-sectional area to body weight in modern humans, the body weights of *A. africanus* and *A. robustus* were estimated to range from 28 to 43 kg and from 36 to 53 kg, respectively (96,97). Different techniques give different results and body-weight estimates have ranged from 30 to 80 kg for *A. afarensis*; 33 to 67 kg for *A. africanus*; 37 to 88 kg for *A. robustus*; and 33 to 88 kg for *A. boisei* (13,98,99). The most recent estimates based on hindlimb joint size are given in Figure 4.2; estimates of height can be determined using similar principles (14,100,101).

If these body weight estimates are reasonable, then encephalization quotients (EQs) can be calculated for early hominids in exactly the same way as they are for nonhuman primates (102,103). Relative brain size calculations are presented in Figures 4.2 and 5.1.

What can we conclude from these EQ data? An obvious difference between modern humans and apes is the relative and absolute size of the brain. In absolute terms, *Homo sapiens* has a cranial capacity about three times that of great apes. However, the EQ values reveal that modern humans have a brain size nearly six to seven times that expected of a similar-sized mammal living today, whereas australopithecines and chimpanzees have a brain size only about two to three times that expected of a similar-sized mammal.

However, it is quite clear from the fossil record that brain expansion per se was not an early trend in human evolution, since brain size in some of the oldest australopithecines, such as *A. afarensis*, was well within the range of extant apes (both in absolute and relative terms). In this regard it is interesting to note that the pelvis of *A. afarensis* has a birth canal whose size and shape show little or no adaptations for passage of an enlarged fetal cranium, adaptations that so clearly dominate the form of the modern human pelvis (see below) (104–106). As we shall see in later chapters when we discuss the evolution of the genus *Homo*, it appears that marked expansion of the human brain took place only within the last 1–2 million years of human evolution (see Fig. 5.5).

BIPEDAL LOCOMOTION: MORPHOLOGY AND BIOMECHANICAL PRINCIPLES

It is self-evident that at some early stage in human evolution a highly unique form of bipedal locomotion evolved from some quadrupedal form of locomotion. The exact type of locomotion employed by the quadrupedal ancestor is still open to debate. Was it like the knuckle-walking of the African ape or the fist-walking of the orangutan, or was it more upright, like that of the gibbon? Or was it something altogether different (107–109)? No matter what type of quadrupedalism was practiced by these "prehominids," it is important to understand what morphological changes were necessary to change a quadruped into a biped (Fig. 5.17).

As we have suggested, the fossil evidence reveals significant postcranial adaptations to bipedalism very early in human evolution, by at least 4.0 to 3.5 mya, and this conclusion receives unequivocal support from the fossilized hominid footprints discovered at Laetoli (110–113) (see Box 5.1 and Fig. 4.14).

In this section we will consider some of the basic biomechanical principles of bipedal locomotion and examine the morphological evidence for bipedalism in australopithecines; in the following section we will consider some of the behavioral pressures that may have contributed to the evolution of this unique mode of locomotion in our ancestors.

There are a number of basic requirements for effective and efficient bipedal posture and locomotion, two of the most important being:
• the body's center of gravity must be lower than it is in quadrupeds and balanced above the points of contact of the feet on the ground not only while standing but also during the "single support phase," that portion of the stride when only one limb is supporting the body
• the lower limb must be able to move quickly through a relatively wide arc to provide propulsive force to the stride

We will shortly see that such adaptations were already underway in the Pliocene.

The ability of humans to maintain trunk balance derives in large part from the large muscles of the vertebral column, the erector spinae group, the abdominal muscles, external and internal obliques, and the muscles of the gluteal region, particularly the glutei medius and minimus. It is important to note that all these muscles attach to the pelvis, specifically to the

Fig. 5.17. A number of anatomical changes are associated with bipedal walking and can be seen when comparing the human skeleton to that of apes. 1) The head is more balanced on the vertebral column and the foramen magnum through which the spinal cord connects with the brain is shifted forward. Because the head is better balanced, there is less need for massive neck muscles to keep it in position. 2) Humans have developed a more barrel-shaped ribcage and 3) secondary curves of the cervical and lumbar vertebral column. 4) The pelvis has become rearranged so that the distance between the sacroiliac joint and the hip joint has been reduced and the iliac blades run in a more sagittal direction. 5) The legs are longer than the arms and constitute a greater proportion of body weight, thus lowering the center of gravity. Numbers indicate percentage of total body weight represented by each postcranial body segment. 6) The knee is brought medially well under the body and closer to the line of action of the body weight. 7) The big toe (hallux) is not opposed to the other toes, so the foot has lost its grasping function. From (234).

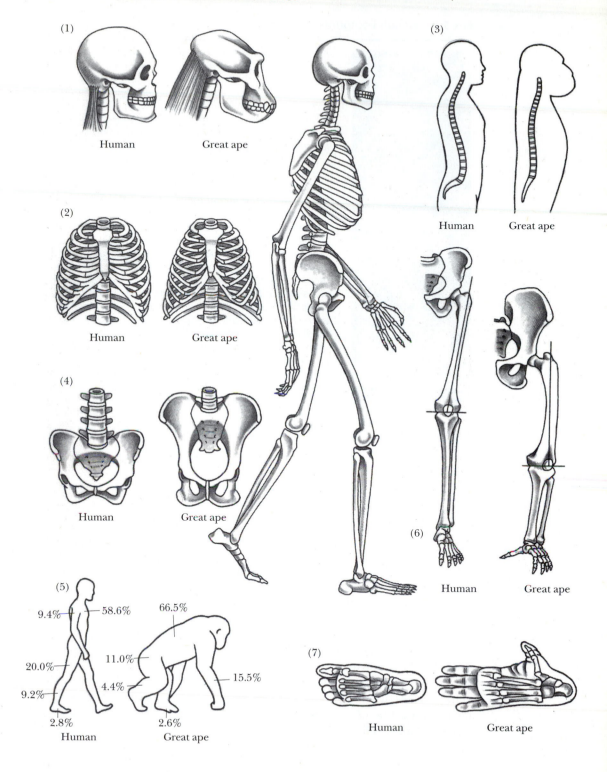

(1) Human   Great ape

(2) Human   Great ape

(3) Human   Great ape

(4) Human   Great ape

(5)
9.4%   58.6%   66.5%
20.0%   11.0%
4.4%   15.5%
9.2%
2.8%   2.6%
Human   Great ape

(6) Human   Great ape

(7) Human   Great ape

Box 5.1.   Laetoli Footprints

From 1977 to 1979 at Laetoli, Tanzania, a team led by Mary Leakey uncovered the trails of four bipedal individuals that had been made in volcanic ashfalls about 3.6 mya. At site G there are two trails representing three individuals. A fourth individual was represented at site A, about 1.5 km from site G. While there is little doubt that the G trails were made by bipedal hominids, there is some question of whether trail A was made by a bear or some other animal. Remarkably, the feet that made the G trail seem indistinguishable from those of modern humans: The great toe, or hallux, was adducted, or aligned with, the lateral toes and left a deep impression in the ash that is typical of the final toeing-off prior to the swing phase seen in human bipedal walking; the four lateral toes were not particularly long and did not project beyond the level of the hallux; the foot was not "flat-footed" as in quadrupedal primates, indicating that a medial longitudinal arch was present. The foot impressions also indicate that the transfer of weight during the stride was fully humanlike in that weight was initially borne by the heel and lateral sole of the foot, then shifted medially onto the ball and hallux before toe-off. Interestingly, it is difficult to reconcile the long, curved pedal phalanges evident in the A. afarensis *foot bones from Hadar with the footprints found at Laetoli (unfortunately, no foot bones have yet been found at Laetoli). Based on comparisons of foot size and height in modern humans, the individual designated as G-1 was probably between 3'8" and 4'4" tall, individual G-3 was probably between 4'4" and 4'11" tall, and the individual from site A was between 2'11" and 3'6" tall.*

iliac blades (Fig. 5.18). If one were to take an imaginary cross section through the pelvis, the resulting picture would look something like a steering wheel and column, the column being the vertebral column at the center and the steering wheel being the iliac blades at the periphery. If the hip bones are twisted like a steering wheel, the vertebral column rotates along its axis as well.

A wheel-and-axle is a simple machine, in a class with levers, pulleys, and inclined planes. The gluteal and abdominal muscles act on the wheel (the ilium) and the erector spinae group acts directly on the axle (the vertebral column). From simple physics it is known that the leverage of the forces acting on the wheel (gluteal and abdominal muscles) will be greater the farther their line of force is from the center of rotation (the axle, or vertebral column). Thus a clear adaptation to improved stability in both lateral

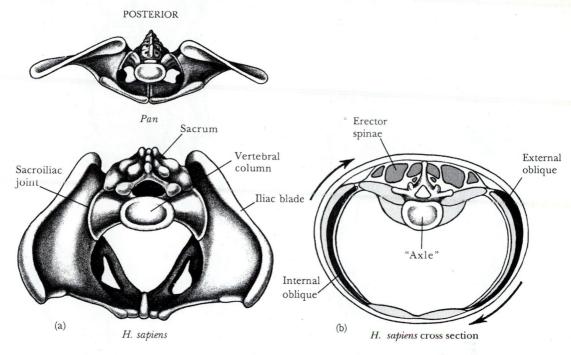

POSTERIOR

Pan

Sacrum

Vertebral
column

Sacroiliac
joint

Iliac blade

(a)

H. sapiens

Erector
spinae

External
oblique

"Axle"

Internal
oblique

(b)

H. sapiens cross section

Fig. 5.18. Wheel-and-axle design of the pelvic region in hominids.   (a) Overhead view of chimpanzee and human pelves. In chimpanzees the external surfaces of the ilia face dorsally (backward), whereas in modern humans they face laterally and "wrap around" the vertebral column, resulting in a more wheellike morphology for muscle attachment. (b) Cross section of the human trunk shown at about the first lumbar vertebra. The force of the erector spinae is applied directly to the vertebral column ("axle"), and the force of the oblique abdominal muscles is applied to the ilia ("wheel").

and front-to-back directions is to "wrap" the ilium around the vertebral column at an ever increasing distance.

If we compare the pelvis of modern hominids and pongids, this is exactly what we see (Fig. 5.19). The pongid ilium is rather long and narrow, and the iliac blades flare out to the sides so that their flat inner surfaces face almost directly forward. Hominids, on the other hand, have short, broad ilia that curve around the vertebral column, so that the flat inner surfaces face more medially.

The most critical muscles for lateral stability in bipedal walking are the lesser gluteal muscles (gluteus medius and gluteus minimus), which run from the lateral surface of the ilium to the greater trochanter of the femur (Fig. 5.19a,b). Their attachments to the femur allow them to function as abductors of the lower limb. Every time a bipedal hominid lifts a foot off the ground to take a step, the gluteal abductors on the opposite side must

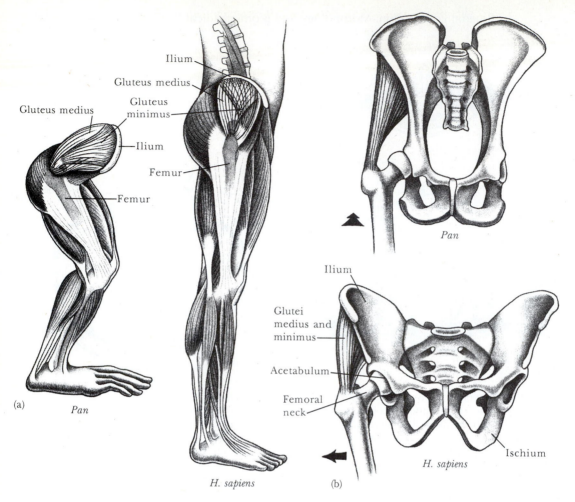

Fig. 5.19. Muscle configuration in the pelvic region of apes and humans. (a)
Lateral and (b) frontal views of the gluteal muscles in *H. sapiens* and *Pan*. In chimpanzees the glutei medius and minimus are extensors and medial rotators of the
hip. In humans, these muscles are critical for maintaining lateral stability during
walking: the abductors on the side of the body supporting the body during a stride
contract to prevent the hip joint from collapsing to the opposite (unsupported)
side. (c) During walking and running the force of body weight times the distance
from its line of action to the center of the hip joint must be balanced by the abductor
muscle force times its distance from the center of the hip joint. Making the femoral
neck longer and/or the distance between the hip joints shorter improves the mechanical advantage of the abductor muscles. But narrowing the distance between
the hip joints decreases the diameter of the birth canal, shown in dashed lines.
Ab = the line of action of the abductor muscles (glutei medius and minimus). From
(105,235). (d) Comparison of the right hip bone in chimpanzees and humans. In
response to increased stresses passing through the bipedal hip joint, the human
pelvis has developed a prominent iliac pillar and anterior and posterior spines not
evident in the chimpanzee. In addition, the human ilium is shorter, to help lower
the center of gravity, and wider, to enlarge the attachment area of flexor and extensor muscles of the hip. This alteration in shape results in a distinctive sciatic
notch. Redrawn from (236).

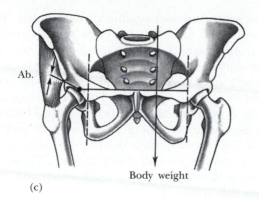

Ab.

Body weight

(c)

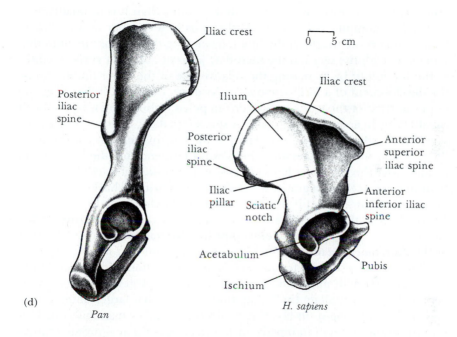

Iliac crest

0   5 cm

Posterior
iliac
spine

Iliac crest

Ilium

Posterior
iliac
spine

Anterior
superior
iliac spine

Iliac
pillar   Sciatic
notch

Anterior
inferior iliac
spine

Acetabulum

Ischium

Pubis

(d)

Pan

H. sapiens

contract to hold the hip steady; if they didn't the hip would collapse to the unsupported side during each stride, and walking would require lurching over sideways (i.e., laterally bending the trunk) to maintain the center of gravity over the leg that is on the ground. This is the type of gait seen today in humans with paralysis of these muscles or with dislocated hips, as well as in apes when they walk bipedally, because in apes the lesser gluteal muscles are positioned to act not as effective hip abductors but rather as extensors and medial rotators of the hip (114,115).

During an individual's lifetime, bones will remodel themselves in response to biomechanical stresses passing through them. The ilium is no exception and will come to reflect the large stresses generated by body weight that are counterbalanced by the lesser gluteal muscles. This stress results in the formation of an iliac pillar, a supporting bony buttress in the form of a thickened outer table of bone along the ilium between the iliac crest and the acetabulum, or hip socket. The presence of this pillar is important osteological evidence of the efficient lateral balance control required by bipedalism. In another bony adaptation to bipedalism, the ilium becomes broader from front to back in order to increase the leverage of hip flexors and extensors around the hip joint. These morphological changes result in the development of a sciatic notch and prominent anterior and posterior iliac spines (Fig. 5.19d).

Another important aspect of balance control in hominids is that the body's center of gravity is closer to the hip joints than it is in quadrupeds (116). The hominid pelvis accomplishes this in a number of ways: by reducing the overall height of the ilium; by moving the part of the ilium that articulates with the sacrum, the sacroiliac joint or auricular surface, closer to the hip joints; by increasing the relative size of the lower limbs; and by the development of a lumbar curve, or lordosis, that effectively brings the upper portion of the trunk back over the pelvis without blocking the birth canal (117). In apes that try to walk or stand bipedally, the center of gravity is well forward of the hip joint (Fig. 5.20a). For this reason, pongid bipedality is very inefficient because the natural tendency for the body to fall forward over the hip joints has to be resisted by powerful muscular activity. In humans the center of gravity has shifted downward and backward relative to overall height, so that it is slightly above and behind the hip joint (Fig. 5.20b). In fact, there is even a slight tendency for the human trunk to fall backward over the hip joint in erect posture; this tendency is easily resisted by the **iliofemoral ligament**, which runs from the anterior inferior spine of the ilium to the proximal femur (Fig. 5.20c). Thus hominids expend little muscular energy in maintaining an erect posture. A general principle of mammalian morphology (including hominids) is that larger animals support their body weight on less bent limbs than smaller mammals do. This shift in posture evident in bipeds further decreases the magnitude of muscle force needed to support the animal while standing or walking (118).

With the assumption of erect posture, more body weight must be supported and propelled by the hindlimbs, increasing the stresses on both the pelvic and hindlimb joints. In bipeds, the lower limbs account for less than one-third of the total body weight, and must alone carry the remaining two-thirds. As a percentage of total body weight, the upper limbs of humans are only 60 percent as heavy as those of chimpanzees, whereas the lower limbs are nearly twice as heavy (119). This redistribution of body weight contributes to a more stable posture, because it shifts the center of gravity lower in the pelvis (see Fig. 5.17).

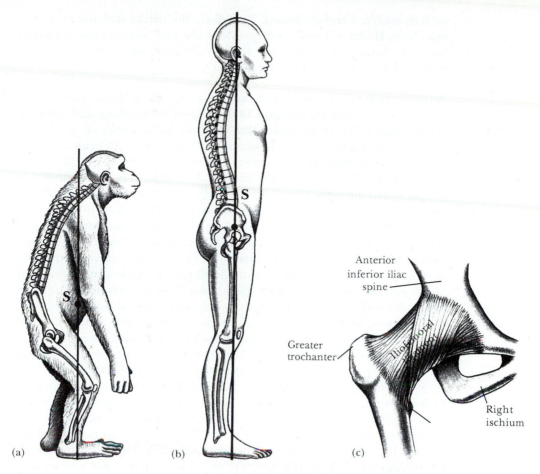

Fig. 5.20. (a) Chimpanzee and (b) modern human in a bipedal posture. Note that in the upright human the line of the center of gravity falls very close to the hip, knee, and ankle joints whereas it is far forward of the hip joint in the chimpanzee. S = center of gravity. From (117). (c) Human hip joint seen from the front; tension in the iliofemoral ligament helps keep the trunk from falling backward when standing upright.

Origins of Bipedalism: The Fossil Evidence

Precise information about the body proportions of early hominids is crucial for accurate functional and phylogenetic interpretations of early human evolution. We shall now examine some of the features of australopithecines that have a bearing on their mode of locomotion. Unfortunately, lower limb specimens associated with the new *A. ramidus* discoveries have yet to be fully analyzed and published. Therefore, the partial skeleton of *A. afarensis* from Hadar ("Lucy") still provides the best information regarding body size, limb proportions, and skeletal allometry in ancestral hominids that predate 3 mya (see Figs. 4.2, 4.12b,c).

Adaptations for Locomotion in A. afarensis   By using allometric relationships between limb lengths and body weights in monkeys and apes for comparison, it has been shown that the limb proportions of *A. afarensis* ("Lucy") are unique among hominoids. *A. afarensis* had already attained forelimb proportions similar to those of modern humans but had hindlimbs that were relatively much shorter. Lucy had very short hindlimbs proportioned most like those of small-bodied African apes and outside the known human range. By contrast, relative humerus length in relation to body size is similar to that seen in a skeletal sample of human pygmies. A similar combination of relative limb lengths appears to exist in the larger individuals of *A. afarensis* and possibly other "gracile" australopithecines as well. Clearly, relative and absolute hindlimb elongation represents one of the striking evolutionary changes in later human evolution. The body proportions of Lucy are not incompatible with bipedal locomotion, but that locomotion was clearly not identical to the bipedal gait of modern humans. Reduced relative stride length in *A. afarensis* probably implies both greater relative energy cost and relatively lower peak velocities of bipedal locomotion in *A. afarensis* than in later hominids (49,50,120).

It has been argued that the upper limb of *A. afarensis* retained a number of features indicating an adaptation to, or retention of, movement in the trees (47,52,121–125). For instance, several of the wrist and metacarpal bones are markedly chimpanzeelike, and the phalanges, or finger and toe bones, are slender and curved as in apes (126,127). These features of the hand suggest well-developed grasping capabilities compatible with suspensory behavior; the fossil hand bones also lack any particular adaptations to knuckle-walking. The hand of *A. africanus*, known from specimens at Sterkfontein, seems similar to that of *A. afarensis*, and both were presumably well adapted for powerful manual tasks, including gripping sticks and stones for vigorous pounding and throwing (121,128,129). The hands do not, however, show any morphological adaptations for humanlike precision grasping (87).

Other upper limb characteristics also suggest that some arboreal adaptations were retained in *A. afarensis*. It is clear, for instance, that the **glenoid cavity**, the socket on the scapula that articulates with the head of the humerus, is directed in a more cranial orientation than is typical in modern humans, which suggests use of the upper limb in elevated positions, as is common during climbing behavior.

When we examine the pelvis and lower limb, *A. afarensis* clearly shows a mosaic of humanlike and pongidlike features (see Fig. 5.8). Some of the distinctly humanlike features of the pelvis include: 1) a low, broad ilium with a deep sciatic notch; 2) a prominent anterior inferior iliac spine for attachment of the rectus femoris muscle, a powerful flexor of the hip; and 3) an ischial surface for the origin of the hamstring muscles that is divided by a vertical ridge into lateral and medial portions (*A. afarensis* had a relatively long hamstring moment arm but one that did not fall outside the range of human variation).

There are also a number of pelvic and lower limb features that differ somewhat from those seen in modern humans (47,52,130,131). For example, the articular surface of the acetabulum lacks the large contribution from the pubic bone that characterizes modern humans (see Fig. 5.19). Functionally, this feature suggests the absence of full, humanlike extension at the hip joint during bipedal locomotion. Other nonhumanlike features of the pelvis and lower extremity include: 1) the extreme width of the pelvis at the level of the iliac crests and at the level of the hip sockets (interacetabular width); 2) the more lateral orientation of the iliac crests; and 3) a relatively shorter femur having a long femoral neck.

The ventral concavity of the sacrum is only slightly developed and the first segment of the sacrum lacks well-developed transverse processes. These features suggest poorly developed sacrotuberous ligaments, which bind together the sacrum and the ischium, and this implies a less well developed mechanism for sacroiliac stabilization when the trunk is in an erect position. The cross-sectional area of the lower back vertebrae, particularly the lumbar and sacral vertebrae, are also extraordinarily small, suggesting that they were not adapted for the bearing of heavy loads associated with full upright postures (48) (Fig. 5.21a).

In *A. afarensis*, the orientation of the iliac blades is similar to that seen in chimpanzees, that is, their external surfaces face more posterolaterally than laterally (47,52,132,133). The ilium also shows the typical australopithecine trait of a laterally flaring anterior superior iliac spine that is far removed from the anterior inferior iliac spine. Taken as a whole, the pelvis of *A. afarensis* reveals that the wrapping of the iliac blades around the vertebral column had already begun but had not yet reached the degree of curvature seen in modern humans (Fig. 5.21b–e). This feature suggests that in *A. afarensis* the mechanism of lateral pelvic balance during bipedalism was more similar to apes than to humans. In addition, the anterior placement of the iliac pillar suggests a bended-knee gait, since electromyographic studies have shown that during such a gait the medial rotators of the hip are important for balance, and they arise from the more anterior aspect of the ilium.

One remarkable feature of Lucy's pelvis is the extreme width of her pelvic inlet, particularly considering her small body size (Fig. 5.21e). The functional significance of this feature is that in combination with horizontal rotation of the pelvis, it minimizes unwanted vertical displacement of the

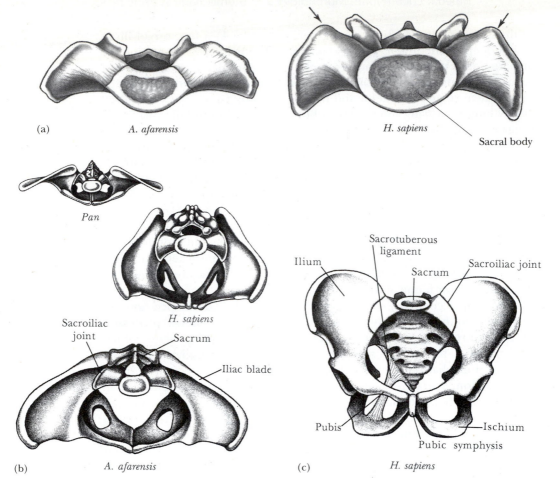

Fig. 5.21. (a) Cranial view of sacrum of *A. afarensis* (left) and modern human (right). In the human note the lateral expanse of the upper lateral angles (arrows) to which powerful sacroiliac ligaments attach. This lateral expansion is greatly reduced in *A. afarensis*. Also note the much larger cross-sectional area of the body of the sacrum in humans. (b)–(e) Comparison of the pelves in *A. afarensis*, *Pan*, and *H. sapiens*. (b) Overhead view. Note that the iliac blades in *A. afarensis* are beginning to curve around the vertebral column, as in the modern human, but the blade angle is still closer to that seen in the chimpanzee. (c) Anterior view of the human pelvis. Strong sacrotuberous ligaments in the human (shown on one side only) help stabilize the sacroiliac joint when the body is erect; features of the sacrum in *A. afarensis* suggest it lacked well-developed sacrotuberous ligaments. (d) Anterior view of the full pelvis in *A. afarensis* with smaller views of *Pan* and *H. sapiens* for comparison. The gluteal muscles are acting as partial abductors in *A. afarensis*, providing some lateral stability; note, however, that the ball-and-socket joint in the australopithecine is shallower than in the human, due to less contribution to the acetabulum from the pubis. (e) *A. afarensis* pelvis (''Lucy'') superimposed on a pelvis of a modern *H. sapiens* female, both scaled to body weight. Note that although the anteroposterior length of the two pelvic inlets is similar, the width of Lucy's pelvic inlet is considerably greater. From (47,134).

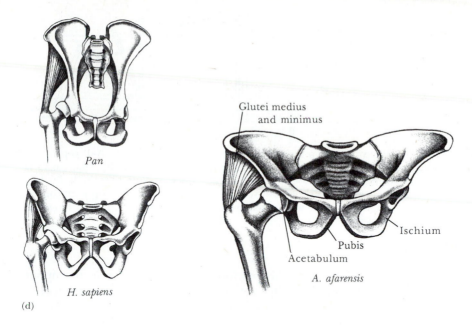

(d)

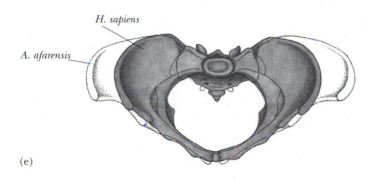

(e)

center of mass during bipedal walking. Later humans reduced this unwanted vertical displacement another way, by elongating the lower limbs (Fig. 5.22). This latter "solution" may have been partly responsible for the reduction of inlet width in later hominids. In the words of one researcher, "Lucy's pelvis . . . does not represent simply an intermediate stage between a chimpanzee-like hominoid and *Homo sapiens*, nor is it essentially a modern human pelvis. Although clearly bipedal and highly terrestrial, Lucy evidently achieved this mode of locomotion through a solution all her own" (134).

Fossil evidence also indicates that the toe bones of *A. afarensis* from Hadar are both longer and much more curved than those of modern hu-

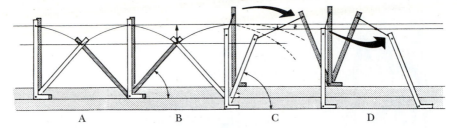

A   B   C   D

Fig. 5.22. Two models of a biped walking the same step length.   A–B represents a condition where the ''hip joints'' are separated by a narrow pelvis whereas C–D represents an individual with a wide pelvis (like ''Lucy''). Note that the individual with the wide pelvis (C–D) shows less vertical displacement of the hip joint for the same stride length. Another way to achieve the same result would be to lengthen the legs. From (134).

mans (Fig. 5.23). For some, this reinforces the evidence from the upper extremity about arboreal activity in *A. afarensis*, since it is easier for feet to grip tree branches with long, curved digits. However, this neglects the obvious point that it is not so easy for feet to grip tree branches without an opposable big toe! Consider this equally valid alternate view: given the loss of the opposable big toe in *A. afarensis*, which mitigates against climbing, any climbing adaptations in Lucy's forelimb should be more accentuated

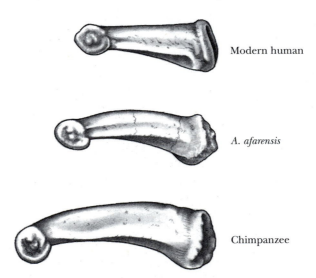

Modern human

A. afarensis

Chimpanzee

Fig. 5.23. Lateral view of proximal pedal (toe) phalanges from the third toe.   Similarities between *A. afarensis* (A.L. 333-115H) and the chimpanzee are seen in their curvatures and overall lateral profiles. The pedal proximal phalanx of humans has a thick base relative to a thin distal portion. From (52).

than in chimpanzees, not less, as they appear to be, for the simple reason that possession of slightly curved fingers and toes by themselves are inadequate adaptations for climbing in an animal lacking opposable, grasping big toes. In other words, without the opposable big toe the lower limbs of *A. afarensis* might have been nothing but dead weight in such arboreal activities! Perhaps they had curved toes for the same reason they had five toes—these are simply primitive features carried over with no particular survival value, positive or negative, from more "apelike" ancestors. And as we noted earlier, there is one other little problem: some workers have suggested that the *A. afarensis* feet typified by the remains at Hadar could not have made the very humanlike Laetoli footprints (109,111,135).

One further piece of evidence used to argue that *A. afarensis* was still a capable climber comes from analyses of the joints of the metatarsals and phalanges. The orientation of these joints indicates that the toes of *A. afarensis* were still capable of significant degrees of plantarflexion, an adaptation for arboreal locomotion (136).

A comparison of the smaller, presumably female, specimens to the larger, presumably male, specimens suggests sexual differences in locomotor behavior linked to marked size dimorphism and has led some to hypothesize that the males were probably less arboreal than females and engaged more frequently in terrestrial bipedalism (47).

A very different viewpoint about *A. afarensis* bipedalism is expressed by several other researchers who consider it to be a fully adapted biped (42–46,105,130). They identify a number of adaptations to humanlike bipedalism found in *A. afarensis*:
- a knee positioned close to the midline to minimize side-to-side shifting of the center of gravity during locomotion
- raised lateral lip of the patellar groove to prevent lateral displacement of the kneecap, or patella, during extension of the leg
- a well-developed iliofemoral ligament, which, as we have noted, helps keep the erect trunk from falling backward
- a long abductor-muscle moment arm for the gluteus medius and minimus for lateral stability in the hip joint during walking
- a posterior position of the gluteus maximus, which acts as an extensor of the lower limb
- and most significantly, the lack of an opposable, grasping big toe or hallux

In the midst of these competing schools of thought, what can we conclude about the locomotor proclivities of *A. afarensis*? We see that Lucy is fundamentally different from apes only in features directly related to bipedalism. We also see more apelike retentions in Lucy than in ourselves. But it would be wrong simply to consider Lucy half-ape, half-human, since the species bears characters that are not present in apes or humans. The essence of the morphological changes we do see in Lucy are in the direction of bipedalism. If it is true that "natural selection, when viewed within the animal's historical context, can be said to have a direction vector'' (46), then we must conclude that such a "direction vector" in *A. afarensis* was clearly pointing toward bipedalism.

Figure 5.8 summarizes the important postcranial features of *A. afarensis.*

Locomotor Adaptations in Other Australopithecines   A good deal of postcranial material of *A. africanus* is available from which to extrapolate locomotor behavior in that species (91,128,130,137–140). In most respects the postcranial skeleton seems generally similar to that described above for *A. afarensis.*

The most complete *A. africanus* specimen, from a mature adult female from Sterkfontein (Sts 14), consists of much of the vertebral column (including the lumbar vertebrae and sacrum), a few ribs, almost the complete pelvis, and much of the femur (see Fig. 4.12d). The ribs, vertebral bodies, and the femoral head, neck, and shaft are all slender, indicating a small, gracile animal. The stature of this individual is estimated at 122 to 137 cm (91). The presence of six lumbar vertebrae is interesting in that modern humans normally have five and African apes no more than three or four (141).[5]

Although the morphology of the australopithecine vertebrae shows some signs of adaptation to the weight-bearing demands associated with terrestrial bipedality, such as the increase in size from proximal to distal vertebral segments (143), the cross-sectional area of the lower back vertebral bodies (lumbar and sacral) is still very small (48). This is an important point. Human vertebrae are characterized by several unique adaptations to bipedal posture: surface areas of the lower lumbar vertebral bodies and cross-sectional areas of their pedicles, the anterior portion of the vertebral arch, are large relative to body size, and lower lumbar pedicles are wider relative to length and to body size than are those of nonhuman, quadrupedal primates. Interestingly, the last lumbar vertebra of Sts 14 does not exhibit either of these humanlike vertebral features—its pedicles and body surface areas are relatively small, and its pedicles are relatively short (144).

All postcranial evidence from Sterkfontein and Makapansgat suggests that *A. africanus* was a gracile animal. However, on the basis of a recently described proximal femur from Makapansgat, it seems that the pattern of sexual dimorphism in *A. africanus* may be similar to that in *A. afarensis* (145). Estimated femur length from one individual (Sts 14) appears about the same relative to overall body length as that in modern humans. From this information some have concluded that in *A. africanus* the lower limbs were about the same length relative to upper limbs as in modern humans (91). If true, this would be in clear contrast to the proportions calculated for *A. afarensis*, with its relatively reduced lower limb length (49).

Recently, however, a new partial skeleton (Stw 431) of *A. africanus* has

[5]Somewhat surprisingly, the new *Homo erectus* skeleton from West Lake Turkana (WT 15000) also has six lumbar vertebrae (142).

been recovered from Member 4, Sterkfontein. Several body proportions of this individual are quite unlike those of earlier *Australopithecus* species like *A. afarensis* or *A. anamensis*. Specifically, forelimb joint sizes of Stw 431 are in the range of modern humans weighing 41–62 kg, whereas hindlimb joint sizes are in the range of modern humans weighing 27–45 kg (in contrast, forelimb and hindlimb joint sizes of *A. afarensis* and *A. anamensis* more closely resemble the human pattern). This new *A. africanus* specimen, if typical of the species as a whole, reveals a primitive pattern of joint size more typical of pongids than hominids. This is particularly interesting in light of the more pongidlike limb proportions in the two known associated partial skeletons of *H. habilis* (OH 62 and KNM-ER 3735—see next chapter) (146).

The *A. africanus* pelvis, similar in many respects to that described for *A. afarensis*, is clearly approaching the modern human pelvis in morphology (Fig. 5.24a). Moreover, *A. africanus* has been described as showing a well-developed, humanlike lumbar curve, which suggests that the posture was more like that found in modern humans than in pongids (91). Another bipedal feature is the carrying angle of the femoral shaft, which demonstrates that the knees, and therefore the feet, were close together during standing and walking. This is important to minimize swaying while striding.

Recently, four articulating hominid foot bones tentatively assigned to *A. africanus* have been recovered from Sterkfontein Member 2 that may be about 3.5 million years old. While the foot clearly belongs to a bipedal hominid, it has been described as having a medially divergent and strongly mobile hallux, as in apes (140). This is taken by some to support the contention that *A. africanus*, like *A. afarensis*, retained some degree of arboreal behavior as part of its total locomotor repertoire. However, one must temper that conclusion by noting the locomotor proclivities of *A. afarensis*, as discussed above.

The postcranial evidence is less satisfactory for *A. robustus*. We know nothing definite about such features as lumbar curvature or body proportions for this species. However, we do know that the ilium shows some important adaptations to bipedalism, such as the reduction of iliac height and the development of an iliac pillar. It also appears that in some features *A. robustus* was a more robust and heavily built creature than *A. africanus* (Fig. 5.24b), although, as noted earlier, body size apparently did not differ much between *A. africanus* and *A. robustus*. As in all australopithecines, the femoral neck is relatively long and the femoral head is small. This suggests greater moment arms for the hip abductors (glutei medius and minimus) and relatively less weight being borne directly on the femoral heads.

A complete metatarsal of the big toe attributed to *A. robustus* has recently been recovered from Swartkrans that has features suggesting humanlike foot postures and ranges of extension. Examination of the toe joints suggests humanlike toe-off, or stride, mechanisms. Most importantly, the great toe in *A. robustus* was a nongrasping structure and incapable of apelike opposition.

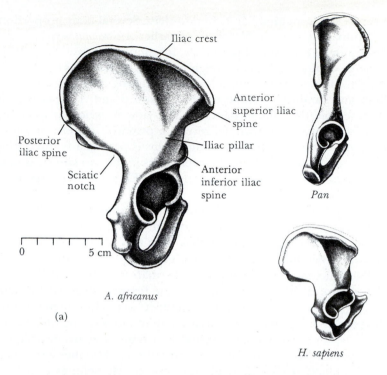

A. africanus

(a)

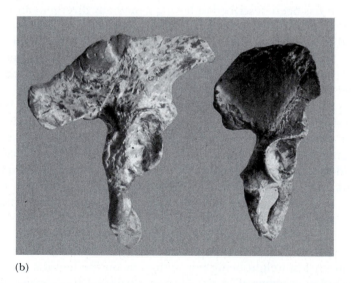

(b)

Fig. 5.24. Pelves of South African australopithecines. (a) Hip bone in *A. africanus*; smaller views of *Pan* and *H. sapiens* are provided for comparison. (b) Lateral view of the right pelvis of *A. robustus* from Swartkrans (left) and *A. africanus* from Sterkfontein (right). Both pelves have broad, short ilia with well-developed sciatic notches (scale about 30 percent natural size). From (91).

Unlike the condition in *A. afarensis*, the broad apical tuft of the distal thumb phalanx is humanlike, not apelike. It has also been shown that the first metacarpal bone of the modern human thumb is characterized by a broad head in relation to its length, a feature found in *A. robustus*, *Homo erectus*, and Neandertals, but, interestingly enough, not in *A. afarensis* (85–87,147). This feature of the thumb may be correlated with toolmaking abilities, and, if so, it is interesting to note that *A. afarensis* spans a time period (about 4–3 mya) that is devoid of any evidence of stone and bone toolmaking.

Taken altogether, evidence from both the hand and foot suggest that *A. robustus* lacked the arboreal component, or phylogenetic baggage, seen in earlier *A. afarensis* and *A. africanus* specimens (83,86).

Even less can be said about the postcranial adaptations of *A. boisei*. As mentioned earlier, few skeletal parts have been found, and few in association with teeth or crania, making attribution tentative at best. However, because *A. robustus* and *A. boisei* are judged to be so closely related, most workers assume similar postcranial adaptations in both species. Fortunately, a fragment of mandible and partial associated skeleton (KNM-ER 1500) has been identified as *A. boisei*, as have several other specimens from the Lake Turkana region (148). The KNM-ER 1500 specimen reveals forelimbs that are relatively large and hindlimbs that are relatively small in comparison to modern humans, and in overall limb proportions most closely resembles A.L. 288-1 ("Lucy").

Another anatomical system that may reveal important clues about bipedal locomotion in australopithecines is the inner ear, specifically the size and shape of the semicircular canals, which, together with their associated neurological structures, mediate perception of angular velocity and balance. The anterior and posterior canals in great apes are smaller than in modern humans and this is presumably the primitive condition for this feature (Fig. 5.25). If so, the larger and characteristically shaped canals of modern humans must have been selected for during the course of the transition from quadrupedalism to bipedalism, and presumably in response to the need for fine neuromuscular control mechanisms of the musculoskeletal system, a crucial adaptation for habitual bipedal locomotion. What is particularly interesting is that the size and shape of the semicircular canals in both *A. africanus* and *A. robustus* are more great-apelike than modern-humanlike,[6] and it is not until we reach the *Homo erectus* stage of human evolution that the semicircular canals take on an essentially modern-humanlike appearance (OH 9, Sangiran 2 and 4). This supports an interpretation drawn from the postcranial evidence that bipedal behavior of australopithecines and (perhaps) early *Homo* was less specialized in terms of obligatory bipedalism than that of modern humans and that the

---

[6]Some specimens referred to *Homo* aff. *habilis*, namely Stw 53, have canal dimensions unlike those seen in any hominids or great apes.

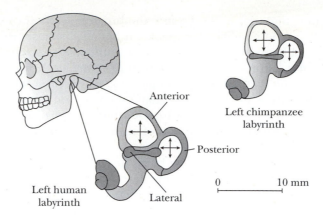

Fig. 5.25.   Relative sizes of semicircular canals in human and great apes.   From (237).

locomotor repertoire of these hominids included a substantial nonbipedal, or arboreal, component (149,150).

Fossil evidence clearly indicates that pelvic reorientation from a typically apelike configuration to a more humanlike one had already commenced several million years ago (105,106,137,151,152). That this pelvic transition to the modern condition was still incomplete in australopithecines, however, is demonstrated by the fact that they had:

- a relatively small area on the sacrum for articulation with the ilium
- relatively small femoral heads
- incomplete rotation of the iliac blades, whose orientation was more dorsolateral than is characteristic of modern humans (this last feature seems to indicate that the hip abductor mechanism discussed earlier did not yet function as it does in modern humans, although this is still a point of contention) (47,105)

What explains some of the morphological rearrangements of the aus-

Box 5.2.   Summary of Trends in Hominid Pelvic Morphology

Since the anatomy of the pelvis is so critical for interpreting locomotor behavior in fossil hominids, let us summarize the salient points. Distinctive features of the modern human pelvis include the following:

- *a low, broad ilium*
- *a short distance from the center of the acetabulum to the articular surface of the sacrum*
- *a deep sciatic notch*
- *a more lateral orientation of the iliac blades*
- *the presence of an iliac pillar*

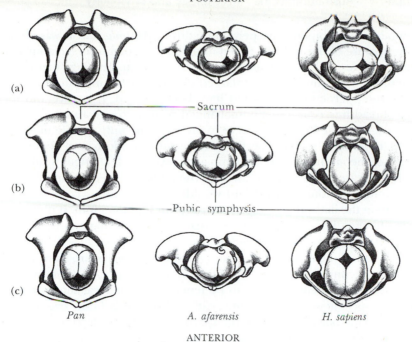

(a)

Sacrum

(b)

Pubic symphysis

(c)

Pan   A. afarensis   H. sapiens

ANTERIOR

Fig. 5.26. Pelvic dimensions, encephalization, and parturition in pongids and hominids. Fetal head is shown passing through (a) inlet, (b) midplane, and (c) outlet of the birth canal seen from below; the membrane-covered soft spot in the infant's incompletely ossified skull, known as the anterior fontanelle, is marked in black to indicate fetal orientation. In *A. afarensis* the birth process was probably more difficult than in the chimpanzee because, although the birth canal was broad, it was constricted from front to back; the infant's cranium could pass through only if it first turned sideways and then tilted. During the human birth process the canal is even more constricted, and a second rotation of the fetal cranium within the birth canal is required. From (105).

tralopithecine pelvis, like the reduction of lateral flare of the ilium, and the commensurate changes in such features as the anterior portion of the iliac pillar, longer femoral neck length, and anterior iliac spine position? One suggested cause is the rapid encephalization, or brain growth, that took place during the Pleistocene (105,137). If this were the case, there would have been significant selective pressure on the female to maintain adequate pelvic breadth both to provide balance during walking and to allow parturition despite the constantly increasing size of the fetal cranium (Fig. 5.26).[7] There is certainly a maximum total pelvic breadth that can be

[7]However, in *A. afarensis* and *A. africanus*, at least, neonatal brainsize (and the corresponding neurocranial dimensions) was smaller than in modern chimpanzees and smaller than in the corresponding pelvic dimensions of A.L. 288-1 ("Lucy") and Sts 14, respectively, indicating little, if any obstetrical constraints in these two early hominid species (153).

maintained in a biped. The pelvic breadth of *Australopithecus* was already great because of the laterally flared ilium and a broad interacetabular distance relative to that in quadrupeds. Because of increasing fetal cranial dimensions, adjustments that enlarged the pelvic opening but did not increase total pelvic breadth would have been favored. If stature and total pelvic breadth were to remain unchanged relative to one another and the dimensions of the birth canal were to increase, the only avenue of change would have been to increase the interacetabular width and reduce the length of the moment arm of the hip abductors. Such changes would have led to increase in the muscle force of the abductor mechanism (because of its reduced moment arm) and would have required a commensurate increase in the iliac pillar and general robustness of the ilium. It is precisely these changes, in addition to those discussed earlier, that can be seen between the hip complex of *Australopithecus* and *H. sapiens*.

Accurate dimensions of the australopithecine pelvis are known from only two specimens: A.L. 288-1 (*A. afarensis*) and Sts 14 (*A. africanus*). Both specimens are usually thought to be females.[8] Obstetrical measurements on these specimens indicate that, relative to newborn brain size, the australopithecine pelvic inlet was more spacious than in modern humans, and thus obstetrical constraints were minimal in early hominids (153). However, pelvic inlet shape does differ between the two species, being more similar to modern humans in Sts 14 but much wider from side to side and narrower from front to back, that is, more **platypelloid**, in A.L. 288-1. A platypelloid shape minimizes the actual space available for fetal entry into and descent through the birth canal and for this reason some have suggested that delivery may have been more difficult in *A. afarensis* than in *A. africanus* (155). In fact, some have even suggested that the obstetrical constraints apparent in the pelvis of A.L. 288-1, in particular the protruding sacral promontory, more likely indicate a male than a female specimen. If A.L. 288-1 was the female of a very sexually dimorphic species, then she would have had to give birth to a child with a neonatal brain size of around 200 g, basically an obstetrical impossibility given her pelvic dimensions. If she was a female of a species with low sexual dimorphism, she would still have had to give birth to a child with a neonatal brain size between about 140 and 160 g, a delivery judged to be more difficult and complicated than in modern humans. If, on the other hand, A.L. 288-1 was the male of a rather small, nonsexually dimorphic early hominid species, then the female

---

[8]Among humans there are a number of anatomical features related to obstetrics by which female pelves differ from those of males: the iliopectineal line is greater in females, reflecting the increased size of the pelvic inlet; the long axis of the sacrum is oriented more horizontally in females, thereby increasing the dimensions of the pelvic midplane and outlet; the ischial spines are everted in females, thereby widening the transverse diameters of the lower pelvic planes; and the inferior border of the ischiopubic ramus is concave in females, which helps widen the subpubic angle. It is interesting to note that, with the exception of the length of the iliopectineal line, all other features of Lucy's pelvis are more typical of males (154).

of this species would have had childbirth difficulties little different from that experienced by modern humans (156).

Behavioral Theories for the Evolution of Bipedalism

As we have seen, australopithecines had evolved unmistakable adaptations to bipedalism by 4.0–3.5 mya. But why did bipedalism develop at all? Are two legs better than four? Bipedalism might seem an unusual mode of locomotion for mammals because it has the disadvantages of reducing speed, agility, and energy efficiency.

Many theories have been advanced to explain the evolution of bipedalism: it frees the hands for tool use; it allows for new feeding adaptations; it allows for behaviors such as carrying food and infants and using the hands for display; it evolved from bipedal threat/appeasement displays; it is more bioenergetically efficient than quadrupedalism; or some combination of these (Fig. 5.27) (157). However, in recent years the fossil record has made it clear that bipedalism predated the use of stone tools, the modern hom-

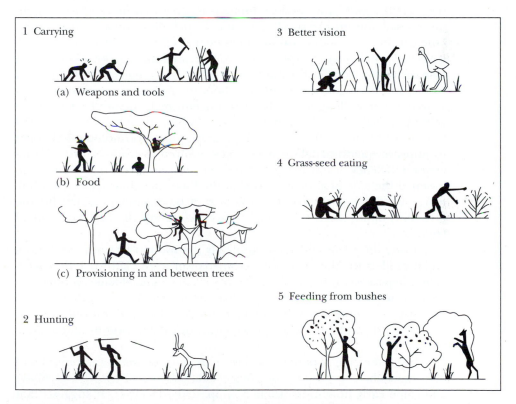

Fig. 5.27. Rival theories to account for the origins of bipedalism. From (238).

inid dental complex, and encephalization above the average levels for other hominoids (158,159).

Could bipedalism be more energy efficient than quadrupedalism? Empirical studies have shown that at maximum running speed, human bipedalism costs twice as much energy per kilogram per kilometer as predicted for a true mammalian quadruped of the same size. It has also been shown that for chimpanzees and capuchin monkeys the energy costs of travelling quadrupedally and bipedally are about the same. Is energy efficiency then not a good argument for the evolution of human bipedalism (109,160,161)?

Of course, there are degrees of bipedalism and varying degrees of energy efficiency: bipedal posture turns out to be an important factor in energetics models of bipedal locomotion. For example, studies using Japanese macaques indicate that these animals expend about 30 percent less energy during upright walking when they shift from postures with deeply flexed lower limb joints and forwardly inclined trunks to more upright postures (humans expend up to 50 percent less energy by walking fully upright rather than with flexed lower limb joints) (162).

It is important to note that while human *running* may be energy intensive, bipedal *walking* in modern humans is somewhat more efficient than quadrupedalism in like-sized quadrupeds, including modern apes (163). One can imagine a scenario in which energy efficiency in terms of food-gathering strategies would actually have increased through bipedalism. The climatic fluctuations in the Miocene resulted in changing distributions of forests and open country. In places where the forests were receding, food sources would no longer have been as concentrated; ancestral australopithecine populations in these marginal areas would thus have had to travel farther to forage for food. One might argue that morphological changes to improve quadrupedalism might have evolved instead, in order to increase efficiency at moving between food sites; however, this would have lessened the ease of gathering food at the food sites themselves. By modifying only the hind limbs, the evolution of bipedalism provided for the possibility of improved efficiency of travel, while still allowing for arboreal feeding.

During the 1970s and 1980s, probably the two most creative and influential models for the evolution of bipedalism were Clifford Jolly's **seed-eating hypothesis** (164) and C. Owen Lovejoy's **sexual-and-reproductive-strategy model** (104). Both have had their critics, yet both stand as landmark attempts to synthesize anatomical and behavioral observations on living primates into plausible scenarios of human origins and adaptations.

The seed-eating hypothesis makes an analogy between anatomical and behavioral characters shared by living gelada baboons (*Theropithecus gelada*) and some early hominids (Table 5.3, pp. 230–31) (164). It suggests that early hominid populations relied on small-object feeding, that this dietary

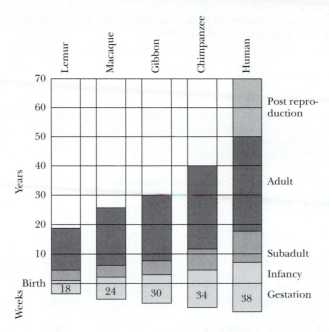

Fig. 5.28. Progressive prolongation of life phases and gestation in primates. Note the proportionality of the indicated phases. The postreproductive phase is restricted mainly to humans and is probably a recent development. From (104,239).

specialization resulted in a suite of adaptations to feeding in grassland savanna, and that bipedalism developed in response to such feeding posture. This model fits quite well some of the dental specializations seen in the "robust" australopithecines, but the more generalized dentition of *A. afarensis* is more difficult to fit, unless of course *A. afarensis* represents the beginning of this new adaptation to savanna living and to small-object feeding, a scenario that is quite possible.

The sexual-and-reproductive-strategy model presents a somewhat different view of human origins based on an undeniable trend toward prolonged life span in the primate evolutionary record (Fig. 5.28) (104). An increased primate life span has implications both for primate physiology and population dynamics and behavior, which bear, as we shall see, on the issue of hominid origins.

Evolutionary Changes in Primate Development

A number of trends in primate physiology such as prolonged gestation, single rather than multiple births, and successively greater periods between pregnancies correlate well with longer periods of infant dependency. Ac-

Table 5.3 Adaptive Characters of Early Hominidae and *Theropithecus* (gelada baboons and their fossil relatives) (from 164)

	A	B	C
Behavior			
Open-country habitat, not forest or woodland	X	—	—
Trees rarely or never climbed when feeding	(X)	—	—
One-male breeding unit	(X)	—	—
Foraging mainly in sitting position	?	—	—
Small daily range	?	—	—
More regular use of artifacts in agonistic situations	X	X	—
Regular use of stone cutting tools	X	X	—
Most food collected by index-pollex precision grip	?	—	—
Postcranial structure			
Hand more adept, opposability index higher	X	—	—
Index finger abbreviated	?	—	—
Hallux short and weak	—	—	X
Hallux relatively nonabductible	X	—	—
Foot double-arched	X	X	—
Phalanges of pedal digits 2–5 shorter	(X)	—	—
Ilium short and reflexed	X	X	—
Sacroiliac articulation extensive	X	X	—
Anterior-inferior iliac spine strong	X	X	—
Ischium without flaring tuberosities	X	X	—
Accessory sitting pads (fat deposits on buttocks) present	(X)	—	—
Femur short compared with humerus	?	—	—
Distal end femur indicates straight-knee "locking"	X	X	—
Epigamic hair about face and neck strongly dimorphic	(X)	—	—
Female epigamic features pectoral as well as perineal	(X)	—	—
Cranium and mandible			
Foramen magnum basally displaced	X	X	—
Articular fossa deep, articular eminence present	X	X	—
Fossa narrow, postglenoid process appressed to tympanic	X	—	—
Postglenoid process often absent, superseded by tympanic	X	X	—
Postglenoid process long and stout	—	—	X

(*Continued*)

cording to Lovejoy's hypothesis, the progressive extension of primate life phases might be accounted for by an evolutionary strategy in which populations devote more energy to the care and survival of fewer young. The increase in primate life span would then be accompanied by both a proportionate delay in the onset of reproductive readiness and greater spacing between births. This requires a female to survive to an older age in order to maintain the same reproductive potential or to give birth to a second

	A	B	C
Basioccipital short and broad	X	—	—
Mastoid process regularly present	X	—	—
Temporal origins set forward on cranium	X	—	—
Ascending ramus vertical, even in largest forms	X	—	—
Mandibular corpus very robust in molar region	X	—	—
Premaxilla reduced	X	—	—
Dental arcade narrows anteriorly	X	—	—
Dental arcade of mandible parabolic, "simian" shelf absent	X	X	—
Dental arcade (especially in larger forms) V-shaped; shelf massive	—	—	X
Teeth			
Incisors relatively small and allometrically reducing	X	—	—
Canine relatively small, especially in larger forms	X	—	—
Canine incisiform	X	X	—
Male canine "feminised," little sexual dimorphism in canines	X	X	—
Third lower premolar bicuspid	X	X	—
Sectorial face of male P_3 relatively small and allometrically decreasing	—	—	X
Molar crowns more parallel-sided, cusps set towards edge	X	—	—
Cheek teeth markedly crowded mesiodistally	X	—	—
Cheek teeth with deep and complex enamel invagination	—	—	X
Cheek teeth with thick enamel	X	X	—
Canine eruption early relative to that of molars	X	—	—
Wear-plane on cheek teeth flat, not inclined buccolingually	X	X	—
Wear on cheek teeth rapid, producing steep M_1–M_3 "wear-gradient"	X	—	—

Column A: Characters distinguishing early Hominidae from *Pan* and other Pongidae.
Column B: Features of the Hominid complex not seen in *Theropithecus*.
Column C: Features of the *Theropithecus* complex not seen in Hominidae.
X indicates presence of character; (X) indicates assumed presence of character.

offspring before the first is independent, thereby producing a "serial litter." However, to accomplish the latter, she would (ideally) need male help. Increased longevity depends on strong social bonds, high levels of intelligence, intense parenting, long periods of postnatal learning, and other such developments to reduce the potential for environmentally induced mortality of the newborn. The emergence of successful hominids in the Pliocene strongly suggests that major changes in reproductive strategies were in fact evolving as hominids came to occupy new environments. Yet neither brain expansion nor significant material culture appear at this time and were presumably not responsible for the shift (unless the material culture was not preserved).

Lovejoy suggests a novel behavioral pattern that could have evolved from typical primate survival strategies in which males and females had nonoverlapping feeding areas and the females and infants had a much-reduced day range to minimize injury to the infants (104,165). Such a division of feeding areas, however, would not genetically favor males unless it specifically reduced competition with their own biological offspring and did not reduce their opportunities for having consort relationships. **Polygynous** mating, the mating of several males with one female, would not be favored by this adaptive strategy, though **monogamous pair–bonding** would be. Sexual division of labor would develop, with the male provisioning the female with the male's biological offspring at some type of **home base**, an area to which hominids return to meet other group members, share food, and make tools. This scenario could also account for a social system capable of supporting multiple dependent offspring rather than, or in addition to, a reproductive strategy of one offspring at a time. In this model such male provisioning is also seen as an impetus to the evolution of bipedalism, since distances would have to be travelled while bearing food.

Lovejoy ascribes the reduced degree of sexual dimorphism in australopithecines (indicated by the lack of sexual dimorphism in A. afarensis canines) to a reduced intensity of sexual selection.[9] Based on analogies with extant primates, this implies a monogamous mating system (166). However, he interprets the evident dimorphism of australopithecine body size as a result of males and females occupying different feeding niches. These findings are not universally accepted. A more recent study indicates a dissociation between body weight and canine size dimorphism in all four species of *Australopithecus* and suggests that different selective forces must have acted on body weight and canine size (167). According to this study there is little evidence in extant primates that body size dimorphism can be linked to males and females occupying different feeding niches. Instead, australopithecine body weight dimorphism is seen as a function of intra- and intersexual competition typical of polygynous, not monogamous, mating systems. This interpretation explains the lack of canine sexual dimorphism in australopithecines as a consequence of a "developmental dental crowding" model in which canine size and canine dimorphism reduction results from selection for increased premolar chewing surface areas accompanied by the space restrictions of tooth sockets for late erupting hominid canines.

[9]This seems to ignore the problem that if all the craniodental and postcranial hominid material from both Hadar and Laetoli are correctly assigned to the single species, A. afarensis, then this species would be one of the most sexually dimorphic primate species known.

There are still other factors affecting canine sexual dimorphism in primates that should be considered in this context. For example, canines are relatively larger in both males and females of those species in which agonistic interactions are most likely to occur. In such cases, the size of the canine teeth of both sexes is influenced by selection of canines as weapons. Conversely, it has also been shown that where aggressive interactions are resolved between coalitions of individuals, selection pressures for enlarged canines are reduced even though agonistic competition can still be intense. That female primates form such coalitions much more commonly than do males may partially explain why canine size is less in females than in males (168).

Lovejoy's model also addresses the critical notion of extended periods for learning and infant dependency. In modern humans the course of development from conception to maturity requires nearly twice the time as in modern apes (169,170). This extended period of maturation in humans is usually regarded as a major evolutionary advance because enhanced learning reduces environmentally induced mortality. This view was best expressed by the prominent population geneticist and evolutionary biologist Theodosius Dobzhansky (171), who stated that

> although a prolonged period of juvenile helplessness and dependency would, by itself, be disadvantageous to a species because it endangers the young and handicaps their parents, it is a help to man because the slow development provides time for learning and training, which are far more extensive and important in man than in any other animal.

Lovejoy's model assumes that relative to monkeys, long periods of learning already existed in the early lifetimes of Pliocene hominids. This assumption relies on the pioneering work of University of Pennsylvania's Alan Mann, who concluded that "a long childhood dependency period, . . . which the evidence . . . seems to indicate for *Australopithecus,* would provide the time necessary for the skills associated with tool-making to be developed in the young" (172).

How can we determine whether long learning periods really occurred in australopithecines? As Mann pointed out, it would be crucial to know how old individual australopithecines were when they died. He estimated their age by examining their teeth. Nearly all mammals have one set of deciduous teeth that are first formed and then replaced by permanent teeth in a predictable sequence. A jaw with some deciduous teeth in it reveals fairly precisely at which point along the way to adulthood the individual died. The key is translating the relative ages of the fossil into actual time spans in years and months. The crucial question is whether australopithecines developed on a humanlike or an apelike timetable. The difference is significant. Based on an analysis of the timing of tooth eruptions in a small sample of mainly *A. robustus* teeth, Mann concluded that australopithecines showed a humanlike pattern of dental development, and so he

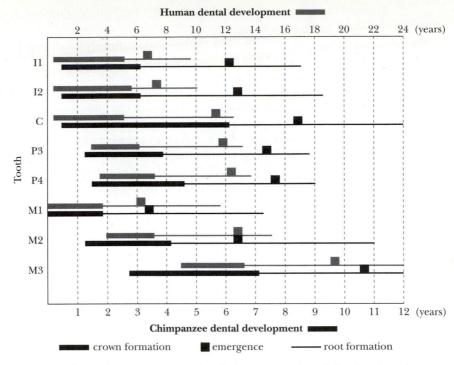

Fig. 5.29. A comparison of human and chimpanzee dental development drawn to same scale of dental completion. Note that while chimpanzee and human first molars erupt at about ages 3 and 6 years respectively, they both erupt at about the same relative time in the total dental development cycle of each species. This is not true of the incisors, canines, and premolars, all of which erupt relatively earlier in humans. From (240).

based his age estimates on the human timetable. Thus it was thought that alteration in the timing of growth and development occurred very early in hominid evolution, indicating that a long maturational period had already evolved in Pliocene hominids older than *A. robustus*.

Mann's work proved to be very influential, and it became widely accepted that humanlike traits of sociality, enhanced intelligence, elaborate communication, and so on, arose very early in the history of the hominid lineage. Recent evidence, however, suggests that the situation may be more complicated than previously thought (58–60,169,173–175).

For example, B. Holly Smith of the University of Michigan, using many more specimens than were available to Mann, aged all the teeth separately for each fossil jaw she studied (175,176). She then statistically compared the dental age ranges of the jaw as determined by the individual teeth to chimpanzee and human dental calibration standards to see which group the fossil most closely resembled. Theoretically, all the teeth in the jaw should follow a standard pattern and rate of development for that species. For example, if the incisors are in a state of maturation that is typical of a six-year-old human, the molars should be as well. Surprisingly, her results showed that only the "robust" australopithecines followed, at least superficially, a humanlike pattern, while *A. afarensis* and *A. africanus* (and *H. habilis*) showed an apelike pattern.

Actually, this "superficially" humanlike pattern in "robust" australopithecines, which concerns the relative rate of eruption of the first permanent central incisors and molars, was first noted by Broom and Robinson back in the early 1950s (177) and has been the subject of periodic debate ever since (178–181). In *H. sapiens*, permanent central incisors and permanent first molars erupt with little time in between. In pongids, eruption of the first permanent incisors is often delayed more than 2.5 years after the permanent first molars erupt (170,182) (Fig. 5.29). Part of the difficulty in resolving this issue is that the developing teeth most crucial to solving this debate, particularly the incisors in some of the fossils, had never been clearly visualized by conventional radiographic techniques because of heavy mineralization. However, recent studies using high-resolution CT scans suggest that patterns of dental development may have differed between *A. robustus* and *A. africanus*, even though the length of time for dental development may have been relatively short in both (Fig. 5.30) (60,169,183).

Several other anthropologists have used a totally independent method

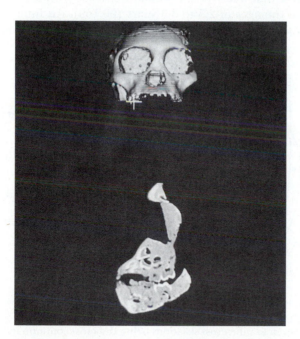

Fig. 5.30. (top) A geometrically accurate three-dimensional image of the Taung skull created from 2-mm thin contiguous CT scans. (bottom) A 2-mm thin CT scan taken through a parasagittal plane of the skull (at the crosshairs in the top picture) showing the state of calcification of the developing teeth. (Image created by G. Conroy and M. Vannier.)

of analysis to age australopithecines at death (173,179,184–187). These studies count the daily microscopic increments, or **cross striations**, and near weekly increments, the **striae of Retzius** or **perikymata**, of enamel laid down as teeth are formed (Fig. 5.31). In modern humans, this technique shows that the lower or cervical third of an incisor tooth crown takes more than three times as long to form as the upper or incisal third, a general pattern that is also seen in *A. afarensis* (LH 2), *A. africanus* (Sts 24), and early *Homo* (KNM-ER 820, OH 6). However, none of these fossil hominids have as great a total number of perikymata on the surface of the tooth as modern humans do. Interestingly, incisor teeth of ''robust'' australopithecines from southern Africa tend to have widely spaced perikymata even at the cervix, unlike the modern human condition. Since lower incisors of ''robust'' australopithecines are similar in height to those of modern humans, their lower total perikymata counts indicate that crown formation must have been much faster in these fossils.

These results independently confirm that many of the earlier australopithecine age determinations using modern human timetables were too old by a factor of about 2; in other words, australopithecines generally followed a pongidlike maturational process, not a humanlike one. These studies suggest that many of the immature australopithecines apparently died between the ages of 2.5 to 3.5 years (60,169). An interesting avenue for future research would be to see whether these new estimates for ages

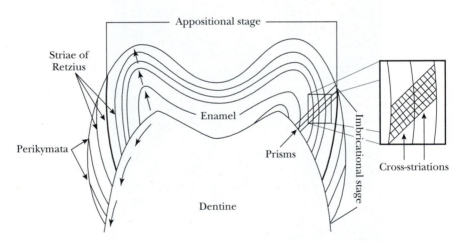

Fig. 5.31. Schematic representation of a molar tooth showing the various incremental growth markers in enamel. Cross striations are produced in enamel formation, with seven to nine cross striations being the most common interval between adjacent striae of Retzius. Striae of Retzius that reach the enamel surface form perikymata, or ridges, on the surface of the tooth. The first stria of Retzius that reaches the enamel surface is taken as the limit between the appositional and imbricational stages of enamel growth. Arrows indicate the two directions of enamel formation. From (241).

at death are related to weaning stresses in australopithecine populations (188). Additionally, obstetrical studies on the australopithecine pelvis provide no evidence of selection for humanlike delayed maturation at this early stage of human evolution (153–155).

It is difficult to be certain just when the modern human maturational pattern finally emerged. The recently discovered *H. erectus* specimen from Nariokotome in West Turkana (see Chapter VII) dated to about 1.5 mya suggests a pattern of maturation that is more like humans than great apes, but one that is probably not fully like extant humans (189,190). Early *Homo* seems to have had maturation rates intermediate between apelike australopithecines and more humanlike *Homo erectus* (191). A fully modern pattern has been discerned in at least one Neandertal (*H. sapiens*) child, a specimen called Gibraltar 2 (175,176).

Another interesting hypothesis for the evolution of human bipedality uses evidence from both primate field ecology and functional morphology to suggest that ecological conditions that produce episodes of bipedal behavior in living chimpanzees may provide clues to the selection pressures leading to hominid bipedalism. More specifically, living chimpanzees seem to adopt bipedal postures much more commonly when feeding on the small fruits of low, open-forest trees. Chimpanzee bipedalism suggests that hominid bipedalism may have evolved in conjunction with arboreal adaptations like arm-hanging as a specialized feeding adaptation permitting more efficient harvesting of fruits among open-forest or woodland trees, an idea that seems compatible with what we know about the anatomy of early hominids. For example, we have seen that *A. afarensis* has features of the hand, shoulder, and torso that relate to arm-hanging postures. And though the australopithecine hip and hindlimb clearly indicate significant advances toward bipedalism, they also indicate a less than optimal adaptation to bipedal locomotion compared to modern humans. This lends support to the idea that bipedalism may have evolved more as a terrestrial feeding posture than as a walking adaptation (192).

We now turn our attention away from bones and teeth to the perhaps more sublime realm of human culture.

BEHAVIORAL AND CULTURAL TRENDS IN AUSTRALOPITHECINES

It is important to recognize that models of human origins must address both the morphological and behavioral differences separating humans and apes. We have already looked at how dietary and/or reproductive behavior has been used to model theories of human evolution. Now we shall examine the emergence of culture: tool use, toolmaking, and the use of fire.

What Is Culture?

What is culture, and when did it begin to play a role in hominid evolution? Definitions of culture have always been elusive and changeable as ethologists and anthropologists learn more about extant and extinct hominids. In a broad sense, **culture** indicates a system of shared meanings, symbols, customs, beliefs, and practices that are learned by teaching or by imitation and used to cope with the environment, to communicate with others, and to transmit information through the generations. Culture also determines the production of human artifacts (193). A behavior is considered culture only if differences in its distribution among populations are independent of any environmental or genetic factors. By these definitions then, the distribution of various nut-cracking behaviors in some populations of West African chimpanzees can be construed as "culture" in these nonhuman primates (194,195).

Most people regard tool use, toolmaking, and the use of fire as three important types of cultural behavior. Certainly they are among the earliest examples of culture among fossil hominids for which there is evidence. It is important to recognize, however, that tool use and even rudimentary toolmaking have been documented among living primates other than humans. For example, chimpanzees are known to adapt thin branches for extracting termites from the ground, to utilize leaf "sponges" for sopping up water in the hollows of trees, and to extract sap from oil-palm trees with a "pestle" and then drink it using a "fibre-sponge." A captive bonobo (*Pan paniscus*) has even been taught the basic skills required to produce usable stone flakes and fragments by hard-hammer percussion (although his stoneflaking skills are not yet as well developed as those exhibited by the earliest known toolmaking hominids) (196–198). Therefore it is not that *H. sapiens* is unique in showing cultural behavior; but we are unique in the complexity and extent of the cultural behavior on which we depend for our survival.

The Evolution of Culture in Hominids

When did hominids begin using tools, and what materials were these tools made of? The use of simple unaltered objects found nearby, which are called **opportunistic tools**, presumably predated the actual physical alteration of an object for one or more specific uses, which is called toolmaking. It is difficult to make inferences about opportunistic tool use from artifacts found at fossil sites because many perishable objects such as wood may have been used long before permanent materials were. Even preserved objects such as stones and fossilized animal bone found in association with fossil hominids are sometimes difficult to assess as opportunistic tools; for example, bones may simply be the refuse of a meal, and stones foreign to the site may have been deposited there through geological activity rather than human intervention.

There is no evidence of tool use or toolmaking associated with any fossil hominoids in the Miocene, nor is it definite which if any australopithecine species made the stone tools found in the numerous Plio-Pleistocene tool sites in eastern and southern Africa. This is because early species of *Homo* are also found in the same areas. However, it is probably safe to assume that in the Pliocene, about 5.0–2.5 mya, early australopithecines were using simple opportunistic tools such as sticks, bones, or stones as well as unaltered objects carried some distance before use, referred to as **manuports**, for collecting plant foods and insects, and for scavenging and killing small animals.

The Oldowan Tradition   The Shungura Formation at Omo, dated to 2.5–2.0 mya, was the first site to yield stone artifacts. Since both early *Homo* and *Australopithecus* are represented in these sediments, it is not certain if one or both groups made tools. Several sites slightly younger than 2 million years at eastern Lake Turkana have also yielded stone tools. Here again, there is no certainty of the identity of the toolmakers. Some of these sites may have been butchery sites; all of them are distinguished by a low density of artifacts, a high frequency of flakes, and a rarity of larger, shaped core tools (199). **Cores** are simply lumps of stone from which flakes have been removed; sometimes a core is the by-product of toolmaking, but it may also be shaped and modified to serve as a tool in its own right. Most of the early stone tools were made from quartz, quartzite, lava, and chert. The stone-tool industry from this time period is referred to as the **Oldowan tradition**, named after Olduvai Gorge, where it was first identified (Fig. 5.32).

Undoubtedly the finest archeological record for early hominids comes from Olduvai Gorge (200). Dozens of occupational sites are found in Beds I and II, which yield artifacts not only of the Oldowan tradition but also of the Developed Oldowan tradition (Fig. 5.33a–d). The latter succeeds the former in lower Bed II and occurs thereafter in Beds II and IV. Oldowan and Developed Oldowan tools have been found at several sites in North Africa (coastal Morocco and Tunisia), East Africa (Olduvai, Koobi Fora, Omo, Hadar), and South Africa (Swartkrans and Sterkfontein). After 2 mya these two traditions often overlap with each other and with later Stone Age industries.

The basic forms of stone tools that predominate from 2.0 to 1.5 mya in the Oldowan tradition include an assortment of choppers, usually made from cobblestones of quartz or quartzite, hammerstones made from pebbles or cobblestones, simple cores, polyhedrals, which are angular tools with three or more intersecting working edges, and flake scrapers (201). The **Developed Oldowan tradition** continues the flake-and-chopper industry seen in the Oldowan tradition. In addition it includes proto-handaxes,

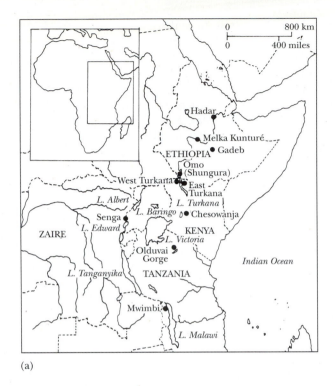

(a)

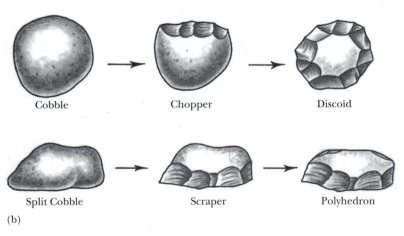

Cobble → Chopper → Discoid

Split Cobble → Scraper → Polyhedron

(b)

Fig. 5.32.   (a) Sites in East Africa, all older than 1.4 mya, where Oldowan tools have been found. From (242–244). (b) Continuities among Oldowan artifact types. Removal of a few flakes transforms a cobble into a chopper and then, if more flakes are struck, into a discoid. Similarly, a split cobble, heavy-duty scraper, and polyhedron form a continuum. (c) A range of Oldowan tools and their traditional classification. 1, hammerstone; 2, subspheroid; 3, bifacial chopper; 4, polyhedron; 5, discoid; 6, flake scraper; 7, flake; 8, core scraper.

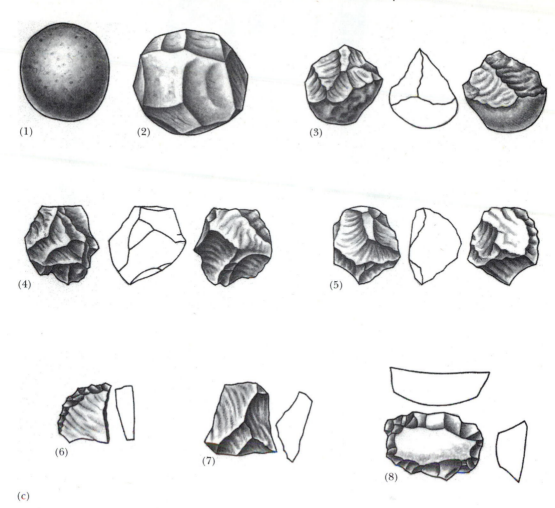

(1) (2) (3)

(4) (5)

(6) (7) (8)

(c)

which are simple pointed choppers, and crude bifacial forms (Fig. 5.33a–d). Rarely present are more sophisticated bifacial forms, such as handaxes, which are bifacial cores with one end pointed for cutting and the other end rounded. These artifacts provide clear evidence of a rudimentary knowledge of working stone for the production of flakes and chipping edges. Some of these archeological occurrences suggest that the species making the tools may have established home bases at some of these sites.

All the sites in eastern and southern Africa yielding Oldowan and Developed Oldowan stone tools also contain remains of *Homo* aff. *H. habilis* and/or *Homo* aff. *H. erectus* (see later chapters). However, one cannot definitely conclude that *Homo* was the sole maker of these tools, since australopithecines have also been found in association with these artifacts: *A. boisei* at Lake Turkana (Koobi Fora), Omo, and Olduvai (Beds I and II) and *A. robustus* at Swartkrans (Members 1 to 3) in southern Africa.

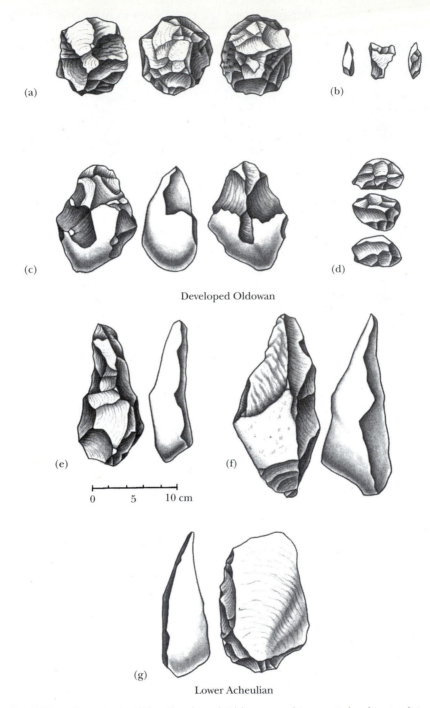

(a)

(b)

(c)

Developed Oldowan

(d)

(e)

0   5   10 cm

(f)

(g)

Lower Acheulian

Fig. 5.33. Stone tools of the Developed Oldowan and Lower Acheulian traditions. Developed Oldowan: (a) multifaceted polyhedral from North Africa, (b) small flake scraper from Olduvai, (c) core scraper from Olduvai, (d) proto-handaxe from Sterkfontein. Lower Acheulian: (e) handaxe from North Africa, (f) trihedral pick from North Africa, (g) cleaver from North Africa. From (245).

The Acheulian Tradition   The most widespread and longest-lived cultural tradition on record is the **Acheulian industry**, a stone-tool tradition predominating in the late Early Stone Age. This tradition was named for St. Acheul, a site near Amiens, France, where artifacts of this style were first identified in the nineteenth century. Its earliest occurrence goes back to approximately 1.5 mya at Olduvai Gorge, Tanzania, and Konso-Gardula, Ethiopia, and it continues in some areas such as Kalambo Falls in northern Zambia to about 60,000 years ago. More sophisticated than the Oldowan and Developed Oldowan traditions, it is sometimes found concurrently with the latter, as at Olduvai, where Acheulian tools have been recovered from the middle of Bed II up through Beds III and IV. The Acheulian tradition is characterized by large cutting tools like true handaxes, cleavers, the axelike stone implements bearing a sharp, somewhat straight cutting edge on one end, and trihedrals, three-sided picklike handaxes (Fig. 5.33e–g).

The Acheulian industry is often associated with *H. erectus*, though the association is sometimes difficult to confirm. For example, *H. erectus* is present at Lake Turkana from at least 1.6 to 1.2 mya, but there is no trace of an Acheulian industry there. In southern Africa some early Acheulian artifacts have been found at Sterkfontein (Member 5), which has yielded *Homo* aff. *H. habilis*. Both *H. erectus* and *A. boisei* fossils have been found at the Acheulian site of Konso-Gardula (202,203). We will discuss early *Homo* in later chapters.

The **Middle Stone Age** in Africa, which is generally dated from over 100,000 to around 40,000 years ago, is characterized by the use of carefully prepared stone cores for the production of flake tools. It is also the time in Africa when regional variation in stone-tool technologies becomes most evident. The **Late Stone Age** in Africa, which generally postdates 40,000 years ago, is characterized by a predominance of blade tools and microliths, tiny geometrically shaped blades often set in handles made of bone or wood. The Middle and Late Stone Ages are both associated exclusively with *H. sapiens* and will be discussed in more detail in later chapters.

In summary, we can say that deliberate stone toolmaking had evolved by about 2.5 mya but that the identity of the toolmakers is inconclusive. Stone tools have not been found in direct association with either *A. afarensis* at Laetoli or Hadar or with *A. africanus* at Sterkfontein or Taung. Although these two species were presumably using some perishable tools, we have no evidence that they were actually making stone tools. The earliest stone tools of the Oldowan and Developed Oldowan traditions have been found at a number of sites yielding *A. robustus* and/or *A. boisei* and *Homo* aff. *H. habilis*, including Koobi Fora, Omo, and Olduvai. *Homo* aff. *H. habilis* is also associated with an early Acheulian industry in both eastern Africa (e.g. Olduvai) and southern Africa (Sterkfontein, Member 5). The more developed Acheulian is generally associated with *H. erectus* and the Middle and Late Stone Age industries with *H. sapiens* (Table 5.4).

Table 5.4   Inferences about Hominid Behavior and Ecology (from R. Potts, 1992)

Hominids and Time Periods (Years Ago)	Inference	Nature of the Evidence
Hominid ancestors (?8–5 million)	Equatorial African origin	Humans are genetically closest to African apes, which today are distributed across equatorial Africa; earliest hominid fossils are in eastern Africa
Earliest hominids (5–3 million)	Habitually bipedal on the ground; occasionally arboreal	Postcranial anatomy of fossils from Hadar in Ethiopia (but disagreements about similarity to modern human bipedalism and degree of arboreality)
	Inhabited a mosaic of grassland, woodland, and thick shrub	Faunas from Laetoli in Tanzania, Hadar, and Makapansgat in South Africa
(3–2 million)	Occupation of open savannas	Fossil pollen and fauna
	Emphasis on a fibrous plant diet in robust australopithecines	Microwear on teeth; large teeth and jaws
	First known manufacture of stone tools	Tools from Ethiopia, Kenya, Malawi, Zaire dated between 2.5 and 2.0 million years
Plio-Pleistocene hominids[a] (2.0–1.5 million)	Increased commitment to bipedalism on the ground	Postcranial anatomy associated with archaic *Homo* established
	Increased dexterity related to tool use and toolmaking, and possibly foraging	Anatomy of hand bones and characteristics of stone tools and cores
	Stones and animal bones carried repeatedly to specific sites	Earliest known complex sites with many stone artifacts and fossils
	Use of tools to procure and process food	Bone and stone tools with distinctive traces of use
	Dietary increase in protein and fat from large animals	Cut marks made by stone tools on animal bones
	Scavenging and possible hunting of large animals; processing of animals at specific spots	Limb bones of animals concentrated at undisturbed archeological sites
	Increased cognitive capacities associated with making tools, foraging, social arrangements and/or developing linguistic skills	Increase in brain size from about a third to a half that of modern humans
	Changes in maturation rate	Implied by brain size increase and possible changes in tooth development
	Increased mobility and predator defence	Large stature evident in skeletal remains of early *Homo erectus* from West Turkana in Kenya

[a]Stone technology and changes in diet, brain size, etc., are usually associated with *Homo*.

No discussion of early hominid culture would be complete without some mention of the cultivation of fire. Evidence from China indicates that *H. erectus* clearly had control over fire by about 500,000 years ago. It has recently been reported, however, that fire was in use at least 1 mya at Swartkrans. The remains consist of altered bones that laboratory analysis indicates were burned at temperatures consistent with campfires rather than natural conflagrations. These bones are found in Member 3 dated at about 1.5 to 1.0 mya (204). Although remains of *A. robustus* and *Homo* aff. *H. erectus* are found in Members 1 and 2, only *A. robustus* is so far known from Member 3; however, *Homo* is presumed to have been present as well. Tools of the Developed Oldowan tradition, usually associated with *Homo*, are found throughout the sequence. It is not clear, therefore, which hominid was using fire at Swartkrans.

PHYLOGENY AND CLASSIFICATION: CURRENT ISSUES AND DEBATES

Thus far we have concentrated on the importance of fossils for unravelling human origins. Equally important is the recognition of a close genetic relationship between humans and the other extant hominoids, especially *Pan* and *Gorilla* (205–211). DNA hybridization experiments indicate at least 98 percent identity in nonrepeated DNA between human and chimpanzee, although these DNA data do not ultimately reveal which of the great apes is phylogenetically closest to humans (212–215).[10] These molecular studies do serve to reinforce, however, more traditional comparative anatomical studies that have emphasized the similarities between humans and African apes for over a century (218).

Attempts to identify direct lineages between Miocene hominoids and present-day apes and hominids have not been particularly successful. The reason for this is quite straightforward: there is simply no decent fossil evidence for hominoid evolution in Africa from the critical time about 12 to 5 mya. Presumably this is when various African Miocene hominoids were differentiating into the African great apes and early hominids (219).

Although no likely Miocene candidates for direct ancestry of the first hominids can be advanced, a number of plausible scenarios for relationships among the various hominid groups have been proposed, and to these we turn next.

---

[10]The question of whether or not mitochondrial DNA data, or any other molecular data for that matter, resolve the human-chimpanzee-gorilla trichotomy is also still open to debate among molecular biologists (210,216,217).

Throughout this chapter we have followed a taxonomically conservative approach by recognizing only one australopithecine genus containing six species: *A. ramidus, A. anamensis, A. afarensis, A. africanus, A. robustus,* and *A. boisei.* However, a debate continues about the actual number of genera and species represented in this fossil sample, and about what their phylogenetic and ecological relationships are to one another and to *Homo* (70,220,221). The significance of the ''gracile-robust'' distinction and its role in hominid evolution has also been controversial. All of these issues will be examined in this section.

Let's first summarize the various competing hypotheses about australopithecine phylogeny that have been offered over the past few years (Fig. 5.34). Unfortunately, not enough is known to speculate with any confidence on the relationship of *A. ramidus* and *A. anamensis* to the other australopithecines, though it seems likely that *A. ramidus* will appear very close to the root of all later hominids in subsequent phylogenetic trees and that *A. anamensis* may be directly ancestral to *A. afarensis.*

• *Hypothesis One:* The hominids from Hadar and Laetoli, which some classify as *A. afarensis,* are really a geographically separate subspecies of *A. afri-*

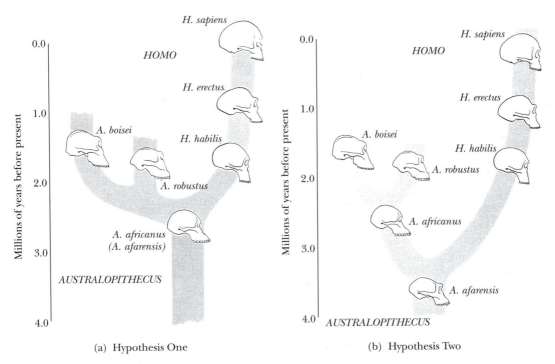

(a) Hypothesis One   (b) Hypothesis Two

Fig. 5.34. The six alternative phylogenetic hypotheses about early hominid evolution discussed in the text. *A. ramidus* would appear very close to the root of all later hominids in these phylogenetic trees and *A. anamensis* may be directly ancestral to *A. afarensis.* From (246).

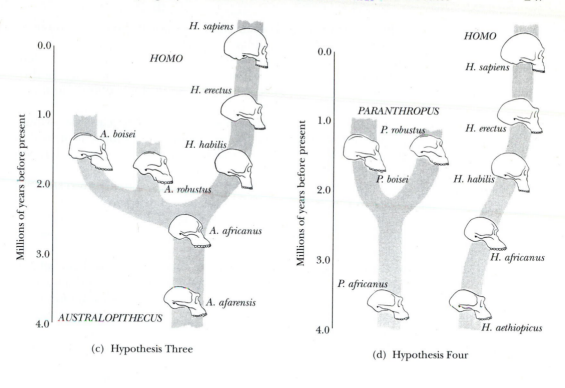

(c) Hypothesis Three

(d) Hypothesis Four

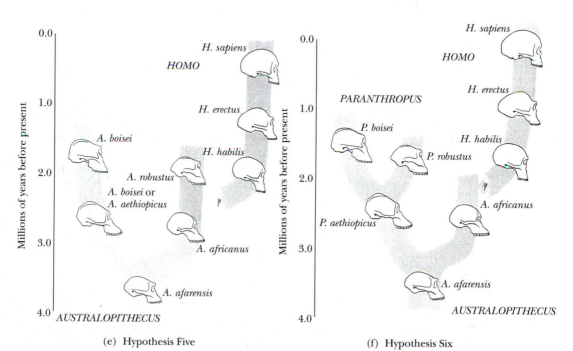

(e) Hypothesis Five

(f) Hypothesis Six

canus, which in turn is the last common ancestor of both the "robust" australopithecine and *Homo* lineages (222).

- *Hypothesis Two: A. afarensis* represents the ancestral species from which both the *Homo* and "robust" australopithecine lineages emerge. In this scenario, *A. africanus* is situated near the base of the "robust" australopithecine lineage (15,36,37).

- *Hypothesis Three: A. afarensis* represents the ancestral species from which *A. africanus* evolved. This latter species, or one very similar to it, is the common ancestor of both later "robust" australopithecine and *Homo* lineages (38,39).

- *Hypothesis Four:* The Hadar and Laetoli hominids represent two species, one related to the "robust" australopithecine lineage (here called *Paranthropus*) and the other to the *Homo* lineage. Therefore, the "robust" australopithecine lineage can be traced back through an *A. afarensis*–like ancestor (23,122,223,224).

- *Hypothesis Five: A. afarensis* represents the ancestral species from which both hyperrobust East African australopithecines and an *A. africanus*–like form evolved. Both *Homo* and *A. robustus* emerge out of this *A. africanus*–like ancestor (88).

- *Hypothesis Six: A. afarensis* is the last common ancestor of a monophyletic "robust" australopithecine lineage (termed *Paranthropus*) and a *Homo* lineage, the latter passing through an *A. africanus*–like stage (225).

The relationship between two of the oldest australopithecines, *A. afarensis* and *A. africanus,* is anything but clear. Are they geographic variants of the same species (Hypothesis One) (1), or is *A. afarensis* the stem hominid species (Hypotheses Two, Three, Five, Six) (37)? The latter is refuted by the new discovery of *A. ramidus,* which now must be considered the most likely candidate for the stem hominid species. Owing to their antiquity, *A. afarensis* and *A. africanus* share, not surprisingly, a number of primitive craniofacial characteristics. Some have argued that the primitive craniofacial plan of *A. africanus* represents a derived morphological composite, making it an excellent structural and phylogenetic intermediate between *A. afarensis, A. robustus,* and *A. boisei* (36,37,226). These authors would exclude *A. africanus* from direct ancestry of *H. habilis* because of the apparent fact that it is specialized in the direction of "robust" australopithecines (Hypothesis Two). Such specializations revolve around the stronger molarization of its premolars, generally increased relative size of its postcanine dentition, and increased buttressing and robustness of its mandibular body. Other features are all closely related to the increased size of the posterior dentition. Larger postcanine teeth are functionally associated with greater mandibular buttressing, more strongly developed muscle attachment areas on the cranium, a shift forward of the center of action of the temporalis muscle, and midfacial buttressing (12).

It has also been pointed out that although *A. afarensis* is remarkably primitive in many features, *A. africanus, A. robustus,* and *A. boisei* more closely resemble *H. habilis* in many of those same features (12). In fact, *H. habilis* and the later species of *Australopithecus* share an extensive suite of derived traits not present in *A. afarensis* at all. This implies that the immediate ancestor of *H. habilis* also probably shared these traits. If *A. afarensis*, rather than *A. africanus*, is the immediate ancestor of *H. habilis*, then a great deal of parallel evolution would have to be postulated. From this point of view it is clearly more parsimonious to assume that the hominid species immediately predating the appearance of *Homo*, *A. africanus*, is the immediate common ancestor not only of *H. habilis* but also of *A. robustus* and *A. boisei* (Hypothesis Three) (38,39).

What is the relationship between *A. africanus* and *A. robustus*? Both are found in South African sites and as we have seen, J. T. Robinson viewed them as occupying separate ecological niches based on dietary preference, *A. africanus* being omnivorous and *A. robustus* vegetarian (90) (Table 5.2). Presumably he considered dating of the fossils to be indeterminate enough that the two species could have overlapped in time as well as geographic area; however, most proposals for dating the South African sediments place the earliest *A. robustus* specimen at least a half million years after the last *A. africanus* specimen. In any case, Robinson considered these two groups distinct enough to assign them to separate genera, renaming the "gracile" hominid *H. africanus* because of its similarity to other *Homo* species.

Some have advocated an ancestor-descendant relationship between *A. africanus* and *A. robustus*, with the latter then giving rise to *A. boisei*. This view is based in large part on an analysis of the structure and function of the australopithecine face (15,226). This follows the evolutionary scheme similar to that shown in Hypothesis Two, in which the origins of the "robust" clade are in *A. africanus*, which is thereby removed from consideration as a human ancestor. To those who see *A. africanus–A. robustus–A. boisei* as a single evolving lineage, the beginnings of specialization characterizing the "robust" australopithecines are already manifest in almost every aspect of the masticatory system of *A. africanus*. Evidence for this viewpoint includes the presence of anterior pillars in both forms. This buttressing is viewed as a structural response to the greater occlusal load arising from the incipient molarization of the premolars. In *A. africanus* this molarization process was just beginning, but the still considerable protrusion of the palate relative to the more peripheral facial frame increased the need for such incipient pillars. The anterior pillars and the advancement of the inferior part of the infraorbital region (where the masseter muscle originated) played a major role in molding the facial topography of *A. africanus*. The presence of such pillars in *A. africanus* is considered evidence linking it to the "robust" australopithecine clade. The absence of the pillars in *A. afarensis* has led some to conclude that its face was the most primitive among the australopithecines (16,226).

This scenario was gaining widespread acceptance before the recent discovery of the 2.5-million-year-old *A. boisei* skull (specimen WT 17000) from west of Lake Turkana (88) (Fig. 5.16). This specimen shows that the *A. boisei* lineage was established prior to the well-dated *A. robustus* specimens from eastern and southern Africa and that, in robustness and tooth size, at least some members of the early *A. boisei* population were as large or larger than the later ones. Previously, most workers had suggested that within the "robust" australopithecine lineage there was a trend toward increasing size and robustness of the skull and jaws. This view is no longer tenable. Two possible phylogenetic schemes involving this new specimen are shown in Hypotheses Five and Six (here labelled as *A.* [or *Paranthropus*] *aethiopicus*).

A. robustus shares with younger examples of *A. boisei* several features that are apparently derived from the condition seen in specimen WT 17000:
- the cresting pattern with emphasis on the anterior and middle parts of the temporalis muscle
- the orthognathic face
- the deep temporomandibular joint with a strong bony projection, or articular eminence, anterior to the mandibular fossa on which the mandibular condyle slides as the jaw opens

Thus, this new specimen shows that *A. robustus* is a related, smaller species that was derived from ancestral forms earlier than 2.5 mya and/or had evolved independently in southern Africa, perhaps from *A. africanus*.

Although the new *A. boisei* specimen shows characteristics of robustness and tooth size usually thought to be typical of later "advanced" "robust" australopithecines, it also has a number of craniofacial features that are more primitive than those in *A. africanus* and similar to those in *A. afarensis*. Some of the primitive features it shares with *A. afarensis* include (3):
- strong upper facial prognathism
- a flat cranial base
- a flat temporomandibular fossa
- extensive pneumatization in the temporal bone
- a large anterior tooth row
- a flat, shallow palate
- a maxillary dental arch that converges posteriorly

In spite of these primitive features, WT 17000 seems clearly to be a member of the *A. boisei* clade. Is it possible that the Hadar sample from which *A. afarensis* comes actually consists of two species, one of which gave rise to *A. boisei*? Features of the nasal region suggest that at least one of the juvenile crania from Hadar has features associated with "robust" australopithecines, while patterns of cranial venous circulation and some postcranial evidence also suggest the same. The phylogenetic implications of this conclusion can be seen in Hypothesis Four. These lines of evidence, however, are not unequivocal and so are also challenged by some researchers (227,228).

In analyzing the differences between the "gracile" and "robust" australopithecines, two related questions come to mind that return us to basic principles of variation. First, how much intra- and interspecific variation can we expect to find in the two forms? Second, are the differences between "gracile" and "robust" forms the product of real functional and biological differences, or are they merely the differences one would predict in two similar animals of different body size? In other words, are "robust" australopithecines merely "blown-up" versions of "gracile" australopithecines, or are they morphologically, behaviorally, and/or ecologically different, as Robinson first suggested? These critical questions are too often ignored in taxonomic arguments about early hominids.

As mentioned earlier, Robinson believed the two forms to be distinct at the generic level and proposed a dietary hypothesis to explain these differences. But how distinct in quantitative terms are these forms? How does their morphological variability stack up against known variability in living hominoids? In postcanine dental areas the "gracile" species are about 88 percent the size of the "robust" species. Is this a great difference? By absolute and percentage measures, "gracile" and "robust" australopithecines are more similar in this dimension than many modern human populations are. According to Robinson's dietary hypothesis, "gracile" australopithecines are supposed to have had smaller posterior dentitions, because of their presumably more omnivorous diet. However, "gracile" australopithecine cheek teeth are not really as small as Robinson implies. After all, their size lies completely within the range of dental variation in modern gorillas in spite of the fact that presumed "gracile" australopithecine body size is only a fraction of that of living gorillas (229).

Another way to look at cheek-tooth size is to ask the question: What is the relative size of the cheek teeth in *Australopithecus* in comparison to body size? As we saw earlier, the megadontia quotient of all australopithecine species (except *A. ramidus*) is large. The sequence *A. afarensis–A. africanus–A. robustus–A. boisei* shows strong positive allometry indicating increasing megadontia through time (11,12,14).

The question of whether "gracile" species and "robust" species were merely allometric variants of one another was first directly addressed by David Pilbeam and Steven Gould of Harvard University, who argued that the three species, *A. africanus*, *A. robustus*, and *A. boisei*, simply represented the "same" animal expressed over a wide range of body size: "In other words, size increase may be the only independent adaptation of these animals, changes in shape simply preserving the function of the smaller prototype at larger sizes" (230). Pilbeam and Gould came to this conclusion after examining the relationships between brain size and body size and between tooth size and body size in the three species. Intraspecific plots of brain size versus body size have been carried out for numerous birds and mammals. (Here "intraspecific" includes not only individual adults or races within a species but also very closely related species displaying the "same" body plan over a wide size range.) The slopes of these plots range from 0.2 to 0.4. The slope for the three australopithecine species calculated by Pilbeam and Gould is about 0.33, well within this "intraspecific" range.

When tooth areas are plotted against body weights, a slope of 2/3 is the expected value of geometric scaling for constant proportions throughout the size range. Any value greater than 2/3 indicates that large animals have relatively larger postcanine teeth than smaller members of the series. The value calculated by Pilbeam and Gould for *A. africanus–A. robustus–A. boisei* is 0.7 and that for pygmy chimpanzee–chimpanzee–gorilla is 0.85. This would confirm that in both these groups the larger species has relatively larger cheek teeth. Based on similar data from other mammals, including rodents, pigs, deer, and monkeys, however, they concluded that positive allometry might be expected in sequences of related mammals that vary in size but not in basic design. Perhaps the observable increase in cheek-tooth size in these species is more closely correlated with increasing metabolic rate than with mere geometric similarity.

With the australopithecines behind us, we emerge on the brink of humanity. As we've seen, it's unclear which, if any, of the currently recognized species of *Australopithecus* gave rise to the earliest known species of *Homo*, although it was most probably a "gracile" form (Fig. 5.35). Although the

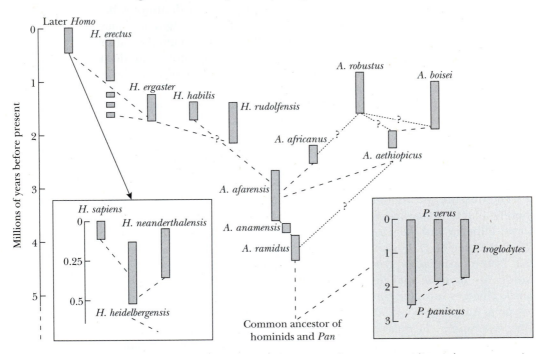

Fig. 5.35. A provisional phylogenetic tree placing *A. ramidus* as the stem species from which all other hominids arose. *A. ramidus* is the most primitive hominid yet discovered. Its many morphological similarities with living chimpanzees confirm molecular evidence that the hominid-chimpanzee clade diverged from each other as recently as 5.5–4.5 mya. The broken line that extends the first appearance of *H. erectus* reflects new evidence that relevant remains from Java date to about 1.8 mya. From (247).

traditional interpretation of the genus *Homo* is that *H. habilis*, *H. erectus*, and *H. sapiens* are chronologically successive species that slowly graded one into another, we shall see in the following chapters that the situation is now thought to be far more complex.

At what point did our hominid ancestors become truly "human"? This question, the subject of the next chapter, remains the most difficult to answer. We can say that many of the biological and environmental forces that helped shape the genetic makeup of modern humans were operating by at least the Pliocene. And whatever the actual selection pressures were for the traits that distinguish us from the other primates—bipedal locomotion, reduced canine teeth, enlarged brains, parental care of the young, home bases, food sharing, verbal communication skills, savanna-adapted diets, cooperative hunting and scavenging, tool use, opposable thumbs, and division of labor, among others—they were certainly in evidence by the mid-Pleistocene.

It is easy to assume that the more recent the fossil being studied, the more confident paleontologists are about its line of descent. And so it may surprise the reader to learn that the source, timing, and area of differentiation—in short, the origin—of our kind, *H. sapiens*, the last bipedal, large-brained primate species to arrive on the scene, is still largely unknown. Although there is no unanimity of opinion on the timing of the *H. erectus*–*H. sapiens* transition, it is probably fair to say that it took place sometime in the Middle Pleistocene, most likely less than 500,000 years ago. Because of the morphological continuity between the two species, the dividing line for humanity will perhaps always remain ambiguous.

These are just some of the interesting issues that we will tackle in the following chapters.

CHAPTER VI

The Origin of the Genus *Homo*

INTRODUCTION

THE DISCOVERY OF "HANDYMAN": *HOMO HABILIS*

MORPHOLOGICAL FEATURES OF *HOMO HABILIS*

Homo habilis: One Species or Two?

EARLY HOMINID LIFESTYLES: TINKER, TAILOR, SCAVENGER, HUNTER?

Because the animal-human boundary is the boundary of the moral universe, the stories that we tell about human origins, even if they are true stories, are myths; and the general point of those stories is explaining—and legitimating—human control and domination of nature.

Matt Cartmill
"Human uniqueness and theoretical content in paleoanthropology"
(*Int J Primatol* 11, 1990)

INTRODUCTION

Our own genus, *Homo*, first appears in the fossil record of Africa some 2.4–2.0 mya. Anthropologists have traditionally divided the genus into three time-successive species, or **chronospecies**, *H. habilis*, *H. erectus*, and *H. sapiens*, reflecting the view that we represent a single, **anagenetic** lineage, i.e., one characterized by a gradual accumulation of changes from ancestor to descendant through time. But does this traditional view of human evolution actually underestimate the number of species of *Homo* that existed at any one time during the Plio-Pleistocene (1,2)?

Over the past two decades an increasing number of fossils ascribed to early *Homo* have been discovered in both eastern and southern Africa (Fig 6.1). However, as the pace of discovery has quickened, so have the inevitable questions such discoveries raise: How can early *Homo* be distinguished from "gracile" australopithecines, particularly *A. africanus* and/or *A. afarensis*? Is the range of morphological variation subsumed under the name *H. habilis* too great for a single species? If so, what other taxa are represented? Does the definition of *Homo* need modification, and if so, how? Is *H. habilis* really ancestral to *H. erectus*? These are just some of the interesting issues facing paleoanthropologists as they study the origins of the genus *Homo*.

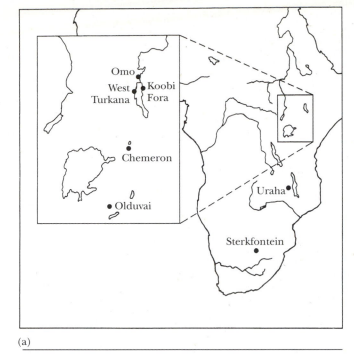

(a)

		Sites	
Mya	Olduvai (OH)	Koobi Fora (KNM-ER)	Omo
1.6	13		
	16		
1.7			
1.8		3891	
	7, 8, 62		
		1805	
	24		
1.9		1470, 1802, 1813, 3732, 3735	L894-1
2.0			

(b)

Fig. 6.1. (a) Location of African sites where *H. habilis*, or similar forms, have been found. (b) Some of the better known fossils often attributed to *H. habilis* arranged in approximate chronological order by site (13).

The starting point for our discussion on the origin of *Homo* is the simple question: "How does one define it?" This is not easy to answer. Our genus, which encompasses such diverse groups as modern humans, Neandertals, and *H. erectus*, is notoriously difficult to define. To be sure, certain evolutionary "trends" are easy to visualize, such as the enlargening of body and brain size and the lessening of sexual dimorphism, particularly during the *H. erectus* stage (3–5). And until quite recently, most descriptions of the genus *Homo* were simply a litany of features, or general trends, characterizing the various species with little emphasis given to the possession of shared derived features that actually define them as members of a genus in the cladistic sense (6–8). For example, Louis Leakey, Phillip Tobias, and John Napier, in their landmark 1964 paper describing the new species, *H. habilis* (8), offered the following:

A genus of the Hominidae with the following characters: the structure of the pelvic girdle and of the hind-limb skeleton is adapted to habitual erect posture and bipedal gait: the fore-limb is shorter than the hind-limb; the pollex is well developed and fully opposable and the hand is capable not only of a power grip but of, at the least, a simple and usually well developed precision grip; the cranial capacity is very variable but is, on the average, larger than the range of capacities of members of the genus *Australopithecus*, although the lower part of the range of capacities in the genus *Homo* overlaps with the upper part of the range in *Australopithecus*; the capacity is (on the average) large relative to body-size and ranges from about 600 c.c. in earlier forms to more than 1,600 c.c.; the muscular ridges on the cranium range from very strongly marked to virtually imperceptible, but the temporal crests or lines never reach the midline; the frontal region of the cranium is without undue post-orbital constriction (such as is common in members of the genus *Australopithecus*); the supra-orbital region of the frontal bone is very variable, ranging from a massive and very salient supra-orbital torus to a complete lack of any supra-orbital projection and a smooth brow region; the facial skeleton varies from moderately prognathous to orthognathous, but it is not concave (or dished) as is common in members of the Australopithecinae; the anterior symphyseal contour varies from a marked retreat to a forward slope, while the bony chin may be entirely lacking, or may vary from a slight to a very strongly developed mental trigone; the dental arcade is evenly rounded with no diastema in most members of the genus; the first lower premolar is clearly bicuspid with a variably developed lingual cusp; the molar teeth are variable in size, but in general are small relative to the size of these teeth in the genus *Australopithecus*; the size of the last upper molar is highly variable, but it is generally smaller than the second upper molar and commonly also smaller than the first upper molar; the lower third molar is sometimes appreciably larger than the second; in relation to the position seen in the Hominoidea as a whole, the canines are small, with little or no overlapping after the initial stages of wear, but when compared with those of members of the genus *Australopithecus*, the incisors and canines are not very small relative to the molars and premolars; the teeth in general, and particularly the molars and premolars, are not enlarged bucco-lingually as they are in the genus *Australopithecus*; the first deciduous lower molar shows a variable degree of molarization.

More recently, a number of anthropologists have begun to analyze the genus *Homo* using cladistic techniques (9–11). One such analysis concluded that the *Homo* clade can only be defined by eight character state changes of a total of ninety cranial, mandibular, and dental characters investigated (10,12,13). These eight are listed in Table 6.1.

Table 6.1   Morphological Features That Define the *Homo* Clade (from 13)

The cladogram presented below is the most parsimonious generated from a set of ninety cranial, mandibular, and dental characters. The resulting *Homo* clade is defined by the following character state changes at Node A:

1. Increased cranial vault thickness.
2. Reduced postorbital constriction.
3. Increased contribution of the occipital bone to cranial sagittal arc length.
4. Increased cranial vault height.
5. More anteriorly situated foramen magnum.
6. Reduced lower facial prognathism.
7. Narrower tooth crowns, particularly mandibular premolars.
8. Reduction in length of the molar row.

The two species comprising the original *H. habilis* hypodigm, *H. habilis* sensu stricto and *H. rudolfensis*, share a hypothetical ancestor with each other that neither shares with any other taxon. That sister group is defined by the five character state changes at Node B, namely:

1. Elongated anterior basicranium.
2. Higher cranial vault.
3&4. Mesiodistally elongated M_1 and M_2.
5. Narrow mandibular fossa.

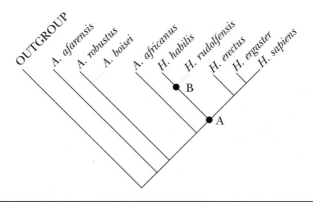

THE DISCOVERY OF "HANDYMAN": *HOMO HABILIS*

In the summer of 1959, just weeks before the discovery of the "Zinj" cranium (*A. boisei*), a left mandibular fragment with M_3 and an isolated lower premolar were found about 8 ft above the basal lava at site MK, Bed I, Olduvai.[1] These teeth (OH 4) were small, narrow, and elongated. However,

---

[1]MK stands for MacInnes Korongo.

in the excitement over the discovery of the "Zinj" cranium a few weeks later, a detailed analysis of the MK teeth was postponed.

The following year some fragmentary postcranial (tibia and fibula—OH 35), calvarial, and dental (OH 6) remains of another small-toothed hominid were found at the same site (FLK)[2] that had yielded the massive-toothed type specimen of *A. boisei* (OH 5). The size and proportions of these smaller teeth clearly ruled out that this was an example of sexual dimorphism. Later that same year, Louis and Mary Leakey's eldest son, Jonathan, discovered additional remains from a nearby occupational site, or **living floor** (FLK NN). These consisted of the greater part of a juvenile mandible with teeth, an isolated upper molar, large parts of two juvenile parietal bones, and a number of wrist, hand, and finger bones. All of these specimens were designated OH 7. At the same locality Mary Leakey found at least a dozen foot bones (OH 8). All the dental remains clearly departed from the australopithecine tendency toward dental enlargement (14).

This "hominizing" trend was not confined to the teeth, however. Even though the parietals belonged to a juvenile, they were far bigger than any australopithecine parietals thus far described. Based on their size and shape, endocranial capacity was estimated at 642–723 cc in this individual, which is greater than in any australopithecine (15,16). Thus, "the same creature which showed hominizing tendencies in its teeth also showed a more hominized brain-size" (17). Over the next few years, several other specimens were found (for example, OH 13, 16) and in 1964 these became the basis for the description of a new species of *Homo* that was formally named *H. habilis* (8) (Table 6.2). The **type** of the new species, i.e., the specimen that serves as the standard for the taxon, became the OH 7 sample mentioned above. Other specimens attributed to *H. habilis* included the skull fragments and teeth (OH 4 and 6), part of an adult foot (OH 8), an incomplete cranium of an adolescent (OH 13), a collection of juvenile cranial pieces (OH 14), and the fragmented cranial vault and dentition (OH 16) of a young adult (8). The name *"habilis"* was suggested to Leakey, Tobias, and Napier by Raymond Dart and in Latin means "handy, skillful, able." The best known specimens from Olduvai include OH 7 (known as "Jonny's Child," after its discoverer, Jonathan Leakey), OH 13 ("Cinderella"), OH 16 ("George"), and OH 24 ("Twiggy"). A possible *H. habilis* specimen from southern Africa, Stw 53 from Sterkfontein, is a partial cranium that has been likened to OH 24 (18). At Sterkfontein, *Homo* aff. *H. habilis* is thus far known only from Member 5, thus postdating the *A. africanus* specimens from Member 4. Several specimens from Swartkrans (SK 847 and SK 45) have also been compared to *H. habilis* at one time or another (19).

Some traditions die hard, and many anthropologists were not amused by the naming of a new species of *Homo*. While two of its describers pro-

---

[2]FLK stands for Frida Leakey Korongo.

Table 6.2   Distinguishing Morphological Features of *H. habilis* (from 8)

Cranial and Mandibular

   Maxilla and mandible smaller than in *Australopithecus*, but equivalent in size to
      H. erectus and *H. sapiens*
   Brain size greater than *Australopithecus*, but smaller than *H. erectus*
   Slight to strong muscular markings
   Parietal bone curvature in the sagittal plane varying from slight (i.e., hominine)
      to moderate (i.e., australopithecine)
   Relatively open-angled external sagittal curvature to occipital
   Retreating chin, with a slight or absent mental trigone

Dental

   Incisors large with respect to those of *Australopithecus* and *H. erectus*
   Molar size overlaps the ranges for *Australopithecus* and *H. erectus*
   Canines large relative to premolars
   Premolars narrower than in *Australopithecus* and within the range of *H. erectus*
   All teeth relatively narrow buccolingually and elongated mesiodistally, especially
      the mandibular molars and premolars

Postcranial

   Clavicle resembles *H. sapiens*
   Hand bones have broad terminal phalanges, capitate and MCP articulations
      resembling *H. sapiens*, but differ in respect of the scaphoid and trapezium,
      attachments of the superficial flexor tendons, and the robusticity and
      curvature of the phalanges
   Foot bones resemble *H. sapiens* in the stout and adducted big toe, and well-
      marked foot arches, but differ in the shape of the trochlea surface of the
      talus and the relatively robust third metatarsal

posed early on that *H. habilis* was both a phenetic and phyletic link between
Australopithecus and *H. erectus* (20,21), this view was not universally shared
(22,23). Critics raised doubts on several fronts, reflecting both the prevailing paradigms and biases of the day (24–26):

- it was believed that the "morphological distance" between *A. africanus*
  and *H. erectus* was too slight to accommodate another species between
  them
- brain enlargement was accepted as a preeminent hallmark of *Homo*; thus,
  hominids with brain sizes smaller than those of *H. erectus* could not be
  called *Homo*
- the definition of the genus *Homo* was held to be immutable and sacro-
  sanct, and some critics were uncomfortable that Leakey, Tobias, and Napier would broaden it to accommodate *habilis*
- behavioral considerations, such as stone-tool culture, were considered
  irrelevant to the definition and diagnoses of hominid species

   The senior author of the new species, Louis Leakey, took another tack
altogether. He concluded that several features of cranial shape shared by
H. habilis and *H. sapiens* were not found in *H. erectus*, and therefore *H.
habilis* should not be regarded as a stage between *A. africanus* and *H. erectus*,
but rather as a form directly ancestral to *H. sapiens* (27)!

By the end of the 1970s, many anthropologists came to recognize the distinctiveness of *H. habilis*, not only from Olduvai but also from other sites in East Africa like Lake Turkana and Omo and possibly from locations in South Africa (Sterkfontein) as well (7,18,19,28–31) (Fig. 6.1a).

As mentioned in the previous chapter, *H. habilis* and *Australopithecus* were contemporaries in East Africa for hundreds of thousands of years. The dates of some of the better known *H. habilis* specimens from East Africa are shown in Figure 6.1b.

MORPHOLOGICAL FEATURES OF *HOMO HABILIS*

The basic morphological features of *H. habilis* are summarized in Table 6.2 and illustrated in Figure 6.2. In general, the cranium of *H. habilis* is more gracile than that of *Australopithecus*, particularly in its less well developed muscular crests. Cranial capacity averages about 650 cc and endocranial casts reveal the first paleoneurological evidence for **Broca's area**, the speech area in the left cerebral cortex (see Fig. 5.10) (32–34). This compares with average cranial capacities of 413 cc for *A. afarensis*, 441 cc for *A. africanus*, 530 cc for *A. robustus*, and 515 cc for *A. boisei* (35). Facial heights and breadths are reduced relative to those in *Australopithecus*, and prominent anterior pillars are absent. In general, maxillae and mandibles are smaller than in *Australopithecus* and are within the size range of *H. erectus* and *H. sapiens*. The sagittal curvature of the parietal bone varies from slight (within the hominine range) to moderate (within the australopithecine range) and the curvature of the occipital bone is less than in *Australopithecus* or *H. erectus*, and within the range of *H. sapiens*.

Regarding the dentition, the canines are proportionately large relative to the premolars. The premolars and molars are within or below the size range found in *A. africanus*, while the incisors are relatively larger. There is a marked tendency toward buccolingual (side-to-side) narrowing and mesiodistal (front-to-back) elongation of most teeth, especially the lower premolars and molars.

H. habilis shows an interesting mosaic of australopithecine and *Homo*-like postcranial features. For example, the foot is humanlike in terms of metatarsal robustness and in having a well-marked longitudinal and transverse arch and a nonopposable hallux. The middle phalanges of the hand are somewhat apelike in being robust and curved with well-marked insertions for powerful muscles of finger flexion; however, the overall length and morphology of the distal phalanges are similar to those of modern humans and, most importantly, the thumb joint, or **carpometacarpal joint**, is distinctly humanlike (36). It would thus seem that *H. habilis* was bipedal but retained a hand capable of powerful grasping.

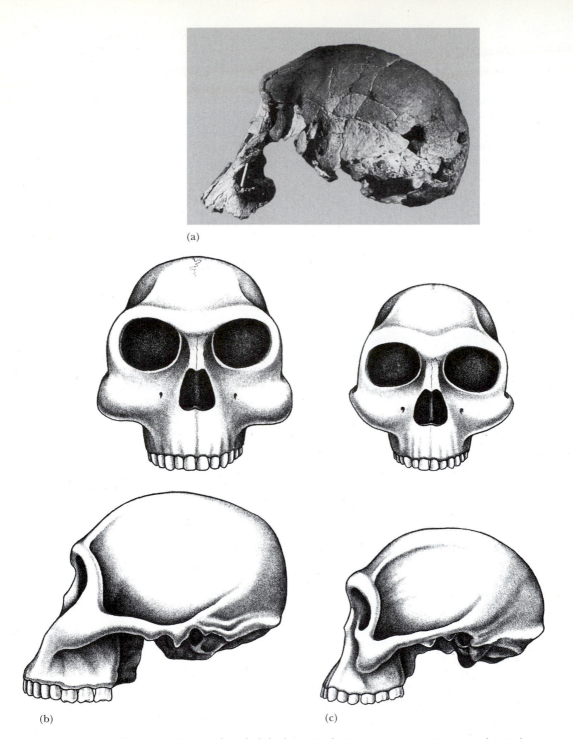

(a)

(b)   (c)

Fig. 6.2. Crania of *H. habilis* from Koobi Fora Formation (Eastern Lake Turkana).
(a) Specimen ER-1470; (b,c) reconstructions based on (b) the same skull, presumably a male, and on (c) specimen ER-1813, presumably a female. Note the reduced
nuchal and sagittal crests and lack of anterior pillars. [a, Courtesy of Alan Walker,
© National Museums of Kenya; b,c redrawn from (7).] (d) Comparison of *H. habilis*
to other early human fossils. From (117).

	Homo habilis (small)	Homo habilis (large)	Homo erectus	Archaic Homo sapiens	Neandertals	Early Modern Homo sapiens
Height (m)	1	c 1.5	1.3–1.5	?	1.5–1.7	1.6–1.85
Physique	Relatively long arms	Robust but "human" skeleton	Robust but "human" skeleton	Robust but "human" skeleton	As 'archaic H. sapiens,' but adapted for cold	Modern skeleton; ?adapted for warmth
Brain size (cc)	500–650	600–800	750–1,250	1,100–1,400	1,200–1,750	1,200–1,700
Skull form	Relatively small face; nose developed	Larger, flatter face	Flat, thick skull with large occipital and brow ridge	Higher skull; face less protruding	Reduced brow ridge; thinner skull; large nose; midface projection	Small or no brow ridge; shorter, high skull
Jaws/teeth	Thinner jaw; smaller, narrow molars	Robust jaw; large narrow molars	Robust jaw in larger individuals; smaller teeth than H. habilis	Similar to H. erectus but teeth may be smaller	Similar to 'archaic' H. sapiens; teeth smaller except for incisors; chin development in some	Shorter jaws than Neandertals; chin developed; teeth may be smaller
Distribution	Eastern (and southern?) Africa	Eastern Africa	Africa, Asia, and Indonesia (and Europe?)	Africa, Asia, and Europe	Europe and western Asia	Africa and western Asia
Known date (years ago)	2–1.6 million	2.4–1.6 million	1.8–0.3 million	400,000–100,000	150,000–30,000	130,000–60,000

(d)

This view of *H. habilis* as essentially human in both form and function was seriously challenged in July 1986, when a partial skeleton (OH 62) was recovered from lower Bed I, Olduvai. The very fragmented remains included pieces of calvaria, maxilla, mandible, ulna, radius, humerus, femur, and tibia (37). Unfortunately, none of the postcranial specimens, except the ulna, preserved any of their articular surfaces (38). The palate and teeth were described as similar to other specimens attributed to *H. habilis*, es-

263

pecially Stw 53 from Sterkfontein, OH 24 from Olduvai, and KNM-ER 1470 and 1813 from Koobi Fora, and for this reason OH 62 was referred by its discoverers to *H. habilis*. However, as we shall see below, some anthropologists now believe that these specimens (and others) are too morphologically diverse to be included in a single taxon called *H. habilis*.

For the time being, if we assume that OH 62 is correctly identified as *H. habilis*, then it reveals details of body proportions that are totally unexpected for this species and raises difficult questions about the place of *H. habilis* in human evolution. For example, the inferred high **humerofemoral index** (length of the humerus divided by the length of the femur multiplied by 100) of about 95 indicates that this individual had relatively long arms. This value is higher than in both modern humans (about 75) and *A. afarensis* (about 85) (39). Moreover, this adult individual is as small, or smaller than, any other known fossil hominid, including the *A. afarensis* skeleton of "Lucy" (A.L. 288-1). This is particularly interesting in that OH 62 is also more similar to African apes in limb-bone proportions than "Lucy" is, and yet "Lucy" is more than 1 million years older than OH 62 and is often considered to be ancestral to *H. habilis*.

This brings up an interesting problem. The juxtaposition in the fossil record of a relatively modern *H. erectus* skeleton (WT 15000) from West Lake Turkana dated to about 1.6 mya (see next chapter) and a postcranially primitive *H. habilis* skeleton (OH 62) dated to about 1.8 mya is perplexing: how could *H. habilis* have evolved so rapidly into *H. erectus* given that their skeletons were so completely different? It is just this type of problem that lends support to those who now view the entire known sample, or **hypodigm**, of *H. habilis* as too diverse to be sensibly encompassed within a single species. If the hypodigm of *H. habilis* needs to be split, there are two interesting possibilities concerning OH 62: 1) OH 62 is not *H. habilis* and on the basis of both its stratigraphic position and limb proportions it would not fit into an evolutionary lineage leading to *H. erectus*; or 2) OH 62 does belong to *H. habilis*, but because of its skeletal features it should be omitted from a role in later human evolution (40). Whatever the final resolution of this problem, the place of OH 62 in human evolution is clearly puzzling.

Homo habilis: One Species or Two?

Two questions that paleoanthropologists must constantly grapple with are: 1) how different do two fossils have to be in order to be considered different species? and 2) how similar must two fossils be in order to be attributed to the same species? It has recently been argued, quite persuasively, that paleoanthropologists probably err on the side of underestimating the amount of taxonomic diversity in the hominid fossil record (1,41). Perhaps in partial reaction to this, there has recently been renewed interest in reevaluating the taxonomic homogeneity of the *H. habilis* hypodigm (42).

Unfortunately, very few authors subdivide the hypodigm in the same

Table 6.3 Multiple Taxon Solutions for Crania and Mandibles Attributed to
H. habilis (from 13)

| Author(s) | Specimens | | Taxon Names |
	OH	KNM-ER	
Robinson (23)	7	—	*A.* aff. *A. africanus*
	13	—	*H.* aff. *H. erectus*
Leakey et al. (28)	7, 16	—	*H. habilis*
	13, 24	—	*H. habilis/Homo* sp.
Groves (43)	7, 13, 16, 24	—	*H. habilis*
	—	1470, 1590, 1802	*H. rudolfensis*
	—	730, 820, 992, 1805, 1813	*H. ergaster*
Stringer (9)	7, 24	1470, 1590, 1802, 3732	*H. habilis* (group 1)
	13, 16	992, 1805, 1813	*H. habilis* (group 2) or *H. ergaster*
Wood (12)	7, 13, 16, 24, 37, etc.	1478, 1501, 1805, 1813, 3735, etc.	*H. habilis*
	—	1470, 1482, 1590, 1802, 3732, etc.	*H. rudolfensis*

way (Table 6.3). For example, of the two most recent monographic studies
of early *Homo*, one (14) concludes that all the Olduvai and Koobi Fora
specimens can be attributed to *H. habilis* as a single **polytypic** species, i.e.,
one comprising several geographical and/or morphological variants,
whereas the other (12) concludes that while the Olduvai fossils can indeed
be attributed to *H. habilis*, two different species are represented in the
Koobi Fora sample, *H. habilis* and a new species, *H. rudolfensis*.

Our whole concept of the taxon *H. habilis* is really based on the fossil
material from Beds I and II at Olduvai and there seems to be a slowly
growing consensus that most, if not all, of this material is reasonably encompassed within a single species, the more important specimens being
OH 7 (the type), OH 13 (cranial parts and mandible), OH 16 (badly fragmented cranium and mandibular dentition), and OH 24 (crushed cranium) (12–14,28,43).[3] So in order to address the question: "*H. habilis*—
one species or two?," we must turn our attention to the specimens from
Koobi Fora, for that is where the problem lies.

Almost from the very beginning of fieldwork at Koobi Fora, a number
of late Pliocene–early Pleistocene hominids were found that could not be
comfortably included within the existing hypodigms of either "robust"
australopithecines or *H. erectus*. Most, if not all, of them were either formally

[3]For differing views see (9,23,44).

or informally allocated to an early species of *Homo* with similarities noted between them and *H. habilis* and/or *A. africanus* (45–50). Some of the better known examples within this group include KNM-ER 992 and 1802 (mandibles), KNM-ER 1470, 1813, 1590 (crania), and KNM-ER 1805 (cranium). The initial describers of this material were cautious in their taxonomic assessments. However, in 1975 the first serious proposal was put forward to formally subdivide the early *Homo* sample into two species, *H. habilis* and *H. ergaster*[4] (51). Others followed suit and this early *Homo* sample was soon being divided in various and sundry ways (9,13,33,52). By the late 1980s it was proposed that *H. habilis* be split into two geographical subdivisions: 1) *H. habilis* **sensu stricto** (in the strict sense) from Olduvai; and 2) *Homo* spp. (several species) from Koobi Fora and southern Africa (10).

Further cladistic analyses of the variations within the cranial vault, face, and dentition of the *H. habilis* hypodigm reinforced the view that multiple taxa were being sampled and that the Koobi Fora and Olduvai early *Homo* samples could be sorted into three species: *H. habilis*, *H. rudolfensis*, and *H. ergaster* (53). According to these studies, the hypodigm of *H. habilis* includes specimens from both Koobi Fora and Olduvai, whereas *H. rudolfensis* and *H. ergaster* are (thus far) restricted to the Turkana Basin. Recently, however, a new specimen attributed to *H. rudolfensis* has been recovered from deposits faunally dated to about 2.4 mya from the Chiwondo Beds of Uraha, Malawi (54–56) (see Fig. 6.1a).

H. rudolfensis is characterized by a large braincase, or **neurocranium**, and *Homo*-like endocranial morphology combined with facial and dental features that resemble, at least superficially, those of "robust" australopithecines. These similarities between *H. rudolfensis* and "robust" australopithecines are regarded as structural resemblances due to parallelisms or convergent evolution, or **homoplasies**, rather than to common ancestry. In this view the clade consisting of *H. habilis* and *H. rudolfensis* is united by five character state changes (10,53) (see Table 6.1).

In this taxonomic scheme, *H. habilis* from Olduvai is regarded as an early species of *Homo* that retains an essentially australopithecine postcranial skeleton and a more hominine masticatory complex, whereas *H. rudolfensis* combines a more *Homo*-like postcranial skeleton with a more "robust" australopithecine craniodental complex (Table 6.4).

Two specimens from Koobi Fora, KNM-ER 1470 and 1813, are particularly instructive in illustrating the taxonomic difficulties involved in sorting out the *H. habilis* hypodigm (Fig. 6.3). Most researchers agree that both

---

[4]The mandible KNM-ER 992 was named the type specimen of the new species, *H. ergaster* (51). "[T]his taxon was inadvertently described under the impression that it was in the public domain, which it was probably not (an unintended breach of ethics); unfortunately, too, it was named before the description of such fossils as 1813 and 3733, with either of which the jaw 992 could perhaps be conspecific" (43). An additional problem with using the nomen *H. ergaster* is that the type specimen, KNM-ER 992, has not been differentiated from *H. erectus* (13).

Table 6.4 Evidence for and Features of *H. habilis* sensu stricto and *H. rudolfensis* (from 13)

	H. habilis *s.s.*	H. rudolfensis
Skull and Teeth		
Absolute brain size (cm^3)	$\overline{X} = 610$	$\overline{X} = 751$
Overall cranial vault morphology	Enlarged occipital contribution to the sagittal arc	Primitive condition
Endocranial morphology	Primitive sulcal pattern	Frontal lobe asymmetry
Suture pattern	Complex	Simple
Frontal	Incipient supraorbital torus	Torus absent
Parietal	Coronal > sagittal chord	Primitive condition
Face—overall	Upper face > midface breadth	Midface > upperface breadth: markedly orthognathic
Nose	Margins sharp and everted; evident nasal sill	Less everted margins; no nasal sill
Malar surface	Vertical, or near vertical	Anteriorly inclined
Palate	Foreshortened	Large
Upper teeth	Probably two-rooted premolars	Premolars three-rooted; absolutely and relatively large anterior teeth
Mandibular fossa	Relatively deep	Shallow
Foramen magnum	Orientation variable	Anteriorly inclined
Mandibular corpus	Moderate relief on external surface, rounded base	Marked relief on external surface, everted base
Lower teeth	Buccolingually narrowed postcanine crowns	Broad postcanine crowns
	Reduced talonid on P_4	Relatively large P_4 talonid
	M_3 reduction	No M_3 reduction
	Mostly single-rooted mandibular premolars	Twin, platelike, P_4 roots, and bifid, or even twin, platelike P_3 roots
Postcranium		
Limb proportions	Apelike	?
Forelimb robusticity	Apelike	?
Hand	Mosaic of apelike and modern humanlike features	?
Hindfoot	Retains climbing adaptations	Later *Homo*-like
Femur	Australopithecinelike	Later *Homo*-like

H. habilis sensu stricto and *H. rudolfensis* have been suggested (12) as species components of the larger *H. habilis* hypodigm. Specimens allocated to the two taxa are as follows:

H. habilis sensu stricto
Olduvai: OH 4, 6, 8, 10, 13–16, 21, 24, 27, 35, 37, 39–45, 48–50, 52, 62.
Koobi Fora: KNM-ER 1478, 1501 1502, 1805, 1813, 3735.

H. rudolfensis
Koobi Fora: KNM-ER 813, 819, 1470, 1472, 1481–1483, 1590, 1801, 1802, 3732, 3891.

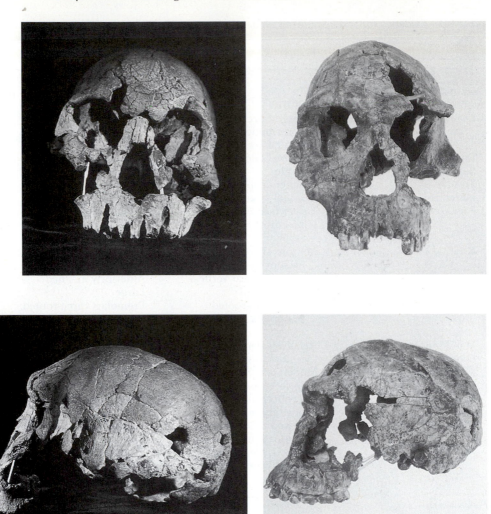

(a)

Fig. 6.3.   (a) Two views of crania KNM-ER 1470 (left) and 1813 (right) (12). (b) Some morphological differences between crania KNM-ER 1470 and 1813 (117). (Photos courtesy of B. Wood and the National Museums of Kenya.)

specimens belong to the genus *Homo*.[5] The question is whether both crania could be drawn from the same species of *Homo*, and if so, would this species be *H. habilis* as defined by the Olduvai fossils? Based mainly on differences in cranial size and shape, particularly in the supraorbital and cheek region, and cranial capacity (about 510 cc for KNM-ER 1813 and about 770

[5]But see (52) for a different view.

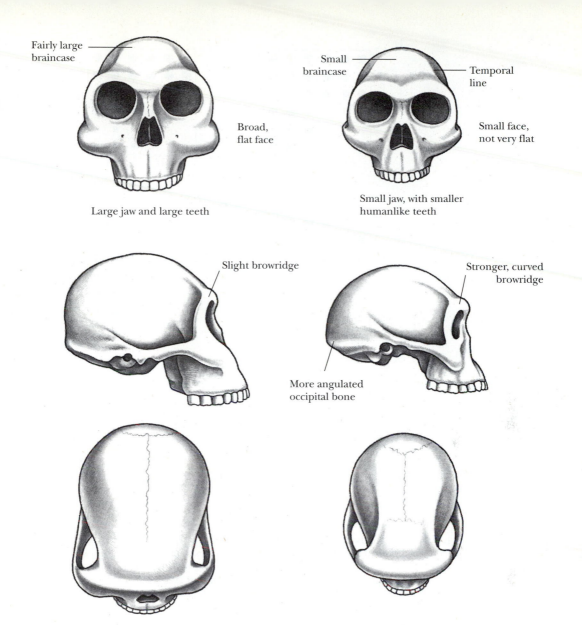

Fairly large braincase

Broad, flat face

Large jaw and large teeth

Small braincase

Temporal line

Small face, not very flat

Small jaw, with smaller humanlike teeth

Slight browridge

Stronger, curved browridge

More angulated occipital bone

(b)   KNM-ER 1470   KNM-ER 1813

cc for KNM-ER 1470), a number of researchers have concluded that these two crania (as well as others) show too much variation to be considered conspecific (9,12,43,44,57,58). In fact, one recent cladistic analysis concluded that the "*H. habilis*" fossils represented by KNM-ER 1813 and the fossils from Olduvai Gorge are most likely the sister group of *H. erectus* whereas the other taxon, *H. rudolfensis*, represented by KNM-ER 1470 and other fossils from Lake Turkana, shares many derived features with austra-

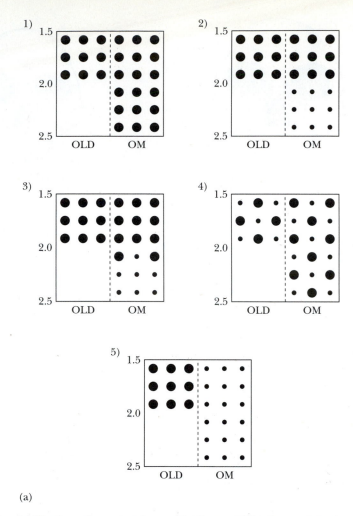

Fig. 6.4. (a) Five hypotheses put forward by Bernard Wood to explain the variation within East African samples of early *Homo*. Each box is divided into the two regional subsets of the fossil evidence: OLD = Olduvai; OM = Omo Group (Shungura and Koobi Fora). The vertical axes represent millions of years (13). Hypothesis 1 represents a single taxon solution; Hypotheses 2–5 all posit more than one early *Homo* taxon. Hypotheses 2 and 3 specify that the two taxa are time successive; Hypotheses 4 and 5 see them as synchronic. Hypotheses 4 and 5 differ in that the latter suggests that the two taxa are geographical variants, i.e., synchronic but allopatric. Note that, in each case, hominids do not appear in the Olduvai fossil record until slightly after 2.0 mya. (b) Diagrams of three most likely taxonomic schemes for early *Homo* in order of descending likelihood. Large dot = *H. habilis*; smaller dot represents a different early *Homo* species, perhaps *H. rudolfensis* (12).

lopithecines (59). This would be fine except that another recent analysis found no good statistical reason, at least based on cranial capacity, to believe that more than one species of *Homo* is being sampled (60). However, we must keep in mind that KNM-ER 1470 was reconstructed from hundreds of pieces and its overall shape is suspect.

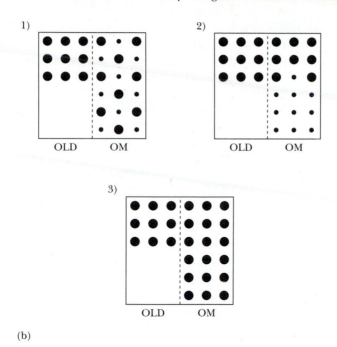

(b)

Some paleoanthropologists have also drawn a distinction between *H. erectus* as defined from the Far East and Koobi Fora specimens sometimes regarded as African versions of *H. erectus* (see next chapter). They attribute such "*H. erectus*–like" specimens from Koobi Fora, for example KNM-ER 730, 992, 3733, 3883, to a different species, *H. ergaster.* Cladistic analyses suggest that *H. ergaster* is the sister group of *H. sapiens* and can be distinguished from *H. erectus* by its retention of primitive features involving the form of the mandible and aspects of tooth crown and root morphology as well as by its sharing with *H. sapiens* such derived cranial features as increased parietal breadth, longer occipital region, broader nasal bones and nasal aperture, shorter cranial base, more substantial basal component of the mandibular symphysis, and buccolingual narrowing of the mandibular canine and first molar (53).

Bernard Wood of the University of Liverpool recently presented five hypotheses about early *Homo* that can be tested by the fossil record (12):
• fossils from Olduvai and the Turkana Basin sample a single species, *H. habilis* (the lack of temporal trends in this model is compatible with the idea of evolutionary stasis in early *Homo,* a view more consistent with punctuated equilibrium models than with gradualistic evolutionary models; see Chapter II (Fig. 6.4a1)
• early *Homo* consists of two time-successive species, the more recent being *H. habilis,* which evolved rapidly (Fig. 6.4a2)

- early *Homo* consists of two time-successive species, the more recent being *H. habilis*, which evolved gradually (Fig. 6.4a3)
- early *Homo* is represented by two **synchronic** (existing or occurring at the same time) and **sympatric** (occurring together in the same geographical area) species, one of which is *H. habilis* (Fig. 6.4a4)
- early *Homo* consists of two synchronic, but **allopatric** (occurring in different geographical areas) species, *H. habilis* at Olduvai and a separate species in the Turkana Basin sites; this model implies that a speciation event took place prior to 2.5 mya (Fig. 6.4a5)

The last four models suggest that variation in early *Homo* warrants recognizing more than one species. Wood's three most likely taxonomic schemes are shown in Figure 6.4b. The two likeliest schemes suggest *H. habilis* at Olduvai and two species in the Turkana Basin, *H. habilis* and *H. rudolfensis*.

EARLY HOMINID LIFESTYLES: TINKER, TAILOR, SCAVENGER, HUNTER?

In order to reconstruct early human behavioral evolution, paleoanthropologists must develop models to organize and interpret an ever-expanding body of paleontological, archeological, and primatological data. The goals of paleoanthropology should be 1) to explain as much as possible about human evolution in terms of animal analogues for the human traits we wish to understand and 2) to seek ''common patterns of adaptations underlying those analogies'' (61). Among the first, and most influential, researchers to apply this reasoning to the study of early hominid behavioral evolution were George Bartholomew and Joseph Birdsell, who proposed that it ''should be possible to extrapolate upward from ecological data on other mammals and suggest the biological attributes of the protohominids and to extrapolate downward from ethnological data on hunting and collecting peoples and suggest the minimal cultural attributes of the protohominids'' (62).

Today, most models of human behavioral evolution can be classified as either conceptual or referential (63,64,65). **Conceptual models** reconstruct early hominid behavior using principles from behavioral ecology and evolutionary theory and information on the behavior of particular primate species, including humans. An example of this type is Lovejoy's model of human behavioral evolution based on pair bonding and ecological separation during foraging, which we discussed in the last chapter (66,67). In contrast, **referential models** use the social system of a particular nonhuman primate species to model early hominid behavioral evolution, examples being the savanna baboon model popular in the 1960s (68) and the pygmy chimpanzee model of the 1980s (69,70).

The savanna baboon model was predicated on the notion that, aside from humans, savanna-dwelling baboons were the most successful ground-living primates. Therefore, study of their adaptations should yield insights into some of the problems that confronted early hominids as they gradually left the trees for more terrestrial habitats on the African savannas. Thus, this model attempted to reconstruct the evolution of human behavior by comparing the social behavior and ecology of baboons with that of living hunter-gatherer groups, including such aspects as troop size and structure, predator defense, home-range size, dietary preferences, and, in particular, the roles of hunting and scavenging.

By contrast, the pygmy chimpanzee model was based more on the close genetic affinity between humans and African apes, and especially on the evidence (mostly molecular) that humans and chimpanzees share a relatively recent common ancestor. This model held that pygmy chimpanzees therefore were the most reliable source of morphological and behavioral data regarding protohominids.

The reconstruction of early hominid behavior is a challenging problem for anthropologists, and any number of both conceptual and referential models have been put forward. A particularly important aspect of any such debate is the evolution of human hunting and what role, if any, scavenging and/or gathering played in the early evolution of this behavior (71,72). This question has led to a sometimes raucous debate among archeologists about the role of scavenging in early hominid behavior (73,74).

Box 6.1. The Debate over "Man the Hunter"

Until relatively recently, most models of human behavioral evolution in general, and the evolution of toolmaking in particular, revolved around the "Man the Hunter" paradigm (75). The intensity of the debate about "Man the Hunter" sometimes made it seem as if the defining image of human nature was at stake (76). The traditional story goes something like this. A successful hunt put a premium on foresight, strategic planning, cooperation, communication skills, and dexterity, all of which in turn selected for larger brains, more efficient bipedalism, and nimbler hands. It envisions that these traits unleashed a technological revolution, raising the payoff for intelligence and augmenting the original selective pressure. In this scenario, hunting becomes the engine that drives a self-sustaining feedback loop of social and intellectual evolution (77). In this hunter's paradise, early hominids lived in social groups characterized by a sexual division of labor in which "Man the Hunter" would return to his monogamously bonded "Woman the Gatherer" at a home base, where he would altruistically share the product of his hunting success with other members of the social group. At one time or another, anthropologists have labored to correlate some or all of the following to a hunting way of life (78):

- *the reduction of canines and increased skill in the manufacture and use of tools and weapons*
- *bipedalism*
- *increasing brain size and human intelligence*

- *sharing of food*
- *sexual division of labor, with males providing sustenance and protection and females providing sexual and reproductive functions*
- *the human nuclear family*
- *continual sexual receptivity of the female, used to attract and hold a provider-male permanently*
- *the incest taboo, used to avoid disrupting nuclear families*
- *exogamy or the exchange of females*
- *cooperation replacing competition among males*
- *male bonding and prominence in social, especially political life*
- *language, used to cooperatively stalk and hunt prey*
- *territoriality, larger home ranges, and increased mobility*
- *aesthetics, developed from the appreciation of beautiful tools*
- *pleasure in killing*

Such testosterone-oriented hypotheses were once defended by appeals to both archeological and primatological observations. For example, behavioral studies on free-ranging chimpanzees at Gombe, Tanzania, showed that males spent significantly more time hunting than females; females, on the other hand, reportedly spent more time "gathering" ants and termites (79). It has even been recently suggested that one "function" of infanticide in chimpanzees might be to "correct" a mother's promiscuity by coercing her into more restrictive mating relationships with high-ranking, adult males (80). Likewise, interpretations of a number of early Pleistocene East African archeological sites have reinforced beliefs that stone tools associated with animal bones unambiguously document early human hunting and butchery practices (81–83) (Fig. 6.5).

But how valid is this "Man the Hunter" scenario? Interestingly, as both primate field studies and archeological methods of analysis expand and mature over the years, the emerging picture is proving to be far more complex than previously thought

(a)

Fig. 6.5. Cartoons illustrating various hypotheses purporting to explain why early hominids disarticulated animal carcasses: (a) to facilitate cooking; (b) for storage; (c) for transporting the carcass back to a camp or home base; (d) for sharing meat with others (118).

(b)

(c)

(d)

*(84). For example, it has recently been reported that chimpanzees living in the trop-
ical rain forest at Tai National Park, Ivory Coast, use tree roots as anvils for cracking
the hard nuts of kola and panda trees with stone or wood hammers selected from
the surrounding forest, some of which are carried up to 100 m for use in cracking
nuts (85). What is most interesting is that females engage in such tool use more
frequently than males and that tools made and used by these chimpanzees are never
used as hunting weapons. While it is true that females participate less often than
males in hunting (4 percent at Gombe and 13 percent at Tai), they are more likely
than males to share meat with other group members when they do hunt (86,87). Such
recent disclosures about chimpanzee behavior have led to a much needed rethinking
about the evolution of early hominid behavior: "Th[ese] observation[s], combined
with the suggestion that tool use may have been a predominantly female activity,
[are] at odds with both early and more recent male-centered models of human social
evolution" (64).*

Scavenging opportunities available to early hominids would be dependent upon two major factors: 1) the kinds of large carnivores in the area
that would compete for the "kill"; and 2) the ecological context in which
the scavenging occurs. Based on analogies with scavenging opportunities
existing today in the Serengeti and Ngorongoro Crater of East Africa, recent studies suggest that early hominids may have regularly encountered
abandoned felid kills, particularly in riparian woodlands during the dry
season. Although most kills would have been of medium-sized adult herbivores, it is unlikely that there would have been much flesh remaining on
such carnivore kills, except for marrow bones and head contents, by the
time hominid scavengers got to them. However, this last point might be
dependent upon the type of carnivore making the kill. For example, it is
hypothesized that large quantities of scavengeable flesh may have remained
if saber-tooth cats had made the kill, since these predators did not have the
masticatory apparatus to crush bones and completely dismember carcasses
that some modern felids do. In this regard, it is important to note that at
least three large saber-tooth felids shared the African continent with early
Homo in the Plio-Pleistocene (77,88,89).

How did early hominids interact with such carnivore communities? One
hypothesis is that saber-tooths may have concentrated their hunting activities in dense woodland and forest localities (closed habitats) while other,
more modern felids may have been active in more open woodland and
savanna habitats. In this scenario, *H. habilis,* with its inferred arboreal abilities, may have scavenged more effectively in forest habitats and may have
been much less susceptible to predation and carcass competition than in
more open habitats. The extinction of saber-tooths in sub-Saharan Africa
coincides with a period of grassland expansion and forest retreat about
1.8–1.6 mya, and perhaps this ecological shift forced *H. habilis* to increase
its use of more open habitats in competition with modern felids. It has
been postulated that such high predation pressure and the need to switch
to more confrontational scavenging and/or hunting strategies may have
contributed to the rapid increase in body size from *H. habilis* to *H. erectus*

and the closely coincident shift in stone-tool technology. The Acheulian tool kit makes its first appearance about 1.6–1.5 mya (90). However, some archeologists speculate that ecological overlap between hominids and large carnivores may have lessened in intensity by the Middle Pleistocene. For instance, the Lower Pleistocene sites at Olduvai Gorge dated to about 1.85–1.70 mya apparently demonstrate that hominids and carnivores exploited similar animal species, were attracted to the same body parts, overlapped spatially, and interacted directly on occasion. However, the Middle Pleistocene sites of Lainyamok and Olorgesailie present a more complex picture. For example, at Lainyamok hominid activities were apparently rare, whereas the mammalian carnivores were diverse and common and hyenas were active collectors and chewers of bones. However at Olorgesailie, where hominid activity was high, carnivore fossils are very rare (91).

One other potential source of scavenged food for early hominids may have been tree-stored leopard kills of small bovids (92).

Archeological sites are also being reevaluated and the view that early Pleistocene "living floors" represented home bases where meat was shared is coming under closer scrutiny. Archeologists use several criteria for recognizing scavenged assemblages in the archeological record, such as: 1) a broad range of prey-animal sizes; 2) a low proportion of juveniles; 3) a broad range of prey-species' habitats; and 4) a skew in the distribution of prey sizes toward the large end of the range (83,93). In a study of the bones at Olduvai, one archeologist at least came to a conclusion about early hominid behavior that shares little with the "Man the Hunter" paradigm (94):

- hominids were scavenging animal kills after most of the other predator-scavengers had abandoned the carcass and scattered some of its parts
- the scavenged parts were mostly leg bones that already had most of the meat removed by other predators, or they were lower leg bones that had little meat on them
- the major, or in some cases the only, usable or edible parts consisted of bone marrow
- hominids were using hammerstones to break open the leg bones in order to expose the marrow
- there is no evidence supporting the idea that hominids removed food to a base camp for consumption or that food was shared

These observations led to the conclusion that: "At the dawn of tool use the early hominids appear to have been scavenging carcasses largely for marginal foods and using tools to gain access to these tiny morsels, mainly bone marrow. That this can be taken as evidence for a 'scavenging' mode of adaptation is highly unlikely, since the tactics indicated must have contributed only slightly to the modal subsistence security of these creatures" (73).

A rather different hypothesis concerning archeological sites at Olduvai was advanced by archeologist Richard Potts of the Smithsonian Institution, who argued that many of these localities were not home bases at all, but rather stone caches where early hominids brought animal carcasses, or parts thereof, for processing. In order to minimize competition with other predators that would be attracted to both kill and processing sites, it was necessary for these early hominids to quickly dismember the carcasses and to abandon the sites as soon as possible. For this reason, they dispersed stone raw material and previously made tools at a number of "caches" within the foraging area. Because these processing sites were revisited over a period of time, numerous stone tools and bones from many different animals would be expected to accumulate. The notion that these sites were abandoned to carnivores helps explain the presence of both stone tool cut marks and carnivore tooth marks on many of the bones (95–97).

But perhaps too much emphasis has been placed on the eating of meat and not enough on the eating of other foodstuffs that would have been available to early hominids. Both the scavenging and the hunting models still have as their central focus the procurement of meat by early hominids as a "high-quality" food. However, because there is an upper limit to the amount of plant or animal protein that a forager can safely consume for calories on a sustained basis, meat may actually have been a relatively minor source of sustenance for early hominids. This upper limit of about 50 percent of total calories means at least half of a forager's total energy needs must be obtained from nonprotein sources, either fat or carbohydrates (98).

Over the past decade or so, a number of anthropologists have questioned the central tenets of the hunting hypothesis, that hunting arose early in human evolution and that meat was the primary food source of early hominids. Instead, these authors contend that a more significant early hominid adaptation was the gathering of plant foods in African savanna environments, which in turn led to the invention of tools for obtaining, transporting, and preparing such foods (99–101). Studies show that even today the diet of so-called "hunter-gatherers" consists mainly of vegetable foods gathered primarily by women (102,103).

We should bear in mind, however, that there are important distinctions between modern hunter-gatherers and early hominids (83):

- modern hunter-gatherers have bigger and more complex brains than early hominids and undoubtedly possess far greater intellectual and linguistic capabilities
- all modern hunter-gatherers know how to use and control fire, whereas early hominids presumably did not, which has obvious implications: fire can be used to keep predators from sleeping quarters and food remains and can also be used to cook or dry meat, thus forestalling spoilage
- modern hunter-gatherers live in ecologically marginal areas that are very different from the environments of early hominids
- modern hunter-gatherers possess tools, implements, and weapons far exceeding those known to early hominids
- modern hunter-gatherers are faced with fewer predator species (besides other humans) than their early Pleistocene ancestors

With these caveats in mind, modern archeological research reinforces the view that early hominids used animal carcasses in less systematic ways than modern hunter-gatherers do and that early humans were predominantly opportunistic meat scavengers and plant food foragers.

One last word of caution is in order about trying to "explain" human evolution as a response to some restricted dietary regime. It has been shown that humans, chimpanzees, and baboons eat a minimum of 333 different plant genera from eastern and southern Africa and that at least twenty-eight of these plants are exploited by all three groups. At least six of these plant genera are recognized in the paleobotanical record: *Acacia* (pods), *Albizia* (flowers and leaves), *Cordia* (fruits), *Diospyros* (fruits), *Ficus* (fruits), and *Ziziphus* (fruits). In addition, woodland savanna nut-producing trees in Africa provide a nutritious mesocarp in addition to edible, oil-rich nut seeds that would have been available as a food resource to early hominids, particularly to those, like *A. robustus* and/or *A. boisei*, that could crack the nuts with either a strong masticatory apparatus or stone tools (104,105).

We remarked earlier that two evident evolutionary trends within the genus *Homo* over the last 2 million years were 1) an increase in mean body size and 2) a reduction in the degree of sexual dimorphism. Let us conclude this chapter by looking at some recent theories that attempt to explain the adaptive advantages of such trends.

It has been suggested that increased terrestrial behavior by early *Homo* may have released a constraint on body size, since it is known that arboreal primate species are generally smaller than their more terrestrial relatives (106). Others have suggested that reproductive and social behaviors (e.g., greater longevity, longer gestation and prenatal periods, lower birth rates, increased sociality, and increased brain size) as well as a number of ecological parameters such as broader dietary niches and increased day- and home-ranges may all be consequences of increased body size (107).

Still others have sought more physiological explanations, one of the most intriguing being that increased body size (and alterations in body proportions) may have helped larger hominids exploit dispersed resources in savanna environments because (all else being equal) they would dehydrate less during the day than smaller individuals with similar levels of metabolic activity. According to this hypothesis, larger hominids would have been able to travel further each day, forage at higher temperatures, and cover a greater home range from a single water source. In fact, three important human attributes, bipedalism, the loss of functional body hair, and increasing body size, all reduce thermal and water stress in open equatorial environments. For example, at normal levels of metabolic activity, a naked skin actually reduces the water requirements of bipedal hominids exposed to temperatures typical of the African savanna, whereas a naked skin confers no such advantage on a quadruped (108–112).[6]

---

[6]But see (113) for a different view.

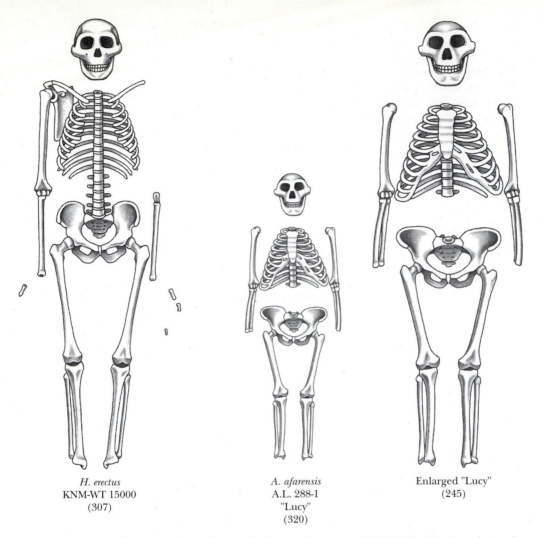

H. erectus
KNM-WT 15000
(307)

A. afarensis
A.L. 288-1
"Lucy"
(320)

Enlarged "Lucy"
(245)

Fig. 6.6. The skeleton of African *H. erectus* (KNM-WT 15000) and *A. afarensis* ("Lucy"). The outline of "Lucy" on the right is her shape if she were enlarged to the same height as *H. erectus*. Approximate ratios of surface area to body mass are given below each figure. The figures show that the evolution of *H. erectus* was accompanied by an increase in both body size and linearity of body form. That is, relative to their height, small australopithecines had broad bodies, whereas early *H. erectus* had narrow ones. This is consistent with thermoregulatory constraints on body shape because in order to maintain the same ratio of body surface area to body mass any increase in height should be accompanied by no change in body breadth (115).

The evolution of body shape can also be analyzed in terms of climatic and thermoregulatory adaptations (114–116). For example, in order to maintain a constant surface area/body mass ratio, absolute body breadth should remain constant despite differences in body height (therefore, pelvic breadth relative to body height actually decreases as later hominids increase in stature). This relationship is illustrated by the fact that while modern human populations living in the tropics vary greatly in stature, they show little variation in body breadth. In contrast, populations living in colder climates have absolutely wider bodies, an adaptation to reduce heat loss by lowering the surface area/body mass ratio. All African early hominids have absolute body breadths within the range of modern human populations inhabiting tropical and subtropical climates. In addition, the taller, more linear body proportions of *Homo* (as opposed to the more ''apelike'' proportions of *Australopithecus*) may have functioned to reduce daytime sweat losses by 20–30 percent in open equatorial environments, thereby reducing daily water requirements by 15–18 percent (Fig. 6.6).

It is now time to leave these early hominids as they scavenge over the landscape of Africa and turn our attention to a more formidable and geographically widespread species, *Homo erectus*.

CHAPTER VII

Quo Vadis *Homo erectus?*

As Voltaire might have said, if *Homo erectus* did not exist it would be necessary to invent him. And, of course, a century ago Ernst Haeckel did just that . . . and named it *Pithecanthropus*. . . .

William Howells
"*Homo erectus* in human descent: Ideas and problems"
(In Homo erectus: *Papers in Honor of Davidson Black*, 1981)

INTRODUCTION

Is *Homo erectus* simply an arbitrarily defined stage, or grade, of human evolution, temporally and morphologically sandwiched between Plio-Pleistocene *H. habilis* on the one hand and upper Middle Pleistocene archaic *H. sapiens* on the other? Or is it a "real" species, with definable boundaries in time and space, a separate evolutionary lineage demarcated from other species of *Homo* by cladogenetic speciation events, and unique (autapomorphic) features? Did *H. erectus* exist only in the Far East, or can it also be identified in Africa and/or Europe? Did *H. sapiens*–like morphology first evolve in Asia and then spread westward to Europe, or was Asian *H. erectus* an evolutionary dead-end, contributing little to modern human evolution? These are difficult questions to resolve, but ones that paleoanthropologists continually grapple with, and ones to which we now turn our attention.

There are three mutually exclusive views about *H. erectus* prevalent among paleoanthropologists today: 1) that the entire known material, or hypodigm of *H. erectus*, represents a single, widespread species that originated in Africa, spread throughout the Old World in the early Pleistocene, and was broadly ancestral to later modern humans; 2) that the hypodigm

Fig. 7.1. Major *H. erectus* and "archaic" *H. sapiens* fossil sites. Some of the European sites may be early Neandertals (82,135).

should be split into several species, with the Far East group considered to have had no significant role in modern human ancestry; and 3) that the name *H. erectus* should be abolished altogether, and all its fossils classified within an anatomically diverse, or polytypic, group of *H. sapiens*.

Table 7.1a Listing of Principal Indonesian and Chinese Localities at Which Remains Attributed to *H. erectus* Have Been Recovered (from 82)

	Trinil	Sangiran	Sambungmachan	Ngandong	Zhoukoudian	Hexian	Gongwangling
Whole crania		X					
Partial braincases	X	X	X	X	X	X	X
Mandibles		X			X	X	
Dentition		X			X	X	
Postcranial parts	X	?		X	X		

Table 7.1b Localities in Northwestern, Eastern, and Southern Africa That Have Yielded Remains Comparable to Asian *H. erectus*

	Ternifine	Sidi Abder-rahman	Thomas Quarries	Salé	Koobi Fora	Nario-kotome	Baringo	Olduvai Gorge	Swartkrans
Whole crania					X	X			
Partial braincases	X		X	X	X			X	X
Mandibles	X	X	X		X	X	X	X	X
Dentition	X	X	X	X	X	X	X	X	X
Postcranial parts					X	X		X	

Fossils are inventoried by body part represented rather than as individual specimens.

Our concept of *H. erectus* as an identifiable stage of human evolution derives from specimens first recovered in Asia toward the end of the nineteenth century. While there is currently debate about whether or not *H. erectus* sensu stricto (in the strict sense of the term, that is, pertaining to the original Javan hypodigm) ever existed in Africa and/or Europe, and about its place in the line of modern human ancestry, there is no doubt that the hypodigm includes a number of fossils from China (for example, Zhoukoudian [formerly Choukoutien], Yunxian, Jianshi, Yuanmou, Lantian) and Java (including Sangiran, Trinil, Modjokerto, Ngandong) (Fig. 7.1; Table 7.1). In order to understand the arguments involved in these debates, we first turn our attention to that part of the world where *H. erectus* was first discovered, defined, and named—the Far East. Then we will examine how the African fossils compare to the Asian *H. erectus* sample. Finally, we will consider the arguments, pro and con, about whether Asian *H. erectus* should be considered directly ancestral to modern humans.

HOMO ERECTUS FROM SOUTHEAST ASIA: CENTRAL AND EAST JAVA

Ernst Haeckel was a German zoologist and philosopher and one of the earliest and most influential supporters of Darwin's theory of evolution. In 1866 he published the first formal phylogenetic tree depicting the course of human evolution and in his treatise predicted the discovery of a "missing" phylogenetic link between humans and apes, to which he gave the name *Pithecanthropus*, meaning "ape man" (Fig. 7.2) (1). Eugene Dubois had a passion for anatomy and natural history, and an obsession with the idea of one day finding Haeckel's imaginary *Pithecanthropus*.[1] This obsession led him to seek out and accept a post as army surgeon in the Dutch East Indies (now Indonesia), a job he hoped would provide opportunities for fossil exploration in remote corners of Asia.

His first stop (in 1887) was Sumatra, but there he only succeeded in finding some fairly recent orangutan teeth. However, as soon as word reached him that part of a fossilized human skull had been found by B. D. van Rietschoten at a place called Wajak (formerly "Wadjak") in Java, he applied for permission to continue his own explorations on that island. The Wajak fossils turned out to be fairly recent—interesting, but no "missing link." By 1890, his searches had brought him to the Solo River in central Java, where his workers soon found a fossilized lower jaw fragment of a juvenile hominid (Kedungbrubus 1)[2] (Fig. 7.1). Then, the following year at Trinil, his workers made the discovery that he would become famous for—a skullcap (Trinil 2) of a primate that was larger than a monkey but smaller than a modern man (Fig. 7.3a). Initially, Dubois thought that he had found a chimpanzee, and thus named the new specimen *Anthropopithecus*. However, by 1893 he concluded that he had actually discovered the missing link between apes and humans, and he renamed the specimen *Pithecanthropus erectus*. Luck continued to come his way. The following year he found a fossilized human femur (Trinil 3) only 35 ft from where the

---

[1]Today most anthropologists would include within the single taxon *H. erectus* virtually all the Javanese and Chinese specimens originally described by Dubois, Black, von Koenigswald, Weidenreich, and others as *Pithecanthropus erectus.* This would encompass specimens previously named *P. robustus, P. dubius, H. modjokertensis, H. soloensis, Meganthropus palaeojavanicus, Sinanthropus pekinensis,* etc.

[2]This specimen, reportedly discovered at Kedung Brubus, was actually found at Kedung Lumbu (2).

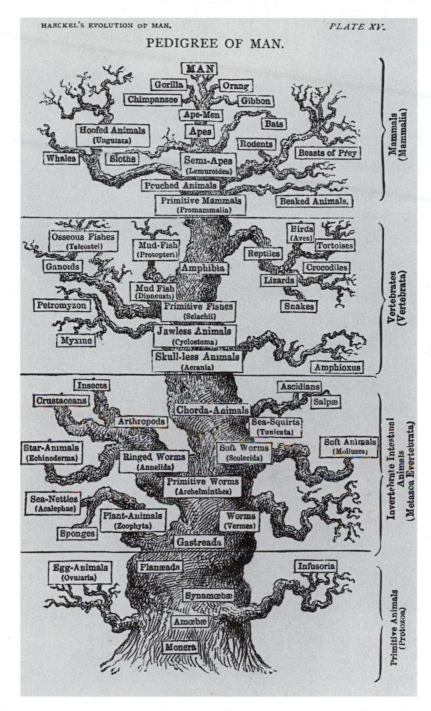

Fig. 7.2. Ernst Haeckel's Pedigree of Man as it appeared in his 1896 book, *The Evolution of Man* (136).

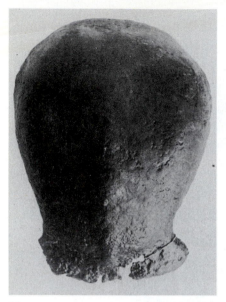

(a)

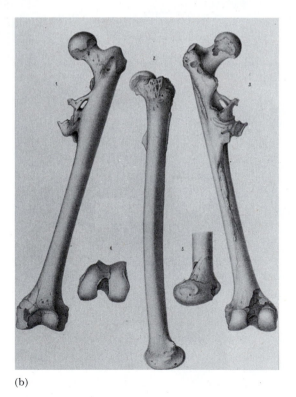

(b)

Fig. 7.3. First discoveries of *Pithecanthropus* from Java.   (a) Eugene Dubois' original photographs of the Trinil 2 skullcap (top and lateral views) and (b) his original
drawings of the Trinil 3 femur (137).

original skullcap was found (five other femoral fragments that were found but never described were rediscovered decades later in the Leiden Museum, boxed up and collecting dust) (Fig. 7.3b). In 1894 he announced his discovery of the skullcap and femur to an astonished world. Haeckel's missing link had at last been found. Dubois christened it *P. erectus*, the "ape man" that walked erect.

The original skullcap, or **calotte**, preserves much of the frontal bone, including a small portion of the left browridge, or supraorbital torus, both parietals, and much of the upper part of the occipital bone. The area just above and behind the browridge, the **supratoral sulcus**, is eroded, exposing the air cavities within the frontal bone, or frontal sinuses, on both sides. Unfortunately, the cranial base is missing. In overall shape, the calvaria is long and narrow, or **dolichocephalic**. The **cephalic index**, the ratio of the greatest breadth of the skull to its greatest length, multiplied by 100, is 70. (Elongated or dolichocephalic skulls have the smallest indices [below 75]; short or **brachycephalic** skulls have the largest indices [above 80]; and **mesocephalic** skulls have intermediate indices [from 75 to 80].) Behind the supraorbital ridge, a continuous bony shelf over the orbits, the forehead is very narrow and receding. The frontal bone also has a slight keel in the midline. Based on the size of the calvaria, brain size is estimated to be 850–950 cc (3).

There was never any doubt that the femur was from a bipedal animal, hence the name *P. erectus*—the erect ape man. The only question was whether or not it was truly associated with the original *H. erectus* skullcap, since its modern features seemed at variance with the primitive nature of the skullcap. The proximal shaft, or **diaphysis**, of the femur has a well-developed **exostosis**, a benign bony growth projecting outward from the surface of a bone. This pathologic condition may have been caused by myositis ossificans, an inflammatory disease of voluntary muscle characterized by aberrant bony deposits or ossification, or by diaphyseal aclasia, an autosomal dominant hereditary disease. Close inspection of the medial epicondyle shows clear evidence of osteoarthritis as well. Unfortunately, chemical (particularly flourine) analyses can only suggest, but not prove, that the skullcap and femur are contemporary with the Trinil fauna (4,5). After a thorough study of the Trinil femur, it was concluded that it could not be distinguished from that of modern *H. sapiens*, and therefore neither its Middle Pleistocene antiquity nor its contemporaneity with the *H. erectus* skullcap from Trinil could be confirmed (4).

It is sometimes said that prophets are seldom recognized in their own time or in their own country. So it was with Dubois. As might be imagined, his discovery caused a sensation, but it soon brought out the detractors as well (a fate that befell Raymond Dart three decades later). In what can only be described as an unfortunate conclusion to an inspired early career, Dubois slowly retreated from the verbal "slings and arrows" fired his way and retired to his home in Holland, a scientific recluse. One story has it that

Dubois took his *Pithecanthropus* and Wajak fossils out of scientific circulation and hid them under the floorboards of his dining room, apparently comforted in the knowledge that his precious fossils were safely hidden beneath his feet at meal time.[3] Although Dubois had discovered the Trinil skullcap in 1891, it was 33 years before he published his first paper with photographs and a detailed description of the specimen (7). Moreover, the Wajak fossils were handed over to Dubois by their discoverer in 1890, but his publication dealing with them did not appear until 31 years later (8).

In a final twist of irony, late in life Dubois became his own worst enemy by claiming that his original *Pithecanthropus* skullcap was not that of a "missing link" after all, but rather that of an animal similar to a giant gibbon. Actually, Dubois believed that gibbons were the missing link based on the notion that the Trinil skullcap was more gibbonlike than great-apelike and that gibbons were the only ape that habitually walked bipedally when on the ground. He also contended that most of the *H. erectus* skulls found later in China (for example, *Sinanthropus pekinensis*) and Java (including the *Pithecanthropus* skulls II, III, IV, and the "Solo Man" skulls) (see below) were all identical to "his" Wajak skulls and thus were all *H. sapiens*.

For over 40 years after Dubois' original discoveries, no further *Pithecanthropus* fossils were unearthed in Java. Fortunately, however, paleontological interest there was rekindled in the 1930s by G. H. R. von Koenigswald, a young paleontologist working with the Dutch East Indies Geological Survey. His initial success came in 1936, when part of a child's braincase was discovered from the Pucangan Formation at Perning near Modjokerto (Fig. 7.1).[4] As we shall see later in the chapter, this skull has recently become

---

[3]The veracity of this story is suspect (6).

[4]Prof. Earnest Hooton (9) of Harvard relates the following tale: "The janitor of the Peabody Museum has passed on to me a crumpled bit of paper that he picked up from the floor in front of the case in which the cast of the baby *Pithecanthropus* is on exhibition. He says that he noticed a frustrated-looking Radcliffe student gazing wistfully and prolongedly at this case and he thinks she may have written this pitiable effort:

Ode to Homo Some-jerktensis

Young Pithy from your Djetis bed
You raise a scarcely human head,
With all its soft spots ossified
And sutures closed that should gape wide.
Your marked postorbital constriction
Would clearly justify prediction
That had you lived to breed your kind,
They would have had the childish mind
That feeds upon the comic strips
And reads with movements of the lips.
They would have had no need for braces
To warp their teeth into their places-
Equipped for general mastication
and not progressive education,
In place of brows a bony torus,
And no ideals with which to bore us."

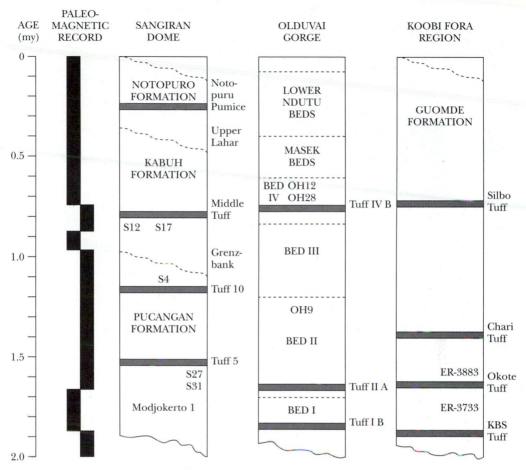

Fig. 7.4. Approximate correlations between *H. erectus* sites in Java (Sangiran), Olduvai Gorge, and Koobi Fora. Only some of the more important fossils attributed to *H. erectus* are shown. Recent ^{40}Ar-^{39}Ar dating suggests that the juvenile calvaria, Modjokerto 1, and two specimens from Sangiran, S27 and 31, may date to 1.8–1.6 mya (10,138).

the focus of great interest because it may be one of the oldest *H. erectus* specimens ever found (10) (Fig. 7.4). The child's cranial capacity was estimated to be 650 cc (11). Von Koenigswald named the new specimen *H. modjokertensis* (later *P. modjokertensis*) and included within this taxon several other specimens from Sangiran, including a partial lower jaw discovered the same year (Sangiran 1b) and several skull fragments with associated upper jaw found a few years later (Sangiran 4ab). He identified a number of dental characters that he considered primitive, or apelike, in this new species (Fig. 7.5):

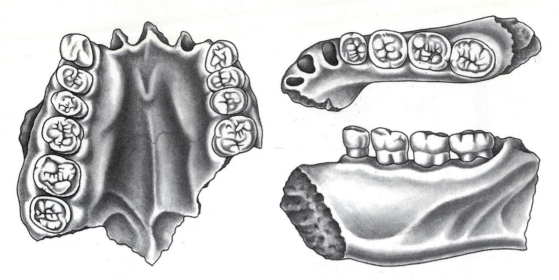

Fig. 7.5.   Upper and lower jaw fragments originally described as *Pithecanthropus modjokertensis* by von Koenigswald but now generally attributed to *H. erectus* (17).

- the largest molar was the M_3
- the P^3 retained three roots
- the upper canine projected slightly beyond the level of the occlusal plane
- the upper incisors were separated from the canine by a small diastema

   Von Koenigswald's efforts were further rewarded in 1937 with the discovery of a calvaria from the Kabuh Formation at Sangiran (Sangiran 2). Unfortunately, von Koenigswald had the habit of paying his fossil collectors by the quantity, not the quality, of the fossils they brought in to him, so perhaps he wasn't too surprised when they brought him the skull in about forty small pieces! When the skull was finally reconstructed, it looked almost exactly like the one discovered by Dubois 40 years earlier, with a low skull contour, sagittal keeling, and a strongly angled occipital bone (see Fig. 7.3). It included a good deal of the braincase, including the frontal, parietals, parts of both temporals and the occipital, part of the left supraorbital rim and browridge, and on the left the zygomatic process, glenoid cavity, tympanic plate, and mastoid process. The endocranial capacity was only a little more than 800 cc. However, as in Dubois' original *Pithecanthropus* calvaria, most of the cranial base was missing in this specimen. The fact that many of the Javanese skulls were found without a cranial base (and, in most cases, facial remains as well) has led some anthropologists to suggest that *H. erectus* may have practiced cannibalism and extracted the brains of their victims through the cranial base (12).
   When the elderly Dubois heard of the discovery of this more complete

Table 7.2 Endocranial Volume Estimates for the More Complete *H. erectus* Crania from Asia and Africa (from 82)

Locality	Specimen Number[a]	Cranial Capacity (cc)
Ngandong	1	1172
Ngandong	6	1251
Ngandong	7	1013
Ngandong	11	1231
Ngandong	12	1090
Hexian		1025
Zhoukoudian	V	1140
Salé		880
Zhoukoudian	II	1030
Zhoukoudian	III	915
Zhoukoudian	VI	850[b]
Zhoukoudian	X	1225
Zhoukoudian	XI	1015
Zhoukoudian	XII	1030
Olduvai	12	727
Sangiran	10	855
Sangiran	12	1059
Sangiran	17	1004
Gongwangling		780
Trinil	2	940
Sangiran	2	813
Sangiran	4	908
Olduvai	9	1067
East Turkana	3883	804
West Turkana	15000	900
East Turkana	3733	848

[a]Specimens are listed in approximate chronological order.
[b]This value for Zhoukoudian VI is estimated.

skull of *Pithecanthropus*, which presumably would have delighted him because it vindicated his original assessment of *Pithecanthropus* as a missing link, he declared that it was probably a fake. In fact, he died without ever bothering to see the new *Pithecanthropus* material collected by von Koenigswald (13).

The overall shape of the *H. erectus* skull has been likened to that of a "fallen soufflé" (14). Adult cranial capacity ranges from about 700 to 1,300 cc, with a mean value of about 883 cc (Table 7.2) (15). Taking body size into account, this is about 87 percent of the cranial capacity in modern humans. Since most of the *H. erectus* material from Indonesia (and China and Africa as well—see below) consists of skulls or skull fragments, it will be useful here to summarize the cranial features that characterize the species, and how *H. erectus* differs from modern humans (Table 7.3; Fig. 7.6).

Table 7.3   General Cranial Features of *H. erectus* (16)

Skull is long and low with greatest cranial breadth situated toward the base of the cranium

Frontal bone is relatively flat and is characterized by pronounced, projecting browridges that are united medially by a distinct glabellar prominence—this whole structure is referred to as the **supraorbital torus**

The boundary between the supraorbital torus and the frontal squama is typically marked by a troughlike depression called the supratoral sulcus

There is a significant degree of postorbital constriction

The frontal bone is characterized by a midline thickening of bone referred to as a **frontal keel**

The parietal bones are characterized by **parasagittal depressions** on either side of the midsagittal keel

The occipital bone has short upper (occipital) and long lower (nuchal) portions that meet at a sharp angle to form a strongly developed **transverse occipital torus**

The superior border of the temporal bone is generally straight and low compared to the highly arched border seen in modern humans

The mandibular (**glenoid**) fossa is deep and narrow

The mastoid process is relatively small and the styloid process is not ossified to the cranial base

Cranial vault bones are nearly twice as thick as in modern humans (averaging 9–10 mm)

Adult cranial capacity ranges from about 700 to 1,300 cc with a mean value of about 883 cc

Orbits are deep and broad and there is no lacrimal fossa

Nasal bones are very broad and the bridge of the nose is relatively flat

There is a marked degree of alveolar prognathism

Mandibles are relatively robust and are distinguished by their large bicondylar breadth, posteriorly inclined symphyseal region, absence of a chin, and broad ascending ramus

Molars tend to have large pulp cavities (**taurodont**) and upper central incisors are typically shovel-shaped

---

In 1941 von Koenigswald made his last discovery in Java, a lower jaw (Sangiran 6) from the Pucangan Formation of Sangiran that was much larger than any of the previous *Pithecanthropus* discoveries. Because of its large size, von Koenigswald named it *Meganthropus palaeojavanicus*. Both he and, later, J. T. Robinson of the Transvaal Museum in Pretoria initially considered it a "robust" australopithecine, a view not taken very seriously by most anthropologists today (see below). The original find consisted of

Fig. 7.6. (a,b) Cranial comparisons between *H. erectus* and modern humans. Note in particular differences in the shape of the forehead, supraorbital tori, orientation of the occipital and nuchal planes, and chin (139). (c–e) Several of the more complete *H. erectus* crania from Java. (c) Posterior views of Sangiran 2 (top left); Sangiran 4 (top right); Sangiran 10 (bottom left); Sangiran 17 (bottom right). (d) Lateral views of Sangiran 4 (top) and Sangiran 10 (bottom). (e) Lateral views of Sangiran 2 (top) compared to East African *H. erectus* KNM-ER-3733 (bottom). (Photos c–e courtesy of G.P. Rightmire.)

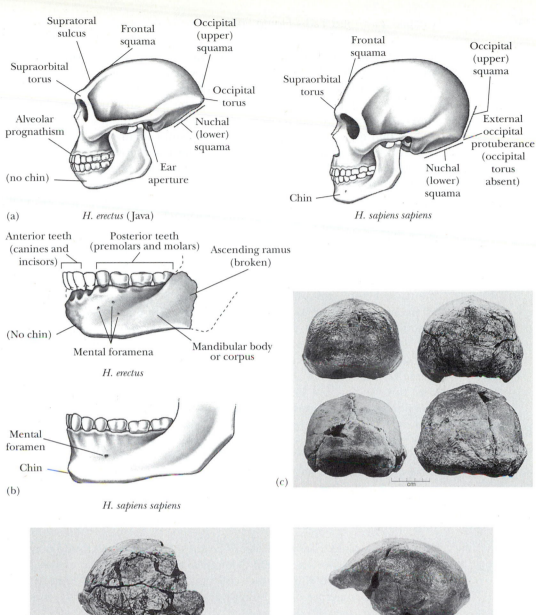

(a)

Supratoral sulcus

Frontal squama

Occipital (upper) squama

Supraorbital torus

Occipital torus

Alveolar prognathism

Nuchal (lower) squama

(no chin)

Ear aperture

H. erectus (Java)

Frontal squama

Occipital (upper) squama

Supraorbital torus

External occipital protuberance (occipital torus absent)

Nuchal (lower) squama

Chin

H. sapiens sapiens

(b)

Anterior teeth (canines and incisors)

Posterior teeth (premolars and molars)

Ascending ramus (broken)

(No chin)

Mental foramena

Mandibular body or corpus

H. erectus

Mental foramen

Chin

H. sapiens sapiens

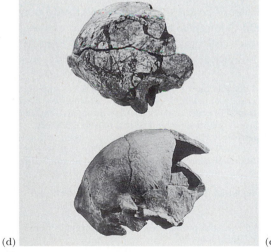

(c)

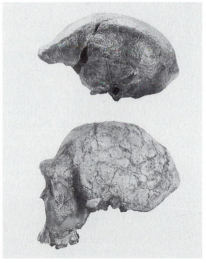

(d)

(e)

a lower jaw fragment preserving P$_3$-M$_1$ and the alveolus for a small canine. In 1952 a second *Meganthropus* jaw fragment was found at Sangiran (Sangiran 8) but this one had only a displaced M$_3$ (17). One of the reasons von Koenigswald considered *Meganthropus* to be an "australopithecoid" was that it came from the same layers as *H. modjokertensis*, and it seemed unlikely to him that two different species of *Homo* would occur side by side.[5] More recently, chemical and mineralogical studies have shown that some of the specimens originally assigned to *M. palaeojavanicus* are more extensively mineralized compared to other Javan specimens attributed to *H. erectus*, presumably a reflection of their longer period of fossilization (20). We shall come back to the implications of this shortly when we discuss the dating of these specimens.

As alluded to above, a minority of anthropologists still hold that some of these Indonesian hominids represent "robust" australopithecines. The five fossils usually mentioned in this regard include four mandibular fragments and one partial cranium all from the Sangiran region of Java and all presumably dating to around 1 mya: 1) the original "Meganthropus A" mandible (Sangiran 6); 2) the Meganthropus B mandible (Sangiran 8); 3) the original "*Pithecanthropus dubius*" mandible (Sangiran 5); 4) a second "*P. dubius*" specimen (Sangiran 9); and 5) a distorted partial cranium (Sangiran 31).[6] However, a thorough phylogenetic analysis has recently shown that this view cannot be substantiated and that all these specimens are morphologically derived toward *H. erectus* and away from *Australopithecus* and even *H. habilis* (21). Specifically, these Javan fossils differ from "robust" australopithecines in a number of ways, for example, in showing no propensity toward molarized premolars, in having much thicker cranial bones, and in having a cranial capacity estimated at 1,000 cc (Sangiran 31), roughly double that of the latest australopithecines!

The Ngandong (Solo River) Sample

One of the most extensive samples of Javanese hominids was found between 1931 and 1933, when the Dutch Geological Survey discovered eleven hominid skulls[7] and two shin bones (collectively referred to as "Solo Man") from the upper terrace of the Solo River near Ngandong (Fig. 7.7). Initially,

[5]Similar arguments resurfaced several decades later (under the name of the "single species hypothesis") with the claim that only one toolmaking hominid species could have lived at any one time in the Pleistocene of Africa: "Because of cultural adaptation, all hominid species occupy the same, extremely broad, adaptive niche. For this reason, allopatric hominid species would become sympatric. . . . The most likely outcome is the continued survival of only one hominid lineage" (18). This debate became a moot point, however, when it was conclusively shown that *Australopithecus* and *H. erectus* were contemporaries at Koobi Fora nearly 1.6 mya (19).

[6]However, recent ^{40}Ar-^{39}Ar dating of Sangiran 31 suggests that it may be closer to 1.6 million years old (10).

[7]A fragment of a right parietal found during the preparation of Solo 3 probably does not belong to it and may indicate a twelfth individual (22).

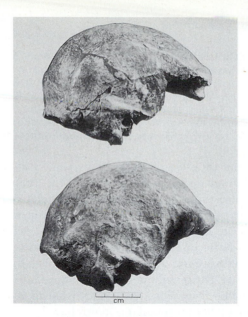

Fig. 7.7. Lateral view of two of the Solo skulls: Ngandong 1 (top) and Ngandong 12 (bottom). (Photo courtesy of G. P. Rightmire.)

some of these skulls were excavated by untrained workers and were shipped back in boxes labelled "tiger skulls" before their true identity was appreciated (22,23). Unfortunately, the geologic age of the Solo skulls has never been satisfactorily determined, although recent preliminary U-S (^{230}Th-^{234}U) dating of vertebrate bone from the same area indicated ages between about 50,000 and 100,000 years (24). Stone tools (mostly chalcedony cores and flakes) have also been found in the area, but there is no definite association of the Solo hominids with the tool industry. The Ngandong tool "industry," lacking handaxes, is distinct from the Acheulian tradition of both Europe and Africa and the absence of the characteristic uni- and bifacial choppers and handaxes also delineates the Ngandong sample from the so-called chopper/chopping-tool complex of the Far East.

The skulls were entrusted to von Koenigswald and moved with him first to the American Museum of Natural History in New York immediately after WW II, then to Utrecht in 1948, Frankfurt in 1968, and finally back to Indonesia in 1976.

There has never been unanimity of opinion on the taxonomy of the Ngandong skulls. Some, like von Koenigswald, Henri Vallois in Paris, and C. Loring Brace of the University of Michigan, considered them "tropical" Neandertals, although in Brace's concept, this stage of evolution is really a link between *H. erectus* and modern humans. Others, like Eugene Dubois, argued that they were not Neandertals, but rather a primitive modern type or "proto-Australian." Franz Weidenreich initially considered the skulls Neandertallike, but ultimately concluded that they were more similar to the older Javanese and Peking *H. erectus*. Finally, in the most recent and thorough study of these crania, A. P. Santa Luca (22) concluded that:

> The entire set of Far Eastern *H. erectus* . . . presents a single morphological "bau-plan": each skull has the same basic shape, with group and individual variations overlaid on this plan. The Ngandong hominids share it with the Peking and Sangiran-Trinil 2 fossils. Absolutely no basis has been found for separating Ngandong as a different species from the latter groups. . . . In morphology, craniometry, and craniography, the Ngandong group agrees with the Far Eastern *H. erectus* specimens . . . and is clearly differentiated from other major hominid groups.

Many of the features of the Solo skulls are similar to those found in *H. erectus*, such as the well-developed supraorbital tori united by a strong supranasal, or **glabellar**, torus, the flat receding forehead, marked postorbital constriction, similar range of cranial capacity, and greatest skull breadth located low down on the skull (22,23,25).

Since independence in 1945, Indonesian anthropologists have continued working in the Sangiran area and have recovered many more skulls, jaws, and teeth. The entire Indonesian *H. erectus* sample now represents parts of approximately forty individuals. What is surprising is that even after all these years, no further postcranial remains have been reported. It is also surprising that very few stone tools have been found in association with Javan *H. erectus* (26).

Recent finds, announced in the summer of 1993, include an important new cranium from Sangiran ("Pithecanthropus IX") that is one of the most complete yet found in Java. Initial reports describe the skull as longer and narrower than other Javan *H. erectus* skulls and as having well-developed and projecting supraorbital tori. The cranial vault bones are also very thick and endocranial capacity has been estimated at 856 cc. What caused the greatest excitement about this discovery was the chance it was the oldest hominid from Java, dating to some 1.4–1.0 mya. However, Sastrohamijoyo Sartono of the Institute of Technology, Bandung, Indonesia, now concludes that the skull may be from the Middle Pleistocene and is about 500,000–700,000 years old (2).

Taxonomic Issues Regarding the Javan *Homo erectus* Sample

There has always been the temptation among taxonomic "splitters" to subdivide the Javanese hominid sample into a number of different taxa and lineages and von Koenigswald did not disappoint in this regard. He recognized no fewer than five hominid species from Java: *H. soloensis* (which he considered a Javanese Neandertal) from the Ngandong fauna; *P. erectus* from the Trinil fauna; *P. modjokertensis* (Sangiran 1B, 4), *P. dubius* (Sangiran 5, 9—so named because Weidenreich initially thought it might be an orangutan), and *M. palaeojavanicus* (Sangiran 6—which he regarded as an "australopithecoid") from the Djetis fauna (27).

This trend to "split" the Javanese hominids continues today among some Indonesian anthropologists (25,28). For example, Teuku Jacob recognizes three distinct groups, or grades, of *H. erectus* from Indonesia (which he still refers to as *Pithecanthropus*): 1) *P. modjokertensis* from the Lower Pleistocene of Sangiran and Perning; 2) *P. erectus* from the Middle Pleistocene of Sangiran, Trinil, and Kedungbrubus; and 3) *P. soloensis* from the Middle Pleistocene of Ngandong, Sambungmachan, and Sangiran.[8] Until recently it was thought that few, if any, of these Indonesian hominids were much older than 1 million years (see below) (30–32). Jacob considers *P. modjokertensis* and *P. soloensis* to be more robust than *P. erectus* in certain features, for example, in their larger cranial capacity (1,000–1,300 cc), thicker cranial vault bones, and more accentuated cranial muscular markings. *P. erectus*, on the other hand, has a cranial capacity of 750–1,000 cc, a more rounded occipital torus, and no external occipital crest. Jacob rejects the idea that these taxonomic groupings simply reflect size differences due to sexual dimorphism. He argues that if this were so, only males would be preserved at Ngandong and only females (with one exception) at Sangiran (Kabuh Formation) (25).

On the other hand, S. Sartono subdivides *H. erectus* into five subspecies: *H. e. dubius*, *H. e. modjokertensis*, *H. e. erectus*, *H. e. pekinensis*, and *H. e. soloensis*. Alternatively, he would subdivide the Javanese *H. erectus* sample into just two subspecies, a small-brained group and a larger-brained group that may have evolved from it. From analyses of cranial size and shape, he concludes that specimens referred to as *Sinanthropus pekinensis* (from China), *H. ngandongensis* (the "Solo Man" skulls), and some *P. erectus* (e.g., *Pithecanthropus* VIII) can be accommodated within his "large-brained" subspecies of *H. erectus*, whereas some other *P. erectus* (e.g., *Pithecanthropus* I, II, III, VII), *P. modjokertensis* (*Pithecanthropus* IV), and *P. dubius* (*Pithecanthropus* C) can be accommodated within his "small-brained" subspecies of *H. erectus* (28).

As mentioned earlier, we now live in an age of taxonomic "lumpers" and most anthropologists today tend to lump all these Javanese specimens within the single taxon, *H. erectus*.

Age of Javan *Homo erectus*

Until recently, most investigations have concluded that most, if not all, of the fossils assigned to *H. erectus* in Asia, including Java, are probably younger than 1 million years (30–32). For most of this century, age estimates of Indonesian *H. erectus* were based on three poorly defined biostratigraphic sequences: 1) a Lower Pleistocene Djetis fauna (Pucangan Formation); 2) a Middle Pleistocene Trinil fauna (Trinil and Kabuh Formations); and 3) a late Pleistocene Ngandong fauna (Notopuro Formation) (Fig. 7.4).

Some of these faunas, particularly the "Trinil," are characterized by highly endemic groups and have few species in common with the Asiatic mainland (33). In fact, such common Eurasian mammals as equids, giraffoids, and camelids are completely absent in the tropical and subtropical

---

[8]Two stone tools (a chopper and a retouched flake) were also found at Sambungmachan, near the same site that yieled the hominid calotte (29).

regions of Pleistocene Southeast Asia generally, thereby testifying to the presence of some biogeographical "filter" affecting mammalian, including human, dispersal. It is thought that these endemic species, and *H. erectus*, could only have reached Java during a period of low sea level when the Sunda Shelf was exposed at about 3.0 mya, 1.25 mya, 0.9 mya, and/or 0.65–0.45 mya (30,32,34). Because water along the Sunda Shelf is so shallow, lowering the sea level to the 40-m isobath would connect Java to Sumatra and Malaysia, thus creating a landbridge to the Asian mainland and to Borneo (Fig. 7.8). Accumulating evidence had suggested that the latter two dates were the most probable for the migration of *H. erectus* into Indonesia, and in fact until recently there was little substantive evidence of hominid occupation in Java prior to about 1.3–1.0 mya. This view was based on a number of radiometric dates (mostly fission-track) indicating that both the Kabuh and Notopuro Formations were younger than 700,000 years. A widely cited earlier radiometric date of 1.9 ± 0.4 mya for some Javanese hominids (*Meganthropus* [Sangiran 8] or *H. modjokertensis*) was considered unreliable, since wherever proper excavations had been carried out on Java, hominids had only been recovered from Middle Pleistocene deposits.

This view has now been dramatically altered by the recent age determination of several *H. erectus* specimens from Java (10). It is now reported, based on ^{40}Ar-^{39}Ar determinations, that the well-preserved juvenile calvaria known as the "Mojokerto child" (Perning 1) from the Pucangan deposits (see above) may be about 1.8 million years old and that several specimens from Sangiran (Sangiran 27 and 31) may be about 1.6 million years old (see Fig. 7.4). If true, this has a number of important ramifications. For example, it would mean that the earliest known hominids from Java are approximately 0.6–0.8 million years older than the type of *H. erectus* from Trinil, at least 0.6 million years older than *H. erectus* from Olduvai Gorge (OH 9), and of comparable age to the oldest specimens of *H.* cf. *erectus* (= *H. ergaster*) from the Lake Turkana region of Kenya (see below). The obvious conclusion would be that *H. erectus* (or *H. erectus*–like hominids) migrated out of Africa into Asia far earlier than anyone had previously thought. As we shall see later in the chapter, there is still considerable debate as to whether or not *H. erectus* was a sidebranch of human evolution restricted to Asia, or whether it appeared in Africa as well.

This reevaluation of the dates for the oldest *H. erectus* from Indonesia also affects the way anthropologists view the "tempo and mode" of Middle Pleistocene human evolution. For example, if the bulk of Javan *H. erectus* were really no older than about 1 million years, as previously thought, then the entire temporal range of *H. erectus* in Asia would not have spanned

Fig. 7.8.   Possible Pleistocene land connections between New Guinea and Australia and the Asian mainland during periods of lowered sea levels, when the Sunda and Sahul land shelves were exposed.   Arrows represent possible early hominid migration patterns and several important early hominid sites from these regions are also shown (140).

Zhoukoudian ●

● Dali

CHINA

● Maba

40°

150°

20°

SOUTH
CHINA
SEA

PHILIPPINES

PACIFIC OCEAN

Tabon Cave ●

SUNDA
SHELF

Long
Rongrien
Cave

● Niah
Cave

BORNEO

SULAWESI

0°

MALAYA

SUMATRA

Leang
Burung
Cave

WALLACEA

BISMARCK SEA

NEW GUINEA

Yuki
●
Nombe ●
Kosipe ●

Huon
Peninsula

Ngandong

JAVA ●

Sangiran

TIMOR

SAHUL SHELF

INDIAN

OCEAN

Malagangerr ●

AUSTRALIA

20°

● Upper Swan
Devil's Lair Cave

● Koonalda Cave

● Mannahill

● Lake Mungo
● Kow
Swamp

Keilor ●

ORS 7 ▷

Bluff rockshelter

Kutikina Cave

Bone Cave

TASMANIA

0   1000 miles

0   1000 km

110°

130°

150°

much more than about 700,000 years, i.e., from about 1.0–0.3 mya, even if the Ngandong crania from Solo were assigned to *H. erectus*. This more restricted temporal range must be kept in mind when evaluating rival claims for "punctuational" or "gradual" models of human evolution and may be one reason why some workers discern little, if any, directed morphological change over time in the *H. erectus* sample from Asia (35) whereas others claim that gradual changes are easily decipherable in cranial capacity and other cranial and dental measures in the temporal sequence of Asian *H. erectus* in Java and China (30,36,37). Thus, let us turn to the other part of Asia that has produced a large *H. erectus* sample, China.

HOMO ERECTUS FROM EAST ASIA: CHINA

In 1919, a relatively unknown Canadian anatomist, Davidson Black, arrived in China to take up his position as professor of neurology and embryology at the newly founded Peking (now Beijing) Union Medical College. Just 9 years later, he found himself an academic celebrity lecturing in North America and Europe. During his lecture tour he wore a specially made gold receptacle tightly secured to his watch chain. In this gold receptacle there was a single fossil hominid tooth (Fig. 7.9).

Fig. 7.9.   In 1919, a relatively unknown Canadian anatomist, Davidson Black, arrived in China to take up the position of professor of neurology and embryology at the newly founded Peking (now Beijing) Union Medical College. Like Eugene Dubois before him, Black was inspired to take up a medical post in Asia because of his interest in human evolution and his belief that humankind first evolved in the Far East. In 1927 he named a new hominid genus from China, *Sinanthropus pekinensis*, which became popularly known as "Peking Man." It is now generally referred to as *Homo erectus*. (Photo courtesy of the Bernard Becker Medical Library, Washington University.)

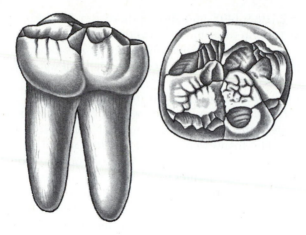

Fig. 7.10. The first tooth of "Peking Man," a lower first molar discovered by Birger Böhlin (13). Davidson Black used to carry this tooth around with him in a specially made gold receptacle tightly secured to his watch chain.

Homo erectus from Zhoukoudian

Like Eugene Dubois before him, Black was inspired to take up a medical post in Asia because of his interest in human evolution and his belief that humankind first appeared in the Far East. And like Dubois, Black was lucky. Coincident with his arrival in Beijing, a Swedish paleontological expedition began excavations at a promising cave site called Choukoutien (now Zhoukoudian), only 30 miles from Beijing. The site had been discovered in 1918 by a Swedish geologist, J. Gunnar Andersson. Paleontologist Otto Zdansky was placed in charge of the 1921 and 1923 excavations. Most of the fossils discovered in these first excavations were shipped back to Sweden for study and curation. Fortunately, however, Zdansky recognized several humanlike teeth from the sample (a right M^3 and a left P_3) and sent them to Black in Beijing for further study and identification. Then, on October 16, 1927, Dr. Birger Böhlin of the Swedish team found another hominid tooth, a left M_1, which he also turned over to Black for study. Black had no doubt that this tooth came from a previously unknown type of fossil hominid and considered it the oldest humanlike fossil yet found on the Asian mainland. Within the year he had formally named it *Sinanthropus pekinensis* (38). This was the single tooth tightly fastened to his watch chain[9] (Fig. 7.10).

Many anthropologists were initially skeptical of Black's claims based on a single tooth, but Black's prescience was soon recognized when W. C. Pei (Pei Wenzhong) discovered the first *Sinanthropus* skullcap at Zhoukoudian

[9]As an historical note, this may not have been the first fossil hominid tooth described from China. In 1903, the German paleontologist Max Schlosser published descriptions of a number of fossil "dragon bones," including a human molar, that had been purchased from Chinese drugstores during the Boxer rebellion at the turn of the century (13,39).

on December 2, 1929 (40), and shortly thereafter found indisputable evidence of stone tools in the same layers as the *Sinanthropus* fossils (41). After Black's death in 1934, excavations continued at Zhoukoudian for 3 more years under the direction of Franz Weidenreich, until war with Japan made further work untenable.[10]

Because of the Japanese threat to the Asian mainland, arrangements were made with United States Marines, who were evacuating North China, to ship the fossils to the American Museum of Natural History in New York for safekeeping. The fossils were packed and sent to the U.S. Marine base at Chinwangtao, where they were stored in footlockers. However, before they could escape, all the Marines were taken prisoner and the fossils were not seen again after December 8, 1941 (42,43). Fortunately, Weidenreich had meticulously described and illustrated most of the Zhoukoudian material and had also made a number of excellent casts that have been preserved in various institutions around the world (44) (Fig. 7.11).

In what can only be regarded as a fit of pique, Dubois never admitted any phylogenetic or taxonomic relationship between his *Pithecanthropus* and Black's *Sinanthropus*. He considered the latter to be a degenerate Neandertal and, as mentioned earlier, the former to be an animal similar to a giant gibbon!

After the upheavals of World War II and the Chinese Revolution, excavations at Zhoukoudian resumed in 1958 and have continued off and on since then under the overall direction of Prof. Wu Rukang.[11] In fact, a frontal and occipital bone found in 1966 actually turned out to be part of the same skull (Skull V) collected by Weidenreich in 1934! The inventory of fossil hominids collected from Zhoukoudian over the past half-century now represents the remains of some forty to forty-five individuals (Table 7.4) (16,37,44,45).

The most famous of the Chinese *H. erectus* sites, the Zhoukoudian (Locality 1) Cave (''Dragon-Bone Hill'') is only about 45 km southwest of central Beijing. Its deposits are more than 40 m thick (the bottom has not yet been reached) and are divided into a number of alternating layers of limestone breccia and nonbreccia consisting mainly of sand, silt, clay, travertine, and ash (Tables 7.4, 7.5) (16,46). The forty-five or so fossil hominids derive from layers 3–11, although three-quarters of those are from layers 8–10 and the majority of the remaining hominids are from layers 3–4. Age estimates have varied for the Zhoukoudian *H. erectus* sample, but it is now generally held that all of the specimens come from sediments well above the Matuyama/Brunhes boundary (from less than 700,000 years ago) and are thus

---

[10]Elwyn Simons tells the story that Black was found dead at his desk early one morning with a *H. erectus* skull firmly clutched in his hands.

[11]Who, like Raymond Dart, was a product of my own Anatomy Department here at Washington University, where he got his Ph.D. under Mildred Trotter, the founding ''mother'' of the American Association of Physical Anthropology.

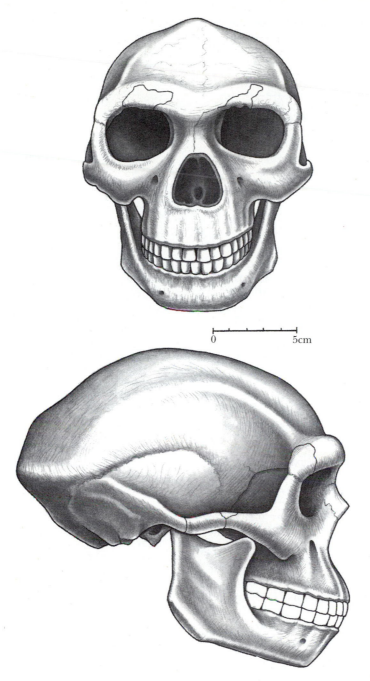

Fig. 7.11. Cranium of *H. erectus* from China.

Table 7.4 Archaic Human Remains from Zhoukoudian (from 16)

Specimen No.	Fossil Hominid Remains	Sex	Age	Locus	Layer	Individual	Year of Discovery
				Locality			
Crania and cranial fragments							
I	fragmentary rt. parietal, lf. frontal	M	A	B	4	B II	1928
II	calvarium (lacking 2 temporals and occipital)	?	A	D	8–9	D I	1929
III	calvarium	M	J	E	11	E I	1929
IV	rt. parietal fragment	M	J	G	7	G II	1931
V	calvarium	M	A	H	3	H III	1934, 1934/36, 1966
VI	frontal frag., lf. parietal frag., rt. temporal frag.	F	A	I	8–9	I I	1936
VII	rt. parietal at mastoid angle	M	AD	I	8–9	I II	1936
VIII	occipital frag.	F?	I	J	8–9	J I	1936
IX	frontal frag., 4 small cranial frags.	M	I	J	8–9	J IV?	1936
X	calvarium	M	A	L	8–9	L I	1936
XI	calvarium	F	A	L	8–9	L II	1936
XII	calvarium	M	A	L	8–9	L III	1936
XIII	lf. maxillary frag. (with I2, P3-M3)	M?	A	O	10	O I	1937
XIV	lf. maxillary frag. (with P3, M1-M3)	M	A	Upper Cave	—	UC?	1933
Facial bones and facial bone fragments							
I	frontal process of lf. maxilla	M	A	L	8–9	Skull X	1936
II	left malar frag.	M	A	L	8–9	Skull X	1936
III	lf. maxillary frag. (with P3-M3)	F	A	L	8–9	Skull XI	1936
IV	rt. palate	F	A	L	8–9	Skull XI	1936
V	cf. Skull XIII						
VI	cf. Skull XIV						
Adult mandibles							
I	part of rt. moiety	F	A	A	S	A II	1928
II	lf. condyle	M?	A	B	4	B II	1928/35
III	3 lf./rt. frags.	M	A	G	7	G I	1931
IV	symphysis and rt. corpus	F	A	H	3	H I	1934
V	symphyseal frag. and lateral bodies	F?	A	H	3	K I	1936
VI	lf. corpus	M	A	K	8–9	K I	1936
VII	lf. frag.	M	A	M	8–9	M I	1937
VIII	lf. hemi-mandible	F	A	M	8–9	M II	1937
IX	lf./rt. frags	F	A	—	10	—	1959

(*Continued*)

Specimen No.	Fossil Hominid Remains	Sex	Age	Locality Locus	Layer	Individual	Year of Discovery
				Non-adult mandibles			
I	symphysis and rt. frag.	F	J	B	4	B I	1928
II	rt. frag.	M	J	B	4	B III	1932/38
III	rt. frag.	F	I	B	4	B IV	1932/35
IV	symphysis and rt. frag.	M	J	B	4	B V	1928/35
V	rt. ramus frag	F	J	C	8–9	C I	1929
VI	rt. frag.	M	J	F	11	F I	1930
				Femurs			
I	proximal half lf. shaft	M	A	C	8–9	C III	1929/36
II	lf. mid-shaft	F	A	J	8–9	J II	1936/38
III	rt. proximal frag.	M	A	J	8–9	J III	1936/38
IV	near complete rt. shaft	M	A	M	8–9	M IV	1937/38
V	lf. proximal shaft	M	A	M	8–9	M IV	1937/38
VI	lf. mid shaft (2 pieces)	M	A	M	8–9	M I	1937/38
				Assorted postcrania			
Tibia I	lf. shaft frag.	—	A	—	—	—	1951
Humeri I	lf. distal frag.	M	A	B	4	B II	1928/35
II	lf. shaft	M	A	J	8–9	J III	1936/38
III	rt. mid-shaft	M	A	—	—	—	1951
Clavicle I	lf. shaft	M	A	G	7	G II	1931
Lunate I	rt. lunate	M?	A	B	4	B II	1928
				Teeth			
	2 specimens; lower LP3, upper RM3						1921/23
1-147	64 isolated specimens; rest in upper and lower jaws; 52 upper, 82 lower, 13 deciduous						1927–37
	5 specimens; upper LI1, upper RP3, upper RP4, lower LM1, lower LM2						1949/50, 1951/53
	lower RP4						1953
	lower LP3 (in jaw)						1959
	lower RP3						1966

Specimen no. refers to the colloquial designation given to the Zhoukoudian remains by the original researchers. Sex and age were attributed by Weidenreich and other primary researchers. Individual refers to the locus from which individual human remains were recovered and the sequential number of the individual with which they are thought to be associated. Year of discovery refers to the year when individual specimens attributed to a single individual were found. A = adult; J = juvenile; AD = adolescent.

Table 7.5   Some Absolute Dates Obtained on the Zhoukoudian Deposits

Layer	Years	Dating Method
1–3	$230,000 \begin{smallmatrix} +30,000 \\ -23,000 \end{smallmatrix}$	Uranium-series
	$256,000 \begin{smallmatrix} +62,000 \\ -40,000 \end{smallmatrix}$	
4	290,000	Thermoluminescence
6–7	350,000	Uranium-series
7	370–400,000	Paleomagnetism
8–9	$420,000 \begin{smallmatrix} +>180,000 \\ -100,000 \end{smallmatrix}; >400,000$	Uranium-series
	$462,000 \pm 45,000$	Fission-track
10	520–620,000	Thermoluminescence
12	>500,000	Uranium-series
13–17	>730,000	Paleomagnetism

Middle Pleistocene in age (Fig. 7.12 pp. 309–10). The original "Peking Man" cranium found in 1929 was recovered from layer 11 and has recently been dated by ESR to about 578,000 years ago. Crania from layers 3–4 and 8–9 give ESR ages of 282,000 and 418,000 years respectively (47). These ages have been generally confirmed by U-S dating methods, which date layers 2 and 4 to 270,000 and 300,000 years ago, respectively, and Skull V from layer 3 to about 290,000 years ago (48,49). Fission-track analysis dates ashes presumably left behind by *H. erectus* from layer 4 to 299,000 years ago.[12]

Thus, it appears that *H. erectus* occupied the cave for about 250,000 years, from about 500,000–250,000 years ago. This is an important consideration when trying to analyze morphological trends within the Zhoukoudian hominid sample. For example, Weidenreich thought that differences in tooth size within Zhoukoudian *H. erectus* simply reflected gender differences, with larger teeth belonging to males and smaller teeth to females. He therefore concluded that there was a long period of morphological stasis within the population through time (53). However, recent dental analyses comparing teeth from upper and lower layers of the cave seem to

[12]Other dates for these layers are as follows: layers 1–3, 0.26–0.23 mya based on U-S dating; layer 4, 0.32–0.29 mya based on fission-track and TL dating; layers 10, 11, 0.610, and >0.417 mya based on TL dating, and <0.592 and 0.340 mya based on U-S dating respectively (50). As for the Upper Cave at Zhoukoudian, radiocarbon dates on amino acids taken from bone give ages of ca. 23,000 and 10,000 years for the upper and lower boundaries of the Paleolithic culture and *H. sapiens* fossils found there (51). Many scholars believe that the strongest fossil evidence for Mongoloid origins derives from these fossils in the Upper Cave at Zhoukoudian [but see (52)].

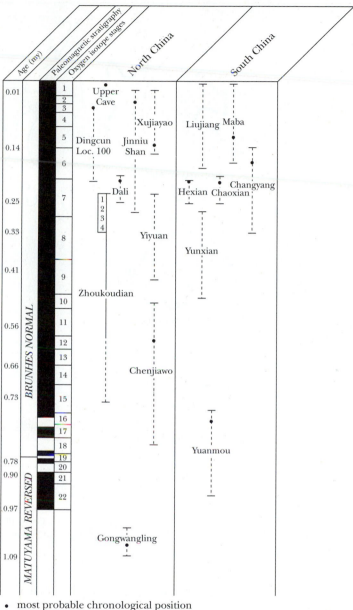

Fig. 7.12. (a) Chronostratigraphic distribution of important hominid sites in China (50).

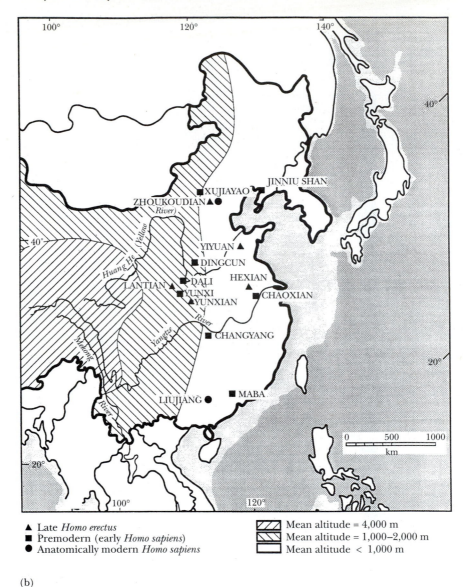

▲ Late *Homo erectus*
■ Premodern (early *Homo sapiens*)
● Anatomically modern *Homo sapiens*

Mean altitude = 4,000 m
Mean altitude = 1,000–2,000 m
Mean altitude < 1,000 m

(b)

Fig. 7.12.   (b) Geographic distribution of important hominid sites in China (50).

show some temporal variation in that lower incisors tend to get larger while lower canines and postcanine teeth get smaller over time (P_3 less than P_4 and M_1 less than other molars), suggesting that the Zhoukoudian sample illustrates dental evolutionary change in the direction toward *H. sapiens* (54). In addition, other Chinese anthropologists have suggested that cranial capacity increased through time in the Zhoukoudian sample, although this is open to debate (37,50).

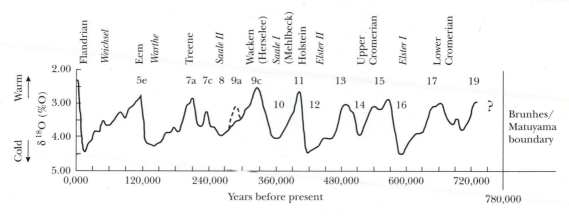

Fig. 7.13.   Chinese geologists have attempted to correlate the various Zhoukoudian layers to the ^{18}O stages of the deep-sea sediment record.   For example, layers 3–4 have been correlated to ^{18}O stage 8, layer 5 to stage 9, layers 6–7 to stage 10, layers 8–9 to stage 11, and layer 10 to stage 12. This signifies that *H. erectus* lived through at least three cold stages (stages 12, 10, 8) and two warm stages (11 and 9) during their occupation of the Zhoukoudian Cave. In the ^{18}O record, even-numbered stages are cold periods and odd-numbered stages are warm periods. Names at top of figure correspond to European glacial stratigraphy (141).

To interpret the paleoclimatological aspects of the site, Chinese geologists have correlated the various Zhoukoudian layers to the ^{18}O stages of the deep-sea sediment record. For example, layers 3–4 have been correlated to ^{18}O stage 8, layer 5 to stage 9, layers 6–7 to stage 10, layers 8–9 to stage 11, and layer 10 to stage 12. If correct, this signifies that *H. erectus* lived through at least three cold stages (stages 12, 10, 8) and two warm stages (11 and 9) during their occupation of the Zhoukoudian Cave (Fig. 7.13). The distribution of loess deposits also supports the view of alternating cold and warm phases. **Loess**, a fine-grained, windblown deposit found downwind of glaciated areas, is generally considered a product of dry, cold climates and has been widespread in China since the early Pleistocene (55). In general, the loess distribution indicates a gradual trend during the Pleistocene toward drier and colder conditions in north China marked by many climatic fluctuations.

Tens of thousands of stone artifacts have been found at Zhoukoudian, mostly made from quartz, flint, and sandstone. The main tool types are choppers, scrapers, points, and burins (Figs. 7.14, 7.15). While some of the flakes were apparently used as tools without further trimming many others were retouched to produce more specialized tools. Three different tool-making techniques were employed by the *H. erectus* toolmakers: **anvil percussion**, in which a large flat stone placed on the ground was used as an anvil for breaking off flakes; **direct percussion**, in which a core flint was held and flakes were detached by striking it with a hammerstone; and **bipolar percussion**, in which an anvil was set on the ground, a piece of quartz

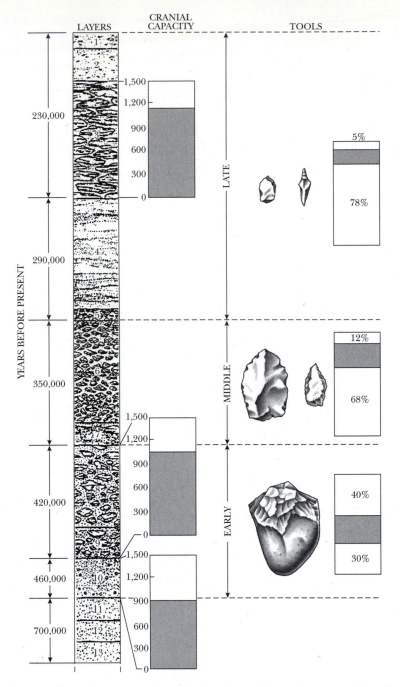

Fig. 7.14. Relationships among cranial capacity, tool manufacture, and time in the Zhoukoudian *H. erectus* sample. Cranial capacity increases from about 915 cc for the earliest cranium to about 1,140 cc for the most recent cranium in the sample. Tools types were mainly larger choppers and scrapers in the lower levels. By later levels the proportion of large and medium tools decreased whereas the proportion of small and more complex tools increased (37).

Chopper   Scrapers

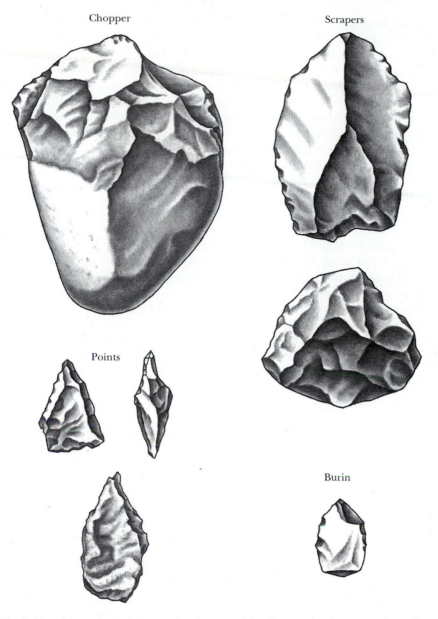

Points

Burin

Fig. 7.15. A representative sample of some of the thousands of stone artifacts that have been found associated with *H. erectus* at Zhoukoudian. The main tool types are choppers, scrapers, points, and burins (37).

held upright on it, and flakes chipped off both ends (bipolar flakes) by striking it with a hammerstone (37).

The stone tools found in the lowest layers of the cave (layers 8–11, dating to about 460,000–420,000 years ago) are mainly large tools (less than 50 g in weight and 60 mm in length) and are made using all three toolmaking techniques. In the middle layers of the cave, from about 370,000–350,000 years ago, the anvil-percussion technique is very rare and the bipolar-percussion method is dominant. This results in a greater proportion of smaller tools (less than 20 g in weight and 40 mm in length). The last stage, dated to about 300,000–230,000 years ago, is characterized by smaller tools of much better quality (37).

Over 50 years ago, Harvard archeologist Hallam Movius first noted a separation of stoneworking technologies in the Old World: the Acheulian handaxe/cleaver complex of Africa and Europe, and the chopper/chopping-tool complex of Asia east of India (Fig. 7.16) (56–58).[13] The geographical division between the Acheulian industries and the chopper/chopping-tool[14] industries of Asia was thought by some prehistorians to correspond to the geographical barriers formed by the Caucasus, the Elburz, the Hindu Kush, and the Himalayas: the so-called "Movius Line." In fact, the archeological tool kit of the Far East was often "defined" more by what it lacked compared to many Western assemblages: the large tools characteristic of the Acheulian, the technique of toolmaking, known as the Levallois technique, in which the core is trimmed to control the form and size of the intended flake, and the patterned changes in standardized tool types seen over time. This led Movius and others to view the Far East as an area of "cultural retardation." It is now known that this characterization is misleading and that the Far East has diverse and rich Paleolithic tool traditions going back into at least the late Lower Pleistocene: nevertheless, there are distinct differences in the tool complexes of East and West (34,58).

Many hypotheses have sought to explain this archeological phenomenon, focusing on different tool requirements of hominid populations in the two regions, the absence of proper stone raw materials, the presence of nonlithic materials for tools, and cultural interruptions during migration. For example, it has been proposed that Asian *H. erectus* may have relied heavily on bamboo in place of stone as a specific adaptation to the heavily forested and cave-filled, or karstic, areas of Southeast Asia (31,60). However, there is another intriguing possibility. We noted earlier that new evidence suggests that *H. erectus* may have first appeared in eastern Asia as early as 1.8 mya. The Acheulian tool kit first appears in Africa about 1.4 mya, some 0.4–0.5 million years after *H. erectus* left Africa for Asia (61). According to this scenario, the reason the Acheulian does not appear in Asia is that *H. erectus* left Africa before Acheulian tools were even developed.

In China, proto-handaxes are made of pebbles and thick flakes, but are not similar to Acheulian handaxes from Europe and Africa. They are large

---

[13]Handaxes and cleavers identified as late Acheulian have been found in association with the *H. erectus*/archaic *H. sapiens* skull from the late Middle Pleistocene of Narmada, India (59).

[14]Technically, choppers are unifacially flaked and chopping tools are bifacially flaked tools.

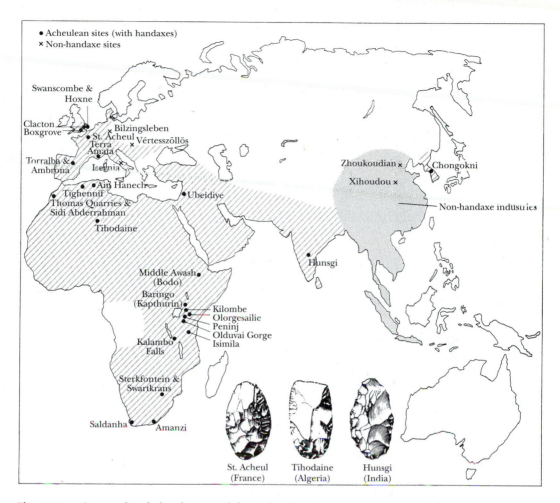

Fig. 7.16. Geographical distribution of the Acheulian handaxe industry and the nonhandaxe industries of East Asia. The geographical division between the Acheulian industries and the chopper/chopping-tool industries of East Asia was thought by some prehistorians to correspond to the geographical barriers formed by the Caucasus, the Elburz, the Hindu Kush, and the Himalayas: the so-called "Movius Line." Three representative Acheulian tools are shown (left to right): a handaxe from France, a cleaver from Algeria, and a handaxe from India (142).

in size and usually irregular in shape and can be classified as bifaces, unifaces, and artifacts with a triangular cross section. They are associated with bolas and other artifacts and together constitute assemblages of large stone implements. Chinese archeologists have described two cultural traditions in the early Paleolithic of China—one is the pebble industry, represented by proto-handaxes, and the other is the flake industry, represented by Zhoukoudian culture (62). It is possible, however, that these different "cultural traditions" simply represent different activity facies or environmental or geographical contexts.

The four thick layers of ash in the cave, the thickest one being over 6 m deep in some places, suggest to some archeologists that the Zhoukoudian hominids had mastered the use of fire, even at the earliest occupation levels, and that they had the ability to control fire and to keep it burning in the cave over long periods of time. A number of plant and animal remains found at Zhoukoudian provide clues to the dietary habits of *H. erectus*. For example, seeds and pollen from Chinese hackberry, walnut, hazelnut, pine, elm, and rambler rose suggest that the fruit and/or seeds of these species may have been part of the *H. erectus* diet (37). Animal bones including those of boar, horse, buffalo, and rhinoceros have also been found, indicating that *H. erectus* was capable of hunting both small and large game. The remains of over three thousand individuals of deer attest to a certain taste for venison!

This conventional view of Zhoukoudian archeology has recently been challenged by archeologist Lewis Binford (63,64). His arguments include the following points:

• since hominids, artifacts, and ash layers are not consistently associated in the cave, they should not be considered unequivocal evidence of hominid occupation
• the ash layers are too thick to be "hearths" and may be the remains of naturally occurring fires that were concentrated in the cave by geological agencies (alternatively, the ash may have resulted from the spontaneous combustion of guano)
• the vertebrate fossils are not necessarily indicative of hominid diets because *H. erectus* may have been just another prey item for animal carnivores responsible for all the fossilized remains

It is fair to say, however, that these arguments have been challenged by other paleoanthropologists who claim that the results were based on questionable statistical techniques that utilized only a small fraction of the total faunal evidence; hence most archeologists believe that the Zhoukoudian Locality 1 assemblage results from, for the most part, repeated hominid occupations (32,50).

Other *Homo erectus* Sites from China: Lantian, Yuanmou, Longgupo, Jianshi, Hexian, Yiyuan, Yunxian

While Zhoukoudian is unquestionably the most famous of the Chinese *H. erectus* sites, similar fossils have now been recovered from numerous other Lower to Middle Pleistocene sites in both northern and southern China (Fig. 7.12b) (50,60,65).

The *H. erectus* material discovered in the mid-1960s from loess deposits at Lantian, Shensi Province, includes an adult mandible with shovel-shaped incisors and congenital absence of the M_3s from Chenjiawo and a partial cranium from Gongwangling (66,67). The two specimens are from deposits about 25 km apart that appear to straddle the Matuyama/Brunhes paleomagnetic boundary (from about 700,000 years ago), although there is still some debate about this (32). The Gongwangling cranium includes the frontal and parietal bones, right temporal bone, most of the orbits, partial remains of the nasal bones, and most of the right maxilla with two teeth. The cranial vault bones are exceedingly thick, supraorbital tori are massive and continuous, the frontal squama is low, and postorbital constriction is well-marked. Endocranial volume is estimated at 775–783 cc. The overall impression is of a cranium even more "primitive" in morphology than any of those from Zhoukoudian or Indonesia (67,68). It is found in reversed polarity sediments (Matuyama) that may be as old as 1 million years and, if true, would make this the oldest hominid from China (Fig. 7.12a) (but see below). The Chenjiawo mandible is from overlying normal polarity sediments (Brunhes) dated to about 650,000 years ago (69). The Gongwangling fauna at Lantian is considered the earliest mammalian fauna associated with *H. erectus* in northern China and suggests that forest environments and warm subtropic conditions existed at the time. This characteristic giant panda–primitive elephant (*Ailuropoda-Stegodon*) fauna slowly gave way to more temperate faunas about 700,000 years ago at Chenjiawo. A small number of chopper/chopping tools have also been found at Lantian.

Dental remains from Yuanmou have assumed some importance, not because of the fossils, which consist only of two incisor teeth (and several stone tools), but because of the date of about 1.7 mya that Chinese anthropologists have given to them. This older age was bolstered by a preliminary amino acid racemization date of 1.54 mya on wild boar (*Sus*) and red deer (*Cervus*) teeth from the site. However, a different interpretation of the paleomagnetic profile of the site suggests that the hominid-bearing sediments may actually be younger than about 900,000 years and possibly closer to 500,000–600,000 years old (Fig. 7.12a) (45,60,70). The incisors are fairly robust and clearly shovel-shaped (68).

However, it has recently been reported that ESR dates combined with a paleomagnetic sequence suggest an age of about 1.7–1.9 million years for a small early *Homo* sample (fragmentary left mandible with P_4 and M_1 and an upper incisor) and associated stone tools from Longgupo Cave, Sichuan, China (71) (Fig. 7.17). If this dating is correct, these would be the oldest hominids and tools from China and would be roughly contemporaneous with the earliest *Homo* from Java mentioned earlier. The Longgupo teeth are said to bear more resemblance to early Pleistocene hominids from East Africa, such as *H. habilis* and *H. ergaster*, than to Asian *H. erectus*, leaving open the possibility that a pre-*erectus* hominid may have entered Asia before

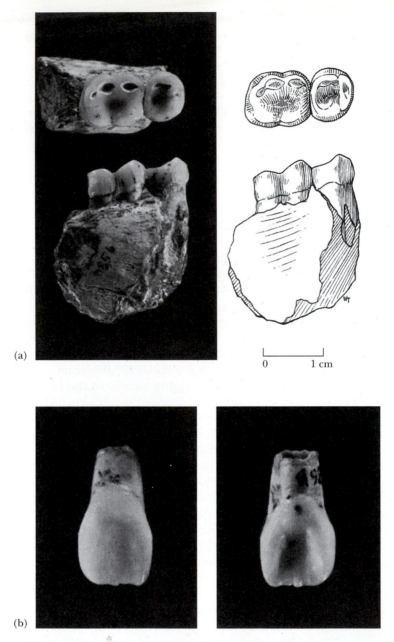

(a)

0   1 cm

(b)

Fig. 7.17.   Longgupo Cave hominids and stone tools.   These may represent the earliest hominids and stone tools from China. (a) Left mandibular fragment with P_4 and M_1; (b) labial view (left) and lingual view (right) of right I^2; (c) (top) elongated, spherical cobble with three relatively discrete areas showing crushing and pitting, suggesting repeated battering; (bottom) lenticular shaped flake tool. (Photos courtesy of R. L. Ciochon, University of Iowa.)

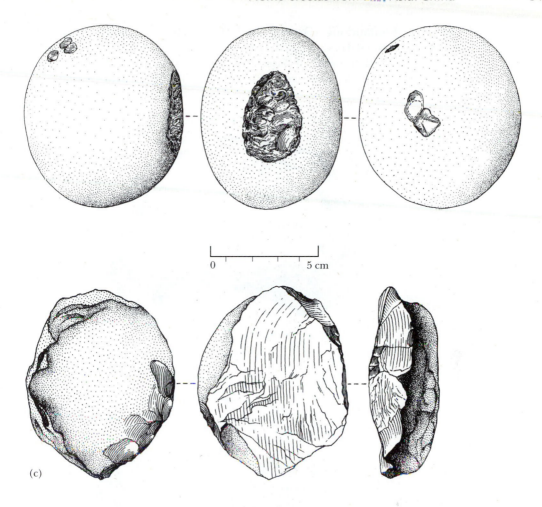

0 |————|————| 5 cm

(c)

2 mya, coincident with the earliest diversification of the genus *Homo* in Africa.[15]

Three hominid molars from Jianshi, variously identified as either *H. erectus* or early *H. sapiens*, are interesting in that they represent one of only three known associations of Middle Pleistocene hominids and *Gigantopithecus* yet found in East Asia (32).[16] These molars have been dated by U-S to about 300,000–200,000 years ago.

In 1980–81, *H. erectus* remains representing several individuals were

[15]The crowns of P_4 in *H. erectus* are generally simple as well as being single-rooted, as in modern humans. By contrast, the Longgupo P_4 root is bifid for most of its length. The M_1 in *H. erectus* usually has six cusps and somewhat thickened and wrinkled enamel. The Longgupo molar, in contrast, has five cusps, and thin, smooth enamel.

[16]The others being one Pleistocene locality in Viet Nam, Tham Om in western Nghe Tinh province, dated to about 500,000 years ago, and Longgupo in China (72).

found at Lontandong (Dragon Pool) Cave, Hexian County (Figs. 7.12, 7.18). The initial Hexian discoveries included a calvaria of a young adult lacking most of the cranial base, a partial left mandibular fragment preserving M_2 and M_3, and five isolated teeth. The next year a weathered

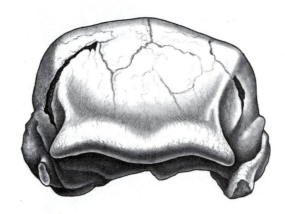

Hexian

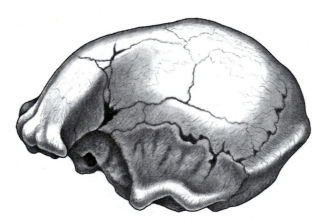

Fig. 7.18.   *H. erectus* calvaria from Lontandong (Dragon Pool) Cave, Hexian County.   Paleomagnetic stratigraphy suggests that the Hexian fossils are younger than 700,000 years and may be as young as 250,000–280,000 years if the correlation of the Hexian fauna to ^{18}O stage 8 is correct. These younger ages are reinforced by various other dating techniques, including TL dates that bracket the calvaria between 0.195 and 0.184 mya, a U-S date of 0.15 mya, and an amino-acid racemization date of 0.3–0.2 mya. These young dates raise the intriguing possibility that *H. erectus* and early *H. sapiens* were contemporaries; a situation, if true, that would thus far be unique to China.

frontal fragment preserving the right supraorbital region and a small part of the squama, a right parietal fragment, and five additional isolated teeth were recovered. These fossils belong to at least three individuals and are particularly significant because they may represent the last known occurrence of *H. erectus* from the Far East. Paleomagnetic stratigraphy suggests that the Hexian fossils are younger than 700,000 years and may be as young as 250,000–280,000 years if the correlation of the Hexian fauna to ^{18}O stage 8 is correct (73,74) (see Fig. 7.12). These younger ages seem to be confirmed by various other dating techniques, including TL dates that bracket the calvaria between 0.195 and 0.184 mya, a U-S date of 0.15 mya, and an amino-acid racemization date of 0.3–0.2 mya. These young dates raise the intriguing possibility that *H. erectus* and early *H. sapiens* were contemporaries; a situation, if true, that would thus far be unique to China (50).

The Hexian calvaria is the first Asian *H. erectus* cranium discovered outside the northern temperate zone of China. Like most *H. erectus* crania, the cranial vault is low and thick and the supraorbital torus is both thick and continuous but both the supratoral sulcus and postorbital constriction are less developed than in the Zhoukoudian *H. erectus* sample. The flattened frontal bone has a sagittal keel. The mastoid process is small and maximum cranial breadth is low down on the skull at the level of the well-developed supramastoid crest. There is marked angulation of the occipital bone. Cranial capacity is about 1,000 cc (cranial capacity averages about 1,050 cc for the Zhoukoudian sample and about 1,100 cc for the Ngandong sample). The body of the mandible is massive and the incisors are characteristically shovel-shaped with well-developed basal tubercles and are morphologically similar to similar teeth from Zhoukoudian and Krapina (45,75,76). Overall, the Hexian material is most similar to Zhoukoudian V. One of the important lessons from this material is that, taken in conjunction with the Zhoukoudian sample, there is no simple continuous decrease in cranial robusticity through time in the Chinese *H. erectus* sample.

Several hominid fragments, including a left and right parietal, frontal and occipital fragments, and seven isolated teeth from at least two individuals, have been recovered from Yiyuan. In general overall morphology, the specimens are similar to those from Zhoukoudian and, along with the Hexian material, could record one of the latest occurrences of *H. erectus* in China (16,50).

Undoubtedly the most significant Middle Pleistocene *H. erectus* fossils to come out of China in many years are two relatively complete crania and artifacts from Yunxian provisionally dated to about 350,000 years ago (Fig. 7.19). Even though it is distorted, the Yunxian II cranium is clearly the largest *H. erectus* cranium ever recovered in China. While they share many of the "typical" *H. erectus*–like cranial features noted earlier, it is interesting that other "typical" *H. erectus* traits like well-developed cranial buttressing and the form of the supraorbital tori are not well expressed in the Yunxian

(a)

(b)

Fig. 7.19.   (a) Frontal and (b) lateral views of EV 9002 and EV 9001, respectively, two of the most complete Middle Pleistocene *H. erectus* skulls from China. Both were discovered at Yunxian and are provisionally dated to about 350,000 years ago. Even though it is distorted, EV 9002 is the largest *H. erectus* cranium ever recovered from China. (Photos courtesy of Li Tianyuan.)

crania, suggesting that such characters are polymorphic within Middle Pleistocene hominids.

What is perhaps more noteworthy is that these two *H. erectus* crania have a number of midfacial features that are often seen in (non-Neandertal) archaic or early modern *H. sapiens* (16,77):

- a more flattened, or orthognathic face with only moderate alveolar prognathism
- a distinct maxillary canine fossa
- the lateral part of the maxilla oriented coronally and highly angled to the zygomatic
- a high origin of the zygomatic root
- a horizontal inferior zygomaxillary border having a pronounced malar notch, or incisure

By way of contrast, many Middle Pleistocene hominids from Europe and/or Africa often classified as *H. erectus* have a different midfacial pattern that is more reminiscent of later-occurring Neandertals such as a pneumatized, obliquely set midface and a low origin of the zygomatic root. If this assessment is correct, it implies that facial structures characteristic of (non-Neandertal) early modern *H. sapiens* were widespread in East Asia at a time when European and African hominids still possessed a morphological pattern distinct from the modern human condition (78). This would have important implications in the debate about the geography of modern human origins (77):

> Given the common occurrence of a mid-facial anatomy characteristic of Late Pleistocene non-Neandertal *H. sapiens* in Middle Pleistocene hominid crania . . . from [E]ast Asia and its less frequent . . . occurrence in Middle Pleistocene Eurafrican hominids, it can be argued that this morphology appears first in Asia and subsequently spread westward.

This view has not gone unchallenged. Several anthropologists have tried to decouple Asian *H. erectus* from any direct role in modern human ancestry by claiming that the "modern" features described for the Yunxian crania also appear in African fossils of equivalent age, the implication being that these features are therefore primitive ones and not indicative of any special phylogenetic relationship. We will come back to this issue in the next section when we address the question of whether or not *H. erectus* can be identified in Africa.

HOMO ERECTUS IN AFRICA?

At the beginning of the chapter we posed the question of whether or not *H. erectus* was a "real" species with definable boundaries in time and space and, if so, whether it could also be identified in the Lower to Middle Pleistocene of Africa and/or Europe. Most anthropologists would answer a definite "yes" to the first question and a definite "maybe" to the second. Let us first review the specimens that have been most consistently classified as *H. erectus* from Africa (we will look at Middle Pleistocene hominids from Europe in the next chapter) and then discuss some of the current controversial issues surrounding *H. erectus.*

A number of fossils from North, East, and South Africa have been described as *H. erectus* over the last half-century (Fig. 7.1). For many years it has been thought that *H. erectus* was present in Africa perhaps as much as 1 million years prior to its occurrence in the Far East. However, as mentioned above, if the new date for Javan *H. erectus* at 1.8 mya is correct, then the earliest known hominids from Java are of comparable age to the oldest specimens of *H.* cf. *erectus* (= *H. ergaster*) from Africa.

Possible *Homo erectus* from North Africa

The first discoveries of *H. erectus* in Africa were from several poorly dated sites in Algeria and Morocco in northwestern Africa associated with variants of the Acheulian tool tradition (79,80) (Fig. 7.1).

The initial discovery in 1933 included part of a cranial vault, the left maxilla, and the lower jaw of a subadult found near Rabat, Morocco. However, because the mandible has a bony chin and the occipital bone lacks a transverse torus, some workers consider the Rabat hominid an early form of *H. sapiens* (81,82). Other more archaic-looking hominids from Morocco include two fragmentary jaws and teeth found in 1955 at Sidi Abderrahman, near Casablanca, a mandible and cranial pieces found between 1969 and 1972 at Thomas Quarries, and a damaged cranial vault, natural sandstone braincast, and part of the left maxilla with I^2-M^2 and lower face found in 1971 at Salé. The Salé cranium is thick-walled and the endocranial volume is estimated at 880 cc (83). It has other typical *H. erectus* features, including pronounced postorbital constriction, frontal keeling, lack of articular tubercle, and greatest skull breadth across the prominent supramastoid crests (79,82). However, it does have some "advanced" *H. erectus* features, such as the development of parietal eminences and a more rounded occipital contour, although the pathological nature of the nuchal area makes measurements of this area suspect.

Between 1954 and 1956, three jaws, a parietal bone, and several teeth were discovered at Ternifine (now Tighennif), Algeria (Fig. 7.20). The Ternifine jaws are described as quite similar in overall morphology and robustness to *H. erectus* jaws from the Far East and from Olduvai (OH 22, OH 23, OH 51) and differ from the Rabat specimen in showing little, if any, development of a bony chin (82). The Ternifine fossils were found in sediments of normal polarity, presumably from within the Brunhes normal epoch less than 700,000 years ago. Tentative correlations of these North African sites with the ^{18}O marine stratigraphic record are given in Figure 7.21.

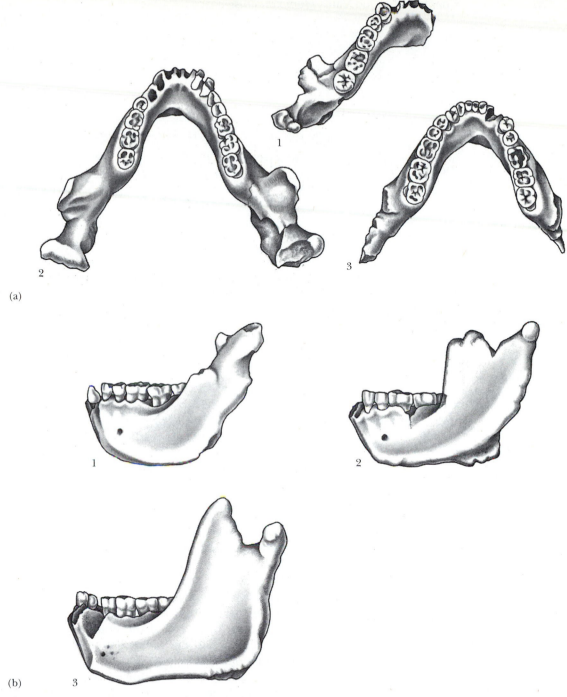

Fig. 7.20. *H. erectus* lower jaws from Ternifine. (a) Occlusal view; (b) lateral view (82).

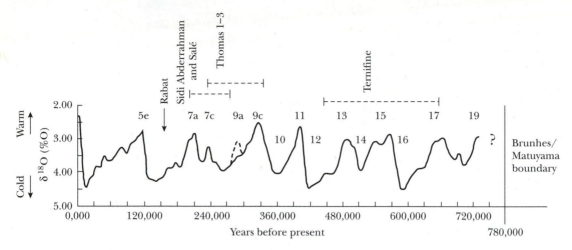

Fig. 7.21. Tentative correlations between fossil hominid sites in North Africa (Rabat, Sidi Abderrahman, Salé, Thomas Quarry, Ternifine) and the oxygen-isotope record (143).

Possible *Homo erectus* from East Africa

By far the most abundant and informative *H. erectus* material from Africa comes from Olduvai Gorge, Tanzania, and Lake Turkana, Kenya.

The first *H. erectus* from Olduvai Gorge was found by Louis Leakey in 1960 at site LLK, upper Bed II (Figs. 7.4, 7.22). The specimen, Olduvai Hominid (OH) 9, is dated to about 1.2 mya and consists of a partial braincase that includes the supraorbital region, occiput, and much of the cranial base. Unfortunately, the face is missing. It shares many of the cranial features that we have already noted for Asian *H. erectus*: 1) a shelflike and robust supraorbital torus that is especially thick above the nose; 2) a low lateral cranial profile with a receding frontal bone (however, unlike many Asian *H. erectus*, the frontal lacks a midsagittal keel); 3) greatest skull breadth low near the mastoid crests; and 4) a reduced degree of basicranial flexion. Endocranial capacity has been estimated at 1,060–1,070 cc (84). In a plane of skull orientation passing through the top of the external auditory meatus and the bottom of the orbit, called the **Frankfurt Horizontal** (FH) plane, it can be appreciated that the rather flattened cranial base contributes to the high position of the occipital condyles, the shallow posterior cranial fossae, and the relatively high position of the occipital protuberance (85) (Fig. 7.23). In overall size, shape, and robustness OH 9 is most similar to *H. erectus* from Java, particularly to Sangiran crania 4, 12, and 17 (3,86).

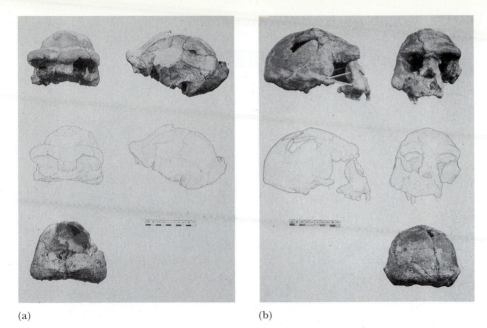

(a)   (b)

Fig. 7.22. The first *H. erectus* discovered at Olduvai Gorge (OH 9) (a) compared to Sangiran 17 (b). Olduvai Hominid (OH) 9 is dated to about 1.2 mya and consists of a partial braincase that includes the supraorbital region, occiput, and much of the cranial base. Note the shelflike and robust supraorbital torus that is especially thick above the nose (glabellar prominence) and the low lateral skull profile with a receding frontal bone. Endocranial capacity has been estimated at 1,060 cc. (Photographs courtesy of G. P. Rightmire.)

Several quartz flakes and other tools were recovered from excavations at the site but are not considered diagnostic and OH 9 is not directly associated with them.

A second *H. erectus* cranium from Olduvai, OH 12, was found in a number of pieces scattered over the surface of site VEK, Bed IV. Upper and lower age estimates for Bed IV are between 620,000 and 830,000 years. Some of the facial skeleton is also preserved, including part of the left maxillary alveolar process with tooth roots and a frontal fragment preserving some of the superior rim of the right orbit (3,86). Brain capacity is estimated at 700–800 cc (84). In many features the cranium is more gracile than OH 9 or any of the Indonesian *H. erectus*. For example, a true occipital torus is not well developed, the cranial vault appears more rounded in posterior view, there is no sagittal keel or parasagittal flattening along the parietals (but there may be traces of slight keeling in the frontal bone), and the temporal lines marking the origin of the temporalis muscle are faint. In addition, the supraorbital torus is lightly constructed (only about 10 mm thick) but there is a distinct supratoral sulcus similar to that seen, for instance, in KNM-ER 3883.

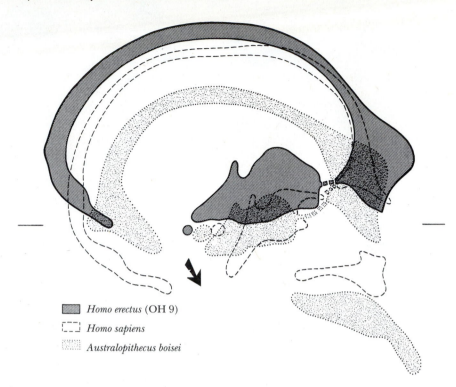

- *Homo erectus* (OH 9)

- *Homo sapiens*

- *Australopithecus boisei*

Fig. 7.23. If OH 9 is oriented in the Frankfurt Horizontal plane, it can be appreciated that the rather flattened cranial base contributes to the high position of the occipital condyles, the shallow posterior cranial fossae, and the relatively high position of the occipital protuberance compared to *H. sapiens* and *A. boisei*. Arrow designates location of the foramen magnum (85).

There are no stone tools directly associated with OH 12, although other skeletal remains attributable to *H. erectus* from upper Bed IV have been found with Acheulian tools (87).

Three mandibular fragments from Olduvai have usually been assigned to *H. erectus* (OH 22, 23, 51) (82). The most complete of the three is OH 22, a nearly complete right mandible preserving P_3-M_2. It probably comes from Bed III or IV and is not younger than about 620,000 years. Its mandibular body is thick and robust, particularly in the symphyseal region, and there is no evidence of any bony chin formation. OH 23 is a left jaw fragment preserving the heavily worn P_4-M_2 from the overlying Masek Beds. OH 51, from Bed III or IV, consists of a partial left mandibular corpus preserving only the worn crowns of P_4 and M_1. The latter two jaw fragments are not too informative, but generally conform to OH 22 in terms of overall shape and robustness.

The first information about the postcranial skeleton of African *H. erectus* also came from Olduvai. In 1970 a hip bone and femoral shaft (OH 28) were discovered at site WK, Bed IV, in association with Acheulian tools (mainly handaxes, cleavers, scrapers) (87). These postcranial fossils, combined with those from Koobi Fora (see below) and those described by Weidenreich from Zhoukoudian, identify a unique *H. erectus* hindlimb morphology that includes 1) a large acetabulum, 2) a robust vertical iliac pillar, 3) a small auricular surface for articulation with the sacrum, and 4) a femur characterized by a large femoral head, anteroposteriorly flattened, or **platymeric**, femoral shaft characterized by thickened cortical bone, narrow medullary cavity, and heavy muscular markings.

In terms of function, there is little doubt that this pelvic-femoral complex is that of a habitual upright biped (5,88,89). Judging from the size of the femur and hip, a body size of 50 kg for this individual has been estimated (82).

A number of beautifully preserved specimens from Koobi Fora have been assigned to *H. erectus*. Two of the best preserved crania, KNM-ER 3733 and KNM-ER 3883, are from the upper Member of the Koobi Fora Formation (Figs. 7.4, 7.24). KNM-ER 3733 is from sediments just below, and KNM-ER 3883 from sediments just above, the Okote Tuff complex dated to approximately 1.6 mya.

KNM-ER 3733 is a relatively complete braincase that includes a partially preserved facial skeleton. The nasal bridge and both zygomatic bones are present, but the maxilla is eroded and all the anterior teeth are missing. KNM-ER 3883 (Fig. 7.24b) also includes part of a face and braincase. While the cranial vault is largely complete only the supraorbital region and right zygomatic bone of the face are preserved. Both specimens have an estimated cranial capacity of 800–850 cc and are somewhat smaller than the heavily built OH 9 braincase from upper Bed II, Olduvai (3).

In lateral view, both KNM-ER 3733 and KNM-ER 3883 exhibit the low cranial profile typical of *H. erectus*. The crania are broad with maximum breadth low on the temporal bones rather than higher up on the parietal vault as in *H. sapiens*. No strong angular process is present and the mastoid process is small. Occipital bones of both East African and Indonesian *H. erectus* are highly angled (between about 100–110 degrees) rather than having the more rounded contour of modern humans (see Fig. 7.6). This occipital angulation is associated with the formation of a transverse torus (less developed in KNM-ER 3883). In KNM-ER 3733 the length of the upper portion of the occipital squama exceeds that of the nuchal plane but in KNM-ER 3883 the upper portion is shorter, which is the usual condition for *H. erectus*.

The Turkana *H. erectus* crania vary in the size and shape of their supraorbital region. The torus in KNM-ER 3733 is especially gracile with only moderate expression of a supratoral sulcus. On the other hand, KNM-ER 3883 has a much larger torus with a more massive glabella region. In this

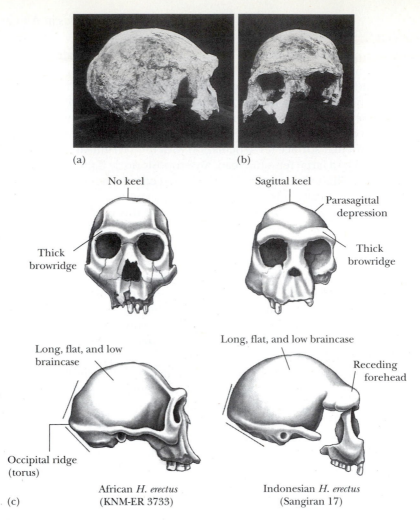

(a)

(b)

No keel

Sagittal keel

Parasagittal depression

Thick browridge

Thick browridge

Long, flat, and low braincase

Long, flat, and low braincase

Receding forehead

Occipital ridge (torus)

(c)

African *H. erectus* (KNM-ER 3733)

Indonesian *H. erectus* (Sangiran 17)

Fig. 7.24. (a) Lateral view and (b) frontal view of one of the most complete *H. erectus* crania, KNM-ER 3883, from the upper Member of the Koobi Fora Formation dated to approximately 1.6 mya. Estimated cranial capacity is 800–850 cc, somewhat smaller than the heavily built OH 9 braincase from upper Bed II, Olduvai. In lateral view KNM-ER 3883 exhibits the low cranial profile typical of *H. erectus*. The cranium is broad with maximum breadth low on the temporal bones rather than higher up on the parietal vault as in *H. sapiens*. In (c) some of the differences between a similar *H. erectus* skull from Kenya, KNM-ER 3733, and Javan *H. erectus* are highlighted. (Photo courtesy G. P. Rightmire.)

it more closely resembles OH 9, even though the overall cranium is smaller. These Turkana crania have frontal bones that show the typical *H. erectus* pattern of postorbital constriction (3).

Several other skull fragments from Koobi Fora are generally similar to comparable parts of KNM-ER 3733 and/or 3883 and are tentatively referred to *Homo* aff. *H. erectus* as well, or to *H. ergaster* (e.g., KNM-ER 730).

Box 7.1   Skeletal Pathology in *Homo erectus*

A partial H. erectus *skeleton (KNM-ER 1808) was recovered in the 1970s from the Upper Member of the Koobi Fora Formation. Unfortunately, most of the bones are pathologically altered, encrusted with a coarse woven bone that is possibly the result of chronic hypervitaminosis A. One possible cause of this pathology is an excessively high dietary intake of animal liver, particularly carnivore liver, by this individual. Such a condition has been documented in early Arctic explorers after ingestion of polar bear, seal, or husky dog liver. Does the ingestion of toxic amounts of carnivore liver reflect a major dietary shift in early human populations marked by increased meat-eating behaviors? In this regard, it may be significant that the first association of stone artifacts and animal bones at Koobi Fora antedates KNM-ER 1808 by only some 200,000 years (90).*

A second interesting hypothesis to explain this skeletal pathology is that a new foraging strategy in early H. erectus *(91) may have resulted in increased ingestion of bee brood (eggs, pupae, larvae) and other immature insects. Bee broods have a high concentration of vitamin A and protracted ingestion of honey and insect larvae could produce the skeletal pathology seen in KNM-ER 1808. The density of nests of the East African bee,* Apis mellifera, *within the foraging area of early* H. erectus *would provide an ample and reliable energy source that could contribute substantially to early hominid nutritional requirements. The human brain is a voracious energy consumer and was expanding rapidly during this phase of human evolution. Even though the brain constitutes only about 2 percent of body weight, it requires about 17 percent of the normal cardiac output and consumes about 20 percent of the oxygen utilized by the entire body. Perhaps a new foraging strategy to secure one of the necessary energy sources, honey, led inadvertently to isolated cases of hypervitaminosis A in early* H. erectus.

The problem in sorting much of this material is due to the fact that both *Homo* and *Australopithecus* occur in deposits above the KBS Tuff, so taxonomic assignments of such isolated and unassociated material are often difficult.

Perhaps the most extraordinary and unique information about *H. erectus* discovered at Lake Turkana pertains to postcranial adaptation. Several partial *H. erectus* skeletons and isolated postcrania from Koobi Fora have been described, including one nearly complete left femur (KNM-ER 1481a) from sediments stratigraphically below the KBS Tuff (89). If the taxonomic assessment of this femur is correct, it would be the oldest *H. erectus* postcranial specimen known.

A more complete and nonpathological *H. erectus* skeleton (WT-15000) was discovered in 1984 on the west side of Lake Turkana (Fig. 7.25) (92). The specimen derives from sediments that immediately overlie a tuff identified as part of the Okote Tuff complex dated to approximately 1.65 mya. Much of the skull and dentition were also recovered and the teeth are similar in size to the Zhoukoudian *H. erectus* sample. Based on standards of modern human dental development, the individual was about 10–12 years old at the time of death (93,94). Both the central and lateral upper incisors are shovel-shaped, a feature often associated with Far Eastern *H.*

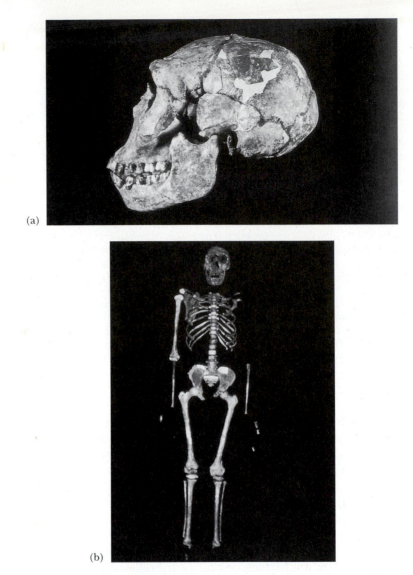

(a)

(b)

Fig. 7.25.   The most complete *H. erectus* skeleton ever found, KNM-WT 15000 from Nariokotome, Kenya.   (a) Lateral view of cranium; (b) the skeleton. (Photographs courtesy of A. Walker and National Museums of Kenya.)

erectus and modern Chinese populations (95). The cranial capacity is estimated at 880 cc and would probably have been just over 900 cc if the individual had lived to maturity (96).[17]

Skull morphology suggests that East African *H. erectus* may have been

[17]Modern humans have about 95 percent of their adult brain size by the age of 10 years.

quite sexually dimorphic. For example, the WT-15000 cranium does not show the exaggerated ectocranial buttressing typical of Asian *H. erectus*, although this may be solely a reflection of its young age at the time of death. In spite of its young age, however, the supraorbital tori are thicker, the palate broader, and the facial skeleton more robust than in KNM-ER 3733 (97).

Probably more informative than the teeth and cranial parts, however, is the extraordinarily complete postcranial skeleton. As noted above, postcranial remains of *H. erectus* are few and far between, and before the discovery of WT-15000, *H. erectus* postcrania were either fragmentary, not definitely associated with skulls or teeth, disputed as to species identification, or diseased (as in KNM-ER 1808). Therefore, the discovery of a virtually complete skull and nonpathological skeleton had been unprecedented.

The height of this individual is estimated to be about 5′3″, and if he had reached maturity would probably have stood over 6′ (98,99). Overall body proportions are similar to those found in equatorial modern people. The vertebral column, while showing a humanlike thoracic and lumbar curvature, differs from modern human vertebral columns in several features, not the least of which is the presence of six lumbar vertebrae (as in *A. africanus*). Modern humans normally have five lumbar vertebrae and African great apes three or four. In addition, the spinous processes are relatively longer and less inferiorly inclined and the laminae are not as broad. This means that the roof-tilelike layering effect of adjacent vertebrae typical of modern humans is not so evident in *H. erectus*. Also, the vertebral (neural) canal for passage of the spinal cord in the cervical and thoracic regions is relatively smaller than in modern humans and the orientation of some of the articular facets differs as well (95,100,101).

Important differences from modern humans are also seen in the pelvis and femur. For example, the ilium is strongly flared laterally but lacks a well-developed iliac pillar (unlike OH 28—see above). This lateral iliac flare is associated with an extremely long femoral neck (85 mm) that is over 3 standard deviations from the average value in modern humans. Moreover, the angle between the femoral neck and shaft is very small (110 degrees) and is 5 standard deviations from the average value for modern *H. sapiens*. The obstetrical conclusion from this and other specimens is that birth canal diameters in early *H. erectus* were quite small and that passage of a modern human–sized, full-term fetus would have been difficult if not impossible. This implies that some growth patterns characteristic of modern humans, such as a continuation of fetal growth rates into the neonatal period, resulting in relatively helpless infants and increased infant dependency, must have already evolved in *H. erectus* by 1.6 mya (95,97,102).

It is interesting to speculate on the functional reasons for the marked postcranial differences in overall size and shape between *Australopithecus* and *H. erectus*. As we have seen, early australopithecines were characterized by relatively short hindlimbs and long forelimbs, a long and bulky trunk having six lumbar vertebrae, and long and curved fingers and toes—all features pointing to retention of some arboreal activity (or to retention of at least this phylogenetic "baggage" from a previous arboreal ancestry). On the other hand, *H. erectus* exhibits postcranial features more conducive to walking long distances, such as relatively long hindlimbs and shortened toes (103,104).

Several specimens assigned to *H. erectus* have been recovered from the Lake Baringo area and from the Ethiopian rift. The Baringo specimens include two mandibles and some postcranial fragments, including a well-preserved ulna, and date to between 700,000 and 230,000 years ago (105–108). The ulna is more gracile than the "robust" australopithecine ulna from Omo (Omo L.40-19) and Neandertal ulnae (109). One bifacial core tool and fourteen flakes were recovered in situ with the hominids, although artifacts are common over the surface near the fossil locality.

Recently, a well-preserved *H. erectus* mandible preserving P_4-M_3 (and an isolated M^3) were discovered in direct association with Acheulian tools (mostly roughly made bifaces and trihedral picks) at the Ethiopian rift site of Konso-Gardula (61). The site is dated to 1.9–1.3 mya. Interestingly, grooves between the mandibular teeth indicate that these early hominids were using some type of wood, bone, and/or sinew for tooth picks. Overall, the tools are most similar to those found from middle Bed II, Olduvai. It seems clear from the cut marks on some of the animal bones that early hominids were using stone tools "to process" them (perhaps cutting off pieces of meat, or breaking bones for marrow). A total of eleven hominids have been found at the site since 1991, and field research indicates the presence of both *Homo* and *A. boisei* (110).

The discovery at Konso-Gardula is particularly informative in showing that the Acheulian appears abruptly in East Africa about 1.4 mya, following about 1 million years of exclusive Oldowan tool manufacture. The first African appearance of *H. erectus* and Acheulian tools date to about 1.7 and 1.4 million years ago respectively, thus calling into question the view that "changes to open and arid conditions may have triggered the origin of *H. erectus* and of his characteristic tool kit" (111), since both these appearances substantially postdate the marked period of global cooling dated to about 2.8–2.4 mya (112).

Possible *Homo erectus* from South Africa

Only one site in southern Africa has yielded hominid fossils that may be attributed to *Homo* aff. *H. erectus.* In 1949, J. T. Robinson discovered a mandible (SK 15) at Swartkrans, South Africa, that he and Robert Broom thought to be an early hominid distinct from *Australopithecus*, which they named *Telanthropus capensis* (113,114). Another mandibular fragment (SK 45), maxillary fragment (SK 80), proximal radius (SK 18b), and P_3 (SK 18a) were subsequently found and all were eventually included within the same genus. By 1961, however, Robinson had formally sunk *Telanthropus capensis* into *H. erectus* (115). In 1969, Ron Clarke of the University of the Witwatersrand recognized that the facial part of a different specimen, SK 847 (originally catalogued as *Paranthropus*), articulated perfectly with the SK 80 maxilla and that they were, in fact, from the same individual. The composite SK 847 cranium and several mandibular pieces (SK 15 and SK 45) are now generally included within the genus *Homo* (116–118) (Fig. 7.26).

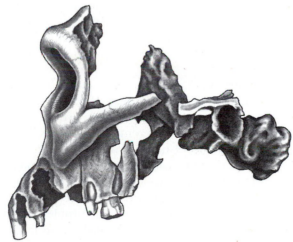

Fig. 7.26. Lateral view of the composite SK 847 cranium. The cranium and several mandibular pieces (SK 15 and SK 45) from Swartkrans are now generally included within the genus *Homo*. The supraorbital torus of SK 847 is pronounced and thickened, but not nearly as much as in other African specimens, and there is a distinct supratoral sulcus separating the torus from the rather steep frontal squama. The specimen lacks the marked postorbital constriction characteristic of Asian *H. erectus*. (Photo by D. Panagos courtesy of the Transvaal Museum, Pretoria.)

A more recent statistical study of SK 847 has cast doubt on its affinities to *H. erectus*, however, by demonstrating that morphological differences between it and two other crania often attributed to *H. erectus*, KNM-ER 3733 and KNM-WT 15000, are greater than would be expected in a single modern human population drawn from eastern and southern Africa (119). Instead, these authors see more similarities to specimens often regarded as *H. habilis* such as KNM-ER 1813 or Stw 53. The supraorbital torus of SK 847 is pronounced and thickened, but not nearly as much as in other African specimens, and there is a distinct supratoral sulcus separating the torus from the rather steep frontal squama. The specimen lacks the marked postorbital constriction characteristic of Asian *H. erectus* (120).

CURRENT ISSUES AND DEBATES

In this chapter we have reviewed the *H. erectus* sample from Asia and Africa, and the Middle Pleistocene hominid record of Europe will be the subject matter of the next chapter. With this information as background, we can now begin to discuss some of the interesting and vexing questions about *H. erectus* that were posed at the beginning of this chapter.

As noted earlier, several anthropologists have recently questioned whether any of the African and European specimens traditionally classified as *H. erectus* should in fact be classified in the same species as Asian *H. erectus*. Indeed, some have even questioned whether Asian *H. erectus* is a valid species and whether it was in the mainstream of modern human evolution (121–126).

But before deciding on what *H. erectus* is not, it is first necessary to decide what it is. One problem in defining *H. erectus* is that it may well represent a grade, rather than a clade, of human evolution. Differences of interpretation generally relate to different philosophies of systematics. As D. T. Rasmussen of Washington University in St. Louis notes, throwing out the notion of grades essentially leads to throwing out anagenesis, which automatically leaves nothing but typological species definitions, and the impossibility of studying gradual change. Over the past decade or so, a number of workers have begun to address this problem by "redefining" *H. erectus* using cladistic analyses that distinguish those features found in hominoids generally (plesiomorphies) from those restricted to various groups within the genus *Homo* (synapomorphies) and those unique to *H. erectus* (autapomorphies).

Starting from the well-founded premise that *H. sapiens*, *H. habilis*, and *H. erectus* are more closely related to one another than to any other species, Bernard Wood of the University of Liverpool considers how these species differ from their hypothetical common ancestor, the possible cladistic relationships among them, and the autapomorphic features of *H. erectus* (Fig. 7.27) (125). As he points out, however, most previous analyses have concentrated on the morphological features that distinguish *H. erectus* from *H. sapiens* and have placed much less emphasis on whether such features distinguish *H. erectus* from *H. habilis* as well. For example, while various morphological indices have been used to highlight skull-shape differences between *H. erectus* and *H. sapiens* (for example, the long, low vault and postorbitally constricted frontal region), these same indices show little difference between *H. erectus* and *H. habilis* crania. Further difficulties depend on which specimens are included in the hypodigm of *H. erectus*. For instance, if massive crania like Bodo, Broken Hill, and Petralona (see follow-

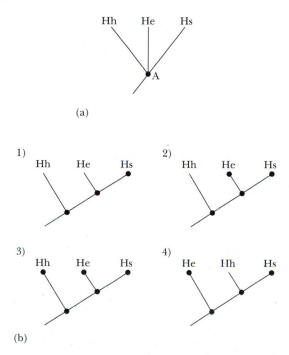

Fig. 7.27. (a) Simplest relationship between the three taxa, *H. habilis*, *H. erectus*, and *H. sapiens* and a hypothetical common ancestor. Examples of possible character states of the common ancestor (A): Primitive (inherited from a common ancestor with *Australopithecus*): 1) absolute brain size greater than 500 cc; 2) emphasis of ectocranial cresting shifted anteriorly with respect to apes; 3) foramen magnum more centrally placed than in the apes; 4) thin cranial vault bones. Derived (with respect to *Australopithecus*): 1) reduced facial prognathism; 2) more discrete mastoid process associated with a reduction in supramastoid breadth; 3) absolute and relative reduction in tooth size; 4) tendency to extra lingual rather than distal cusps on the lower molars. (b) Cladograms depicting possible relationships between the three *Homo* species. Solid circles at the end of a branch indicate the presence of autapomorphic features (125).

ing chapters) are classified in *H. sapiens*, then even some of the character-istic *H. erectus* features like thick cranial vault bones and robust supraorbital tori cannot, by definition, be *H. erectus* autapomorphies. Conversely, Afri-can *H. erectus* crania like KNM-ER 3733 and 3883 have supraorbital tori that are much smaller than those in Asian *H. erectus* and cranial bones that are no thicker than those found in some anatomically modern human popu-lations. The question then becomes, should the "definition" of *H. erectus* be amended to include these specimens or should these specimens be re-moved from *H. erectus?*

Wood offers a philosophy to deal with this conundrum (125):

> [I]t is axiomatic that the definition of a taxon should include all its autapomor-phies, but a definition is not limited to such features. For, while symplesiomorph and shared-derived characters are (by definition) not unique to a taxon, what may be unique is a particular combination of such character states. For example, although individual members of "archaic" *H. sapiens* may have prominent su-praorbital tori and a thick vault, and *H. habilis* a relatively long and low cranium and cranial capacity of around 800 cc, it is only in *H. erectus* that these four features are found in combination. Thus, while as individual characters they have no validity within the definition of *H. erectus*, they are potentially significant in com-bination.

Wood rejects the strict cladistic logic stipulating that if a skull shares even a single autapomorphic feature with *H. erectus*, it must be classified as such. Instead, he prefers the definition emphasizing combinations of prim-itive and shared derived characters (Fig 7.27a)—and using such a defini-tion he feels that KNM-ER 3733 and 3883 should not be automatically placed in *H. erectus*, at least as presently defined (125,127).

Christopher Stringer of the Natural History Museum, London, has also tried to define *H. erectus* in terms of autapomorphic features, and like Wood, he does not intend that any one or two of these characters be used in isolation to identify the species, because "such a typological approach takes no account of individual variation" (123). Instead, he describes a range of characters, most of which would be expected to be present in any member of the species. Like Wood, he also queries the inclusion of the African forms in *H. erectus*, but concludes that they might be considered early representatives of a *H. erectus* grade. If true, their morphological dif-ferences from Asian *H. erectus* would call into question the claim for stasis in the *H. erectus* grade through time.[18]

A much more ideologically extreme cladistic judgment of *H. erectus* is rendered by Stringer's Natural History Museum colleague, Peter Andrews, who argues that "on balance . . . the African crania formerly attributed to *erectus* would have been close to the line leading to *sapiens*" and that "the Asian *erectus* was some way removed from this lineage" (121). Furthermore, he adds that if cladistic analysis confirms that *H. sapiens* is more closely

---

[18]Compare, for example, Rightmire, 1981 (128), and Wolpoff, 1984 (36).

related to *H. habilis* than to *H. erectus*, then the "scenario arising from this is that human evolution bypassed *erectus* in Asia, with a sequence of change from *habilis* through ER 3733 and 3883 and OH 9 and 12, giving rise to a Middle Pleistocene early sapiens . . ." (121). Not surprisingly, these conclusions do not sit well with some, particularly Chinese, anthropologists. How well do they stand up to further analysis?

Andrews' conclusions are based on his interpretation that most of the features used to define *H. erectus* are in fact primitive retentions from a common hominoid and/or hominid ancestor (i.e., plesiomorphies) that are not valid for a species definition. To a strict cladist, if any plesiomorphic character used to define *H. erectus* (maximum skull breadth across the supramastoid crests or marked postorbital constriction, for example) is found in great apes and/or other catarrhines generally, then it cannot be used to define *H. erectus*. Such characters in *H. erectus* should instead be considered assemblages of primitive features.[19] Andrews believes that the only features linking Asian and African forms are primitive features. In contrast, he believes that a number of derived features separate the hominid fossils of the two continents.

For example, the seven autapomorphic features described by Andrews as unique to Asian *H. erectus*, and by definition those not found in European or African Lower to Middle Pleistocene hominids, are the

1) presence of a frontal keel
2) thick cranial vault bones
3) presence of a parietal keel
4) angular torus on parietal
5) inion well separated from endinion
6) mastoid fissure developed
7) the presence of a recess between the entoglenoid and the tympanic plate

Probably the most persistent (and persuasive) critic of this strict cladistic approach has been Günter Bräuer from the Universitèt Hamburg, Germany. He has challenged these conclusions after examining European and African hominids for each of the seven supposedly autapomorphic characters of Asian *H. erectus* (129–132).

1) A frontal keel accompanied by parasagittal flattening is generally present in *H. erectus* crania from Zhoukoudian and Hexian and on some, but not all, of the Indonesian crania. However, the trait is also found in some African hominids usually assigned to *H. erectus* (KNM-ER 3733, OH 12), *H. habilis* (Stw 53), *A. africanus* (Sts 5), early *H. sapiens* (Bodo, Omo 2, Broken Hill, Eliye Springs, Laetoli 18), and in some European specimens like Salé and Arago 21 (see Chapter VIII).

---

[19]However, one may ask (not entirely facetiously) if even a cladist would ever actually confuse the skull of *H. erectus* with that of an early catarrhine like *Aegyptopithecus* in which both shared such similar plesiomorphic traits?

2) Cranial vault thickness is variable and these measures do not differ significantly between East African and East Asian specimens. Some archaic African and European *H. sapiens* have crania as thick, or thicker, than Zhoukoudian *H. erectus.*

3) The midsagittal keel on the parietal is highly variable among East Asian *H. erectus* specimens. In Zhoukoudian Skull XII, it is well developed anteriorly and in others (for example, Skull X and Sangiran 2) it is situated nearer to bregma. KNM-ER 3883 exhibits a slight keel with some parasagittal flatness (the fragmentary bregmatic region of KNM-ER 3733 cannot be evaluated). Slight keeling or midsagittal protuberances also appear in specimens from Ternifine, Omo 2, Petralona, KNM-ER 3883, Ternifine, Bodo, Eliye Springs, and Salé.

4) A tuberlike swelling at the mastoid angle is more or less strongly developed on all Zhoukoudian parietals but is more variable among Indonesian hominids (e.g., absent in Sangiran 2 and 10, slight in Sangiran 4, strong in Sangrian 31). This feature is variable in the African fossils as well. Some swelling in this region occurs in OH 9, OH 12, Ternifine, and Broken Hill. A clear angular torus is present in the Bodo cranium and the Arago parietal shows swelling in this region as well.

5) At least three African hominids, KNM-ER 3733, OH 9, and KNM-ER 1805, exhibit values within the range of East Asian *H. erectus* for this feature.

6) This is a fissure between the petrosal crest of the tympanic and the mastoid process. In both KNM-ER 1813 and OH 12 the petrosal crest is not fused to the mastoid process. Variants of a mastoid fissure are also found in KNM-ER 3884 and OH 24.

7) This is the recess between the convex entoglenoid process and the tympanic plate. A cleftlike morphology occurs in KNM-ER 3883 and possibly in KNM-ER 1813. It is interesting to note that this morphology is quite different on each side of Zhoukoudian Cranium III, thus making its diagnostic value somewhat suspect in any event.

It appears that some of the "autapomorphic" features of Asian *H. erectus* are even found in crania identified as Asian *H. sapiens*. Take, for example, the thick cranial vault bones. The average thickness for some cranial bones of early *H. sapiens* like the crania from Dali and Xujiayao are similar to those of Zhoukoudian *H. erectus* and some bones, like the parietals, are even thicker. Pronounced postorbital constriction is more strongly developed in the early *H. sapiens* Mapa cranium than in Hexian *H. erectus* and frontal keeling is also present in early *H. sapiens* crania from Dali, Yinkou, and Maba. A sharply angulated occipital appears on Dali and Yinkou crania and a prominent angular torus appears on the Dali cranium (these early *H. sapiens* specimens will be more fully discussed in the following chapter).

Thus, if such assessments of *H. erectus* morphology are correct, it would seem that many, if not all, of the "autapomorphies" of Asian *H. erectus* actually occur in other crania from Europe, Africa, and China variably classified as *H. habilis*, *H. erectus*, and/or early *H. sapiens*. In some cases the character in question is present in East African *H. erectus* hundreds of thousands of years before it appears in Asian *H. erectus*. For this reason, most if not all of these characters could just as easily be interpreted as primitive rather than as autapomorphies of Asian *H. erectus*. The hypothesis that Asian *H. erectus* is a highly specialized species on a side branch of human evolution is even more questionable given that it apparently shares many features with later Asian early *H. sapiens* (129,130). Thus, to dismiss Asian *H. erectus* from the mainstream of modern human ancestry based on this type of strict cladistic analysis seems premature at the very least (50). To paraphrase Mark Twain, reports of the death of *H. erectus* are greatly exaggerated.

Other criticisms of an "anywhere but Asia" philosophy of modern human origins have also been offered. For instance, it has been argued that of the seven autapomorphies listed by Andrews, few, if any, are genetically independent and functionally meaningful. For instance, features 1 and 3 may be combined as can features 6 and 7. Even if the function(s) of characters 2, 3, 4, and 5 were known—which they aren't—they may simply reflect the general robustness of the cranium.

If Asian *H. erectus* is not ancestral to modern *H. sapiens*, then it would be necessary to invoke a number of parallelisms and convergences between the two taxa in order to account for such similarities as progressively increasing brain size, more vertical foreheads, thinning of cranial vault bones, and decreasing postorbital constriction. As we shall see in following chapters, those who support a phylogenetic relationship between *H. erectus* and *H. sapiens* in Asia point to the presence in the Far East of temporally and morphologically intermediate specimens such as those from Dali, Ngandong, Narmada, Yunxian, and Jinniu Shan (32,50).

As the hominid fossil record of the Far East improves, it seems apparent that facial morphology of Middle Pleistocene Asian hominids was quite distinct from their European and African contemporaries, with many of these features presaging those found today in modern Asian populations. Such distinguishing facial characteristics include:
- much smaller upper and lower midfacial regions
- more horizontally oriented zygomatic bones
- pronounced and more medially situated malar tubercles bearing a distinct incisura malaris
- more acute and inferiorly situated zygomaticomaxillary angles
- a vertically shorter maxilla

Conversely, European fossil hominids are generally characterized by larger upper and lower facial areas, obliquely oriented zygomatic bones, vertically taller maxillae, and zygomatic bones lacking a malar tubercle and incisura malaris.

Interestingly, some morphological traits characteristic of Far Eastern Middle Pleistocene hominids are now found in all modern human populations (although their frequency is still higher in Asian groups), leading some to conclude that "the world-wide dissemination of morphological traits which first appeared in the Asian fossil record suggests that at least some of the facial traits associated with the emergence of modern humans, resulted not from a single African origin, but from admixture and gene flow between different regions of the Old World" (78).

Other authors (133) have emphasized a mosaic of morphological similarities between Middle Pleistocene *H. erectus* and Late Pleistocene *H. sapiens* from the Far East (for example, the anteriorly oriented anterolateral surface of the frontosphenoidal process of the zygomatic bone; the contour of the lower margin of the zygomatic process of the maxilla and the rounded inferolateral margin of the orbits; the flat nasal region and lower face; sagittal keeling; and the presence of shovel-shaped upper incisors) and use this as evidence that Asian populations of *H. sapiens* evolved directly from Asian populations of *H. erectus*. We will have much more to say on this subject when we discuss the various models of modern human origins in the last chapters.

Earlier mention was made of the two *H. erectus* crania from Yunxian that apparently have a number of midfacial features usually associated with (non-Neandertal) early modern *H. sapiens*. By way of contrast, some of the European and African Middle Pleistocene hominids classified as *H. erectus* and/or archaic *H. sapiens* have a midfacial pattern more reminiscent of later-occurring Neandertals in Europe. If this assessment is correct, it implies that facial architecture characteristic of early modern *H. sapiens* was evident in the Far East far earlier than in Europe or Africa and that *H. sapiens*–like morphology appeared first in Asia and then spread secondarily to the Near East and Europe (77).

This view is diametrically opposed to that which considers Africa the birthplace of anatomically modern humans. Before the evidence from Yunxian was available, supporters of this model could point to the absence of "*sapiens*-like" features in Middle Pleistocene Asian hominids in arguing that modern humans were derived from a non-Asian stock. However, the Yunxian evidence indicates that Middle Pleistocene hominids were highly variable and regionally differentiated, and it now seems reasonable to conclude that *H. sapiens*–like facial morphology appeared at different times in regionally disparate hominid populations—a fine example of what anthropologists call **mosaic evolution**. One might reasonably argue that these are regionally disparate only because of the vagaries of the fossil record. However, if specimens were known from each 100-km interval from Swartkrans to Beijing in 10,000-year intervals, probably most variation would prove to be clinal in space and anagenetic in time.

No one would deny that there are a number of differences between Asian and East African *H. erectus* samples, in particular the less obvious midline keeling and parasagittal flatness along the parietal bone in the East African specimens. But given the fact that fossils attributed to *H. erectus* cover such an enormous geographic and temporal range, such morphological variation seems surprisingly minor. Philip Rightmire of SUNY-Binghamton has detailed over twenty features common to African and Asian *H. erectus* samples that may be used to define *H. erectus* as a "real" taxon and notes that "[w]hile there are obvious differences of size within both Asian and African assemblages, it is apparent that the better preserved crania from these regions are remarkably similar" (82). Some of these features are undoubtedly primitive retentions, whereas others are not. But again, it is important to emphasize the distinctive *combination* of features that together unite these assemblages from China, Java, and Africa.

There is another interesting way to view this problem. If the *H. erectus* sample truly represents a number of different species in Asia and Africa, then human taxonomic diversity must have been significantly pruned since the Middle Pleistocene, as only one hominid species, *H. sapiens*, is extant today. And indeed, if this is the case, what agent could possibly have accomplished such drastic "pruning"? In order to test whether human taxonomic diversity has been significantly pruned over the last several hundred thousand years or whether the number of Lower to Middle Pleistocene hominid taxa have been overestimated by some paleoanthropologists, cranial variation in mixed samples of early fossil hominids, modern humans, and fossils attributed to *H. erectus* must be compared. The results of one such study indicate that the pattern and degree of cranial variation found in *H. erectus* closely approximates that found in the single species, *H. sapiens*, and implies that there is no statistical justification for subdividing the *H. erectus* sample into multiple species (134).

Taken all together, then, the fossil record of *H. erectus* encourages us to view all Middle Pleistocene hominids as essential parts of an evolving lineage that ultimately led to modern humans. This journey continues in the next chapter.

CHAPTER VIII

Almost There—But Not Quite: Archaic *Homo sapiens*

344

when god decided to invent
everything he took one
breath bigger than a circus tent
and everything began

when man determined to destroy
himself he picked the was
of shall and finding only why
smashed it into because
e. e. cummings
100 Selected Poems (1959)

INTRODUCTION

By some 500,000 years ago, *H. erectus* (or *H. ergaster*) populations through-out Africa were being supplanted by, or evolving into, a highly varied group of hominids that began spreading into almost all of Africa's ecological niches, except perhaps for the evergreen tropical forests (see Fig. 7.1). Like many other "intermediate" or "transitional" fossil groups, these hominid populations have been difficult to classify to everyone's satisfaction.[1] For this reason, they are often unceremoniously lumped together under the informal and unflattering designation of "archaic" *H. sapiens* because they had not yet evolved morphological features that can be considered typical of anatomically modern *H. sapiens*. These archaic *H. sapiens* are not to be confused with Neandertals, which are distinct and will be discussed separately in the last chapter.

[1]Of course every fossil group that doesn't become extinct is, by definition, "transitional" between the species it evolves from and the one it evolves into!

Throughout the Old World archaic *H. sapiens* are usually associated with some form of the Developed Oldowan/Acheulian tool complex and are known from such geographically diverse areas as East Africa (Bodo, Ndutu, Kabwe), Europe (Mauer, Steinheim, Arago), the Near East (Zuttiyeh), India (Narmada), Java (Ngandong, Sambungmachan), and China (Dali, Maba, Jinniushan, Xujiayao, Yunxian) (1,2) (Fig. 8.1). As we saw in the previous chapter, in eastern Asia characteristic Acheulian bifaces are not seen; instead there is a core/chopper and flake tradition. While many of these fossils are poorly dated, they probably all fall within a time range of approximately 500,000–200,000 years ago.

An important, and still contentious, issue is whether there was an in situ evolutionary continuum from *H. erectus* to "archaic" *H. sapiens* to anatomically modern *H. sapiens* in these various geographical regions (the so-called **Multiregional Continuity Model**) or whether anatomically modern *H. sapiens* first evolved in Africa and then migrated out of Africa into Eurasia

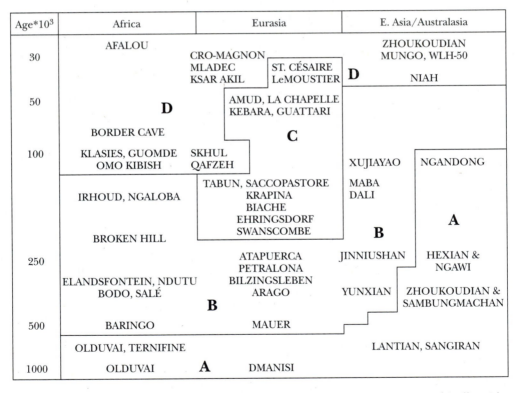

Fig. 8.1. Fossil hominid sites over the last million years are geographically widespread. This is one recent possible classification of fossil hominids during this time period. A = *H. erectus*; D = *H. sapiens*; B and C = those hominids often considered "archaic" *H. sapiens* (classified by some as *H. heidelbergensis* or *H. neanderthalensis*) (72).

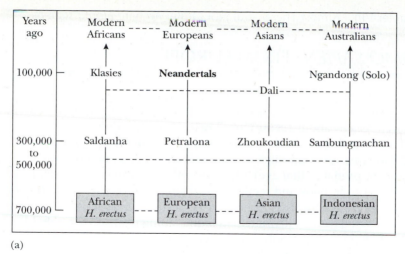

(a)

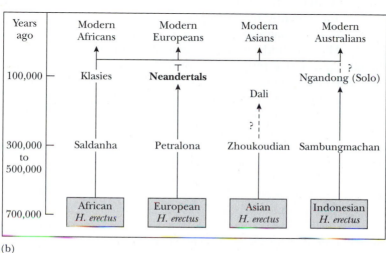

(b)

Fig. 8.2. Graphic representation of two hypotheses concerning modern human origins. Important fossils in different regions are shown at their approximate time levels, starting from *H. erectus.* (a) In this model, each line evolves locally to populations found in the region today; similarity among various geographic populations is explained by gene exchange at all time levels (implied by the horizontal dashed lines). Regional continuity is "demonstrated" by perceived morphological similarities through time within the same geographical regions. (b) In this model, similarity among modern humans is explained by the late expansion of a single modern human population out of Africa that then replaced the local populations existing in other parts of the world (73).

sometime in the Middle/Late Pleistocene, replacing all *H. erectus* and/or "archaic" *H. sapiens* in their path (the so-called Noah's Ark, Garden of Eden, or **Out of Africa Model**) (Fig. 8.2). This is a debate we shall come back to in the next chapter when we consider the emergence of anatomically modern *H. sapiens.*

ARCHAIC *HOMO SAPIENS* FROM EUROPE

Although recent evidence suggests that hominids (*H. erectus*) may have entered Asia by about 1.8 mya, until recently no hominid fossils or securely dated archeological evidence was known from Europe prior to about 500,000 years ago (although it was suggested that some archeological occurrences predated that age) (3).[2] Recently a hominid mandible, preserving most of the body and teeth of the young adult identified as *H. erectus*, was discovered from Dmanisi in East Georgia (Caucasus) with claims that it is associated with a Villafranchian fauna dating to approximately 1.8 mya. Several Oldowan type tools were also recovered at the site (5).

The oldest human fossils and artifacts thus far reported from western Europe are the recently discovered specimens from Gran Dolina, Atapuerca, Spain. Paleomagnetic dating suggests an age of close to 800,000 years (6,7). The hominid sample consists of about thirty human cranial, mandibular, and dental fragments representing at least four individuals. The largest fossil fragment is a piece of frontal bone that is larger than the equivalent bone in early *Homo* or *H. erectus* skulls having cranial capacities less than 1,000 cc, such as ER-3733, ER-3883, and OH-9 from Kenya, Sangiran 2 and Trinil from Java, or the Zhoukoudian sample from China. The frontal bone is relatively thin and has a double arched supraorbital torus rather than the straight, or horizontal, supraorbital shelf characteristic of Asian *H. erectus* and OH-9. Nearly one hundred stone tools have been found with the hominids, mostly cores, pebble tools, and choppers. The absence of handaxes, cleavers, picks, and blades is indicative of a pre-Acheulian level of stone-tool technology. Those who described the fossils consider them ancestors of Late Pleistocene European Neandertals and have provisionally included them in a separate species, *H. heidelbergensis*.

Another early hominid recently reported from western Europe is a tibia discovered in an archeological excavation at Boxgrove, Sussex, southern England. The "Boxgrove man" discovery was initially dated to about 500,000 years ago, although recently some amino-acid racemization dates on fossil marine gastropods that underlie the strata in which the tibia was found suggest an age closer to 362,000–423,000 years. The tibia is associated with early Acheulian tools (8–10). A number of other Middle Pleistocene sites in Europe have yielded fossil hominids that have at one time or another been classified as *H. erectus*, archaic *H. sapiens*, and/or Neandertals. However, the precise number of fossil sites is misleading, as it belies the paucity of good specimens and reliable dates that are actually available

---

[2]It has been recently reported that archeologist Yuri Mochanov of the Russian Academy of Science (4) has found stone tools in Siberia that he claims could be as much as 3.4 million years old, which, if true, would overturn virtually every current scenario of human origins to say the least!

from Europe. Some of the better known localities, with approximate age correlations, are shown in Figure 8.1.[3]

For heuristic purposes it is best to distinguish two archaic Middle Pleistocene hominid groups in Europe, the first of which is sometimes referred to as the older archaic group (from Mauer, Vértesszöllös, Bilzingsleben, Arago, Petralona) and the second, so-called younger archaic group (from Steinheim, Swanscombe, Pontnewydd, Ehringsdorf, Biache, La Chaise, Fontéchevade, Montmaurin, Atapuerca [Sima de los Huesos]). Because members of the "older" group show few, if any, synapomorphic features with later Neandertals and/or modern humans, some regard them as suitable morphological types for the common ancestor of both Neandertals and modern humans. We have already introduced the controversy in the last chapter over whether or not *H. erectus* really existed in Europe at all. For those who argue for its presence, the most oft-cited, if not totally convincing, *H. erectus*–like specimens from Europe are members of this "older" Middle Pleistocene group. By contrast, members of the "younger" group share a number of morphological features that presage those seen in later Neandertals and it is for this reason that some paleoanthropologists refer to them collectively as "anteneandertals" (11,12).

Older Archaic *Homo sapiens* Group

Mauer In 1907 the lower jaw of an early hominid was recovered from fluvial beds near the village of Mauer, just south of Heidelberg, Germany (Fig. 8.3). Its discoverer, Otto Schoetensack, Professor of Paleontology at the University of Heidelberg, described the jaw in 1908 as an early member of the genus *Homo*, thus making Schoetensack the first scientist to ever include such an ancient hominid fossil within *Homo*. The mandible was virtually complete when discovered, but some of the teeth were lost in 1945. As with most of the fossils in the "older" archaic group, the Mauer mandible has a mosaic of features intermediate between *H. erectus* and *H. sapiens*. For example, while the mandible has the robust body and wide, relatively low, ascending ramus and receding chin typical of *H. erectus*, it also has relatively small molars within the size range of modern humans and at the lower end of the size range for the Zhoukoudian *H. erectus* sample. Despite the fact that over five thousand bones, teeth, horns, and antlers of a Middle Pleistocene tropical fauna were recovered from the site before it was closed in 1962, only the single hominid mandible and about twenty bone and pebble fragments that may have been used or altered by hominids were ever found at the site (13). With the possible exception of the recently described hominid specimens from Atapuerca, Spain, and Boxgrove, En-

---

[3]Some of the "archaic" *H. sapiens* sample (e.g., Mauer, Petralona, Arago, Broken Hill, Bodo) share features with both *H. erectus* and *H. sapiens*. For this reason, some regard this sample as a separate middle Pleistocene species *H. heidelbergensis*.

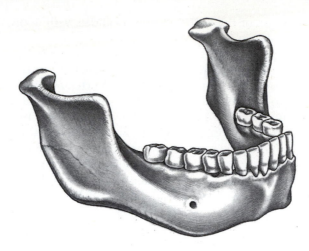

Fig. 8.3.   In 1907 the lower jaw of an early hominid was recovered near the village of Mauer, just south of Heidelberg, Germany.   The Mauer mandible has a mosaic of features intermediate between *H. erectus* and *H. sapiens*. For example, while the mandible has the robust body and wide, relatively low, ascending ramus and receding chin typical of *H. erectus*, it also has relatively small molars within the size range of modern man and at the lower end of the size range for the Zhoukoudian *H. erectus* sample.

gland, this is probably the oldest of the better known archaic European Middle Pleistocene hominids dating to an early Middle Pleistocene interglacial about 500,000 years ago.

Vértesszöllös   Hominid fossils representing the remains of two more archaic individuals were recovered in 1965 from Middle Pleistocene (Inter-Mindel) deposits about 50 km west of Budapest, at Vértesszöllös, Hungary. The hominids were found in association with a pebble/chopper-tool industry said to be similar to that from Zhoukoudian in China. The large mammal fauna from the site suggests a temperate woodland environment. Uranium series dates give inconsistent ages of about 250,000–475,000 years for the archeological/hominid levels (14–16).

The first individual is known from only the crowns of a lower left deciduous canine and fragmentary lower left deciduous molar and the second individual from an adult occipital bone reconstructed from two articulating pieces. The occipital bone has some of the *H. erectus*–like features we have previously identified: a very high and strongly built occipital torus; small cerebellar fossa compared to cerebral fossa, and large nuchal plane relative to occipital plane (Fig. 8.4). On the other hand, the somewhat thinner cranial bones and the estimated cranial capacity of around 1,300 cc are considered more "advanced" features than typically found in *H. erectus* crania. Needless to say, opinions have been divided over the taxonomic and phylogenetic significance of these mosaic features (17–20).

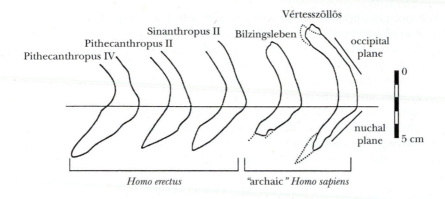

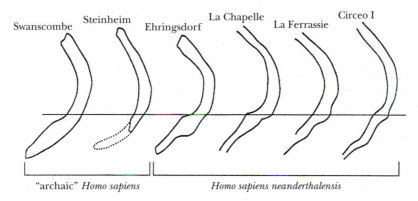

Fig. 8.4. Comparison of the midline profile of the Vértesszöllös occipital bone with those of other Middle Pleistocene hominids from Asia and Europe. Note the sharp angulation between the nuchal and occipital planes in the Vértesszöllös specimen (74).

Bilzingsleben About the same time the first *H. erectus* molars were being discovered from Zhoukoudian, a private naturalist, Adolf Spengler, discovered an equally primitive-looking human molar among the stone tools and animal bones in travertine quarries near the small village of Bilzingsleben, Germany. Unfortunately, the mine quarry closed soon after his 1927 discovery and the human tooth was subsequently lost. However, the site was reopened in 1969 and, as luck would have it, further hominid fossils were discovered there between 1974 and 1977. Radiometric dates have been published for the site, including a date of about 230,000 years ago based on ^{230}Th-^{234}U analysis of associated travertine and an amino acid racemization date of about 340,000 years ago (21–23).

The Bilzingsleben hominid material consists of two connecting occipital fragments, two frontal bone fragments, one parietal fragment, and a right upper molar, all scattered over approximately 400 m^2 of excavated area.

The occipital bone is broad and low with a well-developed occipital torus. In overall size and shape, the Bilzingsleben occipital is more reminiscent of the same bone in such *H. erectus* and archaic *H. sapiens* specimens as *Sinanthropus* III, *Pithecanthropus* VIII (Sangiran 17), OH 9, Vértesszöllös, and Petralona than it is to such "younger" European archaics as Swanscombe, Steinheim, and Ehringsdorf (see Fig. 8.4). These latter crania have smaller occipital tori with curved, rather than highly angled, occipital contours. The frontal bone is described as having a rather "flattish" forehead region and strong supraorbital tori with a broad and smooth glabellar depression between them. The cranial bones are quite thick, averaging about 9 mm in thickness. The Bilzingsleben forehead region is also more similar to such specimens as *Pithecanthropus* VIII and OH 9 than it is to "younger" archaics like Steinheim and Ehringsdorf.

Abundant fauna and flora recovered from Bilzingsleben include macaques, forest elephant, steppe and forest rhinoceros, bison, deer, large horses, wild oxen, bear, and beaver. Larger carnivores such as lion, wolf, panther, and wild cat are rare. Plant remains are indicative of deciduous mixed forest habitats more similar to those found today in the Mediterranean region than to those currently in northern Europe. These plants, along with the remains of Mediterranean-dwelling mollusks, indicate warmer climates than those existing today in the region and are consistent with an interglacial age for this site.

A large number of stone, bone, and antler tools have also been recovered (Fig. 8.5). Animal bones were fashioned into straight and bowed scrapers, knifelike cutting tools, chisels with splintered ends, shaverlike tools, and needle and awllike tools. Antlers were manufactured into picks and clubs. Most of the smaller stone tools are made from flint and are mainly broken cores and flakes; larger and cruder quartzite tools are also known. The numerous holes and cracks found on many of the long bones have

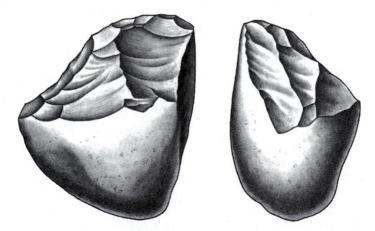

Fig. 8.5.   Quartzite pebble tool from Bilzingsleben (23).

been interpreted to mean that hominids intentionally split them with the aid of small wedges and hammerlike instruments. Burned flint tools and some traces of charcoal suggest the use of fire (23).

Petralona   In 1960 a massive cranium covered in stalagmite was found in a complex cave system near Petralona, Greece (Fig. 8.6). Unfortunately, there have been conflicting views on the dating of the Petralona cranium, ranging from more than 700,000 years ago to less than 100,000 years ago (24,25). ESR age determinations from calcite encrustations and from small bone fragments removed from the cranium yield ages of about 160,000–

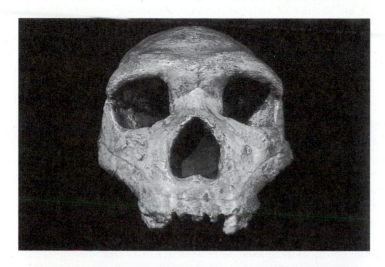

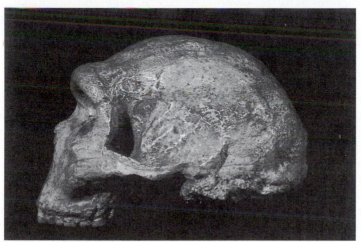

Fig. 8.6.   In 1960 a massive cranium covered in stalagmite was found in a complex cave system near Petralona, Greece.   The Petralona cranium displays a mosaic of *H. erectus* and archaic *H. sapiens* features. (Photos of cast courtesy of E. Delson.)

Fig. 8.7. (a) Lateral view of the Arago 21 (bottom) and Steinheim (top) crania. (b) Frontal view of the same two crania (Arago 21 is on the right). Two of the most informative archaic *H. sapiens* samples are the remains recovered from Arago, France, and Steinheim, Germany. The ruggedly built Arago cranium is characterized by thick supraorbital tori separated from the long, flattish frontal bone by a deep sulcus; low and rectangular orbits; a broad, relatively flat midfacial region; strong alveolar prognathism; and the absence of a canine fossa. Cranial capacity is estimated at 1,100 cc. The Steinheim cranium is distorted but nearly complete, lacking the anterior maxillary region and teeth, and parts of the left side and base. Some of its more archaic features include its overall shape, which is long, narrow, and moderately flattened; low cranial capacity, estimated at 1,100 cc; and pronounced browridges. More modern features include the gracile nature of the cranial vault; the absence of occipital bunning; the well-developed canine fossa; and greatest cranium breadth located high up across the parietals. Because of this mosaic of primitive and advanced features, this cranium, and others like it, are often thought of as transitional forms between *H. erectus* and *H. sapiens*. (Photographs by C. Tarka, courtesy of E. Delson and Institut de Paleontologie Humaine, Paris, and Staatliches Museum für Naturkunde, Stuttgart.)

240,000 years and 127,000 years, respectively. A U-S determination also supports an age of around 160,000–200,000 years for the cranium (26).

As with the other "older" European archaics, the Petralona cranium displays a mosaic of *H. erectus* and archaic *H. sapiens* features. For example, the cranial vault is low with a receding forehead and some of the occipital features and cranial thickness values are more characteristic of *H. erectus*. However, the large cranial capacity of approximately 1,200 cc is in the *H. sapiens* range. In addition, while the supraorbitals are massive they follow the orbital contours as in archaic *H. sapiens* rather than being straight shelf-like structures as in *H. erectus*. The face is large and the maxilla has a "puffed out" appearance, presumably due to an expanded maxillary sinus (reminiscent of the Neandertal condition) (11,20). In fact, several other cranial bones, including the frontal, mastoid, and temporal bones, also show remarkable degrees of pneumatization.

Arago Some of the most informative archaic *H. sapiens* samples are the remains recovered from cave deposits at Arago, France, dated to approximately 400,000 years ago. Cranial and postcranial remains of at least four adults and three children are known from this site. The most important specimens are two mandibles (Arago 2 and 13), a distorted face with associated cranial bones (Arago 21 and 47), and part of a left hip bone (Arago 44) (Fig. 8.7). The mandibles show considerable variability in size and robustness, probably indicative of marked sexual dimorphism in this Middle Pleistocene archaic *H. sapiens* population (see below). They have typical archaic features, such as a receding chin, mandibular bodies that are long and low, and ascending rami that are high and broad (in Arago 2 at least).[4]

[4]The ascending ramus is high and narrow in Arago 13 (E. Trinkaus, pers, comm.).

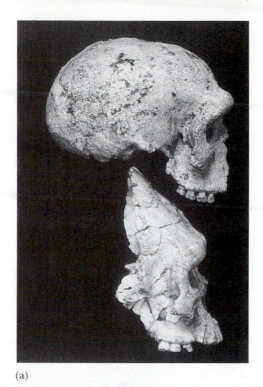

(a)

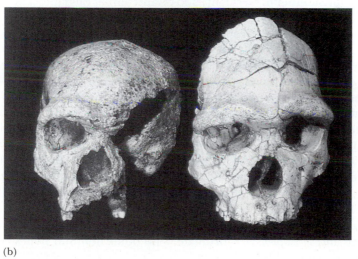

(b)

The ruggedly built cranium is characterized by thick supraorbital tori separated from the long, flattish frontal bone by a deep supratoral sulcus; low and rectangular orbits; a broad, relatively flat midfacial region; strong alveolar prognathism; and the absence of a canine fossa. Cranial capacity is estimated at 1,100 cc (27). Cranial thickness values are similar to Petralona;

however, unlike Petralona, the Arago occipital does have a true angular torus. The hip bone and femoral fragments resemble those of *H. erectus* from Olduvai, Zhoukoudian, and Broken Hill (28).

Some of the similarities between the Petralona and Arago crania, such as the shape of the supraorbital torus and the narrowness of the frontal bone, are probably primitive or plesiomorphic features shared with *H. erectus*. As we will see later, other features, such as the absence of a canine fossa, may be regarded as synapomorphies with Neandertals (29).

Younger Archaic *Homo sapiens* Group

As mentioned above, hominids representing a "younger" archaic group have been recovered from a number of sites in Europe, some of the better known being Steinheim, Swanscombe, Pontnewydd, Ehringsdorf, Biache, La Chaise, Fontéchevade, Montmaurin, and Atapuerca (Sima de los Huesos). Whereas members of the "older" archaic group we have been discussing show many *H. erectus*–like features, this "younger" Middle Pleistocene archaic group seems to be evolving features later seen in more exaggerated form in European Neandertals, hence the designation "anteneandertals" (11,12).

Steinheim   Two of the most famous of these "anteneandertals" are the crania from Steinheim, Germany, and Swanscombe, England. These were, in fact, the first of the European archaic *Homo* crania to be discovered. Dating of both specimens remain problematic, but both clearly seem to be Middle Pleistocene in age. The Steinheim cranium (Fig. 8.7) was found in 1933 by Karl Sigrist in his father's gravel pit. It is distorted but nearly complete, lacking the anterior maxillary region and teeth, and parts of the left side and base (30). Some of its more archaic features include an overall shape that is long, narrow, and moderately flattened; low cranial capacity estimated at 1,100 cc; small mastoid processes; wide nasal aperture; and pronounced supraorbital torus separated from the frontal squama by a broad supraorbital sulcus. More modern features include the gracile nature of the cranial vault; the absence of occipital bunning; the well-developed canine fossa; and greatest cranial breadth located high up across the parietals. Because of this mosaic of primitive and advanced features, this cranium, and others like it, are often thought of as transitional forms between *H. erectus* and *H. sapiens*. Unfortunately, no other hominid bones or tools have been recovered from the site.

Swanscombe   The Swanscombe cranium consists of an occipital, and left and right parietal bones that fit together (Fig. 8.8). Interestingly, the occipital was found in 1935, the left parietal in 1936 and the right parietal in 1955. Since the sutures are clearly open, the cranium probably belongs to a young adult. As in the Steinheim cranium, the occipital is somewhat

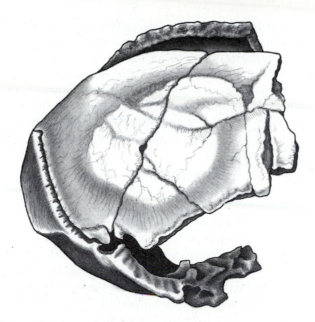

Fig. 8.8. The Swanscombe cranium consists of an occipital, and left and right parietal bones that fit together.   Since the sutures are clearly open, the cranium probably belongs to a young adult. As in the Steinheim cranium, the occipital is somewhat rounded and lacks the marked angulation between occipital and nuchal planes seen in many *H. erectus* crania.

rounded and lacks the marked angulation between occipital and nuchal planes seen in many *H. erectus* crania. However, the parietal bones are quite thick and there is a midline depression on the occipital bone known as a **suprainiac fossa**, a distinctive Neandertallike feature (31) (see next chapter).

Biache   In the 1970s another back half of a cranial vault was found at the site of Biache, France, associated with a maxillary fragment containing the molar teeth and five isolated teeth. The cranium is described as small and gracile (cranial capacity of about 1,200 cc) but rather Neandertallike in overall shape. The occipital bunning, lambdoid flattening, and oval profile (seen in posterior view) with maximum breadth low on the parietals are more reminiscent of features seen in later Neandertals than in the Swanscombe cranium (32) (see next chapter).

Ehringsdorf   Fossils have been known from the quarries at Ehringsdorf, Germany, since 1780. A number of archeological horizons associated with the remains of at least nine hominid individuals are represented in the sample. The geology, fauna, and flora have generally been considered to indicate a last interglacial age but U-S dates give an average age of about 225,000 years (32). Again, these dates are not secure.

Montmaurin   Several specimens are known from two sites and from several levels at Montmaurin, France, including a mandible, several isolated teeth, the mandibular symphysis of a child, an adult maxilla, and a single vertebra. The most important of these, the mandible found in 1949, is similar to other archaic mandibles in that it is robust with a relatively high and broad ascending ramus and is chinless. As with virtually all of the European Middle Pleistocene sites, the age of the Montmaurin hominids is in dispute (33).

Taxonomy and Phylogenetic Relationships among Archaic *Homo sapiens*

There is no shortage of opinions among paleoanthropologists regarding the taxonomy and phylogenetic relationships among these (and other) European Middle Pleistocene hominids. For convenience, these are summarized in Table 8.1 (34). Let us take a closer look at the reasoning behind some of these proposals. In an influential analysis of European Middle Pleistocene hominid crania, Milford Wolpoff of the University of Michigan has suggested that most cranial variation in Middle Pleistocene European

Table 8.1   Four Interpretations of the European Hominid Sequence

Age (ky)	Fossil Hominids	A	B	C	D
30	Early modern	*H. sapiens sapiens*	Modern *H. sapiens*	*H. sapiens*	*H. sapiens*
50	Late Neandertals	*H. sapiens neanderthalensis*			
120	Saccopastore Biache			*H. neanderthalensis*	
220	Ehringsdorf Pontnewydd Reilingen? Swanscombe? Steinheim?	*H. sapiens steinheimensis*	Archaic *H. sapiens*		*H. neanderthalensis*
300	Atapuerca Petralona? Bilzingsleben Vértesszöllös? Arago?	*H. erectus*		*H. heidelbergensis*	
500	Mauer?				

Scheme *A* recognizes two species (*sapiens*, represented by three subspecies, and *erectus*), *B* only one (*sapiens*, in "modern" and "archaic" forms), *C* three (*sapiens*, *neanderthalensis*, and *heidelbergensis*), and *D* two (*sapiens*, *neanderthalensis*).

hominids could be explained by "time, sex and idiosyncrasy" (20). Specifically, he surmised that much of the cranial variation seen in Middle Pleistocene European hominids could be a reflection of marked sexual dimorphism in an evolving lineage rather than indicative of multiple hominid taxa in the sample. He reckoned that where these archaic hominids differed from Neandertals, it was generally in the direction of being more *H. erectus*–like, with the more robust specimens, presumably the males (Petralona, Bilzingsleben, Vértesszöllös), having a greater expression of such features than the smaller, more gracile, and presumably female, specimens (Steinheim, Swanscombe, La Chaise, Biache, Arago 21). Critical to this argument is the contention that these "robust" and "gracile" Middle Pleistocene hominids differ from one another "mainly in metric and morphological features that distinguish males from females in both living populations and in Neandertals." This implies that the group we have referred to as the "older" archaic *H. sapiens* comprises simply the males of this evolving Middle Pleistocene *Homo* lineage, and the "younger" archaic group comprises simply the females.

However, others have argued that the size differences between some of the large specimens (Petralona) and the small specimens (Steinheim) are too great to be males and females of one sexually dimorphic taxon, and therefore require some degree of taxonomic separation (12). In this scenario, as we noted above, the Petralonalike group is regarded as a suitable morphotype for the common ancestor of both Neandertals and modern humans whereas the Steinheimlike group is regarded as "anteneandertals."

What sort of paleontological evidence would help resolve these contradictory viewpoints? Ideally, what is needed to test hypotheses about the degree of sexual dimorphism in Middle Pleistocene hominid populations is a reasonably complete hominid sample from a single site. If such a site could be found, would the hominids from this single population be more, or less, sexually dimorphic than the hominids found between sites like Petralona and Steinheim?

Atapuerca (Sima de los Huesos)   Incredibly, it now appears that just such evidence has finally been uncovered. Over the past few years, the remains of at least twenty-four Middle Pleistocene hominids have been recovered from a cave in Spain (Atapuerca/Ibeas) that represent the most complete Middle Pleistocene hominid sample yet found at a single site anywhere in the world (35,36). This sample, now totalling over thirteen hundred hominid fossils, includes three crania (two of which are more or less complete adult individuals, and one a more fragmentary cranium of an immature individual), nearly seventy isolated teeth, five mandibular fragments, and assorted postcranial remains (Fig. 8.9). Interestingly, the absence of both herbivore bones and stone tools suggests that the site was not a human occupation site or a product of carnivore activity. U-S dating on speleo-

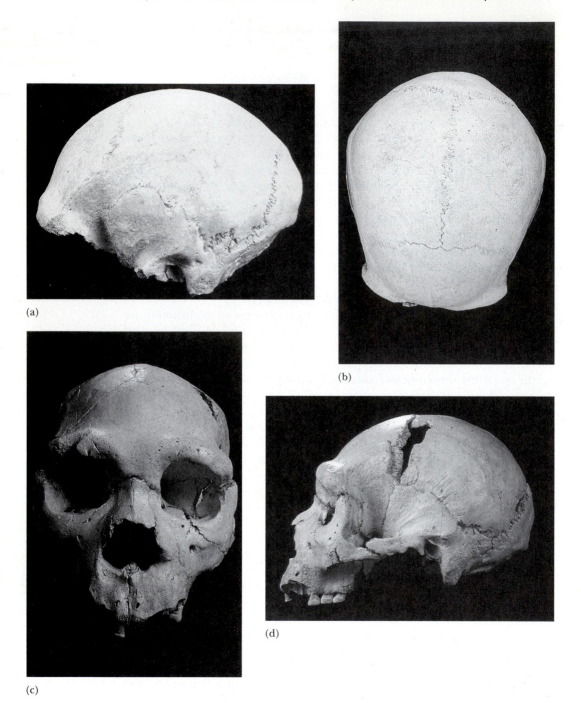

Fig. 8.9. Several views of the "archaic *H. sapiens*" sample from Atapuerca (Sima de los Huesos), Spain.   (a) Lateral and (b) superior views of cranium 4; (c) facial, (d) lateral, and (e) posterior views of cranium 5; (f) lateral view of cranium 6 (36). (Photos courtesy of Madrid Scientific Films.)

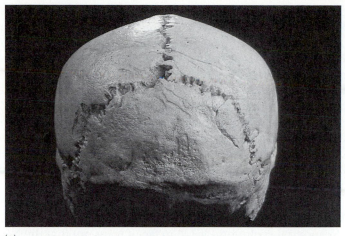

(e)

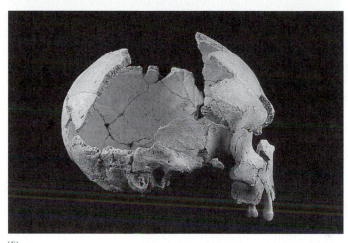

(f)

thems overlying the hominids in the cave have indicated an age of more than 300,000 years.

In answer to the question posed above, it seems that this Atapuerca hominid sample lends more support to the view that extensive variation (presumably due in large part to sexual dimorphism) does indeed characterize Middle Pleistocene hominids. For example, the larger cranium (cranium 4) has a cranial capacity of 1,390 cc whereas the smaller cranium (cranium 5) has a cranial capacity of only 1,125 cc.[5] Thus, in this feature cranium 5 is similar in size to some of the smaller Middle Pleistocene hominids (Steinheim, Ndutu) whereas cranium 4 has one of the largest cranial capacities of any Middle Pleistocene hominid. Somewhat surprisingly, facial

[5]The estimated cranial capacity of the immature individual is 1,100 cc.

architecture in the smaller cranium (Atapuerca 5) shows some resemblances to the Petralona cranium, whereas another facial fragment (AT-404) is more similar to the same region in the Steinheim cranium. Thus, some who once argued that Middle Pleistocene hominid variation reflected taxonomic distinctions now concede that it is indeed possible that two crania as different as Petralona and Steinheim could be encompassed within the variation seen in the Sima de los Huesos sample.

The mosaic nature of the Atapuerca (Sima de los Huesos) sample is remarkable: some features are typical of *H. erectus*, others typical of Neandertals, and still others typical of modern *H. sapiens*. It seems clear from Table 8.2, however, that more features are shared in common with Neandertals than with the other two taxa, and for this reason the Sima de los Huesos sample reinforces the hypothesis expressed earlier that some of these Middle Pleistocene archaic hominids do indeed document an early stage of Neandertal evolution (36). If in fact it turns out that the Neandertal lineage was distinct from our own, then this would also imply an ancient date for the origin of the modern *H. sapiens* clade. Furthermore, if the more fragmentary fossils from Vértesszöllös and Bilzingsleben, which are the most likely candidates for *H. erectus* status in Europe, can be morphologically linked to the Sima de los Huesos sample, then the claims for the presence of *H. erectus* in Europe would likewise be diminished (34).

We should note, however, that these claims do not rule out the possi-

Table 8.2   Some Character Distributions in the Atapuerca Sample (from 34)

	H. erectus	*Neandertal*	H. sapiens
Vault broadest near base	X		
High total prognathism	X		
Laterally thick supraorbital torus	X		
Mandibular morphology	X	X	
Lower limb robusticity	X	X	
Cranial capacity range	X	X	X
Shape of supraorbital torus		X	
Incipient suprainiac fossa		X	
Midfacial projection		X	
Lateral occipital profile		X	X
Tympanic morphology		X	X
High cranial vault		X	X
Shape of temporal squama		X	X
Rear parietal profile	X		X
Adult occipitomastoid morph			X

bility of hominid "grades" in Europe throughout the Middle Pleistocene: the earliest material being *H. erectus*, or *H. erectus*–like, leading to the more transitional, mosaic hominids ("anteneandertals") and resulting in the Classic Neandertals of Europe. Such a view, however, would lead to the exclusion of all early Middle Pleistocene European hominids from the origins of anatomically modern *H. sapiens* if one also believes that the Neandertals were evolutionary dead ends (or that their contribution to the modern human gene pool was minimal). We shall have more to say about Neandertals in Chapter X.

Some Dental Trends in Middle Pleistocene Archaic *Homo sapiens*

Middle Pleistocene archaic hominid populations were characterized by a number of dental trends that are also important to note. For example, there was enlargement of the anterior dentition combined with reduction of the postcanine dentition relative to earlier hominids. Levels of dental sexual dimorphism also exceeded those of modern human populations (20,37). This postcanine size reduction was also associated with a simplification of the molar crowns that involved a reduction and eventual disappearance of the distal major cusps; modification of the so-called Y-5 occlusal pattern of fissures and cusps on the lower molars in which the "arms" of the Y embrace the hypoconid and the "5" refers to the number of well-developed cusps; disappearance of the cingulum; and some reduction of the swelling of the lingual and buccal faces of the crown. In addition to these general dental modifications, archaic hominids from northwest Africa, the Far East, and western Europe all share a number of detailed morphological traits in the permanent postcanine teeth such as a tuberculum molare in P^3, an asymmetric P_3, a strong development of the hypocone in M^1, and enlarged pulp chambers, or taurodontism. However, the Asian and African groups did retain some plesiomorphic dental traits that differentiate them from the European Middle and early Upper Pleistocene hominids, such as the presence of a buccal cingulum; double-rooted lower premolars; strong molarization of the P_4; invariable presence of a hypoconulid in the lower molars; and secondary crenulation or enamel wrinkling that in the Zhoukoudian teeth reaches great complexity (38). These dental similarities between Middle Pleistocene populations of northwest Africa and eastern Asia have been pointed out by a number of authors and have been used to support the notion of two hominid lineages existing in the Middle Pleistocene, one represented by eastern Asian and northwest African populations and the other by western European populations (Table 8.3). Thus, both cranial and dental morphology of the Atapuerca (Sima de los Huesos) material lends support to the notion of regional evolutionary continuity between Middle Pleistocene archaic *H. sapiens* and Upper Pleistocene

Table 8.3   Dental Traits Shared by the Eastern Asian and Northwest African Mid-Pleistocene Hominids[a] (from 38)

(A) Buccal cingulum	Upper and lower canines, premolars and molars
(A) Strong molarization	Lower fourth premolar
(A) Two roots[b]	Lower premolars
(B) Invariable presence of hypoconulid and a Y fissure pattern	Lower molars
(C) Secondary crenulation and fissuration	Upper and lower premolars and molars

[a]These traits are (A) not present in the European Mid-Pleistocene hominids; (B) frequently absent in the European Mid-Pleistocene hominids; (C) sometimes present, but usually less marked, in the European Mid-Pleistocene hominids.
[b]It is possible that this trait has a very low frequency in the European Mid-Pleistocene hominids, since it is present, although rarely, in the European Neandertals.

Neandertals in western Europe (38–40). We will discuss this further in Chapter X.

One other Middle Pleistocene Spanish site near Madrid, Aridos, is worth mentioning because it provides early evidence for organized elephant exploitation by hominids that is somewhat different from the type of marginal scavenging and hunting we noted in early *Homo* in Africa. However, this site does not provide such evidence of elephant hunting as projectile points, spears, or natural traps associated with the elephant remains. The stone tools that are found are of an incipient Levallois technique and some bifaces are of Middle Acheulian type. Evidence of toolknapping and tool resharpening at the site is extensive (41).

ARCHAIC *HOMO SAPIENS* FROM CHINA

Once we move away from specimens that are almost universally regarded as *H. erectus*, we begin to sample Chinese fossils that are sometimes referred to as early *H. sapiens*, or archaic Asians (from Chaoxian, Changyang, Dingcun, Xujiayao, Dali, Jinniu Shan, and Maba) (see Figs. 7.12, 8.10).

Chaoxian, Changyang, Dingcun, Xujiayao, Dali, Jinniu Shan, Maba   The hominid fossils from Chaoxian, consisting of a partial occipital, right maxilla with P³-M¹, and three isolated teeth, were recovered in 1982–83. A U-S date of about 167,000 years ago has been reported from the hominid levels.

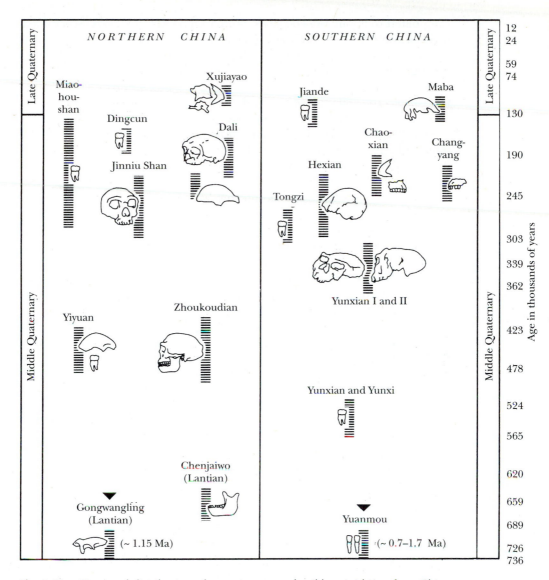

Fig. 8.10.   Temporal distribution of some important fossil hominid sites from China (75).

The relatively thin occipital bone, lack of well-developed ectocranial markings, less pronounced subnasal prognathism, and relatively thin supraorbital tori are all differences from conditions found in *H. erectus*. For this reason the fossils are provisionally regarded as early *H. sapiens*.

In 1956 a partial maxilla and isolated teeth were recovered from Changyang dated to about 195,000 years ago based on U-S methods. Several features of the maxilla suggest affinities to *H. sapiens*, including the anterior position of the incisive foramen, the large maxillary sinus, and the very orthognathic subnasal plane.

Several small isolated teeth from the site of Dingcun provisionally dated to 210,000–160,000 years ago provide some of the earliest evidence of dental reduction in Far Eastern *H. sapiens*.

The largest archaic Far Eastern hominid sample to bridge both the temporal and morphological gaps between *H. erectus* and *H. sapiens* comes from Xujiayao. At least eleven individuals are represented at the site by fragmentary skull bones and isolated teeth. In both size and shape, the cranial bones are described as intermediate between Zhoukoudian and modern humans. As is usual for the Far Eastern sites, dating is problematic, but two U-S dates give ages in excess of 100,000 years and 104,000–125,000 years, respectively. Thousands of stone artifacts have also been recovered, which is sometimes taken as evidence of a kill/butchery or occupation site. The Xujiayao hominids exhibit features similar not only to Chinese *H. erectus*, but also to populations occupying the same region today, and, as we shall see in the next chapter, is one line of fossil evidence used in support of the Mulitregional Continuity Model of modern human origins (42).

One of the better known Chinese specimens, the Dali cranium also shows a number of features transitional between Asian *H. erectus* and living Asians (see Fig. 7.28). The cranium has been insecurely dated by U-S to about 200,000 years ago and correlated to oxygen isotope stages 6–7. Cranial capacity is about 1,120 cc. The face is described as broad and short (possibly due to crushing), with a very broad, bell-shaped nasal aperture and massively developed supraorbital tori. In most midfacial dimensions it resembles such specimens as Steinheim, Arago, and Jebel Irhoud, and has few similarities to Eurasian Neandertals.

Another important early *H. sapiens* specimen from the Far East is the cranium from Jinniu Shan unearthed in 1984. Associated with this cranium were some vertebrae, ribs, pelvis, patella, and limb bones. The cranium may have the largest cranial capacity (about 1,300 cc) associated with the thinnest cranial bones of any archaic *H. sapiens* specimen from the Far East. The hominid cranium is estimated to be about 200,000 years old based on new ESR and U-S dating (43). The significance of this date is that it raises the possibility that *H. sapiens*, as represented by the Jinniu Shan cranium, coexisted in China with *H. erectus*, as represented by Skull V in the upper layer at Zhoukoudian and the Hexian cranium. In addition, Chinese paleoanthropologists believe that some features in the Jinniu Shan cranium, such as the broad nasal bridge, shovel-shaped incisors, and prominent cheekbones, differentiate early Chinese *H. sapiens* from its counterparts in Europe and Africa and therefore best fit the Multiregional Continuity Model of human evolution, which we will discuss more fully in the following chapter (44).

One Chinese specimen that does seem to show some similarities to "classic" Eurasian Neandertals is the Maba cranium dated by U-S to about 169,000–129,000 years ago. Similarities to Neandertals include the shape of the supraorbital tori that are thickest in their medial one-third and the distinctly rounded orbits lacking supraorbital notches.

ARCHAIC *HOMO SAPIENS* FROM AFRICA

About 200,000 years ago, a crucial change took place in the archeological record of Africa that may relate to a major technological breakthrough—the invention of tools with handles by which they could be attached, or hafted, to pieces of wood for use as spears or knives. This is reflected in the disappearance of large bifaces in Acheulian assemblages and their replacement by assemblages of smaller bifaces and Middle Paleolithic flake technology. This foreshadowing of Middle Paleolithic technology in Late Acheulian assemblages indicates that the Middle Stone Age (MSA) of Africa evolved directly out of the terminal Acheulian (called the Fauresmith industry in southern Africa) (2).

Documenting an African transition from archaic to anatomically modern humans depends on the identification of African fossils that are both morphologically and chronologically intermediate between archaic specimens like Broken Hill (Kabwe), Bodo, or Ndutu and modern Africans. Several African fossils often considered for this role include those from Jebel Irhoud (Morocco), Eliye Springs (Kenya), Florisbad (South Africa), Ngaloba (Tanzania), and Omo (Ethiopia) (Fig. 8.1). However, there are a number of formidable problems with this sample (45):

- the sites are few and far between (extending from South to North Africa), and thus preclude any information about regional variation and/or sexual dimorphism in this "transitional" group
- the material is incomplete and fragmentary; for example, the only postcranial specimen for the entire sample is one humerus from Jebel Irhoud (the only mandible, Jebel Irhoud mandible 3, also comes from this site)
- problems of dating exist at four of the five sites

Two of the more complete African Middle Pleistocene archaic crania are those from Kabwe (Broken Hill), Zambia, and Bodo, Ethiopia.

Kabwe (Broken Hill) and Saldanha (Hopefield) Crania   The Kabwe cranium, discovered in 1921 in the Broken Hill mine of what was then northern Rhodesia, became known in anthropological circles as "Rhodesian Man" (Fig. 8.11). The cranium was found with several postcranial bones, including a femur and tibia, and a small number of Sangoan type tools, a terminal Early Stone Age industry (46,47). Opinion has varied over the

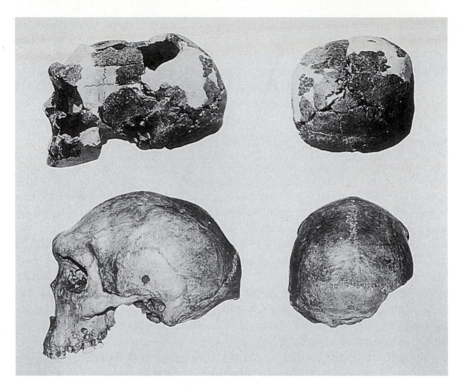

Fig. 8.11. Two archaic *H. sapiens* skulls. (top) The Ndutu cranium, dated to about 400,000–200,000 years ago, was found in association with a number of stone tool-types including spheroids, hammerstones, flakes, cores, and handaxes. It has many of the features found in "typical" Asian *H. erectus*, including the overall form and contour of the occipital with a thickened nuchal torus, the size and shape of the mastoid region, the (inferred) size of the supraorbital torus, and the great thickness of the cranial bones. However, similarities to *H. sapiens* include the presence of pronounced parietal bosses, the more vertical sides of the cranial vault, and the apparent absence of a sagittal keel. Cranial capacity is estimated to be about 1,100 cc. (bottom) The Kabwe cranium, discovered in 1921 in the Broken Hill mine of what was then northern Rhodesia. The cranium is characterized by heavy browridges and a slightly keeled and constricted frontal bone. (Photo courtesy of G. P. Rightmire.)

years about this cranium—some considered it an African Neandertal variant, whereas others, particularly Franz Weidenreich, considered it an enlarged version of "Solo Man" from Java. Indeed, Weidenreich (48) was moved to write: "There is small doubt that the type of Rhodesian man is closer to that of *Homo soloensis* and, consequently, also to his descendants, the Australians, than he is to the European Neanderthal forms and their descendants."

The cranium is characterized by heavy browridges, a slightly keeled and constricted frontal bone, short parietals that show little bossing, acutely flexed occiput with prominent occipital torus, and expansion of mastoid and supramastoid regions, which are more laterally projecting than points higher up on the parietal vault (49). One of the more intriguing features of the cranium is the severe dental decay, which may have been caused by chronic lead poisoning (50).

Dating the cranium has been difficult. Relative chemical dating techniques using fluorine, nitrogen, and uranium initially indicated that it was contemporary with the other human and animal bones at the site, probably of Upper Pleistocene age (51). More recently, however, a combination of archeological and paleontological evidence suggests that both Broken Hill and Saldanha (see below) may date from the later part of the Middle Pleistocene, more than 125,000 years ago (52). The revised older dates for both these specimens have important implications because some anthropologists had previously argued that human evolution was somehow ''retarded'' in sub-Saharan Africa using the ''evidence'' that ''primitive''-looking hominids like Kabwe and Saldhana were only 30,000–40,000 years old (53).

In the 1950s, another important hominid fossil was discovered at Saldanha Bay (near Hopefield), South Africa (49). A diverse fauna and a great number of artifacts have been recovered from the site, initially described as final Acheulian (Fauresmith) and MSA (Stillbay). The Saldanha cranium was originally found in about thirty pieces that, when reconstructed, bore a certain resemblance to the Kabwe cranium in its low, receding forehead separated from large supraorbital tori by a distinct supratoral groove, thickened cranial bones, and prominent occipital crest. A mandible from the same site (but 460 m away) shows a broad ramus much like that seen in the Mauer jaw.

Bodo   Another beautifully preserved Middle Pleistocene hominid is the cranium from Bodo, Ethiopia (54,55) (Fig. 8.12). The cranium was found in 1976 during paleontological, archeological, and geological surveys conducted by the Rift Valley Research Mission in Ethiopia and headed by Jon Kalb. A second hominid's parietal bone was found in 1981 and a distal humerus fragment was recovered in 1990. While the Bodo cranium and isolated parietal bone come from very robust individuals, the humerus is appreciably smaller than many modern human humeri. This suggests that the Bodo hominids may have been quite sexually dimorphic in overall body size (56).

Paleontological and radiometric dating evidence confirms that the Bodo hominids are Middle Pleistocene in age, possibly as much as 600,000 years old. The hominids are associated with a number of Acheulian artifacts, including relatively well-made bifacial handaxes and cleavers. It is interesting to note that a local shift from Oldowan to Acheulian tools occurred within this Middle Awash sequence about this time. While such a shift in tool types occurred elsewhere in Africa by at least 1.5 mya, its occurrence here was much later in time (56–58).

Fig. 8.12.   The Bodo cranium.   One of the most striking features of the face is the great width and overall robustness. A particularly interesting aspect of the Bodo cranium is the identification of cut marks that closely resemble those caused by cutting fresh bone with stone tools. This may by the first documented evidence of intentional postmortem defleshing of bone in the hominid fossil record. (Photos courtesy of T. White.)

The Bodo cranium consists of an almost complete face and partial neurocranium, as well as part of the basicranium anterior to the midline point on the anterior margin of the foramen magnum, known as **basion**. Unfortunately, no tooth crowns are present but the roots and/or alveoli for many of the teeth are preserved. The cranium is large and robust and the cranial vault is exceedingly thick. The nasal root is broad, and the supraorbital ridges are thick, arched, and separated by a prominent glabellar region rather than forming a continuous bony shelf. One of the most striking features of the face is the great depth, width, and robustness of the zygomatic bone, far exceeding that of the Broken Hill or the classic Neandertal of La Chapelle-aux-Saints (see Chapter X). As in the Broken Hill cranium, the zygomatic flares more directly laterally than is characteristic of many classic Neandertal crania. As in most *H. erectus* and archaic *H. sapiens*, a true canine fossa is absent, perhaps due to the extremely large maxillary sinus development. However, unlike most *H. erectus* (including OH 9), the mandibular fossa is not notably deep or narrow, resembling instead that of Broken Hill. Cranial capacity is about 1,300 cc.

In side view the cranium is long and low, with a low, receding forehead. Postorbital constriction is less pronounced than in *H. erectus*. As in most *H. erectus* and archaic *H. sapiens*, there is a slight but distinct keeling of bone along the midsagittal line, especially in the region around bregma.

In overall appearance, the Bodo cranium is most similar to other archaic Middle Pleistocene crania like those from Broken Hill, Petralona, and Arago 21, and is certainly more archaic looking than the undoubted *H. sapiens* crania from the Kibish Formation in Ethiopia (Chapter X). This conclusion is reinforced by the 1981 discovery of a *H. erectus*–like parietal bone from a second individual at Bodo (59).

A particularly interesting aspect of the Bodo cranium is the identification of cut marks that closely resemble those caused by cutting fresh bone with stone tools. This may be the first documented evidence of intentional postmortem defleshing of bone in the hominid fossil record (60,61).

Ndutu Another archaic specimen from East Africa is the cranium found in 1973 at Lake Ndutu, a seasonal soda lake at the western end of Olduvai Gorge, Tanzania (62–65) (Fig. 8.11). The Ndutu cranium, dated to about 400,000–200,000 years ago, was found in association with a number of stone tool types, including spheroids, hammerstones, flakes, cores, and handaxes. Ron Clarke of the University of the Witwatersrand has meticulously reconstructed the cranium and now classifies it as an East African archaic *H. sapiens*, rather than *H. erectus*, mainly because its greatest cranial breadth is high up on the parietal region rather than low down by the mastoids as in "typical" *H. erectus*. Clarke argues that *H. sapiens* evolved in Africa about 1.5 mya from *H. habilis* through an intermediary species he calls *H. leakeyi*. For him, *H. erectus* is strictly an Asian species that arose in, and was confined to, Asia and thus was not ancestral to modern humans.

To be sure, the Ndutu cranium has many of the features found in "typical" Asian *H. erectus*, including the overall form and contour of the occipital with a thickened nuchal torus, the size and shape of the mastoid region, the inferred size of the supraorbital torus, and the great thickness of the cranial bones. It also shows similarity to the Salé cranium from Morocco dated to around 400,000 years ago and possibly to SK 847 from Swartkrans and to KNM-ER 3733. However, the similarities to *H. sapiens* include the presence of pronounced parietal bosses, the more vertical sides of the cranial vault, the presence of an ossified styloid process, the apparent absence of a sagittal keel, the weak development of the supramastoid crest, and the presence of a raised articular tubercle. Cranial capacity is estimated to be about 1,100 cc.

Eyasi   Many years ago, hominid specimens discovered from Lake Eyasi, Tanzania, were initially assigned to *H. erectus* (66,67). These finds were made by the German Ludwig Kohl-Larsen Expedition to East Africa between 1934 and 1940. Lake Eyasi is situated about 50 km south of Olduvai Gorge and the fossils were found in surface or subsurface layers located within 30 to 100 m of the lake shore. The Eyasi hominids consisted of over 250 small pieces, few of which actually fit together. Thus it is not surprising that various attempts to reconstruct the cranium have not met with great success. The fossils were taken to Germany and stored in a farmhouse for protection during World War II. It was thought that they were lost or destroyed during the war but in the late 1960s they were located at Tübingen.

   More recent analysis has concluded that the Eyasi specimens probably belong to an archaic form of *H. sapiens*, not *H. erectus*. In overall morphology the reconstructed Eyasi cranium is more similar to the Saldanha (Hopefield) and Broken Hill crania and is quite dissimilar to *H. erectus* crania like OH 9. For example, it lacks such "typical" *erectus*-like features as a continuous occipital torus, a heavy supraorbital torus, and extensive postorbital constriction. In addition, maximum skull breadth seems high on the parietals, rather than low across the mastoids. The thickness of the cranial bones is within modern limits as is cranial capacity (estimated at 1,220–1,250 cc). One amino-acid racemization study concludes that the specimen may only be about 35,000 years old (68).

Olorgesailie   As mentioned earlier, virtually all Middle Pleistocene *H. erectus* and archaic *H. sapiens* are associated with one form or another of the Developed Oldowan/Acheulian technocomplex. One of the richest examples of this complex is found at the lake margin site of Olorgesailie, Kenya. For well over a million years (about 1.4–0.2 mya), the type of Acheulian technology seen at Olorgesailie was the dominant component of hominid culture throughout much of the Old World. In fact, while an age of 400,000–500,000 years has usually been given for the Acheulian occurrences at Olorgesailie, recent ^{40}Ar-^{39}Ar results indicate that the Olorgesailie Formation may span much of the entire Pleistocene (69).[6] Many of these Acheulian sites have been interpreted as occupation sites, or home bases, of early hominid hunter-gatherer populations; for example, the nu-

---

[6]Dates ranging from 1.0 to 0.5 mya have been attained, and some deposits may be as young as 50,000–220,000 years old.

merous remains of extinct gelada baboons at one Olorgesailie location
(DE/89B) are thought to be the result of systematic hunting and butchery
by early hominids (70). Analyses of the stone flakes associated with elephant butchery sites at Olorgesailie have led to an interesting hypothesis
regarding the "use" of handaxes. It seems that the flakes were derived
from large handaxes, suggesting that one function of handaxes may have
been as "blade tool dispensers" that were carried around by early hominids
but seldom discarded while foraging. On the other hand, the used and
unused flakes made from them were simply left behind at the butchery sites
(69,71).

None of these sub-Saharan Middle Pleistocene "transitional" crania
that we have been discussing resemble European Neandertals in any meaningful way. As we shall see in the next chapter, this observation has most
interesting implications, namely that the emergence of more modern-looking humans in both sub-Saharan Africa and in the Near East over 100,000
years ago took place much earlier than in western Europe, where such
modern-looking populations do not occur until about 40,000 years ago.

CHAPTER IX

Between Apes and Humanity: What the Molecules Say about "Modern" Human Origins

All modern traits . . . need not have had a single geographical origin; different selected traits could arise in different areas and spread by gene flow and selection. Hence, "modern" humans may have no single geographical origin at all.

Alan R. Templeton
" 'Eve': Hypothesis compatibility versus hypothesis testing"
(Am Anthropol 96, 1994)

INTRODUCTION

Our own species name, *sapiens*, which in Latin means "wise," was coined by Swedish naturalist Carolus Linnaeus in the eighteenth century (1) and for many years the taxonomic designation *Homo sapiens* was the first, and only, hominid listed in primate classifications.

Fossils of early modern *H. sapiens* have been recovered from numerous sites in Europe, Africa, and Asia (Fig. 9.1, pp. 377–79), but it is still hotly debated just when and where the first modern representatives of our species evolved, a point we shall consider in more detail later in the chapter.

What kind of mental image is conjured up by the term "modern" *H. sapiens*? More to the point, what do paleoanthropologists mean by the term "anatomically modern human"? This is not as straightforward a question as it sounds because, surprisingly enough, "there appears to be no inclusive definition of our own polytypic species" (2). However, virtually all anthropologists agree that, from the neck up, any anatomical definition of mod-

Table 9.1 Important Cranial Features of Modern *H. sapiens*

Cranial vault enlarged and elevated especially in the frontal and parietal regions; cranial bones reduced in thickness

Biparietal breadth greater than, or equal to, breadth across the ear region, called the biauricular breadth

Occipital region rounded; reduced angulation and reduction of the nuchal, or neck, musculature

Reduction and/or loss of sagittal keeling and parasagittal flattening

Reduction of supraorbital tori into glabellar and supraciliary elements with development of crestlike superior orbital margins

Shortened cranial base with increased flexion of basicranial axis

Reduction of both facial prognathism and height with progressive facial shortening

Reduction of alveolar processes of maxilla and mandible associated with reduction in tooth crown and root size and with development of a canine fossa

Reduction of mandibular robusticity

Development of a bony chin

Brain size averages from 1,300 cc but varies from about 1,000 to 2,000 cc.

Brain and vocal tract fully adapted for speech, including the presence of cerebral asymmetry with language centers predominantly in the left cerebral hemisphere

---

ern humans would include (but not necessarily be limited to) the features listed in Table 9.1 (p. 376).

From the neck down, modern humans are characterized by hip and lower-limb structures fully adapted to a striding bipedal gait and by upper limbs capable of very fine movements of the hand and thumb. The transition from archaic to modern humans saw a pronounced overall reduction in upper-limb muscularity, perhaps correlated with these more precise hand movements. This may account for the increasing numbers of blades relative to flakes and endscrapers relative to sidescrapers that are found in Upper versus Middle Paleolithic assemblages, and for the development of polished bone technology, both of which demonstrate a shift toward elongated tools having greater mechanical advantages (3).

In addition to these anatomical details, we should also note that modern humans have an unusually prolonged life span, a protracted period of childhood dependency, and a pronounced adolescent growth spurt. Perhaps the most distinguishing feature of all, however, is our complete reliance on tools and other forms of material culture for survival.

Now that we know what paleoanthropologists mean by the term ''anatomically modern,'' what do archeologists mean by the term ''behaviorally modern''?

When archeologists talk about the evolution of ''modern'' behavior, they are usually referring to the transition from Middle to Upper Paleolithic

Fig. 9.1. Some of the important sites in (a) Africa and (b) Eurasia where Neandertallike and/or early modern *H. sapiens* have been discovered. (c) Possible classification of some of the fossil hominids of the later Pleistocene (50).

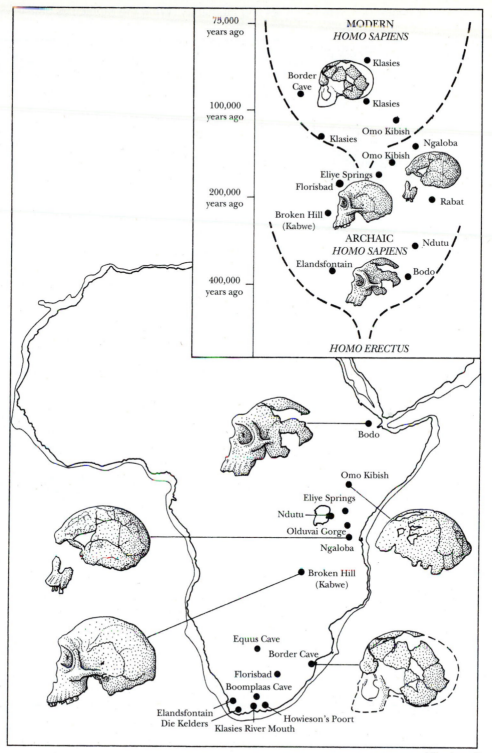

MODERN
HOMO SAPIENS

Klasies

Border
Cave

Klasies

100,000
years ago

Omo Kibish

Klasies

Ngaloba

Omo Kibish

Eliye Springs

Florisbad

Rabat

200,000
years ago

Broken Hill
(Kabwe)

ARCHAIC
HOMO SAPIENS

Ndutu

Elandsfontein

Bodo

400,000
years ago

HOMO ERECTUS

Bodo

Omo Kibish

Eliye Springs

Ndutu

Olduvai Gorge

Ngaloba

Broken Hill
(Kabwe)

Equus Cave

Border Cave

Florisbad

Boomplaas Cave

Elandsfontein
Die Kelders

Howieson's Poort

Klasies River Mouth

(a)

(Continued)

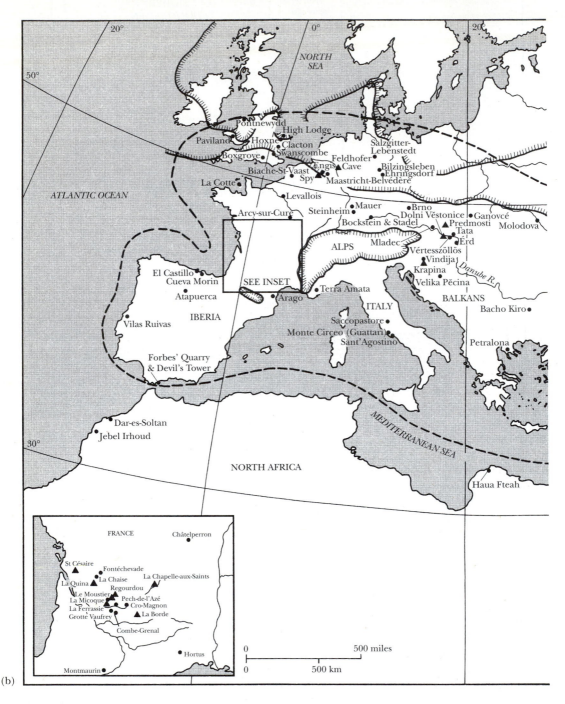

40°
Late Pleistocene
glacial maximum

60°
Middle Pleistocene
glacial maximum

Dnepr R.

Don R.

Dnestr R.

Karatau & Lakhuti
Teshik Tash ▲

Kiik-Koba ▲ • Il'skaya
Staroselye

CASPIAN SEA

• Kudaro

• Dmanisi

BLACK SEA

Shanidar ▲

Tigris R.

Euphrates R.

IRAN

Yabrud
Qafzeh •
▲ Amud & Zuttiyeh
▲ Skhul & Tabun
Kebara

IRAQ

PERSIAN GULF

Nile R.

RED SEA

SAUDI ARABIA

EGYPT

Wadi Halfa •

⬚ ⬚ ⬚	Boundary of the Neandertal world
▲	Supposed Neandertal burials
•	Other hominid sites
⊔⊔⊔⊔⊔	Extent of ice sheets

(Continued)

Years ago	Africa	Eurasia	East Asia/Australasia
30,000	Afalou **Modern Homo sapiens**	Cro-Magnon, Mladeč, Ksar Akil Saint-Césaire, Le Moustier	Zhoukoudian Mungo WLH-50 Niah
50,000	Border Cave	Amud, Kebara La Chapelle, Guattari	
100,000	Klasies, Guomde, Omo Kibish Jebel Irhoud, Ngaloba	Skhūl, Qafzeh, Tabūn **Neandertals** Saccopastore, Krapina, Biache, Ehringsdorf, Swanscombe	Xujiayao, Maba, Dali Ngandong
250,000	Broken Hill **"Archaic" Homo sapiens or Homo heidelbergensis** Elandsfontein, Ndutu Bodo, Salé	Atapuerca, Petralona Bilzingsleben, Arago	Jinniushan, Hexian, Ngawi Yunxian, Zhoukoudian, Sambungmachan
500,000	Baringo Olduvai, Ternifine Olduvai	Mauer Dmanisi	Lantian, Sangiran
1,000,000			**Homo erectus**

(c)

cultures. In western Europe, this cultural transition appears about 45,000–40,000 years ago and is associated with the first appearance of what paleo-anthropologists refer to as anatomically "modern" humans. However, this is *not* the case in other areas of the Old World, such as western Asia or sub-Saharan Africa, where the first appearance of anatomically "modern" humans is associated with Middle Paleolithic or Middle Stone Age assemblages, respectively. In particular, the higher frequencies of blades and bone tools in sub-Saharan MSA (Middle Stone Age) industries give them more of an "Upper Paleolithic" feel than European Middle Paleolithic industries, an observation of particular interest given the early appearance of anatomically "modern" humans in these MSA sites of southern Africa. In western Asia, the cultural transition from Middle to Upper Paleolithic appears slightly earlier than in western Europe and in sub-Saharan Africa the transition appears variably about 40,000–18,000 years ago.[1] However, in both these regions anatomically "modern" humans may first appear approximately 100,000 years ago (Fig. 9.2).

The period of the Middle/Upper Paleolithic transition also witnessed the first human migrations into previously uninhabited areas of the Old World such as Japan and Australia (which imply significant boat-building and navigational skills), and ended with the first human migrations into the New World via Beringia sometime prior to 12,000 years ago (4–6).

[1]In sub-Saharan Africa this transition is from the Middle Stone Age (MSA) to the Late Stone Age (LSA).

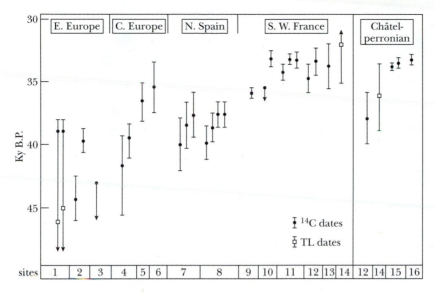

Fig. 9.2. Age determinations for first appearance of Upper Paleolithic industries in Europe (Aurignacian in eastern, central, and western Europe and Châtelperronian in France). Note the general east to west time gradient. Sites: 1, Temnata (Bulgaria); 2, Istallosko (Hungary); 3, Bacho Kiro (Bulgaria); 4, Willendorf (Austria); 5, Geissenklosterle (Germany); 6, Krems (Austria); 7, Castillo (Spain); 8, L'Arbreda (Spain); 9, La Rochette (France); 10, La Ferrassie (France); 11, Abri Pataud (France); 12, Roc de Combe (France); 13, Le Flageolet (France); 14, Saint-Césaire (France); 15, Arcy-sur-Cure (France); 16, Les Cottes (France) (51).

So what kinds of archeological evidence might provide clues to this behavioral revolution from Middle to Late Paleolithic cultures? A partial list would certainly include the following (6,7) (Fig. 9.3):

- Upper Paleolithic assemblages are dominated by blades, particularly ones that are well-designed for hafting, whereas Middle Paleolithic assemblages are dominated by flakes
- Upper Paleolithic tool kits consist mainly of endscrapers, burins (gravers), and points, whereas Middle Paleolithic tool kits consist mainly of sidescrapers and denticulates
- Upper Paleolithic tool types exhibit more regional and temporal distinctiveness compared to the more static tool assemblages of the Middle Paleolithic
- Upper Paleolithic assemblages include more bone, antler, and ivory tools as well as more objects of personal adornment and ''art''
- Upper Paleolithic archeological sites are more complex, i.e., shelters are more elaborate and substantial
- Upper Paleolithic tool kits include more sophisticated weapons, such as the bow and arrow and the spear thrower (earlier than 20,000 years ago)
- the Upper Paleolithic shows more evidence of economic specialization, for example, the hunting of such particular game species as birds, fish, and sea mammals (seals)

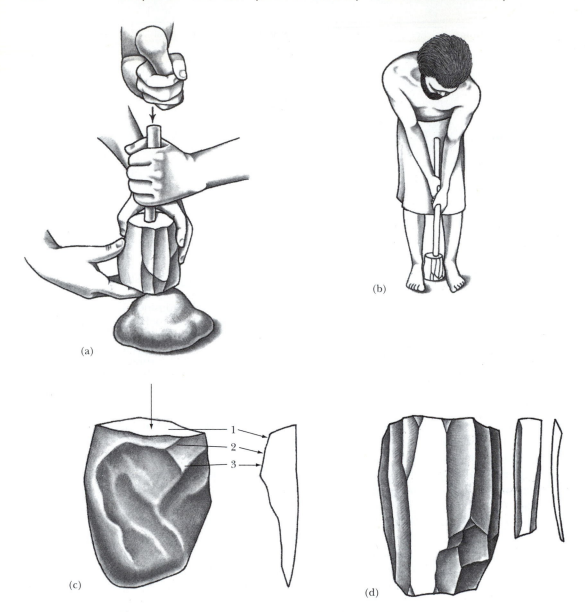

Fig. 9.3. (above) Techniques used by Upper Paleolithic toolmakers. (a) Cores could be placed on a large stone and then a flake detached with a hammer and punch—the indirect percussion or punch technique; (b) blades could be detached by exerting pressure on the core with a pointed tool; (c) characteristic markings of a flake tool; 1, striking platform; 2, percussion cone; 3, small conchoidal bulb of percussion; (d) appearance of prepared core with flake removed. (facing page) Characteristic Upper Paleolithic tools. (a) Aurignacian blade; (b) Gravettian point; (c) Gravettian endscraper; (d) Solutrean point; (e) Magdalenian burin (52).

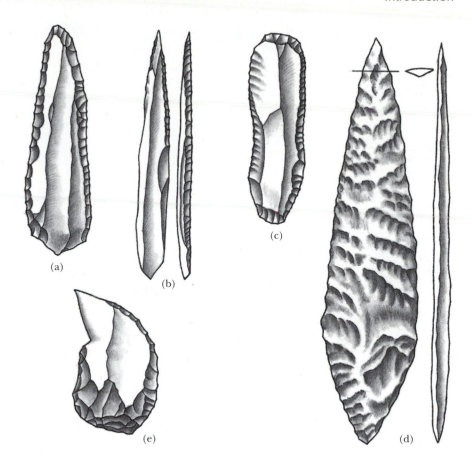

(a) (b) (c) (d) (e)

- Upper Paleolithic populations show more evidence of economic exchange and mobility over large distances, including over water
- Upper Paleolithic graves are more elaborate, suggesting burial rituals or ceremony

The debate over the biological and behavioral origins of "modern" humans remains one of the most contentious, and exciting, issues in contemporary paleoanthropology. Virtually all anthropologists agree that sometime during the Middle/Upper Pleistocene transition, important biological and cultural changes were taking place in human evolution between populations of (what are best called) "late archaic humans" and "early modern humans" (Fig. 9.4). During the Middle/early Upper Pleistocene (approximately 125,000 years ago), only archaic humans are present in the fossil record of the Old World—and these are all associated with what archeologists term Middle Paleolithic assemblages (or Middle Stone Age assemblages in sub-Saharan Africa). However, by about 30,000 years ago, "modern" humans are present throughout much of the Old World and are associated with distinctive Upper Paleolithic assemblages (3,8).

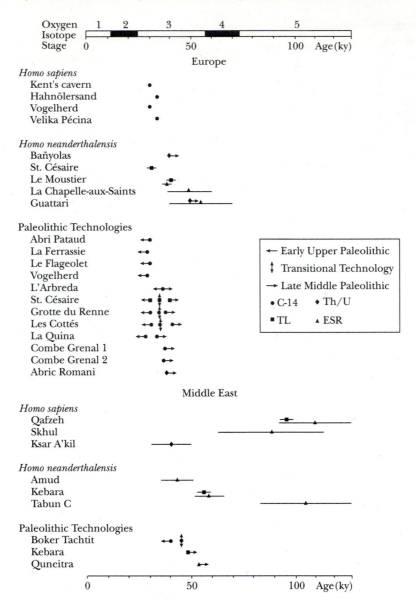

Fig. 9.4. Age estimations for Neandertal and early modern *H. sapiens* and various Paleolithic tool technologies. ky = 1,000 years (53).

Some genetic evidence, provided by mitochondrial DNA studies, also hints that the Middle/Upper Pleistocene transition may be a time of major human population expansion throughout the Old World (9). This is about the extent of the agreement, however. What is not agreed upon is exactly where, when, and how these "modern" humans first arose.

Over the last two decades, there has been a virtual revolution in our thinking about modern human origins. Until then, it had usually been assumed that the emergence of modern humans and Upper Paleolithic assemblages were causally related, virtually synchronous events. Accumulating evidence from a number of Old World sites now undermines this view and suggests that the emergence of early modern humans took place mainly within a Middle, not Upper, Paleolithic cultural context (e.g., Klasies River mouth, Border Cave in South Africa; Dar-es-Soltane in North Africa; Qafzeh and Skhul in the Near East; Krapina A in central Europe) (10,11) (see below). Ironically, only in western Europe do we find a situation in which both archaic and early modern humans are associated with Upper Paleolithic industries, as for example in the Neandertal remains found in an Upper Paleolithic context at Saint-Césaire, France.

We can frame some important questions about the tempo and mode of human evolution around this important transitional period (12). For example, were the dramatic changes in human behavior inferred from the archeological record causally related to changes in morphology, as identified in the human paleontological record? To what extent was the biocultural emergence of modern humans an evolutionary ''revolution,'' or punctuational event, as opposed to a more gradual continuation of previously existing tempos of evolutionary change? Was the biocultural transition from ''late archaic humans'' to ''early modern humans'' restricted in time and space or was it a more universal Old World phenomenon? What were the selective advantages of the biocultural changes in the Upper Paleolithic that allowed early modern humans to become dominant in such a relatively short time span?

There are no easy answers to these questions, but anthropologists have gained valuable insights by amalgamating evidence from a number of separate, but interrelated, fields including paleoanthropology, archeology, geology, and molecular genetics. In fact, one of the most attractive and rewarding aspects of anthropology is its ability to synthesize data from numerous subdisciplines within the biological and behavioral sciences.

CURRENT ISSUES AND DEBATES OVER MODERN HUMAN ORIGINS: OUT OF AFRICA OR MULTIREGIONAL CONTINUITY?

At present, there are two main competing models concerning the evolution of modern *H. sapiens*: the Multiregional Continuity Model and the Out of Africa Model (also sometimes known as the ''Noah's Ark'' or ''Garden of Eden'' Model). In the Multiregional Continuity Model, recent human variation is seen as the product of the Early-to-Middle Pleistocene radiation of *H. erectus* out of Africa and into different regions of the Old World, where these regional populations gradually evolved into the modern populations

Table 9.2 Predictions from Models of *H. sapiens* Evolution (from Stringer and Andrews, 1988)

Aspect	Multiregional Model	Single-Origin Model
Geographic patterning of human evolution	Continuity of pattern from middle Pleistocene to present	Continuity of pattern only from late Pleistocene appearance of *H. sapiens* to present
	Interpopulation differences high; greatest between each peripheral area	Interpopulation differences relatively low; greatest between African and non-African populations
	Intrapopulation variation greatest at center of human range	Intrapopulation variation greatest in African populations
Regional continuity and the establishment of *H. sapiens*	Transitional fossils widespread	Transitional fossils restricted to Africa, population replacement elsewhere
	Modern regional characters of high antiquity at peripheries	Modern regional characters of low antiquity at peripheries (except Africa)
	No consistent temporal pattern of appearance of *H. sapiens* characters between areas	Phased establishment of *H. sapiens* suite of characters: 1) Africa, 2) southwestern Asia, 3) other areas
Selective and behavioral factors involved in the origin of *H. sapiens*	Factors varied and widespread, perhaps related to technology; local behavioral continuity expected	Factors special and localized in Africa; behavioral discontinuities expected outside Africa

found in those same regions today. Obviously, gene flow between these regional populations must have been sufficient to maintain overall "grade" similarities among the various groups (that is, all these regional *H. erectus* populations were evolving into *H. sapiens*) while at the same time allowing regional morphological characteristics to develop and persist (13–15).

The Out of Africa Model is diametrically opposed to the Multiregional Continuity Model. It assumes that there was a relatively recent common ancestral population of *H. sapiens* (most probably in Africa) that had already evolved most of the anatomical features typical of modern humans. This population differentiated regionally in Africa and then expanded beyond that continent to replace all other populations of *H. erectus* and/or other archaic *Homo* species in the Old World over a relatively short period of time. As we shall see, these two models lead to different predictions concerning the evolution of *H. sapiens* that can be tested in the fossil record (Table 9.2).

Actually, many paleoanthropologists working in the later Pleistocene now adhere to an intermediate version (variably present) of the above two models with either: 1) a single origin and major admixture with expansion; or 2) continuity in many but not all geographical regions, with especially the Neandertal regions experiencing replacement through genetic swamping (E. Trinkaus, pers. comm.).

The main characteristic shared by both of these models is that they are both reasonably falsifiable given existing fossil and biochemical evidence. This is the evidence we turn to next.

WHAT DO THE MOLECULES SAY?
ALL ABOUT "EVE"

Based on mitochondrial DNA (mtDNA) studies of modern human populations, some geneticists conclude that the mtDNA of all modern humans
is derived from a single African (woman) ancestor who lived approximately
290,000 to 140,000 years ago (16–18). If this "Mitochondrial Eve" story is
true as stated, the Multiregional Continuity Model is dead and the Out of
Africa Model is alive and well. But is it true?

Mitochondria are organelles in the cell's cytoplasm made up of single,
circular strands of DNA, each having their own genetic coding system. Mitochondrial DNA has several characteristics that make it a potentially powerful tool for human evolutionary studies: 1) unlike nuclear DNA, mtDNA
has a clonal mode of inheritance that is passed down only through the
maternal line, thereby avoiding some of the complexities caused by recombination during sexual reproduction; and 2) mtDNA evolves about five to
ten times faster than nuclear DNA, thus allowing more molecular changes
to accumulate in less time so that more recent evolutionary events can be
studied. The importance of this mode of inheritance to anthropological
studies is that a pair of breeding individuals can only transmit one type of
mtDNA to their offspring, and this is solely through the maternal line (19).

It seems well established that mtDNA variability in modern human populations is relatively low compared to other primates; for instance, variability is less than 10 percent of that found in five orangutans and two crab-
eating macaques, only about 33 percent of that in ten common and two
pygmy chimpanzees, and only about 65 percent of that found in four lowland gorillas sampled from one small area of Africa (16). In addition, it
has been reported that mtDNA haplotypes, or the unique sequence of alleles in the mtDNA, among most (nonaboriginal) human populations are
fairly homogeneous across our species range: about 94 percent of human
mtDNA diversity can be found within any one major geographical population, whereas only about 6 percent distinguishes most human populations
from one another (20). These types of genetic data were immediately seized
upon by Out of Africa enthusiasts to support the claim of a recent common
ancestry of modern *H. sapiens* compared to other primate groups.

As mentioned, it has recently been claimed that all modern human
mtDNA can be traced back to a single common female ancestor (16,21–
23). Why was this proposal so startling? After all, it is hardly surprising that
all mtDNA sequences could be traced back to one woman. As Washington
University population biologist Alan Templeton wrote (24):

All homologous DNA copies in a population must ultimately be traceable to a
common ancestor under the theory of evolution (and) since mtDNA is maternally

inherited in primates, this implies that all copies of human mitochondrial DNA must trace backward to a common female ancestor. The same is true for any species in which mtDNA is maternally inherited, so all such species have a mitochondrial "Eve."

What was startling was the second part of the claim, that molecular biology could pinpoint this mitochondrial "Eve" in time and space. This claim led to a number of secondary hypotheses, dubbed by the press "The African Eve Hypothesis": 1) this common female ancestor lived in Africa around 200,000 years ago (with a range of 290,000–140,000 years ago using mtDNA restriction-site data or a narrower range of 249,000–166,000 years ago using mtDNA sequence data); 2) the mtDNA phylogeny determined by molecular biologists is also a population phylogeny, meaning not only that all mtDNAs in modern humans trace back to this common female ancestor, but also that all modern humans are derived from the same geographical portion of Africa in which this common female ancestor lived; and 3) anatomically modern humans first evolved in Africa and then spread throughout the Old World about 100,000 years ago, driving all other earlier *Homo* populations to extinction without any genetic intermingling.

These hypotheses were originally based on an analysis of mtDNA restriction site maps (representing about 9 percent of the human mtDNA genome) from a sample of 148 humans from five major geographical areas: 20 Africans (18 of whom were African-Americans), 34 Asians, 21 aboriginal Australians, 26 aboriginal New Guineans, and 46 Caucasians (16). From these individuals, 134 distinct mtDNA types were identified. The mtDNA differences within and between each of these five "populations" showed that, in general, variability within a population was greater than variability between populations (suggesting that human races had only recently diverged) and that the particular mtDNA variation *within* the African population (0.47 percent sequence divergence) was greater than that *between* Africans and any other geographical group (Fig. 9.5a). From these data, a genealogical tree of the different mtDNA types was constructed using the

Fig. 9.5.   (a) Intra vs. interpopulational mtDNA divergences in five modern human populations. Values of mean pairwise sequence divergence between individuals within populations are on the diagonal; values below the diagonal are the mean pairwise sequence divergences between individuals belonging to two different populations. For example, mean sequence divergence within African populations is 0.47 percent (on the diagonal); mean sequence divergence between Australian and African individuals is 0.40 (below the diagonal). (b) Genealogy of 134 mtDNA types among 148 people in five different geographic regions. Two (apparent) features of this tree are noteworthy: 1) there are two primary branches, one leading exclusively to African mtDNA types (mtDNA types 1–7) and the other to all other mtDNA types (mtDNA types 8–134); and 2) the data suggest multiple colonization events, since each "population" stems from multiple lineages connected to the tree at widely separated positions (for example, mtDNA type 49 from New Guinea was more closely aligned to mtDNA type 50 from Asia than to the other New Guinea mtDNA types 26–29) (22).

MtDNA Divergence within and between Five Human
Populations

	% Sequence Divergence				
Population	1	2	3	4	5
1. African	0.47				
2. Asian	0.45	0.35			
3. Australian	0.40	0.31	0.25		
4. Caucasian	0.40	0.31	0.27	0.23	
5. New Guinean	0.42	0.34	0.29	0.29	0.25

(a)

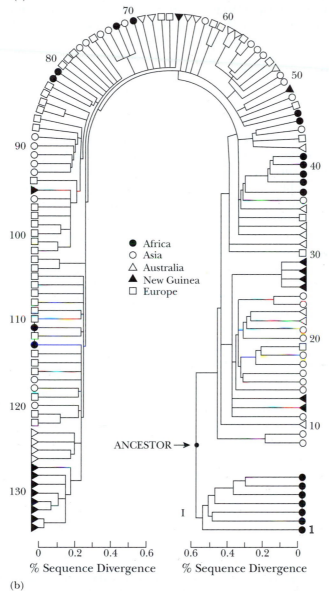

(b)

parsimony analysis computer program PAUP (*Phylogenetic Analysis Using Parsimony*) (25) (Fig. 9.5b). Two (apparent) features of the resulting tree were particularly noteworthy: 1) there were two primary branches, one leading exclusively to African mtDNA types (mtDNA types 1–7) and the other to all other mtDNA types (mtDNA types 8–134); and 2) the data suggested multiple colonization events, since each "population" stemmed from multiple lineages connected to the tree at widely separated positions (for example, mtDNA type 49 from New Guinea was more closely aligned to mtDNA type 50 from Asia than to the other New Guinea mtDNA types 26–29). It was also concluded that Africa was the likely source of the entire modern human mtDNA gene pool because one of the two primary branches led exclusively to African mtDNAs while the other included African mtDNAs as well. Moreover, if the common ancestral mtDNA was considered to be African, then the number of intercontinental migrations needed to account for the geographic distribution of the mtDNA types would be minimized (16,22).

A time scale was affixed to this mtDNA tree by assuming that mtDNA sequence divergences accumulate at a constant rate within lineages and that the main source of mtDNA variation was through neutral mutations (since mtDNA mutations were considered to be largely neutral, their accumulation would be mostly a function of time).[2] If this is the case, then populations having the most divergent mtDNA would, by definition, be the oldest, since more time had elapsed for mutations to accumulate within them. Since the African (African-American) "population" in the original study showed the most mtDNA divergence, they were considered to be the oldest. However, even if this were true, it does not necessarily follow that the various biological and cultural traits by which we define "modern" humans necessarily had an African origin, only that modern mtDNA types had an African origin.

The mtDNA mutation rate was then calculated from what were claimed to be "known" dates of past human migrations into restricted geographical areas: 30,000 years ago for the peopling of New Guinea, 40,000 years ago for Australia, and 12,000 years ago for the New World. By using these dates, the mean rate of mtDNA divergence within humans was determined to be 2–4 percent per million years (see Fig. 3.21b). No reason was given to explain why a narrow 2–4 percent range was used in the original study, given that the true range was reported to be 1.8–9.4 percent (21).

---

[2]This concept is known as "coalescence theory," a theory that holds that all genes (alleles) in any extant population have descended from a single gene, to which they coalesce sometime in the past. In a random mating population at equilibrium, the mean coalesence time is determined by the equation $T = 4N \times [1 - (1/i)]$ where T is the number of generations to coalescence, N is the effective population size, and i is the number of genes under consideration. For example, for any two genes ($i = 2$), the mean coalescence time (T) reduces to $2N$ generations; for a large number of genes, the mean coalescence time (T) reduces to approximately $4N$. Thus, genes in a population with N equal to one million individuals would be expected to coalesce to their one common ancestor four million generations earlier.

Using a figure of 0.57 percent for the average sequence divergence that has accumulated since the common human mtDNA ancestor and a rate of 2–4 percent change per million years, it was determined that the common ancestor of all surviving mtDNA types existed some 290,000–140,000 years ago (these dates were later stretched to 500,000–50,000 years ago) (22). Similarly, it was also calculated that the first migrations out of Africa carrying modern mtDNA types occurred 180,000–90,000 years ago, or even possibly as recently as 105,000–23,000 years ago.

The mitochondrial data also implied that there would have been no interbreeding between African "Eve's" descendants and the indigenous archaic *Homo* populations they encountered throughout the Old World because it was thought that only mtDNA types that can be traced to "Eve" are now found throughout the Old World. If interbreeding had occurred, the mtDNA lineages of the non-African resident populations would have been mixed into the gene pools of the invaders (Fig. 9.6, pp. 391–92). The unavoidable conclusion was that all Old World *H. erectus* and archaic *H. sapiens* populations not ancestral to this African "Eve" were wiped out without interbreeding.

Several other studies based on analyses of nuclear DNA polymorphisms, for example DNA sequence variation at the β-globin locus, purport to show that sequence diversity is greatest in African populations and thereby conclude that European and Asian populations (including aboriginal Americans and Australians) are more closely related to each other than any are

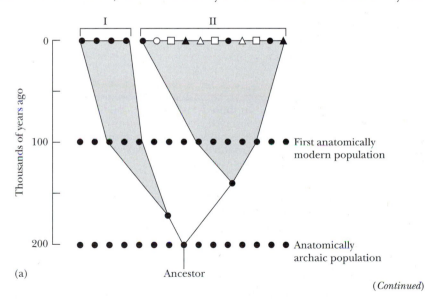

(a)

(Continued)

Fig. 9.6. (a) Scenario relating mtDNA results to an African origin for modern humans. Solid circles represent African mtDNA, and other symbols represent non-African DNA, as in Figure 9.5. The shaded branches I and II represent the two branches seen in Figure 9.5b and encompass the descendants of the common mtDNA ancestor.

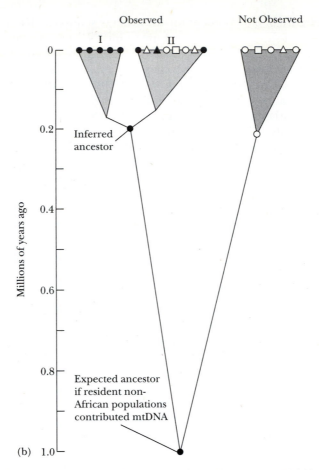

Fig. 9.6. (b) Expected genealogical relationship of human mtDNA if resident populations in Asia and Europe contributed mtDNA to modern populations. The shaded group to the right (''not observed'') shows that if the resident non-African population did contribute mtDNA to modern human populations, then we would expect to observe a third group of non-African mtDNA types approximately five times more divergent than any types observed (22).

to sub-Saharan African populations (26–30). However, a more recent study simultaneously scored nuclear DNA polymorphisms and mtDNA polymorphisms in exactly the same individuals, thereby allowing the *first direct test* of concordance of the mtDNA with the nuclear DNA, which is expected under the Out-of-Africa replacement hypothesis but not under a model with some gene flow. The results of this first, and thus far only, direct test of concordance were quite clear: the two data sets are discordant at the population level (31).

But has molecular biology really solved the question of modern human origins? How ''solid'' are these conclusions drawn from the molecular data? Not very, as it turns out.

Criticisms of the Mitochondrial Eve Hypothesis

Two of the most outspoken critics of the Mitochondrial Eve (or Out of Africa) Model have been University of Michigan anthropologist Milford Wolpoff and Australian anthropologist Alan Thorne (14,32). How do they, and others, parry what seems to be the open and shut case presented by the molecular biologists?

First, they argue that the dates of the first human migrations into New Guinea, Australia, and the New World used by molecular biologist to "calibrate" the molecular mtDNA clock may seriously underestimate the appearance of modern humans in these regions. Moreover, other mtDNA studies suggest that mtDNA mutation rates may not be as constant as presented by proponents of the Mitochondrial Eve Model (33–34). If modern humans arrived in New Guinea, Australia, and the New World much earlier than the assumed 40,000–12,000 years ago, and/or mtDNA mutation rates are proven to be more variable than proponents of the Mitochondrial Eve Model suppose, then this could seriously affect the calculation of mean mtDNA mutation rates for assessing times of divergence. Thus, a more accurate estimate of mean rate of mtDNA divergence within humans may be very different from the 2–4 percent per million years used by proponents of the Mitochondrial Eve Model.

Ultimately, however, their arguments have to explain why there is apparently so little mtDNA divergence in non-African populations if these populations had been evolving in situ for nearly 1 million years. Several possibilities can be entertained:
- such diversity may actually exist but has not yet been discovered
- it is possible that indigenous non-Africans did contribute mtDNA types to the dispersing African populations but they were subsequently lost by either selective or random mechanisms; for example, mtDNA types can be lost through drift (differential mtDNA lineage survival), in which one type slowly replaces all others or through population bottlenecks that reduce the population down to small size and limited genetic diversity (27)
- extremely divergent non-African mtDNA types are not found in modern human populations because they were never contributed by the resident population, leading inevitably to the rather staggering conclusion that the dispersing African population replaced the non-African resident population without any interbreeding—in other words, a complete genetic holocaust!

Wolpoff (14) argues that genealogical "trees" such as those produced by the mtDNA analyses do not necessarily reflect relationships among human populations or their history. This is because tree diagrams assume that population differences arose through population splitting and subsequent isolation. Interpretations of such "trees" assume that the observed differences are the consequence of constantly accumulating random mutations and drift, and that gene flow did not occur. He argues, however, that even minimal gene flow between two populations will greatly reduce the observed magnitude of population differences, thus potentially underestimating the time since population splitting. Because everything we know about recent human migrations and invasions indicates significant amounts of gene flow during and after these events, all populations may appear genetically and morphologically more closely related than they really are.

Another point that casts some doubts on the accuracy of mtDNA data for interpreting splitting events are the apparent contradictions among geneticists in dating the human-chimpanzee split. If one assumes a constant rate of divergence of mtDNA at 2–4 percent (an assumption of dubious validity, as we have seen), one would conclude that humans and chimpanzees diverged about 2 mya, a figure that is clearly at odds with the hominid fossil record. However, by using a rate of 0.71 percent (35), the human-chimpanzee split is calibrated at about 6.6 mya, which is more in line with present paleontological evidence. This same rate gives a divergence time for modern human populations of about 850,000 years, a time period that is not incompatible with the human fossil record, for by that time *H. erectus* populations had emigrated from Africa to Eurasia. Thus, changing the "constant" mtDNA divergence rates by a small amount makes the mtDNA data more compatible with the Multiregional Continuity Model!

More recently, doubts about the Mitochondrial Eve Model have begun to surface even among molecular biologists and systematists as well. As mentioned previously, the original Mitochondrial Eve Model was based on a PAUP analysis, a computer algorithm designed to find minimum length "trees" that can account for the observed differences in the mtDNA sequences. One problem, however, is that for large human mtDNA data sets the computer programs cannot possibly find all the possible trees because there are simply too many.[3] (see Box 9.1). Thus, there is no guarantee that the parsimony analysis would, or even could, find the "best" tree. For this reason, it did not take long before others started coming up with even shorter "best fit" trees using the *same* mtDNA data set—in fact one such study found ten thousand shorter trees, most of which did not even require an African origin (36)! This one study alone demonstrated that the Mitochondrial Eve Model as originally presented was invalid (this, in and of itself, doesn't necessarily disprove an African origin, only that the parsimony test does not resolve the issue). In fact, this study pointed out that an ancient migration into Africa would be just as parsimonious an explanation of the mtDNA data as a migration out of Africa would be.

Because of these types of criticisms, further mtDNA studies were undertaken, but this time the mtDNA genealogical tree was rooted by using mtDNA data from a chimpanzee as an outgroup comparison. The molecular biologists once again concluded that the most parsimonious "tree"

---

[3] For example, the number of unrooted, binary, terminally labelled trees that can be generated for 5 taxa is 15, for 10 taxa is 2×10^6, and for 20 taxa is 2×10^{20} (25)!

Box 9.1. Selecting "Parsimonious" Trees

A central problem in the "mitochondrial Eve" debate is how to interpret nucleotide sequences in human mtDNA so as to construct a tree that reveals human origins. In parsimony analysis the DNA sequences are sequentially arranged to build the most "parsimonious" tree, i.e., the one that considers all the observed sequences and then determines which requires the fewest mutations over the course of evolution. In this example, five DNA sequences, each five nucleotides long, are shown. In the third position, two people have an A nucleotide and three have a G. If comparison to an ancient sequence such as that of a chimpanzee suggests G was originally at that position, then it follows that a mutation must have given rise to the A. Of the two trees shown, the upper tree arranges the sequences in a way that requires only one mutation—therefore, it would be considered a more parsimonious tree than the lower one, which requires two mutations.

The situation can become much more complex. For example, when we consider the fifth position it suggests that individuals I and II are more closely related than I and III (which was the conclusion when we looked only at the third position). With this new information a computer running the PAUP (Phylogentic Analysis Using Parsimony) program could create a different tree that is just as parsimonious as the upper tree. Conflicts like these cause the number of equally parsimonious trees to grow exponentially. With large sample sizes the number of equally parsimonious trees may be in the millions. PAUP goes about the process of finding the best solution by adding sequences to the tree one at a time and then swapping branches around to find better trees. The trees it finds on any one run are necessarily related to the starting tree and the shape of that tree is influenced by the order in which the samples were added. To get the best range of possible trees, one needs to sample trees from many runs with samples added in a different random order.

indicated a relatively recent African origin for modern humans (17,18). This time, the molecular biologists thought they had finally quieted all their critics.

Once again, however, other researchers showed that these studies were still seriously flawed, or at the very least, too simplistic (24,37–40). For example:

- more parsimonious trees could still be generated from the human mtDNA data and furthermore, some of these "more parsimonious" trees still had non-African roots
- the divergence between chimpanzee and human mtDNA was so much greater than that within humans that using the chimpanzee sequence to root the tree may be no more reliable than using a random mtDNA sequence
- to a significant degree, the genealogical tree determined from the mtDNA data was an artifact of the order in which the data had been entered into the PAUP program

Where does all this leave the Mitochondrial Eve Model? A recent thorough critique of the mtDNA data has led one population geneticist, Alan Templeton (24,41), to conclude that:

- the mtDNA data do not resolve the geographical origin of the human mitochondrial common ancestor
- the possible time range within which this common ancestor existed is considerably wider than the 290,000–140,000 years ago commonly cited by the Mitochondrial Eve supporters. For example, using the full 1.8–9.4 percent mtDNA divergence rates, and even assuming a perfect molecular clock, the lower bounds of the 95 percent confidence intervals of the mtDNA ancestor would be as low as 32,000 years ago (using the 9.4 percent rate) and as high as 524,000 years ago (using the 1.8 percent rate). In fact, the most recent analysis of all the mtDNA data concludes that there is a 95 percent probability that the mitochondrial Eve lived between 481,000 and 336,000 years ago assuming a chimpanzee-human split of 4 mya or between 889,000 and 622,000 years ago assuming a human-chimpanzee split of 7.4 mya (42).
- the mtDNA haplotype tree provides evidence only for very recent and geographically limited expansions of human populations, and other than that, the mtDNA haplotype tree reflects restricted gene flow through isolation by distance throughout the entire time period tracking back to the common mitochondrial ancestor
- the mtDNA and nuclear DNA are not inconsistent with a Multiregional Continuity Model
- the claim that Africans have higher levels of mtDNA diversity has never been statistically tested against the null hypothesis of equal mtDNA diversity levels, and until this null hypothesis is rejected there is no basis for the claim of greater diversity in Africans
- there are good reasons for doubting whether or not mtDNA divergence measures are even relevant to the question of population ages

This last point is explained by Templeton (41) in the following way:

> . . . because there is no recombination for mtDNA, even a single selected muta-
> tion arising in a human population can have a major impact on overall diver-
> sity. . . . Diversity measures in DNA regions with little or no recombination often
> display unusual patterns of diversity relative to the remainder of the genome and/
> or to interspecific divergence patterns, and these inconsistencies are explained
> simply by these selective hitchhiking effects. . . . Hence, diversity levels in DNA
> regions with little to no recombination are unreliable indicators of age. Second,
> the diversity level in a geographic area can be greatly influenced by current and
> past gene flow. These human populations are not isolated . . .; hence, diversity is
> not a reliable indicator of age. . . . Thus, relative to testing the hypothesis of an
> African versus non-African origin, diversity measures are irrelevant.

A partial explanation for the conflicting results of various mtDNA studies is that, until recently, the limitations of this molecule for evolutionary
studies have not been clearly presented. First, the mitochondrial genome
is a small fraction of the total genetic makeup of an organism, and thus
may present a deceptively simple picture of overall genetic similarities or
differences within and among populations depending on their social structure. For example, in cases where virtually all males leave the social group
into which they are born and all females remain throughout their lives,
one would expect nuclear genomic variation (which is transmitted by both
sexes and recombined in each succeeding generation) to be spread fairly
homogeneously by male migration. Conversely, in such groups mitochondrial genomic diversity, which is transmitted exclusively by the female parent to the offspring, would be expected to be geographically restricted and
to exhibit large differences between localities. Both of these expectations
are borne out in mtDNA analyses of rhesus macaques (Fig. 9.7) (20).

Second, when considerable intraspecific mtDNA variation exists, failure
to consider this variation may lead to inaccurate estimates of differences
among taxa. It must be remembered that a phylogenetic tree generated
from mtDNA data is first and foremost a "gene tree"—and there is no a
priori reason why it must reflect the underlying "species tree" given that
genes will sort randomly during speciation events (Fig. 9.8) (43).

Third, the notion of a mtDNA "molecular clock" rests on two assumptions, neither of which may be valid: 1) that genetic variation within a taxon
is negligible as compared to the differences among taxa and that therefore
there are virtually no molecular differences between "parent" and "daughter" species at the time of reproductive isolation; and 2) that the rate of
nucleotide substitutions must be calibrated by independent estimates of
divergence and must be approximately the same in all populations or species (so-called rate constancy). The first assumption is belied by the known
fact that intraspecific mtDNA variability is significant in a number of primates (as high as 8.4 percent in populations of the pigtailed macaque,
Macaca nemistrina) (20,44). Therefore, at the time of separation, two incipient species may already have a considerable level of mtDNA divergence,

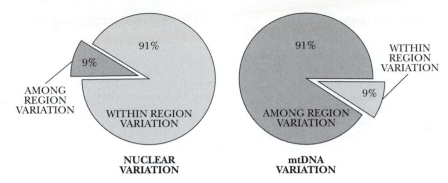

Fig. 9.7. A partial explanation for the conflicting results of various mtDNA studies. The mitochondrial genome is a small fraction of the total genetic makeup of an organism, and thus may present a deceptively simple picture of overall genetic similarities or differences within and among populations, depending on their social structure. For example, in social groups in which virtually all males leave the social group into which they are born and all females remain in their natal groups throughout their lives, one would expect nuclear genomic variation (which is transmitted by both sexes and recombined in each succeeding generation) to be spread fairly homogeneously by such extensive male migration. Conversely, in such groups mitochondrial genomic diversity, which is transmitted exclusively by the female parent to the offspring, would be expected to be geographically restricted and to exhibit large differences between localities. In this figure the portion of total rhesus monkey species diversity in the nuclear and mitochondrial genomes that can be attributed to variation within a geographic region (shaded) and to differences among regions (black) is shown. Note that the distributions are mirror images of one another, in large measure due to the male biased dispersal pattern of this species (20).

the result being that some clock estimates will include significant errors if they assume intraspecific homogeneity at the time of divergence. The second assumption is belied by the fact that several studies have documented differential rates of amino acid and nucleotide sequence evolution in nuclear genes and recent research also casts doubt on the assumption of rate constancy in mtDNA sequences as well. For example, mtDNA genomes of macaque populations from the Malaysian Peninsula and Sumatra are about thirty times more different than would be expected on the basis of the standard molecular clock (20,44). Thus, "[t]he use of mtDNA to date past evolutionary events should be regarded as an extremely crude method—a sundial rather than a chronometer" (20).

While the mtDNA story tells us something about our maternal genealogy, are there any genetic data that can tell us something about our paternal roots? Ideally, for this we need some information from the nonrecombining part of the Y chromosome, whose DNA is inherited paternally. Some clues have recently emerged. For example, a 729-base pair **intron** (a part of a gene that is not translated into a protein) at the ZFY locus on the

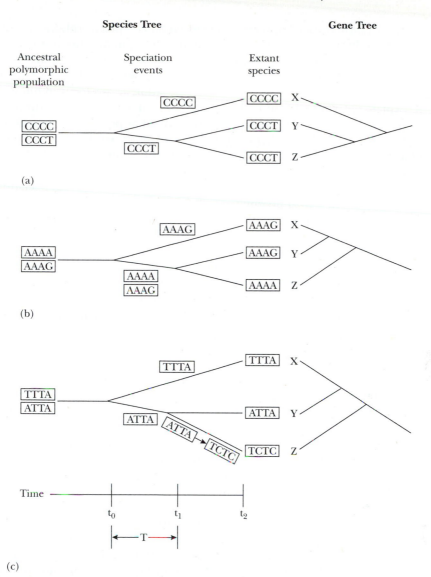

Fig. 9.8. Means by which a species tree may differ from a gene tree. The figure illustrates how alleles may randomly assort during two speciation events (t_0, t_1) involving three lineages from a common ancestral population. In (a) the gene tree reflects the true species relationships. This is because the ancestral alleles, represented by a four-base pair site, segregated into two subpopulations, one of which became fixed along the descent of the species that are most closely related (in this case Y and Z). However, (b) and (c) illustrate two situations in which the gene tree could differ from the species tree depending on how the alleles sort at various speciation events (43). T indicates time between two speciation events measured in generations.

human Y chromosome has recently been sequenced in a worldwide sample of thirty-eight human males (45). Unlike the situation in other nonhuman primates in which phylogenetically informative sequence variability is found in this intron, no sequence variation at all was found in the human sample. How can this lack of intraspecific variation at this locus in humans be explained? There are several considerations. First, nucleotide diversity in species is directly proportional to a quantity that population geneticists refer to as effective population size (N_e). In other words, all else being equal a smaller population will contain less nucleotide diversity than a larger population. There are several ways in which effective population size can be reduced, for example during population bottlenecks and speciation events. A second way to potentially reduce intraspecific variation at a specific genetic locus is if one genetic variant at the locus becomes favored by selection, thereby causing it to sweep through the population carrying along with it all linked nucleotide sequences on the same chromosome (46).

It should be noted that much of the Y chromosome does not recombine, making it particularly vulnerable to such selective sweeps. Hence, inferences based on diversity levels for Y chromosomes and mtDNA may be unreliable, as has been well documented for *Drosophila* in contrasts between regions with and without recombination (A. Templeton, pers. comm.).

According to calculations based on the absence of genetic variability at the ZFY locus in the small human sample, as compared to the amount of variability in nonhuman primates, coalesence of this gene in the ancestral human male lineage occurred 270,000 years ago, but the 95 percent confidence limits of the calculations fall between 0 to 800,000 years (47).[4] Thus, these genetic data may be considered to weakly reinforce the side of the argument that opts for a single, as opposed to a multiregional, recent origin of modern human origins, although the geographical location of this ancestral Y lineage cannot be determined as yet from these data.

More recent data on nuclear DNA may further bolster the Out-of-Africa hypothesis (48). The DNA in question is a piece of chromosome 12, which has a variety of haplotypes in sub-Saharan African populations, loses many of these patterns in Northeast African populations, and is dominated by a single pattern in the rest of the world. One interpretation of these data is that they track a series of small populations moving through population "bottlenecks" as they travel from sub-Saharan Africa through Northeast Africa and ultimately to Eurasia, losing DNA variability along the way. Assuming constant rates of nuclear DNA mutation, this study suggests that this migration out of Africa occurred within the last 100,000 years or so. However, other interpretations are possible. For example, genetic diversity in a population is not necessarily a reflection of when it originated. As

---

[4] In other words, these researchers are telling us that it could take anywhere from 0 to 800,000 years for *no genetic variability to occur*, a rather odd way of looking at things!

supporters of the Multiregional Hypothesis have noted, a small, ancient population existing outside of Africa could create a similar genetic picture since small populations also tend to lose genetic diversity.

CONCLUSIONS

Even though molecular evidence indicates that mtDNA sequences in modern humans coalesce to one ancestral sequence (probably from Africa), it would be incorrect to conclude that this so-called "mitochondrial Eve" was the one mother from whom all humans descended. Instead, "mitochondrial Eve" should be regarded as a mtDNA molecule (or the woman who carried that molecule) from which all modern mtDNA molecules descended. This is a big difference. As University of California biologist Francisco Ayala points out, the notion, popularized in the press, that all humans descend from only one African woman who lived 200,000 years ago is based on a confusion between gene genealogies and individual genealogies (49). Whereas gene genealogies do coalesce toward single ancestral DNA lineages, individual genealogies do not, increasing by a factor of 2 each generation; i.e., each of us has two parents, four grandparents, eight great-grandparents, etc. Therefore, the fact that any one gene coalesces back in time to an ancestral DNA lineage does not preclude many other ancestors existing at the same time from whom other genes were inherited. As Ayala notes: ". . . a person inherits the mtDNA from the great-grandmother in the maternal line, but also inherits other genes from the three other great-grandmothers and the four great-grandfathers (about one-eighth of the total DNA from each great-grandparent). The mtDNA that we have inherited from the mitochondrial Eve represents a four-hundred-thousandth part of the DNA present in any modern human. The rest of the DNA, 400,000 times the amount of mtDNA, was inherited from other contemporaries of the mitochondrial Eve."

The same conclusion holds for the ZFY gene inherited along paternal lines. While this "ZFY Adam" is the individual from whom all humans have inherited this particular gene, he is not our only ancestor in his generation. We have inherited thousands of other genes from many of this "Adam's" contemporaries.

Having reviewed some of the arguments for and against the Out of Africa Model put forward by molecular biologists, we turn in the final chapter to what the fossil evidence has to say on the subject. We begin with the fossil evidence from Africa and then conclude with the evidence from Eurasia.

CHAPTER X

Between Apes and Humanity: What the Fossils Say about "Modern" Human Origins

It is interesting how rapidly and confidently the mitochondrial DNA data have been accepted as the final proof for eliminating the Neanderthals from any contribution to subsequent European populations. At the same time, it is puzzling how a collection of scattered, fragmentary and poorly dated African fossils have been substituted as the ancestors of us all. In many ways, this reflects the tendency in paleoanthropology to prefer sensational catastrophism over mundane gradualism and the willingness of some to accept without criticism (or even suspicion) the results of molecular biology. Thus, if the results of the mitochondrial DNA analysis are correct, the replacement of Neanderthals in Europe was only a minor incident compared to the Old World–wide event in which all archaic human populations were totally replaced by African migrants.

David W. Frayer
"The persistence of Neanderthal features in
post-Neanderthal Europeans" (In *Continuity or Replacement*, 1992)

INTRODUCTION

How do the molecular data discussed in the last chapter fit the fossil data for "modern" *H. sapiens* populations? As we have seen, mtDNA comparisons have been used to support the Out of Africa Model, namely, that *H. sapiens* emerged in Africa about 140,000–100,000 years ago and that all present-day humans are descendants of that African population. Proponents of this model argue that the alternative Multiregional Continuity Model, which posits that *Homo* has been present in Eurasia for nearly 1 million years and that the transition from archaic to modern humans took place in parallel in different parts of the world, is refuted by the mtDNA data. If the Multiregional Continuity Model is correct, they argue, one would expect to see a great deal of mtDNA variation in modern Eurasian populations, which, as we have seen, is apparently not the case. The ap-

Table 10.1 Inferences about Hominid Behavior and Ecology (from R. Potts, 1992)

Hominids and Time Periods (Years Ago)	Inference	Nature of the Evidence
Early Pleistocene hominids (1.5–0.1 million)	Occupation of new habitats and geographic zones	Sites in previously unoccupied areas of eastern Africa; first appearance of hominids outside Africa
	Definite preconception of tool form	Biface handaxes of consistent shape made from rocks of varying original shape
	Manipulation of fire	Indications of fire differentially associated with archeological sites
	Increased levels of activity and stress on skeletons	Massive development of postcranial and cranial bones
Late Pleistocene hominids (100,000–35,000)[a]	Increased sophistication of toolkit and technology; still slow rate of change to tool assemblage	Larger number of stone-tool types than before; complex preparation of cores
	Intentional burial of dead and suggestions of ritual	Preservation of skeletons, some with objects
	Maintenance of high activity levels (locomotor endurance; powerful arms) and high levels of skeletal stress (e.g., teeth used as tools)	Robust skeletons, especially thick leg bones and large areas for muscle attachment on arm bones; prominent wear patterns on incisor teeth
(35,000–10,000)[b]	Decreased levels of activity and stress on skeleton	Decrease in skeletal robusticity (also seen in early modern humans before 35,000 years ago)
	Enhanced technological efficiency	Innovations in stone- and bone-tool production (e.g., blades and bone points)
	Innovations in hunting and other foraging activities, including systematic exploitation of particular animal species	Evidence of spearthrower and harpoon, and trapping netting of animals; animal remains in archaeological middens
	Colonization of previously unihabited zones	For example, sites in tundra in Europe and Asia; colonization of the Americas (Australasia was probably first inhabited around 50,000 years ago)
	Elaboration of artistic symbolic expression and notation	Engraving, sculpting, and painting of walls and figure repetitive marks on bones; jewelery
	Surge of technological and cultural differentiation and change	Variation in toolkits over space and time
	Harvesting and first cultivation of grains; first domestication of animals	Evidence of seeds and fauna from sites dating to the end of the Pleistocene

[a]Neandertals.
[b]Fully modern *H. sapiens*.

parent conclusion, then, is that early Eurasian populations of *H. erectus* and/or archaic *H. sapiens* contributed no surviving mtDNA lineages to the gene pool of modern humans. We wrap up our story of human evolution by examining what the fossil evidence for "modern" human origins has to say on this subject. Table 10.1 provides a summary of the behavioral and ecological inferences that can be drawn from the fossil and archeological record of this latest phase of human evolution.

FOSSIL EVIDENCE FROM AFRICA

South Africa

Some of the most important fossil and archeological sites relevant to the question of modern human origins are in southern Africa (Die Kelders Cave, Equus Cave, Border Cave, Klasies River mouth, and possibly Florisbad) (Fig. 10.1). Of these, the only one to yield a clearly archaic-looking

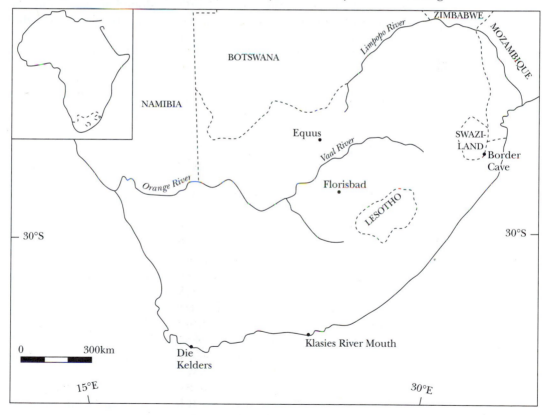

Fig. 10.1. Several of the more important fossil and archeological sites relevant to the question of modern human origins in South Africa (Die Kelders Cave, Equus Cave, Border Cave, Klasies River mouth, and Florisbad) (1).

Homo fossil is the late Middle Pleistocene site at Florisbad, where a hyena-gnawed partial cranium, morphologically similar to such East African specimens as Ngaloba and Omo II dated to about 130,000–120,000 years ago (see below), was recovered. The other South African sites mentioned above contain more modern-looking hominids and date to the earlier part of the Late Pleistocene, some 130,000 to 60,000 years ago (1,2).

Die Kelders   Die Kelders consists of two contiguous caves situated on the southwestern coast of South Africa. The site contains both Middle Stone Age (MSA) and Late Stone Age (LSA) layers separated by a long hiatus of archeologically sterile strata. The LSA layers contain several fully modern adult human bones and a child's partial skeleton dating to about 1,500–2,000 years ago. Excavations in the MSA layers have produced a number of small quartzite artifacts (mainly elongated flakes) and nine human teeth. These levels are tentatively correlated to oxygen isotope stage 4 at the beginning of the last glaciation around 70,000–60,000 years ago (see Fig. 1.3). Micromammals are abundant in the cave fauna and were probably deposited by roosting owls. That these MSA people exploited animal resources less broadly or effectively than did their LSA successors is suggested by the nature of the fauna, particularly the predominance of less dangerous wild game such as eland relative to wild pigs and Cape buffalo, the dominance of penguins over flying birds, and the absence of fish. This has important implications for reconstructing the evolution of early modern human behavior in the Upper Paleolithic. The nine human teeth from the MSA levels represent four to six individuals and provide some sketchy evidence for the anatomical modernity of the MSA inhabitants of southern Africa. Although they are as large as some Neandertal teeth, they are both morphologically and metrically within the range of modern Africans (3,4).

Equus Cave   Equus Cave, located only 500 m from the australopithecine-bearing cave at Taung in the northern Cape Province, has yielded an extensive late Pleistocene fauna that was probably accumulated by hyenas. Both MSA and LSA tools are present. The LSA level, known as layer 1A, is clearly Holocene in age (less than 10,000 years old). Circumstantial geological evidence suggests that layers 1B, 2A, and 2B were deposited about 103,000–32,700 years ago.[1] Thirteen hominid specimens, including twelve isolated teeth and one fragmentary left mandibular corpus containing two molars, have been recovered from these four layers. Unfortunately, since none of the hominid teeth were recovered with in situ MSA artifacts, their exact age is uncertain. These hominid remains are all modern in appearance (5–7).

Border Cave   The hominid fossils from Border Cave in Natal Province include a partial adult cranial vault, two mandibles (one partial and one

---

[1]These dates are uncertain given that radiocarbon dates on organic residues from bones in layer 2B give ages of only about 16,000 years (5).

nearly complete), a largely complete skeleton of a 4- to 6-month-old infant, and some postcranial fragments. The deposits are over 4 m thick (2). At least four of the specimens come from MSA levels. Specimens BC 1 and BC 2, a cranium and a mandible respectively, were recovered from a guano pit and are of unknown stratigraphic provenance (however, BC 1 cannot be younger than 33,000 years, the age of the youngest Stone Age horizon). Chemical analyses associate both specimens with an infant skeleton (BC 3), reportedly a burial, that was excavated from below the third white ash layer (3WA). The infant skeleton was also associated with a perforated *Conus* shell that must have originated from the sea coast at least 80 km to the east. This is one of the only ornaments or ritual objects, and the only grave, known within a South African MSA context (1).

The white ash layer is an important marker bed since it contains the distinctive **Howiesons Poort** artifact assemblage comprising many replaceable bits or inserts specifically designed for hafting in composite tools. Howiesons Poort assemblages are too old to be accurately dated by radiocarbon methods, but an age of 70,000 years is the best estimate (Fig. 10.2). The production of such stone inserts for composite tools is significant at such an early date, since in a European context these are the kinds of artifacts that one finds in much more recent Upper Paleolithic industries associated with anatomically modern populations. ESR dates on bovid enamel from

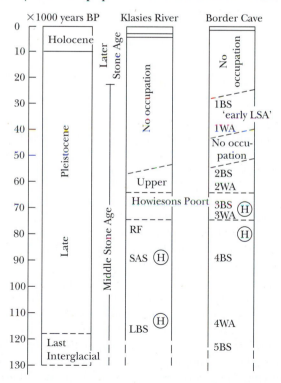

Fig. 10.2. Dating and stratigraphy of Border Cave and Klasies River. H = hominid fossils. From (2).

the site give ages of between 50,000 and 90,000 years for the human remains and a date of about 70,000 years for a mandibular fragment (BC 5) from layer 3WA (the other remains may be of similar age) (8).

Although the Border Cave hominid sample is often described as "anatomically modern," this is by no means uncontested. Multivariate statistical tests show that BC 1 falls outside the morphometric "envelope" of modern Africans and is almost four times as dissimilar from living Africans as the average dispersion within these diverse populations (9,10). In addition, the excellent state of preservation of an infant skeleton (BC 3) and a nearly complete adult mandible (BC 5) warrants caution when assuming great antiquity for some of the Border Cave hominids.

Klasies River   The best evidence for anatomically modern humans in early Late Pleistocene populations of southern Africa comes from the caves at Klasies River mouth situated on the Tsitsikama coast of South Africa (2,11,12) (Figs. 10.1–3). The cave deposits consist of a 20-m thick cone of sediment resting against the cliff face and filling side caverns within the cliff-face. Geological evidence shows that the deposits began to accumulate at the end of the Last Interglacial (about 130,000–118,000 years ago) as sea levels dropped to near their present levels from their maximum interglacial height. Quantities of hearth-ash, shell, animal bones, and human remains have been recovered in association with an MSA industry. The culture-stratigraphy at Klasies River mouth is recognized from the base upward as MSA I, MSA II, Howiesons Poort, and MSA III (13).

It is well established that the site was first inhabited by humans during the Last Interglacial about 120,000 years ago and was apparently abandoned about 60,000 years later. The bulk of the human fossils comes from two strata: the LBS (Light Brown Sand) Member and the overlying SAS (Sands-Ash-Shell) Member. Two maxillary fragments were recovered from the LBS Member and these are the oldest hominids from the site. A Last Interglacial age of approximately 120,000 years for these specimens is supported by oxygen isotope measurements on shell, aspartic acid dating, and U-Th dating (14). These oldest Klasies River hominids are more similar to anatomically modern individuals than they are to such late archaic *H. sapiens* as LH 18, ER 3884, and Jebel Irhoud I (15) (see below).

Most of the hominid fossils come from the overlying SAS Member, for which ESR analysis of associated bovid enamel gives dates in excess of 90,000 years (equivalent to oxygen isotope stage 5c) (16). The human fossil material is fragmentary and consists mainly of upper and lower jaws, isolated teeth, a frontal bone, and other cranial pieces. Postcranial remains are limited to portions of ulna, radius, lumbar vertebra, metatarsal, and clavicle. Possibly as many as ten individuals are represented at the site. The hominid sample shows a degree of robusticity and strong sexual dimorphism that is coupled to a modern facial and dental morphology. There is little resemblance to Neandertal morphology which we will investigate later in this chapter, or to that of more archaic *Homo* because the Klasies River

Description	Location in Chamber Complex	Stratigraphic Level	KRM Designation (1967–68 excavations)
Right mandibular corpus with P_4 to M_2. Three loose teeth probably belong with this individual.	cave 1	SAS member	13400. Also 14691, 14693 14694?
Anterior part of mandibular corpus including symphysis. One loose tooth may belong with this individual.	cave 1	SAS member	14695. Also 14696?
Right mandibular corpus with M_1 to M_3.	cave 1	SAS member	16424
Left mandibular corpus.	cave 1	SAS member	21776
Damaged mandible with M_1 and M_2, right P_4 and M_1.	cave 1B	Base of SAS member	41815
Fragment of left maxilla with alveoli and part of palate.	cave 1A	LBS member	—
Fragment of left maxilla with M^1.	cave 1A	LBS member	—
Frontal fragment, with nasal bones attached.	cave 1	SAS member	16425
Left zygomatic bone.	cave 1	SAS member	16651
Vault fragment, including parts of right parietal and frontal squama.	cave 1A	SAS member	41658
Left clavicle, broken at sternal end.	cave 1	SAS member	26076
Proximal end of left radius.	cave 1	SAS member	27889
Left first metatarsal.	cave 1	SAS member	—
Lumbar vertebra.	cave 1	SAS member	—
Proximal portion of right ulna.	cave 1A	SAS member	—

(a)

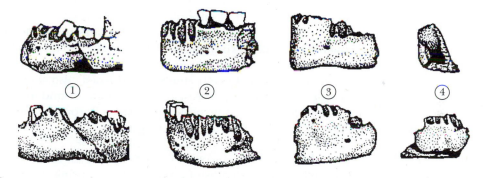

(b)

Fig. 10.3. (a) Some of the more complete hominid specimens from Klasies River. From (17). (b) Lateral and anterior profiles of four Klasies River mandibles. From left to right: 1, no. 41815; 2, no. 13400 (reversed); 3, no. 21776; 4, no. 14695. From (22).

specimens' mandibular bodies tend to be deeper anteriorly than posteriorly, a chin eminence is variably present, and there is no retromolar space. In addition, none of the jaws exhibit a type of internal symphyseal buttressing common to Neandertals. The few postcranial elements are fully modern and, with the exception of the archaic-looking ulna, none show any distinctive Neandertal features (17).[2]

One interesting question that emerges from this fossil material is what constitutes a late archaic from an early modern African face? For example, some late archaics like Florisbad, Ngaloba, and Irhoud I (see below) all have very small faces that would easily fit several of the mandibles/maxillae from Klasies River. Only the Klasies River frontal shows a real contrast with known regions of late Middle Pleistocene African archaics (E. Trinkaus, pers. comm.).

There are few artifacts in the overlying RF (Rockfall) Member, but the Upper Member contains numerous Howiesons Poort and MSA III artifacts and hearths in association with several isolated human teeth and two parietal fragments that are correlated to oxygen isotope stages 4–5a (an age in excess of 60,000 years) (17). The Middle Stone Age people of Klasies ate shellfish, the meat of various sea and land mammals, and plant materials like those with underground buds, called **geophytes**.

The fossils are broken and burnt and show cut marks and impact fractures, perhaps reflecting cannibalism at the site (19). None of the hominids are from deliberate burials. As mentioned, they also show a marked degree of morphological variation and sexual dimorphism. For example, some specimens are quite robust (presumably males) and others quite gracile (presumably females) and two of the four mandibles lack a chin. Because of this, some anthropologists have suggested that designating the Klasies River hominids as "anatomically modern *H. sapiens*" may be misleading unless the phrase is broadened to include a wider morphological range than recent or extant populations would suggest (20–22). However, even with that caveat in mind, the most important thing about Klasies River is that it securely documents the association of certain morphological "trends" characteristic of modern humans with MSA assemblages as early as about 100,000 years ago. As we will see below, new dates from sites in southwestern Asia, particularly Qafzeh and Skhul in Israel, also show that anatomically modern humans were present in that area around 100,000 years ago. Ironically, during this same period in western Europe, as we shall see later in the chapter, only Neandertals were present.

Florisbad   One other pertinent discovery from South Africa is the Florisbad skull, recovered from the depths of a warm lithium spring deposit in the Orange Free State in 1932. The skull consists of frontal and parietal pieces and the incomplete right side of the face. Its major features include a low, broad, prognathous face, rectangular orbital margins separated by a wide, flattened nasal bridge, and rounded, somewhat projecting browridges. The forehead is very broad and rounded, not like the flatter and narrower frontal region of the Kabwe and Saldanha crania (23). A recent reconstruction of the specimen shows it to be intermediate in morphology

---

[2]See (18) for a cautionary view.

between the more archaic Kabwe (Broken Hill) and Saldanha specimens and the more premodern Middle/Late Pleistocene crania from Jebel Irhoud I of North Africa (Morocco), and Eliye Springs, Singa, Ngaloba (Laetoli 18), and Omo 2 from East Africa (24). This latter African group makes a plausible ancestral form for the transitional or early modern populations at Klasies River, Irhoud 2, Omo 1, Dar-es-Soltane 5, and Border Cave, all dated to 120,000–50,000 years ago and associated with Middle Paleolithic industries (25). The Florisbad skull is beyond the range of radiocarbon dating, but may be as much as 100,000–200,000 years old (24).

East Africa

Omo Middle Stone Age assemblages from East Africa (Mumba Rockshelter, Tanzania) may date back to at least 100,000 years ago, and may be substantially earlier if dates from Ethiopia's Gademotta Formation are confirmed (26).

As far as skeletal material is concerned, several important specimens have been recovered from the Omo region of Ethiopia that are relevant to modern human origins. Omo I, consisting of cranial and postcranial fragments, was recovered from the base of Member 1 of Omo's Kibish Formation and is dated to about 130,000 years ago. The skull is said to exhibit some modern-looking features, such as its more rounded occipital region and moderately developed browridges (27). A second calvaria, Omo 2, is thought to be about the same age, although this is uncertain because it was a surface find (Fig. 10.4). Unlike Omo 1, its braincase is long and low and

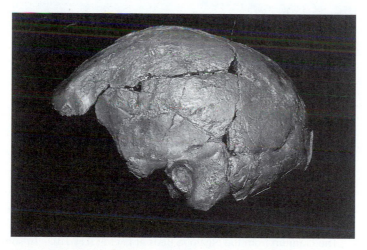

Fig. 10.4. Lateral view of the Omo 2 cranium. Its braincase is long and low and the occipital region is strongly curved as in the more archaic-looking Kabwe (Broken Hill) skull. The frontal bone is relatively broad and flattened but the supraorbital tori are appreciably less thickened than in other specimens of archaic *H. sapiens*. (Photo courtesy of F. Smith.)

the occipital region is strongly curved as in the more archaic-looking Kabwe (Broken Hill) skull. The frontal bone is relatively broad and flattened but the supraorbital tori are appreciably less thickened than in other specimens of archaic *H. sapiens.* The third hominid specimen, Omo 3, consists of only frontal and parietal fragments and is dated to about 30,000 years ago.

Given the anatomical variability expressed in this Omo sample, some anthropologists have suggested that Omo 1 and 2 may represent different populations, with Omo 1 representing a more anatomically modern population and Omo 2 a more archaic one (25,28). Whatever the correct interpretation, the important point is that none of these crania show any significant similarities to the European Neandertals, all being more modern in appearance.

Ngaloba and Eliye Springs   The cranium from the Ngaloba Beds at Laetoli (LH 18), found in 1976, is about the same age as the older Omo Kibish specimens (29) and was excavated in direct association with MSA artifacts and fauna (Fig. 10.5). Two U-S ages for the site are 129,000 ± 4,000 years and 108,000 ± 30,000 years; a date of 120,000 ± 30,000 years ago is based on geological correlations to the Ndutu Beds at Olduvai. In some morphological features LH 18 is reminiscent of the Kabwe skull, but these similarities should not be overemphasized because LH 18 has a number of more modern-looking features as well, including considerable facial size reduction, slight postorbital constriction, a canine fossa, moderately thickened

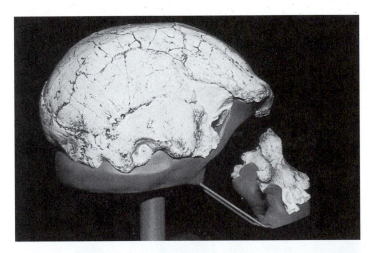

Fig. 10.5.   The cranium from the Ngaloba Beds at Laetoli (LH 18).   In some morphological features LH 18 is reminiscent of the Kabwe skull, but these similarities should not be overemphasized because the skull has a number of more modern-looking features as well. (Photo by E. Delson, courtesy, Department of Antiquities, Dar-es-Salaam, Tanzania.)

(although continuous) browridges, and its greatest breadth between the parietal bones rather than lower down on the side of the skull near the supramastoid crests (18,28).

Another, probably similarly aged, hominid from the west shore of Lake Turkana is the cranium from Eliye Springs, Kenya. Overall, it shares many of the archaic and modern features noted above for the LH 18 skull from Laetoli. For example, while both the low cranial vault and the broad cranial base recall archaic *Homo* morphology, the size and shape of the frontal, parietal, and occipital bones align it more with *H. sapiens* (30).

North Africa

Mugharet el Aliya, Rabat, Dar-es-Soltane, Zouhra   The first early modern humans from North Africa were discovered in 1939 by Carleton Coon at the site of Mugharet el Aliya (Tangier), an isolated M^2 and a left maxillary fragment containing two unerupted premolars and the unerupted canine. They were associated with the **Aterian** stone-tool industry, a North African tool tradition marked by the predominance of tools, known as tanged artifacts, having narrow projections from their base in order to secure them to a haft and endscrapers that seems to have evolved directly out of the underlying Mousterian (31,32).

In 1959 a more complete mandible from Rabat (Temara) was discovered. The Temara mandible was initially thought to be associated with an Acheulian industry, but later excavations have indicated an Aterian level for this fossil as well. In 1975 a partial skull was found at the same site that included the occipital, part of the parietals, and the left supraorbital portion of the frontal. The Temara occipital and supraorbital have been described as essentially modern in appearance.

That same year human fossils were found in a cave at Dar-es-Soltane II. Three individuals were represented: a partial skull preserving part of the upper face and an associated hemimandible (Dar-es-Soltane 5), an adolescent mandible, and a juvenile calvaria. The Dar-es-Soltane 5 cranium is more robust than the Temara specimen, particularly in facial breadth dimensions and in its well-developed browridge and glabella region. However, more modern-looking features are apparent in lateral view, where it can be seen that the face is flattened with only moderate alveolar prognathism and the cranial vault is high. In terms of overall skull morphology, however, these Aterian people are characterized by an enlarged masticatory apparatus (and associated structures) and pronounced postcanine megadonty.

In 1977–78 a mandible and canine, also associated with an Aterian industry, were discovered at Zouhra Cave.

Accurate dating of these hominids is still somewhat problematic since all seem to lie beyond the limits of radiocarbon dating. One TL date of about 41,000 years has been obtained from the cave at Zouhra. Currently, the best age estimates for most of these fossils are about 20,000–40,000 years (31).

Jebel Irhoud   The only North African site that has yielded a reasonable sample of older Mousterian hominids is the cave at Jebel Irhoud, Morocco. Significantly, the associated stone tools, with sidescrapers predominating, were manufactured using the Levallois technique, hinting that the Jebel Irhoud specimens may be older than the fossils from North Africa discussed above. Aterian endscrapers and tanged artifacts are absent from the Irhoud deposits.

The first hominid from the site, the Irhoud 1 cranium, was discovered in 1961 and, once again, shows a combination of archaic and modern features (Fig. 10.6). Its skull is long and wide and the vault is relatively low, within the range of variation seen in Neandertals or other archaic *Homo*. However, the convexity of the frontal bone is more vertical than in Neandertal skulls and lies within the modern range. In addition, the occipital bone lacks the protruding occipital torus that we will see is so typical of Neandertals. Irhoud 1 differs from *H. erectus* skulls in that the lateral sides of the skull are nearly parallel and the parietal swellings are superiorly positioned. The supraorbital tori are moderately developed and the face is broad, but midfacial prognathism does not exceed the modern range. Cranial capacity has been estimated at 1305–1480 cc. A second calvaria (Irhoud 2) was discovered in 1962 that is similar to Irhoud 1.

A juvenile mandible (Irhoud 3) was recovered in 1968 and a juvenile robust humeral shaft was recovered in 1969. While the Irhoud 3 mandible is robust, it does not show any unequivocal Neandertal-derived characters, or **apomorphies**. Its combination of a modernlike chin associated with especially large cheek teeth is reminiscent of the Qafzeh-Skhul hominid sample from the Near East, therefore excluding the Irhoud population from the Neandertal clade and aligning it more with the first modern humans of the Near East.

The Irhoud cave may correlate to oxygen isotope stage 5e; if so, the Irhoud hominids predate the "classic" Neandertals of western Europe. Several ESR dates have recently been run on horse teeth from the site and give ages of 90,000–125,000 years, and perhaps even much older (some dates correlate with oxygen isotope stage 6, 190,000–130,000 years ago) (33). Studies of associated fauna suggest steppe and desert conditions.

In earlier anthropological literature, the Irhoud hominids were often treated as North African Neandertals, or at least Neandertallike, but this view is now changing. It now appears that while there was a steady evolution of Neandertallike features in western European hominids through the Middle to Upper Pleistocene (for example, at Atapuerca), this trend was not so apparent in the North African hominid sample. As a result, some paleoanthropologists believe that by the beginning of the Upper Pleistocene there may have been two very different hominid populations on either side

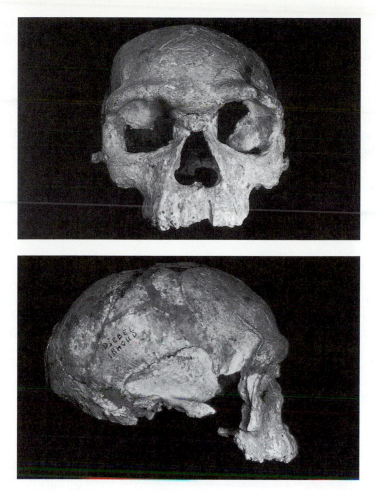

Fig. 10.6. The hominid cranium Jebel Irhoud 1. Its skull is long and wide and the vault is relatively low, within the range of variation seen in Neandertals or other archaic *Homo.* (Photos courtesy of R. Klein.)

of the Strait of Gibraltar, implying that the Mediterranean was a substantial barrier to population migration during this time period. Thus, if the Irhoud population is considered a hominid "grade" immediately preceding the first modern humans, and if Africa is the "cradle" of modern humans, then this cradle was large enough to encompass early modern populations stretching all the way from South Africa to North Africa (31).

As we have now seen, fossil evidence that helps to document the evolutionary sequence from late archaic to early modern *H. sapiens* in Africa continues to accumulate. How do they impact the Out of Africa or Multi-regional Continuity models? Proponents of the Out of Africa Model maintain that at least some of these specimens (Eliye Springs, Omo 1, Dar-es-Soltane 5) show more similarities to Upper Paleolithic modern Europeans (Cro-Magnon 1) than western European Neandertals do, and therefore are more suitable ancestors for modern European populations. Their assumption is that modern humans first evolved in Africa, then spread into the Near East and then to Europe, where they ultimately replaced the local Neandertal populations (34). However, while this simple replacement theory may explain the situation in western Europe, events in central Europe and the Near East are far more complex, as we shall see.

FOSSIL EVIDENCE FROM EUROPE

The "Neandertal Question"

One group of Middle/Upper Pleistocene archaic humans that has received special attention in discussions of modern human origins are the "classic" Neandertals of Europe. Perhaps these early humans, once defined by Aleŝ Hrdliĉka as simply "the man . . . of the Mousterian culture" (35), initially received this special notoriety because the discoveries of their fossilized remains were sympatric (if not synchronous) with the lives of many influential European students of human evolution in the late nineteenth and early twentieth centuries. As Hrdliĉka wrote (35):

> Since Huxley, the Neanderthal skull and Neanderthal man have been written about extensively, but often with but little originality. New finds belonging to the period have become numerous—almost more numerous than legitimate new thoughts. . . . [T]he distressing part is, that the more there is the less we seem to know what to do with it. Speculation there has been indeed enough, but the bulk of it so far has not led into the sunlight, but rather into a dark, blind alley from which there appears no exit.

In Europe, Middle Paleolithic (Mousterian) assemblages are almost invariably associated with Neandertals, whereas Upper Paleolithic (early Aurignacian) industries are almost always associated with anatomically modern humans. Thus far, the only exceptions to these observations come from two sites in France, Arcy-sur-Cure and Saint-Césaire (both dated to about 36,000 years ago), where an Upper Paleolithic (Châtelperronian) industry is associated with Neandertal skeletal morphology (36).[3]

The "Neandertal Question" is probably paleoanthropology's longest running headache, confounding anthropologists ever since fossil Nean-

---

[3]The Châtelperronian is a tool assemblage that probably developed directly out of the preceding Mousterian of Acheulian tradition, a tool tradition that is normally associated with Neandertals. Other Mousterian/Upper Paleolithic mixes occur in the Uluzzian of Italy and the Szeletian/Jerzmanovician of Central Europe (36).

dertals were first discovered and Thomas Huxley's successful 1863 challenge to Rudolf Virchow's contention that they were just the remains of modern pathological idiots. The first Neandertal ever discovered was from Engis Cave in Belgium in 1829–30. There the Belgian physician and anatomist Phillipe-Charles Schmerling discovered the cranial remains of at least three individuals that were associated with extinct animals. One of the skulls soon deteriorated and was lost to science and another was that of a rather robust, essentially modern male dating to only about 8,000 years. Although not recognized as such at the time, the third specimen, a partial cranium, was that of a Neandertal child that was about 2–3 years old when it died. The second Neandertal skull ever discovered was unearthed at Forbes' Quarry on the Rock of Gibraltar in 1848 as a result of construction for British military fortifications there. Like the Engis specimen, the Gibraltar skull was not recognized as a Neandertal until decades later. The name "Neandertal" traces back to the 1856 discovery of a Neandertal calotte, or skullcap, and some postcranial bones from the Feldhofer Cave in the Neander Valley, Germany (37) (Fig. 10.7a) A summary of some of the early, and still most important, Neandertal discoveries is chronicled in Table 10.2 and some of the major sites are shown in Figure 9.1b.

Since Neandertals are now generally regarded as geographic variants restricted to the Middle/Upper Pleistocene of Europe and western Asia, the "Neandertal Question," simply put, is this: "what is their relationship to the succeeding modern European populations" (38)? In other words, were European Neandertals totally replaced by anatomically modern "invaders" from the East, or was there evolutionary continuity between Neandertals and modern human populations in Europe? Conflicting opinions on the subject still bubble to the surface today.[4] To put the question into some perspective, let's briefly outline three of the more historically influential hypotheses on Neandertal phylogeny proposed over the past several decades:

- The first proposes that since Neandertal morphology diverges from that of modern Europeans, Neandertals are peripheral to mainstream human evolution. In this view, they were genetically isolated from the more anatomically modern human populations evolving in the Near East (for example in Qafzeh and Skhul) by Würmian glaciers in western Europe. The ancestry of these "classic" Neandertals were seen to trace back through European "pre-Neandertals," like those from Ehringsdorf, Krapina, and Saccopastore (39–41).[5]

---

[4]It is hard for me to understand why this has been such a vexing and contentious issue in paleoanthropology. To put the question into a more modern context, it would be like asking: "What is the relationship of Australian aborigines to the contemporary population of Australia? Were they totally replaced by English convicts or is there evolutionary continuity between them and modern human populations from Europe?"

[5]Some European Neandertals probably date to the pre-Würm, or end Riss-Würm interglacial (e.g., Krapina (level 5 and below) and Saccopastore, the Würm (e.g., Ganovce, Ochoz), and the Riss (e.g., Fontéchevade, Ehringsdorf).

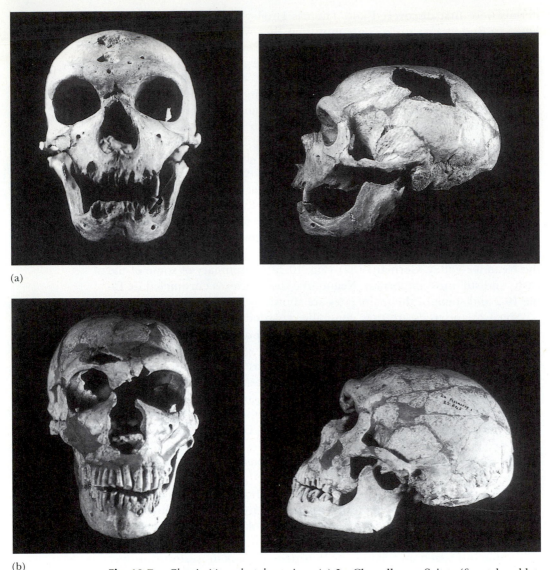

(a)

(b)

Fig. 10.7.   Classic Neandertal crania.   (a) La Chapelle-aux-Saints (frontal and lateral views); (b) La Ferrassie 1 (frontal and lateral views). (Photos courtesy of R. Klein.)

- The second proposes that not only is there evolutionary continuity between Neandertals and modern humans in Europe but that human evolution as a whole went through a worldwide Neandertal stage or phase (35,42–44).
- The third, known as the ''Praesapiens Theory,'' holds that Neandertals are an archaic group that went extinct without issue. Therefore, modern *H. sapiens* cannot be descended from Neandertals, nor can they have passed through a Neandertal stage. Instead, modern humans are envi-

Table 10.2 The First Major Discoveries of Neandertal Remains (from 143)

First Phase, 1914 and Before		Second Phase, 1920–39	
Belgium		Crimea	
Engis	1830	Kiik Koba	1924–26
Gibraltar		Israel	
Forbes' Quarry	1848	Mount Carmel, Tabun Cave	1929
Germany		Italy	
Neander Valley	1856	Saccopastore	1929–35
Belgium		Guattari	1939
Spy Caves	1886	Central Asia	
Croatia		Teshik Tash	1938
Krapina	1899–1906		
Germany			
Ehringsdorf	1908		
France			
Le Moustier 1	1908		
La Chapelle-aux-Saints	1908		
La Ferrassie 1	1909		
La Ferrassie 2	1910		
La Quina	1911		
La Ferrassie 3 & 4	1912		
Le Moustier 2	1914		

sioned as descending from a "praesapiens" type of early human, a contemporary of, but distinct from, the Neandertals. Two arguments are usually put forward to defend this view: 1) the perceived impossibility of deriving Aurignacian Upper Paleolithic Europeans from the underlying archaic Mousterian Neandertals in so short a time span; and 2) discoveries of more modern-looking fossils in Europe that are contemporary with, or even antecedent to, "classic" Neandertals (for example, at Swanscombe and Fontéchevade) (45,46).

Today, the "Neandertal Question" is generally framed in terms of the degree (zero, low, high) of continuity between Neandertals and early modern Europeans in the context of a worldwide process of modern human origins (37).

Now that we have outlined some of the competing hypotheses about the "fate" of the Neandertals, let's examine what they actually looked like.

Virtually all paleoanthropologists agree that "classic" Neandertals are morphologically unique and that this distinctive morphology is best displayed in the western European sample.[6] We will explore some of the func-

[6]Some of the more famous classic Neandertal sites include: Germany (Neandertal); Belgium (Bay-Bonnet, Engis, La Naulette, Spy); Channel Islands (St. Brelade); France (Malarnaud, La Chaise, La Quina, Petit-Puymoyen, La Chapelle-aux-Saints, Genay, Combe-Grenal, La Ferrassie, Le Moustier, Pech de l'Aze, Monsempron, Arcy-sur-Cure); Spain (Banolas, Cova Negra, Gibraltar, Pinar); Italy (Monte Circeo, Santa Croce di Bisceglie).

tional aspects of this morphology a bit later, but first let's look at some of the striking anatomical features that characterize most, if not all, Neandertal skulls (47) (Figs. 10.7, 10.8):

- cranial vaults are long, low (platycephalic) and wide and the cranial base is relatively flat
- the overall facial skeleton is massive, the midfacial region is prognathic, nasal apertures are large, and the maxillary region lacks a canine fossa
- supraorbital tori are well-developed and semicircular in shape—not a continuous bar or "shelflike" structure
- occipital bones are angulated and characterized by occipital ridges, occipital bunning, and the presence of a suprainiac fossa
- molars are characterized by enlarged pulp chambers, or taurodontism
- incisors are large, often shovel-shaped, and often show peculiar wear patterns, indicating they were used as "viselike" tools
- most mandibles are characterized by distinct retromolar spaces, an absence of a true chin, and posteriorly positioned mental foramina

Many of the distinctive Neandertal skull features, such as the elongated vertical facial dimensions, the lack of canine fossae, the large nasal apertures, and the pronounced midfacial prognathism, relate to structures of the midfacial region. Many of the diagnostic Neandertal mandibular features relate to this unique facial profile as well. There have been a number of hypotheses put forward to "explain" Neandertal facial prognathism, for example, as an adaptation to cold, as a passive result of enlarged paranasal sinus development, and/or as a response to increased anterior dental loads. All three factors probably came into play in subtle and interrelated ways. For example, while some facial features, notably nasal morphology, can plausibly be regarded as an adaptation to cold and arid Upper Pleistocene glacial climates, possibly as a physiological response to high-activity levels in regions of moderate to low humidity (48), many other facial features undoubtedly relate to increased loads placed on the anterior dentition by using these teeth as "viselike" tools. The pre- and postcanine teeth have followed somewhat different evolutionary trajectories during the Middle/Upper Pleistocene—the posterior dentition becoming somewhat reduced with the anterior dentition remaining relatively large (49–51). Clearly, Neandertal anterior teeth were responding to different selection pressures than were the posterior teeth.[7]

---

[7]Interestingly, it has been demonstrated that wear striations on the buccal surfaces of the anterior teeth were produced when Neandertals held meat or other matter between their anterior teeth and then cut it with a sharp tool held in the right hand (52). Similar buccal wear striations have been found in several other Middle and early Upper Pleistocene hominids (e.g., Atapuerca/Ibeas, Cova Negra, La Quina). This reinforces an earlier observation that toolmaking techniques from Lower Pleistocene (e.g., Koobi Fora) and Middle Pleistocene (e.g., Ambrona) sites reflect a preferential use of the right hand in early hominids (53,54). As such, these observations strongly suggest that lateralization in the hominid brain has a very ancient history. In addition, in all cases where right and left upper arm bones are preserved, humeral asymmetry of right and left humeri indicates that these Neandertal individuals were right-handed (55).

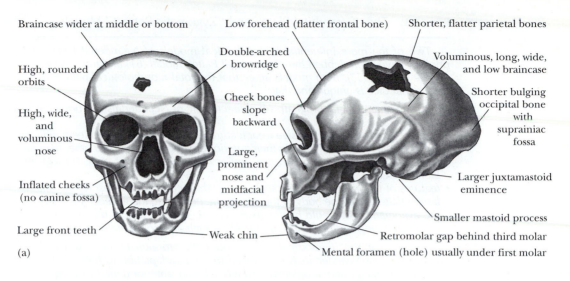

Braincase wider at middle or bottom

Low forehead (flatter frontal bone)

Shorter, flatter parietal bones

High, rounded orbits

Double-arched browridge

Voluminous, long, wide, and low braincase

High, wide, and voluminous nose

Cheek bones slope backward

Shorter bulging occipital bone with suprainiac fossa

Inflated cheeks (no canine fossa)

Large, prominent nose and midfacial projection

Larger juxtamastoid eminence

Large front teeth

Smaller mastoid process

(a)   Weak chin

Retromolar gap behind third molar

Mental foramen (hole) usually under first molar

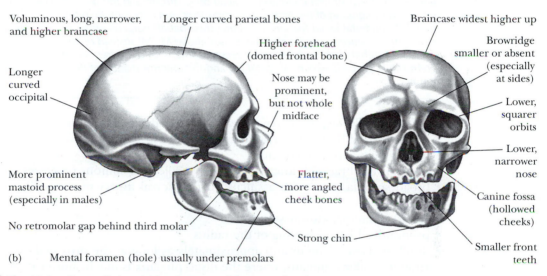

Voluminous, long, narrower, and higher braincase

Longer curved parietal bones

Braincase widest higher up

Longer curved occipital

Higher forehead (domed frontal bone)

Browridge smaller or absent (especially at sides)

Nose may be prominent, but not whole midface

Lower, squarer orbits

Lower, narrower nose

More prominent mastoid process (especially in males)

Flatter, more angled cheek bones

Canine fossa (hollowed cheeks)

No retromolar gap behind third molar

Strong chin

Smaller front teeth

(b)   Mental foramen (hole) usually under premolars

Fig. 10.8. Some distinguishing features of the Neandertal cranium. (a) The Chapelle-aux-Saints skull, with Neandertal features highlighted. (b) The anatomically modern skull of Cro-Magnon 1, with features of *H. sapiens* highlighted (143).

Biomechanical models indicate that the entire Neandertal masticatory apparatus was designed for generating and withstanding high or repeated forces on the anterior dentition, particularly on the incisors. Several lines of morphological evidence support this view, including: 1) relatively large anterior tooth dimensions; 2) excessive amounts of anterior dental attrition; and 3) the presence of dental chipping and pitting on the incisors (56–60).

Box 10.1.   The "Infraorbital Plate" and "Zygomatic Retreat" Models

---

Two of the more influential biomechanical models of Neandertal facial morphology have been dubbed the "Infraorbital Plate" model (61) and the "Zygomatic Retreat" model (57). Both models agree that the total morphological pattern of the Neandertal face is unique and that:

- *the pronounced facial prognathism characteristic of Neandertals is a primitive, or plesiomorphic, feature*
- *both the large size and extensive wear features of Neandertal anterior teeth indicate that they placed heavy loads on their anterior dentition for purposes other than just chewing food, resulting in elevated and/or repetitive levels of stress through the facial skeleton*
- *features of the Neandertal face such as the absence of canine fossae, the anterolateral flattening of the body of the zygomatic bone, and the absence of a notch in the zygomatic root would have maximized the strength of the infraorbital region against bending and/or torsion produced through anterior dental loading*

According to the "Infraorbital Plate" model, the pronounced facial prognathism characteristic of Neandertals is considered to be an adaptation to better withstand sagittally oriented rotary moments induced by heavy anterior dental loading. In the "Zygomatic Retreat" model, the Neandertal face is seen as a compromise between maintaining the ancestral condition of facial prognathism and the derived condition of posterior migration of the masticatory muscle region ("zygomatic retreat"). In this model, Neandertal facial features reflecting this spatial reorganization, or "retreat," include the positioning of the zygomatic root above M^2-M^3 instead of above M^1-M^2, as in most archaic hominids and most recent humans, and the frequent presence of a retromolar space between the distal M_3 and the anterior margin of the mandibular ramus.

The Neandertal postcranial skeleton is just as distinctive as the skull and is characterized by a number of features including (Fig. 10.9):

- heavily built vertebral column
- cervical vertebrae with long, horizontally projecting spinous processes
- broad scapula, most with a sulcus on the dorsal aspect of the axillary border
- robust humerus, with massive head
- pronounced lateral bowing of the radius
- distal phalanx of the thumb approximately as long as the proximal one (unlike modern humans, where the distal phalanx is much shorter than the proximal one); tips, or apical tufts, on the fingers are large and rounded
- pelvis with more dorsally rotated ilia
- thin, elongated superior pubic ramus
- femora with massive, cortically thick cylindrical shafts that lack a distinct pilaster; low femoral neck-shaft angle
- short and strong tibiae with retroverted proximal heads; supplementary facets on the distal tibia for articulation with the talus or ankle bone, known as "squatting facets"
- large and thick kneecaps
- low brachial and crural indices

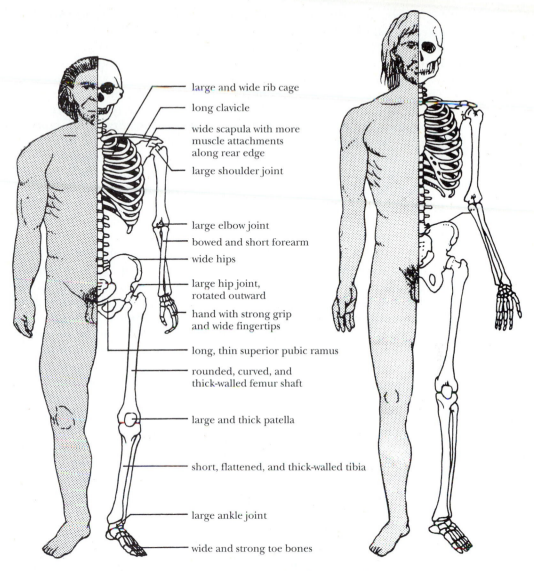

large and wide rib cage

long clavicle

wide scapula with more
muscle attachments
along rear edge

large shoulder joint

large elbow joint

bowed and short forearm

wide hips

large hip joint,
rotated outward

hand with strong grip
and wide fingertips

long, thin superior pubic ramus

rounded, curved, and
thick-walled femur shaft

large and thick patella

short, flattened, and thick-walled tibia

large ankle joint

wide and strong toe bones

Fig. 10.9.   Some distinguishing features of the Neandertal postcranial skeleton (143)
in comparison to modern *H. sapiens* (right).

The most obvious difference between the Neandertal skeleton and that
of later, more modern-looking hominids is the general level of robusticity
in the former. In short, Neandertals were powerfully built. The cervical, or
neck, vertebrae had horizontally long, robust cervical spines. Even the ribs
are particularly thick in cross section. The scapula was very broad with a
peculiar sulcus on the dorsal side of the axillary border, suggesting that the
''rotator cuff'' muscles involved in rotating the shoulder joint were particularly well developed (62). One of the bones of the forearm, the radius, is

highly bowed, giving greater leverage to muscles that help to rotate the forearm. All of the wrist and hand bones are robust with strong muscular markings; thus the hand was not adapted for limp-wristed handshakes (63). Features of the lower limb also display this same level of robustness, particularly in the size and cross-sectional shape of the femoral and tibial shafts. The thickened cortical bones in the femur and tibia reflect overall muscularity of the lower limbs and are obvious adaptations to maximizing torsional and bending strengths within these bones. By contrast, early modern humans do not show such extremes of skeletal and muscular robusticity. In fact, the oldest reasonably complete early modern postcrania from the Near East (Qafzeh and Skhul) are quite gracile by comparison (64).

Neandertal limb proportions also differ substantially from most modern populations in that they tend to have relatively short distal limb segments. For this reason, Neandertal crural (tibia length/femur length) and brachial (radius length/humerus length) indices are low.

What can be the functional explanation for such limb proportions? It turns out that brachial and crural indices are correlated with mean annual temperature in modern populations—those populations living in the coldest climates, for example, Lapps and Eskimos, have the lowest indices as an adaptation to reduce heat loss, whereas those living in hotter regions, for example, Egyptians or equatorial Africans, have higher indices as an adaptation to facilitate heat loss, an example of what is known in biology as Allen's rule. (Two nineteenth-century biological rules relating body form to cold stress are known as Allen's rule and Bergmann's rule. Allen's rule states that in a given species animals living in cold areas tend to have shorter extremities than those in warmer climates. Bergmann's rule states that in a given species the warm-blooded animals living in colder places tend to have greater body bulk than those living in warmer regions.) The shift in limb proportions seen in post-Neandertal populations suggests that these Upper Pleistocene hominids may have been under less thermal stress than Neandertals, possibly because of the first group's better ability to control fire and to make improved clothing and shelters (48,65,66). But Neandertals were not devoid of "culture," as we shall see below.

Cultural Capacities of Neandertals

No hominid group has been more maligned in the history of paleoanthropology than the Neandertals. The trend to dehumanize them has continued right through to the present (67):

> Neandertals have been portrayed as incompetent users of language and symbolic thought, . . . as incompetent hunters, . . . as incapable of anticipating patterned animal movements, . . . as incapable of anticipating future needs for tools and therefore only employing expedient technologies, . . . as incapable of using future tenses or clauses and therefore lacking alliances and even extended families, . . . as incapable of forming ethnic identities, . . . as possibly lacking aggre-

gation sites or even home bases, . . . , as incapable of abstract or realistic artistic expression, . . . as lacking values or symboling ability related to the intentional interment of the dead and by inference lacking any developed religious thought, . . . as lacking the motor and mental conceptual wherewithal to manufacture stone blades and bone tools, . . . and as generally lacking culture as we recognize it . . .

Whew! What a litany of alleged sins.

As Brian Hayden of Simon Fraser University points out in the above quotation, there are two major implications that follow from these views: 1) that Neandertals were genetically incapable of language, symboling, religion, foresight, tool curation, ethnicity, art, hunting, blade and bone tools, which had to wait until the emergence of the genetically superior *H. sapiens sapiens* of the Upper Paleolithic; and 2) that even if Neandertals did have the capacity for these behaviors, they were not a significant part of their world view, thereby failing to avail themselves of this potential. However, Hayden notes that, in contrast to these dehumanizing views, there is a reasonable body of archeological evidence that Neandertals were not significantly different from early *H. sapiens sapiens* in their genetic capacity for cultural behavior and that symbolic behavior was indeed a part of their adaptation in the Middle Paleolithic.

For example, there is now abundant archeological evidence for hafting on Levallois and Mousterian points and scrapers of the Middle Paleolithic (remember, virtually all archeologists agree that that Mousterian assemblages were produced by Neandertals) (Fig. 10.10). Some of this hafted lithic material came from 30–80 km away from the sites where they were found, a strong indicator that hafting involved curation, foresight, and mental templates of tool designs that had to be shaped to certain predetermined specifications. In addition, it appears that at least some Middle Paleolithic populations were already experimenting with the use of bitumen as a glue for hafting handles onto their tools (68). Most important, tool types and patterns of raw material procurement do not necessarily change at the first appearance of anatomically modern *H. sapiens*. It is also clear that both wood and bone tools were manufactured by hominids before the appearance of anatomically modern *H. sapiens*. These tools include a yew spear from Clacton, England, dated to about 300,000 years ago; a spear end found in the rib cage of an elephant at Lehringen, Germany, dating to about 120,000 years ago; and wood tools from the Acheulian at Kalambo Falls. That Neandertals were familiar with working bone and ivory is evidenced by occasional finds of bone points, awls, perforated bones and teeth, cut antlers, ivory rings, and antler digging picks. As far as blade production is concerned, this lithic technology occurs in the Acheulian, as well as the later Mousterian.

In accepting the notion that Neandertals were incapable of art and ritual, some have doubted that Neandertals buried their dead. However, the evidence, particularly from Shanidar, leaves little doubt that not only

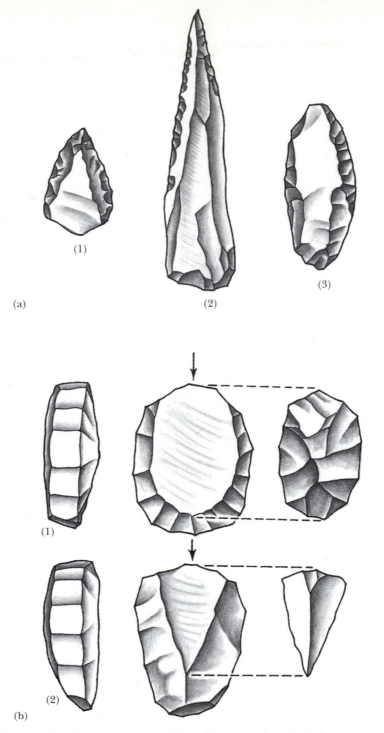

Fig. 10.10. (a) Typical Mousterian tools made by Neandertals. 1) Mousterian point; 2) elongated Mousterian point; 3) sidescraper. (b) Stages in the manufacture of 1) Levallois flake and 2) a Levallois point (144).

were some Neandertals buried, but also that flowers were used in some of these burials—a clear example of symbolic and religious behavior (69). Another indication that an appreciation of art was present even before Neandertals emerged is demonstrated by: 1) a sophistication and beauty in some Acheulian bifaces that far exceeded any possible functional requirements; 2) the selection, in some cases, of particularly attractive fossiliferous chert (a type of flint) or rock crystals for tools; 3) the flaking of handaxes in such a way that prominent single fossils were centrally located in the finished tool; and 4) the transport over long distance of nonfunctional items such as fossiliferous cherts and the teeth of whales and seals (67).

It is also important to note that Neandertals had achieved a level of social caring and responsibility in which disabled members of the community were cared for by other members of the group long after they could have contributed in any substantial way to the group's material welfare. Despite the fact that virtually every reasonably complete skeleton of an elderly Neandertal shows evidence of some trauma, all of these individuals clearly survived for extended posttraumatic periods, as they all show extensive wound healing usually with little or no evidence of infection. It is fascinating to speculate on just what type of indirect value these elderly individuals must have had to the social group that cared for them over such extended periods of time. Perhaps it is not surprising, then, that many of these same individuals were found in intentional burials (70,71).

Finally, we should consider the long-running debate about whether or not Neandertals were capable of fully sapient speech. A most articulate and persistent spokesman for the view that Neandertals lacked "the speech producing anatomy that is necessary for sounds like the vowels (i), (u), and (a), for nasal versus nonnasal distinctions, and certain velar consonants" is Philip Lieberman of Brown University (72,73). Much of Lieberman's argument rests on perceived similarities between the anatomy of the Neandertal supralaryngeal tract based mainly on a reconstruction of the La Chapelle-aux-Saints Neandertal to that of chimpanzees and human newborns. These reconstructions attempt to show that the Neandertal neck could not accommodate the vocal apparatus of modern humans, thereby limiting the sapient quality of speech. More recently, Lieberman's reconstruction of the Neandertal supralaryngeal tract, and the linguistic conclusions drawn from it, has been challenged (74). This more recent interpretation suggests that, while Neandertal craniofacial anatomy is indeed distinctive, there is no osteological evidence to suggest that they could not have had the same linguistic abilities as modern humans. Lending some credence to this is the recent discovery of an intact Neandertal hyoid bone from Kebara (see below), the small bone that anchors some of the tongue muscles. It is virtually indistinguishable from the same bone in modern humans (75–77). This hyoid bone has not settled the debate, however, and the issue of Neandertal linguistic capabilities still generates heated, and mutually contradictory, claims (78,79).

After all the dust has settled, what is our final mental image of Neandertals? It is best summed up in the words of two prominent anatomists who were moved to write (80) that "... a healthy, normal Neanderthalian, ... reincarnated and placed in a New York subway—provided that he were bathed, shaved, and dressed in modern clothing—would [be unlikely to] attract any more attention than some of its other denizens."[8]

The Transition from Middle to Upper Paleolithic

As we have seen, from about 300,000 to 35,000 years ago, the fossil record appears to demonstrate the relatively gradual development and establishment of the Neandertal morphotype in Europe. The time of transition from Neandertal to modern *H. sapiens* in Europe appears to have an east to west gradient, occurring about 34,000 years ago in eastern Europe but several thousand years later (about 30,000–28,000 years ago) in western Europe. Remarkably, Neandertals evolved gradually in Europe for over several hundred thousand years, but then abruptly disappeared over a relatively short time span (25,81) (see Fig. 9.1b).

In Europe, the transition from Middle to Upper Paleolithic assemblages occurred about 45,000–35,000 years ago, much later than in either Africa or western Asia (Near East). Archeological evidence suggests that this transition was associated with the arrival of anatomically modern populations in Europe that were equipped with new technologies—the Aurignacian, named for the assemblage first unearthed at L'Aurignac in France. In some instances, there is evidence for a short period of overlap between these new populations and final Neandertal populations (82–84). As we have previously noted, in both Africa and the Near East, modern human populations first appear in association with Middle Paleolithic (Middle Stone Age) industries.

It is probably fair to say that a majority of Old World archeologists hold that the Out of Africa Model, rather than the Multiregional Continuity Model, best explains the archeological and paleontological data from Europe. Pivotal to this view is the conclusion that all of the earliest modern humans in Europe are associated with Aurignacian assemblages. There seems little doubt that this is the case for such geographically widespread regions as Germany (Vogelherd), Czechoslovakia (Mladeč), Yugoslavia (Velika Pecina), and France (Les Rois). Certainly no evidence in Europe directly associates Aurignacian industries with Neandertals. Of course, the relevant question here is whether the Aurignacion industries reflect the dispersal of an anatomically modern population over the entire continent, or local cultural developments that emerged independently within each region from preceding Middle Paleolithic Neandertal populations. As men-

[8]Is this a commentary on Neandertals or New Yorkers? "New York—A city ... so decadent that when I leave it I never dare look back lest I turn into salt and the conductor throw me over his left shoulder for good luck" (Frank Sullivan).

tioned above, most archeologists favor the former hypothesis (population replacement) based on the following observations (83):

- The Aurignacian seems to be a remarkably uniform technology that extends all the way from western Europe through central, eastern, and southern Europe and even into northern portions of the Near East. This implies that Aurignacian populations maintained social/cultural links over large geographic areas. This pattern of cultural uniformity in the Aurignacian is very different from the highly varied technologies (like the Mousterian of Acheulian tradition in western Europe or the Micoquian, eastern Charentian, and various leaf point industries in central and eastern Europe) found within the same areas of Europe during the preceding Middle Paleolithic.

- A local European origin for the Aurignacian cannot be convincingly demonstrated because the Aurignacian appears relatively suddenly without any clear local Middle Paleolithic antecedents. In any event, it would be difficult to explain how a rather uniform Aurignacian could emerge suddenly from the varied Middle Paleolithic industries. At present, the most likely source of the Aurignacian is in the Middle East (for example at Ksar Akil, Lebanon).

- It is fairly well established that early forms of the Aurignacian were present in most of Europe by 40,000–35,000 years ago and the available radiocarbon dates suggest an overall "cline" of older to younger dates running east to west across Europe (see Fig. 9.2).

- Finally, it is now generally accepted that Aurignacian assemblages include the earliest well-documented occurrences of most, if not all, of the distinctive technological, "symbolic," and other cultural innovations diagnostic of the Upper Paleolithic. The dissemination of such technological breakthroughs throughout Eurasia is hard to imagine without the development of a relatively complex, structured language among these Aurignacian peoples.

If indeed there was replacement of archaic populations by more modern humans, then we should expect to see some chronological overlap between the two. In fact, this appears to be the case from sites in the Perigord and adjacent provinces of southwest France, where two quite distinct technological patterns, the Aurignacian and Châtelperronian (which has clear links to Middle Paleolithic Mousterian technologies), clearly overlap in time and are associated with anatomically modern and Neandertal morphologies (e.g., Saint-Césaire, Arcy-sur-Cure) respectively.

Central Europe   A number of sites in central Europe have yielded remains of early modern human types, the most notable being Mladeč, Zlaty Kun, Vindija, Velika Pecina, Brno, Předmosti, and Dolni Věstonice. As alluded to earlier, these sites are of particular importance to those who argue the case of evolutionary continuity between Neandertals and modern humans.

Upper Paleolithic human fossils and Aurignacian tools were discovered at Mladeč (Moravia) as early as 1881 (Fig. 10.11). Of particular interest is

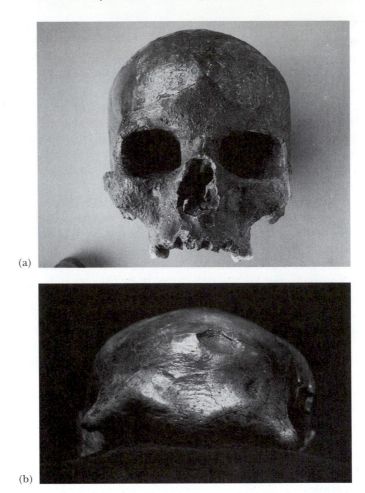

(a)

(b)

Fig. 10.11. Frontal views of (a) Mladec 1 and (b) Mladec 5.   Upper Paleolithic human fossils and Aurignacian tools were first discovered at Mladec (Moravia) in 1881. The skulls still have a number of features reminiscent of Neandertal morphology such as thick cranial bones and massive supraorbitals. These Neandertallike features are found in a number of early Aurignacian modern humans from central Europe. (Photos courtesy of B. Schumann.)

a necklace of drilled animal teeth and numerous distinctive flat bone (Mladeč) points characteristic of the early Aurignacian in the region. The cranial and postcranial material indicates varying degrees of robusticity and size for this population, presumably indicative of sexual dimorphism. The important point about the skeletal biology of this population is that, although they are clearly *H. sapiens sapiens,* some individuals still have a number of features that are reminiscent of Neandertal morphology, including lambdoidal flattening, occipital bunning, thick cranial bones, and massive supraorbitals. These Neandertallike features are found in a number of early Aurignacian modern humans from central Europe (85).

A number of other dental and calvarial fragments from the region, including those from Zlaty Kun (Moravia), Vindija (upper cave), Velika Pecina (Croatia), and Brno (Moravia), reinforce the comments made above about the "mosaic" nature of the Mladeč hominids. For example, the Zlaty Kun and Brno calvarias are also quite robust, with well-developed occipital bunning and thick, projecting supraorbital tori. However, the zygomatics lack the columnar, pillarlike frontal processes so characteristic of Neandertals. In addition, a distinct chin is usually present and the typical Neandertallike retromolar space is less frequent.

From another late Mousterian complex at Kulna, not far from Brno, has come a right maxillary fragment found in 1965 that preserves the canine through M^1. Subsequent excavations have yielded a right parietal fragment and a few isolated teeth.

The largest sample of Upper Paleolithic hominids yet discovered from central Europe comes from the open-air site of Předmosti (Moravia) (Fig. 10.12). Hominids were first found there in 1884. In 1894 a communal grave was discovered containing the remains of eighteen individuals, most with their heads oriented to the north. The grave was covered with limestone

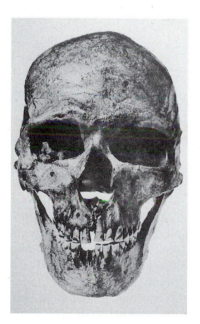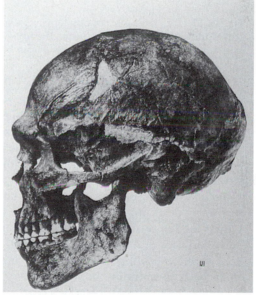

Fig. 10.12. Frontal and lateral views of Předmosti 3, which displays a mosaic of Neandertal and modern human features, such as enlarged browridges combined with a gracile dental size. The largest sample of Upper Paleolithic hominids discovered from central Europe comes from this open-air site at Předmosti (Moravia). (Photos courtesy of F. Smith.)

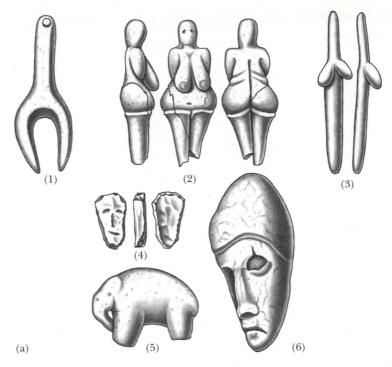

Fig. 10.13.   (a) Examples of clay figurines found at a triple burial at Dolni Věston-ice, Moravia. (b) In the triple burial, the individual in the middle (of undetermined sex) is flanked by two males, both of whom had ivory pendants around their teeth (143,145).

slabs and mammoth bones. There may be as many as twenty-nine individuals represented at the site: 15 subadults ranging from a few months to midteens, 6 adult males, 2 to 4 adult females, and 4 unsexed individuals.[9] The hominids were associated with thousands of stone tools and a diverse bone and antler industry. The predominance of mammoth remains strongly suggests that these animals were the primary prey of the Předmosti hunters. The hominid specimens are quite variable, showing the same mosaic of modern human and Neandertal features noted earlier for this region. One interesting postcranial difference between this population and Neandertals is that the Předmosti population has higher brachial and crural indices, indicating that their distal limb segments were relatively longer than the corresponding bones in classic western European Neandertals.

Dolni Věstonice (Moravia) is a particularly interesting Upper Paleolithic site, dated to about 30,000–25,000 years ago. The site consists of the traces of several tentlike huts, a large collection of mammoth bones, large central hearths, and several burials including one triple burial (Fig. 10.13). A fragment of a charred horse rib in the mouth of one of the skeletons, which

[9]Unfortunately, these were all destroyed in the 1945 fire at Mikulov Castle.

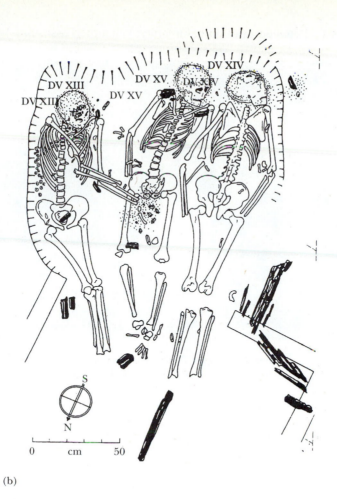

(b)

clearly suffered from some severe illness, may have served as a biting device used to overcome pain. Stone and bone tools, decorative items like beads and pendants, and clay figurines are numerous. One of the clay figurines is of a human head with very asymmetrical left facial features. One of the specimens found at the site (Dolni Věstonice 3) is a virtually complete female skeleton showing severe facial deformation on the left side. Could it be that the clay figurine was an artistic rendering of this individual? If so, it would be the first "portrait" of a human being from the archeological record. Some burials seem to provide evidence of some type of ritual behavior. For example, bodies are often laid on their right sides with knees strongly flexed and are oriented in an east-west direction with the head toward the east; some are placed within a central settlement area facing the hearth; some are associated with perforated carnivore canines and pendants of mammoth ivory; and some have their head and pelvic areas covered by ochre, a dark yellow or reddish pigment (86,87).

As alluded to earlier, those who favor the idea of evolutionary continuity between Neandertal and modern human populations in Europe often turn to the paleontological and archeological record of central Europe for sup-

Fig. 10.14   Frontal view of Upper Pleistocene hominids from (left) Abri Pataud and (right) Cro Magnon. (Photo courtesy of B. Schumann.)

port (38,43,44,85,88,89). They argue that the usual comparisons made between Neandertals and the first anatomically modern western European populations, known as **Cro-Magnons** (Fig. 10.14) after the site where their remains were first identified (''big cliffs'' in French), are potentially misleading because the latter are not necessarily the earliest representatives of post-Neandertal Europeans. According to this line of reasoning, the earliest putative descendants of European Neandertals from eastern and central Europe at Mladeč, Velika Pecina, Vindija, Brno, Předmosti, Dolni Věstonice, and Zlaty Kun predate Cro-Magnons from western Europe and are more archaic-looking as well. These researchers also argue that there is archeological continuity between Middle and Upper Paleolithic assemblages as well, thus further attesting to the continuity of the Neandertal–modern human transition in Europe.

There is little doubt that, historically at least, studies of the ''Neandertal Question'' have overemphasized the western European fossil record at the expense of the central European one, particularly at sites in Hungary, eastern Austria, western Rumania, northern Croatia, and southern portions of Moravia and Slovakia.[10] In fact, some of the first Neandertal fossils ever discovered were from central Europe (at Ochoz and Sipka) and the Krapina fossils still remain the largest sample of Neandertals known from a

---

[10]Important sites in central Europe include: Moravia (Předmosti, Dolni Věstonice, Šipka, Kulna, Mladeč, and Brno); Croatia (Krapina, Vindija, Velika Pecina, Veternica); Slovakia (Sala, Gánovce); Hungary (Subalyuk); Austria (Willendorf, Miesslingstal) (85).

single locality. Similarly, the largest sample of early Upper Paleolithic skeletons comes from Předmosti, yet it has often been overshadowed in the literature by such western European sites as Cro-Magnon and Grimaldi.

Upper Pleistocene hominids from central Europe are associated with both Middle and Upper Paleolithic assemblages. The Szeletian and Aurignacian are the earliest Upper Paleolithic assemblages in the region, with the former being slightly older than the latter. The Szeletian, found mainly in the eastern part of central Europe, is described as having a strong Middle Paleolithic "flavor" and some archeologists believe that it evolved directly out of the local Middle Paleolithic. The Gravettian follows the Aurignacian in central Europe and consists of the usual array of Upper Paleolithic blade tools, including burins, Gravettian points (distinctive small, pointed points with straight blunted backs), extensive and intricate bone and ivory items, and evidence of ritual burials.

As mentioned, one of the earliest Neandertal discoveries was the symphyseal, or chin, fragment found in 1880 at Šipka (unfortunately, this and many other human fossils were destroyed by fire in 1945). Of more anthropological importance, however, are the larger Neandertal samples from a number of central European sites, all apparently dating to the end Riss-Würm or early Würm and all associated with Mousterian assemblages.

The richest of these sites, Krapina, was excavated between 1899 and 1905 and has yielded an extensive faunal and archeological assemblage. The hominid sample consists of over eight hundred fragments, including nearly two hundred isolated teeth representing about eighty individuals, the greatest number of Neandertal remains ever recovered from a single locality (Fig. 10.15). The site is divided into thirteen stratigraphic units, of which the upper nine contain Middle Paleolithic artifacts. Most of the hu-

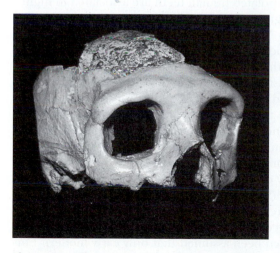
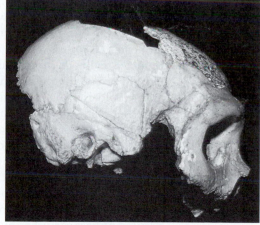

Fig. 10.15. Two views of the Krapina [3] skull. (Photos courtesy of F. Smith.)

man fossils are from levels 3 and 4 and appear to date to the end of the Riss-Würm interglacial. Recently, ESR and U-S dates on hominid tooth enamel from the site indicate that the hominids are about 130,000 years old. Both cranial and postcranial remains show most of the distinctive Neandertal features listed earlier, and clearly align the Krapina hominids with Neandertals from western Europe. One unusual feature of the Krapina Neandertals is the size of their anterior dentition, perhaps the largest of any Pleistocene hominid sample. Estimated stature for the Krapina Neandertals averages 5′ 3″. Interestingly, several specimens from level 8, in particular cranial elements of a 6–8-year-old juvenile (Krapina 1) and a partial occipital bone (Krapina 11) lack features usually found in Neandertals (such as the suprainiac fossa) and suggest to some that these fossils from the upper layers at Krapina may be transitional to anatomically modern hominids (85,90–92).

Because all of the Neandertal remains from Krapina are extremely fragmented, some have suggested that the Krapina Neandertals may have practiced cannibalism, breaking the bones to obtain brains, marrow, and other soft tissues for ritual or dietary purposes. However, careful analysis of the hominid sample reveals that none of the damage patterns can be explained solely as a product of cannibalism and it is just as likely that the damage was caused by normal geological and biological processes (93). More recently the remains of thirteen Neandertals were found near Valence, France, that had cutmarks produced by a flint tool on both skull fragments and a proximal radius (94). Again, it is tantalizing, if unproven, evidence of cannibalism among at least some Neandertals.

Another nearby site, Vindija, is only about 50 km from Krapina and has yielded over eighty Neandertal fragments since 1974. The earliest hominids at the site (from level G_3) date to the lower Würm and are associated with a Mousterian industry. A few isolated human teeth are associated in higher stratigraphic levels with Aurignacian and Gravettian assemblages (95). The G_3 hominid sample is clearly Neandertallike in all relevant features. Interestingly, the Vindija hominids show some features foreshadowing early modern *H. sapiens*, such as the reduction in size of the supraorbital tori, reduced midfacial prognathism, incipient chin development, and the lack of both occipital bunning and lambdoidal flattening. For this reason, some anthropologists suggest that the Vindija sample may be an intermediate form between Neandertals and more modern-looking Europeans (85). Of particular interest is the recent description of two hominid skull fragments from the G_1 level: one, a zygomatic bone that provides the first information about the midfacial anatomy of the Vindija hominids; and two, a frontal/supraorbital torus fragment (96). Both specimens exhibit Neandertallike morphology and both are presumably associated with the Aurignacian industry, based on the presence of a single split-based bone point. This is significant because it has often been assumed that only early modern Europeans produced the Aurignacian.

Another interesting Neandertal fossil comes from the site of Gánovce in northern Slovakia. There, in 1926, a Neandertal endocast with a few adhering segments of the cranial vault was discovered. The endocast reveals that the overall shape of the cranium was distinctly Neandertallike. Estimated cranial capacity is about 1,320 cc, near the average for Riss-Würm Neandertals.

Further information about cranial anatomy of central European Neandertals comes from a frontal bone recovered at Sala in western Slovakia. Interestingly, this individual survived trauma over the right orbit, where there is a healed lesion. This specimen, like some of those from Vindija, also shows more "transitional" features, such as a greater frontal curvature, than is commonly seen in most western Neandertals and Krapina Neandertals.

Another early Neandertal discovery (1905), the mandible from Ochoz, southern Moravia, preserves the alveolar region and complete dentition (except for the right M_3). Further excavations in the 1960s produced two small human skull fragments (portions of a parietal and temporal squama) and an isolated right M_3 found associated with an end Riss-Würm-age fauna. The mandible and teeth have all the features normally associated with western European Neandertals: a retromolar space, large anterior teeth, and taurodont molars.

Similar features are found in a Neandertal mandible from Subalyuk, Hungary. Here, fragmentary remains of a Neandertal adult and child were found in association with a Mousterian assemblage. The adult specimen consists of a mandible preserving the left canine through M_3, the molars on the right side, and a few postcranial elements, including a sacrum and the upper part of the sternum, or manubrium. Western European Neandertals are characterized by a "barrel-shaped" upper thorax, and the ventrally concave Subalyuk manubrium indicates a similar morphology for this central European Neandertal. The Subalyuk child is represented by a calvaria, most of both maxillae, and most of the deciduous dentition. The individual was probably about 3 years old when it died. The calvaria is long, low, and broad and already there is evidence of lambdoidal flattening and an incipient occipital bun. The suture between the frontal bones, or metopic suture, is still present, as it is in most other Neandertal children.

Thus, given the paleontological and archeological richness and complexity of these central European sites, it is easy to see how proponents of both the Out of Africa Model and the Multiregional Continuity Model can manipulate data to support their respective views, the former to argue that the transition from Middle to Upper Paleolithic industries was the result of anatomically modern populations sweeping across Europe from east-to-west and the latter to argue that there was both technological and anatomical continuity between Middle Paleolithic Neandertals and Upper Paleolithic modern populations. To help sort out these issues, we next turn to the important fossils of the Near East.

FOSSIL EVIDENCE FROM THE NEAR EAST

Hominid fossils from the Near East are extremely relevant to the issue of modern human origins. As previously mentioned, Upper Paleolithic cultures first appear in western Asia (the Near East) about 40,000 years ago and the associated hominids, like a child's skull from Ksar Akil, Lebanon, dated to about 37,000 years ago, are anatomically modern. As in western Europe, Middle Paleolithic (Mousterian) assemblages in the Near East are also associated with Neandertals (for example, Tabun, Amud, and Kebara Caves in Israel, Shanidar Cave in Iraq, and Teshik-Tash Cave in Uzbekistan) (Fig. 10.16). However, unlike the situation prevailing in western Europe, anatomically "modern" humans in the Near East are also associated with Middle Paleolithic (Mousterian) assemblages at several sites, the best known being Mugharet es Skhul and Jebel Qafzeh Caves in northern Israel (97,98).

Within the past few years, new advances in dating techniques, particularly TL, ESR, and U-S, have literally revolutionized views of modern human origins. Specifically, these new dates indicate that hominids associated with the Acheulo-Yabrudian and Mousterian industries, such as those at Zutti-yeh, Tabun, Skhul, Qafzeh, Kebara, Shanidar, and Amud, span both the late Middle and Upper Pleistocene and, most importantly, that the archeological "revolution" characterizing the Middle/Upper Paleolithic transition postdated by tens of thousands of years the first appearance of ana-

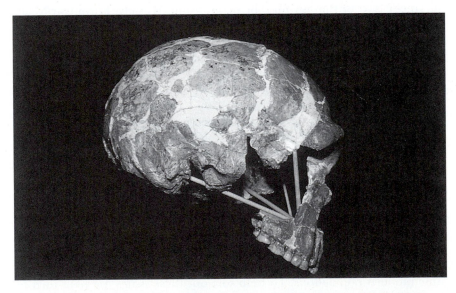

Fig. 10.16. Lateral view of the Tabun 1 skull. (Photo courtesy of F. Smith.)

tomically modern humans in the region (77,99).[11] It now seems apparent that Neandertals and early "modern" humans may have coexisted (or alternated) in Eurasia for tens of thousands of years, perhaps from before 100,000 years ago to just under 35,000 years ago. For example, TL dating of burnt flints and ESR and U-S dating of dental samples at Qafzeh reveal that the early modern *H. sapiens* from this site (the remains of at least twenty hominids are represented), which had previously been assumed to be only about 40,000–50,000 years old, are on the order of about 90,000 years old (97,98,100–104). At the other extreme, Neandertal remains from Saint-Césaire, France, have recently been dated to about 35,000 years ago (105). Proponents of the Out of Africa Model use this type of evidence to bolster the view that Neandertals could not have evolved into anatomically "modern" humans as the Multiregional Continuity Model proposes, but must have been replaced by them instead.

Mt. Carmel Caves (Skhul and Tabun)

When fossil hominids from the Mt. Carmel caves of Tabun and Skhul were first described in the 1930s by Theodore McCown and Arthur Keith, it was thought that the Skhul hominids represented a population characterized by a mosaic of modern and primitive anatomical features and that the Tabun hominids represented a more primitive, "Neanderthaloid" population (Fig. 10.17). Later, they reversed their opinion and concluded that the Skhul and Tabun populations represented the morphological extremes of a single people in the "throes of evolutionary change" (106).

Skhul is one of the most important of the Near Eastern sites from which more modernlike humans have been recovered. However, it should be noted that the Skhul V cranium is usually the one specimen specifically mentioned as being more "modern-looking"—there is a great deal of morphological variation among the Skhul hominid sample with some specimens, like Skhul IV and IX, being much more Neandertallike (9,10). The site consists of three successively older units: Layer A, which contains a mixed assemblage of Middle and Upper Paleolithic artifacts and some potsherds; Layer B, which contains cranial and postcranial remains of at least ten individuals (three of whom were children) associated with a Levallois-Mousterian (Middle Paleolithic) industry; and Layer C, which also has a stone-tool industry similar to Layer B. The hominids from Layer B, most of which appear to have been intentionally buried, represent an early form of what most paleoanthropologists regard as anatomically modern humans. Morphologically, the Skhul hominids are most similar to those from the nearby site of Qafzeh near Nazareth. Recent ESR and U-S dating methods suggest that the Skhul hominids may fall into two faunal ages within Layer

[11]The middle to earlier late Pleistocene archeological sequence in the Near East (Levant) is divided into the Upper or Late Acheulian, the Mugharan (Acheulo-Yabrudian), and the Mousterian traditions.

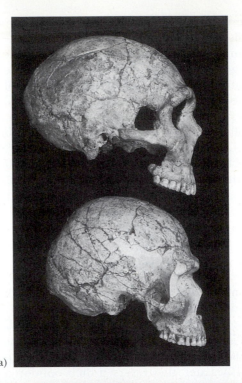

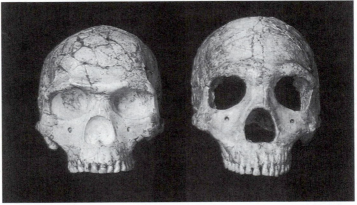

Fig. 10.17. (a) Left lateral view of *Homo sapiens neanderthalensis*, Amud 1 (above), and early *Homo sapiens sapiens*, Skhul 5 (below); (b) frontal view, Amud 1 on right. (Photo by C. Tarka, courtesy E. Delson and Israel Antiquities Authority and Peabody Museum, Harvard University.)

B, an older assemblage of about 80,000–119,000 years and a younger assemblage of about 40,000 years (100,104,107).

It is interesting to note that the stone-tool traditions of these more anatomically modern hominids found in Skhul and Qafzeh are practically indistinguishable from those used at a later date by the morphologically distinct Neandertallike hominids from the same region (for example at Kebara), and both hominid groups apparently practiced intentional burials as well. The only major "cultural" distinctions between the two groups seem to be that the Neandertal assemblages (e.g., Kebara) have a higher percentage of points (presumably hafted to wooden shafts as spear heads) than the Qafzeh assemblages,[12] and that the more anatomically modern human assemblages (e.g., Qafzeh and Skhul) include more evidence of body decorations, such as the use of *Glycymeris* shells, a nonedible molluscan species that must have been brought in from at least 50 km away, for necklaces (Qafzeh and Skhul) and red ochre (Qafzeh) (99).

Although the "cultural" distinctions between the more "modern" Qafzeh/Skhul group and the more Neandertallike Amud/Shanidar/Tabun group may not be so great, some of their morphological differences may reflect subtle, yet significant, biosocial distinctions. For example, the femoral neck-shaft angles in the Near Eastern Neandertallike sample are much lower than in the Qafzeh/Skhul sample. This difference in femoral neck angulation parallels that seen between modern "foragers" and more "sedentary" human populations, with the Qafzeh/Skhul group reflecting the "sedentary" pattern and the Neandertal group the "foragers" pattern. Of course, both of these Middle Paleolithic groups were undoubtedly "foragers," but because the femoral neck-shaft angle decreases with age and level of activity, the suggestion has been made that immature Qafzeh/Skhul individuals may have participated less in foraging-related locomotor activity than the immature individuals of the Neandertallike group. If true, this implies that the immature Qafzeh/Skuhl individuals were being cared for by some of the adult population in or near a primary site location, suggesting in turn a more elaborate social organizational system in this group than in the more Neandertallike groups. Some support for this idea comes from the fact that commensal rodents are much more common at Qafzeh than at "Neandertal" sites like Tabun, Amud, and Kebara, a zooarcheological pattern expected at sites with relatively longer periods of residence at any one time (108).

The nearby cave at Tabun provides one of the best, or at least one of the longest, "yardsticks" of stone tool changes through the Middle/Upper Pleistocene sequence. The dating of the cave deposits has been controversial (Fig. 10.18) (104,109,110). Pre-Mousterian layers at Tabun contain both upper Acheulian levels and Mugharan assemblages (locally referred to as the "Acheulo-Yabrudian" tradition), an industry characterized by the predominance of sidescrapers made from thick flakes with little evidence of Levallois technique. This "Acheulo-Yabrudian" industry is now thought to be older than 200,000 years in the region, and may date back to well over 400,000 years ago. Levallois techniques become more frequent in level Tabun-D, dating back to some 200,000–120,000 years ago; unfortunately,

---

[12]Wooden spears are known from the Lower Paleolithic of Europe, for example at Clacton-on-Sea and at Lehringen.

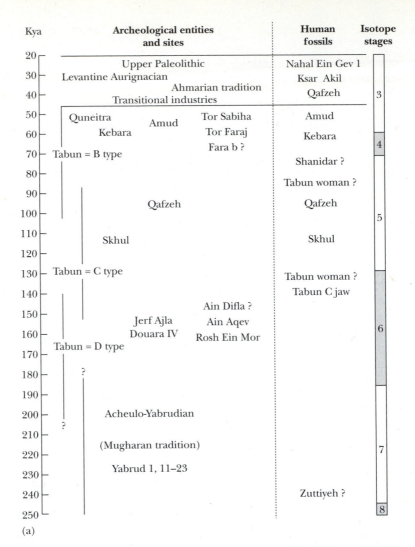

Kya	Archeological entities and sites	Human fossils	Isotope stages
20		Nahal Ein Gev 1	
30	Upper Paleolithic	Ksar Akil	
	Levantine Aurignacian		
40	Ahmarian tradition	Qafzeh	3
	Transitional industries		
50	Quneitra Tor Sabiha	Amud	
60	Amud		
	Kebara Tor Faraj	Kebara	
70	Fara b ?		4
	Tabun = B type	Shanidar ?	
80		Tabun woman ?	
90	Qafzeh	Qafzeh	
100			5
110	Skhul	Skhul	
120			
130	Tabun = C type	Tabun woman ?	
140		Tabun C jaw	
150	Ain Difla ?		
	Jerf Ajla Ain Aqev		
160	Douara IV Rosh Ein Mor		6
170	Tabun = D type		
180	?		
190			
200	Acheulo-Yabrudian		
210	?		
220	(Mugharan tradition)		7
230	Yabrud 1, 11–23		
240		Zuttiyeh ?	
250			8

(a)

Fig. 10.18. (a) Chronology for Near Eastern sites and fossil hominids (99). (b) Comparison of three suggested chronologies for Tabun. Scheme 1 from (109) and scheme 2 from (146) are compared with recent ESR results (110).

no human fossils have yet been discovered in association with this industry. The overlying layer, Tabun-C, is distinguished by more ovate Levallois flakes and a lower frequency of points. Neandertal remains associated with this industry, which date to about 130,000–85,000 years ago, include a nearly complete adult female skeleton (Tabun-C I), a virtually complete adult mandible (Tabun-C II), and some isolated postcranial pieces (the hominids from Qafzeh and Skhul are also associated with this tool industry). An adult femoral shaft and lower molar were also recovered from

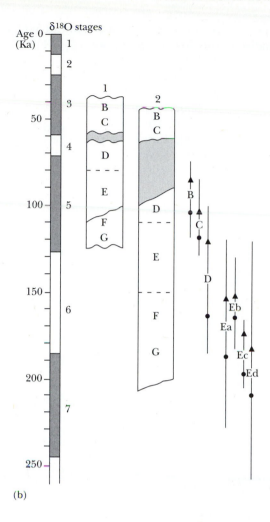

(b)

Layer E. Thus, the estimated age of the Tabun Neandertals is within oxygen isotope stage 5 (see Fig. 1.4b), close to the dates obtained for the more modern-looking hominids from Skhul and Qafzeh. Layer Tabun-B is recognized by the predominance of long, narrow flakes and short, broad-based Levallois points and lasts from about 100,000 to 46,000 years ago. This tool tradition is known from several other sites, including Kebara and Amud, that also yield Neandertallike hominids (99).

Since the stone-tool industries at Tabun seem to show certain progressive changes through time (particularly in the ratio of width to thickness of unretouched flakes), these tool types have been used as a sort of master chronology for correlation of other Near Eastern sites. For example, Tabun-B type Mousterian industries are found in the hominid-bearing layers of Kebara and possibly Skhul, while Tabun-C is found at Qafzeh. ESR dates confirm the relative chronology of these tool types (111):

Tabun E:	154,000±34,000
Tabun D:	122,000±20,000
Tabun C:	102,000±17,000
Tabun B:	86,000±11,000
Qafzeh:	100,000±10,000
Skhul:	81,000±15,000
	46,000±5,000
	93,000±6,000

Qafzeh and Kebara

The site at Qafzeh preserves at least three burials of anatomically modern humans: 1) an adult lying on its right side with knees partially drawn up; 2) a double burial consisting of a young woman lying on her right side with a small child at her feet; and 3) a young boy with deer antlers placed over his hands (Fig. 10.19). Also present are the perforated shells of *Glycymeris*, which were apparently designed for use as amulets or necklaces. As noted earlier, both TL and ESR dates suggest an age for the Qafzeh hominids of about 90,000–100,000 years (98,102)

The Kebara Cave is located on the western side of Mount Carmel. Ar-

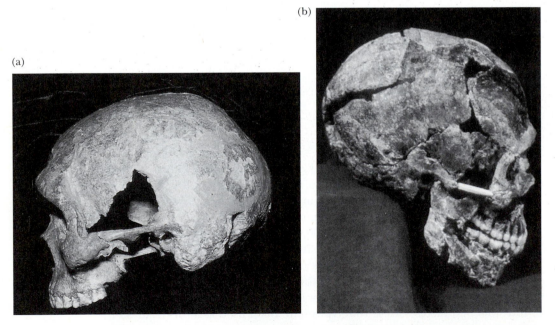

(b)

(a)

Fig. 10.19. The crania of Jebel Qafzeh 6 (a) and 9 (b). (Photos courtesy F. Smith [Qafzeh 6] and E. Delson and Israel Antiquities Authority [Qafzeh 9].)

tifacts from the site resemble those from Tabun-B. Both TL and ESR dating techniques give an age of approximately 60,000 years for the site (97,112). In 1983 an adult male skeleton was recovered from a dug-out grave pit. The skull appears to have been removed from the body after the flesh had decayed, perhaps many months after the individual had died. It is hard to imagine what (religious?) motive might have inspired such an act. Below the well-preserved lower jaw was an intact hyoid bone, the small bone that anchors some of the tongue muscles. The bone is identical in size and shape to the same bone in modern humans and suggests to some that the morphological basis for human speech was fully developed in the Near East by the Middle Paleolithic (74,76,77,113).[13]

All twenty-four of the presacral vertebrae, the 7 cervical, 12 thoracic, and 5 lumbar, are preserved in the Kebara skeleton. These vertebrae are morphologically similar to, and within the size range of, modern human populations. As seen in other Neandertal individuals, the spinous processes of the sixth and seventh cervical (neck) vertebrae are more horizontal than in modern populations. In addition, the cervical segment of the Kebara individual is short relative to thoracic and lumber vertebral lengths, although the functional significance of this feature is unclear.

The pelvis is the most complete of any Neandertal discovered to date and is characterized by an elongated ilio-pubic ramus, a morphology not usually seen in modern humans (see Fig. 10.9). The pelvic inlet is modern in size but the pelvic outlet is confined relative to modern females (114). This supports the view that Neandertals did not have elongated gestation periods or bigger neonates necessitating enlarged pelvic diameters, as had been recently hypothesized (115,116). This peculiar pelvic morphology is restricted to other Neandertal specimens, such as those from Europe and at Shanidar, and does not characterize the more "modern" specimens from Skhul and Qafzeh (75,115–117).

Shanidar

Probably the most informative sample of Near Eastern Neandertal remains comes from the Shanidar Cave in the Zagros Mountains of Iraq, excavated by Ralph Solecki between 1951 and 1960 (Fig. 10.20). This is the largest sample of Neandertal partial skeletons and consists of the remains of seven adults (Shanidar 1–6, 8) and two infants (Shanidar 7, 9) associated with a Mousterian industry. Two radiocarbon dates on charcoal associated with Shanidar crania 1 and 5 range from 50,000 to 45,000 years ago, and the Shanidar 2 cranium may be closer to 60,000 years old. An important lesson to be learned from this sample is how variable Neandertal morphology can be. For example, the Shanidar 1 cranium has the highest cranial vault of any Neandertal, whereas the Shanidar 5 cranium has one of the lowest.

---

[13]For a different viewpoint see (73).

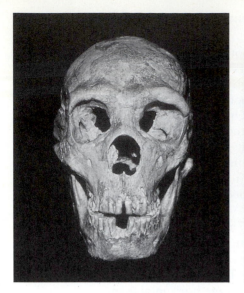
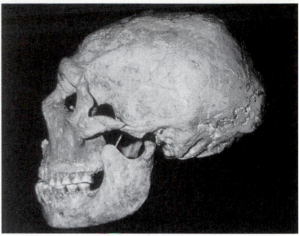

Fig. 10.20. The cranium of Shanidar 1. (Photos courtesy of E. Trinkaus.)

Similarly, Shanidar 5 displays the "typical" Neandertal condition of inflated maxilla containing large air sinuses, whereas Shanidar 1, 2, and 4 have relatively flat maxillae. The Shanidar mandibles are typically Neandertal in morphology in that they posses an anteriorly placed dental arcade to match the corresponding facial projection, mental foramina located posteriorly below the first molar, and large retromolar spaces behind the third molars (66,71,118–120).

There is an extremely high incidence of antemortem trauma in the Shanidar sample (55,70). Of the six reasonably complete adults, four show evidence of past injury and two of them (Shanidar 1 and 3) must have been at least partially incapacitated. Shanidar 1 had injuries to the right side of the head, the right humerus, and the right fifth metatarsal as well as an atrophy of the right clavicle, scapula, and humerus, osteomyelitis of the right clavicle, degenerative joint disease of the right knee, ankle, and first tarsometatarsal joint, and injuries to the left tibia. Shanidar 3 had trauma-induced injuries to the right ankle joint and a penetrating wound in the right side of the rib cage. Shanidar 4 suffered a fracture of the right rib cage, and Shanidar 5 had a scalp wound over the left frontal. The importance of these facts, besides verifying that Neandertal habitats were just as violent as modern urban America seems to be, is that Neandertals had already evolved social mechanisms to care for such disabled members of their group, since many of these injured individuals show evidence of wound healing and apparently lived to old age.[14]

[14]Neandertals clearly had a tough time of it. Trauma has been reported in the original Neandertal specimen (fractured ulna), La Chapelle-aux-Saints 1 (broken rib), La Ferrassie 1 (injury to the right proximal femur), Krapina 180 (nonunion fracture of the ulna), La Quina 5 (injury producing some atrophy of the left humerus), Sala 1 (injury to the right supraorbital torus) (55,70).

Zuttiyeh

The oldest reasonably complete hominid specimen from the Near East is the frontal/facial fragment from Zuttiyeh, Israel. The specimen is associated with the Acheulo-Yabrudian tradition and is estimated to be between 250,000 and 350,000 years old. As the oldest specimen from the region, it assumes great importance in the debate surrounding the Multiregional Continuity and Out of Africa Models of modern human origins. Phylogenetic inferences drawn from the Zuttiyeh specimen have been diverse: some have regarded it as an ancestral Neandertal; others as being uniquely ancestral to "modern" hominids in the Levant and not ancestral to Levant Neandertals; and still others as a more generalized ancestor of all more recent West Asian hominids (121). Most recently, some proponents of the Multiregional Continuity Model have suggested that Zuttiyeh shares significant morphological features with East Asian Middle Pleistocene hominids found in Zhoukoudian, Gongwangling, or Hexian, most of which do not characterize Middle Pleistocene hominids from either Europe or Africa; if true, this would seriously undermine the Out of Africa Model (122).

As we have seen, the Out of Africa Model contends that Middle and/or early Upper Pleistocene Africans are uniquely ancestral to all modern humans. Therefore, it should follow that the earliest Levantine hominids ancestral to the Skhul/Qafzeh "moderns" at Zuttiyeh, for example, should be more morphologically similar to Middle and/or early Upper Pleistocene Africans than to similarly aged hominids from any other geographical region. However, if the above-mentioned analysis of Zuttiyeh is correct, then the East Asian features found not only in Zuttiyeh, but also those from Tabun and Qafzeh, falsify one of the expectations of the Out of Africa Model and support a model of local morphological continuity in the Levant. The Multiregional Continuity Model proponents conclude their study with the following contentions: 1) the "Neandertal" and "non-Neandertal" populations of the Levant are only racially distinct and cannot be differentiated at the species level; 2) the significant levels of East Asian ancestry in the Levant populations (Neandertal, non-Neandertal, or both) demonstrates that "no known African population can be the unique ancestor of all modern populations" (122).

SUMMING UP THE NEAR EAST RECORD

As we have noted above, archeological evidence indicates that the transition from Middle to Upper Paleolithic industries in the Levant occurred about 40,000 years ago and is marked by less reliance on flat unipolar and bipolar Levallois core reduction techniques and increasing use of prismatic cores, ultimately leading to such blade-and-bladelet-dominated industries as the **Ahmarian**. The Upper Paleolithic cultures mainly differ from underlying Middle Paleolithic cultures in their greater production of bone and antler objects, greater use of worked marine shells (possibly for body decorations), production of art objects, more frequent use of red ochre, use of grinding tools, and the practice of encircling hearths with stones and using rocks for reflecting warmth (99).

Before the revised radiometric dates became available for the Near East, anthropologists had thought that the apparent morphological resemblances between early modern humans in Europe (for example, Cro-Magnons) and those from the Near East (Qafzeh and Skhul) reflected a close temporal relationship as well. It was also thought that the Near Eastern ''Neandertals'' from Tabun, Amud, Zuttiyeh, and Kebara were only about 50,000 years old, whereas the earliest anatomically modern humans from Qafzeh and Skhul were younger, perhaps less than 40,000 years old (41,97,98,123). This was used as evidence that the earlier Neandertallike hominids of the area gradually evolved into the more modernlike populations. This view is now no longer tenable, at least as far as the Near East is concerned, because recent TL, ESR, and U-S age determinations show that the Qafzeh hominids date to the earlier part of the late Pleistocene, probably more than 90,000 years ago, and that at least some of the Skhul hominids may date to about 80,000 years ago (98,100,102,104). Conversely, some Neandertallike hominids (Kebara, Amud, Tabun) are associated with the Tabun-B industry dated to between 100,000–46,000 years ago. Thus, some of the more anatomically modern humans, like those from Qafzeh, actually predate some of the Neandertals such as those from Kebara by tens of thousands of years! In fact, new dates from other sites, such as Tabun, now seem to indicate that anatomically modern humans coexisted with Neandertals in the Near East for over 50,000 years. These findings refute not only the view that Neandertals gradually evolved in situ into modern *H. sapiens* in the Near East, but also the notion that the appearance of modern *H. sapiens* coincided with the technological revolution of the Upper Paleolithic, since the cultural traditions of both hominid groups were indistinguishable variants of the Mousterian (77).

Did these Middle Paleolithic Neandertals and early anatomically modern humans from western Asia engage in symbolic behavior? The clear signs of deliberate burials at Qafzeh, Skhul, Amud, Kebara, Dederiyeh, and Shanidar as well as the use of marine shells and red ochre for body decorations at Skhul and Qafzeh strongly suggest that they did (124,125).

Fossil evidence of human populations morphologically and archeologically similar to the Levant sites occurs sporadically throughout adjacent regions, attesting to the fact that these populations were widespread. For example, sites in the Crimea, Kiik-Koba and Tartar provide evidence of human populations associated with Mousterian industries. The Kiik-Koba evidence consists of hand, leg, and foot bones associated with a Mousterian

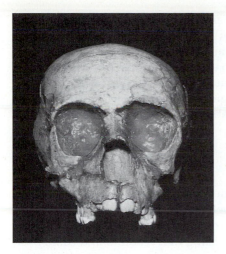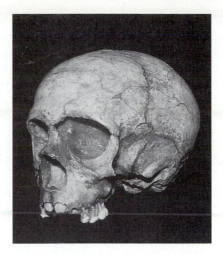

Fig. 10.21.   Frontal and oblique views of the Neandertal child's skull, La Quina 18. (Photos courtesy of F. Smith.)

industry of sidescrapers and small handaxes. The skeletal elements are said to resemble similar bones from Krapina and Tabun. Similarly, the ritually buried child's skeleton from Teshik-Tash in Uzbekistan also differs from that of classic Neandertal children such as that of La Quina (41) (Fig. 10.21).

FOSSIL EVIDENCE FROM AUSTRALASIA

Franz Weidenreich first explored the possibility of regional continuity between Far Eastern *H. erectus* populations and modern Australasian populations over a half century ago, and paleoanthropologists have been arguing the case for and against this concept ever since (126,127). Weidenreich envisioned an "Australoid" lineage passing from Indonesian *H. erectus* to Australian aborigines via intermediaries like Ngandong (Solo) and Wajak. He didn't mince words when he noted (127):

> . . . the ancient Javanese forms, *Pithecanthropus* and *Homo soloensis*, agree in typical but minor details with certain fossil and recent Australian types of today so perfectly that they give evidence of a continuous line of evolution leading from the mysterious Java forms to the modern Australian bushman.

Likewise, he envisioned a "Mongoloid" lineage passing from Chinese *H. erectus* via such "intermediaries" as Dali, Maba, Zhoukoudian Upper Cave, and Liujiang to modern "Mongoloid" populations of East Asia.

If such regional continuity can be proven beyond a reasonable doubt (or what passes for "reasonable doubt" in paleoanthropological circles), then the implications are obvious—anatomically modern Australasians evolved in situ and did not migrate into the region from other geographical areas, as the Out of Africa Model contends. We will shortly examine the arguments, both pro and con, for regional continuity in Australasia, but first we must briefly survey the available fossil evidence bearing on the question.

East Asia

The first appearance of anatomically modern *H. sapiens* in east Asia continues to be problematic. The earliest well-preserved hominids from China that unequivocally exhibit anatomically modern morphology is the Liujiang material. The Liujiang specimens, consisting of a cranium and some postcranial material, were found in association with a characteristic giant panda–primitive elephant (*Ailuropoda-Stegodon*) fauna usually interpreted as being from the Middle Pleistocene. However (as is usual with the Chinese material), the contemporaneity of the hominids and the fauna has not been definitely established. More recently, U-S dates of about 227,000–67,000 years ago have been reported for this site, but again, the stratigraphic relationship between the dated stalactite layers and the hominids cannot be confirmed (128). If the radiometric dating can be believed, it would imply that anatomically modern humans in China were as old, or older than, anatomically modern humans from anywhere else in the Old World (129).

It has been claimed that the Liujiang cranium has many traits that can be traced back to both Chinese *H. erectus* and archaic *H. sapiens,* such as rectangular orbits, frontal bossing, a flat midface with a distinct incisura malaris, a relatively short maxilla, and no lateral alveolar prognathism. As might be expected, the presence of these archaic traits in an otherwise anatomically modern sample has been seized upon by supporters of the Multiregional Continuity Model.

Another important early modern hominid sample from China comes from Zhoukoudian Upper Cave. A series of radiocarbon dates from Zhoukoudian gives ages of about 10,000–18,000 years for the Upper Cave levels. More recent dates, again on nonhuman bone, range from 33,000–13,000 years ago with a suggested age of 24,000–29,000 years for the archeological occurrences. Again however, the stratigraphic relationship between the human burials and the dated faunal material is insecure.

Hominid material from East Asia that may be of early modern *H. sapiens* include the skull from Niah Cave, Borneo; Wajak 1 and II from Java; and Tabon from the Philippines. The fragmentary skull from Niah has been radiocarbon dated on the basis of charcoal possibly associated with the cranium to about 40,000 years ago. The reconstructed cranium is characterized by thin cranial vault walls, a relatively steep supraglabellar region behind which the frontal gently recedes, slightly developed supraorbitals, squarish orbits, prominent parietal bosses, a rounded occipital, and well-marked temporal lines. The face is short, broad, and prognathic with a moderately developed canine fossa. Many of these features are commonly found on Australian aboriginal crania.

The Wajak crania are undated, but are considered Late Pleistocene solely on the basis of perceived morphological similarity with prehistoric Australian aboriginal crania (which is incompatible with faunal analyses that suggest Wajak is essentially recent in age). The Wajak 1 cranium is similar to the Australian cranium from Keilor (see below) in terms of size, proportions, and facial flatness and has been used as evidence documenting regional continuity of fossils from East Asia and Australia (Fig. 10.22).

The Tabon sample consists of the remains of at least five individuals and includes cranial, mandibular, and postcranial elements radiocarbon dated to about 23,000 years ago. The frontal bone is quite gracile and thin, with little postorbital constriction, a relatively steep supraglabellar region, and a gently receding frontal profile. The supraorbitals are only moderately developed and the glabella region is prominent. One mandible shows slight chin development and congenital absence of the third molar. Some features of the mandible, like the three-rooted molars and agenesis of the third molar, suggest "Mongoloid" affinities.

Far East Paleolithic sites older than about 20,000 years are summarized in Figure 7.12. One interesting sidelight to these dates is that if they are anywhere near correct, then *H. erectus* and *H. sapiens* coexisted in China over a substantial period of time (for example, the presence of *H. erectus* at Hexian and *H. sapiens* at Chaohu) (130).

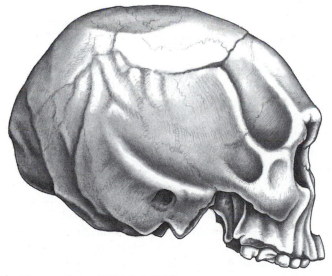

Fig. 10.22.   The cranium of Wajak 1 (142).

Australia

The earliest widely accepted evidence for human occupation of Greater Australia is a radiocarbon date of about 39,000 years ago for charcoal associated with stone tools from western Australia. However, on the basis of TL dates from Malakunanja II rockshelter, some paleoanthropologists argue that human occupation of Australia may actually predate 50,000 years (131) and U-S dates suggest human occupation of Papua New Guinea some 40,000 years ago (132). The oldest dated skeletal remains are the Lake Mungo 1 cremation dated to about 24,700 years ago. It has been argued on geological grounds that the extended burial Lake Mungo 3 may be on the order of 30,000 years. Others have suggested, solely on morphological grounds, that the undated Willandra Lakes specimens (WLH-50) are considerably older than Lake Mungo 1. Kow Swamp is bracketed by radiocarbon dates on shell to about 13,000–9,500 years ago, and the hominids from Coobool Creek, Nacurrie 1, and Keilor all appear to be of a similar age (133).

Cranial material from the terminal Pleistocene of Australia, found in Coobool Creek, Nacurrie, Keilor, Cohuna, Lake Mungo, Kow Swamp, and Tandou, are highly variable but are much larger overall than recent crania from the same region (Fig. 10.23). These crania are dominated by the functional requirements of a large dentition. By the Holocene, a reduction in tooth size and associated alveolar region has resulted in significantly shorter and less prognathic faces.

Because of the great deal of variability in the early hominid sample from Australia, some Australian paleoanthropologists have argued that Australia was populated by two hominid groups, each with a distinct evolutionary origin, that coexisted for long periods of time in the late Pleistocene (134). According to this theory, one group is represented by the robust Talgai, Cohuna, and Kow Swamp specimens that are seen as being derived from Indonesian *H. erectus* through such intermediaries as Ngandong. The second group is represented by the more gracile Mungo and Keilor fossils that are seen as being derived from the Chinese *H. erectus* populations. However, it should be noted that multivariate tests have demonstrated that these so-called "robust" and "gracile" groups are more similar to one another than they are to hominids from any other geographical area (135).

Let us now go back and analyze the fossil data as they pertain to the Multiregional Continuity Model. The crux of the matter is this: if the Multiregional Continuity Model is true, then there must be a number of identifiable and unique "regional features" characterizing both early hominids from Australasia (*H. erectus* or archaic *H. sapiens*) and the later modern sample (prehistoric and modern Australian aborigines). If such regional features cannot be demonstrated to be truly unique to the Australasian sample, i.e., if they can be found in early hominids from other geographical regions, then they cannot be used to support regional continuity.

Weidenreich (127) was one of the first to offer such a list of "regional

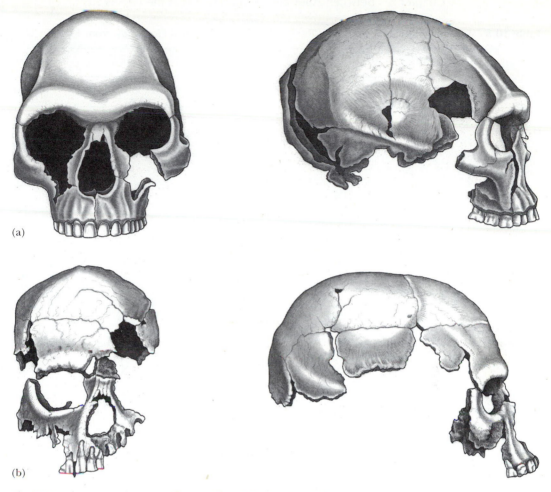

Fig. 10.23. Crania of (a) Kow Swamp 1 and (b) Tandou (142).

features'' linking Indonesian early hominids, specifically Ngandong (Solo) crania, to Australian aborigines:
- well-developed superciliary ridges
- a flat, receding forehead
- a prelambdoid depression
- a sharply angled occipital bone with a toruslike demarcation line between the occiput and the nuchal plane
- a short sphenoparietal articulation in the region where the frontal, temporal, parietal, and sphenoid bones meet on the side of the cranial vault, a region known as pterion
- a deep and narrow infraglabellar notch

Weidenreich's list of ''regional features'' was later expanded to twelve and includes a number of other features linking Indonesian *H. erectus* (based mainly on a reconstruction of Sangiran 17) to Australian hominids (136):

Table 10.3   The Occurrence of Proposed "Regional Features" in Fossil Hominids (from 135)

	Features											
	1	2	3	4	5	6	7	8	9	10	11	12
H. erectus												
KNM-ER 3733	−	−	−	−?	X	X	−	−	−	X	?	?
KNM-ER 3883	X	−	−	−	X	?	−	−?	−	?	?	
Olduvai H9	X	−	X	?	X	?	?	?	?	?	?	?
Sangiran 17	X	X	X	X/−	X	X	X/−	X	X/−	X	?	X
Solo 12	X	X	X	X	X	?	?	?	?	?	?	?
Zhoukoudian reconstruction	X/−	−	−	−	X	X	−	−	X	X	−	X
Australian												
WLH50	X	X	X	−	X	?	X	X	X	?	?	?
Kow Swamp 1	X	X	X	−	X	X	X	X	X	X	X	X
Kow Swamp 5	X	X	X	?	X	X	X	X	X	X	?	X
Kow Swamp 15	−	X?	X	?	?	X	X	X	X	X	X?	X
Cohuna	X	X	X	X	X	X	X	X	X	X	X	X
Talgai	X	X?	X?	?	X	X	?	X?	X?	X	X?	X
Cossack	X	X	?	?	X	X	X	?	?	?	X	X
Mossgiel	X	X	X	−	X	X?	X	X	X	?	X?	X
Lake Nitchie	−	−	X	−	X	X	X	X	X	X	X	X
Keilor	−	−	X	−	X	X	X?	X	X	X	?	X
Lake Mungo 1	−	−	X	−	−?	?	−	?	?	?	?	?
Lake Mungo 3	−	−	X	−	X	?	?	?	?	?	?	?
Lake Tandou	−	−	X	−	X?	X	X?	X	X	?	X	X
Southeast Asia												
Niah	−	?	?	−	?	X	−	−	X	X	?	?
Wajak 1	−	−	X?	−	X	X	−	−	X	X	?	?
Wajak 2	?	?	X?	?	?	?	?	?	?	X	−	X
East Asia												
Maba	−	−	−	?	?	?	?	?	?	?	?	?
Liujiang	−	−	X?	−	−	X	−?	−	X	X	−	X
Upper Cave 101	−	−	X	−	X	X	−?	−	X	X	−	−
Upper Cave 102	X	−	X?	X	X	X	−?	−	X	X	?	?
Upper Cave 103	−	−	X	−	X	X	−?	X	X	X	?	?

(Continued)

1. flatness of the frontal bone in the sagittal plane
2. posterior position of the minimum frontal breadth well behind the orbits
3. a relatively horizontal orientation of the inferior supraorbital border
4. presence of a distinct prebregmatic eminence (bregma being the ectocranial point where the coronal and sagittal sutures intersect)
5. a low position of maximum parietal breadth
6. marked facial prognathism
7. presence of a malar tuberosity
8. eversion of the lower border of the malar

	Features											
	1	2	3	4	5	6	7	8	9	10	11	12
Sub-Saharan Africa												
Bodo I	−?	−	X	?	?	X	−	X	X	X?	?	?
Ndutu	?	−	−	?	X	X	?	−	?	?	?	?
Kabwe 1	X	−	X	−	X	X	X	−	X	X	X	X
Laetoli H18	X	−	X	−	X	X	?	?	?	X	?	?
Omo 1	−	−	?	−	?	?	−?	?	X	?	?	?
Border Cave 1	−	−	−	−	?	?	X?	?	X	?	?	?
Florisbad	−	−	−	−	?	?	−?	?	X	−	?	?
North Africa and Western Asia												
Jebel Irhoud 1	−	−	−?	−	X	X	−	−	X	X	?	?
Wadi Halfa Sample	X/−	−	−	−	X/−	X	X	X	X?	?	−	X
Zuttiyeh	−	−	−	−	?	?	−?	−	−	?	?	?
Skhul 4	−	−	?	?	X	X	−	−	X	X	−	X
Skhul 5	−	−	X	−	−	X	−	−	X?	?	−	X
Jebel Qafzeh 9	−	−	X	?	−	X	−?	−	X	X	−	X
Amud 1	X	−	−	−	−	X	−?	−	−	−?	−	X
Europe												
Petralona	X	−	X	−	X	X	−?	−	X	−	−	X
Arago 21	X	X	−	−	X	X	−	−	X	−	−	X
Steinheim	X	−	−	−	X	X	−	−	X	?	−?	X
La Ferrassie 1	X	−	−	−	−	X	−	−	X	−	−	X
Cro-Magnon 1	−	−	X	−	−	−	?	−	X	?	?	?
Oberkassel 1	−	−	X	−	−	−	X	X	X	?	−	?
Oberkassel 2	−	−	X	−	−	−	−	−	−	?	−	X
Dolni Vestoniče 3	−	−	X	−	−	−	−	−	−	?	X?	X
Předmosti 3	−	−	−	−	−	−	−	−	−	−	−	X
Předmosti 4	−	−	−	−	−	−	−	−	−	−	−	X
Mladeč 1	−	−	−	−	−	−	−	−	−	−	?	?

The numbering of the features follows the text. 'X' = present; '−' = absent; '?' = questionable identification or area not preserved.

9. rounding of the inferolateral border of the orbit
10. the lower border of the nasal aperture lacks a distinct line dividing the nasal floor from the subnasal face of the maxillae
11. marked expression of curvature of the posterior alveolar plane of the maxillae
12. the degree of facial and dental (especially posterior) reduction

However, several paleoanthropologists have argued that many of these same so-called Australasian "regional features" are actually primitive retentions found in many *H. erectus* and archaic *H. sapiens* crania from other parts of the Old World and thus are not indicative of any special cladistic relationship between Indonesian *H. erectus* and modern Australians (135,137,138) As Table 10.3 indicates, if these twelve features are considered individually, then they clearly do not define an Indonesian-Australian clade. However, what if they are considered in combination? That is to say, can the combination of these Australasian features be matched in single specimens outside of Australasia? The answer is, apparently, no. Thus, while it is possible that the presence of a certain *combination* of the above listed traits may support a regional continuity model, the individual traits cannot.

However, two nagging questions further confuse the issue: 1) if "regional continuity" is true, then why do some of the earliest anatomically modern hominids from the region, like Willandra Lakes Hominid (WLH 50), share these "regional features" with earlier Indonesian hominids, whereas others (Lake Mungo 1 and 3, Niah Cave) do not, either individually or in combination? and 2) if the "rapid replacement" model is true, why is there no evidence of an influx of new archeological assemblages into Australia during the late Upper Pleistocene?

Recently, several more rigorous tests of the Multiregional Continuity and the Out of Africa Models have been presented based on the fossil evidence—but unfortunately they come to different conclusions. The first compares several nonmetric features of six *H. erectus* mandibles from Sangiran and Java to modern mandibles from East African and Australian hunter-gatherer populations (139). The Out of Africa Model would predict that the Sangiran mandibles would not display any particular morphological continuity with the modern Australian sample and that the two modern human samples should share more features than either would with the million-year-old *H. erectus* specimens from Indonesia. The Multiregional Continuity Model would predict that the Indonesian *H. erectus* sample should share more features with the modern Australian sample than with the modern African sample. The results of the study favor the Multiregional Continuity Model of regional evolution of *H. erectus* into modern humans in southeast Asia and Australia. Of the seventeen features analyzed, eight supported a grouping of Sangiran and the Australian aborigines to the exclusion of the modern Africans (Kenyans in this case).

The second rigorous morphological test of the Multiregional Model has come to just the opposite conclusion (138)! More specifically, this study addressed two particular hypotheses that should follow from the Multiregional Model: 1) that certain cranial traits should occur exclusively or with a higher incidence in Australia and East Asia, reflecting morphological continuity from *H. erectus* populations in these regions; and 2) that modern *H. sapiens* fossils in each area of the world should strongly resemble modern inhabitants of those same regions. This study rejected those two hypotheses by concluding that: 1) many of the regional features claimed by the Multiregional Model to characterize the East Asian and Australasian evolutionary lines are not exclusive to these regions, with some even occurring at higher frequencies in other populations; 2) some cranial features are clearly related to overall robusticity and related functional demands, and may therefore be of less phylogenetic value; and 3) the differences between some fossil and recent African specimens argue against the maintenance of morphological regional patterns through time, and suggest instead high levels of population differentiation.

The third fossil study employed a sophisticated quantitative test, called matrix correlation, to the question of modern human origins (140). A sample of eighty-three Middle to Late Pleistocene hominid crania were divided into twelve operational taxonomic units (OTUs) based on geographical location and chronological age. Morphological distances were calculated between each pair of samples based on seventy-four metric traits including cranial lengths and breadths, fifty-two discrete traits (defined as present or absent), and thirty-nine angles and indices; these values were then arranged in a morphological distance correlation matrix. When this morphological distance matrix was correlated to design matrices representing both the Out of Africa and the Multiregional Continuity models of modern human origins, it was found that the Out of Africa Model provided a better explanation for cranial variation and refuted the notion of evolutionary continuity in Europe and for the Neandertals of Southwest Asia.

As mentioned earlier, Weidenreich (126) also argued for regional continuity in the Chinese hominid fossil record. Again, his (and others') arguments rest mainly on the identification of what are considered to be "Mongoloid" skeletal features in the Zhoukoudian *H. erectus* sample and in modern northern Chinese:
• midsagittal "crest" and parasagittal depression
• high frequency of metopic sutures
• high frequency of accessory bones that form within the cranial sutures, known as Inca bones
• "Mongoloid" features of the cheek region (i.e., facial flatness)
• mandibular, ear, and maxillary exostoses
• femoral platymeria
• strong deltoid tuberosity of the humerus
• shovel-shaped incisors
• a horizontal course of the nasofrontal and frontomaxillary sutures
• rounded profile of nasal saddle and nasal roof
• rounded infraorbital margin
• reduced posterior teeth
• high frequency of third molar agenesis
• small frontal sinuses

However, in a recent exhaustive survey of the morphological evidence relating to these features, Colin Groves (137) of the Australian National University has questioned the evidence for special likeness of modern "Mongoloids" to Chinese *H. erectus*. Any correlation can be explained by a similarity of Zhoukoudian *H. erectus* to some modern "Mongoloid" populations, but not to others, and perhaps, even in these cases, by retention in some "Mongoloid" groups of primitive character states.

In the final analysis, we must not lose sight of the fact that the great number of facial features clearly distinguishing most fossil Asian hominids from their European and African counterparts cannot simply be wished away. All these features are still found today in higher frequencies among extant ''Mongoloid'' populations than among extant African and/or Eurasian populations. Both European and Australasian samples diverge from the conditions seen in specimens of early hominids from Africa and many of the morphological traits previously restricted only to fossil Asians now occur in all populations of modern humans (however, their frequency remains higher in populations deriving from or occupying the Far East). This worldwide dissemination of morphological traits that first appeared in the Asian fossil record strongly implies that at least some of the facial traits associated with the emergence of modern humans could not have resulted from a single African origin, as extreme versions of the Out of Africa Model propose, but rather from admixture and gene flow between different regions of the Old World (141).

Epilogue

Eventually all things merge into one, and a river runs through it. The river was cut by the world's great flood and runs over rocks from the basement of time. On some of the rocks are timeless raindrops. Under the rocks are the words, and some of the words are theirs. I am haunted by waters.

Norman Maclean
A River Runs through It and Other Stories (1976)

Norman Maclean was haunted by waters; I am haunted by time—time that ranges from the very short durations of unstable elementary particles to the universe's life span of several billion years. This vast range of time is incomprehensible in terms of our everyday experience. Even the limited time span of human evolution reviewed in the previous chapters needs to be expressed on some reduced scale that we can relate to. In order to visualize such a reduced time axis, the Japanese physicist Akiyoshi Wada devised a simple slide rule in time dimensions (1) (see Fig. E.1). The slide rule consists of a main time rule (on the left) that carries a logarithmic time scale on which various historical events are noted and a reference time rule (on the right). Like any slide rule, the left and right sides of the ruler can slide with respect to one another. This so-called Wadaruler is easy to use. Simply photocopy the figure, separate the main rule (left) from the reference rule (right), and mount each part on a stiff card in such a way as to be able to slide the latter against the former. For example, the figure shows an example of time reduction in which the age of the universe ("Big Bang") on the main time rule is set equal to the appearance of Egyptian civilization about 4,000 years ago on the reference time rule. On this scale, australopithecines and early *Homo* first appeared about a year ago and Isaac Newton's *Principia* and the Declaration of Independence were written less than an hour ago. Similarly, if we slide the rule so that the age of the universe is set to 1 year, we would find that Egyptian civilization began less

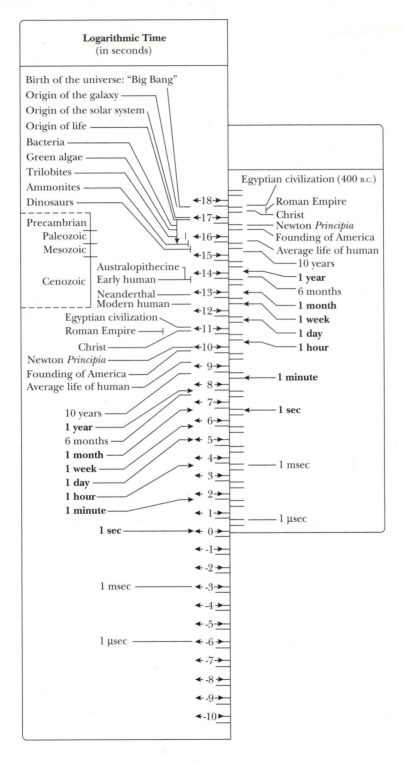

than a minute ago and that Newton's *Principia* and the Declaration of Independence were written less than a second ago.

As we contemplate time—5 million years of human history to be exact—is there any single conclusion to be drawn? Yes, that in both a geological instant and in a restricted Darwinian sense, humankind has been successful, perhaps too much so. As the writer John McPhee expressed it (2):

> For establishing our bearings through time, we obviously owe an incalculable debt to vanished and endangered species. . . . The opossum may be Cretaceous, certain clams Devonian, and oysters Triassic, but for each and every oyster in the sea, it seems, there is a species gone forever. Be a possum is the message, and you may outlive God.

I sometimes imagine the sound of a shot ringing out, and turn in time to see the last elephant, black rhino, or mountain gorilla slowly sink to its knees in the red African dust. In time that will come to pass and on that day an unbearable loneliness will descend over humankind. To all creatures, still wild and free, I dedicate this book. The success of human evolution has not been kind to you.

References

PREFACE

1. Conroy, G. 1990. *Primate evolution.* New York: W. W. Norton.
2. Fields, W. 1990. *What the river knows: An angler in midstream.* New York: Poseidon.

CHAPTER I

1. Linnaeus, C. 1758. *Systema naturae per regna tria naturae, secundum classes, ordines genera, species cum characteribus, differentris, synonymis, locis.* Stockholm: Laurentii Salvii.
2. Owen, R. 1858. On the characters, principles of division, and primary groups of the class mammalia. *J. Linn. Soc. Lond. Zool.* 2:1–37.
3. McCown, T., Kennedy, K., eds. 1972. *Climbing man's family tree: A collection of major writings on human phylogeny, 1699–1971.* Englewood Cliffs, N.J.: Prentice-Hall.
4. Darwin, C. 1859. *The origin of species by means of natural selection or the preservation of favored races in the struggle for life.* London: Murray.
5. Darwin, C. 1871. *The descent of man, and selection in relation to sex.* London: Murray.
6. Mivart, S. G. 1873. On *Lepilemur* and *Cheirogaleus* and on the zoological rank of the Lemuroidea. *Proc. Zool. Soc. Lond.* 1873:484–510.
7. LeGros Clark, W. E. 1959. *The antecedents of man.* Edinburgh: Edinburgh University Press.
8. Martin, R. 1986. Primates: A definition. In *Major topics in primate and human evolution*, ed. B. Wood, L. Martin, P. Andrews, pp. 1–31. Cambridge: Cambridge University Press.
9. Pilbeam, D. 1992. What makes us human? In *The Cambridge encyclopedia of human evolution*, ed. S. Jones, R. Martin, D. Pilbeam, pp. 1–5. Cambridge: Cambridge University Press.
10. Anklin, M. et al. 1993. Climate instability during the last interglacial period recorded in the GRIP ice core. *Nature* 364:203–207.
11. Dansgaard, W., Johnsen, S. J., Clausen, H. B., Dahl-Jensen, D., Gundestrup, N. S., Hammer, C. U., Hvidberg, C. S., Steffensen, J. P., Sveinbjornsdottir, A. E., Jouzel, J., Bond, G. 1993. Evidence for general instability of past climate from a 250-kyr ice-core record. *Nature* 364:218–220.
12. Grootes, P. M., Stuiver, M., White, J. W. C., Johnsen, S., Jouzel, J. 1993. Comparison of oxygen isotope records from the GISP2 and GRIP Greenland ice cores. *Nature* 366:552–554.
13. Taylor, K., Lamorey, G., Doyle, G., Alley, R., Grootes, P., Mayewsi, P., White, J., Barlow, L. 1993. The "flickering switch" of late Pleistocene climate change. *Nature* 361:432–436.

14. Weaver, A. J., Hughes, T. M. C. 1994. Rapid interglacial climate fluctuations driven by North Atlantic Ocean circulation. *Nature* 367:447–450.

15. Field, M. H., Huntley, B., Muller, H. 1994. Eemian climate fluctuations observed in a European pollen record. *Nature* 371:779–783.

16. Kotilainen, A. T., Shackleton, N. J. 1995. Rapid climate variability in the North Pacific Ocean during the past 95,000 years. *Nature* 377:323–326.

17. Johnsen, S., Clausen, H., Dansgaard, W., Fuhrer, K., Gundestrup, N., Hammer, C., Iversen, P., Jouzel, J., Stauffer, B., Steffensen, J. 1992. Irregular glacial interstadials recorded in a new Greenland ice core. *Nature* 359:311–313.

18. Jansen, J., Kuijpers, A., Troelstra, S. 1986. A mid-Brunhes climatic event: Long-term changes in global atmosphere and ocean circulation. *Science* 232:619–622.

19. Shackleton, N. J. 1987. Oxygen isotopes, ice volume and sea level. *Q. Sci. Rev.* 6:183–190.

20. Oerlemans, J., Fortuin, J. 1992. Sensitivity of glaciers and small ice caps to greenhouse warming. *Science* 258:115–117.

21. Bard, E., Hamelin, B., Fairbanks, R. 1990. U-Th ages obtained by mass spectrometry in corals from Barbados: Sea level during the past 130,000 years. *Nature* 346:456–458.

22. Flint, R. 1971. *Glacial and quaternary geology*. New York: John Wiley.

23. Richards, D. A., Smart, P. L., Edwards, R. L. 1994. Maximum sea levels for the last glacial period from U-series ages of submerged speleothems. *Nature* 367:357–360.

24. Jasper, J., Hayes, J. 1990. A carbon isotope record of CO_2 levels during the late Quaternary. *Nature* 347:462–464.

25. Koch, P., Zachos, J., Gingerich, P. 1992. Correlation between isotope records in marine and continental carbon reservoirs near the Palaeocene/Eocene boundary. *Nature* 358:319–322.

26. Van Der Burgh, J., Visscher, H., Dilcher, D. L., Kurschner, W. M. 1993. Paleoatmospheric signatures in Neogene fossil leaves. *Science* 260:1788–1790.

27. Buchardt, B. 1978. Oxygen isotope palaeotemperatures from the Tertiary period in the North Sea area. *Nature* 275:121–123.

28. Raymo, M., Ruddiman, W. 1992. Tectonic forcing of late Cenozoic climate. *Nature* 359:117–122.

29. Zachos, J., Breza, J., Wise, S. 1992. Early Oligocene ice-sheet expansion on Antarctica: Stable isotope and sedimentological evidence from Kerguelen Plateau, southern Indian Ocean. *Geology* 20:569–573.

30. Hays, J., Imbrie, J., Shackleton, N. 1976. Variations in the Earth's orbit: Pacemaker of the ice ages. *Science* 194:1121–1132.

31. Gallup, C. D., Edwards, R. L., Johnson, R. G. 1994. The timing of high sea levels over the past 200,000 years. *Science* 263:796–800.

32. Crowley, T. J., North, G. R. 1991. *Paleoclimatology*. New York: Oxford University Press.

33. Storey, B. C. 1995. The role of mantle plumes in continental breakup: Case histories from Gondwanaland. *Nature* 377:301–308.

34. Romm, J. 1994. A new forerunner for continental drift. *Nature* 367:407–408.

35. Gartner, S., McGuirk, J. 1979. Terminal Cretaceous extinction scenario for a catastrophe. *Science* 206:1272–1276.

36. Herman, Y., Hopkins, D. 1980. Arctic oceanic climate in late Cenozoic time. *Science* 209:557–562.

37. Kennett, J. 1977. Cenozoic evolution of Antarctic glaciation, the circum-Antarctic Ocean, and their impact on global paleoceanography. *J. Geophys. Res.* 82:3843–3860.

38. Molnar, P., England, P. 1990. Late Cenozoic uplift of mountain ranges and global climate change: Chicken or egg? *Nature* 346:29–34.

39. Burbank, D. W., Derry, L. A., France-Lanord, C. 1993. Reduced Himalayan sediment production 8 myr ago despite an intensified monsoon. *Nature* 364:48–50.

40. Turner, S., Hawkesworth, C., Liu, J., Rogers, N., Kelley, S., van Calsteren, P. 1993. Timing of Tibetan uplift constrained by analysis of volcanic rocks. *Nature* 364:50–54.

41. Wang, C., Shi, Y., Zhou, W. 1982. Dynamic uplift of the Himalaya. *Nature* 298:553–556.

42. Coleman, M., Hodges, K. 1995. Evidence for Tibetan plateau uplift before 14 myr ago from a new minimum age for east-west extension. *Nature* 374:49–52.

43. Morgan, M. E., Kingston, J. D., Marino, B. D. 1994. Carbon isotopic evidence for the emergence of C4 plants in the Neogene from Pakistan and Kenya. *Nature* 367:162–165.

44. Lee-Thorp, J., van der Merwe, N., Brain, C. 1989. Isotopic evidence for dietary differences between two extinct baboon species form Swartkrans. *J. Hum. Evol.* 18:183–189.

45. Quade, J., Cerling, T., Bowman, J. 1989. Development of Asian monsoon revealed by marked ecological shift during the latest Miocene in northern Pakistan. *Nature* 342:163–166.

46. van der Merwe, N. 1982. Carbon isotopes, photosynthesis, and archaeology. *Am. Sci.* 70:596–606.

47. Prell, W., Kutzback, J. 1992. Sensitivity of the Indian monsoon to forcing parameters and implications for its evolution. *Nature* 360:647–651.

48. Meehl, G. A., Washington, W. M. 1993. South Asian summer monsoon variability in a model with doubled atmospheric carbon dioxide concentration. *Science* 260:1101–1104.

49. Combourieu-Neubout, N., Semah, F., Djubiantono, T. 1990. The Plio-Pleistocene boundary: Magnetostratigraphic and climatic information from a detailed analysis of the Vrica stratotype (Crotona, Italy). *C. R. Acad. Sci. [III]* 311:851–857.

50. Harland, W., Armstrong, R., Cox, A., Craig, L., Smith, A., Smith, D. 1990. *A geologic time scale (1989)*. Cambridge: Cambridge University Press.

51. Van Couvering, J., Kukla, G. 1988. Pleistocene. In *Encyclopedia of human evolution and prehistory*, ed. I. Tattersall, E. Delson, J. Van Couvering, pp. 459–464. New York: Garland.

52. Faure, G. 1986. *Principles of isotope geology*. New York: John Wiley.

53. Constable, C. 1992. Link between geomagnetic reversal paths and secular variation of the field over the past 5 myr. *Nature* 358:230–233.

54. Langereis, C., van Hoof, A., Rochette, P. 1992. Longitudinal confinement of geomagnetic reversal paths as a possible sedimentary artefact. *Nature* 358:226–230.

55. Jackson, A. 1992. Still poles apart on reversals? *Nature* 358:194–195.

56. Coe, R. S., Prevot, M., Camps, P. 1995. New evidence for extraordinarily rapid change of the geomagnetic field during a reversal. *Nature* 374:687–692.

57. Kappelman, J. 1993. The attraction of paleomagnetism. *Evol. Anthropol.* 2:89–99.

58. Tarling, D. 1980. The geologic evolution of South America with special reference to the last 200 million years. In *Evolutionary biology of the New World monkeys and continental drift*, ed. R. Ciochon, A. Chiarelli, pp. 1–41. New York: Plenum.

59. Baksi, A. K., Hsu, V., McWilliams, M. O., Farrar, E. 1992. 40Ar/39Ar dating of the Brunhes-Matuyama geomagnetic field reversal. *Science* 256:356–357.

60. Butzer, K. W., Isaac, G. L., eds. 1975. *After the australopithecines*. The Hague: Mouton.

61. Szabo, B., Ludwig, K. R., Muhs, D. R., Simmons, K. R. 1994. Thorium-230 ages of corals and duration of the last interglacial sea-level high stand on Oahu, Hawaii. *Science* 266:93–96.

62. Brain, C. 1981. Hominid evolution and climatic change. *S. Afr. J. Sci.* 77:104–105.

63. Brain, C. 1983. The terminal Miocene event: A critical environmental and evolutionary episode. In *SASQUA Int. Symp.*, ed. J. Vogel, pp. 491–498. Rotterdam: A. A. Balkema.

64. Deacon, H. 1983. The comparative evolution of Mediterranean-type ecosystems: A southern perspective. In *Ecological studies: Mediterranean-type ecosystems*, ed. F. J. Kruger, D. T. Mitchell, J. U. M. Jarvis, vol. 43, pp. 3–40. Berlin: Springer-Verlag.

65. Hodell, D., Elmstrom, K., Kennett, J. 1986. Latest Miocene benthic O-18 changes, global ice volume, sea level and the 'Messinian salinity crisis.' *Nature* 320:411–414.

66. Hsu, K., Montadert, L., Bernoulli, C., Cita, M., Erickson, A., Garrison, R., Kidd, R., Melieres, F., Muller, C., Wright, R. 1977. History of the Mediterranean salinity crises. *Nature* 267:399–403.

67. Sugden, D. E., Marchant, D. R., Potter, J., N., Souchez, R. A., Denton, G. H., Swisher III, C. C., Tison, J.-L. 1995. Preservation of Miocene glacier ice in East Antarctica. *Nature* 376:412–414.

68. Larsen, H. C., Saunders, A. D., Clift, P. D., Beget, J., Wei, W., Spezzaferri, S. 1994. Seven million years of glaciation in Greenland. *Science* 264:952–955.

69. Barrett, P., Adams, C., McIntosh, W., Swisher III, C., Wilson, G. 1992. Geochronological evidence supporting Antarctic deglaciation three million years ago. *Nature* 359:816–818.

70. Dowsett, J., Cronin, T., Poore, R., Thompson, R., Whatley, R., Wood, A. 1992. Micropaleontological evidence for increased meridional heat transport in the North Atlantic Ocean during the Pliocene. *Science* 258:1133–1135.

71. Marchant, D. R., Swisher, C. C., Lux, D. R., West, D. P., Denton, G. H. 1993. Pliocene paleoclimate and east Antarctic ice-sheet history from surficial ash deposits. *Science* 260:667–670.

72. Shackleton, N., Backman, J., Zimmerman, H., Kent, D., Hall, M., Roberts, D., Schnitker, D., Baldauf, J., Desprairies, A., Homrighausen, R., Huddlestun, P., Keene, J., Kaltenback, A., Krumsieck, K., Morton, A., Murray, J., Westberg-Smith, J. 1984. Oxygen isotope calibration of the onset of ice-rafting and history of glaciation in the North Atlantic region. *Nature* 307:620–623.

73. Prentice, M., Denton, G. 1988. The deep-sea oxygen isotope record, the global ice sheet system and hominid evolution. In *Evolutionary history of the "robust" australopithecines*, ed. F. E. Grine, pp. 383–403. New York: Aldine de Gruyter.

74. Brooks, A. 1988. Paleolithic. In *Encyclopedia of human evolution and prehistory*, ed. I. Tattersall, E. Delson, J. A. Van Couvering, pp. 415–419. New York: Garland.

75. Oakley, K. 1958. Use of fire by Neandertal man and his precursors. In *Hundert Jahre Neanderthaler*, ed. G. H. R. Von Koenigswald, pp. 267–269. Utrecht: Kemink en Zoon, N.V.

76. Brooks, A. 1988. Middle Paleolithic. In *Encyclopedia of human evolution and prehistory*, ed. I. Tattersall, E. Delson, J. A. Van Couvering, pp. 341–346. New York: Garland.

77. Klein, R. 1992. The archeology of modern human origins. *Evol. Anthropol.* 1:5–14.

78. Brose, D., Wolpoff, M. 1971. Early Upper Paleolithic man and late Middle Paleolithic tools. *Am. Anthropol.* 73:1156–1194.

79. Straus, L. 1995. The Upper Paleolithic of Europe: An overview. *Evol. Anthropol.* 4:4–16.

80. Straus, L. G. 1994. Upper Paleolithic origins and radiocarbon calibration: More evidence from Spain. *Evol. Anthropol.* 2:195–198.

81. Brooks, A. S. et al. 1995. Dating and context of three middle stone age sites with bone points in the Upper Semliki Valley, Zaire. *Science* 268:548–553.

82. Yellen, J. E., Brooks, A. S., Cornelissen, E., Mehlman, M. J., Stewart, K. 1995. A middle stone age worked bone industry from Katanda, upper Semliki Valley, Zaire. *Science* 268:553–556.

83. Binford, L. 1989. Isolating the transition to cultural adaptations: An organizational approach. In *The emergence of modern humans*, ed. E. Trinkaus, pp. 18–41. Cambridge: Cambridge University Press.

84. Soffer-Bobyshev, O. 1988. Late Paleolithic. In *Encyclopedia of human evolution and prehistory*, ed. I. Tattersall, E. Delson, J. A. Van Couvering, pp. 304–309. New York: Garland.

85. Oliva, M. 1988. Discovery of a Gravettian mammoth bone hut at Milovice (Moravia, Czechoslovakia). *J. Hum. Evol.* 17:787–790.

86. Klein, R. 1979. Stone age exploitation of animals in southern Africa. *Am. Sci.* 67:151–160.

87. Klein, R. 1987. Reconstructing how early people exploited animals: Problems and pros-

pects. In *The evolution of human hunting,* ed. M. H. Nitecki, D. V. Nitecki, pp. 11–45. New York: Plenum.

88. Klein, R. 1989. Biological and behavioural perspectives on modern human origins in southern Africa. In *The human revolution: Behavioural and biological perspectives on the origins of modern humans,* ed. P. Mellars, C. Stringer, pp. 529–546. Edinburgh: Edinburgh University Press.

89. Ward, J. 1983. On the antiquity of the Namib. *S. Afr. J. Sci.* 79:175–183.

90. Stanley, S. 1992. An ecological theory for the origin of *Homo. Paleobiology* 18:237–257.

91. Wolpoff, M. 1982. *Ramapithecus* and hominid origins. *Curr. Anthropol.* 23:501–510.

92. Kingston, J. D., Marino, B. D., Hill, A. 1994. Isotopic evidence for Neogene hominid paleoenvironments in the Kenya rift valley. *Science* 264:955–959.

93. White, T. D., Suwa, G., Asfaw, B. 1994. *Australopithecus ramidus,* a new species of early hominid from Aramis, Ethiopia. *Nature* 371:306–312.

94. WoldeGabriel, G., White, T. D., Suwa, G., Renne, P., de Heinzelin, J., Hart, W. K., Heiken, G. 1994. Ecological and temporal placement of early Pliocene hominids at Aramis, Ethiopia. *Nature* 371:330–333.

95. Boesch-Achermann, H., Boesch, C. 1994. Hominization in the rainforest: The chimpanzee's piece of the puzzle. *Evol. Anthropol.* 3:9–16.

96. deMenocal, P. 1995. Plio-Pleistocene African climate. *Science* 270:53–59.

97. Vrba, E. 1988. Late Pliocene climatic events and hominid evolution. In *Evolutionary history of the "robust" australopithecines,* ed. F. E. Grine, pp. 405–426. New York: Aldine de Gruyter.

98. Wesselman, H. 1985. Fossil micromammals as indicators of climatic chage about 2.4 myr ago in the Omo Valley, Ethiopia. *S. Afr. J. Sci.* 81:260–261.

99. Bonnefille, R. 1976. Palynological evidence for an important change in the vegetation of the Omo Basin between 2.5 and 2 milion years. In *Earliest man and environments in the Lake Rudolf Basin,* ed. Y. Copens, F. Howell, G. Isaac, R. Leakey, pp. 421–431. Chicago: University of Chicago Press.

100. Turner, A., Wood, B. 1993. Comparative palaeontological context for the evolution of the early hominid masticatory system. *J. Hum. Evol.* 24:301–318.

101. Kukla, G. 1987. Loess stratigraphy in central China. *Q. Sci. Rev.* 6:191–219.

102. Hooghiemstra, H. 1986. A high-resolution palynological record of 3.5 million years of northern Andean climatic history: The correlation of 26 "glacial cycles" with terrestrial, marine and astronomical data. *Zbl. Geol. Palaont.* 1:1363–1366.

103. Van Valen, L. 1973. A new evolutionary law. *Evol. Theory* 1:1–30.

104. Foley, R. A. 1994. Speciation, extinction and climatic change in hominid evolution. *J. Hum. Evol.* 26:275–289.

105. McKee, J. 1994. Hominid evolution in the context of gradual change among the mammals of southern Africa. *Am. J. Phys. Anthropol.* Suppl. 18:145.

106. Conroy, G. 1990. *Primate evolution.* New York: W. W. Norton.

107. Weaver, K. 1985. Stones, bones, and early man. *Natl. Geogr. Mag.* 168:560–623.

108. Brown, F. 1992. Methods of dating. In *The Cambridge encyclopedia of human evolution,* ed. S. Jones, R. Martin, D. Pilbeam, pp. 179–186. Cambridge: Cambridge University Press.

109. Roberts, N. 1992. Climatic change in the past. In *The Cambridge encyclopedia of human evolution,* ed. S. Jones, R. Martin, D. Pilbeam, pp. 174–178. Cambridge: Cambridge University Press.

110. Stringer, C., Gamble, C. 1993. *In search of the Neanderthals.* New York: Thames and Hudson.

111. Van der Hamman, T., Wijmstra, T. A., Zagwijn, W. 1971. The floral record of the late Cenozoic of Europe. In *The late Cenozoic Glacial Ages,* ed. K. K. Turekian, pp. 391–424. New Haven, Conn.: Yale University Press.

112. Dawson, A. 1992. *Ice Age Earth.* London: Routledge.

113. Sikes, N. E. 1994. Early hominid habitat preferences in East Africa: Paleosol carbon isotopic evidence. *J. Hum. Evol.* 27:25–45.

114. Clark, J. D. 1985. Leaving no stone unturned: Archaeological advances and behavioral adaptation. In *Hominid evolution: Past, present, and future*, ed. P. Tobias, pp. 65–88. New York: Alan R. Liss.

CHAPTER II

1. Effremov, I. A. 1940. Taphonomy: A new branch of paleontology. *Pan-Am. Geol.* 74:81–93.
2. Olson, E. C. 1980. Taphonomy: Its history and role in community evolution. In *Fossils in the making*, ed. A. K. Behrensmeyer, A. P. Hill, pp. 5–19. Chicago: University of Chicago Press.
3. Bishop, W. W. 1980. Paleogeomorphology and continental taphonomy. In *Fossils in the making*, ed. A. K. Behrensmeyer, A. P. Hill, pp. 20–37. Chicago: University of Chicago Press.
4. Brain, C. 1981. *The hunters or the hunted?* Chicago: University of Chicago Press.
5. McKee, J. K. 1993. Formation of geomorphology of caves in calcareous tufas and implications for the study of the Taung fossil deposits. *Trans. R. Soc. S. Afr.* 48:307–322.
6. Weiner, J. 1955. *The Piltdown forgery*. London: Oxford University Press.
7. Spencer, F. 1990. *Piltdown: A scientific forgery*. London: Oxford University Press.
8. Eicher, D. 1976. *Geologic time*. Englewood Cliffs, N.J.: Prentice-Hall.
9. Leute, U. 1987. *Archaeometry: An introduction to physical methods in archaeology and the history of art*. Weinheim: VCH.
10. Gillespie, R. 1984. *Radiocarbon user's handbook*. Oxford: Oxbow.
11. Bard, E., Hamelin, B., Fairbanks, R., Zindler, A. 1990. Calibration of the 14C timescale over the past 30,000 years using mass spectrometric U-Th ages from Barbados corals. *Nature* 345:405–410.
12. Valladas, H., Cachier, H., Maurice, P., Bernaldo de Quiros, F., Uzquiano, P., Arnold, M. 1992. Direct radiocarbon dates for prehistoric paintings at the Altamira, El Castillo and Niaux caves. *Nature* 357:68–70.
13. Russ, J., Hyman, M., Shafer, H., Rowe, M. W. 1990. Radiocarbon dating of prehistoric rock paintings by selective oxidation of organic carbon. *Nature* 348:710–711.
14. Fitch, F. 1972. Selection of suitable material for dating and the assessment of geological error in potassium-argon age determination. In *Calibration of hominoid evolution: Recent advances in isotopic and other dating methods applicable to the origin of man*, ed. W. Bishop, J. Miller, pp. 77–92. Edinburgh: Scottish Academic Press.
15. Faure, G. 1986. *Principles of isotope geology*. New York: John Wiley.
16. Brown, F. 1992. Methods of dating. In *The Cambridge encyclopedia of human evolution*, ed. S. Jones, R. Martin, D. Pilbeam, pp. 179–186. Cambridge: Cambridge University Press.
17. Schwarcz, H. 1992. Uranium series dating in paleoanthropology. *Evol. Anthropol.* 1:56–62.
18. Schwarcz, H. 1992. Uranium-series dating and the origin of modern man. *Philos. Trans. R. Soc. Lond. [Biol.]* 337:131–137.
19. MacDougall, J. 1976. Fission-track dating. *Sci. Am.* 235:114–122.
20. Aitken, M., Valladas, H. 1992. Luminescence dating relevant to human origins. *Philos. Trans. R. Soc. Lond. [Biol.]* 337:139–144.
21. Ciochon, R., Olsen, J., James, J. 1990. *Other origins: The search for the giant ape in human prehistory*. New York: Bantam.
22. Cook, J., Stringer, C., Currant, A., Schwarcz, H., Wintle, A. 1982. A review of the chronology of the European middle Pleistocene hominid record. *Yrbk. Phys. Anthropol.* 25:19–65.
23. Schwarcz, H., Grun, R. 1992. Electron spin resonance (ESR) dating of the origin of modern man. *Philos. Trans. R. Soc. Lond. [Biol.]* 337:145–148.
24. Grun, R. 1993. Electron spin resonance dating in paleoanthropology. *Evol. Anthropol.* 2:172–181.

25. Ikeya, M., Miki, T. 1980. Electron spin resonance dating of animal and human bones. *Science* 207:977–979.

26. Grun, R., Beaumont, P., Stringer, C. 1990. ESR dating evidence for early modern humans at Border Cave in South Africa. *Nature* 344:537–539.

27. Grun, R., Shackleton, N., Deacon, H. 1990. Electron-spin-resonance dating of tooth enamel from Klasies River Mouth Cave. *Curr. Anthropol.* 31:427–432.

28. Grun, R., Stringer, C. B., Schwarcz, H. P. 1991. ESR dating of teeth from Garrod's Tabun cave collection. *J. Hum. Evol.* 20:231–248.

29. Porat, N., Schwarcz, H. P. 1994. ESR dating of tooth enamel. In *Integrative paths to the past*, ed. R. S. Corruccini, R. L. Ciochon, pp. 521–530. Englewood Cliffs, N.J.: Prentice-Hall.

30. Bada, J., Schroeder, R., Carter, G. 1974. New evidence for the antiquity of man in North America deduced from aspartic acid racemization. *Science* 184:791–793.

31. Bada, J. 1985. Amino acid racemization dating of fossil bones. *Ann. Rev. Earth Planetary Sci.* 13:241–268.

32. Brooks, A., Hare, P., Kokis, J., Miller, G., Ernst, R., Wendorf, F. 1990. Dating Pleistocene archeological sites by protein diagenesis in ostrich eggshell. *Science* 248:60–64.

33. Goodfriend, G. 1992. Rapid racemization of aspartic acid in mollusc shells and potential for dating over recent centuries. *Nature* 357:399–401.

34. Miller, G., Beaumont, P., Jull, A., Johnson, B. 1992. Pleistocene geochronology and palaeothermometry from protein diagenesis in ostrich eggshells: Implications for the evolution of modern humans. *Philos. Trans. R. Soc. Lond. [Biol.]* 337:149–157.

35. Turekian, K., Bada, J. 1972. The dating of fossil bones. In *Calibration of hominoid evolution*, ed. W. W. Bishop, J. A. Miller, pp. 171–185. Edinburgh: Scottish Academic Press.

36. Blackwell, B., Rutter, N. 1990. Amino acid racemization in mammalian bones and teeth from La Chaise-de-Vouthon (Charente), France. *Geoarchaeology* 5:121–147.

37. Lincoln, R., Boxshall, G., Clark, P. 1990. *A dictionary of ecology, evolution and systematics.* Cambridge: Cambridge University Press.

38. Ashlock, P. 1974. The uses of cladistics. *Ann. Rev. Ecol. System.* 5:81–99.

39. Ridley, M. 1986. *Evolution and classification: The reformation of cladism.* New York: Longman.

40. Eldredge, N., Tattersall, I. 1975. Evolutionary models, phylogenetic reconstruction and another look at hominid phylogeny. In *Approaches to primate paleobiology*, ed. F. S. Szalay, pp. 218–242. Basel: Karger.

41. Tattersall, I., Eldredge, N. 1977. Fact, theory, and fantasy in human paleontology. *Am. Sci.* 65:204–211.

42. Tattersall, I. 1986. Species recognition in human paleontology. *J. Hum. Evol.* 15:165–175.

43. Hull, D. 1979. The limits of cladism. *Syst. Zool.* 28:416–440.

44. Landau, M. 1984. Human evolution as narrative. *Am. Sci.* 72:262–267.

45. Landau, M. 1991. *Narratives of human evolution.* New Haven, Conn.: Yale University Press.

46. Mayr, E. 1981. Biological classification: Toward a synthesis of opposing methodologies. *Science* 214:510–516.

47. Hennig, W. 1965. Phylogenetic systematics. *Ann. Rev. Entomol.* 10:97–116.

48. Huxley, J. 1958. Evolutionary processes and taxonomy with special reference to grades. *Uppsala Univ. Arssks.* 1958:21–38.

49. Wood, B., Chamberlain, A. 1986. *Australopithecus*: Grade or clade? In *Major topics in primate and human evolution*, ed. B. Wood, L. Martin, P. Andrews, pp. 220–248. Cambridge: Cambridge University Press.

50. Simpson, G. 1975. Recent advances in methods of phylogenetic inference. In *Phylogeny of the primates: A multidisciplinary approach*, ed. W. Luckett, F. Szalay, pp. 3–19. New York: Plenum.

51. Panchen, A. L. 1992. *Classification, evolution, and the nature of biology.* Cambridge: Cambridge University Press.

52. Simpson, G. 1953. *The major features of evolution.* New York: Columbia University Press.

53. Eldredge, N., Gould, S. 1972. Punctuated equilibria: An alternative to phyletic gradual-

ism. In *Models in paleobiology*, ed. T. Schopf, pp. 82–115. San Francisco: Freeman, Cooper.

54. Gould, S. J., Eldredge, N. 1993. Punctuated equilibrium comes of age. *Nature* 366:223–227.

55. Levinton, J., Simon, C. 1980. A critique of the punctuated equilibria model and implications for the detection of speciation in the fossil record. *Syst. Zool.* 29:130–142.

56. Godfrey, L., Jacobs, K. 1981. Gradual, autocatalytic and punctuational models of hominid brain evolution: A cautionary tale. *J. Hum. Evol.* 10:255–272.

57. Cronin, J., Boaz, N., Stringer, C., Rak, Y. 1981. Tempo and mode in human evolution. *Nature* 292:113–122.

58. Gingerich, P. D. 1991. Fossils and evolution. In *Evolution of life: Fossils, molecules and culture*, ed. S. Osawa, T. Honjo, pp. 3–20. Tokyo: Springer-Verlag.

59. Gingerich, P. D. 1993. Quantification and comparison of evolutionary rates. *Am. J. Sci.* 293A:453–478.

60. Tobias, P. 1991. *Oduvai Gorge IV: The skulls, endocasts and teeth of* Homo habilis. Cambridge: Cambridge University Press.

61. White, T. D., Suwa, G., Asfaw, B. 1994. *Australopithecus ramidus*, a new species of early hominid from Aramis, Ethiopia. *Nature* 371:306–312.

62. White, T. D., Suwa, G., Asfaw, B. 1995. *Australopithecus ramidus*, a new species of early hominid from Aramis, Ethiopia. *Nature* 375:88.

63. Kimbel, W. H., Johanson, D. C., Rak, Y. 1994. The first skull and other new discoveries of *Australopithecus afarensis* at Hadar, Ethiopia. *Nature* 368:449–451.

64. Schenk, E. T., McMasters, J. H. 1936. *Procedure in taxonomy*. Stanford: Stanford University Press.

65. Behrensmeyer, A. K. 1992. Fossil deposits and their investigation. In *The Cambridge encyclopedia of human evolution*, ed. S. Jones, R. Martin, D. Pilbeam, pp. 187–190. Cambridge: Cambridge University Press.

66. Weaver, K. 1985. Stones, bones, and early man. *Natl. Geogr. Mag.* 168:560–623.

67. Brain, C. K. 1970. New finds at the Swartkrans Australopithecine site. *Nature* 225:1–7.

68. Brain, C. K. 1993. Structure and stratigraphy of the Swartkrans cave in the light of the new excavations. In *Swartkrans: A cave's chronicle of early man*, ed. C. K. Brain, pp. 23–33. Pretoria: Transvaal Museum.

69. Conroy, G. 1990. *Primate evolution*. New York: W. W. Norton.

70. Patterson, C., ed. 1987. *Molecules and morphology in evolution: Conflict or compromise?* Cambridge: Cambridge University Press.

71. Szalay, F. 1977. Ancestors, descendants, sister groups and testing of phylogenetic hypotheses. *Syst. Zool.* 26:12–18.

72. Simpson, G. G. 1963. The meaning of taxonomic statements. In *Classification and human evolution*, ed. S. Washburn, pp. 1–31. Chicago: Aldine.

73. Martin, R. 1992. Classification and evolutionary relationships. In *The Cambridge encyclopedia of human evolution*, ed. S. Jones, R. Martin, D. Pilbeam, pp. 17–23. Cambridge: Cambridge University Press.

74. Vrba, E. 1980. Evolution, species and fossils: How does life evolve? *S. Afr. J. Sci.* 76:61–84.

CHAPTER III

1. Harland, W., Armstrong, R., Cox, A., Craig, L., Smith, A., Smith, D. 1990. *A geologic time scale (1989)*. Cambridge: Cambridge University Press.

2. Peterhans, J. C., Wrangham, R. W., Carter, M. L., Hauser, M. D. 1993. A contribution to tropical rain forest taphonomy: Retrieval and documentation of chimpanzee remains from Kibale Forest, Uganda. *J. Hum. Evol.* 25:485–514.

3. Bernor, R. L., Flynn, L. J., Harrison, T., Hussain, S. T., Kelley, J. 1988. *Dionysopithecus* from southern Pakistan and the biochronology and biogeography of early Eurasian catarrhines. *J. Hum. Evol.* 17:339–358.

4. Thomas, H. 1985. The early and middle Miocene land connection of the Afro-Arabian

plate and Asia: A major event for hominoid dispersal? In *Ancestors: The hard evidence,* ed. E. Delson, pp. 42–50. New York: Alan R. Liss.

5. Omar, G., Steckler, M. 1995. Fission track evidence on the initial rifting of the Red Sea: Two pulses, no propagation. *Science* 270:1341–1344.

6. Gregory, J. 1896. *The great rift valley.* London: Seeley Service.

7. Holmes, A. 1965. *Principles of physical geology.* London: Thomas Nelson.

8. Bishop, W., Miller, J., Fitch, F. 1969. New potassium-argon age determinations relevant to the Miocene fossil mammal sequence in East Africa. *Am. J. Sci.* 267:669–699.

9. Bishop, W., ed. 1978. *Geological background to fossil man: Recent research in the Gregory Rift Valley, East Africa.* Edinburgh: Scottish Academic Press.

10. Van Couvering, J., Miller, J. 1969. Miocene stratigraphy and age determinations, Rusinga Island, Kenya. *Nature* 221:628–632.

11. Van Couvering, J. A. H., Van Couvering, J. A. 1976. Early Miocene mammal fossils from East Africa: Aspects of geology, faunistics and paleoecology. In *Human origins: Louis Leakey and the East African evidence,* ed. G. L. Isaac, E. R. McCown, pp. 155–207. Menlo Park: W.A. Benjamin.

12. Bishop, W. 1964. More fossil primates and other Miocene mammals from northeast Uganda. *Nature* 203:1327–1331.

13. Bishop, W. 1967. The later Tertiary in East Africa: Volcanics, sediments, and faunal inventory. In *Background to evolution in Africa,* ed. W. Bishop, J. Clark, pp. 31–56. Chicago: University of Chicago Press.

14. Walker, A. 1969. Lower Miocene fossils from Mount Elgon, Uganda. *Nature* 223:591–593.

15. Maclatchy, L. M., Gebo, D. L., Pilbeam, D. R. 1995. New primate fossils from the lower Miocene of Northeast Uganda. *Am. J. Phys. Anthropol.* Suppl. 20:139.

16. Pickford, M., Senut, B., Poupeau, G., Brown, F., Haileab, B. 1991. Correlation of tephra layers from the Western Rift Valley (Uganda) to the Turkana Basin (Ethiopia/Kenya) and the Gulf of Aden. *C. R. Acad. Sci. [III]* 313:223–229.

17. Nengo, I., Rae, R. 1992. New hominoid fossils from the early Miocene site of Songhor, Kenya. *J. Hum. Evol.* 23:423–429.

18. Andrews, P. 1981. Species diversity and diet in monkeys and apes during the Miocene. In *Aspects of human evolution,* ed. C. Stringer, pp. 25–61. London: Taylor and Francis.

19. Evans, E., Van Couvering, J., Andrews, P. 1981. Paleoecology of Miocene sites in western Kenya. *J. Hum. Evol.* 10:99–116.

20. Andrews, P., Meyer, G., Pilbeam, D., Van Couvering, J., Van Couvering, J. 1981. The Miocene fossil beds of Maboko Island, Kenya: Geology, age, taphonomy and paleontology. *J. Hum. Evol.* 10:35–48.

21. Feibel, C. S., Brown, F. H. 1991. Age of the primate-bearing deposits on Maboko Island, Kenya. *J. Hum. Evol.* 21:221–225.

22. McCrossin, M. L. 1992. An Oreopithecid humerus from the Middle Miocene of Maboko Island, Kenya. *Int. J. Primatol.* 13:659–677.

23. McCrossin, M. L., Benefit, B. R. 1993. Recently recovered *Kenyapithecus* mandible and its implications for great ape and human origins. *Proc. Natl. Acad. Sci. U.S.A.* 90:1962–1966.

24. Shipman, P., Walker, A., Van Couvering, J., Hooker, P., Miller, J. 1981. The Fort Ternan hominoid site, Kenya: Geology, age, taphonomy and paleoecology. *J. Hum. Evol.* 10:49–72.

25. Benefit, B. R. 1995. Earliest Old World monkey skull. *Am. J. Phys. Anthropol.* Suppl. 20:64.

26. Gitau, S. N., Benefit, B. R. 1995. New evidence concerning the facial morphology of *Simiolus leakeyorum* from Maboko Island. *Am. J. Phys. Anthropol.* Suppl. 20:99.

27. Benefit, B. R., McCrossin, M. L. 1989. New primate fossils from the Middle Miocene of Maboko Island, Kenya. *J. Hum. Evol.* 18:493–497.

28. Pickford, M. 1981. Preliminary Miocene mammalian biostratigraphy for western Kenya. *J. Hum. Evol.* 10:73–97.

29. Pickford, M. 1983. Sequence and environments of the lower and middle Miocene hom-

inoids of western Kenya. In *New interpretations of ape and human ancestry*, ed. R. Cio-chon, R. Corruccini, pp. 421–440. New York: Plenum.

30. Retallack, G. J., Dugas, D. P., Bestland, E. A. 1990. Fossil soils and grasses of a middle Miocene East African grassland. *Science* 247:1325–1328.

31. Retallack, G. J., Bestland, E. A., Dugas, D. P. 1995. Miocene paleosols and habitats of *Proconsul* on Rusinga Island, Kenya. *J. Hum. Evol.* 29:53–91.

32. Gentry, A. 1970. The Bovidae (Mammalia) of the Fort Ternan fossil fauna. In *Fossil ver-tebrates of Africa*, ed. L. Leakey, R. Savage. Vol. 2, pp. 243–323. London: Academic.

33. Cerling, T. E., Quade, J., Ambrose, S. H., Siles, N. E. 1991. Fossil soils, grasses, and carbon isotopes from Fort Ternan, Kenya: Grassland or woodland? *J. Hum. Evol.* 21:295–306.

34. Jacobs, B. F., Kabuye, C. 1987. A middle Miocene (12.2 my old) forest in the East African Rift Valley, Kenya. *J. Hum. Evol.* 16:147–155.

35. Hill, A. 1987. Causes of perceived faunal change in the later Neogene of East Africa. *J. Hum. Evol.* 16:583–596.

36. WoldeGabriel, G., White, T. D., Suwa, G., Renne, P., de Heinzelin, J., Hart, W. K., Heiken, G. 1994. Ecological and temporal placement of early Pliocene hominids at Aramis, Ethiopia. *Nature* 371:330–333.

37. White, T. D., Suwa, G., Asfaw, B. 1994. *Australopithecus ramidus*, a new species of early hominid from Aramis, Ethiopia. *Nature* 371:306–312.

38. Andrews, P., Van Couvering, J. 1975. Paleoenvironments in the East African Miocene. In *Approaches to primate paleobiology*, ed. F. Szalay, pp. 62–103. Basel: Karger.

39. Kortlandt, A. 1983. Facts and fallacies concerning Miocene ape habitats. In *New interpre-tations of ape and human ancestry*, ed. R. Ciochon, R. Corruccini, pp. 465–515. New York: Plenum.

40. Bernor, R. 1983. Geochronology and zoogeographic relationships of Miocene Hominoi-dea. In *New interpretations of ape and human ancestry*, ed. R. Ciochon, R. Corruccini, pp. 21–64. New York: Plenum.

41. Conroy, G. C., Pilbeam, D. 1975. *Ramapithecus*, a review of its hominid status. In *Paleoanthropology: Morphology and paleoecology*, ed. R. Tuttle, pp. 59–86. The Hague: Mouton.

42. Conroy, G. 1990. *Primate evolution*. New York: W. W. Norton.

43. Walker, A., Teaford, M. F., Martin, L., Andrews, P. 1993. A new species of *Proconsul* from the early Miocene of Rusinga/Mfangano Islands, Kenya. *J. Hum. Evol.* 25:43–56.

44. Harrison, T. 1989. A new species of *Micropithecus* from the middle Miocene of Kenya. *J. Hum. Evol.* 18:537–557.

45. Boschetto, H. G., Brown, F. H., McDougall, I. 1992. Stratigraphy of the Lothidok Range, northern Kenya, and K/Ar ages of its Miocene primates. *J. Hum. Evol.* 22:47–71.

46. Ruff, C. B., Walker, A., Teaford, M. F. 1989. Body mass, sexual dimorphism and femoral proportions of *Proconsul* from Rusinga and Mfangano Islands, Kenya. *J. Hum. Evol.* 18:515–536.

47. Teaford, M. F., Walker, A., Mugaisi, G. S. 1993. Species discrimination in *Proconsul* from Rusinga and Mfangano Islands, Kenya. In *Species, species concepts, and primate evolution*, ed. W. H. Kimbel, L. B. Martin, pp. 373–392. New York: Plenum.

48. Walker, A., Pickford, M. 1983. New postcranial fossils of *Proconsul africanus* and *Proconsul nyanzae*. In *New interpretations of ape and human ancestry*, ed. R. Ciochon, R. Corruccini, pp. 325–352. New York: Plenum.

49. Conroy, G. C. 1987. Problems of body-weight estimation in fossil primates. *Int. J. Primatol.* 8:115–137.

50. Hopwood, A. 1933. Miocene primates from Kenya. *J. Linn. Soc. Lond. Zool.* 38:437–464.

51. Walker, A. 1992. Louis Leakey, John Napier and the history of *Proconsul*. *J. Hum. Evol.* 22:245–2554.

52. Simons, E. L., Pilbeam, D. R. 1965. Preliminary revision of the Dryopithecinae (Pongidae, Anthropoidea). *Folia Primatol.* 3:81–152.

53. Walker, A., Rose, M. 1968. Fossil hominoid vertebra from the Miocene of Uganda. *Nature* 217:980–981.

54. Pilbeam, D. 1969. Tertiary Pongidae of East Africa. Evolutionary relationships and taxonomy. *Peabody Mus. Nat. Hist. Yale Univ. Bull.* 31:1–185.

55. Simons, E. 1972. *Primate evolution.* New York: Macmillan.

56. Walker, A., Falk, D., Smith, R., Pickford, M. 1983. The skull of *Proconsul africanus*: Reconstruction and cranial capacity. *Nature* 305:525–527.

57. Beard, K. C., Teaford, M., Walker, A. 1986. New wrist bones of *Proconsul africanus* and *P. nyanzae* from Rusinga Island, Kenya. *Folia Primatol.* 47:97–118.

58. Begun, D. R., Teaford, M. F., Walker, A. 1994. Comparative and functional anatomy of *Proconsul* phalanges from the Kaswanga primate site, Rusinga Island, Kenya. *J. Hum. Evol.* 26:89–165.

59. Rose, M. 1988. Another look at the anthropoid elbow. *J. Hum. Evol.* 17:193–224.

60. Rose, M. D. 1992. Kinematics of the trapezium-1st metacarpal joint in extant anthropoids and Miocene hominoids. *J. Hum. Evol.* 22:255–266.

61. Ward, C. V., Walker, A. C., Teaford, M. F. 1991. *Proconsul* did not have a tail. *J. Hum. Evol.* 21:215–220.

62. Ward, C. V., Walker, A., Teaford, M. F., Odhiambo, I. 1993. Partial skeleton of *Proconsul nyanzae* from Mfangano Island, Kenya. *Am. J. Phys. Anthropol.* 90:77–111.

63. Ward, C. V. 1993. Torso morphology and locomotion in *Proconsul nyanzae. Am. J. Phys. Anthropol.* 92:291–328.

64. Leakey, R. E., Walker, A. 1985. New higher primates from the early Miocene of Buluk, Kenya. *Nature* 318:173–175.

65. Leakey, R. E., Leakey, M. G. 1986. A new Miocene hominoid from Kenya. *Nature* 324:143–146.

66. Leakey, R. E., Leakey, M. G. 1986. A second new Miocene hominoid from Kenya. *Nature* 324:146–148.

67. Leakey, R. E., Leakey, M. G. 1987. A new Miocene small-bodied ape from Kenya. *J. Hum. Evol.* 16:369–387.

68. Leakey, R. E., Leakey, M. G., Walker, A. C. 1988. Morphology of *Turkanapithecus kalakolensis* from Kenya. *Am. J. Phys. Anthropol.* 76:277–288.

69. Leakey, R. E., Leakey, M. G., Walker, A. C. 1988. Morphology of *Afropithecus turkanensis* from Kenya. *Am. J. Phys. Anthropol.* 76:289–307.

70. Rose, M. D., Leakey, M. G., Leakey, R. E. F., Walker, A. C. 1992. Postcranial specimens of *Simiolus enjiessi* and other primitive catarrhines from the early Miocene of Lake Turkana, Kenya. *J. Hum. Evol.* 22:171–237.

71. Hill, A., Behrensmeyer, K., Brown, B., Deino, A., Rose, M., Saunders, J., Ward, S., Winkler, A. 1991. Kipsaramon: A lower Miocene hominoid site in the Tugen Hills, Baringo District, Kenya. *J. Hum. Evol.* 20:67–75.

72. Martin, L. B. 1995. Oldest known thick-enamelled ape. *Am. J. Phys. Anthropol.* Suppl. 20:144.

73. Leakey, M. G., Leakey, R. E., Richtsmeier, J. T., Simons, E. L., Walker, A. C. 1991. Similarities in *Aegyptopithecus* and *Afropithecus* facial morphology. *Folia Primatol.* 56:65–85.

74. Conroy, G. C. 1994. *Otavipithecus*: Or how to build a better hominid—Not. *J. Hum. Evol.* 27:373–383.

75. Begun, D. R. 1994. The significance of *Otavipithecus namibiensis* to interpretations of hominoid evolution. *J. Hum. Evol.* 27:385–394.

76. Begun, D. R. 1995. Late Miocene European orang-utans, gorillas, humans, or none of the above? *J. Hum. Evol.* 29:169–180.

77. Begun, D. 1992. Miocene fossil hominids and the chimp-human clade. *Science* 257:1929–1933.

78. Begun, D. R. 1994. Relations among the great apes and humans: New interpretations based on the fossil great ape *Dryopithecus. Yrbk. Phys. Anthropol.* 37:11–63.

79. de Bonis, L., Bouvrain, G., Geraads, D., Koufos, G. 1990. New hominid skull material from the late Miocene of Macedonia in northern Greece. *Nature* 345:712–714.

80. de Bonis, L., Koufos, G. D. 1993. The face and the mandible of *Ouranopithecus macedoniensis*: Description of new specimens and comparisons. *J. Hum. Evol.* 24:469–491.

81. de Bonis, L., Koufos, G. D. 1995. Our ancestors ancestor: *Ouranopithecus* is a Greek link to human ancestry. *Evol. Anthropol.* 3:75–83.

82. Andrews, P. 1990. Lining up the ancestors. *Nature* 345:664–665.

83. Leutenegger, W. 1982. Scaling of sexual dimorphism in body weight and canine size in primates. *Folia Primatol.* 37:163–176.

84. Leutenegger, W., Cheverud, J. 1985. Sexual dimorphism in primates: The effects of size. In *Size and scaling in primate biology*, ed. W. L. Jungers, pp. 33–50. New York: Plenum.

85. Raza, S., Barry, J., Pilbeam, D., Rose, M., Shah, I., Ward, S. 1983. New hominoid primates from the middle Miocene, Chinji Formation, Potwar Plateau, Pakistan. *Nature* 306:52–54.

86. Pilbeam, D., Meyer, G., Badgley, C., Rose, M., Pickford, M., Behrensmeyer, A., Shah, S. 1977. New hominoid primates from the Siwaliks of Pakistan and their bearing on hominoid evolution. *Nature* 270:689–695.

87. Barry, J. 1986. A review of the chronology of Siwalik hominoids. In *Primate evolution*, ed. J. G. Else, P. C. Lee. Vol. 1, pp. 93–106. Cambridge: Cambridge University Press.

88. Kappelman, J., Kelley, J., Pilbeam, D., Sheikh, K., Ward, S., Anwar, M., Barry, J., Brown, B., Hake, P., Johnson, N., Raza, S., Shah, S. 1991. The earliest occurrence of *Sivapithecus* from the middle Miocene Chinji Formation of Pakistan. *J. Hum. Evol.* 21:61–73.

89. Pilbeam, D., Smith, R. 1981. New skull remains of *Sivapithecus* from Pakistan. *Mem. Geol. Surv. Pakistan* 2:1–13.

90. Pilbeam, D. 1982. New hominoid skull material from the Miocene of Pakistan. *Nature* 295:232–234.

91. Ward, S., Kimbel, W. 1983. Subnasal alveolar morphology and the systematic position of *Sivapithecus. Am. J. Phys. Anthropol.* 61:157–171.

92. Ward, S., Pilbeam, D. 1983. Maxillofacial morphology of Miocene hominoids from Africa and Indo-Pakistan. In *New interpretations of ape and human ancestry*, ed. R. Ciochon, R. Corruccini, pp. 211–238. New York: Plenum.

93. Rose, M. D. 1989. New postcranial specimens of catarrhines from the Middle Miocene Chinji Formation, Pakistan: Descriptions and a discussion of proximal humeral functional morphology in anthropoids. *J. Hum. Evol.* 18:131–162.

94. Rose, M. D. 1986. Further hominoid postcranial specimens from the late Miocene Nagri Formation of Pakistan. *J. Hum. Evol.* 15:333–367.

95. Pilbeam, D., Rose, M., Badgley, C., Lipschutz, B. 1980. Miocene hominoids from Pakistan. *Postilla* 181:1–94.

96. Pilbeam, D., Rose, M., Barry, J., Ibrahim Shah, I. 1990. New *Sivapithecus* humeri from Pakistan and the relationship of *Sivapithecus* and *Pongo. Nature* 348:237–239.

97. Bernor, R. L., Tobien, H. 1990. The mammalian geochronology and biogeography of Pasalar (Middle Miocene, Turkey). *J. Hum. Evol.* 19:551–568.

98. Martin, L. B., Andrews, P. J. 1991. Species recognition in middle Miocene hominoids. *Am. J. Phys. Anthropol.* Suppl. 12:126.

99. Alpagut, B., Andrews, P., Martin, L. 1990. New hominoid specimens from the Middle Miocene site at Pasalar, Turkey. *J. Hum. Evol.* 19:397–422..

100. Andrews, P., Martin, L. 1991. Hominoid dietary evolution. *Philos. Trans. R. Soc. Lond. [Biol.]* 334:199–209.

101. Martin, L. B., Andrews, P. 1993. Species recognition in Middle Miocene hominoids. In *Species, species concepts, and primate evolution*, ed. W. H. Kimbel, L. B. Martin, pp. 393–427. New York: Plenum.

102. Andrews, P., Tekkaya, I. 1980. A revision of the Turkish Miocene hominoid *Sivapithecus meteai*. *Palaeontology* 23:85–95.

103. Guoqin, Q. 1993. The environment and ecology of the Lufeng hominoids. *J. Hum. Evol.* 24:3–11.

104. Wanyong, C., Yufen, L., Qianli, Y. 1986. On the paleoclimate during the period of *Ramapithecus* in Lufeng County, Yunnan Province. *Acta Anthropol.* 4:88.

105. Woo, J. 1957. *Dryopithecus* teeth from Keiyuan, Yunnan Province. *Vertebrata Palasiatica* 1:25–32.

106. Xu, Q., Lu, Q. 1979. The mandibles of *Ramapithecus* and *Sivapithecus* from Lufeng, Yunnan. *Vertebrata Palasiatica* 17:1–13.

107. Wu, R., Han, D., Xu, Q., Lu, Q., Pan, Y., Zhang, X., Zheng, L., Xiao, M. 1981. *Ramapithecus* skulls found first time in the world. *Kexue Tongbao* 26:1018–1021.

108. Wu, R., Qinghua, X., Qingwu, L. 1983. Morphological features of *Ramapithecus* and *Sivapithecus* and their phylogenetic relationships—morphology and the comparison of the crania. *Acta Anthropol.* 2:6.

109. Wu, R., Qinghua, X., Qingwu, L. 1984. Morphological features of *Ramapithecus* and *Sivapithecus* and their phylogenetic relationships—morphology and comparison of the mandibles. *Acta Anthropol.* 3:9.

110. Wood, B. A., Xu, Q. 1991. Variation in the Lufeng dental remains. *J. Hum. Evol.* 20:291–311.

111. Etler, D. 1984. The fossil hominoids of Lufeng, Yunnan Province, the People's Republic of China: A series of translations. *Yrbk. Phys. Anthropol.* 27:1–55.

112. Schwartz, J. H. 1990. *Lufengpithecus* and its potential relationship to an orang-utan clade. *J. Hum. Evol.* 19:591–605.

113. Wu, R., Qinghua, X., Qingwu, L. 1986. Relationship between Lufeng *Sivapithecus* and *Ramapithecus* and their phylogenetic position. *Acta Anthropol.* 4:1–31.

114. Kelley, J. 1993. Taxonomic implications of sexual dimorphism in *Lufengpithecus*. In *Species, species concepts, and primate evolution*, ed. W. H. Kimbel, L. B. Martin, pp. 429–458. New York: Plenum.

115. Lieberman, S., Gelvin, B., Oxnard, C. 1985. Dental sexual dimorphism in some extant hominoids and ramapithecines from China: A quantitative approach. *Am. J. Primatol.* 9:305–326.

116. Andrews, P., Walker, A. 1976. The primate and other fauna from Fort Ternan, Kenya. In *Human origins: Louis Leakey and the East African evidence*, ed. G. Isaac, E. McCown, pp. 279–304. Menlo Park: Benjamin-Cummings.

117. Leakey, L. 1962. A new lower Pliocene fossil primate from Kenya. *Ann. Mag. Nat. Hist.* 4:689–696.

118. Pickford, M. 1982. New higher primate fossils from the middle Miocene deposits at Majiwa and Kaloma, western Kenya. *Am. J. Phys. Anthropol.* 58:1–19.

119. Conroy, G. C., Pickford, M., Senut, B., Van Couvering, J., Mein, P. 1992. *Otavipithecus namibiensis*, first Miocene hominoid from southern Africa. *Nature* 356:144–148.

120. Conroy, G. C., Pickford, M., Senut, B., Mein, P. 1993. Diamonds in the desert: The discovery of *Otavipthecus namibiensis*. *Evol. Anthropol.* 2:46–52.

121. McCrossin, M. L., Benefit, B. R. 1994. Maboko Island and the evolutionary history of Old World monkeys and apes. In *Integrative paths to the past*, ed. R. S. Corruccini, R. L. Ciochon, pp. 95–122. Englewood Cliffs, N.J.: Prentice-Hall.

122. Leakey, L. 1967. An early Miocene member of Hominidae. *Nature* 213:155–163.

123. Simons, E. L., Pilbeam, D. R. 1978. *Ramapithecus*. In *Evolution of African mammals*, ed. V. J. Maglio, H. B. S. Cooke, pp. 147–153. Cambridge, Mass.: Harvard University Press.

124. Pickford, M., Mein, P., Senut, B. 1994. Fossiliferous Neogene karst fillings in Angola, Botswana and Namibia. *S. Afr. J. Sci.* 90:227–230.

125. Pickford, M., Senut, B., Conroy, G., Mein, P. 1994. Phylogenetic position of *Otavipithecus*: Questions of methodology and approach. In *Current primatology: Ecology and evolution,*

ed. B. Thierry, J. R. Anderson, J. J. Roeder, N. Herrenschmidt, pp. 265–272. Strasbourg: Université Louis Pasteur.

126. Conroy, G. C., Mahoney, C. 1991. A mixed longitudinal study of dental emergence in the chimpanzee, *Pan troglodytes* (Primates, Pongidae). *Am. J. Phys. Anthropol.* 86:243–254.

127. Kuykendall, K., Mahoney, C., Conroy, G. 1992. Probit and survival analysis of tooth emergence ages in a mixed-longitudinal sample of chimpanzees (*Pan troglodytes*). *Am. J. Phys. Anthropol.* 89:379–399.

128. Lydekker, R. 1879. Further notices of Siwalik Mammalia. *Rec. Geol. Surv. India* 12:33–52.

129. Lartet, E. 1837. Note sur la decouverte recente d'un machoire de singe fossile. *C. R. Acad. Sci. [III]* 43:219–223.

130. Lartet, R. 1856. Note sur un grand singe fossile qui se rattache au groupe des singes superieurs. *C. R. Acad. Sci. [III]* 43:219–223.

131. Simons, E., Chopra, S. 1969. *Gigantopithecus* (Pongidae, Hominoidea) a new species from north India. *Postilla* 138:1–18.

132. Frayer, D. 1973. *Gigantopithecus* and its relationship to *Australopithecus*. *Am. J. Phys. Anthropol.* 39:413–426.

133. Ciochon, R., Olsen, J., James, J. 1990. *Other origins: The search for the giant ape in human prehistory*. New York: Bantam.

134. Goodman, M., Baba, M., Darga, L. 1983. The bearing of molecular data on the cladogenesis and times of divergence of hominoid lineages. In *New interpretations of ape and human ancestry*, ed. R. Ciochon, R. Corruccini, pp. 67–86. New York: Plenum.

135. Andrews, P. 1978. A revision of the Miocene Hominoidea of East Africa. *Bull. Br. Mus. (Nat. Hist.) Geol.* 30:85–224.

136. Andrews, P., Cronin, J. 1982. The relationships of *Sivapithecus* and *Ramapithecus* and the evolution of the orang-utan. *Nature* 297:541–546.

137. Sarich, V., Wilson, A. 1967. Immunological time scale for hominid evolution. *Science* 158:1200–1203.

138. Sarich, V. 1971. A molecular approach to the question of human origins. In *Background for man*, ed. P. Dolhinow, V. Sarich, pp. 60–81. Boston: Little, Brown.

139. Sarich, V., Cronin, J. 1976. Molecular systematics of the primates. In *Molecular anthropology*, ed. M. Goodman, R. Tashian, pp. 141–170. New York: Plenum.

140. Sibley, C., Ahlquist, J. 1984. The phylogeny of the hominoid primates as indicated by DNA-DNA hybridization. *J. Mol. Evol.* 20:2–15.

141. Sibley, C., Ahlquist, J. 1987. DNA hybridization evidence of hominid phylogeny: Results from an expanded data set. *J. Mol. Evol.* 26:99–121.

142. Templeton, A. 1984. Phylogenetic inference from restriction endonuclease site maps with particular reference to the evolution of humans and apes. *Evolution* 37:221–244.

143. Templeton, A. 1991. Human origins and analysis of mitochondrial DNA sequences. *Science* 255:737.

144. Andrews, P. 1986. Molecular evidence for catarrhine evolution. In *Major topics in primate and human evolution*, ed. B. Wood, L. Martin, P. Andrews, pp. 107–129. Cambridge: Cambridge University Press.

145. Marks, J., Schmid, C. W., Sarich, V. M. 1988. DNA hybridization as a guide to phylogeny: Relations of the Hominoidea. *J. Hum. Evol.* 17:769–786.

146. Saitou, N. 1991. Reconstruction of molecular phylogeny of extant hominoids from DNA sequence data. *Am. J. Phys. Anthropol.* 84:75–85.

147. Templeton, A. 1985. The phylogeny of the hominoid primates: A statistical analysis of the DNA-DNA hybridization data. *Mol. Biol. Evol.* 2:420–433.

148. Ruvolo, M. 1994. Molecular evolutionary processes and conflicting gene trees: The hominoid case. *Am. J. Phys. Anthropol.* 94:89–113.

149. Rogers, J. 1994. Levels of the genealogical hierarchy and the problem of hominoid phylogeny. *Am. J. Phys. Anthropol.* 94:81–88.

150. Marks, J. 1994. Blood will tell (won't it?): A century of molecular discourse in anthropological systematics. *Am. J. Phys. Anthropol.* 94:59–79.

151. Goodman, M., Bailey, W. J., Hayasaka, K., Stanhope, M. J., Slightom, J., Czelusniak, J. 1994. Molecular evidence on primate phylogeny from DNA sequences. *Am. J. Phys. Anthropol.* 94:3–24.

152. Ruvulo, M. 1995. Seeing the forest and the trees. *Am. J. Phys. Anthropol.* 98:218–232.

153. Rogers, J., Comuzzie, A. 1995. When is ancient polymorphism a potential problem for molecular phylogenetics? *Am. J. Phys. Anthropol.* 98:216–218.

154. Marks, J. 1995. Learning to live with a trichotomy. *Am. J. Phys. Anthropol.* 98:211–213.

155. Green, H., Djian, P. 1995. The involucrin gene and hominoid relationships. *Am. J. Phys. Anthropol.* 98:213–216.

156. Avise, J. C. 1994. *Molecular markers, natural history and evolution.* New York: Chapman and Hall.

157. Britten, R. 1986. Rates of DNA sequence evolution differ between taxonomic groups. *Science* 231:1393–1398.

158. Andrews, P., Martin, L. 1987. Cladistic relationships of extant and fossil hominoids. *J. Hum. Evol.* 16:101–118.

159. Jenkins, F. A., Fleagle, J. G. 1975. Knuckle-walking and the functional anatomy of the wrists in living apes. In *Primate functional morphology and evolution*, ed. R. H. Tuttle, pp. 213–227. The Hague: Mouton.

160. Tuttle, R. H. 1967. Knuckle-walking and the evolution of hominoid hands. *Am. J. Phys. Anthropol.* 26:171–206.

161. Tuttle, R. H. 1970. Postural, propulsive and prehensile capabilities in the cheiridia of chimpanzees and other great apes. In *The chimpanzee: Physiology, behavior, serology and diseases of chimpanzees*, ed. G. H. Bourne, pp. 167–253. Basel: Karger.

162. Schwartz, J. 1984. The evolutionary relationships of man and orang-utans. *Nature* 308:501–505.

163. Darwin, C. 1871. *The descent of man, and selection in relation to sex.* London: Murray.

164. Moya-Sola, S., Kohler, M. 1996. A *Dryopithecus* skeleton and the origins of great-ape locomotion. *Nature* 379:156–159.

165. Wood, B. 1992. Evolution of australopithecines. In *The Cambridge encyclopedia of human evolution*, ed. S. Jones, R. Martin, D. Pilbeam, pp. 231–240. Cambridge: Cambridge University Press.

166. Rose, M. D. 1994. Quadrupedalism in some Miocene catarrhines. *J. Hum. Evol.* 26:387–411.

167. Kelley, J. 1992. Evolution of apes. In *The Cambridge encyclopedia of human evolution*, ed. S. Jones, R. Martin, D. Pilbeam, pp. 223–230. Cambridge: Cambridge University Press.

168. Pilbeam, D. 1979. Recent finds and interpretations of Miocene hominoids. *Ann. Rev. Anthropol.* 8:333–352.

169. Goodman, M. 1992. Reconstructing human evolution from proteins. In *The Cambridge encyclopedia of human evolution*, ed. S. Jones, R. Martin, D. Pilbeam, pp. 307–312. Cambridge: Cambridge University Press.

170. Friday, A. 1992. Measuring relatedness. In *The Cambridge encyclopedia of human evolution*, ed. S. Jones, R. Martin, D. Pilbeam, pp. 295–297. Cambridge: Cambridge University Press.

CHAPTER IV

1. Conroy, G. 1990. *Primate evolution.* New York: W. W. Norton.

2. Tobias, P., von Koenigswald, G. 1964. A comparison between the Olduvai hominines and those of Java and some implications for hominid phylogeny. *Nature* 204:515–518.

3. Kramer, A. 1994. A critical analysis of claims for the existence of Southeast Asian australopithecines. *J. Hum. Evol.* 26:3–21.

4. Stanford, C. B., Wallis, J., Matama, H., Goodall, J. 1994. Patterns of predation by chimpanzees on red colobus monkeys in Gombe National Park, 1982–1991. *Am. J. Phys. Anthropol.* 94:213–228.

5. Stanford, C. B. 1995. The hunting ecology of chimpanzees: Implications for Pliocene hominid behavioral ecology. *Am. J. Phys. Anthropol.* Suppl 20:201.

6. Schrenk, R., Bromage, T. G., Betzler, C. G., Ring, U., Juwayeyi, Y. M. 1993. Oldest *Homo* and Pliocene biogeography of the Malawi Rift. *Nature* 365:833–835.

7. Howell, F., Haesaerts, P., de Heinzelin, J. 1987. Depositional environments, archeological occurrences, and hominids from Members E and F of the Shungura Formation (Omo basin, Ethiopia). *J. Hum. Evol.* 16:665–700.

8. Brain, C. 1988. New information from the Swartkrans cave or relevance to "robust" australopithecines. In *Evolutionary history of the "robust" australopithecines*, ed. F. Grine, pp. 311–316. New York: Aldine de Gruyter.

9. Hill, A., Ward, S., Deino, A., Curtis, G., Drake, R. 1992. Earliest *Homo*. *Nature* 355:719–722.

10. Falk, D., Baker, E. 1992. Earliest *Homo* debate. *Nature* 358:290.

11. Feibel, C. 1992. Earliest *Homo* debate. *Nature* 358:289.

12. Tobias, P. 1993. Earliest *Homo* not proven. *Nature* 361:307.

13. White, T. 1988. The comparative biology of "robust" *Australopithecus*: Clues from context. In *Evolutionary history of the "robust" australopithecines*, ed. F. Grine, pp. 449–484. New York: Aldine de Gruyter.

14. Tobias, P. 1987. The brain of *Homo habilis*: A new level of organization in cerebral evolution. *J. Hum. Evol.* 16:741–761.

15. Toth, N. 1987. Behavioral inferences from early stone artifact assemblages: An experimental model. *J. Hum. Evol.* 16:763–787.

16. Falk, D. 1990. Brain evolution in *Homo*: The "radiator" theory. *Behav. Brain Sci.* 13:333–381.

17. White, T. D., Suwa, G., Asfaw, B. 1995. *Australopithecus ramidus*, a new species of early hominid from Aramis, Ethiopia. *Nature* 375:88.

18. White, T. D., Suwa, G., Asfaw, B. 1994. *Australopithecus ramidus*, a new species of early hominid from Aramis, Ethiopia. *Nature* 371:306–312.

19. Feldesman, M., Lundy, J. 1988. Stature estimates for some African Plio-Pleistocene fossil hominids. *J. Hum. Evol.* 17:583–596.

20. Jungers, W. 1988. New estimates of body size in australopithecines. In *Evolutionary history of the "robust" australopithecines*, ed. F. Grine, pp. 115–125. New York: Aldine de Gruyter.

21. McHenry, H. 1988. New estimates of body weight in early hominids and their significance to encephalization and megadontia in robust australopithecines. In *Evolutionary history of the "robust" australopithecines*, ed. F. Grine, pp. 133–148. New York: Aldine de Gruyter.

22. McHenry, H. 1992. How big were early hominids? *Evol. Anthropol.* 1:15–20.

23. McHenry, H. 1992. Body size and proportions in early hominids. *Am. J. Phys. Anthropol.* 87:407–431.

24. Dart, R. A. 1949. Adventures with *Australopithecus*. *Rationalist Ann.* 1949:15–25.

25. Tobias, P. 1984. *Dart, Taung, and the "missing link."* Johannesburg: University of the Witwatersrand Press.

26. Dart, R. 1925. *Australopithecus africanus*: The man-ape of South Africa. *Nature* 115:195–199.

27. Leakey, L. 1935. *Adam's ancestors*. New York: Longmans, Green.

28. Hooten, E. 1946. *Up from the ape*. New York: Macmillan.

29. Keith, A. 1931. *New discoveries relating to the antiquity of man*. London: Williams and Norgate.

30. Spencer, F. 1990. *Piltdown: A scientific forgery*. London: Oxford University Press.

31. Partridge, T. 1986. Paleoecology of the Pliocene and lower Pleistocene hominids of southern Africa: How good is the chronological and paleoenvironmental evidence? *S. Afr. J. Sci.* 82:80–83.

32. Delson, E. 1984. Cercopithecoid biochronology of the African Plio-Pleistocene: Correlation among eastern and southern hominid-bearing localities. *Cour. Forschunginst. Senckenb.* 69:199–218.

33. Delson, E. 1988. Chronology of South African australopith site units. In *Evolutionary history of the "robust" australopithecines*, ed. F. Grine, pp. 317–324. New York: Aldine de Gruyter.

34. McKee, J. K. 1993. Faunal dating of the Taung hominid fossil deposit. *J. Hum. Evol.* 25:363–376.

35. McKee, J. K. 1993. Formation of geomorphology of caves in calcareous tufas and implications for the study of the Taung fossil deposits. *Trans. R. Soc. S. Afr.* 48:307–322.

36. Tobias, P. V., Vogel, J. C., Oschadleus, H. D., Partridge, T. C., McKee, J. K. 1993. New isotopic and sedimentological measurements of the Thabaseek Deposits (South Africa) and the dating of the Taung hominid. *Quat. Res.* 40:360–367.

37. McKee, J. K., Tobias, P. V. 1994. Taung stratigraphy and taphonomy: Preliminary results based on the 1988–93 excavations. *S. Afr. J. Sci.* 90:233–235.

38. Dart, R. A., Craig, D. 1959. *Adventures with the missing link*. New York: Harper.

39. Berger, L. R., Clarke, R. J. 1994. Eagle involvement in accumulation of the Taung child fauna. *J. Hum. Evol.* 29:275–299.

40. Hedenstrom, A. 1995. Lifting the Taung child. *Nature* 378:670.

41. Broom, R. 1936. A new fossil anthropoid skull from South Africa. *Nature* 138:486–488.

42. Broom, R. 1937. Discovery of a lower molar of *Australopithecus*. *Nature* 140:681–682.

43. Broom, R. 1938. The Pleistocene anthropoid apes of South Africa. *Nature* 142:377–379.

44. White, T. D. 1981. Primitive hominid canine from Tanzania. *Science* 213:348–349.

45. Broom, R., Robinson, J. 1947. Further remains of the Sterkfontein ape-man, *Plesianthropus*. *Nature* 160:430–431.

46. Kuman, K. 1994. The archaeology of Sterkfontein—past and present. *J. Hum. Evol.* 27:471–495.

47. Kuman, K. 1994. The archaeology of Sterkfontein: Preliminary findings on site formation and cultural change. *S. Afr. J. Sci.* 90:215–219.

48. Tobias, P. V., Baker, G. 1994. Palaeo-anthropology in South Africa. *S. Afr. J. Sci.* 90:203–204.

49. Partridge, T. 1978. Re-appraisal of lithostratigraphy of Sterkfontein hominid site. *Nature* 275:282–287.

50. Clarke, R. J., Tobias, P. V. 1995. Sterkfontein Member 2 foot bones of the oldest South African hominid. *Science* 269:521–524.

51. Clarke, R. 1988. A new *Australopithecus* cranium from Sterkfontein and its bearing on the ancestry of *Paranthropus*. In *Evolutionary history of the "robust" australopithecines*, ed. F. E. Grine, pp. 285–292. New York: Aldine de Gruyter.

52. Conroy, G. C., Vannier, M. W. 1991. Dental development in South African australopithecines: Part I: problems of pattern and chronology. *Am. J. Phys. Anthropol.* 86:121–136.

53. Clarke, R. J. 1994. Advances in understanding the craniofacial anatomy of South African early hominids. In *Integrative paths to the past*, ed. R. S. Corruccini, R. L. Ciochon, pp. 205–222. Englewood Cliffs, N.J.: Prentice-Hall.

54. Kimbel, W. H., Johanson, D. C., Rak, Y. 1994. The first skull and other new discoveries of *Australopithecus afarensis* at Hadar, Ethiopia. *Nature* 368:449–451.

55. Clarke, R. J. 1994. On some new interpretations of Sterkfontein stratigraphy. *S. Afr. J. Sci.* 90:211–214.

56. Hughes, A., Tobias, P. 1977. A fossil skull probably of the genus *Homo* from Sterkfontein, Transvaal. *Nature* 265:310–312.

57. Vrba, E. 1982. Biostratigraphy and chronology, based particularly on Bovidae of southern

African hominid-associated assemblages: Makapansgat, Sterkfontein, Taung, Krom-draai, Swarkrans: Also Elandsfontein, Broken Hill and Cave of Hearths. *Pretirage, Prem. Congr. Int. Paleontol. Hum. Nice CNRS* :707–752.

58. Schwarcz, H. P., Grun, R., Tobias, P. V. 1994. ESR dating studies of the australopithecine site of Sterkfontein, South Africa. *J. Hum. Evol.* 26:175–181.

59. Vrba, E. 1980. The significance of bovid remains as indicators of environment and pre-dation patterns. In *Fossils in the making: Vertebrate taphonomy and paleoecology,* ed. A. Behrensmeyer, A. Hill, pp. 247–271. Chicago: University of Chicago Press.

60. Vrba, E. 1985. Ecological and adaptive changes associated with early hominid evolution. In *Ancestors: The hard evidence,* ed. E. Delson, pp. 63–71. New York: Alan R. Liss.

61. PARU. 1994. 28th Annual Report: Palaeo-anthropology research unit (PARU). In *28th Annual Report: Palaeo-anthropology research unit (PARU):* University of the Witwaters-rand.

62. Vrba, E. 1975. Some evidence of chronology and paleoecology of Sterkfontein, Swart-krans and Kromdraai from the fossil Bovidae. *Nature* 254:301–304.

63. Brain, C. 1981. *The hunters or the hunted?* Chicago: University of Chicago Press.

64. Berger, L. R., Menter, C. G., Thackeray, J. F. 1994. The renewal of excavation activities at Kromdraai, South Africa. *S. Afr. J. Sci.* 90:209–210.

65. Vrba, E. 1981. The Kromdraai australopithecine site revisited in 1980: Recent investiga-tions and results. *Ann. Transvaal Mus.* 33:17–60.

66. Dart, R. 1948. An adolescent promethean australopithecine mandible from Makapansgat. *S. Afr. J. Sci.* 45:73–75.

67. Tobias, P. 1967. *Olduvai Gorge.* Cambridge: Cambridge University Press.

68. Dart, R. 1948. The adolescent mandible of *Australopithecus prometheus. Am. J. Phys. Anthro-pol.* 6:391–412.

69. Brain, C., van Riet Lowe, C., Dart, R. 1955. Kafuan stone artefacts in the post australo-pithecine breccia at Makapansgat. *Nature* 175:16.

70. Dart, R. 1957. *The Osteodontokeratic culture of* Australopithecus prometheus. Pretoria: Transvaal Mus. Mem.

71. Ardrey, R. 1961. *African genesis.* New York: Dell.

72. Shipman, P., Phillips, J. 1976. On scavenging by hominids and other carnivores. *Curr. Anthropol.* 17:170–172.

73. Shipman, P., Phillips-Conroy, J. 1977. Hominid toolmaking versus carnivore scavenging. *Am. J. Phys. Anthropol.* 46:77–86.

74. White, T., Johanson, D., Kimbel, W. 1981. *Australopithecus africanus:* Its phyletic position reconsidered. *S. Afr. J. Sci.* 77:445–470.

75. Turner, A., Wood, B. 1993. Taxonomic and geographic diversity in robust australo-pithecines and other African Plio-Pleistocene larger mammals. *J. Hum. Evol.* 24: 147–168.

76. Zavada, M. S., Cadman, A. 1993. Palynological investigations at the Makapansgat Lime-works: An australopithecine site. *J. Hum. Evol.* 25:337–350.

77. Cadman, A., Rayner, R. J. 1989. Climatic change and the appearance of *Australopithecus africanus* in the Makapansgat sediments. *J. Hum. Evol.* 18:107–113.

78. Rayner, R. J., Moon, B. P., Master, J. C. 1993. The Makapansgat australopithecine envi-ronment. *J. Hum. Evol.* 24:219–231.

79. Broom, R. 1949. Another new type of fossil ape-man. *Nature* 163:57.

80. Broom, R., Robinson, J. T. 1950. Man contemporaneous with the Swartkrans ape-man. *Am. J. Phys. Anthropol.* 8:151–156.

81. Clarke, R., Howell, F., Brain, C. 1970. More evidence of an advanced hominid at Swart-krans. *Nature* 225:1219–1222.

82. Olson, T. 1978. Hominid phylogenetics and the existence of *Homo* in member I of the Swartkrans formation, South Africa. *J. Hum. Evol.* 7:159–178.

83. Brain, C. K. 1994. The Swartkrans palaeontological research project in perspective: Re-sults and conclusions. *S. Afr. J. Sci.* 90:220–223.

84. Susman, R. 1988. Hand of *Paranthropus robustus* from Member 1, Swartkrans: Fossil evidence for tool behavior. *Science* 240:781–784.

85. Susman, R., Brain, T. 1988. New first metatarsal (SKX5017) from Swartkrans and the gait of *Paranthropus robustus*. *Am. J. Phys. Anthropol.* 77:7–15.

86. Susman, R. 1989. New hominid fossils from the Swartkrans Formation (1979–1986 Excavations): Postcranial specimens. *Am. J. Phys. Anthropol.* 79:451–474.

87. Susman, R. L. 1993. Hominid postcranial remains from Swartkrans. In *Swartkrans: A cave's chronicle of early man*, ed. C. K. Brain, pp. 117–136. Pretoria: Transvaal Museum.

88. Grine, F. 1989. New hominid fossils from the Swartkrans Formation (1979–1986 Excavations): Craniodental specimens. *Am. J. Phys. Anthropol.* 79:409–449.

89. Grine, F. E., Susman, R. I. 1991. Radius of *Paranthropus robustus* from Member 1, Swartkrans Formation, South Africa. *Am. J. Phys. Anthropol.* 84:229–248.

90. Grine, F. E., Daegling, D. J. 1993. New mandible of *Paranthropus robustus* from Member 1, Swartkrans Formation, South Africa. *J. Hum. Evol.* 24:319–333.

91. Grine, F. E., Demes, B., Jungers, W. L., Cole, T. M. 1993. Taxonomic affinity of the early *Homo* cranium from Swartkrans, South Africa. *Am. J. Phys. Anthropol.* 92:411–426.

92. Grine, F. E. 1993. Description and preliminary analysis of new hominid craniodental fossils from the Swartkrans Formation. In *Swartkrans: A cave's chronicle of early man*, ed. C. K. Brain, pp. 75–116. Pretoria: Transvaal Museum.

93. Grine, F. E., Strait, D. S. 1994. New hominid fossils from Member 1 "Hanging Remnant," Swartkrans Formation, South Africa. *J. Hum. Evol.* 26:57–75.

94. Brain, C. K., Watson, V. 1992. A guide to the Swartkrans early hominid cave site. *Ann. Transvaal Mus.* 35:343–365.

95. Brain, C. K. 1993. Structure and stratigraphy of the Swartkrans cave in the light of the new excavations. In *Swartkrans: A cave's chronicle of early man*, ed. C. K. Brain, pp. 23–33. Pretoria: Transvaal Museum.

96. Brain, C., Sillen, A. 1988. Evidence from the Swartkrans cave for the earliest use of fire. *Nature* 336:464–466.

97. Brain, C. K. 1993. The occurrence of burnt bones at Swartkrans and their implications for the conrol of fire by early hominids. In *Swartkrans: A cave's chronicle of early man*, ed. C. K. Brain, pp. 229–242. Pretoria: Transvaal Museum.

98. Sillen, A., Hoering, T. 1993. Chemical characterization of burnt bones from Swartkrans. In *Swartkrans: A cave's chronicle of early man*, ed. C. K. Brain, pp. 243–249. Pretoria: Transvaal Museum.

99. Clark, J. D. 1993. Stone artefacts assemblages from Members 1–3, Swartkrans cave. In *Swartkrans: A cave's chronicle of early man*, ed. C. K. Brain, pp. 167–194. Pretoria: Transvaal Museum.

100. Brain, C. K., Shipman, P. 1993. The Swartkrans bone tools. In *Swartkrans: A cave's chronicle of early man*, ed. C. K. Brain, pp. 195–215. Pretoria: Transvaal Museum.

101. Vogel, J. 1985. Further attempts at dating the Taung tufas. In *Ancestors: The hard evidence*, ed. E. Delson, pp. 189–194. New York: Alan R. Liss.

102. Watson, V. 1993. Composition of the Swartkrans bone accumulations, in terms of skeletal parts and animals represented. In *Swartkrans: A cave's chronicle of early man*, ed. C. K. Brain, pp. 35–73. Pretoria: Transvaal Museum.

103. Berger, L. R., Tobias, P. V. 1994. New discoveries at the early hominid site of Gladysvale, South Africa. *S. Afr. J. Sci.* 90:223–226.

104. Berger, L. R., Keyser, A. W., Tobias, P. V. 1993. Gladysville: First Early Hominid site discovered in South Africa since 1948. *Am. J. Phys. Anthropol.* 92:107–111.

105. Vrba, E. 1974. Chronological and ecological implications of the fossil Bovidae at the Sterkfontein australopithecine site. *Nature* 250:19–23.

106. Skinner, J., Smithers, R. 1990. *The mammals of the southern African subregion*. Pretoria: University of Pretoria.

107. McKee, J. K., Thackeray, J. F., Berger, L. R. 1995. Faunal assemblage seriation of southern African Pliocene and Pleistocene fossil deposits. *Am. J. Phys. Anthropol.* 96:235–250.

108. Baker, B., Wohlenberg, J. 1971. Structure and evolution of the Kenya Rift Valley. *Nature* 229:538–542.

109. Brunet, M., Beauvilain, A., Coppens, Y., Heintz, E., Moutaye, A., Pilbeam, D. 1995. The first australopithecine 2,500 kilometres west of the Rift Valley (Chad). *Nature* 378:273–275.

110. Hill, A., Ward, S. 1988. Origin of the Hominidae: The record of African large hominoid evolution between 14 my and 4 my. *Yrbk. Phys. Anthropol.* 31:49–83.

111. Hill, A. 1994. Late Miocene and early Pliocene hominoids from Africa. In *Integrative paths to the past*, ed. R. S. Corruccini, R. L. Ciochon, pp. 123–145. Englewood Cliffs, N.J.: Prentice-Hall.

112. Ungar, P. S., Walker, A., Coffing, K. 1994. Reanalysis of the Lukeino molar (KNM-LU 335). *Am. J. Phys. Anthropol.* 94:165–173.

113. Coffing, K., Feibel, C., Leakey, M., Walker, A. 1994. Four-million-year-old hominids from East Lake Turkana, Kenya. *Am. J. Phys. Anthropol.* 93:55–65.

114. White, T. D. 1986. *Australopithecus afarensis* and the Lothagam mandible. *Anthropos* 23:79–90.

115. Patterson, B., Behrensmeyer, A., Sill, W. 1970. Geology and fauna of a new Pliocene locality in north-western Kenya. *Nature* 226:918–921.

116. Behrensmeyer, A. 1976. Lothagam Hill, Kanapoi, and Ekora: A general summary of stratigraphy and faunas. In *Earliest man and environments in the Lake Rudolf Basin*, ed. Y. Coppens, F. C. Howell, G. Isaac, R. Leakey, pp. 163–170. Chicago: University of Chicago Press.

117. Brown, F., McDougall, I., Davies, T., Maier, R. 1985. An integrated Plio-Pleistocene chronology for the Turkana Basin. In *Ancestors: The hard evidence*, ed. E. Delson, pp. 82–90. New York: Alan R. Liss.

118. Hill, A., Ward, S., Brown, B. 1992. Anatomy and age of the Lothagam mandible. *J. Hum. Evol.* 22:439–451.

119. Eckhardt, R. 1977. Hominid origins: The Lothagam mandible. *Curr. Anthropol.* 18:356.

120. Corruccini, R., McHenry, H. 1980. Cladometric analysis of Pliocene hominids. *J. Hum. Evol.* 9:209–221.

121. Kramer, A. 1986. Hominid-pongid distinctiveness in the Miocene-Pliocene fossil record: The Lothagam mandible. *Am. J. Phys. Anthropol.* 70:457–473.

122. Leakey, M. G., Feibel, C. S., McDougall, I., Walker, A. 1995. New four-million-year-old hominid species from Kanapoi and Allia Bay, Kenya. *Nature* 376:565–571.

123. Patterson, B., Howells, W. 1967. Hominid humeral fragment from early Pleistocene of northwestern Kenya. *Science* 156:64–66.

124. Heinrich, R. E., Rose, M. D., Leakey, R. E., Walker, A. C. 1993. Hominid radius from the Middle Pliocene of Lake Turkana, Kenya. *Am. J. Phys. Anthropol.* 92:139–148.

125. Ward, S., Hill, A. 1987. Pliocene hominid partial mandible from Tabarin, Baringo, Kenya. *Am. J. Phys. Anthropol.* 72:21–38.

126. Pickford, M., Johanson, D., Lovejoy, C., White, T., Aronson, J. 1983. A hominoid humeral fragment from the Pliocene of Kenya. *Am. J. Phys. Anthropol.* 60:337–346.

127. Fleagle, J., Rasmussen, D., Yirga, S., Bown, T., Grine, F. 1991. New hominid fossils from Fejej, Southern Ethiopia. *J. Hum. Evol.* 21:145–152.

128. Kappelman, J., Swisher, C., Fleagle, J., Yirga, S., Bown, T., Feseha, M. 1996. Age of *Australopithecus afarensis* from Fejej, Ethiopia. *J. Hum. Evol.* 30:139–146.

129. WoldeGabriel, G., White, T. D., Suwa, G., Renne, P., de Heinzelin, J., Hart, W. K., Heiken, G. 1994. Ecological and temporal placement of early Pliocene hominids at Aramis, Ethiopia. *Nature* 371:330–333.

130. Asfaw, B., Beyene, Y., Haile-Selassie, Y., Hart, W., Renne, P., Suwa, G., White, T., WoldeGabriel, G. 1995. Three seasons of hominid paleontology at Aramis, Ethiopia. Paleoanthropology Society Conference, Oakland, CA.

131. Leakey, R. 1969. Early *Homo sapiens* remains from the Omo River region of southwest Ethiopia: Faunal remains from the Omo Valley. *Nature* 222:1132–1133.

132. Feibel, C., Brown, F., McDougall, I. 1989. Stratigraphic context of fossil hominids from the Omo Group deposits: Northern Turkana basin, Kenya and Ethiopia. *Am. J. Phys. Anthropol.* 78:595–622.

133. Howell, F., Coppens, Y. 1976. An overview of Hominidae from the Omo succession, Ethiopia. In *Earliest man and environments in the Lake Rudolf Basin*, ed. Y. Coppens, F. Howell, G. Isaac, R. Leakey, pp. 522–532. Chicago: University of Chicago Press.

134. Hunt, K., Vitzthum, V. 1986. Dental metric assessment of the Omo fossils: Implications for the phylogenetic position of *Australopithecus africanus. Am. J. Phys. Anthropol.* 71:141–156.

135. Grine, F. 1993. Australopithecine taxonomy and phylogeny: Historical background and recent interpretation. In *The human evolution source book*, ed. R. L. Ciochon, J. G. Fleagle, pp. 198–210. Englewood Cliffs, N.J.: Prentice-Hall.

136. Suwa, G. 1988. Evolution of the "robust" australopithecines in the Omo succession: Evidence from mandibular premolar morphology. In *Evolutionary history of the "robust" australopithecines*, ed. F. E. Grine, pp. 199–222. New York: Aldine de Gruyter.

137. Wood, B., Wood, C., Konigsberg, L. 1994. *Paranthropus boisei*: An example of evolutionary stasis? *Am. J. Phys. Anthropol.* 95:117–136.

138. Semaw, S., Harris, J. W. K., Feibel, C. S., Mowbray, K. M., Renne, P., Bernor, R., Fesseha, N. 1995. New results from the Plio-Pleistocene deposits of the Gona area during the 1994 field season. Paleoanthropology Society Conference, Oakland, CA.

139. Bonnefille, R. 1976. Palynological evidence for an important change in the vegetation of the Omo Basin between 2.5 and 2 milion years. In *Earliest man and environments in the Lake Rudolf Basin*, ed. Y. Copens, F. Howell, G. Isaac, R. Leakey, pp. 421–431. Chicago: University of Chicago Press.

140. Gentry, A. 1976. Bovidae of the Omo Group deposits. In *Earliest man and environments in the Lake Rudolf Basin*, ed. Y. Coppens, F. Howell, G. Isaac, R. Leakey, pp. 293–301. Chicago: University of Chicago Press.

141. Leakey, R., Lewin, R. 1992. *Origins reconsidered: In search of what makes us human.* Boston: Little, Brown.

142. Brown, F., Feibel, C. 1988. "Robust" hominid and Plio-Pleistocene paleogeography of the Turkana Basin, Kenya and Ethiopia. In *Evolutionary history of the "robust" australopithecines*, ed. F. E. Grine, pp. 325–341. New York: Aldine de Gruyter.

143. Brown, F., Feibel, C. 1986. Revision of lithostratigraphic nomenclature in the Koobi Fora region, Kenya. *J. Geol. Soc.* 143:297–310.

144. Brown, F. H. 1994. Development of Pliocene and Pleistocene chronology of the Turkana Basin, East Africa, and its relation to other sites. In *Integrative paths to the past*, ed. R. S. Corruccini, R. L. Ciochon, pp. 285–312. Englewood Cliffs, N.J.: Prentice-Hall.

145. Shipman, P., Harris, J. 1988. Habitat preference and paleoecology of *Australopithecus boisei* in Eastern Africa. In *Evolutionary history of the "robust" australopithecines*, ed. F. E. Grine, pp. 343–381. New York: Aldine de Gruyter.

146. Williamson, P. 1985. Evidence for Plio-Pleistocene rainforest expansion in east Africa. *Nature* 315:487–489.

147. Isaac, G., Harris, J., Crader, D. 1976. Archeological evidence from the Koobi Fora Formation. In *Earliest man and environments in the Lake Rudolf Basin*, ed. Y. Coppens, F. Howell, G. Isaac, R. Leakey. Chicago: University of Chicago Press.

148. Kibunjia, M., Roche, H., Brown, F., Leakey, R. 1992. Pliocene and Pleistocene archaeological sites west of Lake Turkana, Kenya. *J. Hum. Evol.* 23:431–438.

149. Fitch, F., Findlater, I., Watkins, R. 1974. Dating of the rock succession containing fossil hominids at east Rudolf, Kenya. *Nature* 251:213–215.

150. Curtis, G., Drake, R., Cerling, T., Hampel, J. 1975. Age of KBS tuff in Koobi Fora formation, east Rudolf, Kenya. *Nature* 258:395–398.

151. Gleadow, A. 1980. Fission track age of the KBS tuff and associated hominid remains in northern Kenya. *Nature* 284:225–230.

152. McDougall, I., Maier, R., Sutherland-Hawkes, P. 1980. K-Ar age estimate for the KBS tuff, east Turkana, Kenya. *Nature* 284:230–234.

153. McDougall, I. 1981. 40Ar/39Ar age spectra from the KBS tuff, Koobi Fora Formation. *Nature* 294:120–124.

154. Hillhouse, J., Ndombi, J., Cox, A., Brock, A. 1977. Additional results on palaeomagnetic stratigraphy of the Koobi Fora formation, east of Lake Turkana (Lake Rudolf), Kenya. *Nature* 265:411–415.

155. Cooke, H. 1976. Suidae from Pliocene-Pleistocene strata in the Rudolf Basin. In *Earliest man and environments in the Lake Rudolf Basin*, ed. Y. Coppens, F. C. Howell, G. Isaac, R. Leakey, pp. 251–263. Chicago: University of Chicago Press.

156. White, T., Harris, J. 1977. Suid evolution and correlation of African hominid localities. *Science* 198:13–21.

157. Behrensmeyer, A. 1978. Correlation of Plio-Pleistocene sequences in the northern Lake Turkana Basin: A summary of evidence and issues. In *Geological background to fossil man: Recent research in the Gregory Rift Valley, East Africa*, ed. W. Bishop, pp. 421–440. Edinburgh: Scottish Academic Press.

158. Brown, F., Howell, F., Eck, G. 1978. Observations on problems of correlation of late Cenozoic hominid-bearing formations in the North Lake Turkana Basin. In *Geological background to fossil man: Recent advances in the Gregory Rift Valley, East Africa*, ed. W. Bishop, pp. 473–498. Edinburgh: Scottish Academic Press.

159. Haileab, B., Brown, F. 1992. Turkana basin-Middle Awash valley correlations and the age of the Sagantole and Hadar Formations. *J. Hum. Evol.* 22:453–468.

160. Kalb, J., Jolly, C., Mebrate, A., Tebedge, S., Smart, C., Oswald, E., Cramer, D., Whitehead, P., Wood, C., Conroy, G., Adefris, T., Sperling, L., Kana, B. 1982. Fossil mammals and artefacts from the middle Awash valley, Ethiopia. *Nature* 298:25–29.

161. Kalb, J., Oswald, E., Tebedge, S., Mebrate, A., Tola, E., Peak, D. 1982. Geology and stratigraphy of Neogene deposits, middle Awash valley, Ethiopia. *Nature* 298: 17–25.

162. Kalb, J., Jolly, C., Oswald, E., Whitehead, P. 1984. Early hominid habitation in Ethiopia. *Am. Sci.* 72:168–178.

163. Kalb, J. E. 1993. Refined stratigraphy of the hominid-bearing Awash Group, Middle Awash Valley, Afar Depression, Ethiopia. *Newsl. Stratigr.* 29:21–62.

164. de Heinzelin, J. 1994. Rifting, a long-term African story, with considerations on early hominid habitats. In *Integrative paths to the past*, ed. R. S. Corruccini, R. L. Ciochon, pp. 313–320. Englewood Cliffs, N.J.: Prentice-Hall.

165. Johanson, D., Coppens, Y. 1976. A preliminary anatomical diagnosis of the first Plio/Pleistocene hominid discoveries in the Central Afar, Ethiopia. *Am. J. Phys. Anthropol.* 45:217–234.

166. Johanson, D., Taieb, M., Coppens, Y. 1982. Pliocene hominids from the Hadar Formation, Ethiopia (1973–1977): Stratigraphic, chronologic, and paleoenvironmental contexts, with notes on hominid morphology and systematics. *Am. J. Phys. Anthropol.* 57:373–402.

167. Johanson, D., White, T. 1979. A systematic assessment of early African hominids. *Science* 202:321–330.

168. Radosevich, S. C., Retallack, G. J., Taieb, M. 1992. Reassessment of the paleoenvironment and preservation of hominid fossils from Hadar, Ethiopia. *Am. J. Phys. Anthropol.* 87:15–27.

169. Falk, D., Conroy, G. C. 1983. The cranial venous sinus system in *Australopithecus afarensis*. *Nature* 306:779–781.

170. Olson, T. 1985. Cranial morphology and systematics of the Hadar Formation hominids and *Australopithecus africanus*. In *Ancestors: The hard evidence*, ed. E. Delson, pp. 102–119. New York: Alan R. Liss.

171. Senut, B., Tardieu, C. 1985. Functional aspects of Plio-Pleistocene hominid limb bones:

Implications for taxonomy and phylogeny. In *Ancestors: The hard evidence*, ed. E. Delson, pp. 193–201. New York: Alan R. Liss.

172. Hausler, M., Schmid, P. 1995. Comparison of the pelves of Sts 14 and AL 288–1: Implications for birth and sexual dimorphism in australopithecines. *J. Hum. Evol.* 29:363–383.

173. Richmond, B. G., Jungers, W. L. 1995. Size variation and sexual dimorphism in *Australopithecus afarensis* and living hominoids. *J. Hum. Evol.* 29:229–245.

174. Aronson, J., Taieb, M. 1981. Geology and paleogeography of the Hadar hominid site, Ethiopia. In *Hominid sites: Their geologic settings*, ed. G. Rapp, C. Vondra, pp. 165–196. Boulder: Westview.

175. Walter, R. C., Aronson, J. L. 1993. Age and source of the Sidi Hakoma Tuff, Hadar Formation, Ethiopia. *J. Hum. Evol.* 25:229–240.

176. Walter, R. C. 1994. Age of Lucy and the first family: Single-crystal 40Ar/39Ar dating of the Denen Dora and lower Kada Hadar Members of the Hadar Formation, Ethiopia. *Geology* 22:6–10.

177. Clark, J. D., Asfaw, B., Assefa, G., Harris, J. W. K., Kurashina, H., Walter, R. C., White, T. D., Williams, M. A. J. 1984. Palaeoanthropological discoveries in the middle Awash valley, Ethiopia. *Nature* 307:423–428.

178. White, T. D., Suwa, G., Hart, W. K., Walter, R. C., WoldeGabriel, G., de Heinzelin, J., Clark, J. D., Asfaw, B., Vrba, E. 1993. New discoveries of *Australopithecus* at Maka in Ethiopia. *Nature* 366:261–265.

179. White, T. 1984. Pliocene hominids from the Middle Awash, Ethiopia. *Cour. Forschungsinst. Senckenb.* 69:57–68.

180. Asfaw, B. 1987. The Belohdelie frontal: New evidence of early hominid cranial morphology from the Afar of Ethiopia. *H. Hum. Evol.* 16:611–624.

181. Johanson, D., White, T., Coppens, Y. 1978. A new species of the genus *Australopithecus* (Primates: Hominidae) from the Pliocene of eastern Africa. *Kirtlandia* 28:1–15.

182. Protsch, R. 1981. The Kohl-Larsen Eyasi and Garusi hominid finds in Tanzania and their relation to *Homo erectus*. In Homo erectus: *Papers in honor of Davidson Black*, ed. B. A. Sigmon, J. S. Cybulski, pp. 217–226. Toronto: University of Toronto Press.

183. Puech, P.-F., Cianfarani, F., Roth, H. 1986. Reconstruction of the maxillary dental arcade of Garusi Hominid 1. *J. Hum. Evol.* 15:325–332.

184. Weinert, H. 1950. Uber die neuen vor-und fruhmenschenfunde aus Afrika, Java, China und Frankreich. *Zeit. Morphol. Anthropol.* 42:113–148.

185. Leakey, M., Hay, R. 1979. Pliocene footprints in the Laetoli beds at Laetoli, northern Tanzania. *Nature* 278:317–328.

186. Day, M. 1985. Hominid locomotion—from Taung to the Laetoli footprints. In *Hominid evolution: Past, present and future*, ed. P. Tobias, pp. 115–127. New York: Alan R. Liss.

187. Tuttle, R. 1985. Ape footprints and Laetoli impressions: A response to the SUNY claims. In *Hominid evolution: Past, present, and future*, ed. P. V. Tobias, pp. 129–134. New York: Alan R. Liss.

188. Tuttle, R. 1987. Kinesiological inferences and evolutionary implications from Laetoli bipedal trails G-1, G-2/3, and A. In *Laetoli, a Pliocene site in Northern Tanzania*, ed. J.M. Harris, M. D. Leakey, pp. 503–523. Oxford: Clarendon.

189. Tuttle, R., Webb, D., Tuttle, N. 1991. Laetoli footprint trails and the evolution of hominid bipedalism. In *Origine(s) de la bipedie chez les hominides*, ed. Y. Coppens, B. Senut, pp. 187–198. Paris: CNRS.

190. White, T., Suwa, G. 1987. Hominid footprints at Laetoli: Facts and interpretations. *Am. J. Phys. Anthropol.* 72:485–514.

191. Leakey, M., Harris, J. 1987. *Laetoli: A Pliocene site in northern Tanzania.* Oxford: Oxford University Press.

192. Hay, R. 1981. Paleoenvironments of the Laetolil Beds, Northern Tanzania. In *Hominid sites: Their geologic settings*, ed. G. Rapp, C. Vondra, pp. 7–23. Boulder: Westview.

193. Leakey, L. 1959. A new fossil skull from Olduvai. *Nature* 184:491–493.

194. Leakey, L. 1967. *Olduvai Gorge 1951–1961: Fauna and background.* Cambridge: Cambridge University Press.

195. Robinson, J. 1960. The affinities of the new Olduvai australopithecine. *Nature* 186:456–458.

196. Leakey, L. 1960. The affinities of the new Olduvai australopithecine (reply to J.T. Robinson). *Nature* 186:458.

197. Leakey, L., Tobias, P., Napier, J. 1964. A new species of the genus *Homo* from Olduvai Gorge. *Nature* 202:7–9.

198. Walter, R. C., Manega, P. C., Hay, R. L., Drake, R. E., Curtis, G. H. 1991. Laser-fusion 40Ar/39 Ar dating of Bed I, Olduvai Gorge Tanzania. *Nature* 354:145–149.

199. Hay, R. 1973. Lithofacies and environments of Bed I, Olduvai Gorge, Tanzania. *Quat. Res.* 3:541–560.

200. Bishop, L. C., Plummer, T. W. 1995. Modern analogues for Olduvai Bed I environments based on artiodactyl habitat preferences. Paleonthropology Society Conference, Oakland, CA.

201. Hay, R. 1971. Geologic background of Beds I and II. In *Olduvai Gorge*, ed. M. Leakey. Vol. 3, pp. 9–20. Cambridge: Cambridge University Press.

202. Tobias, P. 1980. "*Australopithecus afarensis*" and *A. africanus*: A critique and an alternative hypothesis. *Palaeontol. Afr.* 23:1–17.

203. Vrba, E. 1985. *The Kromdraai australopithecine site.* Johannesburg: University of the Witwatersrand Press.

204. Wood, B. 1992. Evolution of australopithecines. In *The Cambridge encyclopedia of human evolution*, ed. S. Jones, R. Martin, D. Pilbeam, pp. 231–240. Cambridge: Cambridge University Press.

205. Tattersall, I., Delson, E., Van Couvering, J., eds. 1988. *Encyclopedia of human evolution and prehistory.* New York: Garland.

206. Howell, F. 1978. Hominidae. In *Evolution of African mammals*, ed. V. J. Maglio, H. B. S. Cooke, pp. 154–248. Cambridge, Mass.: Harvard University Press.

207. Bonnefille, R. 1994. Palynology and paleoenvironment of East African hominid sites. In *Integrative paths to the past*, ed. R. S. Corruccini, R. L. Ciochon, pp. 415–427. Englewood Cliffs, N.J.: Prentice-Hall.

208. Andrews, P. 1992. Reconstructing past environments. In *The Cambridge encyclopedia of human evolution*, ed. S. Jones, R. Martin, D. Pilbeam, pp. 191–195. Cambridge: Cambridge University Press.

CHAPTER V

1. Tobias, P. 1980. "*Australopithecus afarensis*" and *A. africanus*: A critique and an alternative hypothesis. *Palaeontol. Afr.* 23:1–17.

2. Walker, A., Leakey, R. 1988. The evolution of *Australopithecus boisei*. In *Evolutionary history of the "robust" australopithecines*, ed. F. E. Grine, pp. 247–258. New York: Aldine de Gruyter.

3. Kimbel, W., White, T., Johanson, D. 1988. Implications of KNM-WT 17000 for the evolution of "robust" australopithecines. In *Evolutionary history of the "robust" australopithecines*, ed. F. E. Grine, pp. 259–268. New York: Aldine de Gruyter.

4. Holloway, R. 1983. Human brain evolution: A search for units, models and synthesis. *Can. J. Anthropol.* 3:215–230.

5. Falk, D. 1980. Hominid brain evolution: The approach from paleoneurology. *Yrbk. Phys. Anthropol.* 23:93–107.

6. Falk, D. 1987. Hominid paleoneurology. *Ann. Rev. Anthropol.* 16:13–30.

7. Vrba, E. S. 1994. An hypothesis of heterochrony in response to climatic cooling and its relevance to early hominid evolution. In *Integrative paths to the past*, ed. R. S. Corruccini, R. L. Ciochon, pp. 345–376. Englewood Cliffs, N.J.: Prentice-Hall.

8. Kay, R. 1985. Dental evidence for the diet of *Australopithecus*. *Ann. Rev. Anthropol.* 14:315–341.

9. Demes, B., Creel, N. 1988. Bite force, diet, and cranial morphology of fossil hominids. *J. Hum. Evol.* 17:657–670.

10. Suwa, G., Wood, B. A., White, T. D. 1994. Further analysis of mandibular molar crown and cusp areas in Pliocene and early Pleistocene hominids. *Am. J. Phys. Anthropol.* 93:407–426.

11. McHenry, H. 1984. Relative cheek-tooth size in *Australopithecus*. *Am. J. Phys. Anthropol.* 64:297–306.

12. McHenry, H. 1985. Implications of postcanine megadontia for the origin of *Homo*. In *Ancestors: The hard evidence*, ed. E. Delson, pp. 178–183. New York: Alan R. Liss.

13. McHenry, H. 1988. New estimates of body weight in early hominids and their significance to encephalization and megadontia in robust australopithecines. In *Evolutionary history of the "robust" australopithecines*, ed. F. E. Grine, pp. 133–148. New York: Aldine de Gruyter.

14. McHenry, H. 1992. How big were early hominids? *Evol. Anthropol.* 1:15–20.

15. Rak, Y. 1983. *The australopithecine face.* New York: Academic.

16. McKee, J. 1989. Australopithecine anterior pillars: reassessment of the functional morphology and phylogenetic relevance. *Am. J. Phys. Anthropol.* 80:1–9.

17. Lieberman, P., Laitman, J., Reidenberg, J., Gannon, P. 1992. The anatomy, physiology, acoustics and perception of speech: Essential elements in analysis of the evolution of human speech. *J. Hum. Evol.* 23:447–467.

18. Laitman, J., Heimbuch, R., Crelin, E. 1979. The basicranium of fossil hominids as an indicator of their upper respiratory systems. *Am. J. Phys. Anthropol.* 51:15–34.

19. Laitman, J., Heimbuch, R. 1982. The basicranium of Plio-Pleistocene hominids as an indicator of their upper respiratory systems. *Am. J. Phys. Anthropol.* 59:323–343.

20. Laitman, J. 1984. The anatomy of human speech. *Nat. Hist.* 92:20–27.

21. Laitman, J. 1985. Evolution of the hominid upper respiratory tract: The fossil evidence. In *Human evolution: Past, present, and future*, ed. P. Tobias, pp. 281–286. New York: Alan R. Liss.

22. Gibson, K. R., Jessee, S. A. 1994. Cranial base shape and laryngeal position: Implications for Neanderthal language debates. *Am. J. Phys. Anthropol.* Suppl. 18:93.

23. Falk, D., Conroy, G. C. 1983. The cranial venous sinus system in *Australopithecus afarensis*. *Nature* 306:779–781.

24. Falk, D. 1986. Evolution of cranial blood drainage in hominids: Enlarged occipital/marginal sinuses and emissary foramina. *Am. J. Phys. Anthropol.* 70:311–324.

25. Tobias, P., Falk, D. 1988. Evidence for a dual pattern of cranial venous sinuses on the endocranial cast of Taung (*Australopithecus africanus*). *Am. J. Phys. Anthropol.* 76:309–312.

26. Brown, B., Walker, A., Ward, C. V., Leakey, R. E. 1993. New *Australopithecus boisei* calvaria from East Lake Turkana, Kenya. *Am. J. Phys. Anthropol.* 91:137–159.

27. Falk, D. 1990. Brain evolution in *Homo*: The "radiator" theory. *Behav. Brain Sci.* 13:333–381.

28. Falk, D. 1991. Breech birth of the genus *Homo*: Why bipedalism preceded the increase in brain size. In *Origine(s) de la bipedie chez les hominides*, ed. Y. Coppens, B. Senut, pp. 259–266. Paris: CNRS.

29. Porter, A. M. W. 1993. Sweat and thermoregulation in hominids. Comments prompted by the publications of P. E. Wheeler, 1984–1993. *J. Hum. Evol.* 25:417–423.

30. Wheeler, P. E. 1994. The thermoregulatory advantages of heat storage and shade-seeking behavior to hominids foraging in equatorial savannah environments. *J. Hum. Evol.* 26:339–350.

31. White, T. D., Suwa, G., Asfaw, B. 1995. *Australopithecus ramidus*, a new species of early hominid from Aramis, Ethiopia. *Nature* 375:88.

32. White, T. D., Suwa, G., Asfaw, B. 1994. *Australopithecus ramidus*, a new species of early hominid from Aramis, Ethiopia. *Nature* 371:306–312.

33. WoldeGabriel, G., White, T. D., Suwa, G., Renne, P., de Heinzelin, J., Hart, W. K., Heiken, G. 1994. Ecological and temporal placement of early Pliocene hominids at Aramis, Ethiopia. *Nature* 371:330–333.

34. Asfaw, B., Beyene, Y., Haile-Selassie, Y., Hart, W., Renne, P., Suwa, G., White, T., WoldeGabriel, G. 1995. Three seasons of hominid paleontology at Aramis, Ethiopia. Paleoanthropolgoy Society Conference, Oakland, CA.

35. Leakey, M. G., Feibel, C. S., McDougall, I., Walker, A. 1995. New four-million-year-old hominid species from Kanapoi and Allia Bay, Kenya. *Nature* 376:565–571.

36. Johanson, D., White, T. 1979. A systematic assessment of early African hominids. *Science* 202:321–330.

37. White, T., Johanson, D., Kimbel, W. 1981. *Australopithecus africanus*: Its phyletic position reconsidered. *S. Afr. J. Sci.* 77:445–470.

38. Skelton, R., McHenry, H., Drawhorn, G. 1986. Phylogenetic analysis of early hominids. *Curr. Anthropol.* 27:21–43.

39. Skelton, R., McHenry, H. 1992. Evolutionary relationships among early hominids. *J. Hum. Evol.* 23:309–349.

40. Ryan, A., Johanson, D. 1989. Anterior dental microwear in *Australopithecus afarensis*: Comparisons with human and nonhuman primates. *J. Hum. Evol.* 18:235–268.

41. Kimbel, W. H., Johanson, D. C., Rak, Y. 1994. The first skull and other new discoveries of *Australopithecus afarensis* at Hadar, Ethiopia. *Nature* 368:449–451.

42. Langdon, J., Bruckner, J., Baker, H. 1991. Pedal mechanics and bipedalism in early hominids. In *Origine(s) de la bipedie chez les hominides*, ed. Y. Coppens, B. Senut, pp. 159–167. Paris: CNRS.

43. Latimer, B., Lovejoy, O. 1989. The calcaneus of *Australopithecus afarensis* and its implications for the evolution of bipedality. *Am. J. Phys. Anthropol.* 78:369–386.

44. Latimer, B., Lovejoy, O. 1990. Metatarsophalangeal joints of *Australopithecus afarensis*. *Am. J. Phys. Anthropol.* 83:13–23.

45. Latimer, B., Lovejoy, O. 1990. Hallucal tarsometatarsal joint in *Australopithecus afarensis*. *Am. J. Phys. Anthropol.* 82:125–133.

46. Latimer, B. 1991. Locomotor adaptations in *Australopithecus afarensis*: The issue of arboreality. In *Origine(s) de la bipedie chez les hominides*, ed. Y. Coppens, B. Senut, pp. 169–176. Paris: CNRS.

47. Stern, J., Susman, R. 1983. The locomotor anatomy of *Australopithecus afarensis*. *Am. J. Phys. Anthropol.* 60:279–317.

48. McHenry, H. 1991. First steps? Analyses of the postcranium of early hominids. In *Origine(s) de la bipedie chez les hominides*, ed. Y. Coppens, B. Senut, pp. 133–141. Paris: CNRS.

49. Jungers, W. 1982. Lucy's limbs: Skeletal allometry and locomotion in *Australopithecus afarensis*. *Nature* 297:676–678.

50. Jungers, W., Stern, J. 1983. Body proportions, skeletal allometry and locomotion in the Hadar hominids: A reply to Wolpoff. *J. Hum. Evol.* 12:673–684.

51. Jungers, W. 1991. A pygmy perspective on body size and shape in *Australopithecus afarensis* (AL 288–1, "Lucy"). In *Origine(s) de la bipedie chez les hominides*, ed. Y. Coppens, B. Senut, pp. 215–224. Paris: CNRS.

52. Susman, R., Stern, J., Jungers, W. 1984. Arboreality and bipedality in the Hadar hominids. *Folia Primatol.* 43:113–156.

53. Foley, R. A., Lee, P. C. 1989. Finite social space, evolutionary pathways, and reconstructing hominid behavior. *Science* 243:901–905.

54. Richmond, B. G., Jungers, W. L. 1995. Size variation and sexual dimorphism in *Australopithecus afarensis* and living hominoids. *J. Hum. Evol.* 29:229–245.

55. White, T. D., Suwa, G., Hart, W. K., Walter, R. C., WoldeGabriel, G., de Heinzelin, J., Clark, J. D., Asfaw, B., Vrba, E. 1993. New discoveries of *Australopithecus* at Maka in Ethiopia. *Nature* 366:261–265.

56. White, T. 1984. Pliocene hominids from the Middle Awash, Ethiopia. *Cour. Forschungsinst. Senckenb.* 69:57–68.

57. Dart, R. 1925. *Australopithecus africanus:* The man-ape of South Africa. *Nature* 115:195–199.

58. Conroy, G. C., Vannier, M. 1987. Dental development of the Taung skull from computerized tomography. *Nature* 329:625–627.

59. Conroy, G., Vannier, M. 1988. The nature of Taung dental maturation continued. *Nature* 333:808.

60. Conroy, G. C., Vannier, M. W. 1991. Dental development in South African australopithecines Part II: Dental stage assessment. *Am. J. Phys. Anthropol.* 86:137–156.

61. Conroy, G. 1991. Enamel thickness in South African australopithecines: Non-invasive evaluation by computed tomography. *Palaeontol. Afr.* 28:53–58.

62. Holloway, R. 1984. The Taung endocast and the lunate sulcus: A rejection of the hypothesis of its anterior position. *Am. J. Phys. Anthropol.* 64:285–287.

63. Holloway, R. 1991. On Falk's 1989 accusations regarding Holloway's study of the Taung endocast: A reply. *Am. J. Phys. Anthropol.* 84:81–88.

64. Falk, D. 1983. The Taung endocast: A reply to Holloway. *Am. J. Phys. Anthropol.* 60:479–489.

65. Falk, D. 1985. Apples, oranges and the lunate sulcus. *Am. J. Phys. Anthropol.* 67:313–315.

66. Falk, D. 1989. Ape-like endocast of "ape-man" Taung. *Am. J. Phys. Anthropol.* 80:335–339.

67. Falk, D. 1991. Reply to Dr. Holloway: Shifting positions on the lunate sulcus. *Am. J. Phys. Anthropol.* 84:89–91.

68. Falk, D., Hildebolt, C., Vannier, M. W. 1989. Reassessment of the Taung early hominid from a neurological perspective. *J. Hum. Evol.* 18:485–492.

69. Broom, R. 1938. The Pleistocene anthropoid apes of South Africa. *Nature* 142:377–379.

70. Wood, B. A., Chamberlain, A. T. 1987. The nature and affinities of the "robust" australopithecines: A review. *J. Hum. Evol.* 16:625–641.

71. Rak, Y., Clarke, R. 1979. Aspects of the middle and external ear of early South African hominids. *Am. J. Phys. Anthropol.* 51:471–474.

72. Grine, F., Martin, L. 1988. Enamel thickness and development in *Australopithecus* and *Paranthropus.* In *Evolutionary history of the "robust" australopithecines,* ed. F. E. Grine, pp. 3–42. New York: Aldine de Gruyter.

73. Calcagno, J. M. 1995. Dental crowding in the South African early hominids. *Am. J. Phys. Anthropol.* Suppl. 20:71–72.

74. Grine, F., Kay, R. 1988. Early hominid diets from quantitative image analysis of dental microwear. *Nature* 333:765–768.

75. Kay, R., Grine, F. 1988. Tooth morphology, wear and diet in *Australopithecus* and *Paranthropus* from southern Africa. In *The evolutionary history of the "robust" australopithecines,* ed. F. E. Grine, pp. 427–447. New York: Aldine de Gruyter.

76. Sillen, A. 1992. Strontium-calcium rations (Sr/Ca) of *Australopithecus robustus* and associated fauna from Swartkrans. *J. Hum. Evol.* 23:495–516.

77. Lee-Thorp, J. A., van der Merwe, N. J. 1993. Stable carbon isotope studies of Swartkrans fossils. In *Swartkrans: A cave's chronicle of early man,* ed. C. K. Brain, pp. 251–264. Pretoria: Transvaal Museum.

78. Lee-Thorp, J. A., van der Merwe, N. J., Brain, C. K. 1994. Diet of *Australopithecus robustus* at Swartkrans from stable carbon isotopic analysis. *J. Hum. Evol.* 27:361–372.

79. Sillen, A., Hall, G., Armstrong, R. 1995. Strontium calcium ratios (Sr/CA) and strontium isotopic ratios (^{87}Sr/^{86}Sr) of *Australopithecus robustus* and *Homo* sp. from Swartkrans. *J. Hum. Evol.* 28:277–285.

80. Burton, J. H., Wright, L. E. 1995. Nonlinearity in the relationship between bone Sr/Ca and diet: Paleodietary implications. *Am. J. Phys. Anthropol.* 96:273–282.

81. Thackeray, J. 1995. Do strontium/calcium ratios in early Pleistocene hominids from

Swartkrans reflect physiological differences in males and females? *J. Hum. Evol.* 29:401–404.

82. Clarke, R., Howell, F., Brain, C. 1970. More evidence of an advanced hominid at Swartkrans. *Nature* 225:1219–1222.

83. Susman, R., Brain, T. 1988. New first metatarsal (SKX5017) from Swartkrans and the gait of *Paranthropus robustus*. *Am. J. Phys. Anthropol.* 77:7–15.

84. Susman, R., Stern, J. 1991. Locomotor behavior of early hominids: Epistemology and fossil evidence. In *Origine(s) de la bipedie chez les hominides*, ed. Y. Coppens, B. Senut, pp. 121–131. Paris: CNRS.

85. Susman, R. 1988. Hand of *Paranthropus robustus* from Member 1, Swartkrans: Fossil evidence for tool behavior. *Science* 240:781–784.

86. Susman, R. 1989. New hominid fossils from the Swartkrans Formation (1979–1986 excavations): Postcranial specimens. *Am. J. Phys. Anthropol.* 79:451–474.

87. Susman, R. L. 1994. Fossil evidence for early hominid tool use. *Science* 265:1570–1573.

88. Walker, A., Leakey, R., Harris, J., Brown, F. 1986. 2.5 myr *Australopithecus boisei* from west of Lake Turkana, Kenya. *Nature* 322:517–522.

89. Robinson, J. 1956. *The dentition of the Australopithecinae.* Pretoria: Transvaal Museum Mem.

90. Robinson, J. 1963. Adaptive radiation in the australopithecines and the origin of man. In *African ecology and human evolution*, ed. F. C. Howell, F. Bourliere, pp. 385–416. Chicago: Aldine.

91. Robinson, J. 1972. *Early hominid posture and locomotion.* Chicago: University of Chicago Press.

92. McCollum, M. A., Grine, F. E., Ward, S. C., Kimbel, W. H. 1993. Subnasal morphological variation in extant hominoids and fossil hominids. *J. Hum. Evol.* 24:87–111.

93. McCollum, M. A. 1994. Mechanical and spatial determinants of *Paranthropus* facial form. *Am. J. Phys. Anthropol.* 93:259–273.

94. Rak, Y. 1978. The functional significance of the squamosal suture in *Australopithecus boisei*. *Am. J. Phys. Anthropol.* 49:71–78.

95. Ungar, P., Grine, F. 1991. Incisor size and wear in *Australopithecus africanus* and *Paranthropus robustus*. *J. Hum. Evol.* 20:313–340.

96. McHenry, H. 1975. Fossil hominid body weight and brain size. *Nature* 254:686–688.

97. McHenry, H. 1976. Early hominid body weight and encephalization. *Am. J. Phys. Anthropol.* 45:77–84.

98. Jungers, W. 1988. New estimates of body size in australopithecines. In *Evolutionary history of the "robust" australopithecines*, ed. F. E. Grine, pp. 115–125. New York: Aldine de Gruyter.

99. Hartwig-Scherer, S. 1993. Body weight prediction in early fossil hominids: Towards a taxon-"independent" approach. *Am. J. Phys. Anthropol.* 92:17–36.

100. McHenry, H. 1991. Femoral lengths and stature in Plio-Pleistocene hominids. *Am. J. Phys. Anthropol.* 85:149–158.

101. McHenry, H. 1992. Body size and proportions in early hominids. *Am. J. Phys. Anthropol.* 87:407–431.

102. Martin, R. 1981. Relative brain size and basal metabolic rate in terrestrial vertebrates. *Nature* 293:57–60.

103. Tobias, P. V. 1994. The craniocerebral interface in early hominids. In *Integrative paths to the past*, ed. R. S. Corruccini, R. L. Ciochon, pp. 185–203. Englewood Cliffs, N.J.: Prentice-Hall.

104. Lovejoy, O. 1981. The origin of man. *Science* 211:341–350.

105. Lovejoy, O. 1988. Evolution of human walking. *Sci. Am.* 259:118–125.

106. Rosenberg, K. 1992. The evolution of modern human childbirth. *Yrbk. Phys. Anthropol.* 35:89–124.

107. Tuttle, R. 1974. Darwin's apes, dental apes, and the descent of man: Normal science in evolutionary anthropology. *Curr. Anthropol.* 15:389–398.

108. Begun, D. 1992. Miocene fossil hominids and the chimp-human clade. *Science* 257:1929–1933.

109. Tuttle, R. H. 1994. Up from Electromyography. In *Integrative paths to the past*, ed. R. S. Corruccini, R. L. Ciochon, pp. 269–284. Englewood Cliffs, N.J.: Prentice-Hall.

110. Day, M. 1985. Hominid locomotion—from Taung to the Laetoli footprints. In *Hominid evolution: Past, present and future*, ed. P. V. Tobias, pp. 115–127. New York: Alan R. Liss.

111. Tuttle, R. 1985. Ape footprints and Laetoli impressions: A response to the SUNY claims. In *Hominid evolution: Past, present, and future*, ed. P. V. Tobias, pp. 129–134. New York: Alan R. Liss.

112. Tuttle, R. 1987. Kinesiological inferences and evolutionary implications from Laetoli bipedal trails G-1, G-2/3, and A. In *Laetoli, a Pliocene site in Northern Tanzania*, ed. J.M. Harris, M. D. Leakey, pp. 503–523. Oxford: Clarendon.

113. White, T., Suwa, G. 1987. Hominid footprints at Laetoli: Facts and interpretations. *Am. J. Phys. Anthropol.* 72:485 - 514.

114. Stern, J., Susman, R. 1981. Electromyography of the gluteal muscles in *Hylobates, Pongo,* and *Pan*: Implications for the evolution of hominid bipedality. *Am. J. Phys. Anthropol.* 55:153–166.

115. Tardieu, C. 1991. Etude comparative des deplacements du centre de gravite du corps pendant la marche par une nouvelle methode d'analyse tridimentionnelle. Mise a l'epreuve du'une hypothese evolutive. In *Origine(s) de la bipedie chez les hominides*, ed. Y. Coppen, B. Senut, pp. 49–58. Paris: CNRS.

116. Tardieu, C., Aurengo, A., Tardieu, B. 1993. New method of three-dimensional analysis of bipedal locomotion for the study of displacements of the body and body-parts centers of mass in man and non-human primates: Evolutionary framework. *Am. J. Phys. Anthropol.* 90:455–476.

117. Kummer, B. 1991. Biomechanical foundations of the development of human bipedalism. In *Origine(s) de la bipedie chez les hominides*, ed. Y. Coppens, B. Senut, pp. 1–8. Paris: CNRS.

118. Biewener, A. A. 1990. Biomechanics of mammalian terrestrial locomotion. *Science* 250:1097–1103.

119. Zihlman, A., Brunker, L. 1979. Hominid bipedalism: Then and now. *Yrbk. Phys. Anthropol.* 22:132–162.

120. Jungers, W. 1988. Lucy's length: Stature reconstruction in *Australopithecus afarensis* (AL288–1) with implications for other small-bodied hominids. *Am. J. Phys. Anthropol.* 76:227–231.

121. Marzke, M. 1983. Joint functions and grips of the *Austalopithecus afarensis* hand, with special reference to the region of the capitate. *J. Hum. Evol.* 12:197–211.

122. Senut, B., Tardieu, C. 1985. Functional aspects of Plio-Pleistocene hominid limb bones: Implications for taxonomy and phylogeny. In *Ancestors: The hard evidence*, ed. E. Delson, pp. 193–201. New York: Alan R. Liss.

123. Senut, B. 1989. Climbing as a crucial preadaptation for human bipedalism. *OSSA* 14:35–44.

124. Tuttle, R. 1981. Evolution of hominid bipedalism and prehensile capabilities. *Philos. Trans. R. Soc. Lond. [Biol.]* 292:89–94.

125. Heinrich, R. E., Rose, M. D., Leakey, R. E., Walker, A. C. 1993. Hominid radius from the Middle Pliocene of Lake Turkana, Kenya. *Am. J. Phys. Anthropol.* 92:139–148.

126. Paciulli, L. M. 1995. Ontogeny of phalangeal curvature and positional behavior in chimpanzees. *Am. J. Phys. Anthropol.* Suppl. 20:165.

127. Smith, S. L. 1995. Pattern profile analysis of hominid and chimpanzee hand bones. *Am. J. Phys. Anthropol.* 96:283–300.

128. Ricklan, D. E. 1987. Functional anatomy of the hand of *Australopithecus africanus. J. Hum. Evol.* 16:643–664.

129. Marzke, M. W., Shackley, M. S. 1986. Hominid hand use in the Pliocene and Pleistocene: Evidence from experimental archaeology and comparative morphology. *J. Hum. Evol.* 15:439–460.

130. Lovejoy, O. 1975. Biomechanical perspectives on the lower limbs of early hominids. In *Primate functional morphology and evolution*, ed. R. Tuttle, pp. 291–326. The Hague: Mouton.

131. Berge, C. 1994. How did the australopithecines walk: A biomechanical study of the hip and thigh of *Australopithecus afarensis*. *J. Hum. Evol.* 26:259–273.

132. Stern, J., Susman, R. 1991. "Total morphological pattern" versus the "magic trait"? In *Origine(s) de la bipedie chez les hominides*, ed. Y. Coppen, B. Senut, pp. 121–131. Paris: CNRS.

133. Schmid, P. 1991. The trunk of the australopithecines. In *Origine(s) de la bipedie chez les hominides*, ed. Y. Coppens, B. Senut, pp. 225–234. Paris: CNRS.

134. Rak, Y. 1991. Lucy's pelvic anatomy: Its role in bipedal gait. *J. Hum. Evol.* 20:283–290.

135. Tuttle, R., Webb, D., Tuttle, N. 1991. Laetoli footprint trails and the evolution of hominid bipedalism. In *Origine(s) de la bipedie chez les hominides*, ed. Y. Coppens, B. Senut, pp. 187–198. Paris: CNRS.

136. Duncan, A. S., Kappelman, J., Shapiro, L. J. 1994. Metatarsophalangeal joint function and positional behavior in *Australopithecus afarensis*. *Am. J. Phys. Anthropol.* 93:67–81.

137. Lovejoy, O., Heiple, K., Burstein, A. 1973. The gait of *Australopithecus*. *Am. J. Phys. Anthropol.* 38:757–779.

138. Senut, B., Tobias, P. 1989. A preliminary examination of some new hominid upper limb remains from Sterkfontein (1974–1984). *C. R. Acad. Sci. [III]* 308:565–571.

139. McHenry, H. M. 1994. Early hominid postcrania. In *Integrative paths to the past*, ed. R. S. Corruccini, R. L. Ciochon, pp. 251–268. Englewood Cliffs, N.J.: Prentice-Hall.

140. Clarke, R. J., Tobias, P. V. 1995. Sterkfontein Member 2 foot bones of the oldest South African hominid. *Science* 269:521–524.

141. Schultz, A. 1968. The recent hominoid primates. In *Perspective on human evolution*, ed. S. Washburn, P. Jay, pp. 122–195. New York: Holt, Rinehart and Winston.

142. Latimer, B., Ward, C. 1993. The thoracic and lumbar vertebrae. In *The Nariokotome Homo erectus skeleton*, ed. A. Walker, R. E. Leakey, pp. 266–293. Cambridge, Mass.: Harvard University Press.

143. Ward, C., Latimer, B. 1991. The vertebral column of *Australopithecus*. *Am. J. Phys. Anthropol.* 12:180.

144. Shapiro, L. 1993. Evaluation of "unique" aspects of human vertebral bodies and pedicles with a consideration of *Australopithecus africanus*. *J. Hum. Evol.* 25:433–470.

145. Reed, K. E., Kitching, J. W., Grine, F. E., Jungers, W. L., Sokoloff, L. 1993. Proximal femur of *Australopithecus africanus* from Member 4, Makapansgat, South Africa. *Am. J. Phys. Anthropol.* 92:1–15.

146. McHenry, H., Berger, L. 1996. Ape-like body proportions in *A. africanus* and their implications for the origin of the genus *Homo*. *Am. J. Phys. Anthropol.* Suppl. 22:163–164.

147. Susman, R. L. 1993. Hominid postcranial remains from Swartkrans. In *Swartkrans: A cave's chronicle of early man*, ed. C. K. Brain, pp. 117–136. Pretoria: Transvaal Museum.

148. Grausz, H. M., Leakey, R. E. F., Walker, A. C., Ward, C. 1988. Associated cranial and postcranial bones of *Australopithecus boisei*. In *Evolutionary history of the "robust" australopithecines*, ed. F. E. Grine, pp. 127–132. New York: Aldine de Gruyter.

149. Spoor, C. F. 1993. *The comparative morphology and phylogeny of the human bony labyrinth*, Ph.D. thesis, Universitéit Utrecht.

150. Spoor, F., Wood, B., Zonneveld, F. 1994. Implications of early hominid labyrinthine morphology for evolution of human bipedal bocomotion. *Nature* 369:645–648.

151. McHenry, H., Corruccini, R. 1975. Multivariate analysis of early hominid pelvic bones. *Am. J. Phys. Anthropol.* 43:263–270.

152. McHenry, H. 1975. The ischium and hip extensor mechanism in human evolution. *Am. J. Phys. Anthropol.* 43:39–46.

153. Leutenegger, W. 1987. Neonatal brain size and neurocranial dimensions in Pliocene hominids: Implications for obstetrics. *J. Hum. Evol.* 16:291–296.

154. Tague, R. G., Lovejoy, C. O. 1986. The obstetric pelvis of A.L. 288–1 (Lucy). *J. Hum. Evol.* 15:237–255.

155. Tague, R. G. 1991. Commonalities in dimorphism and variability in the anthropoid pelvis, with implications for the fossil record. *J. Hum. Evol.* 21:153–176.

156. Hausler, M., Schmid, P. 1995. Comparison of the pelves of Sts 14 and AL 288–1: Implications for birth and sexual dimorphism in australopithecines. *J. Hum. Evol.* 29:363–383.

157. Jablonski, N. G., Chaplin, G. 1993. Origin of habitual terrestrial bipedalism in the ancestor of the Hominidae. *J. Hum. Evol.* 24:259–280.

158. Rose, M. 1991. The process of bipedalization in hominids. In *Origine(s) de la bipedie chez les hominides,* ed. Y. Coppens, B. Senut, pp. 37–48. Paris: CNRS.

159. Coppens, Y., Senut, B., eds. 1991. *Origine(s) de la bipedie chez les hominides.* Paris: CNRS.

160. Taylor, R., Schmidt-Nielsen, K., Raab, J. 1970. Scaling of energetic cost of running to body size in mammals. *Ann. J. Physiol.* 219:1104–1107.

161. Taylor, R., Rowntree, V. 1973. Running on two or on four legs: Which consumes more energy? *Science* 179:186–187.

162. Ishida, H. 1991. A strategy for long distance walking in the earliest hominids: Effect of posture on energy expenditure during bipedal walking. In *Origine(s) de le bipedie chez les hominides,* ed. Y. Coppens, B. Senut, pp. 9–15. Paris: CNRS.

163. Rodman, P., McHenry, H. 1980. Bioenergetics and the origin of hominid bipedalism. *Am. J. Phys. Anthropol.* 52:103–106.

164. Jolly, C. 1970. The seed-eaters: A new model of hominid differentiation based on a baboon analogy. *Man* 5:5–26.

165. Lovejoy, O. 1993. Modeling human origins: Are we sexy because we're smart, or smart because we're sexy? In *The origin and evolution of humans and humanness,* ed. D. T. Rasmussen, pp. 1–28. Boston: Jones and Bartlett.

166. Fleagle, J., Kay, R., Simons, E. 1980. Sexual dimorphism in early anthropoids. *Nature* 287:328–330.

167. Leutenegger, W., Shell, B. 1987. Variability and sexual dimporphism in canine size of *Australopithecus* and extant hominoids. *J. Hum. Evol.* 16:359–367.

168. Plavcan, J. M., van Schaik, C. P., Kappeler, P. M. 1995. Competition, coalitions and canine size in primates. *J. Hum. Evol.* 28:245–276.

169. Conroy, G. C., Vannier, M. W. 1991. Dental development in South African australopithecines: Part I: Problems of pattern and chronology. *Am. J. Phys. Anthropol.* 86:121–136.

170. Conroy, G. C., Mahoney, C. 1991. A mixed longitudinal study of dental emergence in the chimpanzee, *Pan troglodytes* (Primates, Pongidae). *Am. J. Phys. Anthropol.* 86:243–254.

171. Dobzhansky, T. 1962. *Mankind evolving.* New Haven, Conn.: Yale University Press.

172. Mann, A. 1975. *Some paleodemographic aspects of the South African australopithecines.* Philadelphia: University of Pennsylvania Publications in Anthropology.

173. Bromage, T., Dean, M. 1985. Re-evaluation of the age at death of immature fossil hominids. *Nature* 317:525–527.

174. Bromage, T. G. 1987. The biological and chronological maturation of early hominids. *J. Hum. Evol.* 16:257–272..

175. Smith, B. 1986. Dental development in *Australopithecus* and early *Homo. Nature* 323:327–330.

176. Smith, B. H. 1994. Patterns of dental development in *Homo, Australopithecus, Pan,* and *Gorilla. Am. J. Phys. Anthropol.* 94:307–325.

177. Broom, R., Robinson, J. 1951. Eruption of the permanent teeth in the South African fossil ape-men. *Nature* 167:443.

178. Wallace, J. 1972. *The dentition of the South African early hominids: A study of form and function*, University of the Witwatersrand, Johannesburg.

179. Dean, M. C. 1985. The eruption pattern of the permanent incisors and first permanent molars in *Australopithecus (Paranthropus) robustus. Am. J. Phys. Anthropol.* 67:251–258.

180. Grine, F. 1987. On the eruption pattern of the permanent incisors and first permanent molars in *Paranthropus. Am. J. Phys. Anthropol.* 72:353–360.

181. Conroy, G. 1988. Alleged synapomorphy of the M1/I1 eruption pattern in robust australopithecines and *Homo*: Evidence from high-resolution computed tomography. *Am. J. Phys. Anthropol.* 75:487–492.

182. Kuykendall, K., Mahoney, C., Conroy, G. 1992. Probit and survival analysis of tooth emergence ages in a mixed-longitudinal sample of chimpanzees (*Pan troglodytes*). *Am. J. Phys. Anthropol.* 89:379–399.

183. Conroy, G., Kuykendall, K. 1995. Paleopediatrics: Or when did human infants really become human? *Am. J. Phys. Anthropol.* 98:121–131.

184. Dean, M. C., Beynon, A. D., Thackeray, J. F., Macho, G. A. 1993. Histological reconstruction of dental development and age at death of a juvenile *Paranthropus robustus* specimen, SK 63, from Swartkrans, South Africa. *Am. J. Phys. Anthropol.* 91:401–419.

185. Dean, M. 1987. The dental developmental status of six East African juvenile fossil hominids. *J. Hum. Evol.* 16:197–213.

186. Beynon, A., Dean, M. 1988. Distinct dental development patterns in early fossil hominids. *Nature* 335:509–514.

187. Ramirez-Rozzi, F. V. 1993. Tooth development in East African *Paranthropus. J. Hum. Evol.* 24:429–454.

188. Shipman, P. 1987. An age-old question: Why did the human lineage survive. *Discovery* April:60–64.

189. Smith, B. H. 1993. Physiological age of KNM-WT 15000. In *The Nariokotome* Homo erectus *skeleton*, ed. A. Walker, R. Leakey, pp. 195–220. Cambridge, Mass.: Harvard University Press.

190. Smith, B. H., Brandt, K. L., Tompkins, R. L. 1995. Developmental age of the KMN-WT 15000 *Homo erectus* in broad perspective. *Am. J. Phys. Anthropol.* Suppl. 20:196–197.

191. Smith, R. J., Gannon, P. J., Smith, B. H. 1995. Ontogeny of australopithecines and early *Homo*: Evidence from cranial capacity and dental eruption. *J. Hum. Evol.* 29:155–168.

192. Hunt, K. D. 1994. The evolution of human bipedality: Ecology and functional morphology. *J. Hum. Evol.* 26:183–202.

193. Jolly, C., Plog, F. 1986. *Physical anthropology and archeology.* New York: McGraw-Hill.

194. Boesch, C., Marchesi, P., Marchesi, N., Fruth, B., Joulian, F. 1994. Is nut cracking in wild chimpanzees a cultural behavior? *J. Hum. Evol.* 26:325–338.

195. Boesch-Achermann, H., Boesch, C. 1994. Hominization in the rainforest: The chimpanzee's piece of the puzzle. *Evol. Anthropol.* 3:9–16.

196. Sugiyama, Y. 1994. Tool use by wild chimpanzees. *Nature* 367:327.

197. Goodall, J. 1976. Continuities between chimpanzee and human behavior. In *Human origins: Louis Leakey and the East African evidence*, ed. G. Isaac, T. McCown, pp. 81–95. Menlo Park: W.A. Benjamin.

198. Toth, N., Schick, K. D., Savage-Rumbaugh, E. S., Sevcik, R. A., Rumbaugh, D. M. 1993. Pan the toolmaker: Investigations into the stone toolmaking and tool-using capabilities of a bonobo (*Pan paniscus*). *J. Archaeol. Sci.* 20:81–91.

199. Howell, F. 1978. Hominidae. In *Evolution of African mammals*, ed. V. J. Maglio, H. B. S. Cooke, pp. 154–248. Cambridge, Mass.: Harvard University Press.

200. Leakey, M. 1981. *Olduvai Gorge.* Cambridge: Cambridge University Press.

201. Toth, N. 1987. Behavioral inferences from early stone artifact assemblages: An experimental model. *J. Hum. Evol.* 16:763–787.

202. Asfaw, B., Beyene, Y., Suwa, G., Walter, R., White, T., WoldeGabriel, G., Yemane, T. 1992. The earliest Acheulean from Konso-Gardula. *Nature* 360:732–735.

203. Asfaw, B. 1995. Progress in paleoanthropology at Konso Gardula. *Am. J. Phys. Anthropol.* Suppl. 20:60.

204. Brain, C., Sillen, A. 1988. Evidence from the Swartkrans cave for the earliest use of fire. *Nature* 336:464–466.

205. Sibley, C., Ahlquist, J. 1984. The phylogeny of the hominoid primates as indicated by DNA-DNA hybridization. *J. Mol. Evol.* 20:2–15.

206. Sibley, C., Ahlquist, J. 1987. DNA hybridization evidence of hominid phylogeny: Results from an expanded data set. *J. Mol. Evol.* 26:99–121.

207. Weiss, M. 1987. Nucleic acid evidence bearing on hominoid relationships. *Yrbk. Phys. Anthropol.* 30:41–73.

208. Rogers, J. 1993. The phylogenetic relationships among *Homo*, *Pan* and *Gorilla*: A population genetics perspective. *J. Hum. Evol.* 25:201–215.

209. Rogers, J. 1994. Levels of the genealogical hierarchy and the problem of hominoid phylogeny. *Am. J. Phys. Anthropol.* 94:81–88.

210. Ruvolo, M., Disotell, T., Allard, M., Brown, W. 1991. Resolution of the African hominoid trichotomy by use of a mitochondrial gene sequence. *Proc. Natl. Acad. Sci. U.S.A.* 88:1570–1574.

211. Ruvolo, M. 1994. Molecular evolutionary processes and conflicting gene trees: The hominoid case. *Am. J. Phys. Anthropol.* 94:89–113.

212. Templeton, A. 1984. Phylogenetic inference from restriction endonuclease site maps with particular reference to the evolution of humans and apes. *Evolution* 37:221–244.

213. Templeton, A. 1985. The phylogeny of the hominoid primates: A statistical analysis of the DNA-DNA hybridization data. *Mol. Biol. Evol.* 2:420–433.

214. Marks, J., Schmid, C. W., Sarich, V. M. 1988. DNA hybridization as a guide to phylogeny: Relations of the hominoidea. *J. Hum. Evol.* 17:769–786.

215. Marks, J. 1994. Blood will tell (won't it?): A century of molecular discourse in anthropological systematics. *Am. J. Phys. Anthropol.* 94:59–79.

216. Ruano, G., Rogers, J., Ferguson-Smith, A., Kidd, K. 1992. DNA sequence polymorphism within hominoid species exceeds the number of phylogenetically informative characters of a HOX2 locus. *Mol. Biol. Evol.* 9:575–586.

217. Bailey, W. J. 1993. Hominoid trichotomy: A molecular overview. *Evol. Anthropol.* 2:100–108.

218. Huxley, T. 1863. *Evidence as to man's place in nature*. London: Williams and Norgate.

219. Conroy, G. 1990. *Primate evolution*. New York: W. W. Norton.

220. Tattersall, I. 1986. Species recognition in human paleontology. *J. Hum. Evol.* 15:165–175.

221. Foley, R. 1991. How many species of hominid should there be? *J. Hum. Evol.* 20:413–427.

222. Tobias, P. 1988. Numerous apparently synapomorphic features in *Australopithecus robustus*, *Australopithecus boisei* and *Homo habilis*: Support for the Skelton-McHenry-Drawhorn hypotheses. In *Evolutionary history of the "robust" australopithecines*, ed. F. E. Grine, pp. 293–309. New York: Aldine de Gruyter.

223. Olson, T. 1985. Cranial morphology and systematics of the Hadar Formation hominids and *Australopithecus africanus*. In *Ancestors: The hard evidence*, ed. E. Delson, pp. 102–119. New York: Alan R. Liss.

224. Zihlman, A. 1985. *Australopithecus afarensis*: Two sexes or two species? In *Hominid evolution: Past, present and future*, ed. P. V. Tobias, pp. 213–220. New York: Alan R. Liss.

225. Grine, F. 1988. Evolutionary history of the "robust" australopithecines: A summary and historical perspective. In *Evolutionary history of the "robust" australopithecines*, ed. F. E. Grine, pp. 509–519. New York: Aldine de Gruyter.

226. Rak, Y. 1985. Australopithecine taxonomy and phylogeny in light of facial morphology. *Am. J. Phys. Anthropol.* 66:281–287.

227. Eckhardt, R. 1987. Hominoid nasal region polymorphism and its phylogenetic significance. *Nature* 328:333–335.

228. Kimbel, W. 1984. Variation in the pattern of cranial venous sinuses and hominid phylogeny. *Am. J. Phys. Anthropol.* 63:243–263.

229. Wolpoff, M. 1971. Competitive exclusion among lower Pleistocene hominids: The single species hypothesis. *Man* 6:601–614.

230. Pilbeam, D., Gould, S. 1974. Size and scaling in human evolution. *Science* 186:892–901.

231. Lieberman, P. 1992. Human speech and language. In *The Cambridge encyclopedia of human evolution*, ed. S. Jones, R. Martin, D. Pilbeam, pp. 134–137. Cambridge: Cambridge University Press.

232. White, T. 1977. New fossil hominids from Laetolil, Tanzania. *Am. J. Phys. Anthropol.* 46:197–230.

233. Tattersall, I., Delson, E., Van Couvering, J., eds. 1988. *Encyclopedia of human evolution and prehistory.* New York: Garland.

234. Martin, R. 1992. Walking on two legs. In *The Cambridge encyclopedia of human evolution*, ed. S. Jones, R. Martin, D. Pilbeam, p. 78. Cambridge: Cambridge University Press.

235. Walker, A. 1993. The origin of the genus *Homo*. In *The origin and evolution of humans and humanness*, ed. D. T. Rasmussen, pp. 29–47. Boston: Jones and Bartlett.

236. Jolly, C., Plog, F. 1986. *Physical anthropology and archaeology.* New York: McGraw-Hill.

237. Shipman, P. 1994. Those ears were made for walking. *New Scientist* July 30:26–29.

238. Isaac, G. L. 1983. Aspects of human evolution. In *Evolution from molecules to men*, ed. D. Bendall, pp. 509–543. New York: Cambridge University Press.

239. Schultz, A. H. 1969. *The life of primates.* New York: Universe.

240. Kuykendall, K. L. 1992. *Dental development in chimpanzees* (Pan troglodytes) *and implications for dental development patterns in fossil hominids.* Washington University, St. Louis.

241. Ramirez-Rozzi, F. V. 1994. Enamel growth markers in hominid dentition. *Eur. Microsc. Anal.* July:21–23.

242. Gowlett, J. 1992. Tools—the Palaeolithic record. In *The Cambridge encyclopedia of human evolution*, ed. S. Jones, R. Martin, D. Pilbeam, pp. 350–360. Cambridge: Cambridge University Press.

243. Potts, R. 1993. Archeological interpretations of early hominid behavior and ecology. In *The origin and evolution of humans and humanness*, ed. D. T. Rasmussen, pp. 49–74. Boston: Jones and Bartlett.

244. Toth, N. 1985. The Oldowan reassessed: A close look at early stone artifacts. *J. Archaeol. Sci.* 12:101–120.

245. Clark, J. 1970. *The prehistory of Africa.* New York: Praeger.

246. Grine, F. 1993. Australopithecine taxonomy and phylogeny: Historical background and recent interpretation. In *The human evolution source book*, ed. R. L. Ciochon, J. G. Fleagle, pp. 198–210. Englewood Cliffs, N.J.: Prentice-Hall.

247. Wood, B. 1994. The oldest hominid yet. *Nature* 371:280–281.

CHAPTER VI

1. Tattersall, I. 1986. Species recognition in human paleontology. *J. Hum. Evol.* 15:165–175.

2. Foley, R. 1991. How many species of hominid should there be? *J. Hum. Evol.* 20:413–427.

3. McHenry, H. 1992. How big were early hominids? *Evol. Anthropol.* 1:15–20.

4. McHenry, H. 1992. Body size and proportions in early hominids. *Am. J. Phys. Anthropol.* 87:407–431.

5. Feldesman, M., Lundy, J. 1988. Stature estimates for some African Plio-Pleistocene fossil hominids. *J. Hum. Evol.* 17:583–596.

6. LeGros Clark, W. 1955. *The fossil evidence for human evolution.* Chicago: University of Chicago Press.

7. Howell, F. 1978. Hominidae. In *Evolution of African mammals*, ed. V. J. Maglio, H. B. S. Cooke, pp. 154–248. Cambridge, Mass.: Harvard University Press.

8. Leakey, L., Tobias, P., Napier, J. 1964. A new species of the genus *Homo* from Olduvai Gorge. *Nature* 202:7–9.

9. Stringer, C. 1986. The credibility of *Homo habilis*. In *Major topics in primate and human*

evolution, ed. B. Wood, L. Martin, P. Andrews, pp. 266–294. Cambridge: Cambridge University Press.

10. Chamberlain, A., Wood, B. 1987. Early hominid phylogeny. *J. Hum. Evol.* 16:119–133.
11. Skelton, R., McHenry, H. 1992. Evolutionary relationships among early hominids. *J. Hum. Evol.* 23:309–349.
12. Wood, B. 1991. *Koobi Fora Research Project IV: Hominid cranial remains from Koobi Fora.* Oxford: Clarendon.
13. Wood, B. 1992. Origin and evolution of the genus *Homo. Nature* 355:783–790.
14. Tobias, P. 1991. *Olduvai Gorge IV: The skulls, endocasts and teeth of* Homo habilis. Cambridge: Cambridge University Press.
15. Tobias, P. 1964. The Olduvai Bed I hominine with special reference to its cranial capacity. *Nature* 202:3–4.
16. Holloway, R. 1965. Cranial capacity of the hominine from Olduvai Bed I. *Nature* 208:205–206.
17. Tobias, P. 1965. *Australopithecus, Homo habilis*, tool-using and toolmaking. *S. Afr. Arch. Bull.* 20:167–192.
18. Clarke, R. 1985. *Australopithecus* and early *Homo* in southern Africa. In *Ancestors: The hard evidence*, ed. E. Delson, pp. 171–177. New York: Alan R. Liss.
19. Clarke, R., Howell, F. 1972. Affinities of the Swartkrans 847 hominid cranium. *Am. J. Phys. Anthropol.* 37:319–336.
20. Tobias, P. 1966. The distinctiveness of *Homo habilis. Nature* 209:953–960.
21. Napier, J. R., Tobias, P. V. 1964. The case for *Homo habilis*. The Times, London, June 5, 1964.
22. Howell, F. 1965. New discoveries in Tanganyika: Their bearing on hominid evolution (reply to Tobias). *Curr. Anthropol.* 6:399–401.
23. Robinson, J. 1965. *Homo "habilis"* and the australopithecines. *Nature* 205:121–124.
24. Tobias, P. 1965. New discoveries in Tanganyika: Their bearing on hominid evolution. *Curr. Anthropol.* 6:391–411.
25. Tobias, P. 1989. The gradual appraisal of *Homo habilis*. In *Hominidae: Proc. 2nd Int. Cong. Hum. Paleontol.*, pp. 151–154. Milan: Editoriale Jaca Book.
26. Tobias, P. 1989. The status of *Homo habilis* in 1987 and some outstanding problems. In *Hominidae: Proc. 2nd Int. Cong. Hum. Paleontol.*, pp. 141–149. Milan: Editoriale Jaca Book.
27. Leakey, L. 1966. *Homo habilis, Homo erectus* and the australopithecines. *Nature* 209:1279–1281.
28. Leakey, M., Clarke, R., Leakey, L. 1971. New hominid skull from Bed 1, Olduvai Gorge, Tanzania. *Nature* 232:308–312.
29. Boaz, N., Howell, F. 1977. A gracile hominid cranium from Upper Member G of the Shungura Formation, Ethiopia. *Am. J. Phys. Anthropol.* 46:93–108.
30. Hughes, A., Tobias, P. 1977. A fossil skull probably of the genus *Homo* from Sterkfontein, Transvaal. *Nature* 265:310–312.
31. Harris, J., Brown, F., Leakey, M., Walker, A., Leakey, R. 1988. Pliocene and Pleistocene hominid-bearing sites from west of Lake Turkana, Kenya. *Science* 239:27–33.
32. Falk, D. 1980. Hominid brain evolution: The approach from paleoneurology. *Yrbk. Phys. Anthropol.* 23:93–107.
33. Falk, D. 1983. Cerebral cortices of east African early hominids. *Science* 221:1072–1074.
34. Falk, D. 1987. Brain lateralization in primates and its evolution in hominids. *Yrbk Phys. Anthropol.* 30:107–125.
35. Tobias, P. 1987. The brain of *Homo habilis*: A new level of organization in cerebral evolution. *J. Hum. Evol.* 16:741–761.
36. Trinkaus, E. 1989. Olduvai hominid 7 trapezial metacarpal 1 articular morphology: Contrasts with recent humans. *Am. J. Phys. Anthropol.* 80:411–416.
37. Johanson, D., Masao, F., Eck, G., White, T., Walter, R., Kimbel, W., Asfaw, B., Manega,

P., Ndessokia, P., Suwa, G. 1987. New partial skeleton of *Homo habilis* from Olduvai Gorge, Tanzania. *Nature* 327:205–209.

38. Johanson, D. 1989. A partial *Homo habilis* skeleton from Olduvai Gorge, Tanzania: A summary of preliminary results. In *Hominidae: Proc. 2nd Int. Cong. Hum. Paleontol.*, pp. 155–166. Milan: Editoriale Jaca Book.

39. Jungers, W., Stern, J. 1983. Body proportions, skeletal allometry and locomotion in the Hadar hominids: A reply to Wolpoff. *J. Hum. Evol.* 12:673–684.

40. Hartwig-Scherer, S., Martin, R. 1991. Was "Lucy" more human than her "child"? Observations on early hominid postcranial skeletons. *J. Hum. Evol.* 21:439–449.

41. Tattersall, I. 1992. Species concepts and species identification in human evolution. *J. Hum. Evol.* 22:341–349.

42. Rightmire, G. P. 1993. Variation among early *Homo* crania from Olduvai Gorge and the Koobi Fora region. *Am. J. Phys. Anthropol.* 90:1–33.

43. Groves, C. 1989. *A theory of human and primate evolution.* Oxford: Clarendon.

44. Walker, A., Leakey, R. 1978. The hominids of East Turkana. *Sci. Am.* 239:54–66.

45. Leakey, R. 1971. Further evidence of lower Pleistocene hominids from East Rudolf, North Kenya. *Nature* 231:241–245.

46. Leakey, R. 1972. Further evidence of lower Pleistocene hominids from East Rudolf, North Kenya, 1971. *Nature* 237:264–269.

47. Leakey, R. 1973. Evidence for an advanced Plio-Pleistocene hominid from East Rudolf, Kenya. *Nature* 242:447–450.

48. Leakey, R. 1974. Further evidence of lower Pleistocene hominids from East Rudolf, North Kenya, 1973. *Nature* 248:653–656.

49. Leakey, R., Wood, B. 1973. New evidence of the genus *Homo* from East Rudolf Kenya. II. *Am. J. Phys. Anthropol.* 39:355–368.

50. Leakey, R., Wood, B. 1974. New evidence of the genus *Homo* from East Rudolf, Kenya. IV. *Am. J. Phys. Anthropol.* 41:237–244.

51. Groves, C., Mazak, V. 1975. An approach to the taxon of Hominidae: Gracile Villafranchian hominids of Africa. *Casopsis SPro Mineralogii a Geologii* 20:225–246.

52. Walker, A. 1981. The Koobi Fora hominids and their bearing on the origins of the genus *Homo*. In Homo erectus: *Papers in honor of Davidson Black*, ed. B. A. Sigmon, J. S. Cybulski, pp. 193–215. Toronto: University of Toronto Press.

53. Wood, B. 1992. Early hominid species and speciation. *J. Hum. Evol.* 22:351–365.

54. Schrenk, R., Bromage, T. G., Betzler, C. G., Ring, U., Juwayeyi, Y. M. 1993. Oldest *Homo* and Pliocene biogeography of the Malawi Rift. *Nature* 365:833–835.

55. Wood, B. 1993. Rift on the record. *Nature* 365:789–790.

56. Bromage, T. G., Schrenk, F., Zonneveld, F. W. 1995. Paleoanthropology of the Malawi Rift: An early hominid mandible from the Chiwondo Beds, northern Malawi. *J. Hum. Evol.* 28:71–108.

57. Wood, B. 1985. Early *Homo* in Kenya, and its systematic relationships. In *Ancestors: The hard evidence*, ed. E. Delson, pp. 206–214. New York: Alan R. Liss.

58. Kramer, A., Donnelly, S., Kidder, J., Ousley, S., Olah, S. 1995. Craniometric variation in large-bodied hominoids: Testing the single-species hypothesis for *Homo habilis*. *J. Hum. Evol.* 29:443–462.

59. Lieberman, D., Wood, B., Pilbeam, D. 1996. Homoplasy and early *Homo*: An analysis of the evolutionary relationships of *H. habilis sensu stricto* and *H. rudolfensis*. *J. Hum. Evol.* 30:97–120.

60. Miller, J. 1991. Does brain size variability provide evidence of multiple species in *Homo habilis*? *Am. J. Phys. Anthropol.* 84:385–398.

61. Cartmill, M. 1990. Human uniqueness and theoretical content in paleoanthropology. *Int. J. Primatol.* 11:173–192.

62. Bartholomew, G., Birdsell, J. 1953. Ecology and the protohominids. *Am. Anthropol.* 55:481–498.

63. Tooby, J., DeVore, I. 1987. The reconstruction of hominid behavioral evolution through strategic modeling. In *The evolution of human behavior: Primate models*, ed. W. Kinzey, pp. 183–237. Albany: SUNY Press.

64. Stanford, C., Allen, J. 1991. On strategic storytelling: Current models of human behavioral evolution. *Curr. Anthropol.* 32:58–61.

65. Moore, J. 1996. Savanna chimpanzees, referential models and the last common ancestor. In *Great Ape societies,* ed. W. McGrew, L. Marchant, T. Nishida, pp. 275–292. Cambridge: Cambridge University Press.

66. Lovejoy, O. 1981. The origin of man. *Science* 211:341–350.

67. Lovejoy, O. 1993. Modeling human origins: Are we sexy because we're smart, or smart because we're sexy? In *The origin and evolution of humans and humanness*, ed. D. T. Rasmussen, pp. 1–28. Boston: Jones and Bartlett.

68. DeVore, I., Washburn, S. L. 1963. Baboon ecology and human evolution. In *African ecology and human evolution*, ed. F. C. Howell, F. Bourliere, pp. 335–367. Chicago: Aldine.

69. Zihlman, A., Cronin, J., Cramer, D., Sarich, V. 1978. Pygmy chimpanzee as a possible prototype for the common ancestor of humans, chimpanzees and gorillas. *Nature* 275:744–746.

70. Zihlman, A. 1983. A behavioral reconstruction of *Australopithecus*. In *Hominid origins: Inquiries past and present*, ed. K. Reichs, pp. 207–238. Washington, D.C.: University Press of America.

71. Hawkes, K., O'Connell, J. F., Blurton-Jones, N. G. 1991. Hunting income patterns among the Hadza: Big game, common goods, foraging goals and the evolution of the human diet. *Philos. Trans. R. Soc. Lond. [Biol.]* 334:243–251.

72. Hawkes, K. 1993. Why hunter-gatherers work: An ancient version of the problem of common goods. *Curr. Anthropol.* 34:341–361.

73. Binford, L. 1985. Human ancestors: Changing views of their behavior. *J. Anthropol. Archaeol.* 4:292–327.

74. Blumenschine, R. J. 1995. Percussion marks, tooth marks, and experimental determinations of the timing of hominid and carnivore access to long bones at FLK *Zinjanthropus*, Olduvai Gorge, Tanzania. *J. Hum. Evol.* 29:21–51.

75. Washburn, S., Lancaster, C. 1968. The evolution of hunting. In *Man the hunter*, ed. R. B. Lee, I. DeVore, pp. 293–303. Chicago: Aldine.

76. Cartmill, M. 1993. *A view to a death in the morning.* Cambridge, Mass.: Harvard University Press.

77. Blumenschine, R., Cavallo, J. 1992. Scavenging and human evolution. *Sci. Am.* Oct.:90–96.

78. Fedigan, L. 1982. *Primate paradigms: Sex roles and social bonds.* Montreal: Edeb.

79. Goodall, J. 1986. *Chimpanzees of Gombe: Patterns of behavior.* Cambridge, Mass.: Harvard University Press.

80. Hamai, M., Nishida, T., Takasaki, H., Turner, L. A. 1992. New records of within-group infanticide and cannibalism in wild chimpanzees. *Primates* 33:151–162.

81. Isaac, G. 1971. The diet of early man: Aspects of archaeological evidence from lower and middle Pleistocene sites in Africa. *World Archaeol.* 2:278–299.

82. Isaac, G. 1978. The Olorgesailie Formation: Stratigraphy, tectonics, and the palaeogeographic context of the middle Pleistocene archeological sites. In *Geological background to fossil man: Recent research in the Gregory Rift Valley, East Africa*, ed. W. Bishop, pp. 173–206. Edinburgh: Scottish Academic Press.

83. Shipman, P. 1983. Early hominid lifestyle: Hunting and gathering or foraging, and scavenging? In *Animals and archaeology*, ed. J. Clutton-Brock, C. Grigson. Vol. 1, pp. 31–49: BAR International Series, Oxford.

84. Hrdy, S. 1981. *The woman that never evolved.* Cambridge, Mass.: Harvard University Press.

85. Boesch, C., Marchesi, P., Marchesi, N., Fruth, B., Joulian, F. 1994. Is nut cracking in wild chimpanzees a cultural behavior? *J. Hum. Evol.* 26:325–338.

86. Boesch, C., Boesch, H. 1984. Possible causes of sex differences in the use of natural hammers by wild chimpanzees. *J. Hum. Evol.* 13:415–440.

87. Boesch, C., Boesch, H. 1989. Hunting behavior of wild chimpanzees in the Tai National Park. *Am. J. Phys. Anthropol.* 78:547–573.

88. Blumenschine, R. 1987. Characteristics of an early hominid scavenging niche. *Curr. Anthropol.* 28:383–407.

89. Lewis, M. E. 1995. Plio-Pleistocene carnivorans and carcass processing in East Africa. Paleoanthropology Society Conference, Oakland, CA.

90. Marean, C. 1989. Sabertooth cats and their relevance for early hominid diet and evolution. *J. Hum. Evol.* 18:559–582.

91. Potts, R., Shipman, P., Ingall, E. 1988. Taphonomy, paleoecology, and hominids of Lainyamok, Kenya. *J. Hum. Evol.* 17:597–614.

92. Cavallo, J., Blumenschine, R. 1989. Tree-stored leopard kills: Expanding the hominid scavenging niche. *J. Hum. Evol.* 18:393–399.

93. Vrba, E. 1980. The significance of bovid remains as indicators of environment and predation patterns. In *Fossils in the making: Vertebrate taphonomy and paleoecology*, ed. A. Behrensmeyer, A. Hill, pp. 247–271. Chicago: University of Chicago Press.

94. Binford, L. 1981. *Bones: Ancient men and modern myths.* New York: Academic.

95. Potts, R. 1984. Home bases and early hominids. *Am. Sci.* 72:338–346.

96. Potts, R. 1987. Transportation of resources: Reconstructions of early hominid socioecology: A critique of primate models. In *The evolution of human behavior: Primate models*, ed. W. G. Kinzey, pp. 28–47. Albany: SUNY Press.

97. Potts, R. 1993. Archeological interpretations of early hominid behavior and ecology. In *The origin and evolution of humans and humanness*, ed. D. T. Rasmussen, pp. 49–74. Boston: Jones and Bartlett.

98. Speth, J. 1989. Early hominid hunting and scavenging: The role of meat as an energy source. *J. Hum. Evol.* 18:329–343.

99. Zihlman, A., Tanner, N. 1978. Gathering and the hominid adaptation. In *Female hierarchies*, ed. L. Tiger, H. Fowler, pp. 163–194. Chicago: Beresford.

100. Tanner, N. 1987. Gathering by females: The chimpanzee model revisited and the gathering hypothesis. In *The evolution of human behavior: Primate models*, ed. W. G. Kinzey, pp. 3–27. Albany: SUNY Press.

101. Fedigan, L. 1986. The changing role of women in models of human evolution. *Ann. Rev. Anthropol.* 15:25–66.

102. Lee, R. B., DeVore, I., eds. 1968. *Man the hunter.* Chicago: Aldine.

103. Bicchieri, M. G., ed. 1972. *Hunters and gatherers today.* New York: Holt, Rinehart and Winston.

104. Peters, C., O'Brien, E. 1981. The early hominid plant-food niche: Insights from an analysis of plant exploitation by *Homo*, *Pan*, and *Papio* in eastern and southern Africa. *Curr. Anthropol.* 22:127–140.

105. Peters, C. 1987. Nut-like oil seeds: Food for monkeys, chimpanzees, humans and probably ape-men. *Am. J. Phys. Anthropol.* 73:333–363.

106. Clutton-Brock, T., Harvey, P. 1977. Primate ecology and social organisation. *J. Zool. Lond.* 183:1–39.

107. Foley, R. 1987. *Another unique species: Patterns in human evolutionary ecology.* New York: John Wiley.

108. Wheeler, P. 1991. The thermoregulatory advantages of hominid bipedalism in open equatorial environments: The contribution of convective heat loss and cutaneous evaporative cooling. *J. Hum. Evol.* 23:107–115.

109. Wheeler, P. 1991. The influence of bipedalism on the energy and water budgets of early hominids. *J. Hum. Evol.* 23:117–136.

110. Wheeler, P. 1992. The influence of the loss of functional body hair on the water budgets of early hominids. *J. Hum. Evol.* 23:379–388.

111. Wheeler, P. 1992. The thermoregulatory advantages of large body size for hominids foraging in savannah environments. *J. Hum. Evol.* 23:351–362.

112. Wheeler, P. E. 1993. The influence of stature and body form on hominid energy and water budgets: A comparison of *Australopithecus* and early *Homo* physiques. *J. Hum. Evol.* 24:13–28.

113. Chaplin, G., Jablonski, N. G., Cable, N. T. 1994. Physiology, thermoregulation and bipedalism. *Am. J. Phys. Anthropol.* 27:497–510.

114. Ruff, C. B. 1991. Climate and body shape in hominid evolution. *J. Hum. Evol.* 21:81–105.

115. Ruff, C. B. 1993. Climatic adaptation and hominid evolution: The thermoregulatory imperative. *Evol. Anthropol.* 2:53–60.

116. Ruff, C. B. 1994. Morphological adaptation to climate in modern and fossil hominids. *Yrbk. Phys. Anthropol.* 37:65–107.

117. Stringer, C. 1992. Evolution of early humans. In *The Cambridge encyclopedia of human evolution*, ed. S. Jones, R. Martin, D. Pilbeam, pp. 241–251. Cambridge: Cambridge University Press.

118. Shipman, P., Rose, J. 1983. Early hominid hunting, butchering, and carcass-processing behaviors: Approaches to the fossil record. *J. Anthropol. Archaeology* 2:57–98.

CHAPTER VII

1. Haeckel, E. 1866. *Generelle Morphologie der Organismen*. Berlin: G. Reimer.

2. Tobias, P. V. 1993. One hundred years after Eugene Dubois: the Pithecanthropus Centennial at Leiden. *J. Hum. Evol.* 25:523–526.

3. Rightmire, G. P. 1984. Comparisons of *Homo erectus* from Africa and Southeast Asia. *Cour. Forschunginst. Senckenb.* 69:83–98.

4. Day, M., Molleson, T. 1973. The Trinil femora. In *Human evolution*, ed. M. H. Day, pp. 127–154. London: Taylor and Francis.

5. Day, M. H. 1984. The postcranial remains of *Homo erectus* from Africa, Asia, and possibly Europe. *Cour. Forschunginst. Senckenb.* 69:113–122.

6. Leakey, R., Lewin, R. 1992. *Origins reconsidered: in search of what makes us human*. Boston: Little, Brown.

7. Dubois, E. 1924. Figures of the calvarium and endocranial cast, a fragment of the mandible and three teeth of *Pithecanthropus erectus*. *Proc. Koninklijke Nederlandse Akad. Wetansch., Amsterdam* 27:459–464.

8. Dubois, E. 1922. The proto-Australian fossil man of Wadjak, Java. *Proc. Sect. Sci., K. Akad. Wetensch. Amsterdam* 23:1013–1051.

9. Hooten, E. 1946. *Up from the ape*. New York: Macmillan.

10. Swisher, C. C., Curtis, G. H., Jacob, T., Getty, A. G., Suprijo, A., Widiasmoro. 1994. Age of the earliest known hominids in Java, Indonesia. *Science* 263:1118–1121.

11. Riscutia, C. 1975. A study on the Modjokerto infant calvarium. In *Paleoanthropology, morphology and paleoecology*, ed. R. H. Tuttle, pp. 374–375. The Hague: Mouton.

12. Roper, M. 1969. A survey of the evidence for intrahuman killing in the Pleistocene. *Curr. Anthropol.* 10:427–459.

13. von Koenigswald, G. 1981. Davidson Black, Peking Man, and the Chinese Dragon. In Homo erectus: *Papers in honor of Davidson Black*, ed. B. A. Sigmon, J. S. Cybulski, pp. 27–39. Toronto: University of Toronto Press.

14. Howells, W. 1973. *Evolution of the genus* Homo. Reading: Addison-Wesley.

15. Holloway, R. 1981. The Indonesian *Homo erectus* brain endocasts revisited. *Am. J. Phys. Anthropol.* 55:503–522.

16. Etler, D. A., Li, T. 1994. New archaic human fossil discoveries in China and their bearing on hominid species definition during the middle Pleistocene. In *Integrative paths to the past*, ed. R. S. Corruccini, R. L. Ciochon, pp. 639–675. Englewood Cliffs, N.J.: Prentice-Hall.

17. von Koenigswald, G. 1971. *The evolution of man*. Ann Arbor: University of Michigan Press.

18. Wolpoff, M. 1971. Competitive exclusion among lower Pleistocene hominids: The single species hypothesis. *Man* 6:601–614.

19. Leakey, R., Walker, A. 1976. *Australopithecus, Homo erectus* and the single species hypothesis. *Nature* 261:572–574.

20. Sighinolfie, G. P., Sartono, S., Artioli, G. 1993. Chemical and mineralogical studies on hominid remains from Sangiran, Central Java (Indonesia). *J. Hum. Evol.* 24:57–68.

21. Kramer, A. 1994. A critical analysis of claims for the existence of Southeast Asian australopithecines. *J. Hum. Evol.* 26:3–21.

22. Santa Luca, A. 1980. The Ngandong fossil hominids. *Yale Univ. Publ. Anthropol.* 78:1–175.

23. Weidenreich, F. 1951. Morphology of Solo man. *Anthropol. Pap. Am. Mus. Nat. Hist.* 43:205–290.

24. Bartstra, G.-J., Soegondho, S., van der Wijk, A. 1988. Ngandong man: Age and artifacts. *J. Hum. Evol.* 17:325–337.

25. Jacob, T. 1981. Solo man and Peking man. In Homo erectus: *Papers in honor of Davidson Black,* ed. B. A. Sigmon, J. S. Cybulski, pp. 87–104. Toronto: University of Toronto Press.

26. Semah, F., Semah, A.-M., Djubiantono, T., Simanjuntak, H. 1992. Did they also make stone tools? *J. Hum. Evol.* 23:439–446.

27. von Koenigswald, G. 1975. Early man in Java: Catalogue and problems. In *Paleoanthropology, morphology and paleoecology,* ed. R. Tuttle, pp. 303–309. The Hague: Mouton.

28. Sartono, S. 1975. Implications arising from *Pithcanthropus* VIII. In *Paleoanthropology, morphology, and paleoecology,* ed. R. H. Tuttle, pp. 327–360. The Hague: Mouton.

29. Jacob, T., Soejono, R., Freeman, L., Brown, F. 1978. Stone tools from mid-Pleistocene sediments in Java. *Science* 202:885–887.

30. Pope, G., Cronin, J. 1984. The Asian Hominidae. *J. Hum. Evol.* 13:377–396.

31. Pope, G. 1983. Evidence on the age of the Asian Hominidae. *Proc. Natl. Acad. Sci. U.S.A.* 80:4988–4992.

32. Pope, G. 1988. Recent advances in Far Eastern paleoanthropology. *Ann. Rev. Anthropol.* 17:43–77.

33. de Vos, J. 1985. Faunal stratigraphy and correlation of the Indonesian hominid sites. In *Ancestors: The hard evidence,* ed. E. Delson, pp. 215–220. New York: Alan R. Liss.

34. Pope, G. G., Keates, S. G. 1994. The evolution of human cognition and cultural capacity: a view from the Far East. In *Integrative paths to the past,* ed. R. S. Corruccini, R. L. Ciochon, pp. 531–567. Englewood Cliffs, N.J.: Prentice-Hall.

35. Rightmire, G. 1988. *Homo erectus* and later middle Pleistocene humans. *Ann. Rev. Anthropol.* 17:239–259.

36. Wolpoff, M. 1984. Evolution in *Homo erectus*: The question of stasis. *Paleobiology* 10:389–406.

37. Wu, R., Lin, S. 1983. Peking man. *Sci. Am.* 248:86–94.

38. Black, D. 1927. On a lower molar hominid tooth from the Chou Kou Tien deposit. *Palaeontol. Sinica. Series D* 7:1.

39. Schlosser, M. 1903. Die fossielen saugetiere Chinas. *Abhandl. Bayerische Akad. Wissenschaften* 22:1–221.

40. Shapiro, H. 1981. Davidson Black: An appreciation. In Homo erectus: *Papers in honor of Davidson Black,* ed. B. A. Sigmon, J. S. Cybulski, pp. 21–26. Toronto: University of Toronto Press.

41. Teilhard de Chardin, P., Pei, W. 1932. The lithic industry of the *Sinanthropus* deposits in Choukoutien. *Bull. Geol. Soc. China* 11:315–365.

42. Shapiro, H. 1974. *Peking Man.* New York: Simon and Schuster.

43. Janus, C. 1975. The Peking Man fossils: progress of the search. In *Paleoanthropology, morphology and paleoecology,* ed. R. H. Tuttle, pp. 291–300. The Hague: Mouton.

44. Mann, A. 1981. The significance of the *Sinanthropus* casts, and some paleodemographic notes. In Homo erectus: *Papers in honor of Davidson Black,* ed. B. A. Sigmon, J. S. Cybulski, pp. 41–62. Toronto: University of Toronto Press.

45. Wu, R. 1985. New Chinese *Homo erectus* and recent work at Zhoukoudian. In *Ancestors: The hard evidence*, ed. E. Delson, pp. 245–248. New York: Alan R. Liss.

46. Liu, Z. 1983. The palaeoclimatic changes inferred from Peking Man cave deposits in comparison with the climatic sequence of other formations. *Acta Anthropol. Sinica* 2:183.

47. Huang, P., Jin, S., Liang, R., Lu, Z., Zheng, L., Yuan, Z., Cai, B., Fang, Z. 1991. Study of ESR dating for burying age of the first skull of Peking Man and chronological scale of the cave deposit in Zhoukoudian site Loc. 1. *Acta Anthropol. Sinica* 10:115.

48. Yuan, S., Chen, T., Gao, S., Hu, Y. 1991. Study on uranium series dating of fossil bones and teeth from Zhoukoudian site. *Acta Anthropol. Sinica* 10:193.

49. Shen, G., Jin, L. 1991. Restudy of the upper age of Beijing man site. *Acta Anthropol. Sinica* 10:277.

50. Pope, G. 1992. Craniofacial evidence for the origin of modern humans in China. *Yrbk. Phys. Anthropol.* 35:243–298.

51. Chen, T., Hedges, R., Yuan, Z. 1989. Accelerator radiocarbon dating from upper cave of Zhoukoudian. *Acta Anthropol. Sinica* 8:221.

52. Kamminga, J., Wright, R. 1988. The upper cave at Zhoukoudian and the origins of the Mongoloids. *J. Hum. Evol.* 17:739–767.

53. Weidenreich, F. 1937. The dentition of *Sinanthropus pekenensis*: A comparative odontography of the hominids. *Palaeon. Sinica* 1:120–180.

54. Zhang, Y. 1991. Examination of temporal variation in the hominid dental sample from Zhoukoudian locality 1. *Acta Anthropol. Sinica* 10:95.

55. Qi, G. 1990. The Pleistocene human environment of North China. *Acta Anthropol. Sinica* 9:340–349.

56. Movius, H. 1944. Early man and Pleistocene stratigraphy in southern and eastern Asia. *Trans. Am. Philos. Soc.* 38:329–420.

57. Clark, J. D. 1994. The Acheulian industrial complex in Africa and elsewhere. In *Integrative paths to the past*, ed. R. S. Corruccini, R. L. Ciochon, pp. 451–469. Englewood Cliffs, N.J.: Prentice-Hall.

58. Schick, K. D. 1994. The Movius line reconsidered. In *Integrative paths to the past*, ed. R. S. Corruccini, R. L. Ciochon, pp. 569–596. Englewood Cliffs, N.J.: Prentice-Hall.

59. Kennedy, K. A. R., Sonakia, A., Chiment, J., Verma, K. K. 1991. Is the Narmada hominid an Indian *Homo erectus*? *Am. J. Phys. Anthropol.* 86:475–496.

60. Schick, K. D., Zhuan, D. 1993. Early paleolithic of China and Eastern Asia. *Evol. Anthropol.* 2:22–35.

61. Asfaw, B., Beyene, Y., Suwa, G., Walter, R., White, T., WoldeGabriel, G., Yemane, T. 1992. The earliest Acheulean from Konso-Gardula. *Nature* 360:732–735.

62. An, Z. 1990. The proto-handaxe and its tradition in China. *Acta Anthropol. Sinica* 9:311.

63. Binford, L., Stone, N. 1986. Zhoukoudien: A closer look. *Curr. Anthropol.* 27:453–460.

64. Binford, L., Ho, C. 1985. Taphonomy at a distance: Zhoukoudian, ''The cave home of Beijing man''? *Curr. Anthropol.* 26:413–443.

65. Wu, X., Poirier, F. 1995. *Human evolution in China.* Oxford: Oxford University Press.

66. Woo, J. 1964. Mandible of *Sinanthropus lantianensis. Curr. Anthropol.* 5:98–101.

67. Woo, J. K. 1966. The skull of Lantian man. *Curr. Anthropol.* 7:83–86.

68. Howells, W. 1980. *Homo erectus*—who, when and where: a survey. *Yrbk. Phys. Anthropol.* 23:1–23.

69. An, Z., Gao, W., Zhu, Y., Kan, X., Wang, J., Sun, J., Wei, W. 1990. Magnetostratigraphic dates of Lantian *Homo erectus. Acta Anthropol. Sinica* 9:7.

70. Wu, R., Qian, F. 1991. The first study of the age of Yuanmou man by the method of amino acid racemization geochronology. *Acta Anthropol. Sinica* 10:199.

71. Wanpo, H., Ciochon, R., Yumin, G., Larick, R., Qiren, F., Schwarcz, H., Yonge, C., de Vos, J., Rink, W. 1995. Early *Homo* and associated artefacts from Asia. *Nature* 378:275–278.

72. Olsen, J. W., Ciochon, R. L. 1990. A review of evidence for postulated middle Pleistocene occupations in Viet Nam. *J. Hum. Evol.* 19:761–788.

73. Liu, T., Ding, M. 1983. Discussion on the age of "Yuanmou Man." *Acta Anthropol. Sinica* 2:48.

74. Xu, Q., You, Y. 1984. Hexian fauna: Correlation with deep-sea sediments. *Acta Anthropol. Sinica* 3:66–67.

75. Wu, R., Dong, X. 1982. Preliminary study of *Homo erectus* remains from Hexian, Anhui. *Acta Anthropol. Sinica* 1:2–13.

76. Wu, M. 1983. *Homo erectus* from Hexian, Anhui found in 1981. *Acta Anthropol. Sinica* 2:115.

77. Li, T., Etler, D. 1992. New middle Pleistocene hominid crania from Yunxian in China. *Nature* 357:404–407.

78. Pope, G. 1991. Evolution of the zygomaticomaxillary region in the genus *Homo* and its relevance to the origin of modern humans. *J. Hum. Evol.* 21:189–213.

79. Hublin, J. 1985. Human fossils from the North African middle Pleistocene and the origin of *Homo sapiens*. In *Ancestors: The hard evidence*, ed. E. Delson, pp. 283–288. New York: Alan R. Liss.

80. McBurney, C. 1958. Evidence for the distribution in space and time of Neanderthaloids and allied strains in northern Africa. In *Hundert Jahre Neanderthaler*, ed. G. H. R. Von Koenigswald, pp. 253–264. Utrecht: Kemink en Zoon N.V.

81. Howell, F. 1978. Hominidae. In *Evolution of African mammals*, ed. V. J. Maglio, H. B. S. Cooke, pp. 154–248. Cambridge, Mass.: Harvard University Press.

82. Rightmire, G. 1990. *The evolution of Homo erectus.* Cambridge: Cambridge University Press.

83. Holloway, R. 1981. Volumetric and asymmetry determinations on recent hominid endocasts: Spy 1 and 2, Djebel Irhoud 1, and the Sale *Homo erectus* specimens, with some notes on Neanderthal brain size. *Am. J. Phys. Anthropol.* 55:385–393.

84. Holloway, R. 1975. Early hominid endocasts: Volumes, morphology and significance for hominid evolution. In *Primate functional morphology and evolution*, ed. R. H. Tuttle. The Hague: Mouton.

85. Maier, W., Nkini, A. 1984. Olduvai hominid 9: new results of investigation. *Cour. Forschunginst. Senckenb.* 69:123–130.

86. Rightmire, G. 1981. *Homo erectus* at Olduvai Gorge, Tanzania. In Homo erectus: *Papers in honor of Davidson Black*, ed. B. A. Sigmon, J. S. Cybulski, pp. 189–192. Toronto: University of Toronto Press.

87. Leakey, M. 1971. Discovery of postcranial remains of *Homo erectus* and associated artefacts in Bed IV at Olduvai Gorge, Tanzania. *Nature* 232:380–383.

88. Day, M. 1971. Postcranial remains of *Homo erectus* from Bed IV Olduvai Gorge, Tanzania. *Nature* 232:384–387.

89. Kennedy, G. 1983. A morphometric and taxonomic assessment of a hominine femur from the lower Member, Koobi Fora, Lake Turkana. *Am. J. Phys. Anthropol.* 61:429–436.

90. Walker, A., Zimmerman, M., Leakey, R. 1982. A possible case of hypervitaminosis A in *Homo erectus. Nature* 296:248–250.

91. Skinner, M. 1991. Bee brood consumption: an alternative explanation for hypervitaminosis A in KNM-ER 1808 (*Homo erectus*) from Koobi Fora, Kenya. *J. Hum. Evol.* 20:493–503.

92. Walker, A., Leakey, R. E., eds. 1993. *The Nariokotome* Homo erectus *skeleton.* Cambridge, Mass.: Harvard University Press.

93. Smith, B. H. 1993. Physiological age of KNM-WT 15000. In *The Nariokotome* Homo erectus *skeleton*, ed. A. Walker, R. Leakey, pp. 195–220. Cambridge, Mass.: Harvard University Press.

94. Smith, B. H., Brandt, K. L., Tompkins, R. L. 1995. Developmental age of the KMN-WT 15000 *Homo erectus* in broad perspective. *Am. J. Phys. Anthropol.* Suppl. 20:196–197.

95. Walker, A. 1993. The origin of the genus *Homo.* In *The origin and evolution of humans and humanness*, ed. D. T. Rasmussen, pp. 29–47. Boston: Jones and Bartlett.

96. Begun, D., Walker, A. 1993. The endocast of the Nariokotome hominid. In *The Nariokotome* Homo erectus *skeleton*, ed. A. Walker, R. E. Leakey, pp. 326–358. Cambridge, Mass.: Harvard University Press.

97. Brown, F., Harris, J., Leakey, R., Walker, A. 1985. Early *Homo erectus* skeleton from west Lake Turkana, Kenya. *Nature* 316:788–792.

98. Feldesman, M., Lundy, J. 1988. Stature estimates for some African Plio-Pleistocene fossil hominids. *J. Hum. Evol.* 17:583–596.

99. Ruff, C., Walker, A. 1993. The body size and body shape of KNM-WT 15000. In *The Nariokotome* Homo erectus *skeleton*, ed. A. Walker, R. E. Leakey, pp. 234–265. Cambridge, Mass.: Harvard University Press.

100. MacLarnon, A. 1993. The vertebral canal. In *The Nariokotome* Homo erectus *skeleton*, ed. A. Walker, R. Leakey, pp. 359–390. Cambridge, Mass.: Harvard University Press.

101. Latimer, B., Ward, C. 1993. The thoracic and lumbar vertebrae. In *The Nariokotome* Homo erectus *skeleton*, ed. A. Walker, R. E. Leakey, pp. 266–293. Cambridge, Mass.: Harvard University Press.

102. Martin, R. 1983. *Human brain evolution in an ecological context*. New York: American Museum of Natural History.

103. Preuschoft, H., Witte, H. 1991. Biomechanical reasons for the evolution of hominid body shape. In *Origine(s) de la bipedie chez les hominides*, ed. Y. Coppen, B. Senut, pp. 59–77. Paris: CNRS.

104. Schmid, P. 1991. The trunk of the australopithecines. In *Origine(s) de la bipedie chez les hominides*, ed. Y. Coppens, B. Senut, pp. 225–234. Paris: CNRS.

105. Leakey, M., Tobias, P., Martyn, J., Leakey, R. 1969. An Acheulian Industry with prepared core technique and the discovery of a contemporary hominid mandible at Lake Baringo, Kenya. *Proc. Prehist. Soc.* 35:48–76.

106. Wood, B., Van Noten, F. 1986. Preliminary observations on the BK 8518 mandible from Baringo, Kenya. *Am. J. Phys. Anthropol.* 69:117–127.

107. Solan, M., Day, M. 1992. The Baringo (Kapthurin) ulna. *J. Hum. Evol.* 22:307–313.

108. Tallon, P. 1978. Geological setting of the hominid fossils and Acheulian artifacts from the Kapthurin Formation, Baringo District, Kenya. In *Geological background to fossil man*, ed. W. W. Bishop, pp. 361–373. Edinburgh: Scottish Academic Press.

109. Feldesman, M. 1979. Further morphometric studies of the ulna from the Omo Basin, Ethiopia. *Am. J. Phys. Anthropol.* 51:409–416.

110. Asfaw, B. 1995. Progress in paleoanthropology at Konso Gardula. *Am. J. Phys. Anthropol.* Suppl. 20:60.

111. Vrba, E. 1985. Ecological and adaptive changes associated with early hominid evolution. In *Ancestors: The hard evidence*, ed. E. Delson, pp. 63–71. New York: Alan R. Liss.

112. Prentice, M., Denton, G. 1988. The deep-sea oxygen isotope record, the global ice sheet system and hominid evolution. In *Evolutionary history of the "robust" australopithecines*, ed. F. E. Grine, pp. 383–403. New York: Aldine de Gruyter.

113. Broom, R., Robinson, J. 1949. A new type of fossil man. *Nature* 164:322–323.

114. Broom, R., Robinson, J. T. 1950. Man contemporaneous with the Swartkrans ape-man. *Am. J. Phys. Anthropol.* 8:151–156.

115. Robinson, J. 1961. The australopithecines and their bearing on the origin of man and of stone tool-making. *S. Afr. J. Sci.* 57:3–16.

116. Clarke, R., Howell, F., Brain, C. 1970. More evidence of an advanced hominid at Swartkrans. *Nature* 225:1219–1222.

117. Clarke, R., Howell, F. 1972. Affinities of the Swartkrans 847 hominid cranium. *Am. J. Phys. Anthropol.* 37:319–336.

118. Olson, T. 1978. Hominid phylogenetics and the existence of *Homo* in Member I of the Swartkrans formation, South Africa. *J. Hum. Evol.* 7:159–178.

119. Grine, F. E., Demes, B., Jungers, W. L., Cole, T. M. 1993. Taxonomic affinity of the early *Homo* cranium from Swartkrans, South Africa. *Am. J. Phys. Anthropol.* 92:411–426.

120. Clarke, R. 1985. *Australopithecus* and early *Homo* in southern Africa. In *Ancestors: the hard evidence*, ed. E. Delson, pp. 171–177. New York: Alan R. Liss.

121. Andrews, P. 1984. An alternative interpretation of the characters used to define *Homo erectus*. *Cour. Forschunginst. Senckenb.* 69:167–175.

122. Clarke, R. 1990. The Ndutu cranium and the origin of *Homo sapiens. J. Hum. Evol.* 19:699–736.

123. Stringer, C. 1984. The definition of *Homo erectus* and the existence of the species in Africa and Europe. *Cour. Forschunginst. Senckenb.* 69:131–143.

124. Stringer, C. 1985. Middle Pleistocene hominid variability and the origin of late Pleistocene humans. In *Ancestors: The hard evidence*, ed. E. Delson, pp. 289–295. New York: Alan R. Liss.

125. Wood, B. 1984. The origin of *Homo erectus. Cour. Forschunginst. Senckenb.* 69:99–112.

126. Kennedy, G. E. 1991. On the autapomorphic traits of *Homo erectus. J. Hum. Evol.* 20:375–412.

127. Turner, A., Chamberlain, A. 1989. Speciation, morphological change and the status of African *Homo erectus. J. Hum. Evol.* 18:115–130.

128. Rightmire, G. P. 1981. Patterns in the evolution of *Homo erectus. Paleobiology* 7:241–246.

129. Brauer, G. 1990. The occurrence of some controversial *Homo erectus* cranial features in the Zhoukoudian and East African hominids. *Acta Anthropol. Sinica* 9:352–358.

130. Brauer, B., Mbua, E. 1992. *Homo erectus* features used in cladistics and their variability in Asian and African hominids. *J. Hum. Evol.* 22:79–108.

131. Brauer, G. 1994. How different are Asian and African *Homo erectus? Cour. Forschunginst. Senckenb.* 171:301–318.

132. Wu, X., Brauer, G. 1993. Morphological comparison of archaic *Homo sapiens* crania from China and Africa. *Z. Morph. Anthropol.* 79:241–259.

133. Wu, X. 1990. The evolution of humankind in China. *Acta Anthropol. Sinica* 9:320–321.

134. Kramer, A. 1993. Human taxonomic diversity in the Pleistocene: does *Homo erectus* represent multiple hominid species? *Am. J. Phys. Anthropol.* 91:161–171.

135. Stringer, C. 1992. Evolution of early humans. In *The Cambridge encyclopedia of human evolution*, ed. S. Jones, R. Martin, D. Pilbeam, pp. 241–251. Cambridge: Cambridge University Press.

136. Haeckel, E. 1896. *The evolution of man.* New York: D. Appleton.

137. Dubois, E. 1894. *Pithecanthropus erectus: eine Menschenaehnliche Vebergangsform aus Java.* Batavia: Landesdruckerei.

138. Rightmire, G. P. 1992. *Homo erectus*: Ancestor or evolutionary side branch? *Evol. Anthropol.* 1:43–49.

139. Klein, R. 1989. *The human career.* Chicago: University of Chicago Press.

140. Stringer, C., Gamble, C. 1993. *In search of the Neanderthals.* New York: Thames and Hudson.

141. Tattersall, I., Delson, E., Van Couvering, J., eds. 1988. *Encyclopedia of human evolution and prehistory.* New York: Garland.

142. Gowlett, J. 1992. Tools—the Palaeolithic record. In *The Cambridge encyclopedia of human evolution*, ed. S. Jones, R. Martin, D. Pilbeam, pp. 350–360. Cambridge: Cambridge University Press.

143. Jaeger, J. J. 1981. Les hommes fossiles du Pleistocene moyen du Maghreb dans leur cadre geologique, chronologique, et paleoecologique. In Homo erectus: *Papers in honor of Davidson Black*, ed. B. A. Sigmon, J. S. Cybulski, pp. 159–187. Toronto: University of Toronto Press.

CHAPTER VIII

1. Kennedy, K. A. R., Sonakia, A., Chiment, J., Verma, K. K. 1991. Is the Narmada hominid an Indian *Homo erectus? Am. J. Phys. Anthropol.* 86:475–496.

2. Clark, J. D. 1992. African and Asian perspectives on the origins of modern humans. *Philos. Trans. R. Soc. Lond. [Biol.]* 337:201–215.

3. Roebroeks, W. 1994. Updating the earliest occupation of Europe. *Curr. Anthropol.* 35:301–305.

4. Morell, V. 1994. Did early humans reach Siberia 500,000 years ago? *Science* 263:611–612.

5. Gabunia, L., Vekua, A. 1995. A Plio-Pleistocene hominid from Dmanisi, East Georgia, Caucasus. *Nature* 373:509–512.

6. Carbonell, E., de Castro, J. M. B., Arsuaga, J. L., Diez, J. C., Rosas, A., Cuenca-Bescos, G., Sala, R., Mosquera, M., Rodriquez, X. P. 1995. Lower Pleistocene hominids and artifacts from Atapuerca-TD 6 (Spain). *Science* 269:826–830.

7. Pares, J. M., Perez-Gonzalez, A. 1995. Paleomagnetic age for hominid fossils at Atapuerca archaeological site, Spain. *Science* 269:830–832.

8. Roberts, M. B., Stringer, C. B., Parfitt, S. A. 1994. A hominid tibia from middle Pleistocene sediments at Boxgrove, UK. *Nature* 369:311–313.

9. Bowen, D. Q., Sykes, G. A. 1994. How old is 'Boxgrove man'? *Nature* 371:751.

10. Roberts, M. B. 1994. How old is 'Boxgrove man'? *Nature* 371:751.

11. Stringer, C. 1984. The definition of *Homo erectus* and the existence of the species in Africa and Europe. *Cour. Forschunginst. Senckenb.* 69:131–143.

12. Stringer, C. 1985. Middle Pleistocene hominid variability and the origin of late Pleistocene humans. In *Ancestors: The hard evidence*, ed. E. Delson, pp. 289–295. New York: Alan R. Liss.

13. Kraatz, R. 1985. A review of recent research on Heidelberg Man, *Homo erectus heidelbergensis*. In *Ancestors: The hard evidence*, ed. E. Delson, pp. 268–271. New York: Alan R. Liss.

14. Kretzoi, M., Vertes, L. 1965. Upper Biharian (Intermindel) pebble-industry occupation site in western Hungary. *Curr. Anthropol.* 6:74–87.

15. Oakley, K. P. 1966. Exhibit: discovery of part of skull of *Homo erectus* with Buda industry at Vertesszollos, north-west Hungary. *Proc. Geol. Soc. Lond.* 1630:31–34.

16. Gamble, C. 1986. *The Palaeolithic settlement of Europe.* Cambridge: Cambridge University Press.

17. Thoma, A. 1978. Some notes on Wolpoff's notes on the Vertesszollos occipital. *J. Hum. Evol.* 7:323–325.

18. Thoma, A. 1981. The position of the Vértessozöllös find in relation to *Homo erectus*. In Homo erectus: *Papers in honor of Davidson Black*, ed. B. A. Sigmon, J. S. Cybulski, pp. 105–114. Toronto: University of Toronto Press.

19. Wolpoff, M. H. 1971. Is Vertesszollos II an occipital of European *Homo erectus? Nature* 232:567–568.

20. Wolpoff, M. H. 1980. Cranial remains of middle Pleistocene European hominids. *J. Hum. Evol.* 9:339–358.

21. Harmon, R. S., Glazek, J., Nowak, K. 1980. 230Th/234U dating of travertine from the Bilzingsleben archaeological site. *Nature* 284:132–135.

22. Howell, F. C. 1981. Some views of *Homo erectus* with special reference to its occurrence in Europe. In Homo erectus: *Papers in honor of Davidson Black*, ed. B. A. Sigmon, J. S. Cybulski, pp. 153–157. Toronto: University of Toronto Press.

23. Mania, D., Vlcek, E. 1981. *Homo erectus* in middle Europe: The discovery from Bilzingsleben. In Homo erectus: *Papers in honor of Davidson Black*, ed. B. A. Sigmon, J. S. Cybulski, pp. 133–151. Toronto: University of Toronto Press.

24. Kurten, B., Poulianos, A. 1977. New stratigraphic and faunal material from Petralona cave with special reference to the Carnivora. *Anthropos* 4:47–130.

25. Poulianos, A. 1978. Correction of the English text on the summary article "Stratigraphy and age of the Petralonian Archanthropus." *Anthropos* 5:264–266.

26. Hennig, G. J., Herr, W., Weber, E., Xirotiris, N. I. 1981. ESR-dating of the fossil hominid cranium from Petralona Cave, Greece. *Nature* 292:533–536.

27. de Lumley, M.-A. 1975. Ante-Neanderthals of western Europe. In *Paleoanthropology: Morphology and paleoecology*, ed. R. H. Tuttle, pp. 381–387. The Hague: Mouton.

28. Day, M. H. 1988. *Guide to fossil man.* Chicago: University of Chicago Press.

29. de Bonis, L., Melentis, J. 1982. L'homme de Petralona: Comparaisons avec l'homme de Tautavel. *Prem. Congr. Int. Paleontol. Hum. Nice* 2:847–874.

30. Adam, K. D. 1985. The chronological and systematic position of the Steinheim skull. In *Ancestors: The hard evidence*, ed. E. Delson, pp. 272–276. New York: Alan R. Liss.

31. Santa Luca, A. P. 1978. A re-examination of presumed Neanderal-like fossils. *J. Hum. Evol.* 7:619–636.

32. Cook, J., Stringer, C., Currant, A., Schwarcz, H., Wintle, A. 1982. A review of the chronology of the European middle Pleistocene hominid record. *Yrbk. Phys. Anthropol.* 25:19–65.

33. Vallois, H. 1956. The pre-Mousterian human mandible from Montmaurin. *Am. J. Phys. Anthropol.* 14:319–323.

34. Stringer, C. 1993. Secrets of the pit of the bones. *Nature* 362:501–502.

35. Arsuaga, J. L., Carretero, J. M., Martinez, I., Gracia, A. 1991. Cranial remains and long bones from Atapuerca/Ibeas Spain. *J. Hum. Evol.* 20:191–230.

36. Arsuaga, J.-L., Martinez, I., Gracia, A., Carretero, J.-M., Carbonell, E. 1993. Three new human skulls from the Sima de los Huesos Middle Pleistocene site in Sierra de Atapuerca, Spain. *Nature* 362:534–537.

37. de Castro, J. M. B., Durand, A. I., Ipina, S. L. 1993. Sexual dimorphism in the human dental sample from the SH site (Sierra de Atapuerca, Spain): A statistical approach. *J. Hum. Evol.* 24:43–56.

38. de Castro, J. M. B. 1988. Dental remains from Atapuerca/Ibeas (Spain) II. Morphology. *J. Hum. Evol.* 17:279–304.

39. Rosas, A. 1987. Two new mandibular fragments from Atapuerca/Ibeas (SH site). A reassessment of the affinities of the Ibeas mandibles sample. *J. Hum. Evol.* 16:417–427.

40. de Castro, J. M. B., Rosas, A. 1992. A human mandibular fragment from the Atapuerca Trench (Burgos, Spain). *J. Hum. Evol.* 22:41–46.

41. Villa, P. 1990. Torralba and Aridos: elephant exploitation in Middle Pleistocene Spain. *J. Hum. Evol.* 19:299–309.

42. Pope, G. 1992. Craniofacial evidence for the origin of modern humans in China. *Yrbk. Phys. Anthropol.* 35:243–298.

43. Chen, T., Yang, Q., Wu, E. 1993. Electron spin resonance dating of teeth enamel samples from Jingniushan palaeoanthropological site. *Acta Anthropol. Sinica* 12:346.

44. Tiemei, C., Quan, Y., En, W. 1994. Antiquity of *Homo sapiens* in China. *Nature* 368:55–56.

45. Smith, F. 1992. Models and realities in modern human origins: The African fossil evidence. *Philos. Trans. R. Soc. Lond. [Biol.].* 337:243–250.

46. Clark, J. D., Brothwell, D. R., Powers, R., Oakley, K. P. 1968. Rhodesian man: notes on a new femur fragment. *Man* 3:105–111.

47. Clark, J. 1970. *The prehistory of Africa.* New York: Praeger.

48. Weidenreich, F. 1943. The skull of *Sinanthropus pekinensis*: A comparative study on a primtive hominid skull. *Palaeontol. Sinica* 10:1–484.

49. Singer, R. 1958. The Rhodesian, Florisbad and Saldanha skulls. In *Hundert Jahre Neanderthaler,* ed. G. H. R. von Koenigswald, pp. 52–62. Utrecht: Kemink en Zoon N.V.

50. Bartsiokas, A., Day, M. H. 1993. Lead poisoning and dental caries in the Broken Hill hominid. *J. Hum. Evol.* 24:243–249.

51. Oakley, K. P. 1958. The dating of Broken Hill (Rhodesian Man). In *Hundert Jahre Neanderthaler,* ed. G. H. R. von Koenigswald, pp. 265–266. Utrecht: Kemink en Zoon, N.V.

52. Klein, R. 1973. Geological antiquity of Rhodesian man. *Nature* 244:311–312.

53. Coon, C. S. 1962. *The origin of races.* New York: Knopf.

54. Conroy, G. C., Jolly, C. J., Cramer, D., Kalb, J. E. 1978. Newly discovered fossil hominid skull from the Afar depression, Ethiopia. *Nature* 275:67–70.

55. Conroy, G. C. 1980. New evidence of Middle Pleistocene hominids from the Afar Desert, Ethiopia. *Anthropos* 7:96–107.

56. Clark, J. D., de Heinzelin, J., Schick, K. D., Hart, W. K., White, T. D., WoldeGabriel, G., Walter, R. C., Suwa, G., Asfaw, B., Vrba, E., Y.-Selassie, Y. 1994. African *Homo erectus*: Old radiometric ages and young Oldowan assemblages in the Middle Awash Valley, Ethiopia. *Science* 264:1907–1910.

57. Kalb, J., Jolly, C., Mebrate, A., Tebedge, S., Smart, C., Oswald, E., Cramer, D., Whitehead, P., Wood, C., Conroy, G., Adefris, T., Sperling, L., Kana, B. 1982. Fossil mammals and artefacts from the middle Awash valley, Ethiopia. *Nature* 298:25–29.

58. Clark, J. D., Asfaw, B., Assefa, G., Harris, J. W. K., Kurashina, H., Walter, R. C., White, T. D., Williams, M. A. J. 1984. Palaeoanthropological discoveries in the middle Awash valley, Ethiopia. *Nature* 307:423–428.

59. Asfaw, B. 1983. A new hominid parietal from Bodo, Middle Awash Valley, Ethiopia. *Am. J. Phys. Anthropol.* 61:367–371.

60. White, T. D., ed. 1985. *Acheulian man in Ethiopia's Middle Awash Valley: The implications of cutmarks on the Bodo cranium.* Netherlands: Joh. Enschede en Zonen Haarlem.

61. White, T. D. 1986. Cut marks on the Bodo cranium: A case of prehistoric defleshing. *Am. J. Phys. Anthropol.* 69:503–509.

62. Mturi, A. A. 1976. New hominid from Lake Ndutu, Tanzania. *Nature* 262:484–485.

63. Rightmire, G. P. 1983. The Lake Ndutu cranium and early *Homo sapiens* in Africa. *Am. J. Phys. Anthropol.* 61:245–254.

64. Clarke, R. J. 1976. New cranium of *Homo erectus* from Lake Ndutu, Tanzania. *Nature* 262:485–487.

65. Clarke, R. 1990. The Ndutu cranium and the origin of *Homo sapiens. J. Hum. Evol.* 19:699–736.

66. Leakey, L. S. B. 1936. A new fossil skull from Eyassi, East Africa: discovery by a German expedition. *Nature* 138:1082–1084.

67. Weinert, H. 1937. Hominidae (Palaeozoolgie). *Fortschr. Palaontol.* 1:337–344.

68. Protsch, R. 1981. The Kohl-Larsen Eyasi and Garusi hominid finds in Tanzania and their relation to *Homo erectus.* In Homo erectus: *Papers in honor of Davidson Black.*, ed. B. A. Sigmon, J. S. Cybulski, pp. 217–226. Toronto: University of Toronto Press.

69. Potts, R. 1989. Olorgesailie: new excavations and findings in early and middle Pleistocene contexts, southern Kenya rift valley. *J. Hum. Evol.* 18:477–484.

70. Shipman, P., Bosler, W., Davis, K. 1981. Butchering of giant geladas at an Acheulian site. *Curr. Anthropol.* 22:257–268.

71. Potts, R. 1993. Archeological interpretations of early hominid behavior and ecology. In *The origin and evolution of humans and humanness*, ed. D. T. Rasmussen, pp. 49–74. Boston: Jones and Bartlett.

72. Stringer, C. B. 1993. New views on modern human origins. In *The origin and evolution of humans and humanness*, ed. D. T. Rasmussen, pp. 75–94. Boston: Jones and Bartlett.

73. Howells, W. 1992. The dispersion of modern humans. In *The Cambridge encyclopedia of human evolution*, ed. S. Jones, R. Martin, D. Pilbeam, pp. 389–401. Cambridge: Cambridge University Press.

74. Klein, R. 1989. *The human career.* Chicago: University of Chicago Press.

75. Etler, D. A., Li, T. 1994. New archaic human fossil discoveries in China and their bearing on hominid species definition during the middle Pleistocene. In *Integrative paths to the past*, ed. R. S. Corruccini, R. L. Ciochon, pp. 639–675. Englewood Cliffs, N.J.: Prentice-Hall.

CHAPTER IX

1. Linnaeus, C. 1758. *Systema naturae per regna tria naturae, secundum classes, ordines genera, species cum characteribus, differentris, synonymis, locis.* Stockholm: Laurentii Salvii.

2. Howell, F. 1978. Hominidae. In *Evolution of African mammals*, ed. V. J. Maglio, H. B. S. Cooke, pp. 154–248. Cambridge, Mass.: Harvard University Press.

3. Trinkaus, E. 1989. The Upper Pleistocene transition. In *The emergence of modern humans*, ed. E. Trinkaus, pp. 42–66. Cambridge, Mass.: Cambridge University Press.

4. Hoffecker, J. F., Powers, W. R., Goebel, T. 1993. The colonization of Beringia and the peopling of the New World. *Science* 259:46–53.

5. Kunz, M. L., Reaniert, R. E. 1994. Paleoindians in Beringia: Evidence from Arctic Alaska. *Science* 263:660–662.

6. Reynolds, T. E. G. 1991. Revolution or resolution? The archaeology of modern human origins. *World Archaeol.* 23:155–166.

7. Klein, R. 1992. The archeology of modern human origins. *Evol. Anthropol.* 1:5–14.

8. Mellars, P. A., Aitken, M. J., Stringer, C. B. 1992. Outlining the problem. *Philos. Trans. R. Soc. Lond. [Biol.]* 337:127–130.

9. Rogers, A. 1995. Genetic evidence for a Pleistocene population explosion. *Evolution* 49:608–615.

10. Thackeray, A. I. 1992. The middle stone age south of the Limpopo River. *J. World Prehist.* 6:385–440.

11. Rigaud, J.-P. 1989. From the Middle to the Upper Paleolithic: Transition or convergence? In *The emergence of modern humans*, ed. E. Trinkaus, pp. 142–153. Cambridge: Cambridge University Press.

12. Trinkaus, E. 1989. Issues concerning human emergence in the later Pleistocene. In *The emergence of modern humans*, ed. E. Trinkaus, pp. 1–17. Cambridge: Cambridge University Press.

13. Wolpoff, M., Wu, X., Thorne, A. 1984. Modern *Homo sapiens* origins: A general theory of hominid evolution involving the fossil evidence from east Asia. In *The origins of modern humans: A world survey of the fossil evidence*, ed. F. Smith, F. Spencer, pp. 411–483. New York: Alan R. Liss.

14. Wolpoff, M. H. 1989. Multiregional evolution: The fossil alternative to Eden. In *The human revolution*, ed. P. Mellars, C. Stringer, pp. 62–108. Princeton, N.J.: Princeton University Press.

15. Frayer, D. W., Wolpoff, M. H., Thorne, A. G., Smith, F. H., Pope, G. G. 1993. Theories of modern human origins: The paleontological test. *Am. Anthropol.* 95:14–50.

16. Cann, R., Stoneking, M., Wilson, A. 1987. Mitochondrial DNA and human evolution. *Nature* 325:31–36.

17. Stoneking, M., Sherry, S. T., Redd, A. J., Vigilant, L. 1992. New approaches to dating suggest a recent age for the human mtDNA ancestor. *Philos. Trans. R. Soc. Lond. [Biol.]* 337:167–175.

18. Vigilant, L., Stoneking, M., Harpending, H., Hawkes, K., Wilson, A. 1991. African populations and the evolution of human mitochondrial DNA. *Science* 253:1503–1507.

19. Weiss, M. L. 1987. Nucleic acid evidence bearing on hominoid relationships. *Yrbk. Phys. Anthropol.* 30:41–73.

20. Melnick, D. J., Hoelzer, G. A. 1993. What is mtDNA good for in the study of primate evolution? *Evol. Anthropol.* 2:2–10.

21. Stoneking, M., Bhatia, K., Wilson, A. 1986. Rate of sequence divergence estimated from restricted maps of mitochondrial DNAs from Papua New Guinea. *Cold Spring Harbor Symp. Quant. Biol.* 51:433–439.

22. Stoneking, M., Cann, R. L. 1989. African origin of human mitochondrial DNA. In *The human revolution*, ed. P. Mellars, C. Stringer, pp. 17–30. Princeton, N.J.: Princeton University Press.

23. Stoneking, M. 1993. DNA and recent human evolution. *Evol. Anthropol.* 2:60–73.

24. Templeton, A. R. 1993. The "Eve" hypothesis: A genetic critique and reanalysis. *Am. Anthropol.* 95:51–72.

25. Swofford, D. L. 1991. *PAUP: Phylogenetic analysis using parsimony, Version 3.1.* Champaign: Illinois Natural History Survey.

26. Wainscoat, J. S., Hill, A. V. S., Thein, S. L., Flint, J., Chapman, J. C., Weatherall, D. J., Clegg, J. B., Higgs, D. R. 1989. Geographic distribution of alpha- and beta-globin gene cluster polymorphisms. In *The human revolution*, ed. P. Mellars, C. Stringer, pp. 31–38. Princeton, N.J.: Princeton University Press.

27. Rouhani, S. 1989. Molecular genetics and the pattern of human evolution: plausible and implausible models. In *The human revolution*, ed. P. Mellars, C. Stringer, pp. 47–61. Princeton, N.J.: Princeton University Press.

28. Mountain, J. L., Lin, A. A., Bowcock, A. M., Cavalli-Sforza, L. L. 1992. Evolution of modern humans: evidence from nuclear DNA polymorphisms. *Philos. Trans. R. Soc. Lond. [Biol.]* 337:159–165.

29. Cavalli-Sforza, L., Menozzi, P., Piazza, A. 1993. Demic expansions and human evolution. *Science* 259:639–646.

30. Fullerton, S. M., Schneider, J. A., Bond, J., Harding, R. M., Boyce, A. J., Clegg, J. B. 1995. DNA sequence variation at the β-globin locus and human evolutionary origins. *Am. J. Phys. Anthropol.* Suppl. 20:94.

31. Jorde, L., Bamshad, M., Watkins, W., Zenger, R., Fraley, A., Krakowiak, P., Carpenter, K., Soodyall, H., Jenkins, T., Rogers, A. 1995. Origins and affinities of modern humans: A comparison of mitochondrial and nuclear genetic data. *Am. J. Hum. Genet.* 57:523–538.

32. Wolpoff, M. H. 1989. The place of the Neandertals in human evolution. In *The emergence of modern humans*, ed. E. Trinkaus, pp. 97–141. Cambridge: Cambridge University Press.

33. Wallace, D. C., Garrison, K., Knowler, W. C. 1985. Dramatic founder effects in Amerindian mitochondrial DNA's. *Am. J. Phys. Anthropol.* 68:149–155.

34. Avise, J. C. 1994. *Molecular markers, natural history and evolution.* New York: Chapman and Hall.

35. Nei, M. 1987. *Molecular evolutionary genetics.* New York: Columbia University Press.

36. Maddison, D. R. 1991. African origin of human mitochondrial DNA reexamined. *Syst. Zool.* 40:355–363.

37. Hedges, S. B., Kumar, S., Tamura, K., Stoneking, M. 1991. Human origins and analysis of mitochondrial DNA sequences. *Science* 255:737–739.

38. Templeton, A. 1991. Human origins and analysis of mitochondrial DNA sequences. *Science* 255:737.

39. Maddison, D. R., Ruvolo, M., Swofford, D. L. 1992. Geographic origins of human mitochondrial DNA: Phylogenetic evidence from control region sequences. *Syst. Biol.* 41:111–124.

40. Goldman, N., Barton, N. H. 1992. Genetics and geography. *Nature* 357:440–441.

41. Templeton, A. R. 1994. "Eve": Hypothesis compatibility versus hypothesis testing. *Am. Anthropol.* 96:141–147.

42. Wills, C. 1995. When did Eve live? An evolutionary detective story. *Evolution* 49:593–607.

43. Bailey, W. J. 1993. Hominoid trichotomy: A molecular overview. *Evol. Anthropol.* 2:100–108.

44. Ruano, G., Rogers, J., Ferguson-Smith, A., Kidd, K. 1992. DNA sequence polymorphism within hominoid species exceeds the number of phylogenetically informative characters of a HOX2 locus. *Mol. Biol. Evol.* 9:575–586.

45. Whitfield, L., Sulston, J., Goodfellow, P. 1995. Sequence variation of the human Y chromosome. *Nature* 378:379–380.

46. Hammer, M. 1995. A recent common ancestry for human Y chromosomes. *Nature* 378:376–378.

47. Dorit, R. L., Akashi, H., Gilbert, W. 1995. Absence of polymorphism at the ZFT locus on the human Y chromosome. *Science* 268:1183–1185.

48. Tishkoff, S., Dietzsch, E., Speed, W., Pakstis, A., Kidd, J., Cheung, K., Bonne-Tamir, M., Santachiara-Benerecetti, A., Moral, P., Krings, M., Paabo, S., Watson, E., Risch, N., Jenkins, T., Kidd, K. 1996. Global patterns of linkage disequilibrium at the CD4 locus and modern human origins. *Science* 271:1380–1387.

49. Ayala, F. 1995. The myth of Eve: Molecular biology and human origins. *Science* 270:1930–1936.

50. Stringer, C., Gamble, C. 1993. *In search of the Neanderthals.* New York: Thames and Hudson.

51. Mellars, P. A. 1992. Archaeology and the population-dispersal hypothesis of modern human origins in Europe. *Philos. Trans. R. Soc. Lond. [Biol.]* 337:225–234.

52. Gowlett, J. 1992. Tools—the Palaeolithic record. In *The Cambridge encyclopedia of human evolution*, ed. S. Jones, R. Martin, D. Pilbeam, pp. 350–360. Cambridge: Cambridge University Press.

53. Stringer, C., Grun, R. 1991. Time for the last Neanderthals. *Nature* 351:701–702.

CHAPTER X

1. Thackeray, A. I. 1992. The middle stone age south of the Limpopo River. *J. World Prehist.* 6:385–440.

2. Deacon, H. J. 1992. Southern Africa and modern human origins. *Philos. Trans. R. Soc. Lond. [Biol.]* 337:177–183.

3. Grine, F., Klein, R., Volman, T. 1991. Dating, archaeology and human fossils from the Middle Stone Age levels of Die Kelders, South Africa. *J. Hum. Evol.* 21:363–395.

4. Klein, R. G. 1975. Middle stone age man-animal relationships in Southern Africa: Evidence from Die Kelders and Klasies River Mouth. *Science* 190:265–267.

5. Klein, R. G., Cruz-Uribe, K., Beaumont, P. B. 1991. Environmental, ecological, and paleoanthropological implications of the late Pleistocene mammalian fauna from Equus Cave, Northern Cape Province, South Africa. *Quat. Res.* 36:94–119.

6. Morris, A. 1991. Biological relationships between Upper Pleistocene and Holocene populations in southern Africa. In *Continuity or replacement: Controversies in* Homo sapiens *evolution*, ed. G. Brauer, F. H. Smith, pp. 131–143. Rotterdam: Balkema.

7. Grine, F. E., Klein, R. G. 1985. Pleistocene and Holocene human remains from Equus Cave, South Africa. *Anthropology* 8:55–98.

8. Grun, R., Beaumont, P., Stringer, C. 1990. ESR dating evidence for early modern humans at Border Cave in South Africa. *Nature* 344:537–539.

9. Corruccini, R. S. 1992. Metrical reconsideration of the Skhul IV and IX and Border Cave 1 crania in the context of modern human origins. *Am. J. Phys. Anthropol.* 87:433–445.

10. Corruccini, R. S. 1994. Reaganomics and the fate of the progressive Neandertals. In *Integrative paths to the past*, ed. R. S. Corruccini, R. L. Ciochon, pp. 697–708. Englewood Cliffs, N.J.: Prentice-Hall.

11. Deacon, H. J., Geleijnse, V. B. 1988. The stratigraphy and sedimentology of the main site sequence, Klasies River, South Africa. *S. Afr. Archaeol. Bull.* 43:5–14.

12. Deacon, H. J., Shuurman, R. 1992. The origins of modern people: The evidence from Klasies River. In *Continuity or replacement: Controversies in* Homo sapiens *evolution*, ed. G. Brauer, F. H. Smith, pp. 121–129. Rotterdam: A.A. Balkema.

13. Singer, R., Wymer, J. 1982. The middle stone age at *Klasies River Mouth in South Africa*. Chicago: University of Chicago Press.

14. Deacon, H. J., Talma, A. S., Vogel, J. C. 1988. Biological and cultural development of Pleistocene people in an Old World southern continent. In *Early man in the southern hemisphere. Supplement to Archaeometry: Australasian studies*, ed. J. R. Prescott, pp. S23–S31. Adelaide: University of Adelaide.

15. Brauer, G., Deacon, H. J., Zipfel, F. 1992. Comment on the new maxillary finds from Klasies River, South Africa. *J. Hum. Evol.* 23:419–422.

16. Grun, R., Shackleton, N., Deacon, H. 1990. Electron-spin-resonance dating of tooth enamel from Klasies River Mouth Cave. *Curr. Anthropol.* 31:427–432.

17. Rightmire, G. P., Deacon, H. J. 1991. Comparative studies of late Pleistocene human remains from Klasies River Mouth, South Africa. *J. Hum. Evol.* 20:131–156.

18. Smith, F. 1992. Models and realities in modern human origins: The African fossil evidence. *Philos. Trans. R. Soc. Lond. [Biol.]* 337:243–250.

19. White, T. D. 1987. Cannibals at Klasies? *Sagittarius* 2:6–9.

20. Caspari, R., Wolpoff, M. H. 1990. The morphological affinities of the Klasies River Mouth skeletal remains. *Am. J. Phys. Anthropol.* 81:203.

21. Wolpoff, M. H., Caspari, R. 1990. Metric analysis of the skeletal material from Klasies River Mouth, Republic of South Africa. *Am. J. Phys. Anthropol.* 81:319.

22. Frayer, D. W., Wolpoff, M. H., Thorne, A. G., Smith, F. H., Pope, G. G. 1993. Theories of modern human origins: The paleontological test. *Am. Anthropol.* 95:14–50.

23. Singer, R. 1958. The Rhodesian, Florisbad and Saldanha skulls. In *Hundert Jahre Neanderthaler*, ed. G. H. R. von Koenigswald, pp. 52–62. Utrecht: Kemink en Zoon N.V.

24. Clarke, R. 1985. A new reconstruction of the Florisbad cranium, with notes on the site. In *Ancestors: The hard evidence*, ed. E. Delson, pp. 301–305. New York: Alan R. Liss.

25. Stringer, C. B. 1989. Documenting the origin of modern humans. In *The emergence of modern humans*, ed. E. Trinkaus, pp. 67–96. Cambridge: Cambridge University Press.

26. Clark, J. D. 1992. African and Asian perspectives on the origins of modern humans. *Philos. Trans. R. Soc. Lond. [Biol.]* 337:201–215.

27. Leakey, R. 1969. Early *Homo sapiens* remains from the Omo River region of south-west Ethiopia: Faunal remains from the Omo Valley. *Nature* 222:1132–1133.

28. Rightmire, G. P. 1989. Middle stone age humans from eastern and southern Africa. In *The human revolution*, ed. P. Mellars, C. Stringer, pp. 109–122. Princeton, N.J.: Princeton University Press.

29. Day, M., Leakey, M. D., Magori, C. 1980. A new hominid fossil skull (LH18) from the Ngaloba Beds, Laetoli, northern Tanzania. *Nature* 284:55–56.

30. Brauer, G., Leakey, R. E. 1980. The ES-1693 cranium from Eliye Springs, West Turkana, Kenya. *J. Hum. Evol.* 15:289–312.

31. Hublin, J. 1992. Recent human evolution in northwestern Africa. *Philos. Trans. R. Soc. Lond. [Biol.]* 337:185–191.

32. Minugh-Purvis, N. 1993. Reexamination of the immature hominid maxilla from Tangier, Morocco. *Am. J. Phys. Anthropol.* 92:449–461.

33. Grun, R., Stringer, C. 1991. Electron spin resonance dating and the evolution of modern humans. *Archaeometry* 33:153–199.

34. Brauer, G., Rimbach, K. W. 1990. Late archaic and modern *Homo sapiens* from Europe, Africa, and Southwest Asia: Craniometric comparisons and phylogenetic implications. *J. Hum. Evol.* 19:789–807.

35. Hrdlicka, A. 1927. The Neanderthal phase of man. *J. R. Soc. Anthropol. Inst.* 57:249–273.

36. Klein, R. 1992. The archeology of modern human origins. *Evol. Anthropol.* 1:5–14.

37. Trinkaus, E., Shipman, P. 1993. Neandertals: Images of ourselves. *Evol. Anthropol.* 1:194–201.

38. Wolpoff, M. H. 1989. The place of the Neandertals in human evolution. In *The emergence of modern humans*, ed. E. Trinkaus, pp. 97–141. Cambridge: Cambridge University Press.

39. Howell, F. C. 1951. The place of Neanderthal man in human evolution. *Am. J. Phys. Anthropol.* 9:379–416.

40. Howell, F. C. 1952. Pleistocene glacial ecology and the evolution of "classic Neandertal" man. *Southwest. J. Anthropol.* 8:377–410.

41. Howell, F. C. 1958. Upper Pleistocene men of the Southwest Asian Mousterian. In *Hundert Jahre Neanderthaler*, ed. G. H. R. von Koenigswald, pp. 185–198. Utrecht: Kemink en Zoon, N.V.

42. Brace, C. L. 1967. *The stages of human evolution*. Englewood Cliffs, N.J.: Prentice-Hall.

43. Brose, D., Wolpoff, M. 1971. Early Upper Paleolithic man and late Middle Paleolithic tools. *Am. Anthropol.* 73:1156–1194.

44. Frayer, D. W. 1992. The persistence of Neanderthal features in post-Neanderthal Europeans. In *Continuity or replacement*, ed. G. Brauer, F. H. Smith, pp. 179–188. Rotterdam: A. A. Balkema.

45. Boule, M. 1923. *Fossil men: Elements of human paleontology*. London: Gurney and Jackson.

46. Vallois, H. V. 1954. Neandertals and praesapiens. *J. R. Anthropol. Inst.* 84:111–130.

47. LeGros Clark, W. E. 1964. *The fossil evidence for human evolution*. Chicago: University of Chicago Press.

48. Trinkaus, E. 1989. The Upper Pleistocene transition. In *The emergence of modern humans*, ed. E. Trinkaus, pp. 42–66. Cambridge: Cambridge University Press.

49. Frayer, D. W. 1978. Evolution of the dentition in Upper Paleolithic and Mesolithic Europe. *Univ. Kansas Publ. Anthropol.* 10:1–201.

50. Brace, C. L. 1979. Krapina, "classic" Neanderthals, and the evolution of the European face. *J. Hum. Evol.* 8:527–550.

51. Anton, S. C. 1994. Mechanical and other perspectives on Neandertal craniofacial morphology. In *Integrative paths to the past*, ed. R. S. Corruccini, R. L. Ciochon, pp. 677–695. Englewood Cliffs, N.J.: Prentice-Hall.

52. de Castro, J. M. B., Bromage, T. G., Jalvo, Y. F. 1988. Buccal striations on fossil human anterior teeth: Evidence of handedness in the middle and early Upper Pleistocene. *J. Hum. Evol.* 17:403–412.

53. Toth, N. 1985. Archaeological evidence for preferential right-handedness in the lower and middle Pleistocene and its possible implications. *J. Hum. Evol.* 14:607–614.

54. Toth, N., Schick, K. 1993. Early stone industries and inferences regarding language and cognition. In *Tools, language and cognition in human evolution*, ed. K. Gibson, T. Ingold, pp. 346–362. Cambridge: Cambridge University Press.

55. Trinkaus, E., Churchill, S. E., Ruff, C. B. 1994. Postcranial robusticity in *Homo*. II: Humeral bilateral asymmetry and bone plasticity. *Am. J. Phys. Anthropol.* 93:1–34.

56. Brace, C. L. 1964. The fate of the classic Neandertals: A consideration of hominid catastrophism. *Curr. Anthropol.* 5:3–43.

57. Trinkaus, E. 1987. The Neandertal face: Evolutionary and functional perspectives on a recent hominid face. *J. Hum. Evol.* 16:429–443.

58. Demes, B. 1987. Another look at an old face: Biomechanics of the Neandertal facial skeleton reconsidered. *J. Hum. Evol.* 16:297–303.

59. Smith, F. H., Paquette, S. P. 1989. The adaptive basis of Neandertal facial form, with some thoughts on the nature of modern human origins. In *The emergence of modern humans*, ed. E. Trinkaus, pp. 181–210. Cambridge: Cambridge University Press.

60. Spencer, M. A., Demes, B. 1993. Biomechanical analysis of masticatory system configuration in Neandertals and Inuits. *Am. J. Phys. Anthropol.* 91:1–20.

61. Rak, Y. 1986. The Neanderthal: a new look at an old face. *J. Hum. Evol.* 15:151–164.

62. Stewart, T. D. 1962. Neanderthal scapulae with special attention to the Shanidar Neanderthals from Iraq. *Anthropos* 57:779–800.

63. Musgrave, J. H. 1971. How dextrous was Neanderthal man? *Nature* 233:538–541.

64. Trinkaus, E., Churchill, S. E., Villemeur, I., Riley, K. G., Heller, J. A., Ruff, C. B. 1991. Robusticity versus shape: The functional interpretation of Neandertal appendicular morphology. *J. Anthropol. Soc. Nippon* 99:257–278.

65. Trinkaus, E. 1981. Neanderthal limb proportions and cold adaptation. In *Aspects of human evolution*, ed. C. B. Stringer, pp. 187–224. London: Taylor and Francis.

66. Trinkaus, E. 1984. Western Asia. In *The origins of modern humans*, ed. F. H. Smith, R. Spencer, pp. 251–293. New York: Alan R. Liss.

67. Hayden, B. 1993. The cultural capacities of Neandertals: a review and re-evaluation. *J. Hum. Evol.* 24:113–146.

68. Boeda, E., Connan, J., Dessort, D. Muhesen, S., Mercier, N., Valladas, H., Tisnerat, N. 1996. Bitumen as a hafting material on Middle Paleolithic artifacts. *Nature* 380:336–338.

69. Leroi-Gourhan, A. 1975. The flowers found with Shanidar IV, a Neanderthal burial in Iraq. *Science* 190:562–565.

70. Trinkaus, E., Zimmerman, M. R. 1982. Trauma among the Shanidar Neandertals. *Am. J. Phys. Anthropol.* 57:61–76.

71. Trinkaus, E., Shipman, P. 1992. *The Neandertals: Changing the image of mankind*. New York: Knopf.

72. Lieberman, P. 1976. Interactive models for evolution: neural mechanisms, anatomy, and behaviour. *Ann. N.Y. Acad. Sci.* 280:660–672.

73. Lieberman, P. 1989. The origins of some aspects of human language and cognition. In *The human revolution*, ed. P. Mellars, C. Stringer, pp. 391–414. Princeton, N.J.: Princeton University Press.

74. Houghton, P. 1993. Neandertal supralaryngeal vocal tract. *Am. J. Phys. Anthropol.* 90:139–146.

75. Arensburg, B. 1989. New skeletal evidence concerning the anatomy of Middle Palaeolithic populations in the Middle East: The Kebara skeleton. In *The human revolution*, ed. P. Mellars, C. Stringer, pp. 165–171. Princeton, N.J.: Princeton University Press.

76. Arensburg, B., Schepartz, L. A., Tillier, A. M., Vandermeersch, B., Rak, Y. 1990. A reappraisal of the anatomical basis for speech in Middle Palaeolothic hominids. *Am. J. Phys. Anthropol.* 83:137–146.

77. Bar-Yosef, O., Vandermeersch, B. 1993. Modern humans in the Levant. *Sci. Am.* 268:94–100.

78. Arensburg, B. 1994. Middle paleolithic speech capabilities: A response to Dr. Lieberman. *Am. J. Phys. Anthropol.* 94:279–280.

79. Lieberman, P. 1994. Hyoid bone position and speech: Reply to Dr. Arensburg et al. (1990). *Am. J. Phys. Anthropol.* 94:275–278.

80. Straus, W. L., Cave, A. J. E. 1957. Pathology and the posture of Neanderthal man. *Q. Rev. Biol.* 32:348–363.

81. Zeuner, F. E. 1958. The replacement of Neanderthal man by *Homo sapiens*. In *Hundert Jahre Neanderthaler*, ed. G. H. R. von Koenigswald, pp. 312–315. Utrecht: Kemink en Zoon, N.V.

82. Reynolds, T. E. G. 1991. Revolution or resolution? The archaeology of modern human origins. *World Archaeol.* 23:155–166.

83. Mellars, P. A. 1992. Archaeology and the population-dispersal hypothesis of modern human origns in Europe. *Philos. Trans. R. Soc. Lond. [Biol.]* 337:225–234.

84. Straus, L. 1995. The Upper Paleolithic of Europe: An overview. *Evol. Anthropol.* 4:4–16.

85. Smith, F. H. 1982. Upper Pleistocene hominid evolution in South-Central Europe: A review of the evidence and analysis of trends. *Curr. Anthropol.* 23:667–686.

86. Svoboda, J. 1987. A new male burial from Dolni Vestonice. *J. Hum. Evol.* 16:827–830.

87. Klima, B. 1987. A triple burial from the Upper Paleolithic of Dolni Vestonice, Czechoslovakia. *J. Hum. Evol.* 16:831–835.

88. Jelinek, J. 1969. Neanderthal man and *Homo sapiens* in central and eastern Europe. *Curr. Anthropol.* 10:475–503.

89. Lindly, J. M., Clark, G. A. 1990. Symbolism and modern human origins. *Curr. Anthropol.* 31:233–262.

90. Smith, F. H. 1978. Some conclusions regarding the morphology and significance of the Krapina Neandertal remains. *Jugoslav. akad. znan. umjet.* 1:103–118.

91. Rink, W., Schwarcz, H., Smith, F., Radovcic, J. 1995. ESR ages for Krapina hominids. *Nature* 378:24.

92. Wolpoff, M. H. 1979. The Krapina dental remains. *Am. J. Phys. Anthropol.* 50:67–114.

93. Trinkaus, E. 1985. Cannibalism and burial at Krapina. *J. Hum. Evol.* 14:203–216.

94. Defleur, A., Dutour, O., Valladas, H., Vandermeersch, B. 1993. Cannibals among the Neanderthals? *Nature* 362:214.

95. Crummett, T. L., Miracle, P. T. 1995. Aurignacian Neandertals? The case of Vindija, Croatia. Paleoanthropology Society Conference, Oakland, CA.

96. Smith, F. H., Ahern, J. C. 1994. Additional cranial remains from Vindija cave, Croatia. *Am. J. Phys. Anthropol.* 93:275–280.

97. Valladas, H., Joron, J. L., Valladas, G., Arensburg, B., Bar-Yosef, O., Belfer-Cohen, A., Goldberg, P., Laville, H., Meignen, L., Rak, Y., Tchervov, E., Tillier, A. M., Vandermeersch, B. 1987. Thermoluminescence dates for the Neanderthal burial site at Kebara in Israel. *Nature* 330:159–160.

98. Valladas, H., Reyss, J. L., Joron, J. L., Valladas, G., Bar-Yosef, O., Vandermeersch, B. 1988. Thermoluminescence dating of Mousterian 'Proto-Cro-Magnon' remains from Israel and the origin of modern man. *Nature* 331:614–616.

99. Bar-Yosef, O. 1992. The role of western Asia in modern human origins. *Philos. Trans. R. Soc. Lond. [Biol.]* 337:193–200.

100. Stringer, C., Grun, R., Schwarcz, H., Goldberg, P. 1989. ESR dates for the hominid burial site of Es Skhul in Israel. *Nature* 338:756–758.

101. Aitken, M., Valladas, H. 1992. Luminescence dating relevant to human origins. *Philos. Trans. R. Soc. Lond. [Biol.]* 337:139–144.

102. Schwarcz, H., Grun, R., Vandermeersch, B., Bar-Yosef, O., Valladas, H., Tchernov, E. 1988. ESR dates for the hominid burial site of Qafzeh in Israel. *J. Hum. Evol.* 17:733–737.

103. Schwarcz, H., Grun, R. 1992. Electron spin resonance (ESR) dating of the origin of modern man. *Philos. Trans. R. Soc. Lond. [Biol.]* 337:145–148.

104. McDermott, F., Grun, R., Stringer, C. B., Hawkesworth, C. J. 1993. Mass-spectrometric U-series dates for Israeli Neanderthal/early modern hominid sites. *Nature* 363:252–255.

105. Mercier, N., Valladas, H., Joron, J.-L., Reyss, J.-L., Leveque, F., Vandermeersch, B. 1991. Thermoluminescence dating of the late Neanderthal remains from Saint-Cesaire. *Nature* 351:737–739.

106. McCown, T., Keith, A. 1939. *The stone age of Mount Carmel.* Oxford: Clarendon.

107. Mercier, N., Valladas, H., Bar-Yosef, O., Vandermeersch, B., Stringer, C., Joron, J. L. 1993. Thermoluminescence date for the Mousterian burial site of Es-Skhul, Mt. Carmel. *J. Archaeol. Sci.* 20:169–174.

108. Trinkaus, E. 1993. Femoral neck-shaft angles of the Qafzeh-Skhul early modern humans, and activity levels among immature Near Eastern Middle Paleolithic hominids. *J. Hum. Evol.* 25:393–416.

109. Jelinek, A. J. 1982. The Tabun cave and Paleolithic man in the Levant. *Science* 216:1369–1375.

110. Grun, R., Stringer, C. B., Schwarcz, H. P. 1991. ESR dating of teeth from Garrod's Tabun cave collection. *J. Hum. Evol.* 20:231–248.

111. Grun, R. 1993. Electron spin resonance dating in paleoanthropology. *Evol. Anthropol.* 2:172–181.

112. Schwarcz, H. P., Buhay, W. M., Grun, R., Valladas, H., Tchernov, E., Bar-Yosef, O., Vandermeersch, B. 1989. ESR dating of the Neanderthal site, Kebara Cave, Israel. *J. Archaeol. Sci.* 16:653–659.

113. Arensburg, B., Tillier, A. M., Vandermeersch, B., Duday, H., Schepartz, L. A., Rak, Y. 1989. A middle Palaeolithic human hyoid bone. *Nature* 338:758–760.

114. Tague, R. G. 1992. Sexual dimorphism in the human bony pelvis, with a consideration of the Neandertal pelvis from Kebara Cave, Israel. *Am. J. Phys. Anthropol.* 88:1–21.

115. Trinkaus, E. 1984. Neandertal pubic morphology and gestation length. *Curr. Anthropol.* 25:509–514.

116. Rosenberg, K. 1992. The evolution of modern human childbirth. *Yrbk. Phys. Anthropol.* 35:89–124.

117. Stewart, T. 1960. Form of the pubic bone in Neanderthal Man. *Science* 131:1437–1438.

118. Stewart, T. D. 1961. The skull of Shanidar II. *Sumer* 17:97–106.

119. Stringer, C. B., Trinkaus, E. 1981. The Shanidar Neanderthal crania. In *Aspects of human evolution,* ed. C. B. Stringer, pp. 129–165. London: Taylor and Francis.

120. Trinkaus, E. 1983. *The Shanidar Neandertals.* New York: Academic.

121. Simmons, T., Falsetti, A. B., Smith, F. H. 1991. Frontal bone morphometrics of southwest Asian Pleistocene hominids. *J. Hum. Evol.* 20:249–269.

122. Sohn, S., Wolpoff, M. H. 1993. Zuttiyeh: A view from the East. *Am. J. Phys. Anthropol.* 91:325–347.

123. Garrod, D. A. E. 1958. The ancient shore-lines of the Lebanon, and the dating of Mt. Carmel Man. In *Hundert Jahre Neanderthaler,* ed. G. H. R. von Koenigswald, pp. 182–184. Utrecht: Kemink en Zoon N.V.

124. Rak, Y., Kimbel, W. H., Hovers, E. 1994. A Neandertal infant from Amud Cave, Israel. *J. Hum. Evol.* 26:313–324.

125. Akazawa, T., Muhesen, S., Dodo, Y., Kondo, O., Mizoguchi, Y. 1995. Neanderthal infant burial. *Nature* 377:586–587.

126. Weidenreich, F. 1939. On the earliest representatives of modern mankind recovered on the soil of East Asia. *Peking Nat. Hist. Bull.* 13:161–174.

127. Weidenreich, F. 1943. The skull of *Sinanthropus pekinensis*: A comparative study on a primtive hominid skull. *Palaeontol. Sinica* 10:1–484.

128. Wu, X. 1990. The evolution of humankind in China. *Acta Anthropol. Sinica* 9:320–321.

129. Pope, G. 1992. Craniofacial evidence for the origin of modern humans in China. *Yrbk. Phys. Anthropol.* 35:243–298.

130. Chen, T., Zhang, Y. 1991. Palaeolithic chronology and the possible coexistence of *Homo erectus* and *Homo sapiens* in China. *World Archeol.* 23:147–154.

131. Roberts, R. G., Jones, R., Smith, M. A. 1990. Thermoluminescence dating of a 50,000-year-old human occupation site in northern Australia. *Nature* 345:153–156.

132. Groube, L., Chappell, J., Muke, J., Price, D. 1986. A 40,000 year-old human occupation site at Huon Peninsula, Papua New Guinea. *Nature* 324:453–455.

133. Brown, P. 1992. Recent human evolution in East Asia and Australasia. *Philos. Trans. R. Soc. Lond. [Biol.]* 337:235–242.

134. Thorne, A. G. 1980. The longest link: Human evolution in Southeast Asia and the settlement of Australia. In *Indonesia: Australian perspectives*, ed. J. J. Fox, R. G. Earnaut, P. T. McCawley, J. A. C. Maukie, pp. 35–43. Canberra: Australian National University Research School of Pacific Studies.

135. Habgood, P. J. 1989. The origin of anatomically modern humans in Australasia. In *The human revolution*, ed. P. Mellars, C. Stringer, pp. 245–273. Princeton, N.J.: Princeton University Press.

136. Wolpoff, M., Wu, X., Thorne, A. 1984. Modern *Homo sapiens* origins: A general theory of hominid evolution involving the fossil evidence from east Asia. In *The origins of modern humans: A world survey of the fossil evidence*, ed. F. Smith, F. Spencer, pp. 411–483. New York: Alan R. Liss.

137. Groves, C. P. 1989. A regional approach to the problem of the origin of modern humans in Australasia. In *The human revolution*, ed. P. Mellars, C. Stringer, pp. 274–285. Princeton, N.J.: Princeton University Press.

138. Lahr, M. M. 1994. The multiregional model of modern human origins: A reassessment of its morphological basis. *J. Hum. Evol.* 26:23–56.

139. Kramer, A. 1991. Modern human origins in Australasia: Replacement or evolution? *Am. J. Phys. Anthropol.* 86:455–473.

140. Waddle, D. M. 1994. Matrix correlation tests support a single origin for modern humans. *Nature* 368:452–454.

141. Pope, G. 1991. Evolution of the zygomaticomaxillary region in the genus *Homo* and its relevance to the origin of modern humans. *J. Hum. Evol.* 21:189–213.

142. Larsen, C. S., Matter, R. M., Gebo, D. L. 1991. *Human origins: The fossil record.* Prospect Heights: Waveland.

143. Stringer, C., Gamble, C. 1993. *In Search of the Neanderthals.* New York: Thames and Hudson.

144. Gowlett, J. 1992. Tools- the Palaeolithic record. In *The Cambridge encyclopedia of human evolution*, ed. S. Jones, R. Martin, D. Pilbeam, pp. 350–360. Cambridge: Cambridge University Press.

145. Coles, J., Higgs, E. 1969. *The archaeology of early man.* New York: Praeger.

146. Bar-Yosef, O. 1989. Geochronology of the Levantine Middle Palaeolithic. In *The human revolution: Behavioural and biological perspectives on the origin of modern humans*, ed. P. Mellars, C. Stringer, pp. 589–610. Edinburgh: Edinburgh University Press.

EPILOGUE

1. Wada, A. 1995. A space-time slide rule. *Nature* 373:xxxv–xxxvi.

2. McPhee, J. 1980. *Basin and range.* New York: Farrar Straus Giroux.

Glossary

absolute dating   methods for determining the age, in years before present, of artifacts, fossils, or rocks, usually based on the amount of radioactive change in the specimen

Acheulian industry   early Paleolithic industry characterized by handaxes and cleavers

aeolian   pertaining to or caused by wind

Ahmarian   a Middle to Upper Paleolithic blade-and-bladelet-dominated industry of the Levant dating to about 40,000 years ago

allopatric   pertaining to taxa occupying different and disjunct geographical areas (see **punctuated equilibrium**)

allopatric speciation   an evolutionary model based on the idea that most evolutionary change is concentrated in comparatively rapid speciation events in small isolated subpopulations of the ancestral species

alpha decay   radioactive decay in which the nucleus of the parent atom loses 2 protons and 2 neutrons; thus its mass number decreases by 4 and its atomic number decreases by 2 (e.g., the decay of ^{238}U to ^{234}Th)

alveolus   tooth socket

anagenesis   an evolutionary process involving the gradual accumulation of changes in ancestor-to-descendant lineages through time (also called phyletic evolution)

analogy   a similarity of form or structure between two taxa that is not shared with their nearest common ancestor; that is, the similar structure has evolved independently in the two taxa and is due to convergent evolution

anterior pillars   two massive bony columns that support the anterior portion of the palate on both sides of the nasal aperture

Anthropoidea   suborder of Primates that includes monkeys, apes, and humans

anvil percussion   a stone toolmaking technique in which a large flat stone is placed on the ground and used as an anvil for breaking off stone flakes

apatite   important mineral component of bones and teeth consisting mainly of calcium phosphate

apomorphy   the evolutionary later state of a character, relative to its ancestral state

appendicular skeleton   the bones of the limbs, including the shoulder girdle

arboreal   relating to life in the trees

association areas   regions of the cerebral cortex involved with complex functions of comprehension, communication, and consciousness

asthenosphere   the layer of the Earth directly below the lithosphere, about 70 to 200 km below the Earth's surface

Aterian   a middle Paleolithic tool industry in North Africa characterized by tools with tanged points and bifacially worked, leaf-shaped points

atomic mass number   total number of protons and neutrons in an atom

atomic number   the number of protons in an atom

autapomorphy   a derived character that arose for the first time in a particular group; autapomorphic characters of a taxon are those not shared by its sister groups or by their most recent common ancestor

axial precession   see **precession**

axial skeleton   the bones of the trunk, including the vertebrae, pelvis, ribs, and sternum

badlands   a complex, stream-dissected topography

basicranium   the base of the skull

basion   the midline point on the anterior margin of the foramen magnum

beta decay   radioactive decay in which one of the neutrons in the nucleus turns into a proton; the atomic number increases by 1 but the mass number remains unchanged (e.g., ^{87}Rb to ^{87}Sr)

bicuspids   premolars

binocular vision   vision in which both visual axes focus on a distant object to produce a stereoscopic (three-dimensional) image

biogenic carbonate   a sediment or rock composed of calcium, magnesium, and/or iron that is produced directly by the life activities or processes of organisms

bipolar percussion   a stone toolmaking technique in which an anvil is set on the ground, a piece of quartz held upright on it, and flakes chipped off both ends (bipolar flakes) by striking it with a hammerstone

blades   a long parallel-sided flake struck from a specially prepared core

brachycephalic   having a disproportionately short head, usually with a cephalic index (breadth/length $\times$ 100) over 80

bregma   the point on the midline of the skull corresponding to the intersection of the coronal and sagittal sutures

Broca's area   the posterior part of the inferior frontal gyrus of the left or dominant hemisphere in the brain; a critical brain area for motor mechanisms governing articulated speech

Brunhes   long interval of geologic time from about 800,000 years to the present in which the polarity of Earth's magnetic field has been (for the most part) normal

buccal   toward the lateral (cheek) side of a tooth

burin   a pointed tool made of chipped flint or stone used to engrave bone, antler, ivory, and wood

calcrete   a limestone precipitated as surface or near-surface crusts and nodules by the evaporation of soil moisture in semiarid climates

calotte   the calvaria without the base of the skull

calvaria   top of the skull; skullcap

canine   the pointed tooth between the incisors and the premolars

carbon isotope analyses   studies comparing the relative abundance of two carbon isotopes, ^{12}C and ^{13}C, in tissues of animals; distinct carbon isotope "signatures" are passed along the food chain from plants to the tissues, including tooth enamel, of herbivores

carpometacarpal joint   articulation between the wrist bones, or carpus, and the metacarpal bones

cave breccia   a term used to describe sediments in caves that are calcified by lime-bearing solutions dripping from the cave roof

cementum   bonelike tissue that covers the external surface of tooth roots

Cenozoic era   that portion of Earth's history covering the last 65 million years or so ("recent life")

cephalic index   the ratio of the maximal breadth to the maximal length of the skull multiplied by 100

character   a morphological feature or trait chosen for study

character weighting   assigning more importance to certain characters than to others to elucidate evolutionary relationships

chronospecies   a species represented in more than one geological time horizon; a time-successive species

cingulum   thickened ring of enamel around the base of a tooth

clade   group comprising all the species descended from a single common ancestor

cladistics   a method of classification employing phylogenetic hypotheses as the basis for classification and using recency of common ancestry as the sole criterion for grouping taxa, rather than data on phenetic similarity (sometimes referred to as "phylogenetic systematics")

cladogenesis   a branching type of evolutionary progress involving the splitting and subsequent divergence of populations (= dendritic evolution)

cladogram   a branching tree diagram used to represent phyletic relationships; also called a cladistic tree

classification   the process of establishing, defining, and ranking taxa within some hierarchical series of groups

clavicles   the collarbones

cleaver   large, usually bifacially flaked artifact with a straight, sharp-edged bit on one end

climatic forcing model   any of several hypotheses that attempt to relate widespread climatic and associated environmental change, in particular the widespread cooling that occurred around 2.5 mya and affected faunas and floras worldwide, to important events in Plio-Pleistocene hominid evolution

conceptual models   models that reconstruct early hominid behavior using principles from behavioral ecology and evolutionary theory and information on the behavior of particular primate species, including humans

continental drift   slow movements of continents (and the crustal plates to which they are attached) over the surface of the Earth

convergent evolution   the independent evolution of structural or functional similarity in two or more unrelated or distantly related lineages or forms that is not based on genotypic similarity

cores   lumps of stone from which flakes have been removed; sometimes a core is the by-product of toolmaking, but it may also be shaped and modified to serve as a tool in its own right

coronal   pertaining to the suture between the frontal and parietal bones

Cro-Magnons   the first anatomically modern western European populations

cross striations   daily microscopic increments of enamel laid down as teeth are formed

culture   a system of shared meanings, symbols, customs, beliefs, and practices that are learned, either by teaching or by imitation, and used to cope with the environment, to communicate with others, and to transmit information through the generations

decay constant   constant rate by which radioactive elements change spontaneously to lower energy states

deciduous   teeth that are shed and replaced by other teeth during the normal course of an animal's lifetime

dendrochronology   dating by tree rings

dental arch   the teeth and their supporting structures

dental comb   the special alignment of canines and incisors for fur grooming in some prosimian primates

dental formula   shorthand notation denoting the numbers and pattern of teeth in each quadrant of the upper and lower jaws

dentine   the avascular tissue forming the core of teeth; 70 percent inorganic (mostly hydroxyapatite) and 30 percent organic (mostly collagen)

Developed Oldowan tradition   a continuation of the Oldowan tool tradition that includes simple pointed choppers, or proto-handaxes, rough bifacial forms, and rare handaxes together with some more evolved scraper forms

diagenesis   the sum of all physical, chemical, and biological changes to which a sediment is subjected after deposition

diaphysis   shaft of a long bone

diastema   space or gap between adjacent teeth in the tooth row

diploic veins   small veins that run between the outer and inner tables of cranial bones

direct percussion   a stone toolmaking technique in which a core flint is held and flakes are detached by striking it with a hammerstone

distal   refers to the side of the tooth or portion of the jaw toward the back of the mouth

dolichocephalic   having a long, narrow skull; usually with a cephalic index below 75

dolomitic   a type of limestone in which magnesium replaces calcite

dryomorph   vernacular term to describe primitive early and middle Miocene hominoids of East Africa and Eurasia characterized by thin enamel on the molar teeth

Early Paleolithic   see **Lower Paleolithic**

East African rift system   an elongated trough in the Earth's crust bounded on either side by faults, stretching all the way from the Red Sea in the north to the southern end of Lake Malawi (bordering Mozambique, Tanzania, and Malawi) in the south

eccentricity of the orbit   the deviation of the Earth's orbit around the sun from near-circularity to more pronounced ellipticity at periods of about 100,000 years and 400,000 years

electron capture   a radioactive decay process in which a proton in the nucleus turns into a neutron, thus decreasing the atomic number by 1; the mass number remains unchanged (e.g., ^{40}K to ^{40}Ar)

electron spin resonance   a method of dating in which the number of trapped electrons is determined by measuring their absorption of microwave radiation; the theoretical age range of ESR dating is from a few thousand years to more than 1 million years ago, but in practical terms most age estimates beyond about 300,000 years are very uncertain

elliptical precession   see **precession**

emissary veins   veins that course directly through the bones of the skull

enamel   the specialized avascular and acellular hard tissue that covers the crowns of teeth

endocranial cast   a naturally occurring (fossilized) or artificially made mold of the external surface of the brain

entoconid   cusp on the lingual rim of the talonid of lower molars

epochs   subdivisions of the Cenozoic era into the Paleocene, Eocene, Oligocene, Miocene, Pliocene, and Pleistocene

estrus   that phase of the sexual cycle of female animals characterized by willingness to permit coitus

evolutionary systematics   a method of classification employing hypothetical reconstructions of evolutionary history incorporating both cladistic data (on the sequence of branching events) and morphological divergence data

exostosis   a benign bony growth projecting outward from the surface of a bone

external auditory meatus   the ear canal and its opening on the lateral side of the skull

flourine test   a relative dating technique based on the fact that bones absorb flourine from surrounding groundwater that then combines with bone calcium to form the compound fluoroapatite; the longer the bone has been in the ground, the more fluoroapatite is present

foramen magnum   large hole in the base of the skull through which the spinal cord passes, joining the base of the brain

Frankfurt Horizontal   plane of orientation of the skull in side view from the superior margin of the external acoustic meatus to the lower portion of the orbit (orbitale)

frontal keel   a midline thickening in the frontal bone

Gauss   long interval of geologic time from about 3.4 to 2.4 mya in which the polarity of the Earth's magnetic field was (for the most part) normal

geomagnetic polarity reversal time scale   the magnetic histories of rocks and sediments

geophytes   plants having underground buds

Gilbert   long interval of geologic time from about 4.4 to 3.4 mya in which the polarity of the Earth's magnetic field was (for the most part) reversed

glabella   area on the frontal bone between the browridges

glacial drift   deposits of rock material transported by glacial ice and then "dumped" by the melting ice on the land surface

glacial periods   portions of geologic time in which the total area covered by glaciers greatly exceeded that of the present

Glacial theory   the idea that extensive glaciers formerly covered much of the Northern Hemisphere

glenoid cavity   the socket on the scapula that articulates with the head of the humerus

glenoid fossa   area on the temporal bone for articulation with the condyle of the mandible

Gondwanaland   see **Tethys Sea**

gracile   describes any slender, lightly built body or body part; often used to categorize the less robust australopithecine species

grade   groups of organisms characterized by a certain level of organization and/or adaptation

graminivorous   grass-eating diet

greenhouse effect   the trapping of heat in the Earth's atmosphere by carbon dioxide

half-life   the time required for half of the atoms of any particular radioactive element to decay

hallux   first toe

handaxe   a large bifacially worked core tool, normally oval or pear-shaped

Haplorhini   suborder of primates that includes the Tarsiiformes and the Anthropoidea

heterodonty   regional differentiation of teeth into incisors, canines, premolars, and molars

home base   an area to which hominids return to meet other group members, share food, and make tools

hominoid primates   the lesser apes (gibbons and siamangs of eastern Asia), the great apes (chimpanzees and gorillas of Africa and the orangutan of Southeast Asia), and humans

homologous   pertaining to structures shared between two species and their common ancestor

homoplasy   any resemblance not due to inheritance from a common ancestry, for example, similarities due to parallel evolution, convergence, or mimicry

Howiesons Poort   a distinctive South African artefact assemblage that contains many tools specifically designed for hafting as replaceable bits or inserts in composite tools

humerofemoral index   the length of the humerus divided by the length of the femur multiplied by 100

hypocone   the main cusp on the distolingual side of the upper molars

hypoconid   cusp on the lateral rim of the talonid of lower molars

hypoconulid   cusp on the middle of the distal margin of the rim of the talonid on lower molars

hypodigm   the entire known material of a species available to a taxonomist for study

hypsodonty   high-crowned teeth

igneous rock   one of the main groups of rocks that make up the Earth's crust, formed of molten material that flows up from the deeper part of the crust

iliofemoral ligament   the ligament that runs from the anterior inferior spine of the ilium to the proximal femur

incisors   the cutting teeth at the front of the upper and lower jaws

inferior transverse torus   the shelflike buttress of bone on the inside of the mandibular symphysis

insolation   the geological effect of solar rays on the surface materials of the Earth

interglacial periods   periods of glacial ice retreat

intermembral index   the length of the forelimb (humerus plus radius) divided by the length of the hindlimb (femur plus tibia) multiplied by 100

interstadials   irregular but well-defined episodes of somewhat milder climatic conditions occurring during glacial periods

intron   a part of a gene that is not translated into a protein

ischial callosities   well-developed sitting pads on the ischium of all Old World monkeys and gibbons

ischial tuberosity   a bony expansion of the ischium that supports ischial callosities

isotopes   two atoms that have the same number of protons but a different number of neutrons

Late Paleolithic   see **Upper Paleolithic**

Late Pleistocene   subdivision of the Pleistocene from about 127,000 to 10,000 years ago (also called Upper Pleistocene)

Late Stone Age   the Upper Paleolithic of southern Africa that generally postdates 40,000 years ago; characterized by a predominance of blade tools and microliths and tiny geometrically shaped blades often set in handles made of bone or wood

Laurasia   see **Tethys Sea**

law of superposition   a geological rule that, assuming strata are relatively undisturbed, fossils contained in lower strata will be older than those higher up in the stratigraphic sequence; it is assumed that fossils found in the same stratigraphic level are roughly contemporaneous, the degree of contemporaneity depending upon how quickly that particular stratum was laid down

Levallois cores   a stone tool core that is extensively preshaped in order to produce one or more flakes having a predetermined shape

lingual   toward the tongue

lithosphere   the top 70 km layer of the Earth, including oceanic and continental crust

living floor   in archeology, an occupation site

loess   an extensive deposit of windblown glacial dust produced by the grinding down of boulders within glacial ice against bedrock

Lower Paleolithic   an archeological subdivision of the Plio-Pleistocene between the first evidence of stone-tool manufacture about 2.6 mya in East Africa and the first appearance, or predominance, of prepared-core flake technologies and flake tools about 200,000–40,000 years ago (also referred to as the Early Paleolithic)

Lower Pleistocene   subdivision of the Pleistocene from about 1.6 to 0.9 mya

mammae   mammary glands, the milk-producing organs characteristic of female mammals

manuports   unaltered objects carried some distance before use as tools

manus   hand

Matuyama   long interval of geologic time from about 2.4 to 0.78 mya in which the polarity of the Earth's magnetic field was (for the most part) reversed

Member   in geology, a rock unit that is a subdivision of a formation

mesial   toward the anterior side of a molar or premolar tooth or to the side of an incisor tooth nearest the midline of the jaw

mesocephalic   having a head shape between dolichocephalic and brachycephalic, usually with a cephalic index between 75 and 80

Messinian salinity crisis   dropping of sea levels worldwide that caused the temporary desiccation of the Mediterranean Sea about 5.3 mya

metacone   the main cusp on the distobuccal side of the upper molars

metaconid   cusp on the distolingual corner of the trigonid

Middle Paleolithic   an archeological subdivision of the Plio-Pleistocene about 200,000–35,000 years ago often referred to (in Europe at least) as the Mousterian, after the site of Le Moustier in France, where it was first recognized; characterized by increasing sophistication of stone-tool technology, particularly in the use of flake tools made from prepared cores (e.g., Levallois cores)

Middle Pleistocene   subdivision of the Pleistocene from about 900,000 to 127,000 years ago

Middle Stone Age   stone-tool tradition in Africa generally dated from over 100,000 to around 40,000 years ago and characterized by the use of carefully prepared stone cores for the production of flake tools; also, the time in Africa when regional variation in stone-tool technologies became most evident

mitochondria   organelles in the cell's cytoplasm made up of single, circular strands of DNA, each having its own genetic coding system; mtDNA has a clonal mode of inheritance that is passed down only through the maternal line

mode   the process of evolution

molars   large grinding teeth at the back of the jaw

molecular clock   a system of dating based on the premise that many molecular differences among taxa are neutral mutations that accumulate at a relatively constant rate when averaged over geologic time

monogamous pair bonding   a social system based on mated pairs and their offspring

monophyletic group   a group containing all the known descendants of an ancestral species; also, a group of species that share a common ancestor that would be classified as a member of the group (clade)

moraines   ridges of glacial drift built up from the material riding on the ice that delineates the melting zones along the margins and bottom of glaciers

morphocline   arrangement of the morphological variations of a homologous character into a continuum of primitive to derived states

mosaic evolution   the appearance at different times of various characters in regionally disparate populations

Mousterian   the tool industry associated most closely with Neandertals, synonymous with the Middle Paleolithic at least in Europe; named for the site of Le Moustier in France, where it was first recognized

Multiregional Continuity Model   the model of modern human origins that holds that the biocultural transition from "late archaic humans" to "early modern humans" developed independently in several different places across the continents

Neogene   in geology, the time-stratigraphic unit composed of the Miocene, Pliocene, and Pleistocene

neurocranium   the portion of the skull enclosing the brain

nitrogen test   a means to measure how long a bone has been in the fossilization process based on the amount of nitrogen remaining in it

nuchal crest   the bony shelf on the back of the skull for the attachment of powerful neck muscles

obliquity   the tilt of the Earth's axis

occipital lobes   the posterior portion of the cerebral cortex, mostly involved with vision

occipital/marginal venous sinus   one pathway for venous blood leaving the brain; typically seen in "robust" australopithecines and *A. afarensis*

occlusal   refers to the surfaces of the teeth that meet during occlusion, or chewing

Oldowan tradition   the oldest formally recognized stone artifact assemblage of the early Paleolithic; originally defined from Beds I and II of Olduvai Gorge, Tanzania

ontogenetic   relating to the growth and development of an individual organism

opportunistic tools   simple, unaltered objects used as tools

optical isomers   two amino acids that have different structures but identical formulae

orthognathous   more vertical, nonprotruding face; opposite of prognathous

Osteodontokeratic Culture   the idea proposed by Raymond Dart that many of the bones and jaws at Makapansgat had been utilized as tools by the early hominids at the cave: teeth as saws and scrapers, long bones as clubs, etc.

Out of Africa Model   the model of modern human origins that holds that the biocultural transition from "late archaic humans" to "early modern humans" was restricted to Africa, after which radiation outward to the rest of the Old World occurred

oxygen-isotope analysis   a measure of the oxygen-isotope ratios in the calcareous shells of deep-sea marine organisms used to determine both ice volume and ocean temperature; it is based on the fact that there are two isotopes of oxygen in ocean water, the heavier ^{18}O and the lighter ^{16}O; since the overall quantity of the two isotopes is unchanging on Earth, more of ^{16}O tends to be locked up in continental ice during glacial periods, making less available in the oceans. Over time this process leads to an increase in the $^{18}O/^{16}O$ ratio of seawater during glacial periods.

paleomagnetic column   the magnetostratigraphic profile of a region

paracone   the main cusp on the mesiobuccal side of the upper molars

paraconid   the cusp on the mesial lingual surface of the lower molars

parallel evolution   the independent acquisition in two or more related descendant species of similar derived character states evolved from a common ancestral condition

paraphyletic group   a group containing some but not all the known descendants of the common ancestor of the group

parasagittal   parallel to the sagittal suture

parasagittal depressions   slight depressions on either side of the midsagittal keel along the parietal bones

perihelion   the point of closest approach of the Earth to the Sun

perikymata   enamel ridges visible on teeth that represent weekly microscopic increments of enamel laid down as teeth are formed (see **stria of Retzius**)

pes   foot

phyletic gradualism   the view of evolution that holds that daughter species usually originate through a progressive series of small, gradual transformations of parental species through anagenesis

phylogenetic systematics   see **cladistics**

phylogeny   the evolutionary or genealogical history of a group of organisms

phylogram   a branching diagram for a set of species that shows their ancestral relationships; one direction, usually the vertical axis, represents time (also called a phylogenetic tree)

plate tectonics   in geology, the movement of segments of the lithosphere that float on the underlying, more gelatinous asthenosphere

platymeric   having an anteroposteriorly flattened femoral shaft

platypelloid   a pelvic shape that is wide from side-to-side and narrow from front-to-back

pliomorph   vernacular term to describe early and middle Miocene hominoids of Eurasia sharing many primitive catarrhine features

pneumatized   filled with air spaces, as in pneumatized portions of the skull

polarity   the direction of a morphocline from primitive to derived

polarity epochs   extended intervals during which the geomagnetic field has predominantly one polarity

polarity events   short-lived geomagnetic polarity reversals occurring within a polarity epoch

polygynous   pertaining to the mating of several males with one female

polymorphic   showing a variety of forms

polyphyletic group   a taxonomic group whose members' resemblances are based on convergences

polytypic   comprising several geographical and/or morphological variants

Pongidae   family of great apes, often including chimpanzees, gorillas, and orangutans

postorbital bar   the bony ring surrounding the lateral side of the orbit in lower primates and many other mammals

postorbital closure   the "walling off" of the orbit posteriorly by means of a bony partition so that the orbit forms a cup-shaped structure, typical of monkeys, apes, and humans

postorbital constriction   narrowing of the skull behind the orbits

precession   perturbations of the Earth's orbit are strongly influenced by gravitational effects of planetary bodies and these perturbations periodically alter the geographic distribution of incoming solar radiation; one of these effects is known as precession, which changes the distance between the Earth and the Sun at any given season (two components of precession are axial precession, in which the Earth's axis of rotation "wobbles" like that of a spinning top, and elliptical precession, in which the elliptical orbit itself rotates slightly)

precession of the equinox   the equinox is the time when the Sun crosses the plane of the Earth's equator, making night and day all over the Earth of equal length (see **precession**)

prehensile   capable of grasping, as hands, feet, and, in some cases, tails

premolars   bicuspids

Primates   order of mammals that includes prosimians (lemurs, lorises, tarsiers), monkeys, apes, and humans

Proconsulidae   family of early Miocene African hominoid primates

prognathism   forward projection of the face and/or jaws

pronograde   quadrupedal locomotion with palms toward the ground

Prosimii   suborder of Primates that includes lemurs, lorises, and tarsiers

protocone   the main cusp on the mesiolingual side of the upper molars

protoconid   one of three main cusps on the trigonid, found on the buccal side of the tooth

pulp cavity   the neurovascular space within the dentine that extends for a variable distance into the roots

punctuated equilibrium   the view of evolution holding that the creation of new species is more often than not a comparatively rapid event and that most evolutionary change is concentrated in comparatively rapid speciation events in small isolated subpopulations of the ancestral species, a process known as allopatric speciation

racemization   the process by which L–amino acids slowly undergo a conversion from the active L–amino acid form to the inactive D–amino acid form over long periods of time

radiometric dating   techniques that make use of the fact that many kinds of atoms are unstable and change spontaneously into a lower energy state by radioactive emission; each radioactive element has one particular mode of decay and its own unique constant rate of decay; measuring ratios of unde-cayed atoms to the products of decay allows one to extrapolate back to the ages of many fossil-bearing rocks

ramamorph   vernacular term to describe middle Miocene hominoids of Eur-asia and East Africa characterized by thickened enamel on the molar teeth

Red Queen Model   the hypothesis that views evolutionary change leading to new species as being driven by competition among populations that share the same habitat, and that sexual recombination is an adaptation to augment a population's capacity to evolve quickly

referential models   models that use the social system of a particular nonhu-man primate species to model early hominid behavioral evolution

relative dating   dating methods that seek to put human fossils and artifacts into a temporal context with other locally associated archeological, faunal, and floral materials

rift valleys   valleys formed by depression of continental crust

robust   describes any large, or heavily built body or body part; often used to categorize the ''robust'' australopithecine species

sagittal crest   the bony crest running along the midline of the skull for attach-ment of enlarged temporalis muscles

scenario   an historical narrative that attempts to describe not only phyloge-netic relationships among taxa but also the ecological and/or evolutionary forces that most directly influenced the character state(s) under discussion

sclerophyllous   refers to vegetation adapted to dry conditions

sectorial   tooth in the lower jaw (usually the anterior premolar) with a honing facet for sharpening the upper canine during occlusion

secular radioactive equilibrium   the condition in any uranium-bearing mate-rial that has lain undisturbed for millions of years, in which the radioactive decay rate of each of the daughter isotopes equals the decay rate of any other uranium isotope in the same sample

seed-eating hypothesis   an hypothesis that makes an analogy between anatom-ical and behavioral characters shared by living gelada baboons (*Theropithecus gelada*) and some early hominids by suggesting that early hominid popula-tions relied on small-object feeding, that this dietary specialization resulted in a suite of adaptations to feeding in grassland savanna, and that bipedalism developed in response to such feeding posture

sensu stricto   Latin term meaning ''in the strict sense''

sexual-and-reproductive-strategy model   a model of human origins based on the trend toward prolonged life span in the primate evolutionary record and its implications for primate physiology, population dynamics, and behavior

simian shelf   distinct mandibular torus that projects posteriorly from the in-ferior surface of the mandibular symphysis (see also **inferior transverse torus**)

single-crystal fusion   a method of potassium-argon dating in which a laser is used to melt crystals to release argon gas; this technique has two important advantages over other methods: 1) the laser beam allows such a localized heating of the crystals that there is much less chance of background atmospheric argon confounding the final age calculations; and 2) it greatly reduces the amount of sample needed for the age determination

sister groups two groups that result from a single split in a cladogram; that is, they (and only they) share the same parent taxon

Siwalik Group the thick sequence of fossiliferous sediments deposited at the base of the rising Himalayas

solstice the time of year when the Sun is at its greatest distance from the Equator

speleothem any one of a number of variously shaped mineral deposits formed in caves by the action of water (e.g., stalagmites, stalactites, and flowstones)

spontaneous fission during spontaneous fission the nucleus within the atomic nucleus of ^{238}U splits into two or more high-energy fragments, and these fragments leave damage tracks within rock crystals that can be enlarged and studied

stasis a time of little evolutionary change

stomata the minute respiratory orifices in the epidermis of leaves

Strepsirhini suborder of primates that includes the Adapiformes and the Lemuriformes

striae of Retzius weekly microscopic increments of enamel laid down as teeth are formed

sulcal pattern the configuration of the grooves on the external surface of the brain

suprainiac fossa a midline depression on the occipital bone

supralaryngeal vocal tract the airspace above the vocal cords

supraorbital torus structure comprising projecting browridges that are united medially by a distinct glabellar prominence

supratoral sulcus troughlike depression between the supraorbital torus and the frontal squama

sutures fibrous joints that connect the several bones of the calvaria

sympatric occurring together in the same geographical area

symplesiomorphy describes a shared primitive character (symplesiomorph)

synapomorphy describes a shared derived character (synapomorph)

synchronic existing or occurring at the same time

talonid posterior heellike portion of lower molars

talus cone sediment, often containing the bones of animals, washed in from the surface in caves where there is a direct passageway between the cave floor and the surface

taphonomy the study of the processes by which animal bones become fossilized

taurodont having large pulp cavities in the teeth

tempo the rate of evolution

temporal fossa the space between the zygomatic arch and the side of the skull through which the temporalis muscle passes to its insertion point on the coronoid process of the mandible

Tethys Sea   a broad waterway that divided the northern supercontinent, Laurasia (consisting of what is now North America, Europe, and Asia), from the southern supercontinent, Gondwanaland (consisting of what is now South America, Africa, Antarctica, India, Madagascar, and Australia)

thermoluminescence   light emitted by trapped electrons as they return to their stable energy states

till   stratified layers of glacial drift

transgression   an incursion of the sea over land that converts initially shallow-water conditions to deeper-water conditions

transverse occipital torus   a transverse bony ridge along the occipital bone where the upper (occipital) and lower (nuchal) portions of the bone meet at an angle

travertine   a crystalline calcium carbonate deposit precipitated in solution by inorganic chemical processes

trigonid   anterior triangular portion of the lower molars

tufas   chemical sedimentary deposits rich in calcium carbonate typically occurring as incrustations around the mouths of springs

tuff   rock composed of volcanic ash cemented or consolidated by the pressure of overlying material

type   in systematics, the specimen that serves as the basis for the name of a taxon

Upper Paleolithic   an archeological subdivision of the Plio-Pleistocene about 45,000–10,000 years ago characterized by the predominance of well-made blades, microliths, distinctive bone points, and the use of burins and other tools to work bone, antler, ivory, teeth, and shells

Upper Pleistocene   see **Late Pleistocene**

varves   layers of glacial till that reflect annual cycles of summer melt-off

Villafranchian   a distinctive mammalian fauna of Europe that includes animals particularly well adapted to highly seasonal, drought-resistant grasslands; recognized by the presence of mammoths (*Mammuthus*), true bovines (cattle, bison, buffalo), and one-toed horses (*Equus*)

xeric   adapted to dry conditions

Index

Page numbers in *italics* refer to figures.